YALE
HISTORICAL PUBLICATIONS
MISCELLANY
XXIV

THE FOURTEENTH VOLUME
PUBLISHED UNDER THE DIRECTION OF
THE DEPARTMENT OF HISTORY ON THE
KINGSLEY TRUST ASSOCIATION PUBLICATION FUND
ESTABLISHED BY
THE SCROLL AND KEY SOCIETY
OF YALE COLLEGE

The Foreign Policy of the United States in Relation to Samoa

By

GEORGE HERBERT RYDEN,

WITH AN INTRODUCTION BY
JOHN BASSETT MOORE

This Essay was awarded the John Addison Porter Prize,
Yale University, 1928

OCTAGON BOOKS

A DIVISION OF FARRAR, STRAUS AND GIROUX

New York   1975

Copyright 1933 by Yale University Press
Copyright renewed 1961 by E. E. Ryden

Reprinted 1975
by special arrangement with Yale University Press

OCTAGON BOOKS
A DIVISION OF FARRAR, STRAUS & GIROUX, INC.
19 Union Square West
New York, N. Y. 10003

Library of Congress Cataloging in Publication Data

Ryden, George Herbert, 1884-1941.
    The foreign policy of the United States in relation to Samoa.

    Reprint of the ed. published by Yale University Press, New Haven, which was issued as Miscellany 24, Yale historical publications.

    Originally presented as the author's thesis, Yale University, 1928.

    Bibliography: p.
    Includes index.

    1. Samoan Islands—Politics and government. 2. United States—Foreign relations—Germany. 3. Germany—Foreign relations—United States. 4. United States—Foreign relations—Great Britain. 5. Great Britain—Foreign relations—United States. I. Title. II. Series: Yale historical publications: Miscellany; 24.

DU817.R9   1975   320.9'96'13   75-17708
ISBN 0-374-97000-9

Manufactured by Braun-Brumfield, Inc.
Ann Arbor, Michigan

Printed in the United States of America

TO MY MOTHER

EMMA SOPHIA RYDEN

PREFACE

My interest in the foreign policy of the United States in relation to Samoa grew out of a study of the career of Thomas F. Bayard as Secretary of State during the first administration of President Cleveland. This interest was further stimulated by the fact that another distinguished native son of Delaware, John Bassett Moore, was closely associated with Bayard as Secretary of the Washington Conference in 1887, a meeting held for the purpose of settling the conflicting claims at that time in Samoa of the United States, Germany, and Great Britain. From a study of the specific problem of 1887, I was led first to go back to the beginning of the whole Samoan problem, and later to proceed to an investigation of its intriguing phases down to 1899, when it was finally settled by the partition treaty among the three powers.

I wish first to acknowledge my particular indebtedness to Professor Ralph H. Gabriel of the Department of History, Yale University, for his unfailing patience and for his sincere and constant endeavor to assist me to find my way through many "entanglements" in the handling of what proved at times to be rather unwieldy material, for his stimulating criticisms of composition during the preparation of the manuscript as a doctoral dissertation, and for helpful suggestions in a subsequent revision of the manuscript.

I wish also to record my profound obligation to one of my first teachers in the Yale Graduate School, Professor Charles McLean Andrews. To me he has been for more than two decades an outstanding example of the true university scholar and teacher. A critic, kind, severe, and inspiring, he has been of inestimable help to me. I am greatly indebted to him for his reading of the whole manuscript of this book and for his many suggestions which have led to significant improvements in the final form of the text.

For the numerous courtesies shown me by members of the staff of the Yale University Library, especially Miss Anne Stokely Pratt, Reference Librarian, I am under many obligations. Dr. Tyler Dennett, formerly of the Department of State, on several occasions generously afforded me every facility to study the diplomatic papers in the archives of that department at Washington, and a member of his staff, Mrs. Natalia Summers, without stint of time or labor, assisted me in locating the documents desired and in having a number of them copied. The authorities in charge of the archives of the Navy Department were equally helpful in giving me access to the original papers relating to the Wilkes Expedition and to other activities of the United States Navy in the Pacific. In conclusion I wish to express my appreciation of the kind assistance of my colleague, Professor W. Owen Sypherd, in the reading of the proof.

G. H. R.

University of Delaware
Newark, Delaware
November 14, 1932

CONTENTS

	PAGE
Preface	vii
Introduction	xi

CHAPTER

I.	The Samoan islands and their explorers	1
II.	United States consular relations with Samoa from 1839 to 1876	19
III.	Commander Meade's treaty of 1872	42
IV.	A. B. Steinberger, special agent to Samoa	83
V.	Steinberger, premier of Samoa	112
VI.	Complications with Great Britain	148
VII.	American-Samoan treaty of 1878	191
VIII.	Beginning of tripartite control in Samoa	207
IX.	German encroachments, and intervention by the United States	264
X.	The Washington Conference, 1887	322
XI.	The Brandeis-Tamasese Régime	367
XII.	Preparations for the Berlin Conference	422
XIII.	The Berlin Conference, 1889	445
XIV.	The *Condominium,* or ten years of entanglement	522
XV.	The partition of Samoa, 1899	558
XVI.	American Samoa	575
Bibliographical Note		582
Index		593

ABBREVIATIONS

For the sake of brevity in the footnotes certain abbreviations have been adopted.

        I.C.   Instructions to Consuls
        C.D.   Consular Despatches
        M.L.   Miscellaneous Letters
        S.R.   Steinberger Report
        S.P.   Steinberger Papers
        F.R.   Foreign Relations

When two or more references are given in a footnote the abbreviation for *ibidem* refers to the primary source, usually a manuscript document in the Archives of the Department of State or the Navy Department in Washington.

INTRODUCTION

TOWARDS the end of a long life Benjamin Franklin, one of the wisest observers of men and of things, sagely wrote: "Experience keeps a dear school." Entrance to it is free, and it is open day and night. Every man, woman, and child is matriculated in it; and, if the pupils would learn their lesson from books, the present volume would suffice for the purposes of graduation. But, unfortunately, the pupils are vain and obdurate. Refusing to profit by the mistakes of others, they insist on paying as tuition the cost of their own perverse or emotional experimentation.

During half a century the United States might have had the Samoan Islands for the asking. At times they were pressed upon it, and, had the proffered honor and responsibility been accepted, the government's action would not have been difficult rationally to justify; for, as sole proprietor, it would have been master of its fate, and not constantly in collision with other powers over an object of relatively slight importance. But, on a fateful day, the United States entered into a "consultative pact." Such things are innocent in appearance and alluring in sound, especially to those who do not stop to consider what the other parties have in mind. Towards the end of 1877 a Samoan chief, called La Mamea, visited Washington. He stood six feet four in his stockings, was good to look upon, and had learned English from missionaries. At White House receptions he towered among the multitude. The mighty men at Washington, few of whom could have told where Samoa was, were good-natured, and were human. They extended to the Big Chief, who had come a long way to see them, the right hand of fellowship; and on January 17, 1878, there was signed a treaty by which it was stipulated that, "if, unhappily, any differences" should have arisen, or should thereafter arise, "between the Samoan Government and any other Government in amity with the United States," the United States would "employ its good offices for the purpose of adjusting those differences upon a satisfactory and solid foundation." The phraseology was faultless, and it appealed to "all benevolent minds"; but it omitted to state the fact that there was no such thing as "the Samoan Government." The Big Chief knew this, but accepted the compliment.

What followed is clearly, faithfully, and impressively detailed in the present volume. The United States, after a succession of bewildering lessons in the school of experience, sought to raise things to a higher plane. Learned writers have argued that, because certain powers have, by contributing small amounts to a common fund, kept a lighthouse burning at Cape Spartel for a number of years, without creating serious international complications, international government is a perfect success. As a matter of fact, it is the worst of all kinds of government. Foreign interests, commercial and missionary, had sought to instil into the Samoan mind the idea that the islands must have a central government, preferably under a king; but, no sooner was a king chosen from among the native chiefs, than some other chief or chiefs rose in rebellion, and, taking to the bush, sallied forth in the cool of the day to fight.

It was in Samoa that Germany made one of her early essays at colonization. That German subjects constituted by far the largest element of bona fide foreign settlers, who occupied land and cultivated it, is clearly shown by the results of the international land commission eventually set up for the adjudication of titles. Out of 134,419 acres claimed by Germans, 75,000, or 56 per cent, were confirmed to them. The British claimed 1,250,270 acres, and obtained confirmation of only 36,000, or 3 per cent; Americans claimed 302,746 acres, and obtained 21,000, or 7 per cent. The Germans, having a preponderant industrial and commercial interest in the group, not unnaturally sought a preponderant voice in local government, such as it was. This principle had been cordially conceded by Prince Bismarck to the United States in the Hawaiian Islands, where Germany had renounced her most-favored-nation clause in recognition of the preponderant interests of the United States. H. A. P. Carter, for many years the highly esteemed minister of Hawaii at Washington, more than once narrated to me the incidents of a night which, while on a special mission to Berlin, he spent by invitation at Friedrichsruhe, where Bismarck, as he smoked his big pipe, assured him that Germany would not stand in the way of the development of the closest relations between Hawaii and the United States. But, in Hawaii, there was a government, by no means perfect, but sole and supreme. In Samoa, there was just enough of a government to make a football for rival foreign groups. Out of this rivalry there grew turmoil and strife; and it was in an atmosphere of contention that the United States, in the exercise of "good offices" under the treaty of 1878, invited Germany and Great Britain to a conference at Washington. As a preliminary, agents were sent out to report on conditions in the islands. The conference took place in the summer of 1887.

In the pursuit of colonial aspirations, Germany had encountered British opposition; and Washington would not have been surprised if a continuance of this condition had been manifested in the conference. But it was not so. The United States presented a programme based on the recognition of native rights. It was natural that Germany and Great Britain should, as actual colonial powers, view this proposal in a severely practical light. The United States has, since those simpler times, occasionally but not continuously, seen things in that light, and has now and then militarily occupied a country that was not its colony. But the Samoan conference had not gone far before it became evident that Germany and Great Britain had come to an understanding, the British representative consistently supporting the German claim that governmental control should follow the preponderance of commercial interests. As the exaltation of native rights and the dominance of preponderant commercial interests were not naturally harmonious, the conference more and more developed points of disagreement, and eventually an adjournment was taken until the autumn. This adjournment was hastened by the intense heat, from which the German minister, who was not physically robust, specially suffered. This I can personally attest. I was present at all the conferences and prepared all the protocols, writing the last and longest of all on July 21, 1887, with the mercury at 103 degrees in the shade.

Soon after the conference adjourned, action was taken by Germany which was regarded in the United States as summary and unjustified. Popular excitement rose to a high pitch. Congress voted money for the defense of American rights. But Prince Bismarck, taking a practical view of the matter, proposed a resumption of the conference at Berlin. This proposal was accepted, but it fell to the administration of President Harrison to carry it out. Commissioners were duly sent to Berlin. Their instructions were originally drafted by William Henry Trescot, an accomplished South Carolinian who had in earlier days seen service in the Department of State of the United States and then in that of the Confederacy, and who, after the installation of President Hayes, was em-

INTRODUCTION

ployed by Republican administrations in various important diplomatic transactions.

The great Berlin Congress of 1878, under the presidency of Prince Bismarck, settled the affairs of Europe in a month. The Samoan conference opened on April 29, 1889, and lasted forty-five days; a treaty, pompously called the General Act of Berlin, was concluded on June 14. As thirty days are to forty-five, so were the affairs of Europe to those of Samoa. It would have been but poetic justice had La Mamea been present. Bismarck had hoped to end the business promptly. He was willing even to restore the unstable Malietoa to the throne. He agreed, in deference to the American delegates, to conduct the proceedings in English; and he presented, through his son Count Bismarck, then minister for foreign affairs, a simple proposal for the protection of the life, property, and commerce of the nationals of the treaty-powers by common action, leaving the matter of native government largely to the natives. The British representative concurred in this proposal. Mr. Kasson, who, although not designated as chairman of the American delegation, really acted in that capacity, seems to have been favorably impressed; but his government would not so have it. In spite of the lesson experience had taught, the United States, still bent on the "consultative pact" or "entangling alliance," insisted on setting up some kind of tripartite foreign authority for the nominal maintenance of a native government. Its prolonged and "vigorous" insistence was duly rewarded. The General Act, in the name of preserving native rights, becomingly set up among the simple islanders an elaborate and complicated foreign mechanism scientifically classified as a *condominium*. This contrivance was specially characterized by things transcending native conceptions and repugnant to native traditions. But the United States insisted that tuition be paid in the school of experience. Chief Justice Ide, one of our own best temporary contributions to Samoa, was not far wrong in saying that the *condominium* substituted several foreign kings for the one native king whom the natives were never willing to have. Experience again repeated itself. No sooner was the native figurehead restored than the other chiefs went into rebellion. The chief rebel this time was Mataafa, in whose behalf the blood and treasure of the United States were on a former occasion ready to be freely and copiously expended. Our duties and responsibilities as a great and enlightened power were not, however, to be shirked. As the proponent of the *condominium,* we joined our copartners in deporting him and certain other recalcitrant chiefs to the Marshall Islands, without taking with them their families.

This transaction, as I can personally testify, peculiarly appealed to the sensibilities of Judge Gresham, a man of warm heart and strong human feelings, who became secretary of state in President Cleveland's second administration. Much that had occurred under the *condominium* was at variance with his views of right and justice as well as of policy; and on May 9, 1894, he made to President Cleveland a report in which he declared that, soberly surveying the history of the relations of the United States with Samoa, nothing had been gained by the departure from our established policy of avoiding entangling alliances beyond the expenses, the responsibilities, and the inconveniences that had so far been its only fruits. Remarking, then, upon the propensity of the imagination to free itself from restraint when contemplating distant objects, he averred that the present entangling alliance had not only failed to correct but had even exaggerated the very evils it was designed to prevent. This clear and unequivocal sentence of condemnation was the beginning of the end. The creaking machinery either refused to work or worked badly. Difficulties accumulated. The three governments virtually superseded the officials of the *condominium* by reversing their decisions and acting directly for themselves. Commissioners were eventually sent out to survey the evils that had been done and to suggest a remedy. They unanimously reported that the defects of the tripartite government were radical and irremediable. The only thing left was a division of the group. The accomplishment of this process is fully detailed in the present volume. It was complicated and prolonged by persistent bargaining by Great Britain, but not by the United States. Formal overtures for a partition were, as I happen to know, preceded by informal soundings which were not reduced to writing. When consulted on the subject, at Paris, in the autumn of 1898, I communicated to Washington my unconditional approval of the principle of partition as the only feasible solution. A year elapsed before the treaty of partition was finally concluded.

A speaker at a peace meeting, when summoned to explain his demand for a big navy, ingenuously replied that he wished to be in the fashion. Combined with this all-pervasive desire is the innate tendency of man, as a reasonable being, to find, as Franklin once remarked, a reason for whatever he wishes to do, and also, as I venture to add, to ascribe to himself higher motives than he does to others for doing it. While the United States was contending for the right of native self-government in Samoa, there was consummated within its own borders the virtual legal disfranchisement of a native element in its own population at least as capable of self-government as were the Samoans. I mention these things not for reproach, but only for reflection. Will the people of the United States heed the lesson? Will they be less disposed than they were half-a-century ago, in the full flush of their first release from two decades of domestic entanglements, benevolently to embark on foreign adventures from which the best that can be hoped for is an escape from disaster? Or will they, scenting the distant aroma, speed o'er land and sea to the romantic rescue of the scorching chestnuts in order that others, having in them a near, definite, and permanent possessory interest, may at a convenient time divide and enjoy them? Should they take such a course, Dr. Ryden may justly exclaim—

> "Thou canst not say I did it; never shake
> "Thy gory locks at me"!

JOHN BASSETT MOORE

New York, February 10, 1933.

CHAPTER I

THE SAMOAN ISLANDS AND THEIR EXPLORERS

THE Samoan archipelago, strictly speaking, consists of fourteen islands.[1] Four of these, however, are mere rocky islets,[2] a fifth is an uninhabited coral atoll,[3] and of the nine remaining only three are of any appreciable size,[4] although the other six are also inhabited and have played important rôles in Samoan history.[5] The group lies some fourteen degrees south of the equator and between the 168th and 173rd degrees west of Greenwich.[6] A little over two thousand miles from Honolulu to the northeast and the same distance from Sydney to the southwest, the Samoan archipelago forms, as it were, the second convenient stopping place between San Francisco and Australia, the distance from the American port being approximately twice that from Hawaii. The exact distance from Panama to the harbor of Pago Pago is 5,656 miles.[7] The most prominent neighboring island groups are the Society Islands to the eastward and the New Hebrides group to the westward, with the Tonga group, named by Captain Cook

[1] W. T. Brigham, "Index to the Pacific Islands," in *Memoirs, B. P. Bishop Museum*, I, No. 2, map no. 15, p. 104.
[2] Fanuatapu, Namua, Nuulua, and Nuutele, off eastern end of Upolu.
[3] Rose, easternmost island of the group.
[4] Tutuila, Upolu, and Savaii.
[5] Manua group (Tau, Olosega, and Ofu), east of Tutuila; Aunuu, off eastern end of Tutuila; and Manono and Apolima, between Upolu and Savaii.
[6] Brigham, "Index to the Pacific Islands," map no. 15, p. 104 as above.
[7] *American Samoa—A General Report by the Governor* (Navy Department, Washington, 1927), p. 2.

the Friendly Islands, only a short distance to the southward,[8] and the Fijis less than seven hundred miles southwest.[9]

An aeroplane view of the Samoan archipelago as a whole would reveal a long string of islands stretching from the uninhabited coral atoll, called Rose Island, on the east, to Savaii on the west. Upon thus approaching the group one would be struck by the height of the three largest islands, Savaii, with the highest peak in Samoa, rising over five thousand feet above the level of the sea;[10] Upolu in the middle, with the next highest mountain, over three thousand feet;[11] and Tutuila to the east, presenting the most rugged aspect of the whole group with four comparatively high peaks, one of them, Mount Matafao, rising to an elevation of over two thousand feet.[12] Far to the eastward one would also descry a prominent cluster of three islands, called collectively, Manua, all of which rise from one thousand to twenty-five hundred feet.[13]

What would also appear as remarkable is the fact that these mountainous islands, except in those regions where the outflow of lava is too recent, are covered altogether with verdure of the most exotic luxuriance.[14] Cliffs rise out of the sea in places, incised here and there by gorges extending to the water's edge with swiftly running streams plunging through them. On account of the water percolating through the many vertical fissures and horizontal hollows of the igneous rocks, these streams, how-

[8] See map of the Pacific Ocean between pp. 436 and 437, vol. 20, *The Encyclopaedia Britannica*, 11th edition.

[9] *American Samoa* etc., p. 2.

[10] Brigham, ''Index to the Pacific Islands,'' p. 144.

[11] *Ibid.*, p. 161.

[12] *American Samoa* etc., pp. 2 and 3.

[13] Brigham, ''Index to the Pacific Islands,'' pp. 97, 123, 124, 153; see also *American Samoa* etc., p. 3.

[14] The clearings along the seaboard for the cultivation of the soil are too insignificant to affect the general appearance of the surface of the group.

ever, may be smaller at the seaboard than inland. Crater formations are especially prominent on the islands of Savaii and Upolu, which, when filled with water and surrounded by virgin bush, present an entrancing scene. In the upper reaches of the hills and mountains waterfalls of surpassing beauty are often to be seen. Where the coast is not steep and rocky, the white sandy fringe makes a striking contrast to the dark green cocoanut trees extending toward the interior.

All the islands, with the exception of Rose, are of volcanic origin, and on the island of Savaii naked patches of lava are prominent physical features along the northern coast. Coral reefs, surrounding practically every island, are also an attractive, and, indeed, useful, feature of the group, making it possible for the Samoans to travel safely in the lagoons from village to village in their boats and canoes, and to carry on their fishing industry. The interior of the islands is almost uninhabited, and since the Samoan villages for the most part are strung along the seaboard, and since the coastlines are frequently gashed by gorges, roads for any great distance are rare, the sole means of communication between villages, in most cases, being by water.[15]

In comparison with other groups in Polynesia the islands of Samoa are not large, and on any ordinary map they appear as mere specks of land. The fact that the largest island, Savaii, is only forty miles long and twenty miles wide, and Upolu, the next in size, has only an average width of eight miles, though its length is the same as Savaii's, while Tutuila has an area of only one-sixth of that of Savaii, indicates the relatively small size of the whole group.

The name of the mariner will probably never be known

---

[15] One exception is the so-called Falealili street, leading from Apia to Vailima, the home of the late R. L. Stevenson, on the island of Upolu.

who first saw the beautiful archipelago once known as "Navigators Islands" and now called by its native name, Samoa. He may have sailed under a Portuguese flag and come around the Cape of Good Hope to reach the South Seas, or he may have been a Spaniard, who had braved the passage around the Horn in search of more lands and fabulous wealth. During the sixteenth and early seventeenth centuries, many islands were discovered by bold sailors, such as the Ladrones, the Philippines, New Guinea, the Carolines, the Solomons, and the Marquesas, and it is quite possible that Samoa was seen by some passing ship belonging either to Portugal or Spain, though no record has been left of any such incident.[16]

The immediate successors of the Portuguese and Spaniards as explorers of the South Pacific were the Dutch. Le Maire, Schouten, and Tasman were leading mariners of that nation in the seventeenth century, and several geographical names, some now obsolete[17] but others still in use, testify to their activities. That an expedition of Le Maire and Schouten was in the vicinity of the Samoan islands in April, 1616, is not improbable.[18] In the account of the expedition, attributed to Le Maire, however, no indication of longitude is given relative to two islands named by these Dutchmen "Cocos and Verrathers," and although a member, named Behrens,[19] of a later expedition

[16] Brigham, "Index to the Pacific Islands," pp. 5 ff. Menezes, a Portuguese, discovered New Guinea, followed by Saavedro, a Spaniard, who came upon the island a few months later. On his return voyage Saavedro saw the Caroline group, which in 1542 was seen again by Villalobos. Mendana discovered the Solomon group in 1567 and toward the end of the century he discovered the Marquesas islands.

[17] Australia was first called "New Holland."

[18] Jacob Le Maire, "Australian Navigations." Translation in Hakluyt Society *Publications*, Second Series, No. XVIII, pp. 195 ff.

[19] Karl Friedrich Behrens, a Mecklenburger by birth, who went with the Roggewein expedition as "Sergeant oder Kommandant von der Miliz" on board the flagship. He wrote an account of the expedition, which appeared in

under the Dutchman, Roggewein, sought to identify these islands as belonging to the Samoan group, the evidence is not very conclusive. Tasman, who by order of Governor Van Diemen sailed in August, 1642, from Batavia to explore the coasts of Australia, and who in the latter part of that year discovered the islands of Tasmania and New Zealand, and in the early part of the next year the Tongan group,[20] may have also cruised in the vicinity of the Samoan islands.[21]

Jacob Roggewein, sent out in 1721 by the Dutch East India Company with three ships,[22] was the first explorer, of whose work there is any clear record, definitely to sight the Samoan islands. According to Behrens the squadron rounded Cape Horn and, having discovered Easter Island, arrived among the islands of Tahiti where one of the ships was lost, May 19, 1722. While steering for the New Britain and New Guinea islands, after departing from Tahiti, the Roggewein expedition came upon the Samoan group on the fourteenth of June, 1722.[23] Behrens says that three islands were discovered at once, "which with trees, herbs, and other plants were very beautiful to

the French language in 1739 and was published in Frankfort and Leipzig in 1757 under the title: *Reise durch die Sud länder und um die Welt.* (See La Pérouse, *A Voyage Round the World,* etc., III, 107, and Augustin Krämer, *Die Samoa-Inseln,* II, 1.)

[20] Brigham, "Index to the Pacific Islands," p. 7.

[21] Bougainville says: "The longitude of these isles [Navigators] is nearly the same in which Abel Tasman was by his reckoning, when he discovered the isles of Amsterdam, Rotterdam, Pylstaart, those of Prince William and the shoals of Fleenskerk." (Bougainville, Lewis de, *A Voyage Round the World,* etc., pp. 283 and 284.)

[22] The ships were: The Admiral's flagship, *Arend,* 110 men, 32 cannon, 120 feet long, commanded by Jan Koster; *Thienhoven,* 80 men, 24 cannon, 100 feet long, commanded by Cornelius Baumann; *Afrikaanshe Galei,* 33 men, 14 cannon, 92 feet long, commanded by Roelof Rosendaal. (See Krämer, *Die Samoa-Inseln,* II, 2, for quotation from *Dagverhaal der Ontdekkingsreis van Mr. Jacob Roggeveen,* etc., which was first published in 1838.)

[23] Krämer, *Die Samoa-Inseln,* II, 2.

see.''[24] The natives approached the ships in their boats, and showed the newcomers fish, cocoanuts, and other articles. Many inhabitants stood on the shore with bows and arrows. Behrens noted in a boat a man who may have been a chief, with many other boats to the right and left; also before and aft. A young woman sitting beside the chief was quite white, as were, more or less, the inhabitants in general. To these early explorers the natives of Samoa appeared handsome and gay and betrayed no indication of being savage in their speech or manners.[25] The tall, brown-skinned, and naked Samoan, skillful as a boatman as well as a builder of picturesque houses in the midst of the luxuriant trees of his South Seas habitat, excited no less interest than the white man with his strange-looking clothes, his great ships, and his ear-splitting cannon. Upon leaving the Manua islands[26] the Roggewein expedition sailed in a northerly direction, and sighted on the next day two more islands, which, according to Behrens, were thought to be the same as those Wylhelm Schouten had discovered and named ''Cocos and Verrathers-Eylande.''[27] Two larger islands were found farther on, the one being named ''Tienhoven'' after Captain Baumann's ship, and the other ''Groeningen'' after the city in Friesland.[28] The island named ''Tienhoven'' is described as very large, very green, and

[24] Krämer identifies these as Tau, Olosega, and Ofu, called collectively Manua, p. 3.

[25] ''Ich fand fast keinen Unterschied zwischen uns und unserer Europaischen Nation, als dass der eine was rother, und der andere was brauner, von der Sonne verbrannt war. Sie schienen redliche Leute zu seyn, freundlich im Sprechen und artig in ihrem Umgang; so dass man gar kein wildes Wesen an ihnen verspuren kunte; auch waren sie nicht bemohlet, wie die andern, die wir vorhin gesehen hatten.'' (Quoted by Krämer, p. 3, from Behrens' *Reise durch die Sud länder und um die Welt*, 1757.)

[26] Named ''Baumann's Land'' after the captain of the *Tienhoven*.
[27] Identified by Krämer as Tutuila and Anuu. See II, 3.
[28] Identified by Krämer as Upolu and Savaii.

covered with trees half way up the mountains. Sailing a whole day along this island, they saw neither its "beginning nor its end," but suspected that an arm stretched close to the second island.[29]

Louis Antoine de Bougainville, the first Frenchman to circumnavigate the globe,[30] was the second known explorer to visit the Samoan archipelago. For a long time he was thought to have been the discoverer of the islands until the publication of Roggewein's Journal[31] made possible a more correct interpretation of Behrens' account.[32] Sailing with two ships from France in December, 1766, and passing through the Straits of Magellan, Bougainville reached Tahiti eight months after the English explorer, Wallis, had visited that group. Taking on board an interpreter there, he sailed northwest, and on the third and fourth of May, 1768, the expedition passed along the north side of the island group of Manua.[33] To quote Bougainville: "The third of May, almost at daybreak, we discovered more land to the northwest, about ten or twelve leagues off. . . . The isle extends two leagues east and west. Its shores are everywhere steep and the whole isle

[29] Krämer, II, 5.

[30] Louis Antoine de Bougainville, *A Voyage round the world, Performed by order of His Most Christian Majesty, in the years 1766, 1767, 1768, and 1769, in the frigate* La Boudeuse *and the store-ship* L'Étoile, trans., London, 1772; two French editions, Paris, 1771 and 1772, Bougainville, Louis Antoine de, *Voyage autour du monde, par la frégate du roi* la Boudeuse, *et la flûte* l'Étoile *en 1766-69.*

[31] "Tagebuch unde Lebensgeschichte des Entdeckers wurden erst 1838 von der Zeeuwsch Genoatschap der Wetenschappen zu Middelburg (Gebroeders Abrahams Verlag) herausgegeben unter dem Titel: 'Dagverhaal der Ontdekkingsreis van Mr. Jacob Roggeveen met de Schepen den Arend, Thienhoven en de Afrikaansche Galei in de jaren 1721 en 1722.'" (See Krämer, II, 7.)

[32] See Krämer, II, 1, and La Pérouse, III, 109. La Pérouse says: "I am justified in believing, that Baumann's Islands are not the same as those, to which M. de Bougainville has given the name of Navigators Islands."

[33] See Krämer, II, 7.

is as it were nothing more than a high mountain, covered with trees up to its summit, without either valleys or plains."[34] Describing the Samoan boats, Bougainville says: "Their periaguas are made with a good deal of skill, and have an out-rigger. Neither the head, nor the stern is raised, but there is a kind of deck over each of them, and in the middle of these decks is a row of wooden pegs ending in a form of large nails, but their heads are covered with a fine shell, which is of clear white. The sail of their periaguas is of a triangular shape, composed of several mats. . . . These periaguas followed us pretty far out to sea." Bougainville called the islands "L'Archipel des Navigateurs," from which designation they were long known as "Navigators Islands." This name was applied to them on account of the skill of the natives in sailing their periaguas.[35]

Neither the Roggewein nor the Bougainville expedition landed on any of the Samoan islands. The first to do so was the ill-fated one of La Pérouse in 1787 with his two ships, *L'Astrolabe* and *La Boussole*.[36] "It is not without reason," says La Pérouse, "that M. de Bougainville has named them *the Navigators*. They [the natives] do not go so much as from one village to another on foot; but perform all their journeys in canoes. Their villages are all situated in creeks by the seaside, and have no paths except to penetrate into the interior of the country.[37] . . . Their only modes of fishing are with the hook and line, and sweep-net. They sold us some of the nets and baits of mother of pearl and white shells, very skillfully wrought.[38]

[34] Bougainville, pp. 278 and 279.   [35] *Ibid.*, pp. 281 ff.
[36] Jean François de Galaup La Pérouse, *A Voyage Round the World in the Years 1785, 1786, 1787, and 1788*, trans., London, 1798, 3 vols. The original was published in 1797 in Paris, *Voyage de La Pérouse autour du Monde*, 4 vols. See also André Bellessort, *La Pérouse*, Paris, 1926, chap. VII.
[37] *La Pérouse*, English trans., III, 117.   [38] *Ibid.*, p. 118.

THE SAMOAN ISLANDS

"... The most lively imagination would find it difficult to figure to itself situations more agreeable than those of their villages. All the houses are built under fruit trees which keep them delightfully cool.[39] ... The islands abound with hogs, dogs, fowls, birds, and fish. They are also covered with cocoanut, guava, and banana trees, as well as another tree bearing a large nut that is eaten roasted and that in taste much resembles a chestnut. Sugar canes grow spontaneously upon the banks of the rivers; but they are watery, and contain less saccharine matter than those of our West India islands; a difference which proceeds, no doubt, from their growing in the shade, without cultivation, and upon too rank a soil."[40]

The La Pérouse expedition, which was destined never to return to France,[41] underwent a sad experience while among the Samoan islands. On December 11, 1787, a detachment of sailors, officers, and scientists, having landed for purposes of exploration, was attacked by a large body of the natives and twelve of the Frenchmen killed. The commander of *L'Astrolabe*, M. de Langle, and seven of its crew, and M. de Lamanon, natural philosopher and naturalist, and three members of the crew of *La Boussole* were the victims.[42] Thenceforth for many years navigators were prone to regard the Samoans as a treacherous people.[43]

The first English account of the Samoan islands was made in the report of the voyage of the *Pandora*, sent out

[39] *Ibid.*, p. 119.   [40] *Ibid.*, p. 120.
[41] La Pérouse sent the first part of his journal to France before his expedition disappeared. Another expedition was sent out from France in 1791, under the command of d'Entrecasteaux, to search for La Pérouse but without success. Not until 1828 were traces found, when Peter Dillon discovered the remains of the wrecked vessels in the New Hebrides group.
[42] *La Pérouse*, III, 84.
[43] Charles Wilkes, U.S.N., *Narrative of the United States Exploring Expedition during the years 1838, 1839, 1840, 1841, 1842*, II, 126.

10   UNITED STATES POLICY IN SAMOA

from England in 1790 under the command of Captain Edward Edwards in search of the mutineers of the *Bounty*. Having visited the Society Islands, and the Hervey and Union groups, the *Pandora* first sighted from the north the island of Savaii on the eighteenth of June, 1791. Supposing "it to be a new discovery, I called it 'Chatham Island'," says Edwards.[44] The *Pandora* also sailed along the northern coast of Upolu and thence to the Friendly Islands. Returning to the Samoan group, the expedition came upon the Manua islands (Ofu, Olosega, and Tau) July 14, later saw Tutuila, and then sailed along the southern coast of Upolu. On the island of Savaii Edwards found a native from the Friendly Islands, who had seen Captain Cook when that navigator visited that group.[45]

The Russian explorer, Captain von Krusenstern, who circumnavigated the globe from 1803 to 1806,[46] evidently made no attempt to reach the Samoan islands, but one of his subordinates, Otto von Kotzebue, who later directed two expeditions to the South Seas, sought the islands on both voyages. The first time, in 1816, on the *Rurick*, he was unsuccessful,[47] but in 1824 he visited the islands when in command of the *Predpriatic*. On April 2 he sighted Rose Island and, not being aware that the French explorer, de Freycinet, had already discovered that atoll,[48] he named it "Kordinoff" after his first lieutenant. On April 3 he passed the Manua group and then turned

[44] *Voyage of H.M.S. Pandora, 1790-91*, Edwards and Hamilton; introduction and notes by Basil Thomson, p. 49.
[45] *Ibid.*, p. 49.
[46] The expedition comprised the ships, *Nadeshda* and *Neva*. See *Voyage Round the World*, etc., Captain A. J. Krusenstern of the Imperial Navy, trans., from German original, London, 1813, 2 vols.
[47] Otto von Kotzebue, *Entdeckungs-Reise in die Sud-See und nach der Berings Strasse, 1815,-'16,-'17,-'18*, Weimar, 1821.
[48] See note no. 51.

THE SAMOAN ISLANDS 11

toward Tutuila. By the fifth he was sailing along the southern coast of Upolu and finally reached Manono.[49]

It fell to the lot of Louis de Freycinet to carry on the work of exploration in the South Seas for France, so auspiciously begun by de Bougainville and La Pérouse. Like von Kotzebue, de Freycinet made two voyages, the first during the Consulate,[50] and the second from 1817 to 1820. On the latter expedition, as alluded to above, de Freycinet discovered, on October 21, 1819, an islet east of the more or less familiar Navigators Islands, which, he says, was not indicated on his maps, and consequently he named it "Rose Island," after his wife.[51] This uninhabited atoll has since been considered as the easternmost outpost of the Samoan group.[52]

Another French expedition, that of J. S. C. Dumont-d'Urville, visited the Samoan islands in the last days of September and the first days of October, 1838.[53] Under the guidance of an English resident on the island of Upolu, named Frazior,[54] and an Anglican missionary named Mills, Dumont-d'Urville and his companions made

[49] Quoted by Krämer, II, 20, from Kotzebue, Otto von, *Neue Reise um die Welt in den Jahren 1823-1826*, Weimar, 1830, I, 143.

[50] *Voyage de décourvertes aux terres Australes exécuté sur les corvettes* le Geographia, le Naturaliste, *et la gëolette* la Casuarina, *pendant les années 1800, 1801, 1802, 1803, et 1804*, etc., Paris, 1807-16, 2 vols.

[51] *Voyage autour du monde—par M. Louis de Freycinet, 1817, 1818, 1819, et 1820 sur les corvettes de S.M.* l'Uranie *et la* Physicienne. Paris, 1839, II, 624; English trans., London, 1823, Arago, J. E. V., *Narrative of a Voyage round the World in the* Uranie *and* Physicienne, etc.

[52] W. T. Brigham, "Index to the Pacific Islands," p. 139.

[53] J. S. C. Dumont-d'Urville, *Voyage au pole sud et dans l'Oceanie sur les corvettes* l'Astrolabe *et la* Zélée, *exécuté pendant les années 1837-1838-1839-1840*, etc., Paris, 1843-54.

[54] Dumont-d'Urville quotes Frazior as estimating the population of the Samoan group at about 80,000 souls, of whom 25,000 were on Savaii and Upolu, 10,000 on Tutuila, 7,000 on Manono, and 3,000 on Apolima. The Manua group was least inhabited. IV, 104.

a number of observations. He agrees with La Pérouse that the Samoan islands are superior to Tahiti for beauty and fertility.[55]

By the middle of the thirties the whaling industry had become so important that efforts were made to induce the United States government to send out into the Pacific an exploring expedition for the purpose of collecting scientific data to make that ocean more safe for the whalemen in which to cruise.[56] "It may be safely alleged," writes Starbuck, "that but for them [the whalemen] the Western ocean would much longer have been comparatively unknown, and with equal truth may it be said that whatever of honor or glory the United States may have won in its explorations of these oceans, the necessity for their exploration was a tribute wrung from the Government, though not without earnest and continued effort, to the interests of our mariners, who for years before, had pursued the whale in these uncharted seas, and threaded their way with extremest care among these undescribed islands, reefs and shoals."[57] And to quote Starbuck further, "so large a portion of our fishing fleet visited the Pacific that the United States was finally forced, when petition after petition had been sent to Congress, to send an exploring expedition to these seas, the ostensible purpose of which was to render the navigation of that ocean more secure as well in respect to the dangers of the land as in regard to those of the sea."[58]

The expedition was authorized by an act of Congress

[55] "Nous rangeant a l'avis de la Péyrouse, nous n'hesitons pas a proclamer ces îles comme bien superieures a Taiti elle-même, et pour leur beauté et pour leur apparent fertilité. La côte est couverte de beaux arbres d'une admirable verdure partout on y distingue de belles plages de sable de jolies auses, des villages populeux et parfaitement ombrages." IV, 95.

[56] Alexander Starbuck, "History of the American Whale Fishery," etc., in *Report of Commissioner of Fish and Fisheries*, p. 97.

[57] *Ibid.*, pp. 2-3.   [58] *Ibid.*, p. 97.

passed May 18, 1836.[59] The command of the expedition was first entrusted to Commodore Thomas ap Catesby Jones and for some time this naval officer directed the preparations at the New York Navy Yard. There was so much delay however, that the secretary of the navy, Mahlon Dickerson, wrote in November, 1837, a letter to Commodore Jones regretting that the expedition had not gotten under way but adding: "I presume you are doing everything in your power to forward the preparations."[60] Commodore Jones left New York in December, presumably after he had resigned his command on account of ill health,[61] and in the following March Lieutenant Charles Wilkes, then in command of the United States brig, *Porpoise*, at Charleston, S. C., and engaged in surveying, was summoned to Washington for "special duty of great importance."[62] The "special duty" implied was the command of the exploring expedition, and despite protests sent to the Navy Department against the appointment of Lieutenant Wilkes on account of his junior rank, orders were issued on March 20 that he take over the command.[63] The preparations completed, Lieutenant Wilkes received his instructions in August, 1838. According to the instructions the expedition was to explore and survey the Southern Ocean "having in view the important interests of our commerce embarked in the whale-fisheries . . . as well as to determine the existence of all doubtful islands and shoals, and to discover and accurately fix the position of

[59] Charles Wilkes, Commander of Expedition, *Synopsis of the Cruise of the United States Exploring Expedition during the years 1838, '39, '40, '41, '42*, p. 6.

[60] Officers of the Ships of War, Navy Department, vol. 25, p. 202, Dickerson to Commodore Jones, Nov. 18, 1837.

[61] *Ibid.*, p. 261, Dickerson to Commodore Jones, May 19, 1838.

[62] *Ibid.*, p. 132, Dickerson to Lieutenant Wilkes, March 2, 1838.

[63] United States Exploring Expedition, Navy Department, vol. 1, p. xiii, Dickerson to Lieutenant Wilkes, March 20, 1838.

those which lie in or near the track of our vessels in that quarter, and may have escaped the observation of scientific navigators."[64] For the extension of "the bounds of science, and to promote the acquisition of knowledge" a corps of scientists were to accompany the expedition. The names of these gentlemen appearing in the instructions were: Mr. Hale, philologist, Messrs. Pickering and Peale, naturalists, Mr. Couthouy, conchologist, Mr. Dana, mineralogist, Mr. Rich, botanist, Messrs. Drayton and Agate, draughtsmen, and Mr. Brackenridge, horticulturist. The investigations and studies in astronomy, hydrography, geography, terrestrial magnetism, meteorology, and physics, however, were entrusted exclusively to the commander of the expedition and the other officers of the navy accompanying him.[65]

With respect to the Samoa and Fiji groups of islands the instructions stated: "It is presumed you will reach the Navigator's Group some time in June, 1839. You will survey this group, and its harbors, with all due care and attention. . . . From the Navigator's Group, you will proceed to the Feejee Islands, which you will examine with particular attention, with the view to the selection of a safe harbor, easy of access, and in every respect adapted to the reception of vessels of the United States engaged in the whale fishery, and the general commerce of these seas; it being the intention of the government to keep one of the squadrons of the Pacific cruising near these islands in future."[66] Enclosed with the instructions were a memorandum and charts concerning certain groups of islands, sent to the Navy Department by the Russian navigator, Admiral Krusenstern;[67] likewise sci-

[64] Officers of Ships of War, Navy Department, vol. 25, pp. 404-412; also printed in Wilkes' *Narrative*, I, pp. xxv-xxxi.
[65] *Ibid.* [66] *Ibid.*
[67] For Krusenstern's Memorandum see Wilkes' *Narrative*, I, 354-359.

entific data, received from the American Philosophical Society of Philadelphia and other scientific societies.[68] The instructions were signed by the new secretary of the navy, J. K. Paulding.

The vessels placed under the command of Lieutenant Wilkes were the sloops of war, *Vincennes* (the flag ship) and *Peacock,* the ship, *Relief,* the brig, *Porpoise,* and the tenders, *Sea-Gull* and *Flying-Fish.* On August 17 sailing instructions and final orders to put to sea were received. Sailing on the 18th from Hampton Roads, the expedition directed its course to the Straits of Magellan via Madeira and Rio de Janeiro, and upon entering the Pacific spent some time in Chilean and Peruvian waters before launching out upon the South Seas.[69] The expedition was engaged in its mission from August, 1838, until the year 1842, its operations extending from the Antarctic regions of the Pacific to the Hawaiian Islands and the coast of Oregon in the North Pacific.

Coming from Tahiti on the *Vincennes,* Lieutenant Wilkes sighted Rose Island on October 7, 1839, and at the same time he "descried the *Porpoise"* which had been separated from the squadron. He found Rose Island a "complete coral reef with the exception of about five acres covered with a clump of large trees." Having made the necessary observations on shore and found the island's situation, the *Vincennes* left Rose Island the same day, sailing to the westward.[70] The first island of the Manua group, Tau, was reached at sunrise on the eighth. The *Porpoise* was this day despatched to survey the islands of Savaii and Apolima while the *Vincennes* pro-

[68] Officers of Ships of War, Navy Department, vol. 25, pp. 404-412; see also Wilkes' *Narrative,* I, pp. xxv-xxxi.

[69] Wilkes' *Narrative,* I.

[70] Wilkes Exploring Expedition, Navy Department, vol. 1, no. 52, Wilkes to Paulding, Oct. 24, 1839; see also Wilkes' *Narrative,* II, 63-65.

ceeded to survey the Manua group. Tau was seen to be "a high island with bold rocky shores, affording no anchorage except for small vessels off the N. W. side." The Americans found the native inhabitants of these islands "well disposed towards strangers," but deserters, many of them convicts from New South Wales, did considerable harm among them.[71] Tau was discovered to be "sixteen miles in circumference, well covered with luxuriant vegetation" with "many cocoanut groves in its northwest side." The other two islands of the Manua group, Olosega and Ofu, had less inhabitants than Tau, although the "king" of the group lived in Olosega "in consequence of its being more easily defended." Olosega "is a narrow ledge of rocks," says Wilkes, "rising nearly perpendicular on both sides and is three miles in length." Ofu, to the westward of Olosega, is, he said, separated from that island by only a small strait a fourth of a mile in width.[72]

On October 11 the *Vincennes* reached Pago Pago harbor in the island of Tutuila. On the 18th the *Peacock* and *Flying-Fish* arrived, but on the next day these two ships were despatched "to make surveys of the islands of Upolu and Manono." "The harbour of Pago Pago" writes Wilkes in his *Narrative*, "is one of the most singular of all the Polynesian isles. It is the last point at which one would look for a place of shelter; the coast near it is peculiarly rugged, and has no appearance of indentations, and the entrance being narrow, is not easily observed."[73] Wilkes found the men of Tutuila "a remarkably tall fine-looking set, with intelligent and pleasing countenances." The women he judged to be "remarkably domestic and virtuous, exhibiting a strange contrast to those of Tahiti."[74]

[71] Wilkes Exploring Expedition, Navy Department, vol. 1, no. 52, Wilkes to Paulding, Oct. 24, 1839.
[72] Wilkes' *Narrative*, II, 65-69.   [73] *Ibid.*, p. 70.
[74] *Ibid.*, pp. 72-73.

THE SAMOAN ISLANDS

During their stay on the island of Tutuila the Americans examined the whole and surveyed the harbor. They found the climate of Tutuila mild and agreeable, particularly at Pago Pago.[75] The surveys on Tutuila completed on October 23, the *Vincennes* left Pago Pago for Apia on October 25, and found the *Peacock* already in the harbor.[76] Wilkes called upon the Rev. John Williams, the founder of the missionary work in Samoa of the London Missionary Society, the British vice consul, Mr. Cunningham, accompanying him to the missionary's cottage.[77]

While the *Vincennes'* officers and men were engaged in surveying Tutuila and Upolu, the *Porpoise* was at the island of Savaii for the same purpose.[78] In fact "every part of the coast of each of the eight islands," wrote Wilkes in a despatch to Paulding, "has been carefully examined. The charts we are now completing . . . will give our results, but owing to the necessary daily duties, are not yet completed, and will not be, in time to forward by this opportunity. Besides making the surveys, the scientific gentlemen and some officers have been sent over the different islands on excursions, by which I have obtained much valuable information relative to their inhabitants. The specimens in the various departments of science obtained, will be preserved and disposed of agreeably to your instructions."[79]

The expedition departed for Sydney on November 10, 1839. Sailing thence to the southward a considerable area of the Antarctic region was surveyed,[80] following which the ships returned to Sydney. New Zealand was later visited and then the Fijis, where commercial regulations

[75] *Ibid.*, p. 81.   [76] *Ibid.*, pp. 87-88.
[77] *Ibid.*, p. 92.   [78] *Ibid.*, p. 108.
[79] Wilkes Exploring Expedition, Navy Department, vol. 1, no. 54, Wilkes to Paulding, Apia, Nov. 9, 1839.
[80] It was at this time that Wilkes Land was discovered.

were agreed to between Wilkes and some Fijian chiefs. Other islands were surveyed and subsequently the expedition sailed for Hawaii. After a sojourn in that archipelago the ships sailed for the northwest coast of North America to survey portions of the Oregon territory.[81]

[81] For accounts of the stay in Samoan waters see despatches 52, 53, and 54, Wilkes to Paulding, in vol. 1 of Wilkes Exploring Expedition papers in archives of Navy Department. For a complete account of all the work of the expedition see volumes 1 to 5 of the *Narrative*, and volumes 6 to 17, 20, and 23 for scientific results. Volumes 18, 19, 21, and 22 were never published.

CHAPTER II

UNITED STATES CONSULAR RELATIONS
WITH SAMOA FROM 1839 TO 1876

ALTHOUGH American whalemen during the half century or more preceding the Civil War had made many contacts with the Samoan islands, and although naval officers such as Captain Wilkes, in exploring and surveying the islands, had acquired much information concerning them which proved of great value to American scientists, and aroused curiosity among the American people, no formal treaty was negotiated between the Samoan people and the United States until the late seventies.

The first representative of the United States in the Samoan group was an Englishman, John C. Williams by name, son of the first London Society missionary on those islands, John Williams. He was appointed acting consul by Captain Wilkes on November 4, 1839,[1] and served as consul, and later as commercial agent by appointment of the Department of State until 1850. In his report from Apia harbor to the secretary of the navy, Captain Wilkes explained that, "deeming it much to the interest to those engaged in the whale fishery" that the United States should have a consular representative at Apia, he had appointed "Jno. C. Williams, Esq., of this island, Acting U. S. Consul until the pleasure of the Government should be known." He added that Williams would "do much to facilitate the supplies required by whaling vessels, and prevent difficulties which occur between them

[1] Wilkes Exploring Expedition, Navy Department, vol. 1, no. 53, Wilkes to Paulding, Nov. 6, 1839, enclosure no. 2.

and the natives, also to prevent desertion and apprehend deserters, as this has become a great evil.''[2] Williams having accepted the appointment on the fifth,[3] Captain Wilkes brought him to a meeting of the chiefs, or *fono*, which had been arranged for the same day, in order to have him recognized by the Samoans as the legal representative of the United States. This recognition was freely given, and then the further business of the meeting was entered upon.[4]

The purpose of the meeting with the chiefs, in addition to securing recognition of Williams as consul, was to get the consent of the chiefs to a code of rules and regulations for the protection of the whalers while in port, and also to insure the natives against imposition. Such a code was considered and adopted by the chiefs, and immediately printed in both the Samoan and English languages so that copies could be furnished to the masters of vessels visiting the islands.[5]

The regulations consisted of sixteen articles. Foreign consuls "duly appointed and received in Samoa" should be "protected and respected." All foreign vessels putting into Samoan ports should likewise be protected. The fullest protection for foreign ships wrecked in the islands should be given, and the property of such vessels should not be stolen but turned over to the consul of the country to which they belonged. "Any person guilty of the crime of murder upon any foreigner," said the fourth article, "shall be given up without delay to the commander of any public vessel of the nation to which the deceased may belong, upon his demanding the same." A port charge of

[2] Wilkes Exploring Expedition, Navy Department, vol. 1, no. 53, Wilkes to Paulding, Nov. 6, 1839.
[3] *Ibid.*, enclosure no. 3, Williams to Wilkes, Nov. 5, 1839.
[4] Wilkes, *Narrative*, II, 102.
[5] Wilkes Exploring Expedition, Navy Department, vol. 1, no. 53, Wilkes to Paulding, Nov. 6, 1839; see also Wilkes, *Narrative*, II, 102-104.

EARLY CONSULAR RELATIONS 21

five dollars for anchorage and water was to be charged; also a charge of seven dollars for pilotage was allowed. Trading in spiritous liquors was forbidden. The apprehension of deserters from foreign vessels by natives was to be rewarded by the payment of five dollars to the individual apprehending the deserter and three dollars to the chief of the district in which the arrest occurred. The regulations were signed by seven chiefs and witnessed by Captain Wilkes, J. C. Williams, acting United States consul, and W. C. Cunningham, the British consul.[6] This was the first agreement ever adopted by a representative of the United States and Samoan chiefs, and from this event may be dated the official relations between Samoa and the United States.[7]

There was, to be sure, no Samoan government exercising authority over the whole group of islands, nor, perhaps, did the chiefs, who accepted the agreement, hold sway over the whole of the one island of Upolu; but, since the chiefs assembled were among the principal ones of the group, a step of the kind taken by them would go far to bring about order and protection for foreigners in Samoa, and at the same time protect the natives from too much imposition on the part of unprincipled whalers and beach combers.

Though Captain Wilkes' principal work was that of directing the exploration and surveying of various island groups, his instructions also called for the establishment of order, and the making of regulations as indicated above. Moreover, he was ordered to take certain punitive measures against natives guilty of cruelties against

[6] *Ibid.*

[7] The first port regulations drawn up by Europeans were those by Captain Drinkwater-Bethune of the English war vessel, *Conway*, together with Chief Pea of Apia harbor. These regulations were dated, January, 1838, almost two years before Wilkes' regulations.

American whalers. One such case in the Samoan group was that of one of the principal chiefs of the island of Savaii, named Popututu, who had "murdered a portion of the crew of a whale boat belonging to the American whale ship, *William Penn*,[8] several years since," and whom Captain Wilkes was extremely anxious to apprehend.[9] It was impossible, after an all-day conference with the chiefs, for Captain Wilkes to prevail upon them to aid him, they alleging that this would bring about civil war, the chief in question having many powerful connections. Although he landed a force on the island of Savaii, Captain Wilkes deemed it too hazardous to send his men into the chief's "native fastness in the mountains" to which he had fled upon learning of the approach of the American sailors.

Previous to Captain Wilkes' arrival in the port of Apia, Captain Hudson, of the *Peacock*, had arrested another native murderer, and the commander of the expedition determined to punish him by banishment upon a far away island, a penalty which was to the natives almost as severe as death. "These proceedings," concluded Captain Wilkes, "I have many assurances to believe, produced a most beneficial effect upon the chiefs and natives and I flatter myself that we have impressed them not only with our justice and desire to cultivate their goodwill and friendship, but at the same time showed them that the lives and property of our citizens are not to be taken or molested with impunity."

Captain Wilkes advised the natives to cultivate their rich soil and to raise live stock for supplying whaling vessels, since the central location of the islands and their

[8] Commanded by Captain Swain of Nantucket.
[9] Wilkes Exploring Expedition, Navy Department, vol. 1, no. 53, Wilkes to Paulding, Nov. 6, 1839.

abundant products, he thought, would make the Samoan group "a general resort for whale ships cruising in their vicinity." As a further sign of good-will, Captain Wilkes invited the chiefs of the Samoan group to visit his flagship, the *Vincennes,* while she was anchored in the harbor of Apia, and in the name of the president he distributed presents "as tokens of friendship."[10]

With the departure of the Wilkes Expedition from Apia, November 10,[11] the American official affairs on the islands were left in the hands of Williams, the acting consul. The confirmation of his appointment as consul did not eventuate. The Department of State seems never to have been informed of Wilkes' action, although the naval archives contain a copy of Wilkes' letter to Williams apprising him of his appointment and a copy of Williams' letter of acceptance as cited above. After an interval of several years, however, John C. Calhoun, secretary of state, wrote in November, 1844, to Williams informing him of his appointment by the president as "Commercial Agent of the United States for the Navigator's Islands," and enclosing among other items a blank bond, which he was instructed to execute and return to the department.[12] This letter was slow in reaching Williams, and since he continued to sign his communications as "U. S. Consul," James Buchanan, the then secretary of state, transmitted on February 19, 1847, duplicates of his predecessor's letter and enclosures,[13] and again wrote Williams on May 12, the same year,[14] which last communication was acknowledged by Williams in a despatch to the Department of State dated June 16, 1848,

[10] *Ibid.*
[11] *Ibid.,* no. 54, Wilkes to Paulding, Nov. 9, 1839.
[12] Instructions to Consuls, vol. 11, p. 307.
[13] I.C., vol. 11, p. 567, Buchanan to Williams, May 12, 1847.
[14] *Ibid.*

as having been received before the original letter of appointment dated November 19, 1844.[15]

As can be readily seen, there was no regular postal service between the United States and the Samoan islands, and consequently letters had to be entrusted to captains of whaling vessels or on rare occasions to captains of warships. As a result, communications were lost or at best delivered many months and sometimes several years after they were written. Therefore, almost nine years after his provisional appointment by Captain Wilkes as acting consul, Williams transmitted his acknowledgment of the receipt of information of his official appointment to office. This letter was sent by the *Henry Aster,* of Nantucket. Evidently the whale ship experienced favorable sailing weather, for the letter was received by the department on October 25, only four months and nine days after it was written.[16] Williams expressed disappointment at not being appointed consul with salary, and stated that if such an appointment could not be made the department could regard his letter as his resignation.[17] The last communication received from him and on file in the Department of State was one dated April 20, 1850, wherein he reported that two hurricanes had recently struck Apia harbor, destroying one English, one French, and two American ships.[18] Williams in all probability sailed for England in the same year.[19]

The first representative of the United States on the island of Tutuila of whom there is any record was Henry Gibbons, who was appointed by Williams to act as commercial agent there "till the pleasure of the United States Government is known."[20] Williams explained, in appris-

---

[15] C.D., Apia, vol. 1.
[16] *Ibid.*
[17] *Ibid.*
[18] *Ibid.*
[19] *Ibid.*, Williams, Jan. 15, 1850.
[20] *Ibid.*, Williams, no date, but probably Oct. 16, 1847, rec'd Feb. 26, 1848.

EARLY CONSULAR RELATIONS 25

ing the department of the appointment, that he had felt obliged to make it on account of the distance of Tutuila from Apia and because it was "frequented by vessels."[21]

With the departure of Williams from the islands, American interests fell into a chaotic state and upon repeated requests from captains of American vessels putting into the port of Apia, and from several residents, the British consular representative, George Pritchard, assumed the duties of representing the United States as well. When the U.S.S. *Falmouth* arrived Commander Pettigru gave him "a written appointment as Consul until the pleasure of the President be known."[22] Pritchard, of course, did not receive a regular appointment by the Department of State, but his bills of exchange, drawn for expenses incurred in giving relief to distressed American seamen, were honored, indicating that the department recognized him as a temporary representative.[23]

The first American citizen to be regularly appointed commercial agent of the United States to the Samoan group was a Virginian named V. P. Chapin, who at the time of his appointment was sojourning in Honolulu.[24] Secretary of State Edward Everett wrote Chapin a letter on February 19, 1853, enclosing a certificate of his appointment, the receipt of which letter Chapin acknowledged from Honolulu in April, adding that he intended to sail for the Samoan islands on or about May first.[25] Chapin arrived in Apia June 3, on board the Hawaiian schooner, *Laurita,* and on June 9 he had a meeting with

---

[21] *Ibid.*

[22] *Ibid.*, "George Pritchard, U. S. Consul," Feb. 26, 1851, rec'd March 9, 1852.

[23] *Ibid.*, Pritchard, April 12, 1852, Dec. 31, 1852, June 30, 1853.

[24] John C. Williams, the first appointee, never accepted his appointment as commercial agent, did not execute a bond, and was not an American citizen.

[25] C.D., Apia, vol. 1, Chapin, April 28, 1853, rec'd June 30, 1853.

the principal chiefs, called for the purpose of the chiefs' granting him the usual *exequatur* preparatory to his entering upon his duties.[26] In the same month Pritchard sent his last despatch, enclosing an account of expenses and stating that he had "delivered over to Mr. Chapin the Flag, Seal, and Official Documents in the Archives of the Consulate."[27]

Upon his arrival, Chapin found the islands in a state of war. There was "no King to rule them and no law to guide them." However, the prospects for trade were good, he thought, as the islands lay directly in line between San Francisco and Australia.[28] Chapin reported in October that the civil war was still going on and there was need of an American or English naval vessel for the protection of foreigners.[29] By the end of the year the war was so seriously interfering with trade that Chapin drew up jointly with the British consul, George Pritchard, a long protest addressed to the principal chiefs against native interference with trade.[30]

Chapin found it necessary to appoint a vice commercial agent at Pago Pago (Tutuila), and his choice fell upon the same man that Williams had appointed in 1847 namely, Henry Gibbons.[31] Chapin established a regular system of keeping records, and with his despatch dated December 31, 1853, were enclosed the first regular reports ever made to the Department of State by a United States representative stationed in Samoa.[32]

[26] C.D., Chapin, June 9, 1853, rec'd March 4, 1854.
[27] *Ibid.*, Pritchard, June 30, 1853, rec'd Nov. 18, 1853. Chapin acknowledged receipt of the property in a letter to the department Oct. 5, 1853.
[28] *Ibid.*, Chapin, June 9, 1853.
[29] *Ibid.*, Chapin, Oct. 5, 1853, rec'd March 6, 1854.
[30] *Ibid.*, Chapin, Dec. 31, 1853, rec'd June 10, 1854. Copy of protest was enclosed with the despatch.
[31] *Ibid.*, Chapin, Oct. 5, 1853, rec'd March 6, 1854.
[32] *Ibid.*, Chapin, Dec. 31, 1853, rec'd June 10, 1854.

No communication from Chapin after his reaching Samoa had been received by the department before a successor was determined upon. Whether this was due to a change in administration, which occurred two weeks after Chapin's appointment, or for other reasons, is not clear.[33] Dr. Aaron van Camp, who had visited the Samoan islands in 1852 as supercargo of the American ship *Orpheus,* of San Francisco, and who had returned to the United States some time in 1853, in all probability made overtures to the department for the post at Apia. Sometime in the latter part of the year he was appointed to succeed Chapin, and on February 16, 1854, he wrote the department from San Francisco that after two months delay he had succeeded in securing a "conveyance to the Islands." He would sail on February 25 on the clipper ship *Rover's Bride*.[34] He arrived in Apia April 12 and presented his orders to Chapin.[35]

Van Camp wrote three days later to the department that although he had reported to Chapin, the latter had refused to deliver the archives until he (van Camp) had been received by the authorities of the islands. Van Camp contended that "this was not necessary from the fact of there being no Government here. I might be received by one Chief, but that would cause jealousy with the others. In the Harbor of Apia there is [sic] five Towns and at least Twenty Chiefs, and all at war with each other." The point van Camp wanted to make was that in being recognized by one chief, he would be at that chief's mercy for the reason that he would want to collect the harbor dues

---

[33] Letter from Edward Everett enclosing certificate of appointment was dated February 19, 1853. Pierce succeeded Fillmore March 4, and the announcement of Marcy's appointment to succeed Everett as Secretary of State was dated March 9.

[34] C.D., Apia, vol. 1.

[35] *Ibid.,* van Camp, April 15, 1854, rec'd Feb. 25, 1855.

for himself.[36] In the month of May, van Camp appointed E. V. C. Ripley as vice commercial agent for Tutuila and the Manua islands,[37] and in July he appointed Elisha L. Hamilton as vice commercial agent for the island of Savaii.[38]

In reply to circular letters from the department respecting conditions in Samoa,[39] van Camp wrote "that the natives of these Islands being at war among themselves, they have not as yet got sufficiently far advanced in civilization to select one of their number as a ruler. They carry on no manufactures or commerce of any kind, their immediate wants for the most part are supplied by the hand of nature, with scarcely an effort at culture. The Samoan Islands are, and have for a number of years been a place of resort for whale ships (mostly American) which come here for the purpose of obtaining wood, water and recruits, such as yams, pigs and poultry, which are obtained in abundance, and for which they give in exchange common cloths, calicoes, axes, hatchets, muskets, powder in at from one to two hundred per cent advance upon home costs." Van Camp reported further that there were no duties or taxes of any kind and the only dues vessels of any nation had to pay was a so-called anchorage fee of six dollars and ten dollars for pilotage. The treaty which Commander Wilkes had negotiated with the principal native chiefs was being pretty generally carried out, van Camp thought. It was the only treaty with the Samoans at the time of writing.

There were very little circulating media among the natives, according to van Camp. The foreigners used mostly the coins of the United States, England, and France. There were five or six mercantile establishments in Sa-

---

[36] C.D.
[37] *Ibid.*, van Camp, May 20, 1854.
[38] *Ibid.*, van Camp, July 20, 1854, rec'd Feb. 27, 1855.
[39] Circular letters, dated Oct. 8, 1853 and March 15, 1854.

moa "through whom the business among the different Islands is carried on." Cocoanut oil was the principal export, most of it going to Sydney, New South Wales. Whalers' drafts sold at twenty-five per cent discount, while consular drafts were discounted thirty-five per cent. Sugar cane, tobacco, nutmegs, cotton, and indigo grew spontaneously on the islands, the report said further, and the native population was estimated at thirty-three thousand inhabitants, the greater portion of them being christianized. The foreign population on the islands was approximately two hundred, of which about fifty resided in Apia.[40]

In April, 1856, the U.S. frigate, *Independence,* Commodore Mervine commanding, anchored in Apia Harbor. Reports emanating from English missionary circles concerning the actions of the American naval officer and those of the American consul, suggest that considerable friction had appeared at the time between the English and American authorities. The Protestant missionary, A. W. Murray, felt constrained to write a letter to the editor of the *Sydney Morning Herald,* charging the two American officers with violating various clauses of Captain Wilkes' treaty, and with high-handed actions in general. Suddenly, in May, the *Independence* sailed away with van Camp on board.[41] But before van Camp left Apia he appointed his predecessor, Chapin, as vice consul during his absence, and in case of accident to Chapin, he also appointed Norman W. Stearns, another American, to act as vice consul.[42] Van Camp's sudden departure seems to have been in connection with his selling the cargo of the bark, *Elvira,* which it was alleged he had ille-

---

[40] C.D., Apia, vol. 1, van Camp, Oct. 1, 1855, rec'd Sept. 27, 1856.

[41] Letter appeared in the *Sydney Morning Herald,* Oct. 3, 1856. (See Consular Despatches, Apia, vol. 1.)

[42] C.D., Apia, vol. 1, van Camp, May 10, 1856, rec'd Dec. 29, 1856.

gally seized while she was bound from San Francisco to Melbourne.[43] Six days later, however, one Jonathan S. Jenkins arrived in Apia with a commission to succeed van Camp,[44] and the next day, May 17, Chapin, whom Jenkins reported as being in charge of the post, ceased his functions as vice consul.[45]

One of Jenkins' despatches reported that a meeting had been held in Apia—probably in August, 1856—at the suggestion of Captain Freemantle of the British man-of-war, *Juno,* to discuss the treaty negotiated by "Commodore Wilkes in 1839 with the people of this Island."[46] This treaty was the only code of rules existing between the Samoans and foreigners, and the British were interested in discussing the various clauses of these commercial regulations for Apia in order to come to some agreement as to which should still be enforced and which should be considered obsolete.

Jenkins left Samoa in December to go to Washington to explain his acts with reference to the property of van Camp, said to have been valued at $200,000, which, it was alleged, van Camp had gained by seizing ships and selling their cargoes. Jenkins left Robert S. Swanston in charge of the post as vice consul during what he supposed would be a temporary absence. The date of Swanston's commission was December 1.[47] Jenkins never returned to his post, tendering his resignation while in Washington the following June.[48] Swanston also sent in his resignation

[43] Claims against van Camp by a Boston firm are to be found in Consular Despatches, Apia, vol. 1.
[44] Jenkins was appointed in Dec. 1855. (See Instructions to Consuls, vol. 5, p. 250, to Jenkins, Dec. 31, 1855.)
[45] C.D., Apia, vol. 1, Jenkins, June 6, 1856.
[46] *Ibid.,* Jenkins, Aug. 15, 1856, rec'd April 6, 1857.
[47] *Ibid.,* Swanston, Dec. 24, 1856.
[48] *Ibid.,* Jenkins to Lewis Cass, dated Washington, June 26, 1857.

EARLY CONSULAR RELATIONS 31

the same month, stating that he wished to go to Sydney.[49] He did not leave Apia, however, until the latter part of August, turning the archives then over to Pritchard, the British acting consul, to be held by him until the arrival of a successor.[50]

During his short tenure of office, Swanston sent to the department some interesting reports. In April he requested advice concerning the half breeds on the islands, that is, "half caste children of American citizens and American negroes by Samoan women." He said there were a great number of these, many of them being "Samoan to all intents, in education and habits"; while others, again, were "comparatively civilized and follow the habits of the people of civilized nations." Questions involving the rights of the half-castes "either as Samoans or as Americans" would very probably arise "at no distant day" and he requested the department to advise him in the matter "in order that all doubts may be settled."[51] In reply to a despatch from Jenkins written in February, 1856,[52] inquiring whether the Act of Congress of August 11, 1848, granting certain judicial powers to consuls and ministers in China and Turkey, would include by implication Oceanica, the department wrote the following April that "the Act of Congress to which reference is made does not allude either in specific or general terms to the Islands in the Pacific ocean."[53] This reply inspired Swanston to write a long despatch describing the anomalous position of a consular officer in the Pacific who did not possess the judicial authority conferred upon his colleagues. "There is no law," he wrote, "and no Govern-

[49] *Ibid.*, Swanston, June 30, 1857, rec'd Jan. 18, 1858.
[50] *Ibid.*, Swanston, Aug. 22, 1857, rec'd May 14, 1858.
[51] *Ibid.*, Swanston, April 13, 1857, rec'd Nov. 6, 1857.
[52] *Ibid.*, Jenkins, Feb. 18, 1856.
[53] I.C., vol. 5, p. 303, to Jenkins, April 12, 1856.

ment, and no remedy for wrong to an American Citizen but in his Consul, . . .; he is *de facto* magistrate, and enshrouded with judicial authority; he is called upon to settle disputes, to preserve order, to enforce justice, and to compel recompense from the wrongdoer." Consular duties in Samoa also expanded "into the field of Diplomacy" since the consul "is called upon to communicate directly with the controlling power, such as it is, of the country where he resides, and with his own Government, on matters which would otherwise devolve on a Minister."[54]

James C. Dirickson, of Maryland, was appointed to succeed Jenkins as commercial agent at Apia, and in September received special instructions rendered advisable by the position of the port of Apia and the fact that the government or governments of Samoa were not recognized by the United States.[55] Dirickson sailed from New York, October 27, 1857, on the *Hellespont*,[56] arriving at Sydney February 28, 1858,[57] where he was detained for two months awaiting an opportunity to proceed to Apia.[58] Although he sailed from Sydney May 1, a month more elapsed before he reached Apia on June 2.[59]

When Dirickson was sent to Apia he was instructed to investigate the controversy between van Camp and Jenkins, and report his findings. He made the report after a twelve months' investigation and cleared van Camp of the charges, speaking of Jenkins as having "acted in a silly, ridiculous, absurd and totally illegal manner." Dirickson thought that van Camp and Chapin had lost from

[54] C.D., Apia, vol. 1, Swanston, April 20, 1857, rec'd Oct. 5, 1857.
[55] I.C., vol. 5, p. 546, to Dirickson, Sept. 25, 1857.
[56] C.D., Apia, vol. 1, Dirickson to Lewis Cass, dated New York, Oct. 25, 1857.
[57] *Ibid.*, Dirickson, dated Sydney, April 7, 1858.
[58] *Ibid.*, Dirickson, dated Sydney, April 29, 1858.
[59] *Ibid.*, Dirickson, dated Apia, June 4, 1858.

sixteen to eighteen thousand dollars by Jenkins' interference.[60]

Dirickson had been on the islands about eighteen months when he resigned on account of ill health. He appointed no temporary consul, but turned the consular property over to the British representative, John C. Williams.[61] Before sailing away on November 25, however, he thought it incumbent upon himself "to correct certain opinions . . . relative to the general character of the Foreign Residents at Apia, as given by my predecessor in office and by some of our Naval officers." Dirickson had "found them to be generally men possessing a liberal education, extremely courteous, and a sense of honor in their business transactions highly commendable, there being no law to enforce the collection of debt." His official career among them had been very pleasant and as proof of the kindly feelings entertained toward him by the residents, he reported that they had presented him with a purse of one hundred dollars on the eve of his departure, the committee signing the letter of presentation including his two colleagues, John C. Williams, British consul, and H. DeBois, Hawaiian consul.[62]

With the departure of Dirickson from Apia in November, 1859, there was no regularly appointed representative stationed in that port until the appointment of Jonas M. Coe, an American resident at Apia, as commercial agent, on March 9, 1864.[63] Samuel M. Wolfe, who was appointed November 2, 1860, to succeed Dirickson, was recalled before he could sail from New York.[64] Daniel

[60] *Ibid.*, Apia, vol. 2, Dirickson, July 1, 1859.
[61] *Ibid.*, Dirickson, Nov. 23, 1859.
[62] *Ibid.*, Dirickson, Nov. 25, 1859, rec'd April 5, 1860.
[63] Coe received his appointment on September 15. (See Consular Despatches, Apia, vol. 2, Coe, Sept. 15, 1864.)
[64] I.C., vol. 7, p. 41, to Wolfe, Feb. 1, 1861.

Ketchum, who was appointed March 25, 1861,[65] wrote no letters to the department, and the reason for his failure to sail is not clear. In his place Captain Edward Gardner was appointed January 15, 1862. He sailed for Samoa via Australia, but was lost in a shipwreck between the Fiji Islands and Samoa while on board a second ship, the *Martha,* out from Sydney. John C. Williams, acting consul, wrote on May 11, 1863, from Apia, that the ship was found water-logged and dismasted at one of the Friendly Islands.[66]

When Coe assumed the post at Apia in September, 1864,[67] the question of the status of the half-castes in Samoa—whether they were to be considered United States citizens or not—gave Coe trouble, and since the department had not replied to Swanston's request for instructions in the previous decade,[68] he had nothing in the consulate files to guide him in the matter. In February, 1867, however, the department supplied the want. Coe was referred to the Act of Congress approved February 10, 1855, which declared "that children born abroad of an American father are citizens of the United States"; and there was no limitation on this provision except "that 'the rights of citizenship shall not descend to persons whose fathers never resided in the United States.'" In other words the citizenship by inheritance enjoyed by the first generation could be retained for life notwithstanding a continued residence abroad, but such inheritance would not descend to the second generation.[69]

In the year 1866, Coe sent a long report[70] describing the political and social conditions in Samoa and stating his

[65] Bureau of Appointments, Department of State.
[66] C.D., Apia, vol. 2.   [67] *Ibid.,* Coe, Sept. 15, 1864.
[68] April 13, 1857.
[69] I.C., vol. 10, p. 63, F. W. Seward to Coe, Feb. 11, 1867.
[70] Virtually copied from Swanston's report of April 20, 1857, with modifications to bring it up to date.

position as commercial agent in relation to them. Lacking the powers granted by Congress to American consular representatives in China and Turkey by the Act of August 11, 1848, he regarded himself as quite helpless.[71] Since the days of Jenkins' and Swanston's appeals for advice in juridical matters, however, an act had been passed by Congress which somewhat clarified the situation of consuls in uncivilized countries and islands; but there is no record that the department sent any instructions concerning the matter to Coe. In "an Act to carry into effect provisions of the treaties between the United States, China, Japan, Siam, Persia, and other countries, giving certain judicial powers to the Ministers and Consuls of the United States in those countries,"[72] there was included a section, which granted certain powers to "consuls and commercial agents of the United States at islands or in countries not inhabited by any civilized people, or recognized by any treaty with the United States." Consuls and commercial agents at such islands or in such countries were "authorized to try, hear, and determine all cases in regard to civil rights, whether of person or property, where the real debt and damages do not exceed the sum of one thousand dollars, exclusive of costs, and upon full hearing of the allegations and evidence of both parties to give judgment according to the laws of the United States and according to the equity and right of the matter in the same manner as justices of the peace are now authorized and empowered where the United States have exclusive jurisdiction. And the said consuls

---

[71] The act referred to is "An Act to carry into effect certain provisions in the Treaties between the United States and China and the Ottoman Porte, giving certain judicial powers to Ministers and Consuls of the United States in those countries." (See United States *Statutes at Large*, 9, ch. CL, pp. 276 to 280.)

[72] United States *Statutes at Large* (1859-1865), 12, ch. CLXXIX, pp. 72 to 79 (Approved June 22, 1860.)

and commercial agents, respectively, are hereby invested with the powers conferred by the provisions of the seventh and eighth sections of this act for trial of offences or misdemeanors."[73]

Section number seven authorized a consul or consular agent "upon facts within his own knowledge, or which he has good reason to believe true, or upon complaint made, or information filed in writing . . . to issue his warrant for the arrest of any citizen of the United States charged with committing in the country an offence against law; and when arrested, to arraign and try any such offender; and upon conviction, to sentence him to punishment in the manner herein prescribed; always meting out punishment in a manner proportioned to the offence; which punishment shall, in all cases, except as is herein otherwise provided, be either fine or imprisonment."[74]

Section number eight provided "that any consul, when sitting alone for the trial of offences, or misdemeanors, shall finally decide all cases where the fine imposed does not exceed one hundred dollars, or the term of imprisonment does not exceed sixty days. And there shall be no appeal therefrom except as provided in section eleven of this Act. But no fine imposed by a Consul for a contempt committed in the presence of the Court, or for failing to obey a summons from the same, shall exceed fifty dollars, nor shall the imprisonment exceed twenty-four hours for the same contempt."[75]

In ignorance of the statute of 1860, or because it lacked "teeth" in the face of the elemental passions of South Sea islanders, Coe, like Swanston before him, participated in several cases as a judge in the Court of Foreign Residents without any authority from the department to

[73] United States *Statutes at Large* (1859-1865), 12, ch. CLXXIX, section 30, pp. 78 and 79.
[74] *Ibid.*, section 7, p. 74.   [75] *Ibid.*, section 8, p. 74.

do so. He did this in coöperation with his colleagues, John C. Williams and Theodor Weber, Hamburg consul, and the arrangement seemed to work well although in one case Coe felt constrained to take exception to a severe sentence on an American citizen.

In the report alluded to above Coe transmitted a list of documents which covered cases upon which he desired advice. The documents are given in outline to indicate the complications always confronting a consular officer where foreigners of various nations are intermingled among a native and barbarous population.[76] The question always arose as to the limits of the respective jurisdictions of the various powers. If an American murdered an Englishman, who should try the case, the British consul or the American representative, or should the consuls coöperate in such a case by bringing it before the Court of Foreign Residents of Samoa? But in the latter situation the American representative would get "entangled" with the representatives of other powers, and this would be contrary to a historic policy of the United States.

Cases on which Coe desired advice involved, for example, an American negro citizen, who had been tried at the British consulate by the Court of Foreign Residents; a complaint of an American citizen against a British subject for debt; a complaint of a German subject against an American citizen for debt; a complaint of a German subject against an American citizen for murderous assault; and various letters of complaints against Samoans by American citizens and *vice versa*. The advice from the department in such cases as these would enable Coe, so he wrote to Washington, "to act unhesitatingly in whatever situation the anomalous state of society existing on these Islands may place me, either as towards Samoans,

[76] C.D., Apia, vol. 2, Coe to Wm. H. Seward, Nov. 15, 1866, rec'd March 23, 1867.

American citizens, or foreigners, resident on these Islands.'"[77]

In the absence of any power to take punitive measures against American criminals and to prevail upon the chiefs to punish Samoans for criminal attacks upon Americans, the only alternative was to have American ships of war visit the islands from time to time to back up the consul. Writing in 1869, Coe declared that no American warship had put in at Apia in thirteen years,[78] and the natives and American beach combers in Samoa had consequently lost all respect for the rights of American citizens. He requested, therefore, that a national vessel be sent to Apia immediately to protect American interests.[79] On September 14, the department informed Coe that the U.S.S. *Jamestown* had sailed for his port on August 21.[80]

Meanwhile, the U.S.S. *Kearsarge* had visited the port of Apia from the fifth to the eleventh of July, while bound for the Friendly Islands and Fiji Islands, but since Commander Thornton had no instructions even to visit Samoa, much less special instructions to investigate matters in connection with the commercial agency at Apia, "he declined entering into any complaints that I might lay before him," wrote Coe on August 1st. The consequence of the visit of the *Kearsarge,* therefore, was that less respect than ever would be "shown by the Samoans to the flag and the rights of American citizens. . . ." There being no system of government or laws on the islands, "the only redress an American citizen can receive for damages to person and property is through the United

---

[77] C.D.

[78] Coe refers to the visit of the frigate, *Independence*, commanded by Commodore Mervine, which anchored in Apia harbor in April, 1856, remaining until the tenth of the following month. See p. 29.

[79] C.D., Apia, vol. 3, Coe, Jan. 25, 1869.   [80] I.C., vol. 12, p. 491.

States Commercial Agency at this port," but since "the representative of the United States occupying the office as commercial agent without judicial powers is unable through the chiefs or so-called authorities to recover damage inflicted on the person and property of an American citizen, then he must await the arrival of a U. S. ship of war, and if nothing then is done for the protection of American interests at these Islands, the flag of the United States will always be disrespected and the rights of American citizens abused."[81] Coe thought, however, that if Commander Thornton had had authority to stop at Apia for the purpose of investigating cases he would have done so. But the situation was serious and by way of illustration Coe related an incident occurring after the departure of the *Kearsarge*. He wrote: "Two boats belonging to an American whaler, the *Emma C. Jones,* of New Bedford, at anchor in this harbor, were sent by the Captain to a distant part of this Island [Upolu] to trade for native provision for the ship's use, [and] were attacked by the Samoans numbering upwards of fifty men in a canoe." The boats were plundered and somewhat damaged, and the trading master, who was an American citizen and a resident of Apia, and who had been employed by the captain of the whaler, was taken by force out of his boat and compelled to go ashore where he was cruelly beaten and detained twenty-four hours before being released. The American representative addressed the chiefs a letter concerning the attack, but they took no notice of it, and of course, with no power to enforce obedience, this case like so many before it, could only be filed in the consulate in the hope that another warship would come along and render assistance to the commercial agent. "This critical state of affairs in the Navigator's

[81] C.D., Apia, vol. 3.

Islands is for many reasons damaging to American trading interests, from it results a feeling of insecurity to person and property, which cramps operations of all kinds and is an obstacle in the way of increasing the facilities whereby our whaling fleet in these seas may be accommodated on their arrival here during the season."

Coe reported further that the islands were in a "complete state of anarchy" and that civil war had at last broken out among the Samoans "much to the disadvantage of agriculture and commerce." It is well to state at this point that the war referred to continued until a truce was effected in 1872, and was the cause of much of the misery which existed in Samoa later. The alienation of much of the land to Germans, Englishmen, and Americans occurred during this war when, for spiritous liquor and for firearms, the Samoans sold their patrimony without realizing the consequences.

Coe was succeeded by S. S. Foster as the chief American representative in the Samoan islands in the early part of the year 1875. Foster's first published report is dated February 28, 1876. In it he discussed the disadvantages under which American trade suffered in competition with that of the Germans and the British. For one thing the latter could more easily finance their undertakings than the Americans, for, although they could borrow money at the rate of three to four per cent, money on the Pacific coast could only be had at ten per cent on good security. The system of long time credits with the Germans and British was more suitable for the bartering business which the ships were engaged in as they went from island to island to pick up their produce. From one to two years were required for a turnover among the Germans and British but their business nevertheless proved profitable on account of their financing. American firms on the other hand demanded payment for goods on the basis of from thirty to ninety days, whereupon interest would be charged upon the unpaid bills. In the third place, the German and British merchants had from long experience learned to supply the islanders with goods that suited their peculiar wants and tastes. Even American traders in the islands found it more profitable to go to the British colonies rather than to the Pacific coast for many of their supplies although the former could not compete with America in lumber and certain kinds of provisions. The fourth reason given by Foster, showing the advantage enjoyed by German and British manufacturers over American in the Samoan market, was the system of bonded goods established by the former. "The trader in the colonies," said Foster, "can pick out parts of packages or patterns of printed cloth to suit him in a wholesale house, and is entitled to a drawback equal to the amount of duties paid, whereas in the United States he must take a whole bale or package, when frequently, through dull colors or bad patterns, one half of the bale is unsalable, thus reducing his profits." The fifth reason for the slackness in American trade was the fact that there was no good market in the United States for copra and cocoanut oil.[82]

[82] H. Ex. Doc. no. 166, 44 Congress, 1 session, pp. 1158-1160.

CHAPTER III

COMMANDER MEADE'S TREATY OF 1872

BEGINNING with Grant's first administration, American governmental activities in the Pacific area, aside from cruises of naval vessels, manifested themselves in several ways, and but for the refusal of Congress to support the president's well-known policy of insular expansion, these activities might have become at that early date even more varied and pronounced.

Just as the Johnson administration was closing, Congress had been prevailed upon to pass an act for the deepening of a harbor in the Midway Islands "to afford a safe rendezvous and port of refuge and resort for the naval and merchant vessels of the United States."[1] A contract for the execution of this work was made in September, 1869, and one of the vessels of the Pacific Fleet, the *Saginaw*, was detailed to aid the contractor by making the necessary surveys.[2] Interest in an Isthmian canal was likewise manifest during Grant's administration. Already in his first report, the secretary of the navy outlined a plan for surveying various routes, and in a subsequent communication to the president he reported that three suggested routes for a canal had been explored and surveyed, but found impracticable.[3] But another expedition, he wrote, had been organized under the provisions of the Act of Congress and it was on its way to survey the so-called Tehuantepec route.[4]

[1] H. Ex. Doc. no. 1, part 3, 41 Congress, 3 session, vol. 3, p. 8, report by Geo. M. Robeson, Dec. 1, 1870.
[2] *Ibid.*   [3] *Ibid.*, p. 9.   [4] *Ibid.*, p. 10.

No canal was dug at this time and work on the Midway Islands project was suspended for lack of sufficient appropriations.[5] A careful perusal of reports of the several secretaries of the navy during the eighteen seventies, eighties, and nineties, however, reveals an ever-recurring concern about American rights along trade routes and a particular interest in our securing control of a base in Hawaii in the North Pacific and also a base in Samoa in connection with the contemplated Isthmian canal and the route to the South Pacific. Hawaii, the Isthmian canal, the Midway Islands, and Samoa were, therefore, closely interrelated in the minds of naval men in Grant's administration, and as a consequence, naval officers acted in various capacities, as surveying officers, diplomats, and treaty makers as well as protectors of our commercial and missionary interests in the Pacific.

This activity is all the more remarkable in view of the apparent apathy on the part of the American people in the matter of foreign affairs and especially with respect to the navy. Reflecting this unconcern for our defense on the high seas, the appropriations by Congress for the navy were constantly declining when Grant took office, a policy which was bound "gradually but surely [to] destroy the navy," as Grant wrote in his annual message to Congress in December, 1870. "It can hardly be wise statesmanship," he added, "in a government which represents a country with over four thousand miles of coastline on both oceans, exclusive of Alaska, and containing forty millions of progressive people, with relations of every nature with almost every foreign country, to rest with such inadequate means of enforcing any foreign policy either of protection or redress. Separated by the ocean from the nations of the Eastern Continent, our

[5] H. Ex. Doc. no. 1, part 3, 42 Congress, 2 session, p. 6, report by Geo. M. Robeson, Nov. 25, 1871.

navy is our only means of direct protection to our citizens abroad, or for the enforcement of any foreign policy.'"6

With respect to the Samoan islands, in particular, it may be said that they came within the field of American diplomatic relations for the first time in 1871. American consular representatives, as we have seen, had had official relations, to be sure, with so-called governments of the islands ever since the middle of the century, and had also coöperated with other consular representatives in joint communications and relationships with the Samoan authorities, but at no time prior to 1871 had the United States been in any way concerned with the political destinies of the archipelago. Then, suddenly, the strategic situation of the islands, as well as their commercial resources, attracted the attention of two groups of Americans, and, simultaneously, the interest of the Department of State in Samoa as a field for diplomatic action may be said to have begun.

One of the groups of Americans which became attracted to Samoa was some land speculators in California. Interested only in profits from lands acquired very often in exchange for firearms and intoxicating liquors, their connection with Samoa and its people produced only baneful results. Many a despatch from American consular representatives at Apia during subsequent years bore testimony of difficulties confronting them on account of these speculators, and at least one of the consuls became corrupted by the ever present possibility of reaping a profit from the iniquitous traffic.

The other group interested in Samoa was headed by the well-known shipbuilder, William H. Webb, of New York City. Webb had built ships since the early years of

6 H. Ex. Doc. no. 1, part 1, 41 Congress, 3 session, vol. 1, p. 16, President Grant to Congress, Dec. 5, 1870.

the eighteen fifties, and during the Civil War he constructed ironclads for the Federal government. One of these vessels, the *Dunderberg,* not being completed before the close of the war, was resold to Webb in 1867 for over one million dollars, the amount which the government had advanced to him on contract.[7] During the war Webb was also interested in the guano business in the Pacific and as a consequence, his attention was later attracted to the possibilities of various trade routes to that ocean, especially across the Central American states. From 1866 onward Webb was president of the Central American Transit Company with a capitalization of $3,000,000. At the same time he was also president of the North American Steamship Company, capitalized at $1,100,000.[8] In 1870 Webb proposed to establish a steamship line between San Francisco and Australia, via Honolulu.

The age of the commercial steamship was just dawning on the Pacific, and Webb was among the first to realize the possibilities of regular steamship service for freight and passengers on that great ocean. Whereas previously only the whaler and clipper ship had maintained sporadic and infrequent communications between the United States and the Pacific world, Webb visualized the day when steamship lines would connect with most of the islands, and when the east coast of the United States through the proposed Isthmian canal, as well as the west coast, would benefit greatly by the trade that was sure to develop. But not only the United States wanted closer communications; Hawaii, and particularly the communities in Australia, were anxious to secure better and more regular markets for their products. Moreover, the postal service,

[7] *Ibid.,* no. 1, 40 Congress, 2 session, p. 20, report by Gideon Welles for the year 1867.

[8] Trow's *New York Directory* for the years 1852 to 1871, in The New York Public Library.

especially between Australia, New Zealand, and England needed decided improvement. With the completion of the transcontinental railway in the United States, it was seen that this service could be speeded up considerably if a regular steamship line between San Francisco and Auckland and Sydney were established. It was estimated that the service by this route would be faster by two weeks than that via the Cape of Good Hope or the Isthmus of Suez. The New Zealand government in particular was anxious to have the service, and when it was learned in 1870 that Webb was planning the establishment of such a line, that government immediately offered him a subsidy. Webb, however, preferred to have the subsidy come from the government of the United States, and an application for such aid was made by him to the forty-first Congress, meeting in its third session in December, 1870.[9]

The field in the Pacific was not entirely clear for Webb. An English line of steamships had already been established in 1870. It made monthly calls at Honolulu to the "great benefit" of the commerce of the kingdom of Hawaii, as the United States minister resident, Henry A. Peirce, reported to the secretary of state in December of that year. Good markets for Hawaiian sugar and other products had thus been secured, he said, and he thought Americans might have a share in the new development. Peirce, therefore, sent Hamilton Fish data in relation to the commercial possibilities between the Hawaiian Islands and Australasia, concluding his despatch by urging that the United States "grant immediately" a subsidy for the proposed line of W. H. Webb to run to and from San Francisco and Australia via Honolulu.[10]

[9] H. Ex. Doc. no. 1, part 4, 42 Congress, 2 session, pp. 13 and 14, report by the Postmaster-General, Nov. 18, 1871.
[10] Despatches, Hawaii, vol. 13, no. 92, Peirce to Fish, Dec. 21, 1870, rec'd Jan. 18, 1871.

That the Department of State was sympathetic toward Webb's venture is clear from the correspondence that passed between Washington and New York. In January, 1871, Hamilton Fish forwarded to Webb[11] an extract from the despatch by Peirce referred to, and Webb immediately replied that he proposed "to request some Senator to ask for any information which the Department has on this subject, with a view to its use in the forthcoming debate in the Senate next Friday."[12] The "forthcoming debate" to which Webb made reference, was to be on four ship-subsidy bills, including Senate Bill no. 1196.

The bill had been reported favorably from the Committee on Post Offices and Post Roads on January 12 by Senator Ramsey of Minnesota, and on the 19th it had been made special order together with three other ship-subsidy bills for Friday, January 27. This was the day on which Webb expected the debate to occur, but when the time arrived, Ramsey failed to insist strongly on the maintenance of the special order, and the four bills lost their privileged position on the calendar. No further action was taken on Senate Bill no. 1196 before the adjournment of Congress.[13] Only one of the other bills was passed by the Senate and even this bill failed to pass in the House, the attitude of Congress toward such legislation being typical of its reticence to embark on any policy that might lead in the direction of expansion beyond the continental territory of the United States. Although attempts to secure a subsidy from the United States government were not immediately abandoned, Webb now turned to the government of New Zealand with favorable

[11] Domestic Letters, Department of State, vol. 88, Fish to Webb, Jan. 20, 1871.

[12] Miscellaneous Letters, Department of State, Webb to Davis, Jan. 21, 1871.

[13] *Congressional Globe*, Senate for Jan. 12, 19, and 27, 1871.

results. The subsidy from that source, while not very large, encouraged the promoters, and the line was started in 1871. Mails were carried regularly every four weeks thereafter between San Francisco, New Zealand, and Australia, via Hawaii.[14]

With the support of the administration, especially the president, the secretary of the navy, and the postmaster-general, Webb and his partners hoped that Congress would eventually follow the example of New Zealand. In referring to the failure of the forty-first Congress to grant the aid at its last session, and in recommending that the subsidy be voted in the opening session of the new Congress, the postmaster-general in his annual report to the president for 1871 said: "A large portion of the heavy traffic and travel between Europe and Australia, which has heretofore taken the routes via Suez and the Cape of Good Hope, will be transferred to the American route via San Francisco, if reliable and rapid steam communication shall be permanently established between that port and the countries of Australasia. Already, since the inauguration of direct steamship service from San Francisco, heavy English mails are being transported across our continent to and from New Zealand and the Australian colonies, the time occupied in their conveyance to destination being less by nearly two weeks than by the Suez route. As manifest considerations of public policy and commercial advantage make it desirable to sustain a first-class line of American steamships upon this route, the question of uniting with the Australian colonies in the support of the existing service by a moderate money subsidy is respectfully submitted to Congress for its consideration and appropriate action."[15]

[14] H. Ex. Doc. no. 1, part 4, 42 Congress, 2 session, pp. 13 and 14, report by the Postmaster-General, Nov. 18, 1871.
[15] *Ibid.*

The recommendation was renewed by the postmaster-general the next year and supported by the president in his annual message.[16] The forty-second Congress, however, showed no greater desire to assist the project than its predecessor, and nothing came of the attempt to secure a subsidy.

Following the appointment of Peirce as minister resident to Hawaii, American interests in the North and South Pacific were cared for with more diligence than before.[17] American expansion in the Pacific seems to have been given a decided impetus by his despatches to the State Department and in his relations with the naval officers on the Pacific Station. On August 5, 1869, he reported having been verbally informed by the Hawaiian minister of foreign affairs "of the intention of the British Government to despatch within a few months a flying or practice squadron of seven vessels of war to touch at this [Honolulu] and other ports on its voyage of circumnavigation around the world."[18] This led Peirce to urge the importance of stationing one of the United States vessels of war at Honolulu for the protection and assistance of American commerce, "especially during the fall, winter, and spring months of the year, when our whaling fleet visits here for supplies and for shipment of their fishery products to the Atlantic ports of the U. States."[19] American naval protection among the islands of the Pacific and a survey of Micronesia was suggested by Peirce the next month[20] and in November of the same year the minister informed Fish that he had had "much conversa-

[16] H. Ex. Doc. no. 1, part 1, 42 Congress, 3 session, p. 17.
[17] Appointed in 1869.
[18] Despatches, Hawaii, vol. 12, no. 9, Peirce to Fish, Aug. 5, 1869, rec'd Aug. 28.
[19] Ibid.
[20] Ibid., despatches nos. 15 and 16, Peirce to Fish, Sept. 11, 1869.

50 UNITED STATES POLICY IN SAMOA

tion" with Admiral Turner[21] with respect to the survey and had "written to him a despatch of twelve pages, accompanied with much manuscript and printed information."[22]

As early as February, 1871, Peirce broached the subject of American annexation of the Hawaiian Islands.[23] Although Fish stated in reply "that it is not unlikely that the President may consult the Senate upon the subject," he was very cautious in making any predictions as to the outcome.[24] In this same year, as was noted, the American line of steamers from San Francisco to Australia via Honolulu was started,[25] and Webb, being desirous of securing a place in the South Pacific in the direct line between Honolulu and Australia where his ships could stop and take coal,[26] instructed an agent, Captain E. Wakeman by name, to visit the Samoan islands, among other duties, and report upon the harbor facilities and the trade possibilities of that archipelago.[27] Pursuant to his instructions, Captain Wakeman left Honolulu on July 20, 1871, on board the mail steamer *Nevada,* arriving in Pago Pago harbor on August 9. "At daylight," he wrote to Webb, "I found myself in the most perfectly land-locked harbor that exists in the Pacific Ocean";[28] and after giving a long description of the harbor, its surroundings, and

[21] When the North Pacific and South Pacific squadrons were united on June 28, 1869, as the Pacific Fleet, Rear Admiral Thomas Turner was placed in command with Commodores Taylor and McDougal commanding the respective divisions. (H. Ex. Doc. no. 1, 41 Congress, 2 session, p. 4.)

[22] Despatches, Hawaii, vol. 12, no. 27, Peirce to Fish, Nov. 26, 1869, rec'd Dec. 17.

[23] *Ibid.*, vol. 13, no. 101, Peirce to Fish, Feb. 25, 1871, rec'd Mar. 20.

[24] Instructions, Hawaii, vol. 2, p. 212, no. 41, Fish to Peirce, April 5, 1871.

[25] United States, New Zealand and Australia Mail Steamship Line.

[26] Henry Erben: "The *Tuscarora's* Mission to Samoa," *Century Magazine,* May, 1889, p. 35.

[27] H. Ex. Doc. no. 161, 44 Congress, 1 session, p. 7, encl. with encl. no. 4.

[28] *Ibid.*

COMMANDER MEADE'S TREATY, 1872   51

the products of Tutuila, Wakeman continued: "There is nothing to prevent a steamer, night or day, from proceeding to her wharf." The agent remained at Pago Pago or in its vicinity for some six days. "Two places," he wrote, "have been secured in the bay of Pago Pago for your ships, the best that could be selected."[29]

On August 17 Wakeman left Pago Pago on board the brig, *L. P. Foster,* for the island of Upolu, arriving in Apia harbor the next day, where he found the United States sloop-of-war, *St. Mary's,* anchored.[30] In Apia Wakeman "called on Mr. Weber[31] and delivered my letters, and found them a Hamburg house of fifteen years' standing." Wakeman found that Weber had in port "two large ships . . . 800 tons each; one nearly loaded" while the other ships would "follow in a few months." The company had four large schooners, which traded "among the various islands down on the equator, and bring their cargoes here, where they are received by the large ships and dispatched for Hamburg." The cargoes consisted chiefly of copra.[32] Wakeman also gave descriptions of the islands of Upolu, Savaii, Rose, and Tau. He was equally enthusiastic concerning Upolu as about Tutuila.

The possibility of a naval station and a coaling station for steamers under the American flag and of even an American protectorate over the Samoan islands did not escape the attention of the vigilant agent. Moreover, the Europeans upon the island of Upolu appeared to be "all in favor of having American law established over the islands." There was a note of urgency in Wakeman's comments. He reported that "Mr. Weber has written some things since to the German government to establish a

---
[29] *Ibid.,* p. 8.   [30] *Ibid.,* p. 9.
[31] Manager of the Godeffroy company, and consul of the North German Confederation until 1871; and subsequently consul of the German Empire.
[32] H. Ex. Doc. no. 161, 44 Congress, 1 session, p. 9, encl. with encl. no. 4.

naval station with a view to a protectorate.'"[33] The Weber recommendation had not been made until after Wakeman's thorough survey in August, 1871, of the commercial possibilities of the Samoan islands, including his examination of the harbor of Pago Pago as a possible place of call for Webb's steamships. Wakeman's report to his employer was dated "At Sea," September 20, 1871. Webb forwarded from his New York office a copy of it to the Navy Department and that department in turn sent it to the Department of State on May 16, 1872.[34] But the latter department had long before been apprised of what Weber was doing or saying in Apia by the United States commercial agent stationed there, Jonas M. Coe, and consequently the chief value of Wakeman's report for the State Department lay in its description of the islands and the attitude of the foreigners in Samoa toward an American protectorate. Wakeman's reference to Weber's plans was merely corroborative of Coe's despatch. It is well, however, to keep Wakeman's information in mind, for upon the basis of his assertions after his arrival in Honolulu, the American minister resident and the naval authorities there subsequently became engaged in certain important activities in relation to Samoa about which more will be said later.

Coe's despatch, dated August 30, had been received by the department as early as October 18. It read as follows: "I have the honor to inform the Department of State that the Consul of the North German Confederation at this port has stated to me of late in confidence (not officially) it is the intention of his Government to lay claim to this Group of Islands for the purpose of having

[33] H. Ex. Doc. no. 161, 44 Congress, 1 session, p. 10.
[34] Executive Letter Book, No. 25, Navy Department, p. 371, Geo. M. Robeson to Hamilton Fish; H. Ex. Doc. no. 161, 44 Congress, 1 session, p. 7, encl. with encl. 4.

a naval station in the Pacific Ocean and he stated to me that he is expecting a steamship of war out from Germany yet this year to explore and examine the harbors at this group. Although the foregoing information has been related to me in confidence, I consider it my duty to acquaint my government of the same.''[35] That the despatch gave the Department of State some concern is clear from the fact that a copy of Coe's despatch was sent to George Bancroft, the American minister to Germany for his information,[36] which elicited the reply from Bancroft that he did not consider the rumor of the acquisition of the Samoan islands by Germany as having any foundation for the reason that the policy of Germany was adverse to colonial possessions.[37] Some ten days later Bancroft stated definitely that Germany did not contemplate the acquisition of the islands,[38] and since we had made inquiries through Bancroft in relation to Germany's alleged ambitions in other directions as well, especially with regard to the purchase by Germany of Samaná Bay from Santo Domingo and the cession of Curaçao in the Dutch West Indies to Germany by the Netherlands, Bancroft wrote the department on December 4 that the German minister at Washington would be instructed to give assurance of the falsity of rumors concerning the acquisition of colonial possessions by Germany.[39] But the department was not satisfied with Bancroft's replies concerning Samoa and on January 8 sent him another instruction saying that it might be well to make further inquiries relative to the reported annexation of the is-

[35] C.D., Apia, vol. 3, Coe, Aug. 30, 1871.
[36] Instructions, Germany, vol. 15, p. 286, no. 399 to George Bancroft, Oct. 30, 1871.
[37] Despatches, Germany, vol. 11, no. 297, Bancroft, Nov. 18, 1871.
[38] *Ibid.*, no. 300, Bancroft, Nov. 29, 1871.
[39] *Ibid.*, no. 304, Bancroft, Dec. 4, 1871.

lands.⁴⁰ Bancroft replied in March that Germany had made an emphatic denial of any desire for colonial possessions⁴¹ and in July another despatch from Bancroft reiterated that Germany did not desire the acquisition of Samoa.⁴²

So the German Empire was hardly born before an expanding America became apprehensive of the Reich's territorial ambitions. Such fears were to be expected in the Caribbean Sea where German annexation of Samaná Bay, St. Thomas, or Curaçao would have meant a distinct thrust at the Monroe Doctrine, but that the Department of State should have betrayed a similar apprehension concerning Germany's intentions in Samoa was a curious development at this early date. But Bancroft was right. Not until 1884 did Bismarck reverse his position relative to German colonies.

The rumor is easily explained by the fact that the German consul's wish was father to his thought of a German protectorate. As the chief representative of the largest foreign interests in the South Seas, the firm of Godeffroy and Son of Hamburg, as well as the representative of the German Reich, he repeatedly urged German protection or annexation in later years. Perhaps he spoke to Coe in order to impress the American commercial agent with the primacy of German claims in Samoa, and also, perhaps, with a view to discouraging any attempts on the part of Americans to secure the annexation of the islands by the United States. The new American line via Hawaii and Samoa meant competition with the German interests. If Captain Wakeman's report were true, moreover, the foreign elements on the island of Upolu were, in the same year that Weber spoke of a German annexation, already

⁴⁰ Instructions, Germany, vol. 15, p. 303, no. 424 to Bancroft, Jan. 8, 1872.
⁴¹ Despatches, Germany, vol. 11, no. 337, Bancroft, March 4, 1872.
⁴² *Ibid.*, no. 386, Bancroft, July 29, 1872.

wishing for American protection. This consideration may have influenced Weber. In any case, here were the representatives of two firms, one a German and the other an American, almost simultaneously suggesting protectorates over Samoa by their respective governments. Without any calculation or deliberation on the part of either government, seeds of future trouble were being sown. The flag of the newly established German Reich met that of the United States in trade rivalry and diplomatic complications first in Samoa, and it can hardly be doubted that Weber's and Wakeman's suggestions for protectorates marked the beginning of the development. As if to clinch his suggestion, Wakeman wrote: "I conclude my limited remarks in regard to the island of Upolu by saying that I know of no other island with the same form of government which all the chiefs are willing and desirous of ceding to the Americans, which would in that event be so valuable. From its commanding position in mid-Pacific, with the control of the commerce of all the islands which are contiguous to this point, with Australia and New Zealand at their door to supply with sugar, coffee, &c., no other group affords equal facility for a naval station as well as a coaling depot for steamers, with a most brilliant future for a most lucrative and extensive commercial enterprise."[43]

At this time Rear Admiral Winslow was in command of the Pacific Fleet, and in pursuance of general instructions, that American commerce and interests among the islands be examined and protected, three ships on the Pacific Station cruised extensively in 1870 and 1871.[44] One of

[43] H. Ex. Doc. no. 161, p. 10, as above.

[44] The demands upon the fleet necessitated the crossing of the limits of the station to reach the Caroline, Kingsmill, and Marshall islands, and on March 7, the Admiral wrote the department that since these islands were "not within the limits of the Pacific Fleet, as marked on the Squadron Chart furnished me by the Bureau of Navigation, I would request to be in-

these ships, the *Narragansett*, by November, 1871, was refitting at the Mare Island Navy Yard, and on the 28th of the month she sailed under the command of Commander Richard W. Meade from San Francisco with the flagship *California* for Honolulu. The admiral wrote the Navy Department from Honolulu on Christmas Eve[45] that the *California* would remain there "for a few days" and then would "sail for Valparaiso, Chile, touching at Tahiti en route," while the *Narragansett* would be directed "to cruise among the Marshall, Phoenix, and other groups of Islands, and thence to Talcahuano, Chile, via Sydney and Auckland."[46] On the fourth of January following, Secretary Robeson telegraphed the commandant of the Mare Island Navy Yard, Commodore E. G. Parrott, to transmit by steamer to Honolulu the following order to Admiral Winslow: "On leaving Sandwich Islands, proceed, direct, to Panama."[47] The commandant acknowledged receipt of the telegram the same day and advised the department that a copy of it was being sent to Admiral Winslow "per steamer, which leaves San Francisco to-morrow, the 5th inst. for Honolulu."[48] Admiral Winslow, however, sailed from Honolulu the same day the order was telegraphed from Washington, and when it reached Honolulu by steamer on January 21, Commander Meade opened it, as he was directed to do by the commandant at Mare Island

formed if it is the intention of the Department to change permanently the cruising limits of this Fleet so as to include the Groups above mentioned." (Pacific Fleet, Rear Admiral J. A. Winslow, Navy Department, vol. 2, p. 136, no. 6, Winslow to Robeson, Valparaiso, March 7, 1871.)

[45] The *California* arrived at Honolulu December 22, and the *Narragansett* the next day.

[46] Pacific Fleet, Rear Admiral J. A. Winslow, Navy Department, vol. 2, p. 127, no. 102.

[47] Letters to Commandants of Navy Yards and Stations, Navy Department, vol. 88, p. 72.

[48] Commandants' Letters, Navy Yard, Mare Island, 1872, Navy Department, p. 4, no. 4.

COMMANDER MEADE'S TREATY, 1872   57

in the event the admiral had sailed, the commandant advising him further in that case, according to Meade, to use his best judgment in the matter of obeying the instructions.[49]

Commander Meade was uncertain as to the exact meaning of the telegram, as to whether or not it indicated that the *Narragansett* should accompany the flagship to Panama. If the *Narragansett* were to be considered as included in the order he would, of course, be confronted with a dilemma. In that case he must either carry out the orders left with him by Admiral Winslow to cruise among the island groups of the South Pacific, or obey the department's order and thus ignore his orders from the admiral. Commander Meade chose the easier course by interpreting the telegram as referring only to the admiral and his flagship. He explained his situation to the secretary of the navy in a letter dated Honolulu, January 21, as follows: "I received the dispatch ordering Admiral Winslow to proceed direct to Panama from this place with instructions 'to use my judgment' in the matter. I do not understand the order as referring to this vessel also and as important American interests are at stake at Tutuila in the Navigator islands shall in obedience to the Admiral's orders proceed thither survey the harbor of Pago Pago and locate a coal depot for the American steamers. I think some kind of treaty with the native chiefs will be necessary to forestall foreign influence which is at present very active in this matter seeking to secure the harbor. . . . With the Dept's telegram before

---

[49] Commanders' Letters, Jan.-April, 1872, Navy Department, p. 51, Meade to Robeson, Honolulu, Jan. 21, 1872, rec'd Feb. 29. In forwarding Meade's despatch to Washington, Parrott wrote the following endorsement thereon February 6: "Respectfully forwarded . . . When I sent the Department's Telegraphic Despatch of Jan'y 4th, 1872 to Rear Admiral Winslow, it was thought best to suggest to Commander Meade, that in case the *California* had sailed, he should open it."

me my judgment advises my going to the Navigator islands first and securing a foot-hold for American citizens. There orders can reach me and future instructions from the Dept't carried out. I have consulted with His Excellency Mr. Pierce, U.S. Minister Resident at these islands and his judgment coincides with mine.''[50] The course adopted by Commander Meade was approved by the department, the notification to him to that effect going forward on the day of the receipt of his despatch, February 29. He was instructed to keep Admiral Winslow and the department advised of his movements and await further orders at Talcahuano upon his arrival at that port.[51]

It is important at this point to say that although the Department of State received the despatch from the commercial agent at Apia about Weber's assertions as early as October 18, 1871, nothing was communicated to the minister resident at Honolulu concerning it, and consequently the only source of the information in Admiral Winslow's and Commander Meade's possession that "important American interests are at stake at Tutuila," must have been what the commander of the U.S.S. *St. Mary's* may have conveyed to Admiral Winslow, or what the minister resident at Honolulu may have learned from various sources and passed on to the admiral after the arrival of the *California* from San Francisco. It will be recalled that Wakeman reported finding the *St. Mary's* in Apia harbor upon his arrival there from Pago Pago on August 18.[52] That ship had arrived ten days before, and sailed for the Fijis and Australia the same day Wakeman arrived, reaching Sydney on November 3.[53] During his ten-

[50] Commanders' Letters, Jan.-April, 1872, Navy Department, p. 51, Meade to Robeson, Honolulu, Jan. 21, 1872, rec'd Feb. 29.
[51] Letters to Commanding Officers, Navy Department, vol. 2, p. 424.
[52] H. Ex. Doc. no. 161, p. 9.
[53] *Ibid.*, no. 1, part 3, 42 Congress, 3 session, p. 26.

day stay at Apia, Commander Harris, the ship's captain, could have been informed by Coe of Weber's conversation, or picked up the information in other ways. That he had no such information, however, to communicate to Admiral Winslow is clear from a reading of the admiral's despatch to the Navy Department reporting the arrival of the *St. Mary's* at Sydney, which he wrote upon his receipt at Honolulu of Commander Harris's despatches. Said Winslow: "The enclosed despatches of Comdr. T. C. Harris will advise the Department of the operations of the *St. Mary's* about the Fiji Islands, and the satisfactory manner in which the orders touching American interests in those Islands have been executed."[54] There is nothing here about a possible German annexation of Samoa, and consequently it must be concluded that Commander Harris's despatches had nothing to say of such a development, and that therefore the only source of information in Honolulu was the minister resident.

Captain Wakeman of the Webb line, for the time being at least, was stopping in Honolulu. He had recently arrived at that port from his tour of the islands in the interests of the new line, and had informed the American minister resident of political and commercial matters relative to the Samoan group. It is not clear whether or not Wakeman arrived in Honolulu before the departure of Admiral Winslow. That the admiral would not have ordered Commander Meade to survey the harbor of Pago Pago and locate a coaling depot there for the use of American ships without the knowledge of Wakeman's visit to Pago Pago and of that agent's securing of "two places" in that harbor for Webb's ships, is a plausible assumption. The only evidence that might be contradictory is a reference to Wakeman's "recent" arrival in Peirce's letter to Meade,

[54] Pacific Fleet, Rear Admiral J. A. Winslow, Navy Department, vol. 2, p. 128, no. 103, Winslow to Robeson, Honolulu, Dec. 24, 1871, rec'd Jan. 19.

dated January 19. Whether an arrival before January 4, the date of the admiral's departure, was considered a *recent* arrival in the mind of Peirce, is the question. However, at the admiral's request as well as at that of the commander, the minister resident composed a letter to Meade designed to clarify for him the objects of his contemplated cruise. That portion of the letter relating to Samoa reads as follows: "It is of great importance to the future interests of our country in the South Pacific, and I may say in this *Hemisphere* that you should proceed as soon as possible even before visiting Micronesia, to the *Navigators islands,* for the purpose of promoting by all legal and proper means, American interests and enterprises, present and contemplated at that group. The aboriginal population is about 35,000, who are very intelligent and virtuous, and desirous of placing themselves under the influence and guidance of American people, who may settle there. The port of Pago Pago, island of Tutuila is by far the best and most commodious harbour in the South Seas, and will soon be the Coaling station for our line of steamships running between San Francisco, New Zealand and Australia."

"In view of the future domination of the U. States in the N. & S. Pacific Oceans; it is very important that the Navigator islands should be under American control—ruling through the native authorities.—Capt. E. Wakeman, an American recently arrived from the Navigators, having informed you of matters political and commercial, relating to those valuable islands, it is unnecessary for me to dilate thereon. You will no doubt take such action there, for the protection and promotion of American interests as may seem to you just and proper." The action intimated by Peirce as desirable was the negotiation of a treaty, and he found a precedent therefor in the treaty that Commodore Jones, commanding the U.S.S. *Peacock,* made in 1826 "with the ruling *chiefs* of the Hawaiian Islands." Though that officer was unauthorized to make the treaty, and though it was never ratified by the Senate of the United States, "nevertheless," wrote Peirce, "its binding powers were recognized by both Governments until the Treaty of 1849 was made." Such a procedure could also be followed to advantage for the United States with respect to the Samoan islands, thought Peirce. "A treaty or convention, if made by you with acknowledged, legitimate rulers of the Navigator or Samoan Archipelago," he wrote in conclusion, "or with those of the respective islands composing it—granting to citizens of the U.S. all proper rights and privileges, would no doubt receive the approval of our Government."

"If otherwise; time would be gained by such a treaty— people of other nationalities or their governments, would be anticipated in present designs in regard to those islands, and our own citizens in the meanwhile, enabled to secure by purchase from the native authorities Coaling Stations, Harbour lands and agricultural tracts. In my judgment, the U.S. Government is not prepared to accept the sovereignty of the Islands in question—nor to rule them by a Protectorate government."[55]

In forwarding on January 22 a copy of the above quoted letter to Hamilton Fish, Peirce wrote that the letter conveyed his "views of affairs in the regions named; with suggestions as to the course he [Meade] should pursue, to be of most service in promoting the interests of the U. States, and that the situation demands." Peirce further informed the secretary of state that "Comdr Meade received on yesterday, instructions to proceed immediately to Panama—but has concluded under the discretion given, to proceed on the cruise as marked out to

[55] Despatches, Hawaii, vol. 14, no. 136, Peirce to Fish, Jan. 22, 1872, received Feb. 26, enclosing despatch Peirce to Meade, Jan. 19, 1872.

him by Admiral Winslow; and I am of opinion that he will act wisely in so doing."[56]

Peirce's despatch was received at the Department of State on February 26, and the next day, according to a superscription, it was directed that it be sent to the secretary of the navy. This was done on March 1, the letter with enclosures not being received by Robeson, however, until March 5.[57] If the secretary of the navy knew of the contents of Peirce's despatch to the secretary of state before writing his own despatch of February 29 to Meade, approving that officer's course, it would explain his prompt action in replying to Meade on the same day as Meade's despatch to himself of January 21 was received. In other words, the receipt by the Department of State of Peirce's letter of January 22 on February 26, and the Navy Department's receipt of Meade's letter of January 21 on February 29, certainly brought the two departments into immediate touch with each other relative to Commander Meade's action. Secretary Robeson's approval of Commander Meade's course, therefore, must have been conditioned on the approval of the Department of State, even though, as stated above, the formal letter from the Department of State to the Navy Department enclosing Peirce's despatch was not dated until March 1 and not received by the latter department until March 5.

Commander Meade sailed away from Honolulu January 28, arriving at Pago Pago on February 14.[58] While preparing to make a re-survey of the harbor and its approaches,[59] he was obliged to sail for Apia to investigate

[56] Despatches, Hawaii, vol. 14, no. 136.

[57] Executive Letters, Jan.-June, 1872, Navy Department, p. 84, Fish to Robeson, March 1, 1872.

[58] H. Ex. Doc. no. 1, part 3, 42 Congress, 3 session, appendix, p. 26, report by George M. Robeson, Nov. 26, 1872.

[59] It will be recalled that the first survey was made by Wilkes in 1839.

COMMANDER MEADE'S TREATY, 1872

the case of one W. H. Hayes, master of the American brig *Leonora,* accused of depredations in the Gilbert group.[60] He returned to Pago Pago, however, on the 23rd, and the re-survey of the bay and also the survey of the coral bank between the harbor and the small island of Aunuu were reported on March 12 as completed.[61]

Before he sailed for Apia Commander Meade had taken the precaution, however, of drawing up an agreement with the leading chief at Pago Pago, Mauga, and thus followed the advice of the minister resident at Honolulu. The document was short and dealt with only one subject, namely, the granting by Chief Mauga to the United States of "the exclusive privilege of establishing in the said harbor of Pago Pago, island of Tutuila, a naval station, for the use and convenience of the vessels of the United States Government." Chief Mauga further agreed not to "grant a like privilege to any other foreign power or potentate." For this concession the chief and his successors and their people were "to have the friendship and protection of the great Government of the United States of America."[62]

Upon his return to Pago Pago Meade also drew up in the name of Chief Mauga commercial regulations for the port.[63] These were promulgated on March 2, Meade adding an endorsement thereto, that a copy of the same would be sent to the United States government with his approval "for the information of all masters of vessels visiting Pago Pago." The regulations consisted of nine

[60] Commanders' Letters, Jan.-April 1872, Navy Department, p. 111, Meade to Robeson, Feb. 29, 1872.

[61] *Ibid.,* p. 125½, Meade to Robeson, Pago Pago, March 12, 1872.

[62] H. Ex. Doc. no. 161, pp. 6-7, encl. in encl. no. 4, Hamilton Fish to A. B. Steinberger, March 29, 1873.

[63] These regulations were the second of their kind drawn up for a Samoan port by an American naval officer. As we have seen, Captain Wilkes drew up the first regulations in 1839 for the port of Apia.

articles. By the first article the chief promised to protect all foreign consuls duly appointed, "and all foreigners settling on the island. . . ." The second article provided for the protection of foreign ships wrecked on the island to prevent their cargoes from being stolen. It also protected the property of deceased foreigners, providing that said property should be delivered up "to the Consul of the nation of the person so deceased."

The third article read as follows: "Every vessel entering Pago Pago shall pay a port charge to the Chief, to be regulated by agreement between the Chief, the Agent of the California and Australian Steamship Company and the foreign Consuls. Pilots shall be appointed by the same persons. The Agent of the Steamship Company to be the Pilot Commissioner *ex officio,* and the charge for pilotage for men-of-war and merchant vessels to be $1.00 per foot of draft and $1.00 per day for detention on board. Where pilots are declined, half-pilotage will be paid. Each pilot to be furnished with a copy of Port Regulations and to show the same to the Master of each vessel which he may bring into port."

Article four prohibited the employment of natives on Sundays by foreigners either on shore or on board vessels "except under circumstances of absolute necessity, such as aid in case of the wreck of a vessel, or the coaling of the Steamship obliged to proceed on time on her voyage North or South." The fifth article forbade "all trading in distilled or spiritous liquors, or any kind of intoxicating drink," and any person found guilty of so offending "before a mixed court composed of U.S. Consul, H.B.M. Consul and the Chief of the Bay," should be fined $100.

Article six was designed to discourage the prostitution of native women, and article seven provided for the apprehension of deserters by the chief and their surrender to the consul whose jurisdiction extended over such deserters. All fines according to article eight should "be paid in specie or its equivalent, or be commuted at the rate of one month's labor on roads for $10.00 ten dollars." The ninth and final article read as follows: "Should any Master of any Merchant vessel refuse compliance with the local regulations the cause to be referred to the Consul of the Nation to which the vessel belongs and redress sought thence."[64]

On the same day the regulations were promulgated, March 2, Chief Mauga also raised a new Samoan flag, which Commander Meade "saluted with 15 guns, from our howitzer on shore, landed by us with the Battalion for drill." The flag was probably the work of Commander Meade also, although he did not say so in his report to the department, contenting himself with merely enclosing a description of it. The flag consisted of nine stripes representing nine islands of Samoa: Tau, Olosega, Ofu, Anuu, Tutuila, Upolu, Manono, Apolima, and Savaii. Four white stripes and four white stars represented the four large islands, Savaii, Upolu, Tutuila, and Tau, and five blue stripes represented the small islands. In concluding the description Commander Meade wrote: "The moon (an ancient emblem in Samoa) is shown in the first and last quarters . . . representing the letter S or Samoa."[65]

Commander Meade next turned to politics by making an address to the chiefs and people of the island of Tutuila. This was done in an effort to unite the chiefs of the island and secure a confirmation from them of the port regulations of Pago Pago. In his address the commander, moreover, rather naïvely explained the purpose of his visit to Pago Pago, and, reading it, one easily discovers what was occupying his mind at the time. The address as

[64] H. Ex. Doc. no. 161, enclosure A with despatch, Meade to Robeson, March 12, 1872.
[65] *Ibid.*, enclosure C.

reported by Meade to the department began as follows: "The Government of the United States of America is about to establish commercial relations with the Samoan Islands by means of the line of Steamers now plying between California, Hawaii, New Zealand and Australia, and wishes in its own interest as well as that of its citizens to secure a convenient port in the Samoan islands to use as a coaling station and resort for its ships of war which are to cruise in the South Seas to protect commerce. I have come to Pago Pago as it is the finest harbor in the islands and the key to Samoa, to survey and examine it for that purpose and to secure from the Chief of Pago Pago such rights and privileges as will prevent other Nations from acting in a way adverse to the interests of American citizens or to your injury as a free people and the rightful owners of the soil." Meade assured the chiefs that the United States did "not seek an inch" of their territory nor "the control" of their affairs. The United States, he said, would "from time to time send ships of war (and they have many) to your islands and also no doubt wise persons to assist you in framing good laws for yourselves and the foreigners who may settle among you and will aid you by its influence and protection to establish a sound and stable form of Government under which the Samoan people can grow prosperous and happy."

Meade decried the disunion that was prevalent among the Samoans and advised "the Chiefs and people of Tutuila . . . to set the example to the rest of Samoa by uniting under one Chief elected in Council by all the other Chiefs on Tutuila, raising a flag as an emblem of his Government and framing such simple laws as will conduce to the happiness and welfare of the people of this beautiful island." Having accomplished this, he was certain that the people of Upolu, Savaii, and the other islands would

COMMANDER MEADE'S TREATY, 1872

follow their example. Meade then proceeded to describe the structure of American state governments and thought that they were good patterns for the Samoans to imitate in setting up their own governments of districts or states. Finally Meade referred indirectly to the possibility of other powers annexing the islands when he said: "The Government and people of the United States seek your friendship and welfare and will aid you to establish yourselves as a nation by peacefully exerting its great influence to prevent your independence from being taken away from you by any foreign power. . . .' "[66]

As a result of Commander Meade's appeal for peace and unity on the island of Tutuila, articles of confederation were framed on March 9 by the chiefs of the northern and the eastern parts of the island. The native leaders "having met in council this 9th day of March A.D. 1872," says the document, "do hereby agree to form a league and *confederation* for our mutual welfare and protection and *to unite our several districts* under the *Flag raised* at Pago Pago on the Second day of March A. D. 1872.

"And we hereby do *solemnly bind ourselves* to carry out this covenant *faithfully* as far as our *jurisdiction extends* and to *maintain peace* with each other and to carry out in our several districts the *Commercial regulations* of Pago Pago promulgated the 2nd March A. D. 1872 and recognized by *Commander Richard W. Meade, U. S. Navy, Commanding United States Steamer "Narragansett."*[67]

In reading the address of Commander Meade to the chiefs and people of Tutuila, and in noting some of the terms of the commercial regulations for Pago Pago, it becomes clear that the activities of Wakeman on behalf of the Webb line, and the willing support which the American minister resident at Honolulu rendered in behalf of

[66] H. Ex. Doc. no. 161, enclosure D.   [67] *Ibid.*, enclosure B.

the same project, were at the bottom of the whole movement. The Navy Department had given no order to Admiral Winslow to send the *Narragansett* to Pago Pago. In fact, had the admiral been at Honolulu when the department order of January fourth arrived, directing him to proceed direct to Panama, he would probably have cancelled his own order to Meade to make a re-survey of Pago Pago harbor, and ordered the *Narragansett* to accompany the *California*. We have seen, also, that Commander Meade was himself somewhat dubious as to which course to pursue, carry out the orders of Admiral Winslow or sail for Panama. Hence, it must be concluded that the whole movement had its origin in Honolulu.

Peirce was fully aware of the Webb line project. In fact, as has been noted, he advocated in a despatch to the Department of State that a subsidy be voted by Congress in support of it. Wakeman in all probability was in touch with Peirce before he left Honolulu to go to Pago Pago, and Peirce's letter to Meade shows that Wakeman had talked with them both upon his return from Samoa. That the admiral ordered Meade to make a re-survey of the harbor of Pago Pago and to establish a coaling station there is attested to by Meade in his letter to the Navy Department before leaving Honolulu, but it seems that it was Peirce who first suggested to Meade the negotiation of a treaty for the exclusive use of Pago Pago harbor as a naval station, although Meade in his letter to the department before his departure for Pago Pago would have it appear that the idea originated with himself and that Peirce's views coincided with his own. In all probability Wakeman had suggested the need of such a treaty to Peirce. At all events, he furnished the news about Weber's attempts to secure a German protectorate and both Peirce and Meade regarded the matter of Meade's immediate departure for Pago Pago to secure a foothold for the

United States as urgent enough to justify the commander's ignoring the order from Washington to proceed to Panama.

The presence of the *Narragansett* in Samoan waters was known to the German consul as early as the eighteenth of February when Commander Meade arrived at Apia to try the case of the master of the *Leonora*. While it is improbable that he learned at this time that Commander Meade had the day before signed the agreement with the chief of Pago Pago for the exclusive use of the harbor as a naval station, the promulgation of the commercial regulations for Pago Pago after Meade's return to Pago Pago was soon the common knowledge of all foreigners in Samoa. The fact that a special favor was shown the Webb line in the regulations, providing, as they did, for the participation of an agent of that line in any agreement with the native chiefs and the foreign consuls concerning port charges and the appointment of pilots, could not be overlooked by the German consul. Moreover, the definite exclusion of himself from membership in the mixed court at Pago Pago, which was designed to try cases of illegal barter or sale of intoxicating liquors to natives by foreigners, was not a favorable omen of future German prestige in Pago Pago harbor. The re-surveying of the harbor and its approaches by Meade naturally caused rumors to fly thick and fast as to the ultimate meaning of the operations, but Consul Weber, it is certain, entertained no illusions. Furthermore, Commander Meade's efforts to bring about the union of the chiefs of Tutuila in support of the commercial regulations and, if possible, a confederation of all the islands under one government, could be interpreted by Consul Weber as indicating only one thing, namely, that an American protectorate might follow the acquisition of Pago Pago harbor. Already the natives were talking about it, and as early as

April 9, less than forty days after the commercial regulations for Pago Pago were promulgated, the chiefs at Apia signed a petition to the president praying for annexation of the whole group of islands by the United States.[68]

The *Narragansett* sailed away from Pago Pago on March 12 after a short visit to Leone at the west end of the island the previous day. In less than two weeks Consul Weber arrived in the harbor on a German warship. Learning of the American naval station project, the consul made representations to Chief Mauga on the spot. Later he wrote him a letter from Leone dated March 26, confirming his protest. In the letter he reminded the chief that a German subject had purchased a certain strip of land along the shores of the harbor of Pago Pago from a Samoan native named Maee. He requested the chief, therefore, "not to allow any sale of these lands by other parties, as I shall protect for the present Maee's sale, reserving all German rights and claims." He also would have Mauga know "that the port regulations of Pago Pago are not yet legalized, and will not be recognized by me for the present."[69] Chief Mauga thereupon requested the United States commercial agent, Jonas M. Coe, to send to Rear Admiral Winslow a translation of a letter from himself informing the admiral of the German consul's protest against the commercial regulations. "I have, therefore," wrote the chief, "to beg that you will take the necessary measure to have them legalized."[70]

Upon receipt of Commander Meade's despatch of

[68] H. Ex. Doc. no. 161, p. 4, encl. in encl. no. 2, J. B. M. Stewart to W. H. Webb, June 28, 1872.

[69] *Ibid.*, p. 7, encl. in encl. no. 4, Fish to Steinberger, March 29, 1873.

[70] Commanders' Letters, Jan.-April, 1872, Navy Department, p. 125½, Meade to Robeson, March 12, 1872, encl. E., Mauga to Winslow, March 31, 1872. Attached to foregoing letter, although not mentioned therein. Doubtless forwarded by Admiral Winslow to the Navy Department and there filed with Meade's letter.

COMMANDER MEADE'S TREATY, 1872   71

March 12, enclosing the commercial regulations, the address of the commander to the Tutuilans, and the articles of confederation agreed upon by the chiefs, Secretary Robeson on May 14 submitted a copy of the correspondence to the Department of State.[71] The next day he transmitted "an additional paper relative to the Navigator Islands, addressed to W. H. Webb, Esqr., under date of Sept. 20, 1871 by E. Wakeman." This was the report which Captain Wakeman had sent to his employer concerning his investigations in the Samoan islands the previous summer, and which Webb had forwarded to Secretary Robeson.[72] The Meade treaty of February 17 had in the meantime been forwarded by Robeson to Fish on April 10 without Meade's covering despatch, the secretary of the navy stating that it had not yet reached the department, but that as soon as it was received, he would transmit it also.[73] At the time of the receipt of Meade's despatch of March 12, the covering letter for the treaty was still being awaited.[74]

Secretary Fish, with Meade's despatch of March 12 clarifying for him the circumstances surrounding the signing of the treaty, and also with Captain Wakeman's report describing the commercial possibilities of the islands, the strategic value of Pago Pago harbor, and the desire of the Europeans on the islands for American protection, promptly recommended to the president that the agreement of February 17 between Commander Meade and Chief Mauga be ratified. President Grant just as

[71] Executive Letter Book, No. 25, Navy Department, p. 369, Robeson to Fish, May 14, 1872.

[72] *Ibid.*, p. 371, Robeson to Fish, May 15, 1872; see also encl. in encl. no. 4, Fish to Steinberger, March 29, 1873, in H. Ex. Doc. no. 161, pp. 7-11.

[73] *Ibid.*, p. 328, Robeson to Fish, April 10, 1872.

[74] No such letter has been found in the archives of the Navy Department. Perhaps it was never written, or if so, it probably went astray. How the treaty was sent by Meade to the Navy Department is not known.

promptly transmitted the agreement to the Senate on May 22 for ratification.[75] Said the president in his message to the Senate: "This instrument proposes to confer upon this Government the exclusive privilege of establishing a naval station in the dominions of that chief for the equivalent of protecting those dominions." Secretary Robeson's letter to Secretary Fish, dated May 15, with Wakeman's report, was enclosed with President Grant's message; and also Consul Weber's protest to Chief Mauga against the commercial regulations, dated March 26.[76] The president explained that no report had "yet been received from Commander Meade on the subject." He continued: "Although he was without special instructions or authority to enter into such agreement, the advantages of the concession which it proposes to make are so great, in view of the advantageous position of Tutuila, especially as a coaling station for steamers between San Francisco and Australia, that I should not hesitate to recommend its approval but for the protection on the part of the United States which it seems to imply. With some modification of the obligation of protection which the agreement imports, it is recommended to the favorable consideration of the Senate.'"[77]

Thus it has been seen that the work of Meade was approved by the secretary of the navy, the secretary of state, and finally by the president. Whether the Senate would likewise approve it was a mooted question. Through the whole proceedings, from Peirce's recommendations in Honolulu to the president's message enclosing Wake-

[75] Secretary Fish returned the Meade correspondence to Secretary Robeson the next day, May 23. (See Executive Letters, Jan.-June, 1872, Navy Department, p. 195.)

[76] Executive, L, 42 Congress, 2 session, Grant to the Senate, May 22, 1872, enclosures; H. Ex. Doc. no. 161, pp. 7-11.

[77] *Ibid.;* see also H. Ex. Doc. no. 161, p. 6.

COMMANDER MEADE'S TREATY, 1872   73

man's report, it is clear that the interests which the United States government wished at that moment to support were those of the Webb steamship line. This is brought out again in a letter from Secretary Robeson to Webb in June, at the time the treaty was before the Committee on Foreign Relations. Said Robeson: "In reply to your letter of this date, it gives me pleasure to say that this Department naturally takes a strong interest in all measures which tend to increase our commerce in the Pacific Ocean, either with the countries of China and Japan or with the newer and growing colonies of Australia and New Zealand, also with the islands lying between the coasts of the United States on the West, and those countries. Among such measures your line of Steamers from San Francisco to Australia and New Zealand via the Sandwich and Navigators Islands, deserves, in the estimation of this Department, all the aid and encouragement from the Government of the United States which can with propriety be rendered, and you may rely upon all the support we can properly give you. The Department is fully aware of the convenient position of the Navigator's islands as a stopping place between San Francisco and New Zealand and Australia and also of the advantages of the land locked harbor of Pago Pago as a place for a naval and coaling station, repairing ships and generally as a mercantile port, and of its natural capacity for defence, in which it has the preference over the reef locked harbors in its vicinity or any harbor in that portion of the Pacific.''[78]

Again, in his annual report to the president for 1872, Secretary Robeson wrote with regard to the desirability of the ratification of the Meade agreement as follows: "It is by no means the province of this report to discuss ques-

[78] General Letter Book, No. 56, Navy Department, p. 218, Robeson to Webb, June 12, 1872.

tions of foreign policy or to present any event even of the plainest interests or requirements of national commerce, but I cannot forbear to say that if we are not prepared to ignore wholly the imperative commercial needs as well as the splendid commercial opportunities of our Pacific States, and to yield also the opening avenues of the Pacific trade to the comprehension and courage of more liberal though more remote people, we should not neglect the opportunity thus afforded at least to protect, if not encourage, some of the American interests which are there struggling to establish themselves.'"[79]

The Meade agreement was never ratified by the Senate. The only record of what action was taken on it is to be found in the executive journal of the Senate, and there it states that the agreement was read for the first time on May 22—the day it was transmitted by President Grant—and "on motion by Mr. Cameron ordered, that the said agreement be referred to the Committee on Foreign Relations, and, together with the message and accompanying documents, be printed in confidence for the use of the Senate."[80] If any minutes of the Committee on Foreign Relations were kept, they have not been found, and consequently it is uncertain what was done with the agreement in the committee.[81] It was never reported back to the Senate.

Although there undoubtedly was strong opposition in Congress to the assumption by the United States of any obligations in relation to the Samoan islands (just as there was opposition to the annexation of Santo Domingo

[79] H. Ex. Doc. no. 1, part 3, 42 Congress, 3 session, pp. 13-14, report by George M. Robeson, Nov. 26, 1872.

[80] Executive Journal, United States Senate, vol. 18, pp. 254-255.

[81] Although the records of the Committee on Foreign Relations were not filed before 1890, it is possible that the records concerning the Meade agreement may be found among uncatalogued papers of the Senate in the attic of the Capitol.

COMMANDER MEADE'S TREATY, 1872   75

and the purchase of the Virgin Islands in the Caribbean) two members, at least, favored the granting of protection to Samoa. Both of these members, let it be noted, Sherman Houghton of the House and Cornelius Cole of the Senate, were from California. On March 7, 1872, Mr. Houghton, by unanimous consent, submitted the following resolution, which was agreed to: "Resolved that the President of the United States be, and is hereby, requested to transmit to Congress any and all correspondence, and documents received by him relating to the application of the inhabitants of the Navigator Islands, in the Pacific ocean to have the protection of the Government of the United States extended over said islands."[82] Some two months later Senator Cole submitted the following resolution in the Senate, which was agreed to: "Resolved that the Committee on Foreign Relations be instructed to inquire into the expediency and policy of the United States Government affording protection to the independent group of islands in the South Pacific ocean known as the Navigators Islands, such protectorate being desired by the inhabitants."[83]

It is interesting to note in connection with the Grant administration's efforts to acquire exclusive right to Pago Pago harbor, that the rumor of German expansion in the Pacific also stimulated the government of New Zealand to endeavor to ward off the alleged danger even a little earlier. But for Downing Street's opposition to embarking upon new colonial ventures during the years prior to its reversal of the policy in the British annexation of the Fijis in 1874, this movement would no doubt have been far more effective than Consul Weber's at-

[82] *Congressional Globe*, part 2, 42 Congress, 2 session, House, March 7, 1872, pp. 1509-10.
[83] *Ibid.*, part 4, 42 Congress, 2 session, Senate, May 13, 1872, p. 3352.

tempts to interest the German Empire in the protection of the Samoan group. As a matter of fact, from 1870 to 1875, and again in 1883, New Zealand was much more interested in acquiring the archipelago as a part of her political system than was Germany at any time during those years.

It is curious, also, to note that New Zealand's desire for bringing the Samoan group within the British Empire at the particular time under discussion was, moreover, partly due to the completion of the transcontinental railway in the United States in 1869, and to the consequent stimulation that that event gave to efforts for better commercial and mail connections with the mother country. As was noted above, New Zealand was ready to grant the proposed Webb line a subsidy even before the application for such aid was made to the United States Congress in 1870, and after the failure of the subsidy bill in the Senate, we saw that Webb turned a favorable ear to New Zealand's offer and started his line in 1871. With this steamship line operating under the patronage of New Zealand, and making regular calls at Pago Pago, the Samoan group had become relatively much nearer to New Zealand than had ever been the case when only irregular communications with those islands by sailing vessels were maintained. Consequently, any rumor that a foreign power like Germany was likely to cut New Zealand's new line of communication with the mother country, and might also absorb all the new trade by getting control of Pago Pago and the rest of Samoa, would naturally react sharply upon the commercial and political interests of New Zealand, if not, indeed, upon those of all British possessions in Australasia.

Furthermore, there was the question of defense. With Germany endeavoring to protect in the South Seas German commercial interests, such as those of the Godeffroy company, certainly the fears entertained by New Zealand for her own safety were much more disturbing than any feeling of insecurity the United States, for example, may have felt when rumors were afloat that the newly born empire was threatening to expand into the Caribbean Sea. New Zealand was in effect evolving a Monroe Doctrine of her own, and the Samoan group in the new age of steamships seemed more necessary to her as an outpost of defense than at any previous time. Finally, it must be remembered that the whole missionary movement in Samoa had its origin in England. There were no American missionaries there, and except for infrequent communications with the United States through the whalers, the earliest connection of Samoa with the outside world was through the English missionary activities begun in 1830 by John Williams. Consequently the oldest foreign population in Samoa was English in sympathy and understanding.

The reasons for New Zealand's interest in Samoa were, therefore, substantial, and far more important than those of the United States at the time. Consequently it is not surprising to find the New Zealand premier, Julius Vogel, and two of the governors of that colony, Sir G. Bowen and Sir James Furgusson, all three strongly pressing the matter of annexation from 1870 to 1875. In 1871 the legislative council of New Zealand sent an address to the queen praying for British control in Samoa. The legislative council desired to submit to Her Majesty's "consideration," read the address,

"That, with a view to the better prevention of the iniquitous traffic in Polynesian labor, and to the better protection of British commerce in the Pacific, and especially the postal and commercial connection with Great Britain, through the United States of America, which this Colony has made great sacrifices to create, it is of the greatest importance that Your Majesty's authority should, as speedily as possible, be established in the Navigator Islands.

"That, in the event of the annexation or assumption of a protectorate over these islands by a foreign power—a contingency which, from reliable information, appears to be imminent—British interests in the Australian Colonies would in time of war become seriously endangered.

"That, as these islands appear to be well suited for settlement, and the population desirous of being more closely connected with Your Majesty's Empire, it is highly desirable that the group should be attached as a dependency to such one of the Australian Colonies as Your Majesty may select.

"And we humbly pray that Your Majesty will be pleased to create a naval station as early as possible in the group, which we believe to possess an excellent harbor and to be otherwise well suited for the purpose."[84]

But as stated, the British Foreign Office at the moment showed no enthusiasm for acquiring new territory and early in 1872 sought to discourage the movement in New Zealand. Indeed, it was during the very days that Commander Meade was surveying Pago Pago harbor that Lord Kimberley sent a despatch dated February 23, from the Colonial Office in London, stating "that Her Majesty's Government have had under consideration the despatch transmitting a memorandum with a copy of the resolution adopted by the Legislative Council of New Zealand on the subject of the Navigator Islands. Her Majesty's Government are not insensible to the fact the increase of commerce in the Pacific, and the constant advance of European settlement in those regions, must ren-

---

[84] Quoted in despatch no. 64, Canisius to Adee, Oct. 1, 1883, Consular Despatches, Apia, vol. 12.

COMMANDER MEADE'S TREATY, 1872

der the South Sea Islands of far greater interest than formerly. They are not, however, prepared to advise Her Majesty to take upon herself further direct responsibilities, such as would be entailed upon her by the assumption of sovereignty or of a protectorate over the Navigator Islands."[85]

There is no doubt that the British authorities in London knew that Germany did not contemplate any expansion in the Pacific at this time; in fact Downing Street, after the completion of the American transcontinental railroad to the west coast, could be expected to be more interested in knowing what the United States was planning to do in the Pacific world than the Reich recently established in the year 1871. In the opinion of the Foreign Office, it was the United States just then, not Germany, that needed watching. Downing Street had already learned of the petition the Samoans had sent to the president asking for the protection of the United States. In fact, Sir E. Thornton, the British minister at Washington, as early as June 22, 1872, was instructed by Earl Granville to inquire what the decision of the United States would be with regard to the petition. This occurred even before the petition was received in Washington, for Mr. Hale, the acting secretary of state, in reply to Thornton, said "that he was under the impression that no such petition had been received, and referred to an answer given some time ago to an inquiry made by the House of Representatives, in which Mr. Fish stated that no such request had been received."[86] Later Mr. Fish confirmed Mr. Hale's statement, but informed Thornton of Meade's treaty, say-

[85] *Ibid.*
[86] H. Ex. Doc. no. 201, 42 Congress, 2 session, Grant to House of Representatives, March 16, 1872, enclosing Hamilton Fish's letter of same date in compliance with House resolution of March 7.

ing that it was made "without any previous instructions or powers"; but that "the President had deemed it expedient to transmit it to the Senate for its sanction."

When Thornton alluded to newspaper reports concerning Meade's alleged declaration of a protectorate over the island of Tutuila, Fish said "that the Government had received no information of such an act, and that, if it had taken place, it had been done without instructions." Thornton enclosed with his despatch to Earl Granville "three printed copies of some documents relating to the island of Tutuila, which were forwarded to the Navy Department by Captain Meade, and subsequently submitted to the House of Representatives." In describing these documents Thornton continued: "They include some commercial regulations for the harbor of Pago Pago, signed by the chief of Tutuila, which Captain Meade forwards 'with his approval,' and a somewhat grandiloquent address which he makes to the chiefs and people of that island."[87]

Evidently the Foreign Office had become satisfied that there was no present danger of American expansion in the Pacific, and consequently the next year Lord Kimberley again dampened the ardor of the New Zealand annexationists by sending the governor on November 18, 1873, a negative reply to his communication expressing the wish of the New Zealand government that the islands be annexed. Her Majesty's government, he wrote, would not "be disposed to sanction any steps which would lay this Government under obligation to interfere in the affairs of these islands."[88] Again, on February 10, 1874, Lord Kimberley wrote in the same vein with reference to

[87] Quoted from despatch, Thornton to Granville, July 18, 1872, as reported in despatch no. 64, Canisius to Adee, Oct. 1, 1883, C.D., Apia, vol. 12.

[88] Kimberley to Furgusson, Nov. 18, 1873, as quoted in despatch no. 64, from Canisius as above.

COMMANDER MEADE'S TREATY, 1872

the Fiji group, and referred to his despatch of November 18 in connection with the Samoan islands.[89]

The Meade treaty was not, however, regarded so lightly by the New Zealand people as by the British authorities in England. This was particularly true after the United States government sent a special commissioner, named A. B. Steinberger, to Samoa in 1873, for thereupon the New Zealanders became much concerned about the policy of this government. Therefore, Kimberley's despatch of February 10, 1874, did not stop the agitation in New Zealand for annexation. Despatches, memoranda, and addresses of the public men of that colony show conclusively how alarming the appearance of the United States as a possible contender in Samoa for the possession of Pago Pago seemed to them, and the situation only spurred them on to further efforts to annex the islands. Julius Vogel, formerly premier, now commissioner of New Zealand in London, in communicating with the Colonial Office, stated that New Zealand's postmaster-general had suggested some arrangement with the government of the United States with respect to Pago Pago harbor. "The group is too near New Zealand," said Vogel's memorandum, "to make it desirable that the islands should be subject to such an arrangement as was clearly contemplated by Captain Meade, or that they should be annexed to any foreign power. Ministers are of opinion that immediate action in the matter is extremely desirable."[90] Again, on March 11, 1874, the governor of New Zealand, Sir James Furgusson, sent a despatch to the Colonial Office, saying: "It is now considered certain that the Government of the United States have accepted the tender of the protectorate of the Navigator (Samoan) group, and especially the

[89] *Ibid.*, Feb. 10, 1874, as quoted in despatch no. 64 from Canisius as above.

[90] Quoted in Canisius' despatch no. 64 as above.

concession of the excellent harbor of Pago Pago as a naval station, which the chiefs had previously offered to Her Majesty's Government, an event which can hardly be regarded otherwise than a misfortune to this community.'"[91]

Thus had begun the diplomatic game between the United States, Germany, and Great Britain over Samoa, a game that was not to end until 1899.

[91] Quoted in Canisius' despatch no. 64 as above.

CHAPTER IV

A. B. STEINBERGER, SPECIAL AGENT TO SAMOA

THE petition from the natives of Samoa, which had occasioned the inquiry from the House of Representatives in March, and which had also caused the British foreign office through the minister in Washington to inquire of the Department of State in July what action would be taken upon it, finally reached the president some time in August. The document was dated April 9, 1872, and the translation was certified by Dr. G. A. Turner, a medical missionary of the London Missionary Society. "We, the chiefs and rulers of Samoa," it read, "deem it necessary for our future well-being and better establishment of Christianity, free institutions, fellowship of mankind, protection of life and property, and to secure the blessings of liberty and free trade to ourselves and future generations, do petition the President of the United States of America to annex these our islands to the United States of America."[1]

Curiously enough the appeal was not sent directly to the president, but seems to have been entrusted to one J. B. M. Stewart, who, writing from New York on June 28, 1872, enclosed it in a letter to the shipbuilder, W. H. Webb, of New York, wherein he said: "I shall look upon it as a favor if you will present it to the President upon his return to Washington."[2] This Stewart was a sea cap-

[1] H. Ex. Doc. no. 161, p. 4, encl. 1.1 encl. 2, Stewart to Webb, June 28, 1872.
[2] *Ibid.*, pp. 3 and 4, encl. 2.

tain, and is known to have commanded in later years an American bark named the *Menshikoff*, which sailed between San Francisco and the Fijis. He was associated with a shipping firm in California, and together with a group of Californians was interested in Samoan lands on the island of Tutuila. The group had organized a company under the name, Polynesian Land Company, and during the civil war which kept the Samoan islands in a turmoil from 1869 onwards for some three years, the company had acquired considerable areas of land on options, the consideration being for the most part firearms and ammunition.

This company looked with favor upon the Webb proposal to use Pago Pago harbor for a coaling station, since this would enhance the value of the company's lands, but the group of investors saw in an American protectorate an even greater advantage for the reason that such a political relationship between the United States and Samoa would tend to protect their holdings against possible repudiation of contracts by the island chiefs as well as provide a free market in the United States for the products of the plantations which the company apparently was planning to establish. Captain Stewart, therefore, on one of his periodical visits to Samoa, taking advantage of the very recent sojourn of Commander Meade in Samoan waters, may very easily have persuaded the impressionable Samoan chiefs to petition the president for protection. The peace between the factions was hardly more than a truce, and the danger of a renewed conflict was ever present. This may have influenced the foreigners the previous August to intimate to Captain Wakeman their desire for protection at that time, and by April 1872, immediately after Commander Meade's departure from Samoa, this wish was no doubt quite as strong among them, especially the missionaries, as among the natives.

In any case, whether Captain Stewart had anything to do with the drawing up of the petition or not, it was entrusted to his care, and on June 28, as already stated, two months and nineteen days after it was signed, he was in New York writing a letter and enclosing the petition to Webb for his transmittal to the president on the first occasion when a personal interview between the president and Webb might be obtained.

The next actor on the scene appeared then in the person of Colonel A. B. Steinberger. A man of considerable education, and apparently of some means, Colonel Steinberger seems to have enjoyed the personal friendship of President Grant. Steinberger was also a friend of Webb, and in August, 1872, an understanding had been reached between them that President Grant should be approached by the latter with a view to securing for Steinberger a special commissionership to Samoa. Webb was still hoping for a subsidy from the United States, as was noted in the last chapter. He, moreover, had in his possession the petition for a protectorate which Captain Stewart had sent him some seven weeks before to present to the president. There is no doubt that he was interested in a protectorate as well as a subsidy. If Congress could be prevailed upon to extend protection to Samoa, the subsidy might be forthcoming as well, and *vice versa*. But it was necessary to obtain official information concerning the political situation in Samoa to lay before Congress, and in Webb's opinion it was highly desirable, therefore, to impress President Grant with the importance of sending Colonel Steinberger to Samoa as special commissioner. The president had already shown his interest in Samoa in recommending in May of that year the ratification of Meade's treaty with reservations, and the administration had also supported Webb's efforts to secure a subsidy and would continue to do so. Hence it was thought that the Steinberger proposal would also elicit the president's support.

Accordingly, on the evening of August 16, Steinberger met the president personally at Long Branch, New Jersey. That the interview was cordial is evident from the fact that Steinberger wrote to the president the next day thanking him for his "kindly expression of last night." Webb's name was probably mentioned in the course of the conversation, for in the same letter Steinberger wrote: "Mr. Webb will present full facts relating to the Navigator's Islands." Confirming, no doubt, what had passed between the president and himself, Steinberger continued: "In the interests of the Government and yourself, I wish to go thither [Samoa] under the mantle of authority and report personally to yourself, and can only pledge my earnestness and good faith."[3] Webb had his conference with the president some time between August 17 and August 20, and on this occasion probably presented to the president the petition from the Samoan chiefs for annexation of the islands. That he recommended Steinberger for the special mission to Samoa is clear from an endorsement on Steinberger's letter of August 17 by Horace Porter, the president's private secretary, in referring this letter to the secretary of state. Porter wrote from Long Branch on August 20, as follows: "Mr. Webb strongly recommends Mr. Steinberger as a competent person to visit the Navigator's Islands and report upon their condition. He proposes to serve without pay. Of course it is not the intention to annex these islands, but if, in your judgment, it would be well to send a commissioner to report upon their condition with a view of sending such information to Congress, you might commission Mr. Steinberger for this duty."[4]

[3] Miscellaneous Letters, Department of State, Steinberger to the President, Aug. 17, 1872.
[4] *Ibid.*

STEINBERGER, SPECIAL AGENT

Months went by and no action was taken in the matter by the State Department. Finally, in March, 1873, negotiations between Secretary Fish and Steinberger began. In reply to a request from the secretary for a brief statement of Steinberger's purpose in desiring to visit the islands, Steinberger wrote in Washington on the fourteenth in part as follows: "Tutuila, the third island in area, is noted for its harbor of Pago Pago, known to be one of the best in the Pacific Ocean, affording for years a refuge for our men and the commerce of other nations." Steinberger said he wanted to "examine the more important islands and report upon the same, their advantageous position as bearing upon our growing commerce with the British colonies, the character of the natives, the soil, climate, products, and capacity." He concluded by "asking for such powers and instructions, with such aid and comfort as the Department may accord to a special commissioner."[5]

Almost immediate action was now taken by the department. On March 29 Fish wrote a letter of instructions to Steinberger enclosing therewith in confidence President Grant's communication to the Senate of May 22, 1872, which, as was noted in the last chapter, was the covering letter for Meade's treaty and with which was also enclosed the Wakeman letter and the Weber protest.[6] The information concerning the Samoan islands was so inadequate, said Fish, "that an ample field is there afforded for the observations and reports of an intelligent special agent. You have accordingly been selected as such. . . . The points to which you will specially direct your attention are—

1. The number of islands constituting the group and the extent of each.

[5] *Ibid.*, Steinberger to Fish, March 14, 1873.
[6] H. Ex. Doc. 161, encl. no. 4, pp. 5-11.

2. The number of inhabitants, both aboriginal and from abroad.

3. The nature and quantity of the agricultural and other productions.

4. The harbors suitable for vessels engaged in long voyages by sea."

The document is significant, moreover, as indicating that the administration was not unmindful of the future need of a naval station. Said Fish: "It is not unlikely that perhaps in the not distant future the interests of the United States may require not only a naval station in the Samoan group, but a harbor where their steam and other vessels also may freely and securely frequent. Full and accurate information in regard to the islands will be necessary to enable the Government here to determine as to the measures which may be advisable toward obtaining that object."[7]

In view of the future difficulties in Samoa over land holdings of foreigners, the next two paragraphs in Fish's instructions are of interest: "In the course of your communication with the chiefs in the islands, you will caution them against making grants of their land to individual foreigners. The European nations, who colonized this hemisphere, have usually regarded such grants from the aborigines as invalid, and in all probability the rule will be held to apply to the Samoan group." Steinberger was cautioned "to avoid conversation, official or otherwise, with any persons respecting the relations between this and any other country." He was to remember, moreover, that he was "not a regular diplomatic agent, formally accredited to another government, but an informal one, of a special and confidential character, appointed for the

[7] This would indicate pretty clearly that Secretary Fish regarded as final the failure of the Senate to ratify the Meade treaty.

sole purpose of obtaining full and accurate information in regard to the Navigators' Islands." Steinberger was to be paid twelve dollars a day for expenses from the time of his departure from Washington until his return, the time limit, however, being fixed at December first. No other compensation was to be paid him.

Almost three months elapsed before Steinberger was ready to sail for Samoa. He explained in letters to the president and the secretary of state dated San Francisco June 24, that finding no ship for the islands he had been compelled to furnish his "own means of conveyance." He planned to leave on the twenty-sixth, accompanied by "a proper artist," and he thought he would "gain in time and effectiveness" by having his own boat.[8] No naval vessel was available for the long journey to Samoa, and even if there had been, the department might have thought it the better policy not to give the mission the publicity that Steinberger's arrival on such a vessel would have occasioned. As a matter of fact, Steinberger did not sail from San Francisco until June 29. His craft was a chartered pilot-boat named *Fanny,* "a schooner," he wrote, "of forty-three tons, new measurement. . . . The care necessary in selecting a proper vessel for such a journey and its adaptability for the prosecution of my duties when at the islands, and also the adequate fitting out of the same, must be my apology for delay before sailing." Steinberger was gone from the United States until December, about five and one-half months, and the account of his visit to Samoa is based on the very full and illuminating report which he wrote at sea while returning to America.[9]

[8] M.L.

[9] Steinberger, A. B., "Report on Samoa or Navigator's Islands," in Steinberger Papers, Department of State. The report is not dated, but it was sent by Steinberger to Hamilton Fish under covering letter, dated February 13, 1874. Forwarded by Fish to President Grant, April 21, 1874, and transmitted by the President to Congress on the same day. Referred to Committee

The crew of the *Fanny* "consisted of a Scotch captain, a Swedish mate, and Russian, Finnish, and Swedish sailors. The artist was a man from Boston who also served as secretary to Steinberger.[10] In compliance with "an oral suggestion" from the secretary of state that he might be "an observer" in the Hawaiian islands as well, Steinberger, *en route* to Samoa, touched at Honolulu. That his mission had aroused considerable curiosity is evidenced by the fact that San Francisco papers, which had preceded him to Hawaii, contained articles suggesting that Steinberger had been sent as a United States representative to the Hawaiian government. "Hence I took immediate occasion," he says, "to assure His Majesty, King Lunalilo, that I was in no wise accredited to his government, and that news-vendors in this, as in many other cases, were irresponsible agitators." But Steinberger "accepted an invitation to visit Pearl River Harbor, and homeward bound again touched at Honolulu, and while awaiting repairs to vessel, availed myself of the opportunity to visit sugar-estates and learn something of the Hawaiian Islands."[11]

The Steinberger expedition sighted Manua on August 6, but as there was no harbor there the vessel sailed on until Pago Pago harbor was reached the next morning, Thursday, August 7, at eight o'clock.[12] "In a few minutes our vessel was crowded with natives," wrote Steinberger, "among them one who could speak a little English, John

on Foreign Relations in the Senate, April 22, 1874. See also Senate Ex. Doc. no. 45, 43 Congress, 1 session, pp. 1-58, or House Ex. Doc. no. 161, 44 Congress, 1 session, pp. 13-69. The report embraces some fifty-eight printed pages, and in addition to giving an account of political conditions in the islands, it contains considerable scientific data in relation to the geology, flora, etc., of the group.

[10] Steinberger's report to Fish as above; see also S. Ex. Doc. no. 45, 43 Congress, 1 session, p. 35 and p. 2.

[11] S.R.   [12] *Ibid.*; S. Ex. Doc. no. 45, p. 34.

Sine, an intelligent but knavish fellow, really the hereditary chief of the bay, educated by Rev. Dr. Powell." The next day at three o'clock Steinberger, his artist-secretary, and his interpreter called upon Mauga, the chief with whom Commander Meade had negotiated the agreement of the year before. The meeting took place in the village assembly house of Pago Pago, and the chief made it clear that he regarded himself as under the protection of "Amerika". On the ninth the chief returned Steinberger's call, bringing his wife and young daughter also on board the *Fanny*. Steinberger described the chief's family as dressed in European clothes and exhibiting "no little dignity and propriety." While the party dined in the cabin of the *Fanny*, the natives crowded the decks.[13]

On the tenth a council was held with the chief for the purpose of coming to some agreement for the modification of the harbor regulations made by Commander Meade with the chief at the time the agreement for the exclusive use of Pago Pago harbor by the United States was drawn up.[14] "These regulations provided for harbor commissioners," reported Steinberger, "consisting of Mauga, the agent of the Australian Steamship Company, and a foreign consul; this commission to fix rates. There being no agent of said company or foreign consul in the bay, and Mauga not fairly comprehending such a paper, was apt to exercise arbitrary rule, claiming United States protection or even authority.'"[15]

When Steinberger entered the harbor of Pago Pago, there was no pilot available and he "found that the buoy which Commodore Meade had put upon Whale Rock was

---

[13] *Ibid.*

[14] Unless Steinberger received oral instructions to treat with the chief, as though the Meade treaty had been ratified, there was no justification for his having any dealings with Mauga.

[15] S.R.; S. Ex. Doc. no. 45, p. 34.

gone, and no facilities provided for water."[16] Since no harbor dues had been fixed by the commission provided for in Commander Meade's regulations, Steinberger in agreement with Mauga made an appendix to these regulations fixing the harbor dues at three cents per ton in Pago Pago harbor, "water being free and proper facilities given for same; this sum not subject to change until such time as we may buoy and mark out harbor and construct and maintain lighthouse; this sum being paid by American ships as a precedent."[17] This appendix was approved by S. F. Williams, the British acting consul at Apia on October 6, 1873.[18] The appendix agreed to, Steinberger "paid the pilot full charges and the harbor dues at the rates mentioned in the appendix, taking receipts and leaving him blank forms of receipts."[19]

Mauga promised to "buoy the harbor, and open a boat-passage at the upper end of the bay to the small stream, thus giving facilities for ships in the harbor to take fresh water as compensation for harbor-dues."[20] Mauga failed to keep his promise.[21] In fact, shortly after Steinberger's departure from Pago Pago, August 15, the chief "seized a boat belonging to the English schooner, *Dauntless,* demanding an unlawful sum of money as harbor-dues, which was paid." Upon complaint by the captain, the English consul imposed a heavy fine upon the chief, which was remitted, however, when Steinberger refunded to the cap-

[16] S.R.

[17] *Ibid.;* S. Ex. Doc. no. 45, p. 55, encl. L 1, appendix to Pago Pago harbor regulations agreed to Aug. 14, 1873.

[18] *Ibid.,* encl. L 2. [19] *Ibid.;* S. Ex. Doc. no. 45, p. 34.

[20] *Ibid.*

[21] Upon his return to Pago Pago in October, Steinberger found that Mauga "had not buoyed the harbor nor opened the boat passage for water. He begged that I would do this work for him. Finally, with the pilot, we arranged for this work, and there is a reasonable hope that it will be done." (S. Ex. Doc. no. 45, p. 41.)

tain the money paid over three cents per ton. "I did this to get a practical recognition of Commodore Meade's action. Whatever may be the avarice and ignorance of Mauga or his farcical estimate of the importance to himself of Commodore Meade's treaty, yet that treaty and the harbor-regulations with the intelligent and dignified action of this officer, gave to the United States a powerful influence, made a lodgment among the people without a fixed government, attracted and attached all the natives to us, and compelled upon the part of foreigners a tacit acknowledgment of the priority of America in its right to treat with the Samoans."[22]

Steinberger left Pago Pago on August 15 for Apia, landing on the island of Aunuu on the way. The chief at Aunuu, Faumuina by name, expressed the "earnest hope, that Samoa would establish a government, or that the United States would take them under her wing." Arriving at Apia August 17, Steinberger found that Coe, the American commercial agent, had gone to San Francisco. He called upon Williams, the English consul, and found him "an intelligent gentleman, the son of the martyr missionary, and born in Samoa, created a chief by the natives, and endeared to them." When Steinberger stated to Williams the object of his visit the consul had "lent his hearty co-operation." Upon his arrival in Apia the chiefs of the islands of Upolu, Manono, and Savaii were assembled at the so-called capital of Samoa, Mulinuu, immediately to the westward of Apia, "for the purpose of making laws and establishing a stable government for the whole group."

Steinberger met the chiefs by appointment on the nineteenth at the home of a Mr. Collie, having the English consul for interpreter, and informed them that the pur-

[22] S.R.; S. Ex. Doc. no. 45, pp. 34 and 35.

pose of his mission was to gather information about the islands and their inhabitants. He was not "clothed with diplomatic powers to treat with them," he told them, but it was his "desire to meet and confer with them." He moreover advised them that he "was accredited to Samoa and the Samoans, not to the white foreign residents." He then touched upon an extremely delicate subject, as far as the foreigners in Samoa were concerned, when he said he was aware of the fact that they [the natives] "now felt keenly the transfer of lands to the whites which was the result of their own tribal feuds, and the advantage taken of their necessities; and that the Prime Minister of America had instructed me to advise the natives against the sale of land to foreigners."[23] Thus, with one stroke, had Steinberger, so he felt, gained the confidence of the natives and "from that day till the hour of my departure from the islands," he reported, "the chieftains would seek me, asking advice, and detailing their plans for the creation of government and establishment of laws. . . . For the first time they felt they had met a white man other than missionaries, who advised them against the sale of their land and mingled freely with them without sinister motives. . . . Pages of specific instructions could not have evinced greater forethought or accomplished more by the Secretary of State than that one sentence, 'Advise the natives against the sale of property.' It was at once a pathway to their confidence."

Steinberger was repeatedly called upon by the foreign residents to tell them what his advice to the natives would be "with regard to land-sales." He could not but say to them, he wrote, that he "thought the Samoans had been imposed upon, but that land-titles must be a matter for future investigation by recognized and legal tribunals,

[23] S.R.; S. Ex. Doc. no. 45, pp. 35 and 36.

and that I could not assume to arbitrate upon any specific question." Continuing, he reported: "I found myself in an anomalous position, and determined to avoid issues, but adhere to the natives."[24]

Steinberger found representatives of the Polynesian Land Company both in Pago Pago and Apia. He knew very little of the originators of the scheme of land speculation, he wrote, but he thought the scheme not creditable. "The San Francisco stockholders and one, James McKee, of Sandwich Islands," he understood, were "innocent and highly respectable gentlemen, whose money has been squandered and their reputation stained by adventurers representing them on the islands." The company had established trading-posts at Pago Pago and Apia, Steinberger wrote further, and with a supply of arms and ammunition had made contracts with the warring natives "for immense tracts of land at nominal prices." Money was to have been paid within two years, but the time had elapsed without any such additional payments being made, and since the natives had ceased fighting, the impossibility of holding them to these contracts appeared to Steinberger as quite apparent.[25]

On the twenty-fourth a conference or "talk," as the natives called it, was held. A large number of prominent chiefs were present. Wrote Steinberger, "The government's 'talking man,'[26] Prime Minister Tupai, of Atua, delivered a lengthy address, recapitulating the history of the war, expressing their desire for the permanent peace, commenting upon the loss of their lands, their helpless positions if foreigners should unjustly demand fines, and an English or German war-vessel should come to collect,

---

[24] Ibid.; S. Ex. Doc. no. 45, p. 36.   [25] Ibid.
[26] Official orator. An important personage in the Samoan governmental organization.

and closing with an earnest prayer that 'Amerika' would extend its protection over them and instruct them in law making."[27]

The "prime minister" having concluded his speech, another chief of the island of Upolu, Saga by name, "a tall, grave, gray-haired man," presented to Steinberger "the government 'Staff' and 'fly-flap,' representing the unity of all their people, saying that they sent them to 'Amerika' as pledges of their desire to be ruled by that great Government; that these were the recognized symbols of the people and their language; that the great chiefs in council had determined upon this, and there was not a dissenting voice in Upolu, Manono, and Savaii; also that in one week every Samoan would know that the emblems of their nationality had passed into the hands of 'Amerika.'"[28]

A great meeting or *fono* was held at Mulinuu on August 27 to celebrate the peace of Samoa, the Atua, Manono, and Savaii chiefs and warriors being fed and entertained by the Tuamasaga and Aana people.[29] Steinberger described the assemblage as follows: "The guests were seated in a large, deep circle, with an opening toward Apia. Soon the long files of the Tuamasaga began to approach through the cocoa-nut groves, singing Christian hymns, the warriors in gorgeous head-dress of blonde human hair, preceded by a 'talking man,' who assigned them places; these were followed by others bearing live and roasted pigs and poultry; then followed deep lines of young girls chanting, all in native dress of 'fine mats' and 'siapo' with wreathes and flowers in their hair, each bearing fruit, yams, and taro. It seemed as though the whole population had poured out. Provisions in great

[27] S.R.; S. Ex. Doc. no. 45, p. 37.   [28] *Ibid.*
[29] Atua, Tuamasaga, and Aana were the three political districts of Upolu.

piles surrounded them; speeches were made, and peace reigned in Samoa."³⁰

Not only were the natives desirous of protection but also the more respectable white element as well. On the nineteenth of August immediately after his first conference with the native chiefs, Steinberger received an address signed by Messrs. Williams, Collie, Turner, Deane, Barnard, Parker, Blackwood, and others. The writers assumed that Steinberger had been "delegated by the President of the United States of America to visit these islands in answer to a petition signed in April, 1872, by a large and influential majority of high chiefs and rulers, praying that the protection of the United States of America be extended to this group of islands," and they expressed their "hope that the prayer of the natives may be granted by the President and Government of the United States." Both factions of the natives had endeavored since the war to frame a code of laws. But, in the words of these foreign residents, the natives "have found themselves unequal to the performance of legislative duties in framing such a code of laws as will prevent civil strife and of involving them in trouble with foreign powers. It is not incompatible with the welfare of both races that whites and natives should live side by side and in amity with each other; but to conduce to and insure this desirable and practicable end it is necessary that a sound code of laws should be established for the government of natives and whites irrespective of rank or condition of both races." These foreigners, therefore, hoped that Steinberger would give their request for a protectorate his "favorable consideration."³¹

Steinberger delayed his answer until he was about to leave the islands and until he had had time to study the

---

30 S.R. 31 *Ibid.*, encl. C 1.

Samoan people and the islands. That he was sympathetic toward the proposal for an American protectorate is clear from the following passage in his letter of reply dated Apia, October 6: "I am deeply sensible of the necessity for law and an established government upon these islands. I regard it as being necessary for the salvation of the Samoans that some government extend to them power and protection. . . . Your petition I will present to our Government of the United States. I will carry with me your hopes; your prayer will be in my mind and heart."[32]

Going to the island of Manono on August 28, in an open boat with the Reverend George Brown and a number of natives, Steinberger talked with the chiefs and natives there. Then he went to the island of Apolima, whence he returned to Apia on September 1.[33] September 5 Steinberger sailed for the island of Savaii, where he remained about three weeks, going around the island by open boat and penetrating the interior; meeting the people and chiefs in church, in school, and in council.[34] Toward the latter part of the month he returned to the island of Upolu.[35]

The chiefs having formed a code of laws, principally based on "the Huahine laws of Tahiti and Tonga" they presented the code in a crude form to Steinberger for his approval. Steinberger called "the English, American, and German consuls together; also the Protestant and Roman Catholic missionaries; and after consultation, the laws were modified and returned to the chiefs." Steinberger reported that he experienced "no little difficulty" in obtaining the coöperation of the German consul and other white residents for the reason that they "had been purchasers of land, and demanded that all past land-

[32] S.R.; encl. C 2.
[34] *Ibid.*
[33] *Ibid.;* S. Ex. Doc. no. 45, p. 37.
[35] *Ibid.;* S. Ex. Doc. no. 45, p. 38.

sales should be ratified by the government, debarring future investigation." Steinberger thought "this was too palpably unjust, and coming from a consciousness of non-validity of title," and he, therefore, "could not accede to it."

October 2, 1873, was an eventful day for the Samoan people. With their code of laws ready, they now raised their flag as a symbol of union at Mulinuu and the flag was officially saluted by the foreign consuls. In describing the event Steinberger said: "With the missionaries and foreign representatives on either hand I saluted the flag and addressed the people. Previous to this ceremony, I was much concerned to know what would be the action of the German consul.[36] While our relations were of the most agreeable character, yet, knowing his control of a great monopoly, I had doubts about his recognition of the Samoan government and their laws; hence I was the more gratified to have him present and all the vessels displaying national bunting. I felt that I was not only eminently successful, but that every element was harmonized."[37]

The next day, October 3, Steinberger, in company with Dr. Turner, visited Malietoa Laupepa some two miles above Apia, where he was living in retirement with his aunt, Patocine (Emma). Steinberger described him as "a young man, educated by the missionaries, preferring retirement to politics, ambition and strife—his great name a sure protection."[38] In referring to Malietoa's interests Steinberger wrote: "He expressed his great joy that peace had come, and laws were created for his people; he was earnest in his desires for American jurisdiction; he knew much of our country, our civil war, the freedom of

[36] Theodor Weber was also the representative in Samoa of the firm of Godeffroy and Son of Hamburg.
[37] S.R.; S. Ex. Doc. no. 45, pp. 38 and 39.
[38] *Ibid.;* S. Ex. Doc. no. 45, p. 39.

the negroes, and our paternal care of the Indians.''[39] The next day, October 4, Malietoa, his wife, and Emma were received on board the *Fanny*, with the Reverend George A. Turner for dinner. Malietoa on this occasion said he would send Steinberger a letter for the president of the United States.[40] He kept his promise, and the letter was as follows:

House of Malietoa
Moatoa, Oct. 4, 1873.

Chief:

This is my letter of love to you, the chief who rules America. I am very much pleased with regard to the union between our governments. My desire is that good arise for this land. Now, this is my opinion and my wish, be pleased to appoint for us the chief Colonel Steinberger.

It is very proper for that chief to come here, to make things straight in this land.[41]

To prevent jealousies arising on account of his visit to Malietoa, Steinberger went to the Atua chiefs' headquarters at Matautu the next morning, October 5, as previously arranged with the government's "talking man," Prime Minister Tupai. Chiefs from Atua had been sent for, and in council in Atua they had come to the conclusion to present Steinberger with the "great sacred mat of Tui Atua, a piece of cloth held in great reverence by them, older than their history, known to most of the other islands in the Pacific, having the power of life and death, and which would ransom their nation." The mat was presented by Tupai with much ceremony. Steinberger then placed it upon his own head and made a formal reply.[42]

[39] S.R.

[40] *Ibid.* There were two missionaries named George A. Turner. The younger was a medical missionary and was referred to by the natives as Dr. Turner, Jr. He was evidently the son of Rev. George A. Turner.

[41] *Ibid.*, encl. E.   [42] *Ibid.;* S. Ex. Doc. no. 45, p. 39.

STEINBERGER, SPECIAL AGENT

At this meeting Steinberger learned that Chief Mauga of Pago Pago was universally hated by the Atua chiefs, who maintained that the whole island of Tutuila belonged to their district of Atua. They were particularly anxious to let Steinberger know that they did not recognize Mauga's flag, which Commodore Meade had designed for him. Fearing that Mauga might attack Steinberger upon his return to Pago Pago in order to obtain so great a prize as their mat, the Atua chiefs, moreover, offered to send a chief with the American representative in order to protect him and the mat. Steinberger, however, declined to accept this offer.[43]

On October 6 Steinberger "accompanied by the foreign consular boats, with flags flying," proceeded to Mulinuu to meet for the last time the representatives of Samoa. It was a momentous occasion; everyone hoped that a new day had dawned for Samoa. Even the Protestant and Roman Catholic missionaries were present. Never before had they mingled in politics, nor had they met before in any public meeting. Advantage of Steinberger's presence was taken by the native leaders to read for the first time their newly formulated constitution and laws.[44] The constitution provided for a government based on the Taimua and Pule which on August 21, 1873, had organized the same. Seven chiefs or rulers were to be chosen from the Taimua and Pule to be the head of the government, each of the seven to rule one year. These seven rulers and judges were to have the power to decide all questions, and make treaties and agreements with foreign powers, and to receive ambassadors and commissioners from them. They were, moreover, to adjust all disputes arising in the islands, and should also frame whatever laws would be

---

[43] *Ibid.;* S. Ex. Doc. no. 45, pp. 39 and 40.
[44] Constitution and code of laws appear in Steinberger's report as enclosures F and G.

necessary for the government of the islands. In addition to the seven rulers there should also be chosen four rulers by the government "from among the people, who by their wisdom and intelligence" were to "form the pillars of the edifice of government, and aid the Taimua by their superior judgment," and see to the execution of the laws. They were to be called governors, and their duties consisted of overseeing "the work of the judges, the scribes, and all the government work of Samoa." The constitution also outlined the duties of judges and provided for an oath of office to be taken by the members of the Taimua. Freedom of religion was provided for; likewise trial by jury. The Samoan laws, which had also been adopted on August 21, were classified under twenty-five heads. These laws related to murder, theft, marriage, adultery, perjury and false accusation, slander, rebellion, the selling of lands, tattooing, drinking by government officers, the Sabbath, four-footed animals, trespass, assault, weapons, schools, public roads, great journeying parties, obscene night dancing, vessels, trading, weights and measures, money, and revenue.

Following the promulgation of the Samoan constitution and laws Steinberger addressed the assemblage in part as follows: " 'I came with greeting, and the earnest friendship of our people and my Great Chief. I have spoken the views of my chiefs. I have counseled you as to your interests, advised you against the sale of lands, deprecated recognition of liquor-shops, and told you of the industry of our people. I have found you to be a brave, earnest, and honest people; you tell me that you are a simple people, and that you believe in my people, and hope for guidance from them. I will carry this in my heart and my mind; my Great Chief shall see you through me. . . . I have the letter of the Government of Samoa (Taimua) to his Excellency the President of the United States, which I will in person present.' "[45]

The letter alluded to by Steinberger had been read by the government secretary. It referred to the fact that harmony and the laws had been established, and that the flag had been raised. "And yet, notwithstanding that we have set up laws for the government of Samoa," said the letter, "it is as though the body is whole, but it is only lying on the ground; it has no living breath in it. As is the story in the Bible: God made man, then the body was whole, but it was only a lying down, there was no living health in it. Then God breathed into it, and that is the cause of its moving about and being alive. In the same way Samoa and the laws are the person. We are exceeding desirous that you should breathe into Samoa. Be pleased to bring your wisdom, and the goodness and beauty of the American Government to teach our government and to aid Samoa in the matter of laws. We have shown the details of our government to the chief that came from the American Government, Colonel Steinberger. He will let your excellency and the American Government know all about it. We also know the object for which he was appointed, and the reason for which he came to Samoa; that is, the union between the government of Samoa and America. We very much desire that affair to be confirmed." The letter concluded with a wish that the president would be pleased to send Steinberger back to Samoa as an official American governor.[46] Referring to his reply to the government anent the appeal for aid, Steinberger reported: "I told the government of officials and chiefs that I had no power to treat with them; that my instructions were to gather facts and report the same, and that this I hoped faith-

[45] S.R., encl. D 2.
[46] *Ibid.*, encl. D 1, Taimua and Pule to President Grant, Oct. 3, 1873.

fully to do, but that I had no pledges upon the part of my Government to make; and our meeting ended.'"[47]

On the next day, October 7, Steinberger sailed from Apia homeward bound. He brought several letters with him from representative missionaries expressing their views regarding a protectorate. These gentlemen were the Rev. George A. Turner and the Rev. S. J. Whitmer of the London Missionary Society, Father L. Elloy, Roman Catholic bishop, and the Rev. George Brown, Wesleyan missionary. A personal letter by Mr. Turner, dated Apia, read in part: "You came at a very appropriate time, when the native chiefs were all assembled for the purpose of endeavoring to establish law. . . . You leave us in order to fulfill the most important part of your mission. . . . The Samoans have expressed an earnest desire that you should return and dwell among them and aid them in the capacity of first United States representative in Samoa. . . ."[48]

Messrs. Whitmer and Turner, chairman and secretary, respectively, of the Samoan District of the London Missionary Society, wrote Steinberger in part as follows:

1. That we believe the expressed desire of the Samoans for a United States protectorate is a *bona fide* wish on the part of the chiefs and people generally of Upolu, Savaii and Manono.
2. That we, and our mission generally, heartily concur in the desire of our people for the protectorate, believing not only that it will be a great benefit to the Samoan people, but that it will be the saving of the race.
3. That should your Government see fit to accede to the wish of the existing Samoan government for your own appointment as first United States representative in Samoa, we shall be most happy to welcome you in that capacity; feeling sure, from what we have seen of you, that you will do

[47] S.R.; S. Ex. Doc. no. 45, p. 40.   [48] *Ibid.*, encl. I 1.

justice to the Samoan people, and aid them in every possible way, in all their laudable efforts for social and political improvement.[49]

The French Roman Catholic bishop congratulated Steinberger on the wisdom "shown in fulfilling the delicate and important mission credited to your care by your government toward our poor and so disturbed Samoan people. Since the last war," he continued, "our Samoan chiefs seem unable to govern their country without the help of a strong hand, which might keep them saved from miserable effects of jealousy between themselves." Even now for fear of renewed disturbances the power was not placed in proper hands, he added. Such leaders as Mataafa of Atua and Malietoa of Tuamasaga were not included in the Taimua for fear that their appointment might have been mistaken by rival districts as a nomination for the title of king. "Some intervention is necessary," the bishop concluded, "to bring that unsettled state to an end. Providence seems to show us that the Government of the United States is to take interest in that matter; may it be, as I hope, for the glory of God, and the happiness of the Samoan people, to which's welfare we are to give, my collaborators and I, our strength and life until death."[50]

While Steinberger was on the island of Savaii the Wesleyan leader, Reverend George Brown, also gave the American representative a letter. Mr. Brown probably understood the conditions in Samoa as well as any foreigner, and his letter therefore gives a very illuminating account of the actual situation. In this communication dated Saleaula, Savaii, September, 1873, he corroborated what the other missionaries had written. He wrote in

[49] *Ibid.*, encl. I 2. Letter dated Oct. 4, 1873.
[50] *Ibid.*, encl. I 3, L. Elloy to Steinberger, Sept. 29, 1873.

part: "I have long felt that the only hope of any settled government being formed in Samoa, or of any real progress in the arts of civilization must be either in alliance with or a protectorate from some power apart from themselves. I have now lived in Samoa for nearly thirteen years, and am, with one exception, the senior missionary of any now residing in the group. I have lived almost entirely among the natives, and have had very good opportunities for observing their customs and for judging their character. . . . They are now engaged in an attempt to form a government for the whole of the group, but I have little or no hope of their ever being able to establish one which would be either permanent or effective. I fear, also, that difficulties will soon spring up between the natives and the whites, arising from the land sales which have been effected during the late war. Should these lands be occupied, many difficulties will arise not only from disputes about the titles, but also from the relations between the two races. The Samoans will consider themselves as the rulers of the country, and in that capacity will, in all probability, pass laws to which the whites cannot agree, and the enforcement of which they will undoubtedly resist. Hence I fear that unless there exists some authority to which both whites and natives must be amenable, we shall soon have a state of enmity existing between the two races, which would prove disastrous to both, but more especially to the Samoans. For these reasons I rejoiced when I heard of the petition sent by the chiefs, asking for a protectorate from the Government of the United States, and I earnestly hope that their petition will be favorably received. I have often spoken about it to the natives, and I believe that they are now unanimous in their desire for a protectorate."[51]

[51] S.R., encl. I 4.

Steinberger landed at Leone, Tutuila, on October 8, sending his vessel around to Pago Pago, while he with Meredith, United States vice commercial agent at the former place, visited chiefs Tuiteli and Sateli, with whom he had long interviews. "They were waiting to receive the Government emissaries, and expressed their joy at the establishment of a government and assured me of their hearty co-operation," wrote Steinberger.[52] From Leone Steinberger went by foot to Pago Pago, arriving late at night on the ninth, where he found Chief Mauga on board the *Fanny* awaiting his arrival. The next day, October 10, Steinberger met Mauga and some of his council. "I gave them a history of the government at Mulinuu," he wrote, "and the desire for unity and concord among all Samoans."[53] Steinberger then reminded Chief Mauga of Commander Meade's agreement with himself. "Commander Meade," he said, "with one of our great war-ships, has made a treaty with you, and you have given us the right to your beautiful harbor. Commander Meade also made for you a flag and hoisted our own, believing that at no distant day your harbor would afford refuge to our vessels, and create such general commerce and commercial relations as would more nearly bring the Samoan and the American into close relation and bonds of fellowship." Then, as if to impress Chief Mauga with the importance of this relationship between himself and the United States, he continued his address: "In our country we have many tribes of natives, but they are not so peaceable or honest as yourselves; only a few are Christians; but it is cold in winter; the earth gives them but little (you have every thing), but my Government gives them lands, farmers, tools, teachers, clothing, and provisions,

[52] *Ibid.;* S. Ex. Doc. no. 45, pp. 40 and 41.
[53] *Ibid.;* S. Ex. Doc. no. 45, p. 41.

and makes laws for them. Some tribes are rich and happy, but they have made farms, built churches and schoolhouses, and live as their white brethren.'"[54]

After reading his address to Mauga, Steinberger received a letter in return directed to the president of the United States in the following words:

"We know that you are a great people, with many ships and many warriors, but that you are all united in peace; that you cultivate the soil, build great houses, make great roads, and talk to each other through the air. We want the same, and pray for the aid, protection, and friendship of the President of the United States.

"Your men-of-war and your people's vessels have come into our harbor. We have made agreements with them, and your flag is joined to ours. We gave to you exclusive right to our harbor, and we want you to use it.

"We are poor, but we are happy in our peaceful island. Our Samoan brethren in the other islands are divided, and their hands raised against each other. We all want peace; we want unity and laws, and beg you to come and instruct us in concord and law-making, extending to us the protection of your excellency's great Government.'"[55]

The next morning, October 11, Steinberger weighed anchor and sailed for Manua. He landed on the twelfth at the village of Tau-Nanna, where he found the native missionary teacher could speak English, and with him he met Tui-Manna, the king, the same day. Steinberger found the king to be a blind old man of eighty or more years. The American talked with him over an hour.[56] The next day, October 13, the *Fanny* left Manua and Samoa.[57] Steinberger's voyage homeward was by way of Hawaii. He reported from San Francisco on December 13, 1873,[58] and

[54] S.R., encl. A 2.
[56] *Ibid.*; S. Ex. Doc. no. 45, p. 41.
[58] M.L.
[55] *Ibid.*, encl. A 1.
[57] *Ibid.*

again wrote from St. Louis, February 9, 1874, that he would arrive in Washington in a few days,[59] but was sending on his written report in advance. Whether Steinberger went directly to Washington or stopped at Baltimore is not clear, but on March 4 he wrote from Baltimore, saying that he was remaining there "to avoid newspaper reporters" while at the same time he was "hoping for an expression of the sense of the Department and Government. . . . I am earnest in my desire," he continued, "to serve the Samoan people, and feel a sense of obligation to them, foreseeing also the great advantage to our Government."[60]

Secretary Fish acknowledged the letter the same day, saying that Steinberger's report concerning his visit to the Samoan islands had reached Washington "in due season, and has been read with lively interest." He added: "It is replete with novel and valuable information, and shows that you must have been a diligent and judicious observer."[61] There were no suggestions as to what line of policy the United States intended to follow. The letter was merely a noncommittal one of acknowledgment.

There can be no doubt that Steinberger, during his two months' stay in Samoa, captivated both the foreign residents and the natives with his charming manners, as much as by his ability. It has been noted that his coming to the islands was assumed by the foreign residents as the answer of the United States to the petition from the natives for a protectorate. As a matter of fact, they were not far wrong. It will be remembered that when Webb had his conference in August, 1872, with the president, with the view of endorsing Steinberger's proposal to go

---

[59] *Ibid.*   [60] *Ibid.*
[61] H. Ex. Doc. no. 161, p. 69, encl. 10, Fish to Steinberger, March 4, 1874. Steinberger's report was sent to the department under covering letter dated Feb. 13, 1874. (See Miscellaneous Letters, Department of State.)

to Samoa as a special commissioner, he in all probability brought with him the petition for a protectorate, which Captain Stewart had entrusted to him for transmittal to the president. The interest of President Grant was gained, and but for the cautious Hamilton Fish, Steinberger would probably have gone to Samoa in that very year of 1872. In other words, both Steinberger and Webb had gone around Fish, as it were, to reach the president and had gained his consent to Steinberger's going to Samoa. With the information Steinberger might obtain, the interest of the Senate in the islands might be aroused to the extent of securing its ratification of Meade's treaty, and possibly Congress might be persuaded to vote a subsidy for Webb's ship line as well. Whether Grant was impressed by the petition for protection of the islands is not clear. He never submitted it to Congress, but in view of the fact that he had already transmitted Meade's treaty to the Senate for ratification, and was known to favor a subsidy for Webb, in addition to being an expansionist as far as the Caribbean Sea was concerned, it is hardly likely that he would have stood in the way of the annexation of Samoa if the sentiment in the country at the time had favored expansion in any direction beyond the continental area of the United States. Steinberger went to Samoa, nevertheless, as the president's special commissioner, and while Hamilton Fish was careful to instruct him that he was not a diplomatic officer, he could not prevent Steinberger from taking advantage of the peculiarly favoring circumstances that prevailed in Samoa when Steinberger arrived.

The natives had just come through a devastating civil war and were attempting for the first time in their history to frame a constitution and a code of laws for the whole group of islands with a view to preventing, if possible, future tribal wars. Steinberger made no effort to discourage either the natives or the whites from believing that eventually the United States would take over the islands, and in one case he intervened between the natives and the German consul in a way that would easily lead the natives to suppose that the United States had already accepted the responsibility of protecting them against rapacious land grabbers. His dealings with Chief Mauga with a view to the enforcement of the Meade treaty despite the fact that no action had been taken on it by the Senate, and his attempt to secure that rather independent chief's adherence to the government recently proclaimed at Mulinuu, were just so many more moves to keep the United States in a primary position politically in Samoa. Finally, his conferences with Malietoa, the Atua chiefs, and the missionaries, and his obtaining from all of them letters recommending protection and containing requests or suggestions that he be returned to Samoa as the first governor or diplomatic agent to the new government, clearly prove that he sought in various indirect ways to bring to bear upon the authorities in Washington such influences that not only they, but eventually Congress as well, would become convinced of the desirability of annexing the archipelago.

CHAPTER V

STEINBERGER, PREMIER OF SAMOA

IN order to keep Steinberger informed relative to developments in Samoa subsequent to his departure from the islands, two of the missionary leaders, Turner and Brown, wrote to him in October and November; the former, two letters, and the latter, one. These letters are further evidence that Steinberger had created the impression in Samoa that he expected to return to Samoa and direct the government, perhaps as an American governor.[1] In enclosing the letters Steinberger wrote to Secretary Fish from Baltimore on March 14, 1874: "... I can with facility control these people; and to me it would be a labor of love, and I await the action of the Department. I shall write to my friends in Samoa and propose an address to the Samoan government, which I will submit to yourself. If approved, it should have an official air. Each movement of myself, even in detail, will be faithfully submitted to the Secretary of State."[2]

That Steinberger wanted to return to Samoa either as a governor of the islands or as minister or commissioner is indicated in another letter written to Fish from Baltimore on April 8. "The Samoan letters submitted by myself will nearly express the views of this people. They seek protection. If the extending of an American protectorate over them is not at this moment deemed advis-

---

[1] H. Ex. Doc. no. 161, pp. 70 and 71, enclosures 1, 2 and 3 in enclosure 11.
[2] Miscellaneous Letters, Department of State, Steinberger to Fish, Mar. 14, 1874.

able by the Government, it then seems to be a matter of moment that our Government will send a minister or commissioner, with plenipotentiary power to recognize their government and treat with them as an independent people. The government which I was mainly instrumental in creating has been recognized by the commander of the English Australian squadron flag-ship, *Pearl*.[3] The resources of the Samoan Islands are embodied in my report. The native chiefs are now devoted to America, and every foreign missionary seeks American protection. After spending some months with these people, it is my judgment that the United States extends a protectorate over the group, appoint a governor and secretary, equipment for, say, one hundred men as a native guard, clothing, muskets, a battery of four field-pieces (brass) with ammunition, and a scientific corps consisting of a botanist, taxidermist, photographic artist, and surgeon; the latter to be a microscopist." Steinberger apparently was not content merely to be a governor of the Samoan group. He seems to have had visions of a veritable little island empire for in continuing his letter he said: "The islands north and adjacent to Samoa, Eilbut, Ellier, and Kingsmill group, speak a tongue analogous to the Samoan. These islands are nearly depopulated by South American slavers, and in a few months would be tributary to a Samoan government. Any expenditure upon the part of the United States could be refunded by direct tax." Steinberger presented "these views with the hope," he wrote, "that my report, with accompanying documents, will be submitted to the Senate Committee, with message from

[3] On November 14 Dr. Turner had written Steinberger that the British warship *Pearl*, the new flagship on the Australian Station, had just visited Apia, and that Commodore Goodenough had recognized the Samoan government by inviting the Taimua on board, hoisting the Samoan flag and firing a salute of seven guns. (See H. Ex. Doc. no. 161, p. 70, encl. 1 in encl. 11.)

his Excellency the President, and that I may be called upon to express the desire of the Samoans, as I feel to have their interest also in mind."

Steinberger's return to the United States had, of course, aroused considerable interest, and newspapers were publishing accounts of adventurers on the West coast planning to go to Samoa in search of gold. Steinberger commented on this. "Nothing could be more damaging," he wrote, "than a rush of adventurers to these islands; there is no gold or other precious metals in Samoa; this particular matter I have thoroughly investigated. In my address to the Samoan government I shall caution them against any such excitement. This paper I will first forward to the Department."[4] On April 14, Secretary Fish acknowledged receipt of Steinberger's two letters of March 14 and April 8, writing in a noncommittal vein: "The subjects of which the letters treat are under consideration."[5]

Three days later, April 17, Steinberger wrote again from Baltimore to Fish enclosing his proposed letter to the Samoan government and suggesting "that the Department officially indorse the paper, and acknowledge receipt of their letters, also the 'fly-flap' and 'staff' and that the American consul at Apia be advised of the transmission of such papers and defer to the same."[6] Secretary Fish acknowledged receipt of Steinberger's letter almost immediately, expressing regret, however, that it was not deemed expedient to comply with his request that his proposed address to the Samoan government be endorsed by the department "as it would be contrary to the usual practice of the Department."[7] The real reason for the department's refusal to endorse Steinberger's

[4] M.L., Steinberger to Fish, April 8, 1874.
[5] H. Ex. Doc. no. 161, p. 72, encl. 13.   [6] M.L.
[7] H. Ex. Doc. no. 161, p. 74, encl. 15.

proposed letter to the Samoans was the fact that its contents would have placed the department in the position of endorsing Steinberger's desire to return to Samoa and to carry on there a sort of quasi-intervention on behalf of the United States, if not govern the islands under a protectorate. On the same day, April 21, Secretary Fish forwarded Steinberger's report to the president, who forwarded it promptly to the Senate and the House of Representatives with no comments or suggestions.[8]

Though Steinberger's efforts for the time being had been vetoed by Secretary Fish's letter, he continued to act as though the Samoan government would sooner or later come under the protection of the United States, and that consequently he would be sent to the islands as the first commissioner or governor. If that were the case, his future position in Samoa, it appeared to him, would be one of real power, and the possibility of his realizing something financially from his favored situation did not escape his attention. He accordingly went to Hamburg and negotiated with the firm of Godeffroy & Son a secret agreement on September 16, 1874, wherein he promised to exert his influence to secure favors from the Samoan government for the German company; in fact, give it a monopoly of the copra trade in return for a considerable financial consideration in the form of commissions. Steinberger was to receive, for example, two dollars per ton weight of copra and cocoanut fibre sold by the government of Samoa to the establishment of J. C. Godeffroy & Son, and ten per cent upon the amount of purchases made by the Samoan government for material, etc., from the same company. The land held by the company would be guaranteed by Steinberger. This clause of the agreement is interesting in view of the warnings Steinberger had uttered to the natives during his stay among them the

[8] S. Ex. Doc. no. 45, p. 1.

previous year that they should not sell their lands, and especially because of what his report had said in regard to section eight of the new laws with respect to the selling of land. In the report he wrote: "When section eight, 'law for selling land', was read,[9] it was at once opposed by the German consul and agent of Godeffroy & Co., and our acting commercial agent, Mr. Hamilton. They wished a clause inserted which would forever debar investigation into past land-sales, and that the titles be ratified . . . I at once insisted that the law should be accepted, and opposed addition or modification . . . This was the single extra official and arbitrary act upon my part during my intercourse with the Samoans." Steinberger's change of heart is easily discerned, however, when one reads on the other hand in section A of article 4 of the Steinberger-Godeffroy agreement that Steinberger was "to procure for the establishment of J. C. Godeffroy & Son at Apia the Samoa government recognition and counter signature of all land sales heretofore made to the managers of the same by the natives." The faith of the Godeffroy people in Steinberger's ability to do this, and the value they placed upon his services in general, was due to his convincing them that he was soon returning to Samoa with enhanced authority from the government of the United States. This is shown in the first article of the agreement where it was expressly stated that Steinberger would proceed "to the Samoa Islands as United States Commissioner in order to establish there a fixed and substantial government upon the principles of good administration." It is also seen in the second article where Steinberger, who, "because of his future position at Samoa and the home endorsement, will evidently exercise a paramount influence in the Samoan Islands," pledged himself to the interests of the Godeffroy company altogether, promis-

---

[9] At the great meeting at Mulinuu on October 6, when the new laws for Samoa were proclaimed by the Taimua and Pule.

ing "to avoid all other business connections in toto in America, Europe, and Samoa."[10]

Upon his return from Germany, probably in October, 1874, Steinberger resumed his negotiations for the annexation of the Samoan islands by the United States and, without divulging his secret arrangement with the Godeffroy company, he secured permission from the government to return to Samoa for the purpose of further observation. Before his instructions were issued, however, he wrote to Fish on November 19, making certain suggestions. A war vessel conveying him to Samoa, he wrote, "should salute their flag and receive their chief officers of government at Apia, and visit Pago Pago, if only to show appreciation of the tender of this bay without cost to the United States." The receipt of the "staff" and "fly-flap," and "sacred mat" of Atua should be acknowledged by the president because by these symbols "they virtually tender their country." Continuing he said: "Future legislation will determine the action of the United States in this, but I am confident of my ability and the devotion of the natives to make Samoa valuable, creditable and popular." Steinberger wrote about having conferred with Messrs. Godeffroy at Hamburg, but his duplicity is seen in that he said nothing about his agreement with the German company. He also wanted precedence "over the American and other consuls." He reverted to the subject of armament when he said: "A few presents would gain much for us, such as two small guns (brass), a Gatling gun, a 12-pounder Parrott, to give dignity to their government-house; also a small lot of light clothing and small arms for guards."[11]

Finally on December 11, Steinberger received instructions from Fish for a second visit to the Samoan islands,

[10] H. Ex. Doc. no. 44, 44 Congress, 2 session, pp. 128-130, encl. 1 with encl. 25.
[11] *Ibid.*, no. 161, p. 75, encl. 16.

the president having determined that he was to go again in the character of a special agent. A man-of-war was to bring him to the islands, as he had requested, but the expense of the mission must be borne entirely by himself. This time not even expense money was available.[12] A letter from President Grant to the Samoan government was entrusted to him wherein the chief executive acknowledged receipt of their symbols: "staff" and "fly-flap," and "sacred mat" of Atua. "You may be assured," the president said, "that I am duly sensible of the significance of these gifts." The president made no promise concerning protection, but said: "Being, then, as you are, much nearer to us than to any European nation, on this account alone it would be natural, were there no other reasons, that we should take a lively interest in your welfare and in all that concerns you." Colonel Steinberger, the president added, had, so far, acted acceptably, and therefore he had "authorized him again to visit you, for the purpose of informing me of the progress of your affairs since he left you."[13]

In continuing his instructions to Steinberger the secretary of state said there was no doubt of the natural fertility of the Samoan soil and of many other resources. He thought, moreover, the position of the Samoan group in the Pacific commanding "and particularly important to us." He added, however, that it was "more than doubtful . . . whether these considerations would be sufficient to satisfy our people that the annexation of those islands to the United States is essential to our safety and prosperity. In any event, supposing that the general sentiment should be favorable to such a measure, I am not aware that it has received such an expression as would require an acknowledgment by the Government and warrant measures on our part accordingly. It is deemed in-

[12] H. Ex. Doc. no. 161, p. 76, encl. 17. [13] *Ibid.*, p. 77, encl. with encl. 17.

STEINBERGER, PREMIER OF SAMOA

expedient without such a call from the public to originate a measure adverse to the usual traditions of the Government, and which, therefore, probably would not receive such a sanction as would be likely to secure its success. Under these circumstances, your functions will be limited to observing and reporting upon Samoan affairs, and to impressing those in authority there with the lively interest which we take in their happiness and welfare.'"[14]

Thus the various appeals from Samoa for annexation or protection were answered in the negative and Colonel Steinberger went back neither as a diplomatic agent, because we had made no treaty with Samoa, nor as a commissioner or governor, since we neither had annexed the islands nor taken them under our protection. But he was not definitely told to decline the appeals from Samoa, and hence, as we shall see, he was about to lead them for sometime to believe that he had authority to give them protection; and indeed his coming to them on board an American naval vessel, and also his bringing gifts to the Samoan government such as he had asked for, namely, guns and ammunition, would necessarily prolong the illusion.[15] The administration, especially the Navy Depart-

[14] *Ibid.*, p. 76, encl. 17.
[15] *Ibid.*, p. 78, encl. 19. List of articles furnished by the War and Navy Departments for presentation to the Samoan government:
    ARMY: 100 Springfield muzzle-loading rifle muskets cal. .58; 10,000 cartridges.
        1 Gatling gun and carriage, cal. .1 inch; 1,000 cartridges.
        2 twelve-pound bronze guns and carriages; 200 rounds of ammunition.
        1 three-inch Parrott gun and carriage; 100 rounds ammunition.
    NAVY: 1 Brozle boat howitzer, with ammunition.
        1 forge complete.
        100 suits sailors' flannel clothing, with caps.
        3 United States flags, and extra bunting.
        Some band instruments.
        12 revolvers, with ammunition.

ment, wanted Pago Pago harbor, and perhaps all the islands, but when it was impossible to secure the ratification of the Meade treaty by the Senate, the chances of finding sufficient support for an annexationist policy in Congress at this time were, as Secretary Fish suggested in his second instructions to Steinberger, non-existent. And yet the authorities permitted Steinberger to return to the islands without having called his attention to the fact that his relations with the Pago Pago chief were illegal without the ratification. Perhaps they expected that the Senate might some day ratify it, and therefore thought it would be well not to be too punctilious in the matter. On February 2, 1875, Steinberger informed Secretary Fish from the U.S.S. *Pensacola* in San Francisco harbor that "all material is on board excepting 'flags, bunting and band instruments.' " He intended to avoid publicity, but would do his duty.[16]

A month before his departure Steinberger had also entered into an agreement with John H. B. Latrobe, Jr., of Baltimore, who was to go to Samoa with him and render all assistance possible to carry out contracts made by Steinberger. For these services Latrobe was to receive "twenty-five per cent of all commissions and pecuniary profits of every description of all undertakings in which the said Steinberger may be engaged." Moreover, since Steinberger might "have it in his power to establish and organize a form of government for said islands, or some of them, under which it may so happen that the said Steinberger may hold office, and be able to provide office through his influence for his friends" he promised to "use his influence, both official and personal, to procure for the said Latrobe the best and most honorable and lucrative office under said government after he, the said

[16] H. Ex. Doc. no. 161, p. 78, encl. 20.

Steinberger, shall be himself provided for." Latrobe should also have twenty-five per cent of any income Steinberger received in connection with a contract with one Walter S. Wilkinson, of Baltimore.[17] And should Steinberger also receive any compensation from the United States government "for past or future employment in connection with said islands" Latrobe should share in the same proportion in this income. The agreement was to be terminated only in the event that Latrobe should want to leave Samoa.[18]

Steinberger arrived in Honolulu February 15 on the *Pensacola,* which had left San Francisco February 2. The king of Hawaii, who had visited the United States for a space of two months, returned to his homeland on the same warship.[19] The fact that he was on the same ship as the king, Steinberger wrote, set in circulation rumors that he was accredited to the Hawaiian government, which rumors he immediately denied. Since the *Pensacola* was to remain in Hawaiian waters, Steinberger secured passage on the U.S.S. *Tuscarora,* Captain Henry Erben, which had been engaged in deep-sea soundings from San Francisco to Honolulu, but which "left the latter port on the 4th of March for the Samoan group for the purpose of conducting, at the instance of the Department of State,

[17] According to the agreement between the firm of Godeffroy and Steinberger, "the government of Samoa [was] to grant a monopoly for the exportation of the bark of the *ua* or Chinese paper mulberry to the establishment of J. C. Godeffroy and Son at Apia, for Europe, and to Walter S. Wilkinson, of Baltimore, Md., for America for a period of twenty years from the date of the establishment of intended Samoan government." (See section [1] article 4 of Steinberger-Godeffroy agreement, p. 130, H. Ex. Doc. no. 44.)

[18] H. Ex. Doc. no. 44, p. 135, encl. 3 with encl. 25.

[19] *Ibid.,* no. 1, part 3, 44 Congress, 1 session, p. 8. The king had recently been recognized by the United States government, and soon upon his return to Hawaii the treaty of 1875, reserving certain privileges to the United States, was negotiated.

an inquiry into the claims, or complaints of American citizens against the natives of that group."[20] The *Tuscarora* arrived at Apia April 1, 1875.[21]

Steinberger's arrival was hailed with delight by the natives, and when he presented the Samoan government the guns and ammunition from the United States government his place in their confidence became well-nigh impregnable.[22] During Steinberger's absence from Samoa the natives had come to the conclusion that their government with seven chiefs (Taimua) and four higher chiefs (Pule) was not as effective as one with a king at its head. But being unable to make a choice, they felt obliged to elect two kings, Malietoa Laupepa and Pulepule, the latter belonging to a rival family to that of Malietoa, known as the Tupua family. These two were vested jointly with the office and title of king on January 2, 1875. When Steinberger returned to Samoa he persuaded, however, the chiefs to give up their two-king régime and select Malietoa Laupepa as their sole king. A new constitution was adopted on May 18 which provided for a legislative branch of two houses, the Taimua and the Faipule,[23] and also a premier, it being understood, of course, that Steinberger would be named the first premier by King Malietoa. The monarchy thus established was a sort of duplex hereditary one. A king was to be elected every four years alternately from the "two great houses of Malietoa and

[20] H. Ex. Doc. no. 1, part 3, 44 Congress, 1 session, p. 8.
[21] *Ibid.*, no. 161, p. 90, encl. A 2 with encl. 24.
[22] See article by Henry Erben: "The *Tuscarora's* Mission to Samoa" in *Century Magazine* for May 1889, pp. 34-37. This article contains three letters from the Taimua which do not appear in the printed government documents. One dated May 12, 1875 is addressed to President Grant; one on the same day addressed to Captain Erben; and one on May 13 addressed to Col. Steinberger.
[23] *Taimua* in the Samoan language means a leader; *Faipule* is a compound word from *fai*, to do, or to make, and *pule*, a command, or an order.

Tupua." The premier, who was to be the counselor of the king, should preside over the Taimua and should have the right to take the floor in either the Taimua or Faipule. No act by the king should be valid without the countersignature of the premier.[24] In the opinion of George H. Bates, a United States special commissioner sent to Samoa in 1886, the government established for Samoa by Steinberger, while "rather elaborate for a people so primitive in all respects" nevertheless contained "much that is worthy of consideration in any scheme for the future government of the country." Bates declared further that the government inaugurated under the revised constitution was "the only really stable and efficient one which the islands have had since there has been a considerable foreign population." He admitted, however, that the government was "a personal government by Steinberger, the Premier acting through the instrumentalities and forms of a constitutional native government." Steinberger "originated everything," declared Bates, "and, without doubt, his will was law." All foreigners in Samoa whether they were friendly or opposed to Steinberger agreed "that it was *his* government."[25] A perusal of the clauses of the constitution instantly betrays its origin. But for those clauses relating to the king and the prime minister, and the peculiarly Samoan names, the reader might easily conclude that they had been copied from some state constitution in the United States. It is evident that Steinberger wrote the whole instrument. He furthermore sent a copy of the constitution to the Department of State on

[24] Special Agents, vol. 2, Department of State, report by Geo. H. Bates, dated Dec. 10, 1886; see also H. Ex. Doc. no. 238, 50 Congress, 1 session, appendix A, pp. 194-198, encl. B 1.

[25] Special Agents, vol. 2; see also H. Ex. Doc. no. 238, appendix A, p. 142.

May 23 with a letter from the Samoan government to the president.[26]

Before the constitution was drawn up by Steinberger, he wrote to the London Missionary Society on May 5, requesting their advice with respect to certain urgent laws, etc.[27] Their answer, dated June 12, was a long statement in which they took up *seriatim* the points raised by Steinberger. The missionaries were particularly anxious that an effective liquor law be enacted to bring to an end the large volume of unlicensed selling of liquor which the traders were carrying on among the islands. They also wanted a law as effective as that in Hawaii with respect to the prevention of the prostitution of native women at the ports. They promised that one of them would act as interpreter between Steinberger and the Samoan government. They also promised the use of their printing press for the printing of government documents. They designed for Steinberger a national coat-of-arms, a private seal for the king, and a royal decoration order.

Steinberger was not satisfied with King Malietoa's manner of dress and living and in compliance with a request from him, the missionaries stated further: "We have already acted on your suggestion, and have advised the King to adopt, as fast as he can, a style of dress becoming his position; to try and obtain from the Government a house in which he could live with his family in a style suitable to the King of the entire group. He received our advice in good part, and promised at once to attend to it." Steinberger also wanted assistance from the missionaries in a proposed investigation of labor conditions on German plantations. This they promised to

[26] Miscellaneous Letters, Department of State.
[27] Steinberger Papers, Department of State, Steinberger to Fish, July 4, 1875, rec'd Aug. 30, enclosing letter from Steinberger to London Missionary Society, May 5, marked enclosure 3.

give him. The registration of marriages on the islands had been extremely lax and the missionaries also advised Steinberger to effect an immediate change.[28]

The letter from the missionaries to Steinberger referred to above was addressed to him as United States commissioner to Samoa; and the understanding that he was acting under instructions from his superiors when he intervened to reform the government of Samoa, is borne out even more clearly in a letter from S. F. Williams, British acting consul, who, on July 3, requested Steinberger to inform him "when the laws will be proclaimed as I wish to give British subjects notice that they are amenable to your Government and laws."[29]

Steinberger accepted the premiership of Samoa on July 4, 1875,[30] and on the same day notified the State Department of the step. Although he wrote later, October 28, that he had had no opportunity since July to send in his resignation as special agent, it is very likely that when he took over the Samoan post he hoped to hold both offices until such time perhaps when Congress should act favorably on the petition for protection. Steinberger wrote to Fish on July 4 that he had "publicly announced" that he "could receive no pay, emoluments, or title of nobility" in view of the fact that he was an American citizen. He appeared to be somewhat dubious, however,[31] of the legality of his holding two offices, one as special agent of

---

[28] *Ibid.;* see also H. Ex. Doc. no. 161, pp. 93-94, encl. A 5, S. J. Whitmer, George Turner, Henry Nisbet, and George A. Turner to Col. A. B. Steinberger, June 12, 1875.

[29] *Ibid.,* encl. 1.

[30] Steinberger wrote July 14 as the date of his appointment when he reported to the department on October 28, but on July 4 he reported that he had then accepted the position. Evidently July 4 is the correct date. Compare enclosures 23 and 24, pp. 81 and 89 respectively, in H. Ex. Doc. no. 161.

[31] S.P., Steinberger to Fish, July 4, 1875.

the United States, and the other as premier of the Samoan government; and hence he asked "the assistance of the Department in the passage of a bill by Congress permitting me, as an 'American citizen,' to hold office here under a foreign government. So much does America fill the hearts and minds of these people that any treaty for harbors, naval stations, coaling depots, or other privileges draughted in Washington would receive prompt recognition here."[32] This letter was received by the department August 30, but no action was taken upon it and no request for Steinberger's resignation was made. The department was waiting for a reply from Steinberger to an inquiry it had sent him on May 6. This inquiry had been prompted by two despatches sent by Foster, the American consul, a few days after the departure of Steinberger from San Francisco on his second journey to Samoa. In his first despatch Foster had said: "There is still some danger of war, but not until they hear definitely from the United States in regard to a protectorate, which they consider has been promised them with the speedy return of Colonel A. B. Steinberger with the presents promised and until this is settled little can be done in regard to claims or any other affairs with them."[33] In the other despatch Foster complained that Steinberger had "assumed the right without consulting one foreign consul in Apia, to levy tonnage-dues, and gave a native chief the right to examine a ship's register" when entering Pago Pago harbor.[34]

Secretary Fish wrote Steinberger that Foster's despatches "lead to the apprehension that although, pursuant to the instructions of this Department your functions

[32] S.P.
[33] C.D., Apia, vol. 3, no. 6, Foster, Feb. 8, 1875, rec'd April 16.
[34] *Ibid.*, no. 7, Foster, Feb. 8, 1875, rec'd April 16.

as special agent to the Samoan Islands were limited to obtaining information in regard to that group, the rulers there consider that you have promised them the protection of this Government." If this was true, continued Fish, "it is much to be regretted, as no such promise was made, nor any hope of such protection was held out by warrant of this Government, and such promise, if made, was one which this Department, in the absence of a formal treaty, or of the sanction of Congress, had no right to authorize you to make." Fish wrote further: "It is also stated by the consul that you assumed the right to levy tonnage-dues in that quarter, and professed to give a right to a native chief to examine registers without, on your part, having consulted a single foreign consul upon the subject. This would present a case of the assumption and exercise of arbitrary and unauthorized power quite inconsistent with your instructions, which would be equally surprising and painful to the Department, but which, it is hoped, is susceptible of explanation, which will consequently be acceptable."[35]

Foster's despatches, dated February 8, were not received in Washington until April 16. Secretary Fish's communication to Steinberger, dated May 6, was not answered by the latter until October 18, and this despatch did not reach Washington until December 6. Hence ten months elapsed between the date of Foster's despatches and the time of the receipt by the department of Steinberger's explanation. In his reply Steinberger denied the charges or insinuations by Foster saying that "at no time, by word or action, have I ever held out a hope to the people of Samoa of protection or annexation; to the contrary my every act has been to convince the native chiefs of the necessity of supporting and protecting them-

[35] H. Ex. Doc. no. 161, p. 79, encl. 21, Fish to Steinberger, May 6, 1875.

selves." To support his position Steinberger referred to two of his letters, one to the white residents on August 19, 1873, the other an address, which, he said, he delivered to the Samoans in the presence of the consuls and American naval officers on April 22, 1875, after his return to Samoa, and during the course of which he said: "America is great, rich, and prosperous. From Samoa they wish for nothing but to have our ships enter your harbors and their people protected. We have millions of square miles of territory, and our tradition, policy, and feeling are opposed to the acquisition of distant lands, etc."[36] With respect to his relations with Mauga on his first visit to Samoa Steinberger wrote: "When in Pago Pago Harbor, in August, 1873, I found that Mauga, the high chief of the bay, had become imbued with simple notions of his importance through the treaty with Commander Meade, and was charging pilotage and harbor-dues for which he was to buoy the harbor and furnish fresh water free to all ships, my only action was the appendix to Commander Meade's harbor regulations."[37]

Foster, of course, was in error in saying that Steinberger had not consulted "one foreign consul" upon the subject of levying tonnage-dues. S. F. Williams, the British acting consul, as a matter of fact, signed a statement of approval of the rates of tonnage-dues fixed by Steinberger.[38] However, in view of the fact that the Senate had not ratified Commander Meade's treaty, there was no occasion for Steinberger's paying any attention to its terms and to Mauga's alleged violations of them. Rather than restrain Mauga from charging exorbitant harbor dues and from becoming "imbued with simple notions of his importance through the treaty," Steinberger's action in

[36] S.P., Steinberger to Fish, Oct. 18, 1875, rec'd Dec. 6.
[37] *Ibid.*
[38] H. Ex. Doc. no. 45, p. 55, encl. L 2 with Steinberger's report.

enforcing the treaty and recognizing its validity had the effect of accentuating the evil and causing the chief's estimation of his importance to increase. Instead of becoming less independent of the other chiefs and joining whole-heartedly with them in forming a general government, the temptation was ever present in the Pago Pago chief's mind to remain independent, since he alone of all the chiefs had negotiated a treaty with a naval officer of the United States, which treaty also had been recognized by a special representative of the United States, Steinberger himself.

Even before the arrival of Steinberger the second time, April 1, 1875, Foster had received information concerning Steinberger's limited status. A letter from Secretary Fish, dated November 14, 1874,[39] to Foster's predecessor, Jonas M. Coe, in reply to a despatch from Coe dated August 28,[40] inquiring concerning the status of Steinberger during his first visit to the islands, was forwarded to the Taimua of the Samoan government by Foster on March 24, 1875, just eight days before the second arrival of Steinberger.[41] Fish said in this letter: "In reply, I have to state that Col. A. B. Steinberger was appointed a special agent to inquire into and report upon the condition and resources of the Samoan Islands. He was not authorized to make any treaty with the authorities of those islands or in any way to pledge this Government for the protection of that group."

Since Secretary Fish had Coe's letter in his possession before Steinberger returned to Samoa, and in fact sent the above quoted reply to Coe almost a month before he wrote his second instructions on December 11 to Steinberger, it seems reasonable to suppose that Steinberger

[39] S.P., Fish to Coe, Nov. 14, 1874.
[40] C.D., Apia, vol. 3, Coe, Aug. 28, 1874.
[41] *Ibid.*, Foster to the Taimua, Mar. 24, 1875.

had convinced the secretary of state that Coe's insinuations or charges were unfounded; otherwise we have again proof that the department had at first ignored Steinberger's loose interpretation or even violation of its instructions. That the State Department in harmony with the Navy Department would have favored annexation or protection, and was merely waiting for a change in sentiment in Congress is evident from the attitude it assumed toward Steinberger. But whatever may have occurred after the department sent the answer to Coe, Foster knew that Steinberger's status, on his first visit at least, was a limited one, and he had reason to suspect from Fish's letter that if the government had no intention as late as November 14 to pledge its protection over the islands, Steinberger upon his arrival the second time on April 1, could not bring with him instructions that would warrant him to act as he actually did.

Open friction between Foster and Steinberger did not begin, however, immediately upon Steinberger's arrival in Samoa, even though, as has been noted, the American consul, shortly after assuming his post and after Steinberger had sailed from San Francisco the second time for Samoa, had complained to the secretary of state concerning Steinberger's pretensions and alleged pledges to the Samoans during his first visit to the islands. The presence of the *Tuscarora* at Apia during April and most of May with its commander, Captain Erben, assisting Steinberger in reforming the Samoan government, kept Foster from displaying unfriendliness all at once toward the special agent. As a matter of fact, the consul reported to Washington on May 22 that Steinberger had been "very well received by the natives of these Islands. . . ." There were, to be sure, some three or four American landholders who, according to Foster, opposed Steinberger. But on the other hand, he declared there were forty-four other Americans in the island group, who were "in favor of good government, and good laws, and will cheerfully obey them when made." Malietoa had been chosen king the day before he wrote, and saluted by the guns of the *Tuscarora*. "As all the missionaries and well-disposed residents here support the new Government," Foster continued, "it is to be hoped it will be permanent and prevent future wars. It will also enable them to develop the resources of these Islands so rich in soil and all kinds of tropical vegetation and thus cause a large accession to the trade and commerce of the Pacific, of which no doubt the Americans will get their share."[42] That Foster even looked to Steinberger for aid is clear from a letter dated June 3 informing Steinberger of a threatened assault upon himself by one, H. C. Edwards. "I wish the Taimua," wrote Foster, "to have this man arrested and tried. . . ."[43]

Trouble between Foster and Steinberger arose in the course of time over the land question. On May 1 Foster had sent a claim of the former American commercial agent, J. M. Coe, to the Taimua for fifty dollars per month as rent for lands at Mulinuu used for government purposes, but which Coe claimed he had purchased from a chief named Toomalatai on June 1, 1874. The rent was to begin on the day Foster forwarded the claim,[44] even though in July of the previous year Coe had notified the government of his purchase, and that he was prepared to make an agreement with them to pay him rent for occupying his land, or that if they wanted to purchase the

[42] C.D., Foster to Hunter, May 22, 1875. Foster evidently sent this despatch by the *Tuscarora*, which was to sail "to-morrow."

[43] S.P., Steinberger to Fish, July 4, 1875, encl. 2, Foster to Steinberger June 3, 1875; see also H. Ex. Doc. no. 161, pp. 111-112, encl. D 1, with encl. 24, Steinberger to Fish, Oct. 28, 1875.

[44] *Ibid.*, Steinberger to Fish, Oct. 28, 1875, rec'd Dec. 6.

land, he would sell it to them.[45] Perhaps through the influence of Steinberger, the Taimua either made no replies to Foster's communications or their answers were evasive. Finally, in answer to Foster's latest demand on October 16 for a settlement of the Coe claim, Steinberger notified Foster on the same day that a joint land commission would "be appointed to adjudicate land claims, disputed titles, and fix boundaries." In concluding his notice Steinberger reminded Foster that the British and German consular representatives addressed their communications to the premier, a hint that Foster should do the same, and thus recognize Steinberger in his official capacity in the Samoan government, something that Foster had consistently avoided doing, his communications having nearly always been directed to the Taimua.[46] Within three days after sending his notice to Foster, Steinberger had in his possession letters from two chiefs, one from Tamasese saying that he was the real owner of the "Sogi" land, and that Toomalatai "had not the slightest claim to this land,"[47] and the other from Toomalatai himself, denying that he had ever sold the land to Coe. He admitted, however, that he had placed the land "under the protection of Mr. Coe, the American Consul, for fear some one might sell it secretly, or some one of our family might steal it and sell it." Coe had given him "forty dollars to bind the contract," he admitted further, but added, "I did not sell it at all."[48]

On October 30 Steinberger as premier notified Secretary Fish that it had "just come to the notice of the government that large tracts of land, claimed to be owned by the 'Polynesian Land Company' will be sold at public auction under the authority of S. S. Foster, agent." He

[45] S.P.
[46] Ibid.
[47] Ibid.
[48] Ibid.

added: "Titles to some of this land may be good, but such sale, without consultation with the government, is likely to result in grave complications, especially as the name of the American consul is given to it."[49] The day before Steinberger wrote the above despatch, he sent in his resignation from the position of special agent.[50]

Meanwhile, Foster had written a despatch to the Department of State dated October 3, stating that the Roman Catholic bishop, Father Louis Elloy, and the Reverend Messrs. G. A. Turner, Jr., S. I. Whitmer, G. A. Turner, Sr., and George Pratt, of the London Missionary Society (all of whom except the last two had given Steinberger on his first visit letters favoring annexation and his speedy return to the islands) were inquiring as to "the present status of Col. A. B. Steinberger in regard to the Government of the United States, and its future protection of Samoa; and whether he was authorized to form a government here; and whether it is their intention to sustain him by the power of the United States Government." Continuing, Foster wrote: "A full board of the London Missionary Society is ordered to be convened in November next, to take into consideration what steps ought to be taken to prevent the utter demoralization of the natives now going on since May last. If the bishop and members of the board of missions are assured Colonel Steinberger is not acting under authority of the United States Government, or that the United States Government will not retain him in power by force, he will be sent off the island by their influence with the high chiefs. In consideration of the high character of these worthy men, and their desire not to mix themselves with political affairs of the country, and also their desire to

[49] *Ibid.*, Steinberger to Fish, Oct. 30, 1875, rec'd Dec. 6.
[50] M.L., Steinberger to Fish, Oct. 29, 1875, rec'd Dec. 6.

still try and improve this people, that they regard still in their infancy, I have made this request for them, and respectfully beg an answer at your earliest convenience."[51]

Foster's despatch was received on December 31, and on January 12, 1876, the third assistant secretary, J. A. Campbell, replied in part as follows: "In December, 1874, he [Steinberger] was directed to proceed to the islands again, in the capacity of special agent, for the purpose of presenting a letter from the President, and a number of presents from this Government to the Taimua of Samoa. He has fulfilled his mission, made his report, and tendered his resignation as special agent, which has been accepted, and any official or semi-official connection he may have had with this Government is terminated. His first visit to the islands was merely for the purpose of observing and reporting upon their condition; his second visit was to fulfill certain duties in regard to which he was specially instructed, and which have been fulfilled. On neither occasion did his visit have any diplomatic or political significance whatever. Colonel Steinberger was not authorized or empowered by the United States to sustain, in any way, directly or indirectly, any government that he might form or assist in forming. The United States consul is the only representative of the United States in the Samoan Islands, and you will so inform the missionaries and others interested."[52]

The day after Steinberger resigned as special agent of the United States, he notified the Department of State, as premier of the kingdom of Samoa,[53] that His Majesty King Malietoa had "been pleased to select a representa-

[51] C.D., Apia, vol. 4, Foster to Hunter, Oct. 3, 1875, rec'd Dec. 31.
[52] I.C., vol. 81, Campbell to Foster, Jan. 12, 1876.
[53] S.P., Steinberger to Fish, Oct. 30, 1875, rec'd Dec. 6.

STEINBERGER, PREMIER OF SAMOA 135

tive near the capital at Washington, in the person of Walter S. Wilkinson, Esq., whose commission has been forwarded."[54] Steinberger also enclosed a draught of a proposed treaty between Samoa and the United States consisting of fifteen articles.[55] Steinberger's plan was that Wilkinson should negotiate with the United States for a treaty, and the draught he sent to Fish was to serve as a model for both Fish and Wilkinson. The draught was received by the department on December 6, but nothing seems to have been done with it. The proposed treaty was a good one, and if promptly negotiated would have prevented much trouble later for the reason that it would have served to stabilize the government in Samoa. It provided for freedom of trade between the United States and Samoa with the "most favored nation" clause, and permitted the use of Samoan harbors freely by United States steam-vessels without charge. No special rights were granted to the United States in Pago Pago harbor but on the other hand no protection of Samoa was asked for.

On the same day that the treaty draught was sent to Washington, a letter from the Taimua to President Grant also went forward. They informed the president that they were "still very pleased with Col. A. B. Steinberger. . . ." But there was "something else" which they wanted to explain to His Excellency. The land which had been "sold anyhow [for little or nothing] during our wartime to different people" was to be auctioned off by order of the United States consul, S. S. Foster, the coming January. They desired the president's advice. They

[54] According to Steinberger's contract with the Godeffroy firm, Walter S. Wilkinson of Baltimore was to have the monopoly on the exportation of the bark of the Chinese paper mulberry from Samoa for a period of twenty years.
[55] S.P.

thought there should be an investigation into land titles before any more sales should be permitted.[56]

In the same month, October, 1875, when relations between Steinberger and Foster became acute and when the missionaries were beginning to question Steinberger's authority from the United States to intervene in Samoan affairs, the British acting consul began openly to oppose the premier.[57] According to Steinberger, his opposition at first consisted of presenting old, trivial, and worthless claims to the government of Samoa. The turn of his fortunes in Samoa, however, Steinberger attributed to influences behind the British consul and outside of Samoa, that is, in Fiji. It was in this very year of 1875 that the annexationists in New Zealand and Australia had finally persuaded the British government to annex the group of Fiji. Early in July of the same year, according to Steinberger, an English planter of Fiji named Young came to Samoa and fraternized freely with the British acting consul and the missionaries. Steinberger suspected he was an observer for the British administration of Fiji and that his sudden appearance was due to an interest among the British of Australasia in what the United States, as represented by Steinberger, was doing in Samoa. Young's "industry as a reporter," wrote Steinberger, "attracted some attention." After a month's sojourn in Samoa, Young went back to Fiji, but returned in October.

Prior to Young's second coming to Samoa, the British consul's attitude toward Steinberger had been most friendly and the London Missionary Society people had been very helpful to him in suggesting laws and in translating Samoan native laws.[58] Even the brother of the British acting consul was Steinberger's confidential sec-

[56] S.P., the Taimua to President Grant, Oct. 30, 1875.
[57] *Ibid.*, Steinberger to Fish, Jan. 8, 1876.
[58] H. Ex. Doc. no. 44, p. 29.

retary. Immediately after Young's second arrival, however, the secretary left Steinberger without notice, and as has been noted, S. F. Williams, the British acting consul, began to oppose the government. Moreover, "the London Missionary Society made decided war upon myself," wrote Steinberger, and his suspicions were aroused as to the ultimate meaning of the change in his former friends' attitude. He assumed that the British colonials, especially in Fiji, desired the annexation of Samoa by the empire. Steinberger was right in his diagnosis of the situation. It was noted in a previous chapter that the New Zealanders in particular clamored for the annexation of Samoa from 1870 to 1875. With the reversal of Downing Street's policy with reference to Fiji in 1875, the annexationists in Australasia had won a great victory and could look forward to annexations elsewhere. Friction between the United States and Great Britain over Samoa may be said to date, therefore, from 1875. It lasted with varying intensity until the Anglo-Samoan treaty of 1879, and even as late as 1883 the annexation movement in New Zealand was strong enough to attract the attention of Washington. The interest that the negotiation of Meade's treaty had aroused in New Zealand was accentuated, of course, by the two missions of Steinberger, and when the British became suspicious of Steinberger's real status in Samoa they found a willing tool in Foster, the United States consul, in disposing of Steinberger.

Nothing of moment, however, happened until the arrival on December 12, 1875, of the British warship, *Barracouta* under the command of Captain Stevens. According to Steinberger, the British acting consul then became more arrogant in his demands on the Samoan government, and English subjects were upheld in their violation of laws of Samoa. The consul and Captain Stevens in fact were reported as having done everything in their power to annoy and harass the Samoan authorities and particularly Steinberger. Consul Foster boarded the *Peerless*[59] on December 17 and seized her in the name of the United States. Foster, after the arrival of the *Barracouta*, had been in consultation with the British consul, and Steinberger charged them with a conspiracy to destroy the government, and that the seizure of the *Peerless* was but one act in the furtherance of their schemes. Steinberger protested against this seizure. When Foster took possession of the *Peerless* he found some of the arms and ammunition which the United States government had presented the Samoan government. Foster also took possession of Steinberger's personal belongings including some of his correspondence.[60]

Consul Williams and Captain Stevens called a meeting of the king, the other Samoan authorities, and the foreign consuls to take place on December 24. Three protracted sessions were held, the other two coming on December 27 and December 29.[61] The meetings turned out to be an examination of Steinberger, and demands were made upon him to produce his credentials. During these sessions Foster continually prompted Captain Stevens, and was in constant consultation with the British consul. After the third session Captain Stevens proclaimed that English subjects should not obey the laws and that they should be exempt from taxation. At the second session the

[59] Three days after Steinberger made his agreement with the Godeffroy firm in Hamburg, the latter instructed their agents in San Francisco to advance Steinberger credit for the purchase of a vessel to be used by himself in Samoan waters. Such a vessel was purchased shortly after Steinberger sailed for Honolulu, and, having been registered as an American craft, and named the *Peerless*, it proceeded to Samoa.

[60] H. Ex. Doc. no. 44, p. 33.

[61] Steinberger Papers, proceedings of the meeting at Mulinuu or the *Barracouta* investigation; see also H. Ex. Doc. no. 44, pp. 7-22, enclosures 4 and 5.

king made a speech containing some thirty points, some designed to protect Steinberger, others to expose the methods of Captain Stevens, and the British and American consuls. "You have examined our premier," he declared, "for the purpose of having him show his papers from the American Government. We now wish to impress truly on you that he is neither an adventurer nor a schemer, but he is a gentleman whom we requested the President of the United States to send to us, in our petition to him, to assist us in establishing our government."[62]

On January 8, when Steinberger reported the investigation to Secretary Fish, he declared that he was not only supported by the king, all the branches of the government, and the natives, but by almost all the Americans as well. He was opposed, he said, by the American and British consuls and by the London Missionary Society. In this report Steinberger asked for "immediate action of the Government." He evidently referred here to the several petitions sent by the king and the Samoan authorities to the president requesting the recall of Foster and protection for himself.[63]

On January 10, 1876, Steinberger sent another despatch to Hamilton Fish enclosing a statement signed by all Americans in Samoa with the exception of six and Foster. These twenty-five signatures included those of Coe, Meredith, and Parker, former American consular

[62] *Ibid.*, speech by King Malietoa in answer to Captain Stevens on December 27, 1875; see also H. Ex. Doc. no. 44, pp. 20-22, encl. 5.

[63] *Ibid.*, Steinberger to Fish, Jan. 8, 1875; see also H. Ex. Doc. no. 44, p. 36, encl. 8. The petitions were brought to the United States by Steinberger's secretary, Frank Platt, and are to be found in the unbound Steinberger Papers in the Department of State. They consist of four letters to President Grant: from King Malietoa, January 7; from the Taimua, January 10; from the Faipule, January 10; and from the district governors, January 10, 1876. These petitions have not been printed.

representatives in Samoa. The statement was one of "approbation" and "cordial support" of Steinberger. "Having under the rule of the new Samoan government experienced more of law and order, peace and quietude, than ever before known in the history of the port of Apia," read the statement, the signers took pleasure in affixing their names, and in sending the original to the United States.[64]

A notice signed by the three consuls, Williams, Poppe,[65] and Foster, and by Captain Stevens, on January 13, withdrawing recognition of the laws of the Steinberger government, drew from King Malietoa a protest on January 21. "We . . . desire to know," the king asked them, "whether you were appointed by your respective governments to come to Samoa to make laws for our people, and compel them to obey such laws in preference to laws made by us, who have been appointed by the people to rule this realm, and to create laws for the proper government of all our islands."[66]

As the British had chartered a special boat to bring the news to Fiji of what had transpired in Samoa, Steinberger got the king to commission his private secretary, Frank Platt, as special commissioner to take despatches to Washington.[67] Among these despatches were the petitions requesting Foster's recall, referred to above, and a personal letter from Steinberger to President Grant informing him that Foster and the "English officers" had failed "to reach your kindly letters to myself. . . ."[68] Platt's departure was delayed ten days on account of the detention of an English merchant vessel on which he had

[64] S.P., Steinberger to Fish, Jan. 10, 1876, encl.
[65] German acting consul and Apia representative of the Godeffroy company.
[66] S.P.
[67] *Ibid.*, Steinberger to Fish, Jan. 24, 1876, enclosing Platt's credentials.
[68] *Ibid.*, Steinberger to Grant, Jan. 23, 1876.

taken passage, whereupon the Samoan government chartered a German schooner to convey Platt to Hawaii.[69]

Following the departure of Platt for the United States, measures were taken by the conspirators to arrest Steinberger. According to a letter from the Taimua to President Grant, the scheme was first "concocted" by Captain Stevens of the *Barracouta,* which was still anchored in Apia harbor, and Dr. Turner of the London Missionary Society. It was necessary, however, to obtain Malietoa's consent. Malietoa was accordingly persuaded to board the vessel in secret at night, and there under the influence of the captain and the missionary he agreed to request Consul Foster and the captain to arrest Steinberger. "Malietoa consented to this wrong and was led astray by these people," wrote the Taimua. On the morning of February 8 "a file of marines and one hundred armed sailors from the ship of war, and a few officers, accompanied by Captain Stevens, S. S. Foster, United States consul, Mr. Turner, missionary, and S. F. Williams, acting British consul, all came into our seat of government and arrested the premier. . . . He is now a prisoner in the British ship of war the *Barracouta.*" Evidently only Malietoa was prevailed upon to join the English party at this time, for in the evening of the day Steinberger was arrested, the king was forced to resign by the Taimua and Faipule and the same night, under a guard of soldiers, he was sent to another island of the Samoan group. "He is no longer our King and will never be again," wrote the Taimua to President Grant. A week later the *Barracouta* with Dr. Turner on board brought Malietoa back to Upolu but though strong efforts were made to have Malietoa reinstated, the Taimua and Faipule steadfastly refused to accept him. The chiefs, moreover, informed the president that although they had been pressed to accept a British

[69] *Ibid.,* Steinberger to Fish, Jan. 24, 1876.

protectorate and give up their "desire to be protected by the United States of America," they had declined to do this also and would "await patiently for a United States ship of war to assist us to investigate the meaning and cause of this persecution they are bringing on us."[70] From this time until the summer of 1879, a period of over three years, the Samoan government was without a king. The United States eventually recognized the government by negotiating the first ratified treaty in Samoan history in January, 1878.

The *Barracouta* remained in Apia harbor over a month after the arrest of Steinberger, the premier being kept on board the whole time. On February 29, Jonas M. Coe, who had resided at Apia for over thirty years and who, it will be recalled, was United States commercial agent at that place for ten years, was also arrested by English marines and blue-jackets and taken on board the *Barracouta* by order of Captain Stevens. This was done for political reasons, it being alleged that he was responsible for the Samoan government's refusal to reinstate Malietoa. When the chiefs remained adamant Captain Stevens, accompanied by the British and American consuls, brought sailors to the capital on March 13 for the purpose of seizing the guns of the government. A fight ensued in which two Samoan chiefs and six warriors were killed and three Englishmen mortally wounded.[71] This information was sent to President Grant on May 1 after Steinberger and Coe had been taken to Fiji on the *Barracouta*. In the meantime the U.S.S. *Tuscarora,* now commanded by Captain J. N. Miller, had come to Apia to investigate the

[70] S.P., the Taimua to the President, Mulinuu, Feb. 24, 1876; see also H. Ex. Doc. no. 44, pp. 70 and 71, encl. 13.

[71] Consul Foster reported March 20 that the casualties were: Samoans, ten killed and eighteen wounded; English, three dead and seven wounded. (See H. Ex. Doc. no. 44, p. 140, encl. 27.)

situation. "We think he knows everything about the troubles that have been brought upon our government," the Taimua informed the president. They further requested the president to send Colonel Steinberger back to them "so that he can work again with us in our government as he did when we had him with us."[72]

Steinberger was confined on the *Barracouta* almost two months, being released together with Coe at Levuka in the Fijis on April 5. He informed Fish that during his imprisonment he had been "assigned a servant's room in a deck-house in the after part of the ship, eight feet by six feet, without windows or ventilation, with a thermometer ranging from eighty-four to ninety-five degrees, and under an armed guard with ball-cartridge."[73] Coe was sent from Levuka to the United States for trial. Evidently Sir Arthur Gordon, governor of Fiji, did not approve of Captain Stevens' actions against Steinberger and invited the latter to visit him if he had any communication to make to the governor.[74] Steinberger did not avail himself of the invitation but proceeded to Auckland as he had learned that a court-martial of Captain Stevens would be held. He arrived there April 28, and learned "that Commodore Hoskins considered the matter of such grave importance that he would not treat with it, although four English war-ships were in port, but referred the case to the home government." Oddly enough, although the United States vice consul at Auckland fraternized with Captain Stevens and declined to assist Steinberger even in such a small matter as cashing a draft for him, the press of Auckland and the people generally condemned the course of Cap-

[72] S.P., the Taimua to the President, Mulinuu, May 1, 1876; H. Ex. Doc. no. 44, pp. 71-72, encl. 14.
[73] *Ibid.*, Steinberger to Fish, June 1, 1876, rec'd July 6.
[74] *Ibid.*; see also H. Ex. Doc. no. 44, p. 81, encl. 16 and p. 99, encl. Y with encl. 16.

tain Stevens.[75] The officers on the *Barracouta,* moreover, "revolted" at the captain's treatment of Steinberger while he was a prisoner, and invited him "to mess with the wardroom-officers."[76]

A shipbuilder in San Francisco, R. L. Ogden, wrote the president remonstrating against the actions of Foster and suggested that Coe be appointed to succeed him. Ogden said further: "The alacrity with which the honorable Secretary of State declared Mr. Steinberger in no way accredited by the United States was construed into an intimation that he would receive no protection that an ordinary American citizen might expect, and went far to bring about the present condition of affairs."[77]

At the time of Steinberger's arrest all his personal belongings, as we have seen, were seized, including his letters, documents, and library, by Consul Foster. Steinberger's contract with the Godeffroy firm was thus discovered together with his communications with President Grant and Hamilton Fish. These private documents Foster caused to be published in the English papers throughout Polynesia and Australasia, and sent a copy of the Godeffroy contract, with the Godeffroy-Steinberger correspondence, to the Department of State as justification of his arrest of Steinberger.[78] He also sent a transcript of the so-called *Barracouta* investigation of Steinberger. He justified his seizure of the *Peerless* on the ground that it was violating the neutrality laws of the United States in carrying guns in Samoan waters. He was powerless, he explained, to prevent Steinberger's "flagrant" violations of United States laws until the arrival of the *Barracouta.* He was then enabled "to put a check to the arrogant as-

[75] H. Ex. Doc. no. 44, pp. 80-81. [76] *Ibid.,* pp. 79-81.
[77] Steinberger Papers, Ogden to the President, San Francisco, May 5, 1876.
[78] C.D., Apia, vol. 4, Foster to Hunter, Mar. 18, 1876, rec'd May 13.

sumptions of power claimed by the premier over foreign residents in Samoa."[79] Foster ordered the condemnation and sale of the *Peerless*—claimed by Steinberger as his property—but according to the department's instructions to Foster's successor, his despatches in regard to the seizure and sale were "meager and unsatisfactory."[80]

While in Auckland, Steinberger sent a special messenger to Samoa to secure evidence for himself, and then proceeded to England to confront Captain Stevens. He requested the president to send him duplicates of his credentials which were seized in Samoa.[81] This was done, and in acknowledging receipt of the duplicates, Steinberger wrote the president from London in November that the action of the English government with reference to his case would depend upon whether or not the acts of Foster were repudiated and his own integrity as an ex-United States official be maintained.[82]

On receiving a note from Steinberger, his brother, John, wrote him in reply from San Francisco that although copies of papers containing accounts of the attack had been sent to Secretary Fish, Senator Ingalls, and others, he had very little hope that the government would take any steps in his behalf for the reason "that the Administration is in such trouble that they are afraid to do any thing." This reference was to the secretary of war and other cabinet officers who were accused of fraud and whose actions were under investigation.[83]

The administration, however, did support Steinberger's cause. On May 15, 1879, instructions were sent to

[79] *Ibid.*, Foster to Hunter, Jan. 5, 1876.
[80] I.C., vol. 82, Campbell to Griffin, June 23, 1876.
[81] Steinberger Papers, Steinberger to President Grant, Suez, Egypt, Pacific and Oriental Steamship *Mongolia*, Aug. 18, 1876.
[82] *Ibid.*, Steinberger to the President, London, Nov. 14, 1876.
[83] C.D., Apia, vol. 4, Foster, Sept. 25, 1876, rec'd July 6, 1877, enclosure 2, John Steinberger to A. B. Steinberger, San Francisco, Mar. 20, 1876.

the United States minister at London, John Welsh, to present the "claim of A. B. Steinberger versus Great Britain for [an] outrage in Samoa at the hands of the officers and crew of H.M.S. *Barracouta,* including his deportation from Samoa."[84] Upon receipt of the instructions Welsh cabled the department desiring further instructions before presenting the claim, stating that he was convinced that indemnity was due Steinberger from the United States rather than from Great Britain since the British officials acted at the request of the United States consul.[85] Evarts cabled Welsh to insist on the claim,[86] but on August 11 Welsh informed the department that Great Britain denied responsibility for the acts of Captain Stevens as he acted at the request of the United States consul and the king of Samoa. Nevertheless the government had caused the naval officer to be dismissed from the service.[87] No further action seems to have been taken on behalf of Steinberger by the United States government.

The arrest and deportation of Steinberger caused considerable discussion in Congress. Individual members were curious to know what powers were conferred upon Steinberger by the president, and in response to a resolution of the House of Representatives of March 15, 1876, President Grant sent to that body on May 1 a report from the secretary of state with all the Steinberger correspondence then in the possession of the department.[88]

---

[84] Instructions, Great Britain, vol. 25, p. 405, no. 289, Evarts to Welsh, May 15, 1879.

[85] Despatches, Great Britain, telegram, Welsh to Evarts, June 24, 1879.

[86] Instructions, Great Britain, vol. 25, p. 471, telegram, Evarts to Welsh, June 26, 1879.

[87] Despatches, Great Britain, no. 342, Welsh to Evarts, Aug. 11, 1879.

[88] At this time Steinberger's report relative to his first visit to Samoa was also sent to the House, although two years before it had been transmitted to the Senate and published. (See H. Ex. Doc. no. 161, 44 Congress, 1 session, "A. B. Steinberger" pp. 1-125.)

STEINBERGER, PREMIER OF SAMOA

The interest in Steinberger continued, and on February 24, 1877, the president transmitted another report on the special agent with accompanying correspondence, to the House in response to a resolution by that body of January 25.[89]

There can be no doubt that Steinberger was an adventurer, and that if he did not expressly disobey his instructions from the Department of State, he went beyond them and placed not only himself but also the United States government in a compromising position in relation to the natives as well as to the foreign inhabitants in Samoa. He had visions of playing the part of a benevolent despot in the South Seas. At the same time he hoped to secure a fortune through his contract with the Godeffroy company, feeling no doubt that President Grant would in all probability assume an indulgent attitude toward him. Meanwhile, if the English and German interests did not interfere, he might eventually secure an impregnable position and perhaps persuade the Washington authorities to seek to have the islands annexed. He was in a fair way to succeed with the natives and, but for the fact that the Grant administration had enough to think about at home in warding off political attacks, might have received enough support to prevent the collapse of his grandiose dream when the English intervened.

[89] H. Ex. Doc. no. 44, "The Agency of A. B. Steinberger in the Samoan Islands," pp. 1-159.

CHAPTER VI

COMPLICATIONS WITH GREAT BRITAIN

GILDEROY W. GRIFFIN was appointed consul at Apia in June, 1876.[1] In order to assist him in avoiding the pitfalls that would certainly confront him upon his arrival in Samoa, the department informed him concerning conditions in the islands and particularly about the Steinberger-Foster difficulty.[2] There would doubtless be many "partisans of contending factions, representing conflicting interests on the islands," who would approach him and appeal to him to use his "influence for the benefit of their particular party as against other factions." He was instructed, therefore, to hold himself "aloof from all entangling alliances either with any of the different factions on the islands or with [his] colleagues, the representatives of other governments." The Samoan authorities, moreover, were to be informed that Steinberger, when serving as their premier, had "no official status or connection" with the United States government and that the government declined "to accept any responsibility" for his acts. Foster's course in deporting Steinberger, however, "was illegal and unauthorized" and was "disapproved by the Government." Consequently, the president had removed the consul.[3]

Griffin took over the consulate from Foster September 28,[4] and a week later he sent a long report to the depart-

[1] I.C., vol. 82, p. 699, to Griffin, June 6, 1876.
[2] *Ibid.*, p. 595, to Griffin, June 23, 1876; H. Ex. Doc. no. 44, pp. 153-155, encl. 31.
[3] *Ibid.* [4] C.D., Apia, vol. 4, Griffin, Sept. 28, 1876, rec'd Dec. 2.

ANGLO-AMERICAN COMPLICATIONS 149

ment concerning conditions in Samoa as he had found them.[5] He had learned upon his arrival that various factions on the islands were contending with the government of Samoa for the control of affairs, and that the German consul, Theodor Weber, had advised the Samoan government to substitute its old flag for the one adopted during the Steinberger régime, because the latter was "offensive to a majority of the people on the islands." Weber wanted Griffin to join him in advising the government to the same effect, but this he refused to do, citing his instructions not to interfere in the political affairs of Samoa. On the same day this interview was held, Griffin was invited to visit the Taimua and Faipule for an official welcome. At this reception he was told by the official speaker that "Commodore Haskins, and the English acting consul, Williams, and the German consul had advised them to take down their flag but that they had declined to do so." The speaker then "spoke of the great services of Col. Steinberger . . . and expressed a desire to have him returned to them." Griffin then told the assembly that he had instructions not to interfere in Samoan affairs. Steinberger's status was also explained to them.

On the next day, October 1, the German man-of-war *Hertha,* commanded by Captain Knorr, arrived in Apia, but refused to salute the "Steinberger" flag. When a Samoan delegation informed him that their flag had been accepted by all the foreign consuls and by the missionaries, and that it had been saluted by the French and American men-of-war, "the captain said, 'perhaps when you reflect further you may wish to change your flag.' The delegation replied, 'We are prepared to give you a final answer, and that is, we cannot and will not consent to change the flag adopted by the Samoan people.'"

Griffin informed the department further that he thought

[5] *Ibid.,* Griffin, Oct. 6, 1876, rec'd Dec. 2.

150   UNITED STATES POLICY IN SAMOA

the native population was satisfied with its government and that their troubles were due to interferences by the foreign consuls and missionaries. They looked forward to the return of Steinberger because he had protected them, and were pleased to know that Foster had been removed. Foster had "found it more agreeable and profitable," said Griffin, "to act in concert with the English consul and the London society of missionaries than to obey his instructions and to discharge properly the duties incumbent upon him as an officer of the United States Government." In obedience to his instructions, Griffin requested from Foster more information concerning the sale of the *Peerless,* but Foster declined to say more than was divulged by him in his despatches to the department. When questioned further Foster had explained that the sale of Steinberger's personal effects was to satisfy a claim of a George F. Waters. Finally Griffin reported that the Samoan Land Company had appointed a new agent, J. G. Colmesnil, but that Foster had refused to turn over the property to him.[6]

From the above report by Griffin it is quite evident that the so-called "Steinberger" government was still being opposed by the Germans and English, and that it looked steadily to the United States for assistance. The German consul was angry because he could negotiate no treaty with the Samoan government for the protection of the Godeffroy interests, and, therefore, hoped to set up another government more amenable to German demands. The English were still smarting under the alleged insult they suffered in the *Barracouta* affair. Some of the missionaries in particular were anxious to see overthrown what appeared to them to be only a rump government. They had lost all confidence in it since its deposition of

[6] C.D., Apia, vol. 4, Griffin, Oct. 6, 1876, rec'd Dec. 2.

ANGLO-AMERICAN COMPLICATIONS 151

their favorite, King Malietoa. Griffin, on the contrary, became almost immediately impressed with the claims of the government party, and remained loyal to it during his entire connection with the Apia consulate.

Griffin had not been in Samoa a full month before he was reporting difficulties with the German consul. He informed the department that after his refusal to join the German consul in advising the Samoans to give up their flag, the consul had written him an official letter bearing date October 12 inviting Griffin to join him and Captain Knorr and "to coöperate with them for the alleged purpose of establishing 'an independent Government in Samoa represented by all Samoa.'" The German consul—who also represented the firm of Godeffroy and Son—went on to explain in his letter that the unsettled state of affairs caused great damage to German interests, but he wanted to assure Griffin that the German government had no intention of interfering with the independence of Samoa. Griffin replied to Weber's letter the next day, October 13, informing the German consul that he had no authority to coöperate with his colleagues "or with any other persons in such an undertaking." Upon receipt of Griffin's reply, Weber, together with Captain Knorr, wrote straightway the same day to the Taimua and Faipule, explaining that the German man-of-war had been sent to Samoa to protect German interests, and that it was the desire of the German government to assist in establishing a stable government. They added that the English consul had consented to coöperate in the undertaking, but not the American representative. Five days elapsed. Then, when no reply to the German communication seemed to be forthcoming, another letter was sent on the eighteenth by the two Germans, setting forth certain points, six in number, upon which the factions should agree, and threatening pressure if the Taimua and Faipule failed to comply with the German demands. One of the points forbade war between the government party and the opposition (Puletua); another provided for the convocation by the consul and captain of a grand deliberative assembly of Samoa. They informed the government party, moreover, that they were going to leave Samoa on the *Hertha* for a short trip of three weeks and then return for their answer.[7] That would give the Samoans time in which to deliberate, but in the absence of the *Hertha* no assembly should be held.

While the answer of the Taimua, October 19, was couched in diplomatic language, it made clear that that council was opposed to German interference. The Taimua, moreover, on October 23, handed to Griffin a long letter addressed to the president of the United States, appealing for aid against the encroachments of Germany and Great Britain. In commenting on this letter which he promptly sent to the department, Griffin said the Samoans "fully believe that the cause of the hostility to them on the part of the German and English Governments is the fear that treaties of friendly relations will soon be perfected between the Samoan Government and that of the United States. The governors and rulers have a large lot of copra, which they refuse to sell to the German consul, who is connected with the firm of Godeffroy and Son."

Foster, the former American consul, who was now living on the island of Tutuila, seems to have maintained his connection with the Germans and English after his dismissal by the department, and was at that moment promoting discord by supplying guns to the opposition and advising the natives on that island to hoist the old flag

---

[7] The *Hertha* went to the Tonga Islands, where the German consul and Captain Knorr negotiated a treaty with the king of Tonga, acquiring thereby a coaling station for Germany.

ANGLO-AMERICAN COMPLICATIONS 153

and not to believe in the friendly expressions of the president of the United States. This gave the Samoan government additional cause for alarm, and they complained to Griffin. As a matter of fact, Griffin was becoming somewhat disconcerted himself and, in reporting these events, asked the department for additional instructions. His health, moreover, had broken down, and he requested a leave of absence.[8]

It does not appear that any instruction was sent by the department in reply to the above despatch. Its receipt over two months after it left Apia perhaps precluded any answer that might be effective. Nevertheless, a memorandum by Mr. Campbell, third secretary of state, written January 4, relative to it, noted that there "is an unaccountable interference on the part of representatives of the German Government in Samoan affairs and Mr. Griffin was right in refusing to have anything to do with the matter. The Samoans appear to have some reason for their fear of German domination."[9]

About three weeks after the above despatch was sent, Griffin was waited upon by the Taimua and Faipule and offered a commission by them to negotiate a treaty between the United States and Samoa. Griffin declined to accept the commission, informing the Samoan officials that as an officer of the United States he was unable to do so. In describing the incident the consul wrote: "On the 12th of November, in the night, and after a continuous session of many hours, the two Houses of the Government, and nearly all the Governors of Districts came to my home in a body, bringing with them the staff and other insignia of office. The Secretary of the two Houses addressed me in a lengthy speech, expressing a desire that I should go to the United States as their representa-

[8] C.D., Apia, vol. 4, Griffin, Oct. 24, 1876, rec'd Dec. 29.
[9] *Ibid.*, memorandum by Mr. Campbell dated Jan. 4, 1877.

tive and be accompanied by some of their great chiefs.'"[10] Upon receiving Griffin's refusal, the chiefs renewed their request, whereupon Griffin informed them that he intended to go to the United States on account of ill health and would advise the government at Washington of their desires, and at the same time exhibit the warrant of authority to represent them, which he received from them.[11] The document was signed by the members of the Taimua and Faipule and countersigned by the Samoan secretary of state, Le Mamea. The seal adopted by the government during the Steinberger régime was affixed.[12] Whether Griffin engineered this move so as to provide himself with an excuse to depart immediately for Washington in an effort to secure a treaty between the United States and Samoa before the Germans or British could negotiate one, or whether the commission was a spontaneous offer on the part of the Samoan government is not clear. From a careful reading of Griffin's correspondence, it would seem that the natives had been so impressed by Steinberger's personality, that the political influence of some of the English missionaries and the German consul over them had for the time practically disappeared, and that they looked to the United States alone for protection or at least for benevolent guidance. They were not ignorant of the close relations existing between the United States and Hawaii and according to Griffin they attributed Hawaii's "prosperity to the favoring influences of the American Government." In fact, before Griffin's departure for the United States the secretary said to him: " 'The Government of the Hawaiian Islands has the moral support

[10] C.D., Apia, vol. 5, confidential memorandum, Griffin to Hamilton Fish, dated Washington, Feb. 17, 1877, p. 36.

[11] *Ibid.*, p. 37.

[12] Commission enclosed with Griffin's letter dated Washington, February 2, 1877, in Consular Despatches, Apia, vol. 5; H. Ex. Doc. no. 44, p. 159, encl. with encl. 32.

ANGLO-AMERICAN COMPLICATIONS

of the United States, and that support is stronger and greater than the protectorate of any other country. Why not extend the same support to us? Are the inhabitants of those islands more worthy than we? Is their love for your country any greater than ours? You have treaties with them, why not have treaties with us?' "[13] Upon his arrival in Washington Griffin explained that his selection by the Samoans as their unofficial agent was "not the result of any direct or indirect solicitation on my part or of any intrigue to that end," but that it was difficult for them to believe "that a consular officer of the United States who shows consideration for them, and courtesy and regard in his conduct toward them, is not also charged with instructions to advise and assist them and even to use what influence he may have to protect them," and that when it became known that he was about to leave Apia for the United States, the Samoan government thought "they saw a special opportunity of establishing some international relations between the two countries."[14]

On November 13 Griffin appointed D. S. Parker, an American merchant, to act as vice consul during his absence, and lost no time in leaving Apia.[15] That Griffin left Apia on the same day is evident, for on the sixteenth he was at the Tonga Islands where he obtained a copy of a "Treaty of Friendship" between Germany and Tonga signed on behalf of Germany on November 1 by his colleague, Theodor Weber, and Captain Knorr of the *Hertha*.[16] Parker had some difficulty in obtaining recognition from the two American captains who commanded vessels belonging to the firm of Stewart, Cooper & Com-

[13] C.D., Apia, vol. 5, Griffin's memorandum dated Washington, Feb. 17, 1877, p. 33.
[14] *Ibid.*, pp. 35-36.
[15] *Ibid.*, vol. 4, Griffin, Nov. 13, 1876, rec'd Jan. 23.
[16] *Ibid.*, communication A from Griffin, dated Va Vau, Friendly Islands, Nov. 16, 1876, rec'd Jan. 23.

pany of San Francisco. One of the captains was none other than J. B. M. Stewart of the *Menshikoff,* who in 1872 at the time of Meade's treaty, brought to America the appeal of the Samoan chiefs to President Grant for protection. For the reason that Griffin had shown dislike for the methods of the land company of which Stewart was a member, the name of the American consul had become anathema to Stewart, and Griffin's nomination of Parker was, therefore, not recognized by him. When, consequently, Parker demanded Captain Stewart's ship papers, the latter refused to give them up and advised the captain of another ship belonging to his firm, which was also in Apia harbor, to do the same. Parker reported, moreover, that Captain Stewart was circulating false statements concerning Griffin's character and integrity during the latter's absence in the United States, one falsehood being that Griffin had accepted bribes from the Samoan authorities to go to the United States and negotiate a treaty for them.[17]

While Griffin was on his way to the United States, a reply to his despatch of October 6 was sent by the department to Apia, approving his action in declining to join in the protest against the flag adopted by the Samoan government. The department expected the consul to preserve his neutrality in all purely local affairs of Samoa, and also to cultivate cordial relations with his colleagues, because it might be advisable for the foreign consuls to coöperate in matters affecting trade and commerce.[18]

On January 15, 1877, while Parker was still acting as United States vice consul, there arrived at Apia a new British consul, E. A. Liardet, to succeed Acting Consul Williams, whom the British government had removed on account of the Steinberger scandal.[19] The change had been

[17] C.D., Apia, vol. 5; Parker, Dec. 28, 1876, rec'd March 16.
[18] I.C., vol. 84, p. 416, to Griffin, Dec. 20, 1876.
[19] C.D., Apia, vol. 5, Parker, Feb. 8, 1877, rec'd May 11.

ANGLO-AMERICAN COMPLICATIONS 157

made in deference to the letter of protest against the Steinberger arrest, which the Taimua and Faipule had sent to the British government on July 22 the previous year. Lord Derby's reply to the letter of protest did not, however, reach Apia until April 4, but in it he explained that the trouble had been caused by the Samoan government's failure "to attend to well founded grievances of certain British Subjects," and because of an attack on the crew of the *Barracouta*. But (it added) as evidence of the good will of Her Majesty's government, a new consul would be sent to Samoa.[20]

Not many days after Liardet's arrival in Apia, he succeeded in meeting the native chiefs of both parties, and gaining their consent to haul down both flags—the government standard adopted during the Steinberger régime and the older emblem, now claimed by the Puletua or opposition party. The two parties were also prevailed upon to try to form a new government. At the same time Weber desired aid from Parker and Liardet in securing a treaty for Germany. He was to have a meeting with the chiefs and desired his colleagues' attendance for their moral support. They declined to do this, whereupon Weber threatened the natives with claims amounting to $14,000 if they did not consent to a treaty.[21]

On February 10, James G. Colmesnil arrived in Apia to serve as a regularly appointed American vice consul, and, finding Griffin absent, he took over the archives from Parker.[22] On the thirteenth, upon being received by the chiefs, Colemesnil made a speech defending Griffin against his detractors, stating that the consul had returned to the

[20] *Ibid.*, Colmesnil, April 7, 1877, rec'd Aug. 3.
[21] *Ibid.*, Parker to Campbell, Feb. 8, 1877, rec'd May 11.
[22] Shortly after Griffin reported to the department the difficulties between Colmesnil and Foster the previous October, he nominated Colmesnil for the permanent position of vice consul at Apia. Colmesnil proceeded to Washington, and on December 8 the nomination was approved and the appointment made. He served as acting consul until Griffin's return to Apia,

United States on account of ill health and not because his credentials were imperfect. The next day he posted a warning to all American citizens to abstain from meddling in the political affairs of the natives.[23]

The chances for a complete understanding between the two factions seemed bright during the spring of 1877, a situation largely due to the coöperation of the American representative with the plans of his colleagues. On March 7 the government party and the Puletua held a meeting to settle their differences. The meeting lasted all day and adjourned until the next day with no results on either occasion. But they were going to have a general meeting "tomorrow" wrote Colmesnil on the twelfth. Colmesnil attended only as a spectator at the first two meetings. Both factions were agreeable to changing the constitution and the laws; they were also ready to agree about elections; but as for the flag, neither side was willing to withdraw.[24]

When at a general meeting of the two factions on the thirteenth of March the situation became again critical and war seemed about to break out, the parties appealed to the representatives of America, England, and Germany to advise them how to solve their problem. Colmesnil thereupon agreed to join with the other consuls in signing a letter addressed to the natives.[25] The letter of the consuls suggested the following points for reconciliation: "(1) That new elections shall take place in all districts in Samoa in about two months. (2) That only the Taimua [members] of Atua, Ituatane, and Ituafafine re-

but due to the fact that he failed to file a bond, the department was obliged to ignore his communications officially, though they were read and annotated.

[23] C.D., Apia, vol. 5, Colmesnil, Feb. 14, 1877.
[24] *Ibid.*, Colmesnil to Campbell, March 12, 1877, rec'd May 11.
[25] *Ibid.*, Colmesnil, April 2, 1877, rec'd Aug. 3.

ANGLO-AMERICAN COMPLICATIONS 159

main to act as a provisional government until the elections are over. (3) All other points to be decided by the new government [i.e.,] flag, constitution, etc."

This compromise came nearer to the wishes of the opposition than to those of the government faction, for the former had demanded a general election, whereas the latter had previously only agreed to an election in three districts where they said the people were divided. But both factions agreed to accept the proposal and, said Colmesnil, "they have been hard at work since that time electioneering among themselves, and it is to be hoped that they will finally agree."[26] Colmesnil was satisfied that the Taimua and Faipule party was "the strongest by far," but the Puletua had purchased Snider rifles in large quantities from one of the German firms (Ruge-Hedleman & Co.) and were supported by the German interests in general, "which makes them bold." The American representative realized that his intervention went beyond the policy of the United States but he hoped nevertheless to receive the department's approval of what he had done.[27]

The above events are recounted somewhat fully for the reason that Colmesnil's intervention on March 13 and certain of his subsequent acts indicate a change in American policy in Samoa and mark the first feeble beginnings of a movement that finally culminated in the treaty of Berlin of 1889 with its tripartite arrangement for the government of Samoa. While Colmesnil was never recognized by the Department of State as a vice consul, due to his failure to file a bond, the events occurring during his occupancy of the post at Apia while Griffin was absent, really brought the department to the point of considering a modification of its policy in the direction of more definite coöperation.

[26] *Ibid.*   [27] *Ibid.*

At about this time the British officials in Fiji were much exercised over rumors that Steinberger was fitting out a filibustering expedition destined for Samoa.[28] This was particularly alarming, thought Colmesnil, for the reason that the British were making strong efforts to annex the Samoan islands to the Empire, and "unless some nation takes a protectorate over the group," he continued, "they will belong to England in less than 12 months." The British vessel, *Beagle,* had been in Samoan waters for two months waiting for a settlement of the Samoan problem and was expected to sail for Fiji with the news. "Her presence," added Colmesnil, "has an effect on the natives in favor of England." As for the Germans, Colmesnil did not think they wanted the islands, being content with a treaty containing a "most favored nation" clause[29] but favored the Puletua hoping that a treaty from that faction would be the easier to secure.

The natives might have settled their troubles under the compromise if left alone, but the Germans, more concerned about securing a favorable treaty than about a peaceful solution of the native quarrel, brought pressure to bear with threats of fines upon the government party and in so doing forced that party to seek a further compromise with the Puletua and to ask Great Britain for protection against German encroachments. The Puletua willingly listened to the government's advances in this matter, for although they were receiving arms from the

[28] This news was brought by the American bark, *Menshikoff,* arriving from Fiji March 11. The report became the subject for a representation to the State Department on April 23 by the British minister in Washington, Sir Edward Thornton. He said that the report was that Steinberger was to be aided by a Captain Hayes and G. A. Woods. He stated that the success of the expedition might prejudice interests of the British colony of Fiji and of legitimate commerce in the Pacific.

[29] C.D., Apia, vol. 5, Colmesnil, March 12, 1877, rec'd May 11.

ANGLO–AMERICAN COMPLICATIONS 161

Germans against the governmental faction, they nevertheless, with the two Malietoas as their leaders, enjoyed the sympathy of the English residents, particularly the missionaries. It was not difficult, therefore, to get them to approach the British government for protection. The party that was really humbling itself under the circumstances, was the government or "Steinberger" party, for at the very moment it sought reconciliation and protection from Great Britain, the British consul at Apia had authority to demand an indemnity for the *Barracouta* incident. Liardet, who did not like Weber's methods and saw a danger to British interests in the German threats, was probably instrumental in bringing the two factions together in a common appeal to Great Britain.

But the government party was much concerned as to how the United States, the power that had sent them Steinberger, would receive the news of their intended action. And so, on the evening of April 2, the Taimua and Faipule waited upon Colmesnil for advice. They wanted, moreover, to know if the United States would be "angry" with them, and if it would invalidate their claims upon the good will of the United States should they ask Great Britain for protection. Although Steinberger had helped them a great deal, he had not been recognized by the United States as its representative after his appointment as their premier. But now it was rumored that a German man-of-war was expected and that the Germans were threatening to force their claims for nearly $20,000. Therefore, they needed protection immediately. Colmesnil assured them "that they had a perfect right to ask any nation for protection" but that he could not advise them either for or against the step.

They then left him and the next day, April 3, addressed a petition to Her Majesty the Queen, a petition to Sir Arthur Gordon, governor of Fiji, and a letter to the

British consul, Liardet. The following day, April 4, the German ship *Augusta* arrived to relieve the *Hertha*. "The Germans have made Apia a naval station," reported Colmesnil. "It will be seen that the natives are very anxious to have a protectorate and, since the United States does not take any action, they are appealing to Great Britain to prevent their falling in the hands of Germany. . . . That the natives can carry on a government without the aid of some foreign country is impossible, due to the varied foreign interests."[30]

While Germany and Great Britain were quarreling for supremacy in Samoa, why should not the United States retain her favorable position with the party which was governing Samoa? Another appeal from the natives to the United States would serve to keep our country in the forefront as one of the interested powers, and why should not the United States at least share with Great Britain the protectorate over Samoa? Such thoughts, no doubt, impressed Colmesnil with the importance of taking some action himself after the visit at his house of the Taimua and Faipule. Liardet might be congratulated by Englishmen throughout the South Seas for bringing the two factions together to agree upon an appeal to Great Britain, but Colmesnil, by making the appeal a joint one, and for protection not annexation, could be equally shrewd in the effort to prevent what looked to him as the beginning of an annexation movement on the part of Great Britain.

The American bark, *Menshikoff*, Captain J. B. M. Stewart, from San Francisco, was soon leaving for Fiji, and a Samoan delegation arranged to take passage in her in order to present their petition to Sir Arthur H. Gordon, governor of Fiji. A petition to the United States for protection could of course be sent through the mails by

[30] C.D., Apia, vol. 5, Colmesnil to Campbell, April 7, 1877, rec'd Aug. 3.

ANGLO-AMERICAN COMPLICATIONS 163

the same vessel, and, consequently, one was drawn up addressed to the president, and signed on the thirteenth of April by Le Mamea, the secretary of state, and a long list of chiefs.[31] The Taimua and Faipule wanted the American, Jonas M. Coe, to go with the Samoan delegation to Fiji as their official interpreter,[32] and Colmesnil replied that since Coe was a free agent he could do as he wished.[33] Coe went with the delegation when it sailed to Fiji on the thirteenth. That Colmesnil was pleased at the prospect of an American penetrating into the inner circles of the approaching conference in Fiji goes without saying. Coe's presence there would make it possible for Colmesnil to learn what transpired in the conference between the Samoans and Sir Arthur. The petition to the president of the United States likewise went forward, and in commenting on it, Colmesnil wrote in the covering despatch: "If the United States is willing to take action in conjunction with Great Britain, it will help in establishing a strong independent nation." The petition to the United States, however, did not reach Washington until August 3, and Colmesnil in the course of time came to the conclusion that he could not wait for the answer.

A month after the departure of the Samoan delegation for Fiji, and prior to its return to Samoa, Liardet and Colmesnil clashed. The British consul on May 14 presented a document to the Taimua and Faipule for their signatures, which would give him the control of the revenues of the government of Samoa and also mortgage to him all the lands of the people in order to secure a fine put upon the Samoans by the English government for the killing of part of the crew of the *Barracouta*. Prior to

[31] *Ibid.*, Colmesnil, April 13, 1877, rec'd Aug. 3, petition enclosed.
[32] Dr. Turner, one of the English missionaries, seems to have been the interpreter for the Malietoa party.
[33] C.D., Apia, vol. 5, second despatch, Colmesnil, April 13, 1877.

this action, Liardet had been indiscreet enough to disclose to Colmesnil that the British government had left the matter entirely in his hands whether the fine should be collected or not, and that it would not amount to more than $6000. Colmesnil promptly wrote to the Taimua and Faipule "stopping the proceedings" by advising the government to wait with their answer until they had heard from Great Britain and the United States about the protectorate. Again Colmesnil acknowledged to the Department of State that he was aware of the policy of the United States against interference in foreign political affairs, but added significantly that "a United States representative is a non-entity if he cannot interfere on occasion and for all practical purposes might as well have his office in Washington City."[34]

The Samoan delegation presently returned on the bark, *Menshikoff*, from Fiji, having found Sir Arthur Gordon and the other British officials interested only in the annexation of the Samoan group. Though the Samoans steadfastly refused to accede to Sir Arthur's wishes,[35] it was reported to Colmesnil by a delegation of Samoans that the English consul, the missionaries, and British business interests in Samoa, rather than accept the outcome as final, were working secretly for a speedy annexation. The delegation waited upon the American representative on the evening of May 23 and asked for permission to hoist the American flag to protect them against interference by various whites working "under secret instructions of persons in authority." When Colmesnil pointed

[34] C.D., Apia, vol. 5, Colmesnil, May 20, 1877, rec'd Sept. 15.

[35] It was said that the Samoans acquired a dislike for the British administration of Fiji at the time of their visit. This might explain somewhat their attitude toward annexation. In any case their appeal to the president for a protectorate would have prevented their acting favorably on Sir Arthur's proposal or intimation.

ANGLO-AMERICAN COMPLICATIONS 165

out to the delegation that they represented only a part of the government, they left at nine o'clock and returned at midnight with the whole government and repeated their request. Colmesnil then gave his consent to their hoisting the United States flag over their own as long as they did not fight among themselves.[36] In reporting this incident, Colmesnil repeated his reasons for a United States protectorate, namely, that most of the people wanted it, and that the petition he had forwarded to Washington was their fourth request for such a relationship with the United States.[37] A week later Colmesnil reported that the political affairs of the islands were much improved and reiterated "that but for the continual interference of some whites here who are under the instructions of persons in some authority, the question [peace between the factions] would have been settled long ago."[38]

While these significant events were transpiring in Samoa, Griffin was absent in the United States. After his arrival home he wrote the department on February 2 informing his superiors of the desires of the Samoans to negotiate a treaty and also of his refusal to accept a position under their government.[39] His action relative to the Samoan commission was approved by the department. As for the treaty, the department thought it would probably be mutually beneficial, but, owing to the uncertainty as to

[36] C.D., Apia, vol. 5, Colmesnil, May 25, 1877, rec'd Sept. 15.

[37] In recounting the incident nine years later to George H. Bates, United States special commissioner to Samoa, E. L. Hamilton stated that Captain Stewart of the *Menshikoff*, for whose American associates Colmesnil acted as agent, was intimately connected with Colmesnil in the flag-hoisting episode, and that Weber, the German consul, was also cognizant of the move and approved it as a means of forestalling a British annexation. (See p. 198, H. Ex. Doc. no. 238, 50 Congress, 1 session.)

[38] C.D., Apia, vol. 5, Colmesnil, June 2, 1877, rec'd Sept. 15.

[39] *Ibid.*, Griffin, Washington, Feb. 2, 1877; H. Ex. Doc. no. 44, pp. 155-159.

the stability of the government of the islands, it was desirable to proceed with caution. The department desired, however, any information the consul could give on the subject. Meanwhile the matter would be held under consideration.[40] Griffin replied from Louisville, Kentucky, on April 13, that he was glad the government was considering a treaty, and emphasized the importance of such an agreement because the American citizens in the islands were complaining bitterly of the scant protection afforded their property.[41] On the twenty-sixth of April, however, the department informed Griffin that there was no present necessity for negotiating a treaty as proposed, the letter concluding with a request to know when Griffin would return to his post.[42] In acknowledging receipt of the department's latest communication, Griffin insisted on the need for a treaty and expressed his desire of going to Samoa in the capacity of United States commissioner to negotiate a treaty of commerce and friendship.[43] A week later Griffin repeated his request for a commissionership to Samoa, but this time he emphasized the need of reporting fully upon the character of the government of Samoa and its ability to carry out any relations it might enter into with the United States. In reply to the department's reference to the lack of stability of the Samoan government, he explained that "both the German consul and Acting Consul Williams[44] have been unremitting in their attempts to overthrow the Steinberger Government and will continue to do so until the United States negotiates a treaty." He also called attention to the attacks upon him-

[40] I.C., vol. 85, p. 392, to Griffin, March 29, 1877.
[41] C.D., Apia, vol. 5, Griffin to Campbell, Louisville, April 13, 1877.
[42] I.C., vol. 85, p. 589, to Griffin, April 26, 1877.
[43] C.D., Apia, vol. 5, Griffin to Campbell, Louisville, May 2, 1877.
[44] Williams was the British representative when Griffin departed from Apia the previous November, and Griffin did not know in May that Liardet had succeeded Williams the previous January.

ANGLO-AMERICAN COMPLICATIONS 167

self by Captain Stewart of the Polynesian Land Company because of his opposition to that company's schemes to unload on the Samoan Government its land deeds in return for government bonds. He referred also to Consul Weber's failure to bribe him to divert trade from the United States to the Godeffroy company, and denied all charges of bribery against himself, referring particularly to his refusal to accept gifts from the Samoan government before departing for the United States.[45]

The department answered both letters on May 18 by referring to its instruction of the twenty-sixth of April, and stated further that "late advices from Samoa only confirmed the opinion expressed in that instruction, namely, that that government was unstable and about to undergo a change. The department did not look with favor upon Griffin's request for an appointment as commissioner to Samoa, and instructed him to "continue to carry out the policy of non-interference with the governmental officers of the islands" upon his return to Apia as consul.[46] These definite instructions relative to non-interference were no doubt inspired by the receipt on May 11 of Colmesnil's despatch concerning the first two attempts between the factions in March to reach a peaceful solution and also of Colmesnil's despatch concerning his cautioning the American citizens in February not to mix in the political affairs of the Samoan people.

But a month after it had instructed Griffin "to continue to carry out the policy of non-interference," the department was ready to modify its position. It informed him "that later advices received from the Islands indicate the possibility that some concerted action on the part of the consular representatives of civilized powers in Samoa may perhaps be necessary to prevent revolution, anarchy,

[45] C.D., Apia, vol. 5, Griffin to Campbell, Washington, May 9, 1877.
[46] I.C., vol. 86, p. 52, Campbell to Griffin, May 18, 1877.

and bloodshed among the natives. In view of this state of affairs and in consideration of the interest this Government has in the peace and prosperity of the Islands, it may become necessary for the Department to so far modify your instructions as to have you coöperate with your colleagues in such efforts as they may make to produce harmony and establish a firm government. Immediately upon your arrival at your post you will report to the Department a statement of the condition of affairs in the Islands in order that the Department may be enabled to judge what course it will be proper to pursue."[47]

Griffin did not receive this communication, however, until after his arrival in Apia, for, two days after it was sent, he was writing the department from San Francisco informing it that he intended to sail for his post of duty the same day on the schooner *Dreadnought*. He reported "that the German and British consuls with the assistance of the agents of the Polynesian Land Company in Apia . . . have succeeded in inducing the people of Samoa to change their form of government, to which they were much devoted."[48] He reported further that the president of the land company, who resided in San Francisco, had called upon him that day (June 20) and "begged" him to join the company. The president said "that it had been arranged to sell all the land claimed by the company to the new Government, and to take interest-bearing bonds in payment." Griffin continued: "He said that he did not expect the new Government to pay the bonds but it was agreed that the Land Company should be allowed to col-

[47] I.C., vol. 86, p. 255, to Griffin, June 18, 1877. When and from whom the "later advices" had been received by the department is not clear, for Colmesnil's despatches concerning his intervention for American protection and the flag-hoisting episode were not received until August 3 and September 15, respectively.

[48] This information was erroneous.

ANGLO-AMERICAN COMPLICATIONS 169

lect an import duty upon every article brought to the Islands. He offered me one-fourth of the entire proceeds for my coöperation and support in his scheme, which of course I declined to accept. I am satisfied that the German and British consuls and the agents of the Land Company have practiced a great fraud upon the unsuspecting natives and that their conspiracy will result disastrously to the prosperity and happiness of the people of Samoa and materially injure our trade and commerce with the Islands." In conclusion Griffin expressed himself as desirous of further instructions.[49]

Griffin, in his despatch from San Francisco, expressed also the desire that Colmesnil be removed from the post of vice consul at Apia. Doubtless Colmesnil's connection with the land company as its agent in Samoa could no longer be looked upon with favor in view of the machinations of that company. As a matter of fact, the department had written Griffin before he returned to Samoa that Colmesnil could not be recognized as vice-consul at Apia for the reason that he had failed to file a bond.[50] A second letter received by Griffin after his return to Apia was of the same tenor, although the department expressed regret that it could not take cognizance of the despatches it had received from Colmesnil as acting consul.[51]

While Griffin was still on the high seas, events in Samoa took a serious turn. Colmesnil reported that the Taimua and Faipule, having despaired of bringing the Puletua to terms, had called upon him on July 10 and informed him that they would haul down the American flag until the trouble was over; that they hoped they would be

[49] C.D., Apia, vol. 5, from Griffin, San Francisco, June 20, 1877, rec'd June 28.
[50] I.C., vol. 86, p. 23, to Griffin, May 15, 1877.
[51] *Ibid.*, vol. 87, p. 181, to Griffin, Oct. 3, 1877.

able to hoist their own flag alone when it terminated, without the intervention of foreigners; and that they would be recognized by the different great nations as an independent state. Colmesnil enclosed in his despatch copies of two documents indicating clearly that the English residents were definitely behind the Puletua. The documents were letters by one George Pritchard, the first directed to the Puletua and the second presumably to the younger Malietoa. In the former letter, dated June 12, Pritchard regretted the fact that there were no guns available, the government party having enforced strictly its embargo on the importation and sale of them. In the letter to Malietoa, the writer referred disparagingly to the German consul, Weber, regretting that, for the moment, he [Weber] had "despaired of Samoan conditions." He thought Weber a "weak man." Continuing, Pritchard informed Malietoa: "I have talked with Mr. Weber, and have shown him the right of your doings. I am very much pained with that gentleman. Mr. Weber has a weak mind. I have endeavored to induce him to lend you assistance in your work, and he thus states to me, that he is disgusted with the whole of Samoa, that he is much vexed with chiefs of the Tuamasaga that they should be so long up and doing."[52]

The same day, July 15, Colmesnil sent another despatch to Washington informing the department that on July 12 at three o'clock in the afternoon a fight had occurred between the Samoan government and the Puletua and that the Taimua and Faipule party had been victorious after about two hours fighting. This encounter, like so many others in Samoa, would not deserve even a passing mention but for the fact that a previous agreement had been made between Colmesnil and the Taimua and Fai-

[52] C.D., Apia, vol. 5, Colmesnil, July 15, 1877, rec'd Sept. 15.

ANGLO-AMERICAN COMPLICATIONS 171

pule to respect the neutrality of Apia and Mulinuu, a suburb of Apia and the seat of the government. The German consul, moreover, had agreed with Colmesnil to enforce the neutrality of the municipality, and, consequently, when six hundred of the Puleuta warriors had escaped into the neutral district after their defeat, the German and American consuls disarmed them in order to save their lives, turning them over to the government as prisoners of war. The British consul on the other hand took no part in the establishment of the neutral zone, but on the contrary afforded an asylum for about forty of the Puletua and refused to surrender them to the government.[53] For the moment, therefore, the German and American representatives were acting together without British support, and their action in providing for a neutral municipal zone was the beginning of a movement which developed in 1879 into the important municipal convention negotiated by the representatives of the three powers for the neutralization of Apia and for its government by the consuls.

On July 21 Colmesnil reported that the Samoans were then "at work forming their laws" and expected to crown their king on the Tuesday following. He enclosed a letter from the Taimua and Faipule to the president of the United States wherein they informed him that the rebellion had been put down, and that they were engaged in selecting their king and making their government more complete. Only one nation caused them fear, namely, Great Britain. The actions of the United States' representative they commended. The letter was countersigned by Le Mamea, and had the "Steinberger" seal affixed.[54] This letter no doubt was requested by Colmesnil as a support for his various acts of intervention in Samoa.

[53] *Ibid.*, second despatch from Colmesnil, July 15, 1877, rec'd Sept. 15.
[54] *Ibid.*, Colmesnil to Evarts, July 21, 1877, rec'd Sept. 15.

Griffin arrived at his post for his second sojourn in Samoa on July 26,[55] and on the thirtieth he wrote a general report of conditions as he found them after an absence of over eight months.[56] He was warmly welcomed by the government and people of Samoa. At the formal reception by the Taimua and Faipule he was told of the various efforts of the German and English consuls to overthrow the government during his absence, and learned that the British consul was still protecting the forty members of the Puletua on the premises of the consulate, and that he would continue to do so until the arrival of Sir Arthur Gordon, who was expected from Fiji "any day." The British consul was threatening punishment of the Samoan government, Griffin added, and concluded his despatch by repeating the desire of the Samoan government to make a treaty. After an investigation, he thought the government was strong enough faithfully to carry out the provisions of a treaty.

In course of time Griffin received an answer to his request from San Francisco for further instructions. The department wrote the consul that he should keep himself "clear from entangling alliances of all kinds," but to do all in his power "to aid in maintaining a good and permanent government on the Islands." Upon the receipt of further advices from Griffin after his arrival at his post, the department would be able to give him the fuller instructions he might desire.[57] Griffin's report of July 30, written after his arrival in Apia, did not reach Washington until September 29, but the department promptly replied to it on October 3, approving his course since his return to his post, though still declining to open negotiations for a treaty with Samoa. In explanation of its posi-

[55] C.D., Apia, vol. 5, Griffin, July 27, 1877, rec'd Sept. 29.
[56] *Ibid.*, Griffin, July 30, 1877, rec'd Sept. 29.
[57] I.C., vol. 86, p. 361, to Griffin, July 5, 1877.

tion the department refused to believe "that affairs in the Islands were sufficiently settled at the date of your despatch to justify the Government in negotiating the desired treaty."[58]

It is important to note at this point that while Griffin had failed to secure a treaty for Samoa during his visit in America, and while the department as late as October 3 thought that the situation in Samoa had not changed for the better sufficiently to justify the negotiation of a treaty, the latter had distinctly modified its attitude relative to intervention in Samoan affairs to the extent of suggesting aid in the maintenance of a good and permanent government on the islands. Moreover, from a careful study of the despatches and instructions, it may be inferred that the change was taken not so much with reference to the German operations in Samoa as against the encroachments of the British. The department sent no communication to Colmesnil either commending or reprimanding him. In fact, it sent him no instructions at all. Yet, while the United States ignored Colmesnil's flag-hoisting exploit, it is quite clear that the authorities in Washington did not fail to see that he had probably prevented the British annexation movement from gaining headway, and that the government of Samoa had received another lease of life in the face of the attacks of the Puletua. In response, therefore, to many appeals from the "Steinberger" government for aid, and stimulated no doubt by the crisis in Samoa and Colmesnil's intervention on several occasions to prevent anarchy and possible British annexation, the department initiated a policy which developed into the Berlin Act of 1889.

The United States was not yet ready to accede to the many appeals for annexation or even protection, but

[58] *Ibid.*, vol. 87, p. 181, to Griffin, Oct. 3, 1877.

it was prepared to help the authorities in Samoa in maintaining a stable government. This decision almost amounted to a benevolent interest in the welfare of the government of Samoa, and prepared the way for the decision of our government, in January, 1878, to recognize that government in a formal way, and to make a treaty with it containing a clause providing for the advice and help of the United States whenever the Samoans requested it.

But any American consul endeavoring to solve the problem of intervention in Samoa without entangling his country was bound to be confronted sooner or later by a dilemma. If he intervened alone, he would be opposed by the other two consuls, who, as a matter of course, would interpret his step as meaning eventually a protectorate, whereas if he coöperated with his colleagues he could do nothing less than enter into agreements and even negotiate treaties with them, if the action of intervention were to be effective. But the latter course would tend to entangle his country with the other powers in the affairs of a distant, half-civilized people, and such a step would reverse an historic policy of the United States.

Such was the problem confronting Griffin upon his return to Apia. He was obliged to do one or the other thing. There apparently was no middle ground. Being above all interested in a prominent position for the United States in the islands, he adopted the policy of intervention without entangling alliances, with the result that, not excepting Steinberger, he became the American most cordially hated by the foreigners, who ever represented the United States in Samoa. On the other hand, the Samoan government clung to him as their best foreign friend. On August 9 Griffin forwarded to Washington a despatch[59] enclosing

[59] C.D., Apia, vol. 5, Griffin, Aug. 9, 1877, rec'd Nov. 16.

ANGLO-AMERICAN COMPLICATIONS 175

a letter from the Taimua and Faipule, dated August 7, to President Hayes, expressing again their desire for a treaty, and also a letter from the same bodies to William Evarts, secretary of state, thanking him for his letter of May 21[60] and expressing appreciation of the return of Griffin to his post.

On August 14 Griffin established a consular court against the "most determined opposition" of the white population in Apia. On the seventeenth, judgment for upwards of two hundred dollars was entered against an American citizen named Dunn, in favor of the Roman Catholic Mission, which Dunn had tried to defraud. Because Dunn assembled an armed force to resist the collection of the money, Griffin did not call upon the local authorities to carry out the judgment. The American consul had more serious trouble with a case involving an American citizen and a British subject. The British consul, Liardet, defied Griffin's authority as a magistrate and personally informed him that he could not understand how he could claim the right to exercise criminal and civil jurisdiction. On the eighteenth he also wrote to Griffin that the case would be referred to Sir Arthur Gordon, "who would be expected shortly."[61] But the British consul went further. He ordered the arrest of the United States marshal and deputy marshal on one particular occasion,[62] and apparently encouraged an assault upon the American consul and his ejectment from the consulate on September 21 by a band of ruffians led by an Englishman named Hunt. Only the timely arrival of the French man-of-war, *Le Signelay*, and the protection afforded the con-

[60] Notes to Minister for Foreign Affairs, Samoa, Department of State, from Evarts, May 21, 1877, requesting recognition of G. W. Griffin as consul at Apia.
[61] C.D., Apia, vol. 5, Griffin, Aug. 28, 1877, rec'd Nov. 16.
[62] *Ibid.*, Griffin, Sept. 14, 1877, rec'd Nov. 16.

sul and the United States flag by her commander, Captain Aube, seems to have prevented even more serious trouble for Griffin.[63] As a matter of fact, Griffin only left his asylum on board the French warship when conditions in Apia had somewhat abated. Then the French escorted him ashore and he took up his residence at Mulinuu under the protection of the Samoan government,[64] where he remained until the following summer and until he finally left for home.

In his fear or rage over the turn of events, Griffin, at the time of the greatest excitement, requested the department to transfer him to "some consulate in a civilized country." There is in the archives of the Department of State a long summary of the Anglo-American consular conflict in Samoa as reported by Griffin, and the conclusions put down in the memorandum indicate that the cause of the attack upon the consul was not yet clear to the department, although it was strongly inferred that the officers of the British consulate were connected with the assault. There were also "grave questions involved as to the official jurisdiction of the two consuls, which will doubtless give rise to international controversy between the governments of the United States and Great Britain." For these reasons and "in view of the violently partisan and personal character of Mr. Griffin's testimony," it seemed desirable to the department that "an impartial investigation of the facts on the spot" should be carried on "before taking up any line of international action."[65] In the course of time Griffin was informed that his charges on account of the outrage committed upon himself would receive consideration.[66]

[63] C.D., Apia, vol. 5, Griffin to Evarts, Sept. 29, 1877, rec'd Nov. 14.
[64] Ibid., Griffin, Sept. 29, 1877.
[65] Ibid., memorandum on Griffin's despatches nos. 20, 21, 25, and 26.
[66] I.C., vol. 87, p. 447, to Griffin, Nov. 20, 1877.

ANGLO-AMERICAN COMPLICATIONS

By December 3 the United States was ready to make representations to Great Britain. The legation in London was informed by the department of the recent outrages on the United States consul and consulate and that the British consul abetted the assault, and the American minister was instructed to advise the government of Great Britain thereof.[67] Some weeks later the legation was informed of the outrages perpetrated upon the marshal and deputy marshal of the United States consulate by an armed force acting under the authority of the British consul, and the minister was further instructed to bring this matter also to the attention of the Foreign Office and request an investigation.[68] Ten days later more papers were sent to the legation dealing with the latter case.[69] John Welsh, the American minister, reported on January 12 that he had made representations to the Foreign Office pursuant to the department's instructions,[70] and on March 7 he was able to advise the department that the Foreign Office had expressed regret at the connection of the British consul with the outrages on the United States consular officers, and stated that he had been called home to make explanation of his conduct.[71] At the same time the British government desired to know what legislative and judicial powers were conferred by the United States on its consul in Samoa, "being apprehensive that if they were different from those generally conferred upon consuls con-

[67] Instructions, Great Britain, vol. 25, p. 44, no. 234, Evarts to Pierrepont, Dec. 3, 1877.
[68] *Ibid.*, vol. 25, p. 53, no. 244, Evarts to Pierrepont, Dec. 18, 1877.
[69] *Ibid.*, vol. 25, p. 59, no. 250, Evarts to Pierrepont, Dec. 28, 1877.
[70] Despatches, Great Britain, vol. 133, no. 17, Welsh to Evarts, Jan. 12, 1878.
[71] The British consul, Liardet, died suddenly in Apia, February 10, but the Foreign Office in London evidently had not received the news, due to lack of cable communication with Samoa. (See Consular Despatches, Apia, vol. 5, Griffin, Feb. 11, 1878.)

tinual difficulties would result.'"⁷² The United States expressed satisfaction at the prompt action taken by Great Britain and supplied the Foreign Office with the information it desired.⁷³

Thus was closed an incident which might have brought on serious consequences but for the recognition by Great Britain as much as by the United States of the fact that under the peculiarly difficult conditions prevailing in Samoa the bitter quarrels between consuls which occurred there from time to time could not be interpreted as symptoms of a fundamental conflict between the two powers on those distant islands. The incident, however, had more implications. Before the matter was finally settled by the British government's apology to the United States, it had disturbed somewhat the relations between France and Great Britain. The British government was irritated because of the aid rendered Griffin by Captain Aube. With a view to placating Great Britain the French admiralty ordered that Captain Aube be relieved of his command and sent home. Information concerning this phase of the situation came to the Department of State indirectly.

Early in December and simultaneously with the first representation to Great Britain concerning the Griffin assault, the department had instructed the American minister in Paris, Noyes, to hand to the French foreign minister, Waddington, a customary letter of thanks from the United States government to Captain Aube for his aid to Griffin, with the request that the Quai d'Orsay forward the letter to Captain Aube.⁷⁴ This instruction Noyes com-

⁷² Despatches, Great Britain, vol. 133, no. 39, Welsh to Evarts, March 7, 1878.

⁷³ Instructions, Great Britain, vol. 25, p. 97, no. 48, Evarts to Welsh, March 26, 1878.

⁷⁴ *Ibid.*, France, vol. 19, no. 18, Evarts to Noyes, Dec. 5, 1877.

plied with on the eighteenth of December and, since there was nothing more for him to do, the matter so far as he was concerned seemed ended. Late in January, 1878, however, Noyes received an unofficial and personal letter from the French naval officer informing him that in consequence of his action on behalf of Griffin, "he had been relieved of his command by the Admiral commanding the squadron and ordered to return to France." The captain added that he had received an unofficial communication from a friend stating that the United States government had thanked him for his aid, and he inquired if that were true. Before writing an answer, Noyes thought it would be prudent to interview the French minister for foreign affairs and inquire why the letter of thanks had not been forwarded, and when he did so he learned for the first time of Great Britain's attitude with respect to the action of the French captain. Waddington requested delay before replying to Noyes' inquiry, and in reporting the interview to the department Noyes said: "It now appears that serious complications with the English Government resulted from this affair, which have for a month and more been the subject of diplomatic negotiations." Days and weeks intervened without any reply from Waddington, during which time Noyes sent his secretary twice to the Quai d'Orsay for information. Finally, Noyes called in person again on March 6 to explain his embarrassment in keeping Captain Aube waiting for an answer. Waddington begged for further delay and said he had "the best of reasons to believe that everything would be satisfactorily arranged, when the thanks of our Government would be communicated to Captain Aube and he again be assigned to a command." The minister for foreign affairs added "that Captain Aube was a brave and excellent officer, but a little rash and precipitate sometimes, that in this instance he had acted from good impulses, but that he transcended his authority and violated his orders, resulting in great trouble and embarrassment.'"[75]

It was noted that Welsh advised the department from London on March 7 that the British Foreign Office had expressed regret at the British consul's actions against Griffin. It is plausible to suppose that the French foreign minister's statement to Noyes on March 6, that he had "the best of reasons to believe that everything would be satisfactorily arranged," was founded on knowledge of what Great Britain's answer to the United States would be, and that the relations between France and Great Britain in consequence thereof would soon become normal enough to preclude any offense on Great Britain's part should the letter of thanks be finally forwarded. The relations between France and Great Britain did become normal again within a month after Downing Street's apology to the United States minister, and on April 5 Noyes informed the department that the thanks of the United States government which Noyes on December 18 had requested Waddington to convey to Captain Aube, had been officially communicated to that officer and that he would be assigned again to an active command.[76]

The actions of Griffin in Samoa caused a slight reaction in the German Foreign Office as well, although at this time Germany had no colonial ambitions and was merely interested in the welfare of German commercial interests in the South Seas as represented in particular by the firm of Godeffroy and Son of Hamburg. On May 17, 1877, Baron von Thielmann, German chargé d'affaires at Washington, wrote the Department of State expressing Germany's opinion that the political dissensions in Samoa, which were endangering commerce there, were fostered by the belief of one of the parties that it would re-

[75] Despatches, France, vol. 83, no. 74, Noyes to Evarts, March 8, 1878.
[76] *Ibid.*, no. 84, Noyes to Evarts, April 5, 1878.

ANGLO-AMERICAN COMPLICATIONS 181

ceive material support from the United States, and that this belief had been encouraged by the action of the United States consul in declining to coöperate with his colleagues for a settlement of these dissensions. Germany, therefore, requested that the United States aid in the promotion of peace by announcing to the Samoans that it favored neither of the parties but desired the establishment of order.[77] But on one occasion the German consul had spoken disrespectfully of the United States and this was regretted and disapproved by the German government, as that government's minister in Washington informed the department early in 1879.[78] This apology was coupled with the expression of a desire by Germany that the United States consul in Samoa be instructed to assist the representatives of Germany in concluding a treaty with Samoa, the German government thereby recognizing the influence which the United States had acquired in Samoa by that time as a result of her own treaty with the Samoan government.[79]

It was noted that when Griffin left the French warship he took up his residence at the capital of the Samoan government for protection, and that he remained at Mulinuu during the rest of his stay in Samoa. While he thus enjoyed protection, he was placed in a favorable position to enjoy the confidence of the government and to act as adviser when occasion demanded. In December he forwarded to Washington a copy of a letter from Sir Arthur Gordon to the Taimua and Faipule, wherein the governor of Fiji informed the Samoans that he would arrive in

[77] Notes from German Legation, vol. 14, Thielmann to Evarts, May 17, 1877.
[78] Memorandum of interview between Kurt von Schlözer and F. W. Seward, Jan. 23, 1879. (Notes from German Legation, vol. 15.)
[79] The treaty between United States and Samoa was concluded January 17, 1878. See next chapter.

Samoa in January or February and that he would then have some suggestions to make to them concerning their government. The Taimua replied that they wanted no suggestions.[80] Simultaneously the Samoans were being threatened in a less subtle way by the German consul, who, Griffin reported, levied a new fine upon the Samoan government on December 22 amounting to $13,000 for alleged destruction of property belonging to German citizens. On January 4 Weber called upon the government to pay the balance of a former fine of $16,000 and threatened them with the guns of the *Augusta*. These were fines for trivial offenses, said Griffin, but the government was making arrangements to pay the first fine in full because the German consul had informed them that for every day's delay there would be $500 added to the fine.[81] In spite of the difficulties confronting the Samoan government, it was nevertheless able to bring the war with the Puletua to a victorious end by defeating the remaining forces of opposition on the island of Tutuila. Despite the aid and encouragement they had received from the renegade Foster, erstwhile United States consul, the forces of Mauga had surrendered their arms and ammunition to the government warriors.[82]

Sir Arthur H. Gordon, H.B.M. high commissioner for the Western Pacific and governor of Fiji, finally arrived on February 10 on board the *Sapphire,* accompanied by the Honorable John Gorrie, chief justice of Fiji and judicial commissioner for the Western Pacific, and other prominent officials.[83] The British consul, Liardet, died suddenly the same morning, and thus there was no opportunity for Sir Arthur to hear in court his side of the con-

[80] C.D., Apia, vol. 5, Griffin, Dec. 26, 1877, rec'd March 19, 1878.
[81] *Ibid.*, Griffin, Jan. 10, 1878, rec'd March 4.
[82] *Ibid.*, Griffin, Jan. 16, 1878, rec'd March 4.
[83] *Ibid.*, Griffin, Feb. 25, 1878, rec'd May 29.

troversy with Griffin.[84] Nevertheless, the high commissioner in a communication to Griffin suggested that he permit the case of the attack on the consulate to be taken up before Judge Gorrie, but Griffin refused, saying in his reply that he had no instructions that would authorize him to allow such a case to be tried in a British court, as it was a matter for international inquiry.[85]

In communicating with the Samoan government Sir Arthur referred to its appeal the previous spring for British protection and emphasized the reason for its rejection by the queen. The high commissioner also referred to British fines and the pledge they had made of the whole islands as security and wanted the Samoans to state reasons why these fines should not be demanded.[86] To the Taimua and Faipule, according to Griffin, it appeared that the speech indicated an attempt on the part of Sir Arthur to secure some kind of an agreement from them, but they disclosed to Griffin that this would be impossible before the return of Le Mamea from the United States.[87]

Realizing Griffin's influence over the government, Sir Arthur then tried to induce the consul to advise the Taimua and Faipule to sign an "obnoxious" agreement, and when he refused, the German consul joined the British high commissioner in requesting him to associate with them in an agreement, informally if not formally, for coöperative action in Samoa. But Griffin steadfastly remained aloof. Thereupon Sir Arthur began to use pressure upon the Samoan government by threatening fines. The guns of the *Sapphire* were fired to impress the

[84] *Ibid.*, Griffin, Feb. 11, 1878, rec'd May 29.
[85] *Ibid.*, Griffin, Feb. 25, 1878, rec'd May 29.
[86] *Ibid.*
[87] Le Mamea, the Samoan secretary of state, left Apia in September to request American protection or negotiate a treaty.

Samoans with British power, British marines were paraded on shore, money was employed for corrupting the chiefs, and reports were circulated that another rebellion was being organized. This was the information Griffin forwarded to Washington. Finally, the Samoan war vessel, *Mulinuu,* was seized and the British threatened to take it to Levuka and sell it at auction to pay the claims for the *Barracouta* attack. This was a distinct blow at the stability of the Samoan government, for the reason that the *Mulinuu* had been used by them to transport warriors between the islands to put down rebellious forces. The high commissioner then gave the government until four o'clock of the afternoon of February 23 to come to terms.

Great excitement prevailed, according to Griffin, and the Taimua and Faipule were ready to fight. In order to prevent bloodshed Griffin hoisted the American flag at the Samoan capital on the evening of February 22. On the afternoon of the twenty-third, when the time limit set by Sir Arthur was fast approaching, Griffin addressed a letter to the high commissioner informing him of negotiations in the United States for a protectorate and requesting him to give up the Samoan war vessel. This Sir Arthur refused to do and took it with him to Fiji. What the high commissioner had in mind to do when the clock struck four is problematical. He could easily have seized the islands, for no American war vessel was in the harbor to support Griffin's pretensions. Virtually living under Samoan protection as he was, Griffin could not have appeared very formidable to Sir Arthur, who had a warship and marines to carry out his orders. But the British had been in trouble with Griffin before, and that incident was now the subject of American representations to Downing Street. Perhaps the high commissioner, advised by the chief justice of Fiji as he must have been, decided, therefore, that it would be unwise to risk another international

ANGLO-AMERICAN COMPLICATIONS 185

incident. Instead of doing anything to the Samoan government at four o'clock, the high commissioner, with his staff and the judicial commissioner, Chief Justice Gorrie, went on board the *Sapphire* at that hour and sailed away to Fiji.[88]

But the *Sapphire* was not long absent from Apia. When she returned on March 12 she had A. P. Maudslay, the newly appointed acting consul for Samoa, and deputy commissioner for the Western Pacific, on board.[89] Maudslay lost no time in addressing a letter to the government requesting an interview for the thirteenth. This granted (though reluctantly, for the reason that Sir Arthur had threatened, when the *Sapphire* returned, to enforce his demands), the matter of a treaty was brought up, and it was agreed that the Taimua and Faipule should meet Maudslay at the British consulate the next day.[90] Nothing being accomplished at this meeting, the British representative announced on the fourteenth that he would give the Samoan government twenty-four hours to come to terms and, if by the end of that time they had failed to comply with his demands, he would place the matter in the hands of the captain of the *Sapphire*. The Samoans, no doubt under the inspiration of Griffin, thereupon requested the British consul to eliminate from the proposed agreement article two, which, if allowed to remain would constitute a breach of good faith with the United States. The article read as follows: "The subjects of Her British Majesty shall always enjoy in Samoa whatever privileges may be accorded to those of the most favored nations and no right shall be granted to any foreign state which shall not be equally enjoyed by Great Britain."

[88] C.D., Apia, vol. 5, Griffin, Feb. 26, 1878, rec'd May 29.
[89] *Ibid.*, Griffin, March 13, 1878, rec'd May 29.
[90] Evidently the British colonials wanted to forestall the American treaty negotiations, but the American-Samoan treaty had already, on January 17, been signed in Washington.

On the fifteenth and before the twenty-four-hour period had elapsed, Griffin informed Maudslay that a treaty between the United States and Samoa had been negotiated on January 17 and cited article V of that treaty wherein the United States undertook to assist Samoa in her difficulties. "In view of this fact," he wrote to Maudslay, "the Government of Samoa has requested me to inform you that it peremptorily declines to enter into any agreement with other governments for the settlement of differences without first consulting the Government of the United States." March 15 was a difficult day for both consuls. In addition to the above quoted letter Griffin wrote to Maudslay two other letters. Maudslay wrote two replies, allowing his third communication of the day to be a mere formal acknowledgment of Griffin's third contribution to a very heated correspondence. In Maudslay's reply to Griffin's first letter he said: "I have not received any instructions from my government directing me to refer for settlement to the United States any matter in dispute between Her Majesty's Government and the Taimua and Faipule of Samoa." To which Griffin retorted in his second letter that his "authority for placing the Samoan Islands under the protection of the United States flag is of such a character as not to admit of any question by the British Acting Consul." Maudslay understood Griffin here to mean that article V of the American treaty provided for a protectorate. His answer to Griffin, though he may not have known it, was the same as the Department of State would have made. He wrote: "I am unable in this case to admit that a clause in a treaty by which the United States offers assistance to the Samoan Government in settling differences . . . can be understood as placing the Samoan Islands under the protection of the United States." This answer brought forth from Griffin the flat assertion that "The Samoan Islands are now under the protection of the

United States." To this Maudslay made no rejoinder, and the fruitless argument was brought to a close.

By the sixteenth the matter was in the hands of Captain Murray of the *Sapphire*. But Maudslay had evidently come to the conclusion that to force a treaty upon an unwilling people would be a valueless procedure, and consequently the captain's ultimatum said nothing about a treaty. His demands were a $1000 fine as an indemnity for the killing of some of the *Barracouta's* crew in Steinberger's time, the formal and legal surrender of the Samoan war schooner, *Mulinuu*, which Sir Arthur Gordon the previous month had taken to Fiji and renamed the *Elizabeth*, and protection for the Puletua refugees who were still lodged in the British consulate. At the same time the captain issued his ultimatum, he warned Griffin about the impending bombardment. "Every care," he wrote the consul, "will be taken of the Samoan hut in which you reside, but as you have no consular flag to mark it I shall not be responsible for your safety." Griffin from his "hut" replied on the same day that the United States flag "is hoisted both for the protection of this consulate and the Government of Samoa." Captain Murray then wound up the discussion for that day by replying: "Your protest will not have the slightest influence with regard to my intended proceedings against the Samoan Government should they refuse my demands."

By this time the Taimua and Faipule had come to the conclusion that the British captain meant to shoot, and since Griffin could provide no American vessel at the moment to protect them and himself from the guns of H.M.S. *Sapphire*, some of the government officials ventured to go out to the warship and have a talk with its captain, Murray. Having again no doubt been coached by Griffin, these officials were adamant against showing the Puletua refugees any consideration. But the captain apparently was ready for a compromise in order to escape from an embarrassing situation. He contented himself with the payment of the *Barracouta* indemnity and the surrender of the *Mulinuu*. Then the *Sapphire* sailed away.[91]

Two days later, under Griffin's inspiration, the Samoan government drew up a protest against the acts of the British representatives, which was sent by Griffin to Washington. The Samoans asked the United States to adjudicate the matter, avowing that they paid the fine of $1000 to Captain Murray with fear and dread and that it was an unjust act to fine them and to take away their two masted vessel, the *Mulinuu*, to Fiji.[92]

For his later actions in Samoa Griffin had not the slightest authority. He had received no official information concerning the treaty that had been negotiated by the Samoan secretary of state at Washington the previous January. This is clear from a reading of his despatch of May 8, almost two months after he wrote Maudslay so grandiosely about the treaty and its meaning for Samoa. He no doubt knew the contents of the treaty from private sources or from the reading of newspapers, but on the above mentioned date he informed the department that he had not received any "official communication in regard to the conclusion of a treaty between the United States and Samoa."[93]

Griffin's despatch of March 21, concerning his clash with the British consul and captain, reached Washington May 29. The department wrote the consul in reply on June 8 "that the whole subject will be enquired into and will receive careful consideration" but the department

[91] C.D., Apia, vol. 5, Griffin, March 21, 1878, with enclosures, rec'd May 29.
[92] *Ibid.*, enclosure.
[93] *Ibid.*, vol. 6, Griffin, May 8, 1878, rec'd July 26.

would await the reports of Thomas M. Dawson and Gustavus Goward before discussing the subject further. The former, it was explained, was on his way to Samoa to succeed Griffin, who was to be transferred. Goward, Griffin was also informed, was accompanying the Samoan secretary of state, Le Mamea, on the U.S.S. *Adams* with the newly negotiated treaty between the Samoan government and the United States, having also been appointed commercial agent for Pago Pago for the purpose of establishing American rights in that harbor as provided for in the treaty.[94]

The department, however, did discuss "the subject further" with Griffin before the arrival of Dawson and Goward in Samoa, for, only six days after the first communication, Secretary Evarts thought the matter important enough to take it in hand personally, writing as follows: "A careful perusal of your despatch No. 46 of the 21st of March last, respecting the proceedings of the British Acting Consul and Naval Commander at Mulinuu with respect to the exaction of an indemnity alleged to be due, and transmitting the correspondence between yourself and those officers in reference thereto leaves doubt in my mind as to the warrant for all your proceedings in the premises." He, therefore, wanted more information before expressing an opinion and continued: "It is desirable to a full understanding of the case that any correspondence which may have taken place between yourself and the Samoan Government relative to the protection vouchsafed by you in your official capacity, as well as the protest and request for arbitration mentioned by you as placed on record in your consulate should be transmitted to the Department."[95]

Dawson did not sail on the *Adams* from Panama with

[94] I.C., vol. 89, p. 326, to Griffin, June 8, 1878.
[95] *Ibid.*, p. 365, Evarts to Griffin, June 14, 1878.

Goward, but left on a commercial steamer from San Francisco on May 13. Due to the captain's inability to land him at Pago Pago on account of a storm, Dawson was carried all the way to Auckland,[96] and because of the infrequent communications between that port and Apia, he did not reach his journey's end until August 13.[97] Griffin continued at his post until the arrival of Dawson and was in charge of the consulate, therefore, when the Samoan secretary of state, La Mamea, and Goward, a month before Dawson's arrival, came to Apia on board the *Adams* with the treaty.

With the knowledge of the successful negotiation of a treaty between the United States and the Samoan government, the British and German officials had ceased for a time to importune the Taimua and Faipule to change their government,[98] and, until the arrival of Le Mamea, bringing definite information concerning the terms of his treaty, the situation in Samoa remained, therefore, comparatively peaceful. By the time the two communications of the department requesting explanations from Griffin concerning his so-called protectorate, arrived, Griffin had departed from Samoa, and Dawson was in charge.[99]

[96] C.D., Apia, vol. 6, Dawson, Auckland, June 25, 1878.
[97] *Ibid.*, Dawson, Aug. 20, 1878, rec'd Nov. 16.
[98] *Ibid.*, Griffin, May 8, 1878, rec'd July 26.
[99] *Ibid.*, Dawson, Sept. 13, 1878, rec'd Dec. 12.

CHAPTER VII

AMERICAN-SAMOAN TREATY OF 1878

GRIFFIN's failure to secure a treaty in Washington was merely a spur to the persistent Samoans to try again. It has been noted that Griffin, shortly after his return to Apia, forwarded to Washington on August 9 another request from the Samoan government for a treaty. Undoubtedly under the inspiration of Griffin and without waiting for an answer to their communication, the Samoan government in September appointed an agent in the person of its secretary of state, M. K. Le Mamea, with full powers to proceed to the United States and negotiate a treaty. Colmesnil, the acting consul during Griffin's absence from Samoa, was commissioned by the Taimua and Faipule to accompany Le Mamea as adviser.[1]

The "Tatooed Prince," as the *San Francisco Chronicle* described Le Mamea, arrived at San Francisco on board the *Isabel* in the early part of November, 1877,[2] and in a few days he continued his journey together with Colmesnil to Washington.[3] The coming of Le Mamea attracted considerable notice in the American press[4] for the reason that the first news concerning the British attack on Griffin in September came from passengers on the same vessel. The general opinion expressed in the press was that Le Mamea was going to ask for American protection. This

---

[1] C.D., Apia, vol. 5, Griffin, Sept. 18, 1877, rec'd Nov. 16.
[2] *New York Times*, Nov. 9, 1877 (page 5, column 2).
[3] *Ibid.*, Nov. 18, 1877 (page 9, column 7).
[4] *Ibid.*, Nov. 9, 1877 (page 5, column 2).

opinion was stimulated by representations made by the passengers on the *Isabel,* to the effect "that the sentiment of the natives is almost unanimously in favor of some connection with the United States."[5]

Upon their arrival in Washington, Le Mamea and Colmesnil called first upon the assistant secretary of state, Frederick W. Seward. To the secretary Le Mamea appeared as "a tall, fine-looking, swarthy-complexioned man," who "spoke English easily and fluently, but with some quaint idioms that seemed to render it more impressive." Le Mamea's credentials being "in proper form, and as the business which brought him to Washington," wrote Seward, "was so important, it had been deemed wise that he should come on himself, instead of entrusting it to any diplomatic or consular representative, I duly presented him to the Secretary of State, Mr. Evarts."[6]

On November 28 Le Mamea was presented to President Hayes by Secretary of State Evarts, Colmesnil, his counsel, having accompanied him.[7] The next day the *New York Times* in an editorial uttered a warning against "entangling alliances." It said in part: "From the time of Steinberger's ill-starred and wholly unauthorized mission until now, the entire Samoan business has appeared very much like a job. If the Polynesians now in Washington, who profess to represent their own people at home, are not really the agents of more artful men than they, no harm can come of concluding a treaty with them. But the chances are that an annexation or 'protectorate' scheme lurks somewhere in this new and plausible project. The State Department will not commit the Government to any

[5] *New York Times,* Nov. 9, 1877 (page 5, column 2).
[6] F. W. Seward, *Reminiscences of a War-Time Statesman and Diplomat, 1830-1915,* p. 437.
[7] *New York Times,* Nov. 29, 1877 (page 1, column 3).

new departure from our well-settled policy of avoiding entangling alliances."[8]

In their endeavors to secure a favorable issue to their mission, the Samoan representatives in Washington knew how to take advantage of the proneness of Americans to be jealous of Great Britain. A despatch from Washington of December 9 to the *New York Times* stated: "The Samoan Ambassador and Mr. Colmesnil, his counsel, have had several interviews with the Secretary of State in regard to the negotiation of a treaty of friendship and commerce. Mr. Colmesnil says, that in case no treaty should be negotiated, the result would be the same as in the case of Fiji a few years ago, namely, English annexation. Samoa has asked England for a protectorate but has been refused. Sir Arthur Gordon told those who made the application that he did not understand the word 'protectorate,' and advised them to go home, think over the matter and conclude to give England the control of Samoa. He would then negotiate with them.'"[9]

Indicating, as it did, his general policy, it is important to see what President Hayes said concerning the Samoan islands in his first annual message on December 3, some five days after Le Mamea had been presented to him. "The government of the Samoan Islands", he wrote, "has sent an envoy, in the person of its Secretary of State, to invite the Government of the United States to recognize and protect their independence, to establish commercial relations with their people, and to assist them in their steps toward regulated and responsible government. The inhabitants of these islands, having made considerable progress in Christian civilization and the development of trade, are doubtful of their ability to maintain peace and independ-

[8] *Ibid.*, Nov. 29, 1877, editorial (page 4, column 4).
[9] *Ibid.*, Dec. 10, 1877 (page 1, column 3).

ence without the aid of some stronger power. The subject is deemed worthy of respectful attention, and the claims upon our assistance by this distant community will be carefully considered."[10]

After the formal presentation Seward was authorized to "discuss matters" with Le Mamea on the part of the United States and was officially informed by the Samoan ambassador that "with the increase of intercourse and trade, the Samoan Islanders had perceived that they might become the object of some intrigue, or perhaps fall under the sway of some one of the maritime powers of Europe, whom they would be powerless to resist. Doubtful of their ability to maintain peaceful and stable existence," continued Seward, "they wished the United States to recognize and protect their independence, to establish commercial relations with their people, and to assist them in their step toward regulated and responsible government."

As a matter of fact Le Mamea had come to Washington to ask for nothing less than the protection of the flag of the United States, "either by formal annexation or under a protectorate, in such form as the American Government might prefer." In offering their islands to the United States they "hardly anticipated," continued Seward in his interesting account, "that there would be any hesitation on our part in accepting such an offer."[11]

Seward explained to Le Mamea "that, while the American people had in former years been willing and desirous of extending their national domain on the continent, yet there had now come a decided change in public opinion. Extension of the national boundaries was now looked upon with disfavour." The secretary amplified his state-

[10] Richardson, *A Compilation of the Messages and Papers of the Presidents, 1789-1897*, VII, 469.
[11] F. W. Seward, *Reminiscences*, etc., p. 437.

ment by saying that this opposition to the extension of American territory was especially strong with reference "to the acquisition of any islands, near or remote, inhabited by any race but our own," and cited as examples of this opposition the shelving or summary rejection of the proposed treaties for naval stations in the West Indies and for the acquisition of St. Thomas, Santo Cruz, and Santo Domingo. "Even the Panama canal," Seward told Le Mamea, "had been allowed to pass into the hands of a European power; and the purchase of Alaska was still a subject of reproach and ridicule, and pronounced a gigantic folly." Seward having had a hand himself "in the negotiation of these treaties could foresee," he said, "the difficulties in the way of the mission he [Le Mamea] had undertaken." Seward added, however, as though to give Le Mamea some hope, that he believed "this dread of national expansion was a passing phase and an unreasonable and unnatural one. But, while it lasted it had to be reckoned with."[12]

Seward laid the Samoan proposals before Secretary Evarts, who in turn presented them to the president and cabinet. "Both President Hayes and Mr. Evarts believed that my father's policy in this regard [national expansion]," continues Seward in his narrative, "had been wise and judicious. But they saw also that it would now encounter the same opposition that it had during the administration of President Johnson and subsequently under that of President Grant.'"[13] Seward found the Navy Department "warmly" favoring the Samoan proposition, as it had long "desired the establishment of naval outposts in the Pacific." But upon sounding the leading members of the committees on foreign relations in both Houses, as well as the important Republican leaders in Congress, it was found that while there "were differences of opinion

[12] Ibid.   [13] Ibid.

among them, . . . practically all were agreed that the times were inauspicious for the consideration of any such project." It would have been impossible to secure the Senate's "consent to any treaty that involved expense or obligation" and the opposition of the House to any proposal from a Republican administration was certain on account of the Democratic majority. "It seemed to be considered a mark of patriotism," concluded Seward, "to oppose any addition to our own country."[14]

Having finally come to the realization that no annexation or protectorate of the Samoan islands would be possible under the prevailing conditions, the Samoan envoy said that Seward might "draw up the treaty in any form" he thought best, and that "he believed his people would agree." The Samoan people would agree to grant to the United States "their best harbour, that of Pago Pago, which fortunately," said Seward, "was as yet unoccupied, and in return would ask nothing, except our assurance of peace and friendship."[15]

In an endeavor "to meet the various Congressional and popular objections," Seward says that he "drafted a treaty, and then another and yet another." "It seemed as if the Senate might be induced to consent to the acceptance of a harbour, provided the country was not to pay anything for it, or even to agree to protect or defend it."[16]

A treaty of commerce and friendship was finally signed on January 17, 1878, by the secretary of state and Le Mamea, and transmitted to the Senate by President Hayes the same day.[17] The treaty provided in the first place for perpetual peace and friendship. The second article guaranteed to the United States a site for a naval station at Pago Pago on the island of Tutuila, and freedom of com-

[14] F. W. Seward, *Reminiscences*, etc., p. 437.
[15] *Ibid.*   [16] *Ibid.*
[17] Executive Journal, United States Senate, vol. 21, p. 202.

AMERICAN-SAMOAN TREATY OF 1878

merce in all Samoan ports. It is important to note in this connection that the United States was not promised the exclusive use of Pago Pago, as was the case in the Meade treaty of 1872. That part of the article covering this matter is as follows: "Naval vessels of the United States shall have the privilege of entering and using the port of Pago Pago, and establishing therein and on the shores thereof a station for coal and other naval supplies for their naval and commercial marine, and the Samoan Government will hereafter neither exercise nor authorize any jurisdiction within said port adverse to such rights of the United States or restrictive thereof.''[18] It will be seen that when Great Britain negotiated her treaty with Samoa in August of the next year, she was quick to take advantage of the fact that the United States did not have the exclusive rights in Pago Pago harbor.[19] United States vessels were freed from all import and export duties in Samoan ports, but a tonnage duty of one-half of one per cent per ton actual measurement was provided for in the treaty. All disputes between citizens of the United States in Samoa should be heard by the United States consul, and disputes between citizens of the United States and citizens of Samoa should be heard by the consul and a Samoan official.

Article V of the treaty is important for the reason that all subsequent interventions by the United States in behalf of Samoa were based on this article, and on account

[18] H. Ex. Doc. no. 238, p. 124.

[19] Article VIII of the Anglo-Samoan treaty of August 28, 1879, reads in part: "Her Majesty the Queen of Great Britain may, if she think fit, establish on the shores of a Samoan harbor, to be hereafter designated by Her Majesty, a naval station and coaling depot; but this article shall not apply to the harbors of Apia or Saluafata, or to that part of the harbor of Pago Pago which may be hereafter selected by the Government of the United States as a station under the provisions of the treaty concluded between the United States," etc.

of it the United States went so far as to negotiate the treaty of 1889, whereby it became not only formally engaged to protect Samoa but joined two other powers in a tripartite control of Samoan affairs. The article is in full as follows: "If, unhappily, any differences should have arisen, or shall hereafter arise, between the Samoan Government and any other Government in amity with the United States, the Government of the latter will employ its good offices for the purpose of adjudicating these differences upon a satisfactory and solid foundation."[20] This statement was as far as the United States would go in the matter of protection for Samoa. Benevolent interest in the welfare of the islands was the maximum that could be secured from the Senate. "Even the phrases rendering our good offices in case of disputes with other powers were objected to," writes Seward, "but were finally allowed to stand."[21] The "most favored-nation" clause was included in the treaty. The seventh article provided for a renewal or cancellation of the treaty after ten years.[22]

After its submission to the Senate by the president, that body on January 18, 1878, referred the treaty to the Committee on Foreign Relations and ordered that it be printed in confidence for the use of the Senate.[23] On January 29, Senator Hamlin from the committee reported the treaty without amendment.[24] The next day the treaty was read a second time in the Committee of the Whole, and with only two slight amendments introduced by Senators Edmunds and Christiancy, the treaty was reported to the Senate in practically the same form as when it left the president's hands. Senator Hamlin then submitted a resolution advis-

[20] H. Ex. Doc. no. 238, p. 125.   [21] Seward, *Reminiscences*, etc., p. 437.
[22] Original treaty in Department of State. For text of treaty see William M. Malloy, *Treaties, Conventions*, etc., vol. 2, pp. 1574-1576.
[23] Executive Journal, United States Senate, vol. 21, p. 202.
[24] *Ibid.*, p. 218.

AMERICAN-SAMOAN TREATY OF 1878

ing and consenting to the ratification of the treaty with the two amendments.[25] The resolution by unanimous consent was then considered and passed unanimously in the affirmative.[26] In pursuance of the Senate's advice the president ratified the treaty on February 8. The ratifications were exchanged on February 11, and the treaty proclaimed on February 13.[27]

In a long editorial on April 10, under the caption "Our Foothold in the South Pacific" the *New York Times* said in part: "The tidings of the successful completion of the treaty . . . presumably have by this time reached Samoa in season, no doubt, to anticipate the diplomatic flank movement of Sir Arthur Gordon, Governor of Fiji, for the annexation of the Samoan Islands as a British colonial possession. The intrinsic importance of the naval and supply station acquired by the treaty, and the precedent it creates in our history as a nation will cause its practical attainment to be watched for with curiosity and interest."[28] Suspicious as the *Times* had appeared relative to the negotiations at Washington, it is interesting to note that the writer of this particular editorial saw no danger in article V to our existing foreign policy of "no entangling alliances". Wrote the editor further: "Article fifth provides that in any dispute between the Samoan Government and any other Government in amity with the United States, our Government shall 'employ its good offices for the purpose of adjusting those differences upon a satisfactory and solid foundation.' We cite this provision because it has been said that our Government has

---

[25] *Ibid.*, p. 220.   [26] *Ibid.*, p. 221.

[27] Malloy, *Treaties, Conventions*, etc., p. 1574. A memorandum was attached to the treaty on February 9 and signed by Le Mamea as follows: "The words 'one-half of one per cent per ton actual measurement' in Article III are understood to mean at the rate of one-half cent on each ton and they are not deemed susceptible of any other meaning." (*Ibid.*, p. 1575.)

[28] *New York Times*, April 10, 1878 (page 4, column 3) editorial.

undertaken a protectorate of Samoa. This fifth article is the only one that could give color to that interpretation, and it will be seen that nothing of the sort has been done. As therefore, without 'entangling alliances' or any troublesome pledges, a valuable naval and coaling station has been acquired in what Admiral Wilkes long ago pronounced the best harbor of the South Pacific, we may look with satisfaction for the practical carrying out of the treaty now to be attempted."[29]

In the meantime rumors had been abroad in the latter days of February and in early March that the British contemplated either a protectorate or an annexation of Samoa. A despatch from London of March 1, for instance, quoted the *Standard* as saying: "We understand that Sir Arthur Gordon, Governor of the Fiji Islands, has been ordered to proceed to the Samoan authorities for British protection."[30] On the next day the *San Francisco Alta* published a denial of the truthfulness of the news from London, basing its assertion upon statements made by Le Mamea, when the Samoan envoy was in San Francisco.[31] When on April 12 Le Mamea called at the Department of State and at the White House to bid farewell, the assistant secretary of state, Seward, betrayed his interest in England's intentions in Samoa by asking Le Mamea "whether there was any truth in the report that England had seized Samoa." Le Mamea replied that "he could not believe there was, as circumstances and his latest information were against such a conclusion. The report, he said, might have risen from the fact that Sir Arthur Gordon, the Governor of Fiji, recently went to the Samoan

[29] *New York Times*, April 10, 1878 (page 4, column 3) editorial.
[30] *Ibid.*, March 1, 1878 (page 5, column 2) news despatch from London, March 1.
[31] *Ibid.*, March 2, 1878 (page 1, column 5) news dispatch from San Francisco, March 1.

Islands for the purpose only of establishing a consular court."[32]

Although the British government before 1875 had been apathetic toward the question of the annexation of Samoa, and had rebuffed the New Zealanders on several occasions, it cannot be said that Downing Street was altogether indifferent after 1875 and subsequent to Sir Arthur Gordon's becoming governor of Fiji and high commissioner for the Western Pacific. It has been noted that Steinberger's assumption of power in Samoa in 1875 was responsible for a reaction in British colonial circles, especially in Fiji, in favor of British annexation of Samoa, and it can be confidently asserted that Griffin's troubles in Samoa were also due to his running afoul of this same growing tendency toward British expansion. Le Mamea was, of course, ignorant of Sir Arthur's communication to the Taimua and Faipule, requesting a treaty, and that "there was apprehension," according to Bates, "that Sir Arthur Gordon intended to force the acceptance of the treaty at the point of the bayonet."[33] Neither he nor Seward knew, moreover, that at this juncture Griffin had felt it his duty to raise the United States flag on February 22, to protect the government of Samoa from a possible annexation by Great Britain.

Seward, nevertheless, instinctively felt that it was Great Britain who might take advantage of the failure of the United States to make a treaty, and article V, wherein the United States undertook to assist Samoa when in political difficulties, was perhaps drawn up with Great Britain in view more than Germany. As a matter of fact, Seward sounded the British minister as to what Great Britain might do in the event of the failure of the treaty

[32] *Ibid.*, April 13, 1878 (page 1, column 3) news despatch from Washington, April 12.
[33] H. Ex. Doc. no. 238, p. 145.

negotiations then going on between Le Mamea and himself. Seward writes: "When I mentioned to the British Minister, Sir Edward Thornton, that the Samoans might perhaps ask Queen Victoria for a protectorate, in case their negotiations with us should fail, he smiled and said, 'Well, I suppose we should take them, but I do not think we should care to enter into any quarrel about it.' "[34]

As was seen in the last chapter, the German government (for reasons of commerce) was even more interested than Great Britain in securing a treaty, and, as will be seen in the next chapter, Theodor Weber finally negotiated a treaty on January 24, 1879, a year after the American-Samoan treaty. When this had been consummated the German minister to the United States, Dr. von Schlözer, could not help showing his pleasure one day when calling upon Seward. The colloquy that ensued betrayed a trace of envy, however, with reference to the success of the United States in obtaining Pago Pago harbor for a naval station. Said the German minister: " 'Aha! Also we have a harbour in Samoa. Not the best—no, you have the best. You have Pago Pago. But we have the next best.' " " 'What one have you, mein Herr?' " " 'Apia—Apia Harbour.[35] It is a good harbour. It is where the people are, and the trade. We shall use our harbour. You do not use yours—no. But you will, some day. Some day, you will.' " "And in so saying," writes Seward, "the cheery envoy proved himself a prophet."[36]

The treaty with Samoa having been ratified by the United States Senate, Gustavus Goward was commissioned to accompany Le Mamea and represent the United States when the treaty was presented to the Samoan gov-

[34] Seward, *Reminiscences*, etc., p. 437.
[35] Schlözer was mistaken about the harbor. Saluafata harbor east of Apia was the one granted to Germany for a naval station.
[36] Seward, *Reminiscences*, etc., p. 437.

AMERICAN-SAMOAN TREATY OF 1878

ernment. He received his instructions from Seward on April 6, 1878, his official title being: "United States Commercial Agent at the United States Commercial Agency at Pago Pago."[37] Later Goward was instructed to take passage with Le Mamea on a vessel from New York to Panama, the United States government defraying the expenses of both.[38] The U.S.S. *Adams,* Commander Rodgers, brought the Samoan and American representatives to Samoa from the Isthmus of Panama, arriving in the port of Apia on June 28. Following mutual courtesies on board the vessel between a delegation from the Samoan government and the American officers, Le Mamea took his leave of Commander Rodgers and Goward, having arranged for official calls by the Americans upon the Taimua and Faipule for July 3. The American consul, Griffin, also came on board to pay his respects, and to give information concerning political conditions on shore. On the third he accompanied Goward and Commander Rodgers to the official reception.[39]

The Samoan assemblage on the third must have presented to the Americans a somewhat ludicrous appearance. "Upon entering there," wrote Goward, "we found assembled the Taimua and Faipule and other rulers and distinguished chiefs arrayed, for the most part, in European habit, the most prominent of which were the navy uniform coats of various nations."[40] All three of the Americans delivered speeches. Commander Rodgers spoke

[37] I.C., vol. 88, p. 642, Seward to Goward, April 6, 1878; see also S. Ex. Doc. no. 2, 46 Congress, 1 session, p. 5.
[38] *Ibid.*, vol. 89, p. 23, Seward to Goward, April 16, 1878.
[39] C.D., Apia—Pago Pago, vol. 13, report by Gustavus Goward Nov. 27, 1878; see also S. Ex. Doc. no. 2, 46 Congress, 1 session, p. 2. Goward made three reports to Seward, Nov. 27, 28, and Dec. 28, 1878. These reports were transmitted by Secretary Evarts to President Hayes, March 20, 1879, and forwarded to the Senate by the president on the same day in compliance with a Senate resolution of March 3.
[40] *Ibid.*

first. Goward made the significant statement that the United States "recognizes your assembled rulers and chiefs, the Taimua and Faipule, as the Samoan Government, and Samoa itself as an independent nation among other nations of the earth, such as England, Germany, and France, entitled with them to the courtesies and rights known to international law. Other people like yourselves, struggling for independence and national position, have in vain sought for her powerful aid and recognition. You have the honor to be the first to induce her to extend her good offices and active influence to islands so far distant." Consul Griffin brought the speech making to a close by remarking "that they [the Samoans] now had what they had asked for, and that everything had come to pass as he had foretold them, they could always rely on the American Government as sure to keep its promise and as bearing good will towards them."[41] The treaty was thereupon proclaimed the same day.[42] On the occasion of the proclamation Goward was presented with a fine mat as a covering for the copy of the ratified treaty which he would bring back to the United States. The new name of the Samoan government was shown on the mat as follows: *Le Malo Sooso o Samoa,* that is, "The United Government of Samoa." The mat was valued by the natives at £5000 and was the ransom of Mauga, the late owner, the chief of Pago Pago with whom Meade made his treaty.[43] Chief Mauga had joined the Puletua movement against the Taimua and Faipule during Le Mamea's absence in the United States and though aided by the English under Liardet and also by the former United States consul,

[41] C.D., Apia—Pago Pago, vol. 13, report by Gustavus Goward Nov. 27, 1878; S. Ex. Doc. no. 2, 46 Congress, 1 session, p. 3.

[42] The ratification was advised by the Taimua and Faipule with amendments July 3, 1878, and proclaimed at Mulinuu the same day.

[43] C.D., Apia—Pago Pago, vol. 13, report by Gustavus Goward Nov. 27, 1878; S. Ex. Doc. no. 2, 46 Congress, 1 session, pp. 7 and 8.

AMERICAN-SAMOAN TREATY OF 1878   205

Foster, had been defeated in January, 1878. His famous mat now went to the United States as a gift from the government he had recognized only because he had been defeated by it.

A series of *tololos* (popular meetings) were held during five days to celebrate the ratification of the treaty. The *tololos* began on July 17 and it was estimated that from 15,000 to 18,000 natives were assembled, showing the popularity of the treaty. In company with the officers of the *Adams,* Goward and Griffin were placed "in the posts of honor" at Mulinuu, the capital, and "for many hours each day," wrote Goward, "we received the delegations from the various districts into which the Samoan Islands are divided." Every band from the districts vied with the others to display their warlike movements on parade. The maidens brought gifts of yams, taro, and chickens, and the men carried pigs as presents, "all of which was thrown at our feet."[44]

The festivities at an end, the *Adams* left Apia on July 30, having on board Messrs. Goward and Griffin, and a commission appointed by the Samoan government for the purpose of officially transferring the rights in the harbor of Pago Pago as provided in the treaty. "On the following morning [July 31] at daylight," reported Goward, "we were coasting along the southern shores of Tutuila, and before noon were safely moored in the quiet waters of the land-locked harbor of Pago Pago, the finest and most capacious in the South Seas." On August 5 the Samoan commission signed the deed whereby the government transferred to the United States "the privilege of using the port of Pago Pago and the shores thereof, in accordance with the provisions of the treaty."[45] In connection

[44] *Ibid.,* p. 4.
[45] The deed of transfer will be found printed in S. Misc. Doc. no. 58, 50 Congress, 2 session.

with the transfer, naval men from the *Adams* "erected on Goat Island at a point commanding the view of the entire harbor, a flag-staff some fifty-four feet high, and raised thereon the American flag." Two *tololos* were held in honor of the Americans on the island of Tutuila, one at Laulii and the other at Leone.

CHAPTER VIII

BEGINNING OF TRIPARTITE CONTROL IN SAMOA

IMMEDIATELY upon his arrival in Apia on August 13, Dawson, the newly appointed American consul, requested an *exequatur* from the Samoan government, but for more than a week this was not accorded him. Moreover, Griffin, though promising from day to day that he would do so, failed to transfer the consulate with its archives to Dawson, saying at last to his successor, on the eve of his sailing away on the *Adams,* that he intended to transfer the consulate to Goward. Dawson was mystified by his failure to secure an *exequatur* from the government. He attributed the whole situation to a rumor Griffin had caused to circulate among the Samoans, namely, that Dawson had come to Samoa as an agent of the American landowners, and therefore, could not represent the United States in a disinterested manner.[1]

After the *Adams* had sailed (August 20), and a week after his arrival in Apia, Dawson asked Goward if Griffin had transferred the archives to him, and when Goward replied in the negative, Dawson entered the consulate and took possession of them. Presently there fell into Dawson's hands a letter which Griffin had written to the Tai-

[1] C.D., Apia, vol. 6, Dawson, Aug. 20, 1878, rec'd Nov. 16. Though Dawson did not know it, Griffin perhaps got the rumor from Goward, who apparently was envious of Dawson. Even before the *Adams* left Panama for Samoa with Le Mamea and Goward on board, Goward sent a despatch to Washington in which he insinuated that Dawson, who was then in California awaiting a ship for Samoa, was associated with the California land speculators.

208 UNITED STATES POLICY IN SAMOA

mua and Faipule stating that he (Griffin) would turn the American archives over to them to be kept until they recognized his successor. This he did, he explained, despite the fact that Dawson had presented a letter to him from the Department of State directing that he should receive the archives, because he (Dawson) had not been recognized by the Samoan government. Griffin wrote, "as he has not been recognized by your honorable body I do not see how he can enter upon his duties and therefore the delivery of the archives to him would be entirely useless. You of course have a right after the conclusion of the treaty to correspond direct with the Government of the United States and are the best judges whom you shall recognize as representatives of the United States."[2] This appeared to be a brazen attempt on the part of Griffin to keep Dawson from being recognized, so as to compel the department to make a change and perhaps send Griffin back to Samoa. For Griffin had changed his mind about the desirability of staying in Samoa. The negotiation of the treaty, the consummation of which was to some degree at least due to his own efforts, had made Griffin a veritable oracle to the Samoan government. He regretted exceedingly the necessity of leaving. When he sailed away on the *Adams* he carried with him a letter from the Taimua and Faipule to the department expressing their great appreciation of his services to them and their hope that he would be returned to them.[3]

The attitude of the foreigners toward Griffin, on the other hand, especially the English, was well expressed in a news item appearing in the *Samoan Times* of Apia for August 22: "On Wednesday last, G. W. Griffin, ex-American Consul, took his departure in the United States war steamer *Adams,* and we sincerely hope that we have seen

[2] C.D., Apia, vol. 6, Dawson, Aug. 22, 1878, rec'd Nov. 16.
[3] *Ibid.*, Griffin, Washington, Nov. 22, 1878.

the last of him.'"⁴ And on August 24 in an article welcoming Dawson the writer said: "Mr. Consul Dawson has a very ugly battle to fight in consequence of the chicanery, low cunning, and disgraceful conduct of Griffin, who was not satisfied with bringing the American flag in bad odour, but put himself out of the way to insult his successor.

> Sir, the man of honour's come
> Newly alighted,—
> Is the loud music I gave order for
> Ready to receive him?"⁵

Dawson having learned the true situation lost no time in going to a meeting of the Taimua and Faipule with a view to securing recognition. He was well received, the government having the previous day decided to recognize him. What was equally important, he had met with a cordial reception from all the white population.⁶

The new American consul had not been at his post long before the question of carrying out properly article IV of the treaty was raised. A criminal case (Williamson *versus* Asa) was to be tried, and since the principals were an American and a Samoan, the treaty provided that two judges should sit on the case, the American consul, and a native judge appointed by the Samoan government. The native judge insisted on holding the court at Mulinuu, the Samoan capital. Dawson objected, stating that there was no United States authority to hold any court outside of the consulate. The Samoan government thereupon agreed to meet Dawson's wishes. In reporting this incident Dawson stated that unless otherwise ordered he would main-

---

⁴ *Ibid.*, Dawson, Aug. 22, 1878, rec'd Nov. 16; clipping enclosed with despatch.
⁵ *Ibid., Samoa Times*, Aug. 24, 1878; clipping enclosed with despatch.
⁶ C.D., Apia, vol. 6, Dawson, Aug. 22, 1878.

tain the same position in all future cases that might come up.⁷ The department approved his action.⁸

Dawson was not favorably impressed with the Samoan government, which he thought very inefficient in the discharge of its functions. There was no legal code, he reported, "everything being left to the discretion of the judges." Moreover, the government was "unwilling to use coercive measures," he declared, "and consequently many fines imposed are never collected." Dawson did not approve of flogging as a form of punishment, and although it was practiced by other foreigners, he would not impose such punishment unless otherwise instructed.⁹ Another case which came up during the autumn indicated clearly the difficulties confronting the consul in interpreting the treaty in such a way that neither ill will among the natives would be aroused nor the legitimate rights of American citizens go unprotected. Colmesnil, the former acting consul, and the late adviser to Le Mamea in the United States, was suing the Samoan government for the payment of his expense account for the journey to the United States and return and his professional fee. A Samoan judge sat with Consul Dawson on the case and a deadlock ensued when Colmesnil's claim of $4,130.50 was pared down by Consul Dawson to $3,366.13 and by the Samoan judge to only $1000.¹⁰ The consul declined to accept the lower figure. The matter was discussed so often by Dawson in his despatches to Washington that the department finally ordered him to desist, leaving Colmesnil to the mercy of the Samoan government. Earlier in the month Dawson wrote to the department asking whether he should press the claims against native Samoans, which had been al-

⁷ C.D., Apia, vol. 6, Dawson, Sept. 2, 1878, rec'd Nov. 18.
⁸ I.C., vol. 90, p. 543, to Dawson, Nov. 23, 1878.
⁹ C.D., Apia, vol. 6, Dawson, Oct. 1, 1878, rec'd Nov. 27.
¹⁰ *Ibid.*, Dawson, Oct. 31, 1878, rec'd Dec. 31.

lowed by the Court of Inquiry of the *Tuscarora* in May, 1875.[11] The department replied, March 3, that the subject would receive its attention but gave no clue as to what the decision would be.[12]

The department explained to Dawson during the following January what the judicial powers of a consul in Samoa were, and sent him general instructions as to the powers conferred by the laws of the United States and the recent treaty. There being no diplomatic officer in Samoa, the consul's powers were supreme, but his decisions were subject to review by the secretary of state.[13] Not being a lawyer Dawson was naturally puzzled at times as to the course he should pursue. On one occasion he accepted a power of attorney from Messrs. B. Wellman, J. K. Hobbs, and other landowners in Samoa, in order to protect their interests. He informed the department, however, that he would surrender this power if it were thought that this connection would conflict with or prejudice his official duties.[14] The department replied that in view of the judicial powers with which the consul was clothed it was the desire of the department that he surrender his power of attorney "to the proper persons."[15] Before the department received Dawson's despatch, however, the consul had himself come to the conclusion that questions might arise requiring his official and unbiased attention in connection with his clients' land claims, and consequently he advised the department that he had returned the power of attorney.[16]

Following the defeat by the Samoan government of the opposition party on the island of Tutuila in January, the

[11] *Ibid.*, Dawson, Oct. 17, 1878, rec'd Dec. 31.
[12] I.C., vol. 91, p. 437, to Dawson, March 1, 1879.
[13] *Ibid.*, vol. 91, p. 151, to Dawson, Jan. 22, 1879.
[14] C.D., Apia, vol. 6, Dawson, Dec. 12, 1878, rec'd March 17, 1879.
[15] I.C., vol. 91, p. 584, to Dawson, March 24, 1879.
[16] C.D., Apia, vol. 6, Dawson, Feb. 25, 1879, rec'd May 2.

relations between the native factions had been unusually peaceful. This was to some extent due to a general curiosity among the natives as to whether the United States was actually going to declare a protectorate over the islands, and also to the fact that after the payment of the *Barracouta* indemnity to the British in March, the British and German consuls refrained from interfering. The German representative in fact changed his tactics altogether after the American-Samoan treaty was negotiated. Instead of favoring the Puletua or trying to set up a new government by getting the factions to agree, Weber followed the lead of the United States and frankly sought a treaty from the government party. He even went so far as to suggest to his government that it request the Department of State to instruct the American consul to coöperate with him to that end.[17] The German ambitions in Samoa at this time were entirely commercial.

The attitude of Germany, as well as the new relationship of the United States toward the islands as a result of the American-Samoan treaty, aroused some discussion in the European and American press in the autumn of 1878. A statement in the Paris journal, *Estafette,* that the German government was definitely committed to annexation of the entire Samoan group, was declared in a despatch from London to the *New York Times* to be "highly improbable." Germany had merely "invited England to co-operate in demanding from Samoa equal rights for traders, settlers and mariners, with any other nation, probably on account of the treaty between Samoa and the United States. Germany professes to desire no more than equality under some agreement embodying the 'most favored nation' clause.''[18] A few days later the German

[17] Notes from German Legation, vol. 15, Schlözer to F. W. Seward, Jan. 23, 1879.
[18] *New York Times,* Nov. 14, 1878 (page 1, column 5).

official *Gazette* also contradicted the report appearing in the *Estafette,* the *New York Times* publishing a despatch from Berlin stating that "the *Gazette* declares that Germany does not contemplate acquiring or founding colonies beyond the Atlantic. The dispute in regard to the Samoan Islands will naturally be settled by a treaty, which will secure to Germany, and other States interested, the privileges granted to the most favored nation."[19] In commenting upon the *Estafette* article and the denials emanating from Berlin and London, the *New York Times* said editorially: "A few years ago it would have made very little immediate difference to our country whether any or all of these statements were true. But early in the present year a treaty was made between our Government and the Samoan, which puts the matter in a different light. Under that treaty, rights were given in part of Samoa (Pago Pago Harbor) which are probably to a certain extent exclusive. In return, guarantees were given by the United States (Article V) which might call for early fulfillment, in the precise contingency which has now arisen. There is not much doubt that the present difficulty in the islands has risen out of this treaty, and accordingly it becomes interesting to know what rights and obligations were mutually conferred and assumed. . . . It is clear that such obligations of counsel or assistance as we have assumed should be freely and fully discharged at the proper moment."[20] From an attitude of ridicule toward all things Samoan, the *Times* had thus reversed its policy. It thereby reflected perhaps a growing interest among the American people in the fate of the Samoans, as well as in the rights of the United States in these islands.

Though 1878 was notable for internal peace in Samoa, the old government, set up in Steinberger's day, began to

[19] *Ibid.*, Nov. 19, 1878 (page 1, column 3).
[20] *Ibid.*, Dec. 9, 1878 (page 4, column 4).

disintegrate in the later months of the year. Dissatisfaction among the people seemed to be general. The reason for this state of affairs was said to be the failure of the government to secure a protectorate from the United States. In a joint letter to the consuls[21] the Taimua and Faipule therefore announced that the government was about to disband so as to enable the representative chiefs to return to their districts and get fresh mandates from their constituents. The government would resume its functions on December first.[22] Dawson wrote immediately a letter to the Taimua and Faipule remonstrating with them against the suspension of governmental functions until after the elections, and suggested their leaving some individual or a committee with plenary powers to act. This advice the Taimua and Faipule expressed a willingness to accept and appointed three members of the Taimua to carry on the government.[23]

Le Mamea also informed Dawson that the government intended to negotiate a treaty "with Weber and with other nations," but action was being postponed, he said, until one "General" J. J. Bartlett, could be placed in the government. This person was none other than an American adventurer, of less ability than Steinberger to be sure, but nevertheless recommended to Le Mamea by Steinberger during the former's sojourn in the United States.[24] Le Mamea had desired Steinberger to return with him to Samoa, but the latter had thought it better that a "military" man should precede him and perhaps prepare the way for his own more triumphant return later. As a

[21] September 30, 1878.
[22] C.D., Apia, vol. 6, Dawson, Oct. 1, 1878, rec'd Nov. 27.
[23] *Ibid.*, Dawson, Oct. 1, 1878.
[24] The negotiations between Le Mamea and Steinberger probably gave rise to the rumors referred to in the previous chapter, namely, that Steinberger was fitting out a filibustering expedition in the interest of the old government in Samoa.

TRIPARTITE CONTROL IN SAMOA   215

matter of fact the "General" was already in Samoa when Dawson first arrived, and Le Mamea was now endeavoring to make a place for him in the government.[25]

Although the anti-American feeling among the better class of English residents had disappeared, a persistent bitterness among the beach comber element of Apia remained. This fact Dawson soon learned to his near undoing, for, on one night in October, he was attacked by a drunken Englishman named Bell, and narrowly escaped death. The case was taken up promptly by the British consul and a satisfactory apology made by the assailant whom Dawson later prudently thought it best not to prosecute.[26]

By October, 1878, the relations between the Samoan officials and the German consul were friendly enough to permit an agreement to be made between the Samoans and Consul Weber and Captain Werner of the *Ariadne*, concerning a treaty. It was decided to open negotiations on January 1, when another German warship was expected to arrive at Apia.[27] However, there was still a lingering hope among the Samoan authorities as late as December that the United States might be prevailed upon to establish a protectorate, and Dawson was requested to forward to Washington their petition.[28] It was the last appeal from the old government.

The return of the members of the Taimua and Faipule to their respective districts for fresh mandates from their constituents did not result in the establishment of a more stable government. In fact, this very confession of weakness by the "Steinberger" government brought on a quarrel in the ranks of the Puletua as to which of their

[25] C.D., Apia, vol. 6, Dawson, Oct. 1, 1878, rec'd Nov. 27.
[26] *Ibid.*, Dawson, Oct. 16, 1878, rec'd Dec. 31.
[27] *Ibid.*, Dawson, Oct. 18, 1878.
[28] *Ibid.*, Dawson, Dec. 19, 1878, rec'd Mar. 27.

greatest chiefs, Malietoa Talavou or Malietoa Laupepa, Talavou's nephew, should be elected king of the new government which they were determined to establish on the ruins of the old.[29] For a time, therefore, a three-cornered fight threatened, and, as if the situation was not complicated enough, a report circulated freely that Great Britain was entertaining a scheme for consolidating the Samoan and Tonga islands with her Fiji group into an empire in the Pacific.[30] In fact so rapidly was a serious situation developing, that Dawson sent a despatch to the department requesting that a United States war vessel be ordered to Samoa to protect American interests.[31] Shortly after the receipt of Dawson's latest communications, the secretary of state brought the matter up in a cabinet meeting, April 11, stating that the information received from the islands indicated "great danger of an outbreak there, which would imperil the lives of the foreign residents."[32] The Department of State had already communicated with the Navy Department, and on April 10 the secretary of the navy replied that a war vessel had been sent to Samoa.[33]

In an effort to save their government from complete collapse,[34] the Samoan officials in the month of January invited Bartlett—who had been waiting six months or more for just such an invitation—to enter their service as an adviser, principally to instruct them as to the laws

[29] C.D., Apia, vol. 6, Dawson, Jan. 1, 1879, rec'd Mar. 27.
[30] *Ibid.*
[31] *Ibid.*, Dawson, Jan. 4, 1879, rec'd Mar. 27.
[32] *New York Times*, April 12, 1879, (page 5, column 2).
[33] I.C., vol. 92, p. 36, to Dawson April 15, 1879.
[34] The weakness of the government was very evident in the month of January. At that time Malietoa Talavou, the uncle of Laupepa, "took up his abode unmolested" at Mulinuu, the Samoan capital, and after living there undisturbed for four months he was elected king by his adherents on May 3. (See Bates' report, appendix A, in H. Ex. Doc. no. 238, p. 147.)

and customs prevailing in the United States.³⁵ While Bartlett was awaiting his opportunity, which, as stated, came in January, the German consul began to fear that perhaps this American, like Steinberger before him, would so insinuate himself into the Samoan government that his (Weber's) plans for negotiating a treaty with them would again be frustrated. This danger was particularly imminent after Bartlett's appointment. When, therefore, the negotiations for the treaty in January seemed to lag, the German consul again threatened Samoa with penalties should the deliberations result in a disagreement.³⁶ Sensational reports again circulated in Europe as to Germany's real intentions in Samoa. The *Pall Mall Gazette's* Berlin correspondent telegraphed that "The German Government in consequence of the refusal of the Samoans to comply with its demands has instructed the corvette *Ariadne* and the gunboat *Nautilus* to exact satisfaction by force if necessary."³⁷ But in a despatch to the *New York Times* from Berlin it appeared that "*The North German Gazette* denies the sensational reports relative to Germany's intended action toward the Samoan Islanders, and states that Germany will merely keep sufficient naval force in the neighborhood to retain possession of two small ports on the Island of Upolu, which she seized and will hold as a pledge until the Samoan Government grants Germany her treaty rights."³⁸

On January 24 Germany's long desired treaty was finally concluded.³⁹ It was signed by Captain Werner of the German corvette, *Ariadne,* Theodor Weber, the consul,

---

[35] C.D., Apia, vol. 6, Jan. 23, 1879, rec'd Mar. 7, and Feb. 14, 1879, rec'd May 2, both from Dawson.
[36] *Ibid.*, Dawson, Jan. 23, 1879, rec'd Mar. 7.
[37] *New York Times,* Jan. 17, 1879 (page 1, column 3), quoted in London despatch of Jan. 16.
[38] *Ibid.,* Jan. 20, 1879 (page 1, column 3).
[39] C.D., Apia, vol. 6, Dawson, Jan. 25, 1879, rec'd Mar. 7.

and three representatives of the Samoan government, and consisted of thirteen articles. In transmitting an official copy of the treaty to the department, Dawson pointed out an ambiguous feature in the clause dealing with land titles.[40] The clause occurred in article VI of the treaty, and read as follows: "Especially does the Samoan Government hereby guarantee to the German subjects peaceable possession of all lands in Samoa, which they have hitherto bought from Samoans in a regular manner and in accordance with the custom at the time, and all further interference with regard to such lands is therefore excluded by this confirmation by the Samoan Government of the ownership of the German subjects. The Germans shall therefore be at liberty to make use of all their lands in Samoa without interference, to establish plantations thereon, and to procure and employ the necessary laborers as well for such purpose as also in general for their wharves, business premises, and houses."[41] Under this clause the German landowners (and this meant in particular the firm of Godeffroy & Son), were guaranteed all the land which had been acquired "from Samoans in a regular manner and in accordance with the custom at the time."

This as a matter of fact settled nothing, and as Bates, special commissioner to Samoa, reported to the department in 1886, "paved the way for future trouble."[42] Much of the land had been deeded to the Germans in return for firearms and intoxicating liquor during the troubled times prior to the Steinberger régime. No matter how determined the succeeding Samoan governments might be

[40] C.D., Apia, vol. 6, Dawson, Feb. 13, 1879, rec'd May 2.
[41] Official copy enclosed with Dawson's despatch, Feb. 13; H. Ex. Doc. no. 238, encl. no. 90, p. 128.
[42] Bates' report in Special Agents, vol. 2, Department of State; H. Ex. Doc. no. 238, appendix A, p. 146.

in urging the recovery of these lands on the plea that they were obtained fraudulently, the Germans would defend the transaction as carried out "in a regular manner and in accordance with the custom of the time." The land question in fact was at the bottom of all the conflicts between the Samoans and Germans in subsequent years as they had been previously to the treaty, and the opposition of prominent chiefs to the alienation of such large tracts of land by treaty was not long in developing, for in transmitting the treaty to Washington, Dawson also enclosed their letters of protest.[43] Bates' report states that on February 26, just a month after the treaty was signed, a meeting was held in Apia by the chiefs of the district of Tuamasaga to protest. "This district," he said, "containing about two-fifths of the population of Upolu, was the seat of the most determined opposition to the existing Government, and the meeting was made the occasion, not only of criticism of the new treaty, but of assault upon the Government (Malo) for its concessions. Three of the Taimuas were in attendance to explain their action, and were interrogated with the keen sarcasm which distinguishes the Samoan orators."[44]

Another important point of objection to the treaty was the provision that the German citizens should not pay tonnage duties. This concession appeared in the fourth article and in addition to no tonnage duties the Germans were not to submit "to any restrictions with regard to their vessels."[45] In the American treaty there was a provision that "a tonnage duty of one-half of one per cent per ton actual measurement" should be levied on Ameri-

[43] C.D., Apia, vol. 6, Dawson, Feb. 13, 1879, rec'd May 2.
[44] Bates' report in Special Agents, vol. 2, Department of State; H. Ex. Doc. no. 238, appendix A, p. 146.
[45] Official copy enclosed with Dawson's despatch, Feb. 13; H. Ex. Doc. no. 238, encl. no. 90, p. 127.

can vessels entering Samoan harbors, but by this clause neither did the United States concede much nor could Samoa hope to gain much, for the reason that American shipping at the time was not very important. But with Germany it was different. Vessels of the Godeffroy firm were coming and going frequently, due to the fact that Apia was the headquarters of that firm's important operations throughout the South Seas. That this firm should escape the payment of tonnage dues was considered another big concession to Germany with consequent loss of revenue to the Samoan government.

In article V the Samoan government granted to Germany the use of the harbor of Saluafata as a naval station. While mercantile and naval vessels of other nations might enter Saluafata harbor, the government of Samoa undertook not to grant "to any other nation such rights with respect to the harbor of Saluafata and its shores as those granted to the German Government." In other words, only Germany might use Saluafata harbor for a naval station, a distinct advantage over the rights acquired by the United States in Pago Pago harbor in the American-Samoan treaty of the previous year. In that treaty the United States had received no exclusive use of Pago Pago harbor for a naval station.[46]

Curious inequalities of course were bound to appear in the treaty, showing how impossible it was for white men and the primitive races to stand on a basis of absolute equality. While the Samoans—if any should ever go to Germany—were bound by the treaty "to submit to the laws and regulations of the country, and to observe the respective manners and customs, as also the religious propriety," the Germans in Samoa would only be held

[46] Compare article II of the American treaty with article V of the German, pp. 124 and 127 in H. Ex. Doc. no. 238, enclosures nos. 89 and 90 respectively.

"to observe such laws and regulations as may be, in future, agreed upon between the two Governments, but meanwhile they shall not do anything which would trespass upon the laws and regulations of their own country."[47] This provision clearly envisaged a municipal pact for Apia in the future which would keep order there, at the same time regulating the relations between native and German, while the rights of extraterritorial jurisdiction would be reserved. Article VI provided for the payment of taxes by Samoans in Germany according to the laws of that country, but the Germans in Samoa should only "pay such taxes and duties to the Samoan Government as may hereafter be agreed upon between the two Governments." Germany also was to enjoy the rights in Samoa of the "most favored nation." In article X, moreover, the government of Samoa undertook not to grant "any monopolies, indemnities, or real advantages to the disadvantage of German commerce or of the flag and subjects of the German Empire." This clause was, of course, vague and susceptible of all sorts of interpretations with the opportunities for future troubles multiplied, especially if the stronger party should interpret any favor granted by Samoa to other nationals as injurious to itself.

On February 24 Dawson sent the Department of State a communication from the Taimua and Faipule expressing their views relative to the treaty, and he stated that there was nothing in it conflicting with the one concluded with the United States.[48]

The opening made for "General" Bartlett in January to associate himself with the Samoan government was sufficient to enable him to attain the same position Steinberger had held in 1875, namely, that of premier. His ap-

[47] See article III in H. Ex. Doc. no. 238, p. 126, encl. no. 90.
[48] C.D., Apia, vol. 6, Dawson, Feb. 24, 1879, rec'd May 2.

pointment and installation in the latter position occurred in March, and his address on that occasion was significant enough to attract the attention of the British and German consuls, who inquired of Dawson whether Bartlett could claim United States protection.[49] In fact it became increasingly clear to Dawson that these foreign representatives were adopting a hostile attitude toward Bartlett, making again delicate the situation of the American consul.[50] In June the British and German consuls issued a protest to the government against the position assumed by Bartlett, claiming that he was not clothed with military powers but only with those of a law officer.[51] Dawson declined to associate himself with his colleagues in this protest since such action on his part would mean intervention in the affairs of the government which the United States had recognized in the American-Samoan treaty. The position of Bartlett somewhat mystified Malietoa Laupepa of the opposition as well, and he sent a note to Dawson inquiring what attitude the United States would take should Bartlett be killed during the hostilities. Dawson assured Malietoa that Bartlett was not an agent of the United States, but advised him to make Bartlett a prisoner rather than kill him.

The reason for the protest of the consuls was the fact that Bartlett, who was endeavoring to strengthen the military power of the tottering "Steinberger" government, now being menaced from various directions, was expected to take the field. During the spring there was uneasiness. In the beginning of May the government gave orders for the protection of the harbor at Mulinuu, the capital, as the opposition was then planning to elect a

[49] C.D., Apia, vol. 6, Dawson, Mar. 28, 1879, rec'd June 26.
[50] *Ibid.*, Dawson, Mar. 29, 1879, rec'd June 26.
[51] *Ibid.*, vol. 7, Dawson, June 19, 1879, rec'd Aug. 22.

king and install him there.[52] A few days later the government requested the consuls to guarantee the neutrality and protection of Mulinuu pending the civil war that was expected.[53] The consuls promised to comply, but extended the territory in which they would maintain order and neutrality to the whole municipal area of Apia occupied by foreigners.[54] Both the Taimua and Faipule on the one side and the adherents of Malietoa on the other were agreeable to the plan, and an agreement was entered into with the consuls. Dawson reported this agreement to the department on June 4,[55] and on June 11 he informed the department that the Samoan government had empowered the foreign consuls to enforce the laws in the neutral territory.[56] The consular representatives thereupon assumed the responsibility of governing the neutral territory as well as preserving peace and order there, and a proclamation was issued by them stating to the foreign and native residents their authority.[57]

It is important to note the steps taken at this time by Dawson for the reason that they were preliminary to the so-called treaty of September 2, 1879, which was the beginning of that tripartite control in Samoan affairs which later developed into the *condominium* of 1889. These informal arrangements made by Dawson in June with the other consuls were approved by the department in two communications to Dawson dated August 28,[58] while on the same day the department also approved his action in

[52] *Ibid.*, vol. 6, Dawson, May 9, 1879, rec'd July 26.
[53] *Ibid.*, Dawson, May 13, 1879, rec'd July 26.
[54] *Ibid.*, Dawson, May 19, 1879, rec'd July 27.
[55] *Ibid.*, Dawson, June 4, 1879, rec'd Aug. 22.
[56] *Ibid.*, vol. 7, Dawson, June 11, 1879, rec'd Aug. 22.
[57] *Ibid.*, Dawson, June 19, 1879, rec'd Aug. 22.
[58] I.C., vol. 93, p. 387, no. 29 to Dawson, August 28, in answer to Dawson's despatch no. 67; vol. 93, p. 388, no. 31 to Dawson, Aug. 28 in answer to Dawson's despatches nos. 70 and 73.

relation to Bartlett, namely, his refusal to join the other consuls in a protest to the Samoan government against the assumption by Bartlett of military powers.[59]

The willingness on the part of the United States to coöperate informally with the two other powers for the protection of foreigners in Apia did not go so far, however, as to recognize the jurisdiction of the British high commissioner's court for the Western Pacific in cases where United States citizens were suing British subjects. Efforts were made in June, 1879, by the British consul to secure Dawson's recognition of the court, but, like his predecessor, he regarded this step as merely preliminary to British protection or annexation, and, therefore, declined. To have recognized the code of a court which had its seat in the Fijis under the high commissioner would have meant the tying up of part of the American consular jurisdiction in Samoa with a British jurisdiction, the head of which was quite outside of the island group. Dawson reported his refusal to recognize the court on June 5, and gave the added information that the British consul consequently had declined to entertain complaints of United States citizens against British subjects. He furthermore asked for instructions.[60] On June 16 Dawson advised the department that further efforts had been made and even insults offered to compel him to recognize the court.[61] In reply to these despatches the department informed Dawson that his action in withholding recognition of the high commissioner's court, or of the right of Great Britain to establish such independent tribunal was approved.[62]

In the month following the consular arrangements for

[59] I.C., vol. 93, p. 388, no. 32 to Dawson, August 28.
[60] C.D., vol. 7, Dawson, June 5, rec'd Aug. 19.
[61] *Ibid.*, Dawson, June 16, rec'd Aug. 22.
[62] I.C., vol. 93, p. 553, to Dawson, Sept. 9, 1879.

the protection and government of Apia, rumors were afloat again that Great Britain was contemplating an annexation of the islands. Dawson discussed with the department the possibilities of such an attempt being made, and also the advisability of a joint protectorate in order to prevent it.[63] In the meantime the U.S.S. *Lackawanna* arrived on June 26 in response to Dawson's request in January for naval protection, and for the time being American interests were secure.[64] There had been no change in the military situation since the consuls had issued their joint proclamation placing Apia under their control, but through an inadvertence of Captain Chandler of the *Lackawanna*, the immediate breaking out of civil war between the Malietoa adherents and the "Steinberger" government, "which the Consuls had long been trying to avert by carefully steering between Scylla and Charybdis," was everywhere expected.

The captain, immediately upon his arrival in Apia harbor, had been advised by the American consul, despite the latter's poor opinion of the authority of the Taimua and Faipule, against showing any official recognition of that government's opponent, Malietoa, although "kindly treatment of him and his people" was recommended. Accordingly, when on June 30 the captain received Malietoa and his chiefs on board the *Lackawanna*, they had "a friendly interview," and then the captain "quietly dismissed them." On the afternoon of the same day a committee from the Taimua and Faipule came on board to call upon the captain and "when the delegation left the ship they received a salute of seventeen guns." "This discrimination between the two parties," wrote Dawson, "was so marked, and considered such an open insult to Malietoa and his people, as to produce the most intense

[63] C.D., Apia, vol. 7, Dawson, July 26, rec'd Oct. 17.
[64] *Ibid.*, Dawson, June 26, rec'd Aug. 22.

excitement I have ever witnessed in Samoa. The news immediately spread far and wide that the American man-of-war had come to fight for the Taimua and Faipule, . . . while the Chiefs and principal Samoans passed Americans on the streets without speaking to those with whom they had been most friendly."[65]

Everyone thought the war would begin at once. Dawson reported that the consuls "deemed it necessary to call a special meeting and invite the American and German[66] Captains of men-of-war with H.B.M. Acting Consul General to be present, which we did on the 2 inst." At this meeting it was the unanimous opinion "that the apparent error could only be corrected by a similar salute to Malietoa, which might place things on the same basis as before. This Captain Chandler agreed to give and did so the following day when Malietoa went on board, and things again resumed their ordinary course." At the meeting of the consuls on July 2 there was also drawn up a manifesto "to the Chiefs and Rulers of the different districts of Samoa" wherein the consuls "let it be distinctly understood by both parties that neither might expect foreign aid in the settlement of their internal difficulties by force." The manifesto brought an end to "the circulation of false reports on both sides that either would receive such aid.'"[67]

Dawson's despatch irritated the department somewhat, and on October 25 a communication was sent reprehending the consul for what the department thought was interference in the political affairs of Samoa. Attention was further called to the fact that he was not a diplomatic officer.[68] It is clear that the department still recog-

[65] C.D., Apia, vol. 7, Dawson, July 11, 1879.
[66] Captain Deinhard of the *Bismarck*.
[67] C.D., Apia, vol. 7, Dawson, July 11, 1879.
[68] I.C., vol. 93, p. 696, to Dawson, Oct. 25, 1879.

TRIPARTITE CONTROL IN SAMOA 227

nized the old "Steinberger" government and that it considered a salute to Malietoa was a mistake as long as he was not recognized as the rightful successor of the Taimua and Faipule. Upon receipt of this communication Dawson expressed himself as regretting that his "part in connection with the salute to Malietoa July 3d . . . was not approved by the Department." He disavowed having given any advice to Captain Chandler, saying that although at the meeting of July 2 it was his opinion "in common with that of my colleagues . . . that a salute similar to that given the old party's delegates was the only thing that could allay the existing agitation," he had "absolutely refused to advise Captain Chandler to give such a salute . . ." The captain on August 25, as a matter of fact, "distinctly stated that he gave it on his own judgment."

The department's reprimand "greatly perplexed" the consul. He had given no advice to Malietoa and his adherents. In fact he had "refrained as far as it seemed possible from anything that appeared . . . like diplomatic intercourse with the Samoans of either party." What he had done was "done in conjunction with my colleagues, and fully reported to the Department. I have concealed nothing." Dawson's position was indeed difficult. There being no diplomatic officer accredited to the Samoan government, he must naturally act at times in ways that bordered on diplomatic functions. He then called attention to his participation in the agreement concerning the neutralization of Apia, and said, "if, indeed, I have in anything acted the part of a diplomat it seems to me that I did so, when, in connection with my colleagues, I entered into an agreement with the Taimua and Faipule, and Malietoa establishing the Neutral Territory, which action was approved by the Department. . . ." He further called attention to the fact that his entering into the convention of September 2, 1879,[69] for the government of Apia was necessarily a diplomatic act although he signed the agreement conditionally, "subject to the approval of the United States Government."[70]

All the public regulations for Apia which until July 11 had been issued by the consuls were forwarded to the department,[71] and Dawson informed the Washington authorities further that the consuls had appointed policemen for Apia and "licensed seven publicans at $10 per month each." Dawson sent the department an interesting description of the embryo consular government at Apia. "For the purpose of carrying on the Consular Government we meet twice a week, Tuesdays and Saturdays at 1 P.M., and sit as local magistrates week about; i.e., the Senior Consul one week, the next in order the next, and the Junior Consul the third week. Each Consul sitting as local magistrate deals with all the cases brought before him for violation of local regulations irrespective of the nationality of the accused, except he be a Samoan, and then the Samoan judge, there being two in the Neutral Territory, sits with him. In a case of great importance all the Consuls sit together. In a case affecting international rights each Consul deals with his countrymen, or in any case beyond the violation of the simple local regulations. Thus far everything has gone on smoothly, and Apia was never before so free of rows, and characterized by so much order. The foreign population all coöperate thus far with the Consuls, and it is to be hoped that this step will be the dawning of a better day in the way of Government for Samoa. Of course the Consuls receive no compensation for these extra and responsible duties, which are entirely *pro bono publico.*"[72]

[69] See page 235.
[70] C.D., Apia, vol. 7, Dawson, Jan. 19, 1880, rec'd April 1.
[71] Enclosed with Dawson's despatches, nos. 73 and 81.   [72] *Ibid.*

In the previous February, Dawson had reported to the department that Sir Arthur H. Gordon, high commissioner, was expected from Fiji the following April on a mission to conclude a treaty with Samoa.[73] This move was a natural reaction to the news that the Germans had finally obtained their treaty. But Sir Arthur delayed his coming to Samoa. Perhaps he was awaiting the time when chaos would reign there, and when the British might step in to restore order. He was still harboring ideas, of course, of British annexation, but he was careful to avoid, if possible, the mistakes of the past. The British high commissioner finally arrived the latter part of August.[74] Before he could negotiate a treaty he must know with what party he should treat. Should it be with the Taimua and Faipule, with whom both the United States and Germany had negotiated treaties, or with Malietoa, the pretender to the kingship? For this reason he sent a note on August 23 to Dawson advising him "that he had been commissioned by the Queen of Great Britain to make a treaty with Samoa, and requesting me to meet with him and the other foreign representatives before he entered into negotiations, in order that he might receive our counsel and coöperation." To this request Dawson assented.[75] Two days later, on the 25th, Dawson received another note from Sir Arthur informing him that the queen had also commissioned him to enter "into treaty negotiations with the government of Samoa for the erection of Apia into a municipality, and asking me to join in a discussion of the subject. . . ." This invitation Dawson also accepted.[76]

The first meeting with the British high commissioner

[73] C.D., Apia, vol. 6, Dawson, Feb. 14, 1879, rec'd May 2.
[74] *Ibid.*, vol. 7, Dawson, Aug. 22, 1879, rec'd Nov. 13.
[75] *Ibid.*, Dawson, Sept. 3, 1879, encl. no. 1, rec'd Nov. 13.
[76] *Ibid.*, encl. no. 2.

was held at the German consulate on the same day that Dawson received the second communication. The three foreign consuls were present, also the commanders of the British, German, and American war vessels and Mr. Alfred P. Maudslay, British deputy commissioner and late acting consul at Apia. Sir Arthur informed the meeting that he wanted advice as to which Samoan party he should turn to negotiate a treaty. As the Old Party, i.e., the acephalous "Steinberger" government, had been in the bushes, as it were, ever since May 28, there could be no thought of negotiating with them. Malietoa Talavou, his nephew Laupepa having stood aside, was the head of the *de facto* government at this time. He had been crowned at Mulinuu on May 3 by his adherents and although the Taimua and Faipule were invited on that occasion to witness the ceremony—a sign of the rebels' contempt for the Old Party's strength—they were driven away from the capital in the latter part of the month.[77] While civil war had been threatening all summer, the Old Party being now in the opposition, nothing so serious had happened, and it was concluded that the Malietoa party was firmly entrenched. Hence the meeting unanimously advised the British high commissioner to negotiate his treaty with Malietoa.[78] This was done on August 28.

The treaty consisted of ten articles and was signed by Arthur Gordon, Alfred P. Maudslay, Malietoa Laupepa, and Saga Leauauna.[79] In the second article the Samoan government (Malo) engaged not to grant to any other "Sovereign or state any rights, privileges, authority, or predominance in Samoa in excess of such as are or may be accorded to Her Britannic Majesty." Thus a protectorate by a single power was at the start ruled out unless,

[77] H. Ex. Doc. no. 238, p. 147, appendix A, (Bates' report).
[78] C.D., Apia, vol. 7, Dawson, Sept. 3, 1879, encl. 3, rec'd Nov. 13.
[79] H. Ex. Doc. no. 238, pp. 130-131, encl. 91.

TRIPARTITE CONTROL IN SAMOA   231

of course, that power be Great Britain. In the second paragraph of the same article Great Britain was granted the "most favored nation" treatment. In article III British subjects were guaranteed possession "of all lands heretofore purchased by them from Samoans in a customary and regular manner." But should a dispute arise provision was made for its settlement in a fair manner. Article IV was definite in stating that a British subject "charged with a criminal offense cognizable by British law" should "be tried by Her Britannic Majesty's high commissioner for the western Pacific Islands, or other British officer duly authorized by Her Britannic Majesty in that behalf." The expression "British law" was to include "any rules duly made and issued by Her Britannic Majesty's high commissioner for the western Pacific Islands for the government of British subjects within his jurisdiction." Article V provided for the trial of civil suits also by the high commissioner's court, or other British officer duly authorized where a British subject was the defendant. Article VI was remarkable for the fact that "every summons or warrant to appear as a witness before Her Britannic Majesty's high commissioner . . . directed to a Samoan subject, shall have the same authority, and may be enforced in like manner as if such summons or warrant had been directed to a subject of Her Britannic Majesty." Article VII provided for future regulations "to enforce the observance by British subjects of the existing municipal laws and police regulations of Samoa . . . and for the due observance of quarantine by British subjects."

By comparing the above provisions with those in the United States (art. IV) and German (art. VII) treaties,[80] it is seen that in the latter two instruments in all

[80] See enclosures nos. 89 and 90, pp. 125 and 128 respectively in H. Ex. Doc. no. 238.

cases, civil or criminal, where an American or a German on the one hand and a native on the other were involved, an officer of the Samoan government should sit in judgment together with the consul of the foreigner in the case. In the United States treaty a convicted American should be punished according to the laws of the United States, and a Samoan according to the laws of Samoa. The British treaty was silent concerning cases where Samoans were defendants and British subjects were plaintiffs, but it is improbable that such cases were understood as coming under the jurisdiction of Samoan courts. The British could no doubt try such cases together with a representative of the Samoan government in the same manner as obtained in the United States and German consular jurisdictions. The main point the British treaty stressed was that in all cases, civil or criminal, where British subjects were defendants against Samoan plaintiffs, they should be tried in a British court without a representative of the Samoan government sitting as an associate judge.[81]

Article VIII provided for a naval station and coaling depot for Great Britain in Samoa on the shores of any harbor except Apia or Saluafata—the latter being reserved to Germany exclusively by her treaty of January 24, 1879—and that part of Pago Pago harbor which might in the future be selected by the United States under the provisions of that power's treaty of January 17, 1878. In other words Pago Pago harbor not having been secured by the United States for its exclusive use as a naval station and coaling depot, might also be selected, without the

[81] A British order in council in 1875 created the office of high commissioner for the Western Pacific to govern British island possessions such as the Fijis. For the protection of British subjects scattered throughout Polynesia and Micronesia another order in council in 1877 extended the operation of the original order to embrace within the high commissioner's jurisdiction some fifteen groups of islands including the Samoan group.

TRIPARTITE CONTROL IN SAMOA 233

Samoan government's violating its treaty with the United States, by Great Britain for the same purpose, provided the United States had previously made its choice of site.[82]

On August 30, when the three consuls were holding one of their business sessions, Sir Arthur desired to see the consuls for the purpose of communicating some important intelligence to them. He was received at once, and informed them "that he had just been waited upon by Malietoa and fourteen of his Chiefs, who offered the Samoan Islands to the Queen of Great Britain." Coming as it did only two days after the treaty was signed, the offer of the chiefs was a surprise even for Sir Arthur, but not unpleasing to him, if he was still entertaining the hopes he cherished in 1877 and 1878. "This intelligence was like a bomb in our midst," continued Dawson in his despatch, "and seemed likely to destroy that unanimity which had hitherto prevailed in our councils. Most of us said nothing but thought there must have been some mistake. His Excellency said Malietoa had declared his purpose to write a letter to the Queen to the same effect as his statement. But on Monday the first instant when the letter was received His Excellency frankly admitted that it was very different from what he had expected, and it was found besides that both the German Consul and myself had received precisely similar letters from Malietoa addressed to His Excellency the President of the United States and the Emperor of Germany, asking for a joint protectorate of the three great Governments over Samoa, instead of offering the Islands to any one of those Powers."[83]

[82] It was seen that by the Meade agreement of 1872 the United States would have been entitled to the exclusive use of the shores of Pago Pago harbor. The treaty of 1878 granted no exclusive use.

[83] C.D., Apia, vol. 7, Dawson, Sept. 3, 1879, rec'd Nov. 13.

Evidently after making their offer to the high commissioner, the Samoan government had come to believe that by so doing they would violate their treaties with the United States and Germany, for in their letter to the president they said: "We are of opinion that we shall have no peace until we give our own authority to some great Government. But what causes us difficulty is the Article in the treaties entered into with your Excellency, the President of the United States, and the Government of Germany and the Government of Great Britain to the effect that we will not befriend one Government more than another; that we shall treat in a precisely similar manner all great Governments who have entered into treaty relations with Samoa."[84] For this reason the only solution of their difficulties lay in a joint protectorate. In other words the "most favored nation" clause in all three treaties prevented the Samoan government from offering the islands to one power. "These letters to the three powers," wrote Dawson in conclusion, "restored harmony among the foreign representatives."[85]

Dawson became very much intrigued with the idea of a joint protectorate over Samoa and on the second of September he and Captain Chandler negotiated an agreement with the British and German representatives for the government of the district of Apia as a preliminary measure to a joint control of the whole group of islands. As a matter of fact, a joint protectorate appeared to Dawson as very essential in order to prevent further disturbances and at the same time to conserve the rights of the United States as well as those of the other powers. The idea must have struck Sir Arthur and Weber in the same way, and perhaps Dawson was influenced by them to believe that

[84] C.D., Apia, vol. 7, Dawson, Sept. 3, 1879, encl. no. 4, Malietoa to the President, Aug. 31, 1879.
[85] *Ibid.*

the United States would have to forego its historic policy of isolation and participate in the protectorate. In any case Dawson did not want the British high commissioner to set up a municipal government alone for the protection of British subjects as he was authorized to do in article VII of the treaty of August 28, for such a procedure would have meant the driving in of a wedge of British influence in the islands that certainly would have resulted in a British protection of all Samoa. Consequently, the interesting municipal convention of September 2 was drawn up, which formed the legal basis for the tripartite control of the Apia district. Although this convention was never submitted to the Senate for ratification, it was nevertheless accepted by the Department of State as a necessary arrangement, and until it came to an end by the withdrawal of the German consul therefrom in 1887, the American consuls were instructed to assist in its enforcement as though the convention had been ratified by the Senate. The executive department, therefore, acting on its own responsibility and without authority from the Senate, established a precedent of eight years' duration leading to the "entanglement" of the Berlin Act of 1889.

The convention, consisting of thirteen articles, was signed by Arthur Gordon and Alfred P. Maudslay representing Great Britain, Captain Mensing, commander of the German war vessel *Albatross,* and Theodor Weber, the German consul, Captain Chandler, commander of the U.S.S. *Lackawanna,* and Consul Dawson, and two representatives of the Samoan government, Malietoa Laupepa and Saga le Auauna. Only Great Britain looked on the convention as a treaty; Germany accepted it as an agreement in accordance with article VIII of her treaty of January 24, 1879, with Samoa.

The first article stated what the boundaries of the district were to which the treaty should apply. Article II stated that the town and district so described should "be placed under the government of a municipal board, consisting of those foreign Consuls resident in Apia whose nations have entered into treaty relations with Samoa." The powers of the board, as expressed in the third article, related to police power, public works, sanitary regulations, the issue of licenses, harbor regulations, and the prevention of the sale "of spiritous liquors to Samoans and other islanders of the Pacific Ocean." The fourth article granted to the board the right of taxing houses and lands within the district of Apia for the purpose of defraying governmental expenses. A municipal magistrate, to be appointed by the board, and authorized to try all offenses against the municipal regulations, was provided for in article V. The sixth article stated that subjects or citizens of the contracting parties in Apia, who were charged with offenses against the laws of their own country, should be tried according to these laws and in accordance with the stipulations in the treaty between the Samoan government and their own. "Every Samoan subject," said article VII, "charged with a criminal offense within the limits of the district of Apia, other than an offense against the municipal regulations, shall be liable to trial by the magistrate appointed under the provisions of Article V, in conjunction with a Samoan magistrate."

The territorial integrity of Samoa was preserved in the eighth article "and the Samoan flag shall be hoisted at such place of meeting of the municipal board as may be permanently adopted." Not only the neutrality of the town and district of Apia in case of civil war was provided for in the next article, but also the adjacent districts of Letogo, Tiapepe Point, and Siusega were considered neutral territory and subject to "such regulations as may be considered necessary for the support and maintenance of such neutrality."

The tenth article provided that the convention should "be revised at the end of four years from its date" and, if the internal conditions permitted it, the powers granted to the board of consuls should then cease "and the district again pass under the control and authority of the Samoan Government." In the eleventh article the German representative accepted the convention subject to the conditions of article VIII of the treaty of January 24 between Germany and Samoa, and the twelfth article stated that "the representatives of the United States government provisionally accede and assent to the present Convention, on behalf of the government of the United States subject to the approval of that government." The last article provided for the exchange of ratifications within a year from the date of the treaty.[86]

Ten days after Dawson wrote his first despatch concerning the convention, he wrote again, explaining his position and giving reasons for his actions subsequent to the arrival of Captain Chandler in the *Lackawanna*. In the first place he described the old government of Samoa as no government at all. Its representatives "talked, wrote letters, and made treaties" but when they attempted to enforce their laws their authority was nil. The so-called government imposed no taxes, collected no revenues, and was without resources. It could not afford protection "to either the lives or property of its own subjects and much less to foreigners." Dawson very much doubted if the new government, which the people of Samoa decided should have a king at its head, would be "any improvement on the old" because the Samoans were "utterly incapable of establishing or maintaining any form of government in the presence of the large foreign interests

[86] The original copy of convention is catalogued among unperfected treaties in the Department of State; for printed copy see H. Ex. Doc. no. 238, pp. 132-134, encl. no. 92.

here, and [because of] the determination of the foreign population not to respect or observe the authority of those so far beneath them in culture and intelligence." Dawson wrote further that the Old Party had forfeited all respect when it abandoned its capital "before a blow had been struck on either side, and by requesting the foreign Consuls to establish and conduct the only government in existence in Samoa."

In supporting his action in relation to the convention, Dawson said that he and Captain Chandler had found it absolutely necessary to associate themselves with it in order to prevent the consular government of Apia from being broken up. If they had declined to act "Chaos and Anarchy would have assumed sway once more in Apia and would have been the only Government in Samoa, as they had been for a long time before to the great peril of the lives and property of all foreign residents." "Moreover [Dawson continued], if we had not acted in concert, the English representatives would have acted alone in the establishment of a municipality in Apia, and thus secured a foothold which would have been the key to the control of these Islands. It seemed much better, therefore, to share than to lose all interest in the outside or foreign authority exercised here. In fact, it was my own conviction that I would be severely censured by the Department if I should allow the United States Government to lose an equal part in the control of affairs here with other Governments." He hoped therefore, that the course he had pursued would "be deemed worthy of approval."[87]

As a result of the recognition of the new régime in Samoa, Dawson had no further interest in the welfare of the American adventurer, Bartlett. In fact, he caused the arrest in September of this erstwhile premier of the Old

[87] C.D., Apia, vol. 7, Dawson, Sept. 13, 1879, rec'd Nov. 17.

TRIPARTITE CONTROL IN SAMOA

Party government for inciting the natives to civil war,[88] but a few days later ordered the case dismissed.[89] That he had been put in one delicate position after another by the presence in Samoa of Bartlett is evident from a reference to "adventurers" in his despatch of September 13, quoted above. "I beg respectfully to state," said Dawson, "that a Consul has enough to contend with here to get on with the natives and his colleagues, and ought not to be exposed to a constant fire in the seas from adventurers whose only interest in the Samoans is the money they hope to make out of them."[90] But Dawson's antipathy toward American adventurers did not prevent his doing a kind deed for Bartlett's wife. During the summer, it being found that the "General" was destitute, the consul arranged to have Mrs. Bartlett sent to the United States as an act of public charity.[91]

The recognition of Malietoa's party by the powers as the *de facto* government was a signal for the beginning of the long expected civil war. Dawson reported on September 30 that it had then begun,[92] and the next day wrote another despatch to the department suggesting that the great powers take steps to end the struggle.[93] The war continued unabated throughout the months of October and November, Dawson reporting its progress on the average once a week.[94] What troubled him most was the fact that in the midst of the turmoil Captain Chandler found it necessary to sail away from Apia, and he urged

[88] *Ibid.*, Dawson, Sept. 20, 1879, rec'd Nov. 17.
[89] *Ibid.*, Dawson, Sept. 24, 1879, rec'd Dec. 11.
[90] *Ibid.*, Dawson, Sept. 13, 1879, rec'd Nov. 17.
[91] *Ibid.*, Dawson, Aug. 13, 1879, rec'd Oct. 17.
[92] *Ibid.*, Dawson, Sept. 30, 1879, rec'd Dec. 11.
[93] *Ibid.*, Dawson, Oct. 1, 1879, rec'd Dec. 11.
[94] *Ibid.*, Dawson's despatches, nos. 108, 109, 110, 112, 117, 118, 120, 121, 123, 124.

the necessity of the presence of another war vessel as soon as possible.[95]

Some two weeks after the departure of the *Lackawanna,* the German man-of-war, *Bismarck,* arrived with the German consul general from Sydney on board.[96] About the fifteenth of November the British man-of-war, *Emerald,* arrived with Sir Arthur Gordon, and the *Bismarck,* which had gone away temporarily was expected to return together with a second German war vessel, the *Nautilus.*[97] The Old Party warriors had been violating the neutral territory, and plantations and other foreign property had suffered to such an extent that Malietoa appealed to the foreign consuls for protection.[98] Upon the arrival of Sir Arthur, therefore, efforts were made by the foreign representatives to bring about peace among the natives, while at the same time maintaining the neutral territory inviolate. The government of the district of Apia was just being established and Dawson was requested to accept the position of first magistrate of Apia by the German and British consuls.[99]

The foreign consuls soon determined to resort to forcible means for the purpose of securing the neutrality of the district.[100] When therefore the violations continued, the German man-of-war, *Bismarck,* proceeded down the coast, demanding the razing of the forts erected by the natives at Falula and the payment of a fine, and causing them to surrender their war boats. This action, Dawson thought, virtually brought the war to an end.[101] His prediction proved true. On November 28 he was able to re-

[95] C.D., Apia, vol. 7, Dawson, Oct. 14, 1879, rec'd Jan. 7, 1880.
[96] *Ibid.,* Dawson, Nov. 1, 1879, rec'd Jan. 7.
[97] *Ibid.,* Dawson, Nov. 15, 1879, rec'd Feb. 6.
[98] *Ibid.,* nos. 117 and 118 from Dawson, Nov. 6, Nov. 13, respectively.
[99] *Ibid.,* Dawson, Nov. 17, 1879, rec'd Feb. 6.
[100] *Ibid.,* Dawson, Nov. 19, 1879, rec'd Feb. 6.
[101] *Ibid.,* Dawson, Nov. 24, 1879, rec'd Mar. 4.

TRIPARTITE CONTROL IN SAMOA   241

port that hostilities had ceased and that Malietoa was probably elected king by both factions. Dawson thought, moreover, that at last peace and a permanent government had been secured.[102]

Immediately after the conclusion of hostilities Dawson reverted to the idea of a joint protectorate as the best arrangement under the circumstances for the interests of the United States as well as for the welfare of the natives.[103] The following extracts give his point of view. "Now, if the three home Governments will unite in protecting and guiding the Government there ought to be a good and stable Government here. . . . I should indeed regret to have the United States allow these Islands to pass under the control of any other foreign Government. . . . Probably neither Germany nor England will desire to lose their hold here, and the only remedy I can see to prevent anarchy is a joint protectorate by the three powers, making this neutral ground in case of war between any of them."

Two weeks after Dawson sent to Washington the above quoted despatch, the situation in Samoa steadily improved, and on December 15 the representatives of both Samoan parties were prevailed upon by Captain Deinhard to meet on board the *Bismarck* and sign a treaty of peace. This treaty contained four articles.[104] There should be no more war in Samoa, and arbitration, instead of appeal to arms, was to settle all future difficulties. The chiefs of both parties accepted and ratified the treaties with the three powers including the Apia municipality convention. The contracting parties engaged to have appointed by each province two chiefs who should meet together at the

[102] *Ibid.*, Dawson, Nov. 28, 1879, rec'd Mar. 4.
[103] *Ibid.*, Dawson, Dec. 1, 1879, rec'd Mar. 4.
[104] H. Ex. Doc. no. 238, appendix A, pp. 199-202, encl. B 5 in report by Geo. H. Bates. Copy of treaty of peace sent to Washington by Dawson with despatch no. 128, Dec. 17, 1879.

call of Captain Deinhard for the purpose of making settlement for damage to property during the war and for the establishment of a government to be recognized by all Samoa. Thirteen chiefs of the Old Party and twelve of Malietoa's adherents signed the treaty in the presence of Captain Deinhard, Theodor Weber, and Captain Chuden of the German war vessel *Nautilus*.

The provinces of Samoa, which were entitled to send two chiefs to the next meeting, were eight in number, three on the island of Upolu, and three on Savaii, the islands of Manono and Tutuila each constituting a single province. The sixteen chiefs now representing all Samoa met on board the *Bismarck* on December 23 at Captain Deinhard's invitation. An agreement, virtually a constitution, was then drawn up.[105] Malietoa Talavou was recognized as king during his lifetime. The king being old, his nephew, Malietoa Laupepa, was appointed regent to carry on the duties of the kingship. All flags theretofore recognized in Samoa were abolished, and a new emblem "to show the unity of Samoa" was adopted.

The legislative department of government, the Taimua and Faipule, was reëstablished. Each province should be entitled to two chiefs in the Taimua, and unless the provinces elected others to the Taimua on or before January 21, 1880, the present chiefs who were assisting in drawing up the agreement should regard themselves as members of the Taimua. The Taimua members were to be elected for four years and the Faipule members for three years, their terms to begin on "the day of their first meeting at the seat of Government." Three of the largest provinces were to elect five members each of the Faipule, four smaller provinces, including Tutuila, were to elect four

[105] H. Ex. Doc. no. 238, appendix A, pp. 202-206, encl. B 6 in above report. Copy of agreement sent by Dawson with despatch no. 130, Dec. 29, 1879.

members each, and the island of Manono, three members. The two houses should sit separately and vote separately by the majority rule. In cases of disagreement between the two houses the king (regent) should "decide which decision shall be valid or whether the deliberations on the matter in dispute shall be postponed." The two houses should assemble once a year but not remain in session more than three months. One member of the Taimua from each province should remain at the capital between sessions to assist the king (regent) in enforcing the laws. This smaller king's council should conduct all foreign affairs in connection with the treaties, and should consult the foreign representatives in Samoa concerning ways and means for prohibiting or regulating "the sale and supply by foreigners to Samoans and also to other people in Samoa, of intoxicating drinks, arms, and ammunition of war."

The constitution provided for the election in each province of a governor, all election disputes being referred to the Taimua and Faipule. Should there be disagreement between the two houses also as to who should be governor in a particular province, the final decision should rest with the king (regent). The term of office for the governor should be two years and six months. The governor should have the power to appoint judges, police, and minor officials in the province, and should supervise the enforcement of the laws.

The date of the assembling of the Taimua and Faipule should be determined by the king or regent in each year. One-half of the present chiefs should remain at Mulinuu and assist the king to carry on the government temporarily until January 20, 1880, when the first meeting of the Taimua and Faipule should assemble for the purpose of framing further constitutional provisions and new laws as found necessary. These chiefs while thus assisting temporarily should meet the foreign representatives for the purpose of discussing the question of war damage to the property of foreigners.

The agreement of December 23, like that of December 15, was witnessed by Captains Deinhard and Chuden of the German navy and the German consul, Theodor Weber. Since neither Dawson nor the British consul had had any part in either the proceedings of December 15[106] or of December 23,[107] they "purposely refrained," Dawson wrote to the department on January 19, "from expressing any approval of the action of Captain Deinhard in the reestablishment of a Government in Samoa, . . . [their] approbation of his course being limited to the termination of the war." Dawson and the British consul were of the opinion, he continued, "that it would at least have looked much better if the meetings of December 15 and 23 had been held on shore instead of on board the *Bismarck*, and that it would have been courteous at least to have invited the Consuls to be present, and looked less like a German settlement of the matter, though so far as I can ascertain the delegates acted voluntarily, and composed the greater part of the agreement of December 23d, making Malietoa King and Malietoa Laupepa Regent. I shall have only so much to do with the new Government as may seem absolutely necessary to me till I can hear from the Department."[108]

Almost simultaneously with Dawson's writing the above despatch, in fact just four days before, the department sent to him its reply concerning the events of the latter part of August and early September, approving his acts in connection with the municipal convention,[109] and, in another despatch five days later, his provisional recogni-

[106] C.D., Apia, vol. 7, Dawson, Dec. 15, 1879, rec'd March 4.
[107] *Ibid.*, Dawson, Dec. 23, 1879, rec'd March 4.
[108] *Ibid.*, Dawson, Jan. 19, 1880, rec'd April 1.
[109] I.C., vol. 94, to Dawson, Jan. 15, 1880.

TRIPARTITE CONTROL IN SAMOA 245

tion of Malietoa's government as *de facto,* instructing him at the same time to recognize the new government as *de jure.*[110] These instructions, written on January 15 and January 20 respectively, did not reach Dawson for some two months, and the statement in his despatch of January 19, that he would have only the most necessary relations with the new régime until he heard from the department, is understood if the dates of the two instructions and Dawson's despatch are kept in mind.[111]

Thus the United States in its turn withdrew its recognition of the Old Party government, which had been without a head ever since the day when the British persuaded Malietoa Laupepa in 1876 to banish Steinberger and the Taimua and Faipule, in retaliation, had deposed Malietoa. This government, which the United States had formally recognized by entering into a treaty with it in January, 1878, and which in return for rights in Pago Pago harbor had gained from the United States the promise contained in article V of employing "its good offices" for the purpose of adjusting differences that might arise "between the Samoan government and any other government in amity with the United States," was now a thing of the past. The Washington authorities, in deciding upon recognition of Laupepa's government, knew that civil war had broken out, for Dawson's despatch, number 117, written as late as November 6, was in the possession of the department[112] before the instruction to recognize Malietoa's government had been sent, and all the information that it

[110] *Ibid.,* p. 643, to Dawson, Jan. 20, 1880.
[111] Dawson wrote in the same despatch of January 19: "In regard to the recognition of Malietoa as King of Samoa, . . . of course all my acts are provisional till I can receive instructions from the Department. This has been well understood by him and my colleagues throughout. He is undoubtedly King of Samoa without a rival Government, and I think by the will of the great majority of Samoans, and most foreigners. But in making him such I do not consider that I have taken any active part whatever."
[112] Received Jan. 7, 1880.

and previous despatches contained about the civil war and the arrival of the German consul general from Sydney was at hand. Therefore it is clear that the department believed the Old Party was engaged in a forlorn cause, and that since both Sir Arthur Gordon and the German consul general for the Pacific had visited Samoa and recognized the new régime, it was necessary to back up Captain Chandler and Dawson in their provisional recognition by making that régime *de jure*. The irritation that the department had felt in October on learning of the salute given Malietoa the previous July, had worn off to some extent, but it is evident that it was disappointed at the disappearance of the old "Steinberger" government.[113] As yet it knew nothing, of course, of the peace treaty of December 15; nor did it know that the new government, in the agreement of December 23, had recognized the treaty of the former government with the United States as well as the other pacts with Germany and Great Britain. It was March 4 before this news reached Washington.[114] The department's instruction to recognize Malietoa Talavou as king reached Dawson by the middle of April, and on the fifteenth Dawson reported that the king was much gratified.[115]

With the coming of peace to Samoa, Dawson was relieved of two American adventurers, "General" Bartlett

[113] On October 25 Charles Payson, third assistant secretary, had written Dawson with reference to the Malietoa salute as follows: "In the course which you pursued you appear to have lost sight of the important fact that this Government, by virtue of a treaty concluded with the Taimua and Faipule, recognizes that authority as the governing power over the Samoan Islands, and cannot properly recognize any other until satisfied that the present Government no longer exists, but a new one has actually been established in its place." (Instructions to Consuls, vol. 93, p. 696, to Dawson, Oct. 25, 1879.)

[114] See superscriptions on despatches from Dawson, nos. 126 and 129, dated Dec. 15 and 23 respectively.

[115] C.D., Apia, vol. 8, Dawson, April 15, 1880, rec'd June 25.

and a certain Thomas A. Lord, a land speculator, who at the time of near-anarchy in Apia had assaulted him. Both of these men having fought for the old régime, were now of course repudiated by their old friends, and in the same despatch that Dawson sent to the department about the treaty of peace, he could also say that Messrs. Bartlett and Lord had departed from the islands. Thus faded away from Samoa the last echo of the Steinberger régime, and except for the institution of a suit by Bartlett after his return against the United States for alleged injuries sustained when he was arrested and imprisoned in 1879 by Captain Chandler and Consul Dawson, the name of Bartlett disappears altogether from the consular correspondence anent Samoa.[116] Upon his arrival in California Lord stirred up the speculators there who were interested in Samoan lands. Criticisms against Dawson flew thick and fast, but in the end, since Dawson proved the falsity of the charges of irregularities, he was upheld by the department.[117] The whole controversy hinged on what Dawson called the attempt of the "San Francisco land ring" to exchange their Samoan lands, which had cost them virtually nothing, and which yielded them virtually nothing, for Samoan government bonds. They sought Dawson's removal on account of his having frustrated their scheme.[118] Dawson also informed the department that the land speculators of San Francisco were working in the interest of English annexation of the islands, hoping that thereby they might secure a settlement of their difficulties.[119]

In the following March the peace of December 15 was

[116] *Ibid.*, vol. 7, Dawson, Jan. 12, 1880, rec'd April 1.
[117] See Dawson's despatches, nos. 147 (April 14, 1880), 150 (April 22), 151 (April 23), 161 (May 26), 162 (June 2) in Apia vol. 8.
[118] C.D., Apia, vol. 8, Dawson, June 15, 1880, rec'd Sept. 15.
[119] *Ibid.*, Dawson, July 13, 1880, rec'd Sept. 15.

again disturbed by certain elements of the Old Party who refused to support the new government. Through the intervention of the foreign consuls, however, an amicable understanding was soon brought about.[120] It was now thought advisable by the consuls—since the stability of Malietoa's government was not all that they could wish for—that some arrangement should be made whereby the aid of the consuls in strengthening the native government might most effectively be given. It was thought best to make some radical constitutional changes, and not be content merely to intervene from time to time when crises arose. This proposal was agreed to by Dawson the more readily because he was advised by the new German consul general for Samoa, Captain Zembsch, that he had instructions from the German imperial government, dated January 12, 1880, informing him that the governments of Great Britain and the United States had accepted the proposals of the German government, and ordering him to recognize Malietoa and enter into an agreement with his colleagues for the protection of his government by the three powers.[121] Moreover, the British government on January 14 had ordered H.B.M.S. *Danae* to proceed to Samoa, her commander, Captain Purvis, having instructions to recognize Malietoa, and protect his government in conjunction with the naval forces of Germany and the United States.[122] Dawson, therefore, without instructions from the Department of State and without information as to whether his part in the negotiation of the municipal convention of the previous September was approved, entered into another agreement with the representatives of Germany and Great Britain, this time for a tripartite control of the islands. It was a logical step from the tri-

[120] C.D., Apia, vol. 8, Dawson, Mar. 11, 1880, rec'd May 26.
[121] *Ibid.*, Dawson, April 9, 1880, encl. no. 2, rec'd May 26.
[122] *Ibid.*

TRIPARTITE CONTROL IN SAMOA 249

partite control of Apia, and he believed that the German consul had been correctly informed concerning the desire of the United States to adhere to a joint protectorate. He was quite certain that conversations had been going on between the three powers after their receipt of Malietoa's appeal for a joint protectorate, and on March 13, he wrote the department: "I have to state that Sir A. Gordon is expected here again the first of next month. I sincerely hope we may have a man-of-war here then, as I am inclined to think efforts are being put forth in the direction of English annexation, though I hope the question has already been settled by a joint protectorate of the three Governments."[123]

Accordingly, the representatives of the three powers met on the twenty-fourth of March and drew up an agreement of four articles which was signed by Malietoa Talavou, the king, Malietoa Laupepa, the regent, and Chief Mataafa. The foreign representatives who signed the document were Captain Zembsch, German consul general, Thomas M. Dawson, and J. Hicks Graves, British consul.[124] In the preamble reference was made to the king's request on August 31, 1879, that the powers take joint action for the preservation of peace in Samoa; to the termination of the war by the treaty of peace of December 15; to the agreement of December 23, whereby Malietoa Talavou was elected king for life; to the German government's instructions of January 12, 1880, to the consul general to recognize the king and together with the representatives of the United States and Great Britain to negotiate an agreement for the protection of his government; to the orders of January 14, 1880, instructing Captain Purvis of H.B.M.S. *Danae* to proceed to Samoa and

[123] *Ibid.*, Dawson, March 13, 1880, rec'd May 26.
[124] H. Ex. Doc. no. 238, appendix A, Geo. H. Bates' report, pp. 207-208, encl. B 7.

recognize Malietoa Talavou and in conjunction with the United States and Germany naval forces to protect the Samoan government. Finally, the preamble stated that the king and government, being earnestly desirous of protection, willingly entered into this agreement with the foreign representatives.

The first article provided for the recognition of Malietoa Talavou as king during his lifetime, and the selection of his successor "by the three protecting powers." The second article stated that there should be an executive council of three members to assist the king and government of Samoa, "consisting of a citizen of the United States of America, a German and a British subject and they shall hold the offices, respectively, of minister of justice, minister of finance, and minister of public works." The ministers should be nominated from among the residents of Samoa by their respective consuls, according to the third article, but though they should hold office from the date of their nomination, the nomination must be confirmed by the home government. The concluding article provided for the continuance in office of the members of the executive council until their successors were nominated, and that their salaries should be agreed upon by the Samoan government "and the consular representatives of the three protecting powers."

During the month of April Dawson sent a series of despatches concerning, first, the agreement of March 24, second, his carrying out the department's instruction to recognize the king, and, third, the nomination of Jonas M. Coe as minister of justice for the newly protected government.[125] By June 21 all of these despatches had been received by the department, which on July 1 was ready to take a definite position in relation to the tripartite pro-

[125] See despatches nos. 145 (April 9), 148 (April 15), 149 (April 21), and 151 (April 23), Apia, vol. 8.

tectorate, for on that day it directed Dawson to report the circumstances which led him to believe that a protectorate had been agreed upon by the powers and added that no such protectorate was contemplated on the part of the United States.[126]

To this communication Dawson sent an answer on September 10. He referred again to the information he had received from Consul General Zembsch and Captain Purvis, information which he had sent in his first despatch of April 9 when he had given the intelligence about the agreement of March 24. He also referred to his despatch of August 17, which of course was written after the department's inquiry, but which contained additional information from Consul General Zembsch to Dawson concerning the alleged willingness of the United States to assist in establishing the protectorate.[127] He referred in particular to the department's instructions of January 20 wherein he was informed that "with regard to the proposed concurrent action of the Powers having commercial interests in Samoa further instruction will in due time be addressed to you."[128] This was the communication in which the department had instructed Dawson to recognize Malietoa. Furthermore, just five days before, it had informed Dawson that his action in connection with the convention of September 2, 1879, was approved.[129]

For a more complete understanding of the position of the United States in 1880 in relation to the other two powers it is necessary to digress somewhat in order to obtain a view of what was transpiring in Germany. Simultaneously with the change of régime in Samoa, the German firm of Godeffroy got into financial difficulties

[126] I.C., vol. 96, p. 500, to Dawson, July 1, 1880.
[127] Despatch no. 183, Apia, vol. 8.
[128] I.C., vol. 94, p. 643, to Dawson, Jan. 20, 1880.
[129] *Ibid.*, to Dawson, Jan. 15, 1880.

and suddenly went bankrupt. The persistence with which Theodor Weber, the German factotum of the South Seas, had urged the tottering Old Party government to give him a treaty is partly explained by the fact that what little trade the Americans had in Samoa was protected by treaty, whereas the much larger interests of the Germans, especially the Godeffroy firm, were not protected at all. Weber got his treaty, but just as civil war was threatening, and when it broke out the following September, the Godeffroy property suffered very much from the depredations of the opposing war parties. This turn of events explains the sudden appearance of the German consul general from Sydney and the subsequent efforts of Captain Deinhard to bring the war to an end. To make restitution for the destruction of the property of foreigners was one of the main immediate duties of the temporary organization effected on board the *Bismarck* in December. But this did not help, for there were other causes, as well, operating to bring on the collapse of the house of Godeffroy, one in particular the fact that that company had wide ramifications throughout the South Seas. In January, Dawson advised the department that rumors relative to the bankruptcy of the firm had caused a sensation in Apia. This event prompted him to suggest that an opportunity was now afforded for enterprising Americans to step in and capture the business.[130]

With the failure of the Godeffroy firm also fell the powerful official, Theodor Weber, the consul. He did not quit Samoa, except perhaps to go to Germany to assist in reorganizing the old firm, but his combining in himself both German commercial interests and the authority of the German Reich was henceforth impossible. Though Weber might still endeavor to dominate those of the German government's representatives who might be pos-

[130] C.D., Apia, vol. 7, Dawson, Jan. 4, 1880, rec'd March 3.

TRIPARTITE CONTROL IN SAMOA

sessed of weaker personalities than his own, he no longer enjoyed the monopoly of representing the German Empire and the Godeffroys at the same time. The first representative of Germany at Apia who was not connected with the commercial interests there was Captain Zembsch, one of the signers of the agreement of March 24 for the tripartite control of the Samoan government and the first foreign representative in Apia to be a consul general.

The collapse of the firm of Godeffroy caused considerable chagrin among the German expansionists at home. Especially was this true when it was learned that English bankers had acquired control of the assets of the defunct company to cover a mortgage. This intelligence caused a great effort to be made in Germany to obtain a subvention from the government to redeem the property. In fact it was considered a patriotic duty to prevent, if possible, the absorption by the English of the one large firm that had carried the German flag into all the harbors of the South Pacific. An appeal was made to Prince Bismarck, who accepted the cause of the redemptionists as his own, and caused a bill to be introduced in the Reichstag for governmental aid, to the delight of all supporters of colonial expansion.

Their joy was, however, short-lived, for opposition to the scheme soon developed. The ultramontanes and anti-centralization members, constituting the Central party under the leadership of Dr. Windhorst, bore down heavily upon the bill and defeated Prince Bismarck. The defeat of the bill brought on a heated "post mortem" discussion and the United States minister in Berlin, Andrew D. White, thought the matter significant enough to warrant the sending of two despatches concerning it. The question arose as to what was at the bottom of the opposition. White's view as expressed in his first despatch of May 3, 1880, was that the majority of the Reichstag preferred not to embark upon a colonial policy with Prince Bismarck, and feared that government aid for the rehabilitation of the Godeffroy firm would be a first step in that direction.[131]

During the week following his sending the first despatch he secured proofs of the correctness of his view from two sources, and on the tenth he sent his second despatch. In this he informed the department that the semiofficial organ of the Prince Chancellor, the *Nord-Deutsche-Allgemeine Zeitung,* "has already published two or three articles from newspapers in various parts of Germany condemning the course of the Reichstag, especially on the ground that with the defeat of the same measure the chance of a colonial development of the German Empire is indefinitely postponed." But what he regarded as "the most striking proof of the correctness of the view I have given is to be found in the reply of Dr. Windhorst to the very remarkable speech—the only speech in fact during this session—made by the Imperial Chancellor on Saturday last. In his speech the Chancellor had complained among other things, in very strong terms, of the conduct of certain members regarding the Samoan question, alleging that personal feeling toward himself was at the bottom of the opposition to the measure." Dr. Windhorst in his reply to this speech disclaimed any personal bias and said "that his opposition and the opposition of those who voted with him on the Samoan bill was entirely due to a dread of beginning a colonial policy. While Germany, he declared, was supporting with such great difficulty the army essential to her existence in Europe, it would be quite impossible to think of developing a colonial system for the support of which a large and powerful navy would be absolutely necessary." White then concluded significantly: "Our own Government may rely upon it, I think

[131] Despatches, Germany, no. 118, White to Evarts, May 3, 1880.

it is certain, that any attempt to begin a colonial policy in the Pacific by the German Government, even with the Chancellor at its head, will be defeated. It is perfectly clear that the vast majority of the German nation has an unconquerable distrust of it.''[132] White was right in his diagnosis but wrong in his forecast. Temporarily prevented from entering upon a new phase in the development of the German Empire in 1880, Prince Bismarck in 1884 not only embarked upon a colonial policy in Africa, but in the Pacific as well, the German flag being raised in New Guinea and Consul General Stübel attempting to establish a German protectorate over Samoa in the same year.

The information that White furnished the department came at a time when there was uncertainty as to how far the United States should coöperate with Germany and Great Britain in giving stability to the Samoan régime. On January 15 the department had approved Dawson's actions in signing the municipal convention of September 2, 1879, but was undecided whether that convention should be regarded as a treaty to be ratified by the Senate or merely an agreement for the tripartite government of the district of Apia to meet a temporary emergency. We know that Dawson regarded the convention as a treaty and that the negotiation of it was the first step in a joint protectorate of the whole archipelago. Was the department ready to follow Dawson or would it reprimand him for assuming that the United States would want to become "entangled."

It is quite certain that the department wavered for some months. Should the frequent visits of Sir Arthur Gordon to Samoa and the activities of Captain Deinhard and Consul Weber seem to presage an attempt on the part of either the British or Germans to establish a single pro-

[132] *Ibid.*, no. 121, White to Evarts, May 10, 1880.

tectorate, the United States, in order to keep its hold on Pago Pago harbor, might be obliged to enter a joint protectorate. Furthermore, Prince Bismarck's attempt to assist the bankrupt firm of Godeffroy in the spring of 1880 caused just as much uneasiness in Washington as the rumored German attempt at annexation of Samoa in 1871 and 1872. Consequently, when White's second despatch arrived the department felt relieved and thanked the minister on June 1 for his "important despatch."[133] In the meantime, on May 26, Dawson's communication of April 9, informing the department of the agreement of March 24, had arrived, and on June 19 and June 21 two more messages were received, advising the department of the nomination of Jonas M. Coe as minister of justice under the tripartite control of the Samoan government. When, therefore, on July 1, in a reprimanding tone, the department directed Dawson to report the circumstances which led him to think that a joint protectorate of Samoa had been agreed upon, we can only interpret the action as due to its belief in the sincerity of the German and British representatives in acceding to the wishes of the Samoan government for a joint protectorate, and that the danger of a single protectorate was not so great as Dawson had feared. Furthermore, the reassuring news from Berlin of the defeat of the Samoan bill and White's assurance of the improbability of German colonial expansion in the Pacific gave the United States government a feeling of security in regard to its rights in Samoa, and dampened any ardor that might have existed for a joint protectorate. July 1, 1880, therefore, must be regarded as a date when the United States again decided to remain aloof from formal entangling alliances, although it is quite clear that the government had no intention of withdrawing from the

[133] Instructions, Germany, vol. 16, p. 575, no. 108, Evarts to White, June 1, 1880.

TRIPARTITE CONTROL IN SAMOA

convention of September 2, 1879, if it were regarded as an agreement and not as a treaty. In other words, the United States would remain "entangled" informally as far as the district of Apia was concerned.

Since the department's inquiry of July 1 did not reach Dawson before September, he continued during the summer to coöperate with his colleagues in the control of the Samoan government. On May 12 he reported that a rebellion at Lufilufi had been brought to an end by the intervention of the consuls, in whose behalf Captain Purvis of the British war vessel *Danae* had landed and punished the offenders.[134] Another rebellion, which had broken out in the harbor of Saluafata,[135] had likewise been stopped by foreign intervention.[136] On May 18 Dawson informed the department that the consuls had called upon the king and demanded the passage of laws prohibiting the importation of firearms and the sale and supply of intoxicating liquors to natives, and that he had complied with all demands.[137] On July 1, the same day that the department sent to Dawson the inquiry referred to above, Dawson again reverted to the incapacity of the Samoans for self-government, adding that only the annexation of the islands by some great power would insure permanent peace.[138] Then again on July 22 he returned to the idea of a joint protectorate. He described the vacillating policy of his colleagues with respect to their joint assistance to the government, and explained it as due to their uncertainty with respect to Malietoa's grip on the political situation. He believed, however, that the Malietoa party was still in the ascendancy, but thought that the salvation

[134] C.D., Apia, vol. 8, Dawson, May 12, 1880, rec'd July 22.
[135] *Ibid.*, Dawson, May 15, 1880, rec'd July 22.
[136] *Ibid.*, Dawson, June 4, 1880, rec'd July 23.
[137] *Ibid.*, Dawson, May 18, 1880, rec'd July 22.
[138] *Ibid.*, Dawson, July 1, 1880, rec'd Sept. 15.

of the islands lay only in a joint protectorate of the three treaty powers.[139] A week later he reported that he had had an interview with some of the Old Party chiefs who declared their adherence to the peace policy and endorsed his views of the situation.[140] In reply to the last two despatches the department said that the vacillating policy of Dawson's colleagues relative to Malietoa could not be commended, and instructed the consul to give the government of Malietoa his moral support as long as he was actually king.[141]

In the beginning of August Dawson reported that the king had begun to war upon his enemies and that the consuls had again endeavored to restore order.[142] The principal chiefs of the Old Party were seized by the king's warriors and a request had come from the regent that the neutral boundaries of the district of Apia be extended, all of which indicated to Dawson nothing less than the prospect of another civil war.[143] By the middle of the month the war seemed imminent, for several villages of the Old Party had been burned. What made things worse was the fact that concerted action on the part of the consuls, Dawson thought, could no longer be expected.[144] The disturbances brought Sir Arthur Gordon again to Samoa. His coming resulted in the deportation of an English adventurer named W. J. Hunt, who had wormed his way into the confidence of Malietoa as chief secretary, and who had endeavored to turn the king against Dawson after the latter had protested against his admission into the government.[145] The king apologized to Dawson for

[139] C.D., Apia, vol. 8, Dawson, July 22, rec'd Oct. 14.
[140] *Ibid.*, Dawson, July 29, 1880, rec'd Oct. 14.
[141] I.C., vol. 97, p. 571 to Dawson, Oct. 29, 1880.
[142] C.D., Apia, vol. 8, Dawson, Aug. 6, 1880, rec'd Oct. 14.
[143] *Ibid.*, Dawson, Aug. 11, 1880, rec'd Oct. 14.
[144] *Ibid.*, Dawson, Aug. 17, 1880, rec'd Oct. 14.
[145] *Ibid.*, Dawson, Aug. 29, 1880, rec'd Oct. 14.

TRIPARTITE CONTROL IN SAMOA   259

Hunt's actions. After Hunt had gone, Dawson was asked to appoint the new chief secretary. This he declined to do.[146]

The next month the U.S.S. *Alaska* arrived in Apia and remained for a week, during which time Captain Brown had several interviews with the king.[147] By the first of October Dawson thought that after the deportation of Hunt the king had shown a greater disposition toward peace,[148] but on October 19 he was again expecting war and said that in his opinion the consuls would be powerless even to protect the neutral district should such a calamity befall Samoa again.[149]

The old king died suddenly on November 8. The question now arose as to who should be his successor.[150] Dawson was doubtful whether the so-called rebels would recognize the deceased king's nephew, Malietoa Laupepa, as king, although he had been acting as regent since the peace negotiations on board the *Bismarck* the previous December. As a matter of fact the German consul general was already advocating a division of the government between the two parties, an old scheme of Weber's.[151] By the twentieth of the month civil war had begun in earnest,[152] and Dawson urged the presence of a man-of-war, Captain Chandler being suggested as a suitable officer to come to Samoa. It was thought that he and the consul, together with the missionaries, might succeed in bringing peace.[153] In another despatch, dated December 1, Dawson

[146] *Ibid.*, Dawson, Aug. 31, 1880, rec'd Nov. 10.
[147] *Ibid.*, despatches nos. 190 and 192 from Dawson, dated Sept. 13 and 20 respectively, rec'd Dec. 4.
[148] *Ibid.*, vol. 9, Dawson, Oct. 1, 1880, rec'd Dec. 9.
[149] *Ibid.*, Dawson, Oct. 19, 1880, rec'd March 3, 1881.
[150] *Ibid.*, Dawson, Nov. 10, 1880, rec'd Feb. 7, 1881.
[151] *Ibid.*, Dawson, Nov. 15, 1880, rec'd Feb. 7.
[152] *Ibid.*, Dawson, Nov. 20, 1880, rec'd Feb. 7.
[153] *Ibid.*, Dawson, Nov. 28, 1880, rec'd March 3.

again urged the sending of a warship, on the ground that the Old Party was guilty of cruelties toward non-combatants.[154] By Christmas, however, the king's party had gained several victories,[155] and two days after New Year's day Dawson could report that the war was practically over.[156] By that time Malietoa Laupepa had control of Savaii and by the end of February the chiefs of Tuamasaga and Manono had declared in his favor. In the same month, however, the Samoan prime minister withdrew from the Malietoa government and went over to the Old Party side, thus affording the German consul general again the opportunity to declare himself in favor of two governments for Samoa.[157] In fact with the coming of peace early in January the German representative had expressed himself as fearful of Dawson's acquiring too much power in Malietoa's government, and, therefore, two governments, one of which at least might be dominated by the Germans, appeared to Captain Zembsch a better arrangement than a single government gradually slipping away from German influence and coming under American or British guidance.[158]

On March 19, 1881, Malietoa Laupepa was crowned king by his adherents, and both the American and British representatives recommended recognition of him by their respective governments. At the same time efforts were made to effect a reconciliation between the two parties by suggesting that a vice king be appointed from the Old Party.[159] This arrangement, however, was not acceptable to the Old Party chiefs, and a few days later they crowned Tamasese of the house of Tupua as king of Atua and

[154] C.D., Apia, vol. 9, Dawson, Dec. 1, 1880, rec'd March 3.
[155] *Ibid.*, Dawson, Dec. 23, 1880.
[156] *Ibid.*, Dawson, Jan. 3, 1881, rec'd April 11.
[157] *Ibid.*, Dawson, Feb. 7, 1881.   [158] *Ibid.*, Dawson, Jan. 3, 1881.
[159] *Ibid.*, Dawson, March 24, 1881, rec'd June 22.

TRIPARTITE CONTROL IN SAMOA   261

Aana at Leulumoega. Neither Dawson nor the other consuls were present at this ceremony, and took no action regarding it.[160] Although Captain Zembsch never ceased to have official relations with Malietoa's government, Dawson was suspicious of his attitude, and as far back as October 26 discussed the German consul general's peculiarities.[161] The local English newspaper of Apia was quoted by Bates a few years later as saying with reference to Tamasese's elevation to his petty kingship: " 'We understand the Consuls were invited to attend the meeting at Leulumoega, but declined, a course which we believe will have the approval of all the foreign residents in Apia and probably in the group. It is to be regretted, however, that the consuls do not take a more definite position in regard to Samoan affairs. We think that if they were to proclaim boldly (which we believe they are in a position to do) that Malietoa is the only sovereign in Samoa recognized or likely to be recognized by their Governments, and that they cannot countenance any other power in Samoa, the difficulties in this group would be nearer a solution.' "[162]

Tamasese, who now appeared in the public eye of Samoa for the first time, was the same chief whom Germany was later to support as king in 1887, 1888, and until the Berlin Conference of 1889. At this time, however, the German representative was not ready to desert Malietoa, and on April 28, the latter was received by the captain of the German corvette, *Hertha,* on board the ship, and given the gun salute as king.[163]

Preparations for war continued, but according to Bates, "there was no fighting, other than some trifling skir-

[160] *Ibid.,* Dawson, March 29, 1881.
[161] *Ibid.,* Dawson, Oct. 26, 1880, rec'd Jan. 6.
[162] H. Ex. Doc. no. 238, appendix A, report by Geo. H. Bates, p. 150.
[163] *Ibid.,* appendix C, report by J. B. Thurston, p. 273.

mishes, until the latter part of June, when, the United States steamer *Lackawanna* being in port, Captain Gillis visited both parties at their forts and addressed the chiefs.''[164] The chiefs of the Old Party, now the adherents of Tamasese, expressing a desire for a peace conference, Captain Gillis agreed to arrange one with the understanding that Malietoa was already recognized by the United States as king. A meeting was arranged between representatives of both parties and the consuls by Captain Gillis for June 26, when the captain placed before the chiefs "four articles, which he thought would meet the difficulties." An armistice of ten days duration was effected, during which time the articles were to be discussed. Thereupon the *Lackawanna* sailed away for a visit to Pago Pago, returning to Apia at the end of the armistice. The two parties then reassembled on board the *Lackawanna* on July 9, and the articles were discussed again. Although the articles contained no reference to the question as to who should be king, the Malietoa people now came forward and "offered to compromise by electing Tamasese vice king." Again the assembly adjourned, this time for three days, to give time for full consideration, and on the twelfth the chiefs met for the third time on board the *Lackawanna*. Another "long discussion ensued, which resulted in the acceptance of the conditions as laid down, and the agreement was signed by the chiefs present, and also by Captain Gillis and the three Consuls as witnesses.''[165]

The peace that was now established remained practically unbroken for three and a half years until the reversal of Prince Bismarck's colonial policy brought on the

[164] H. Ex. Doc. no. 238, appendix A, report by Geo. H. Bates, p. 150.

[165] *Ibid.*, despatches from Dawson numbers 244 and 248, dated July 12 and July 16, respectively, give the full particulars of the "Lackawanna Peace." They are to be found in Consular Despatches, Apia, vol. 10.

TRIPARTITE CONTROL IN SAMOA

diplomatic difficulties with the United States that continued until the Berlin Conference of 1889. The "Lackawanna Peace," as the settlement has been called, is important in Samoan history and in the diplomatic relations of the United States, Germany, and Great Britain, because it formed one of the principal bases for the final agreement between these three powers in the Berlin Act of 1889.

The Lackawanna agreement of July 12 was as follows:

"1. On this day assembled on board the U. S. S. *Lackawanna,* in this harbor, the Samoan chiefs whose names are hereto signed. They are all true representatives of the war party of Malietoa and of the war party of Tupua, and concerning this matter this is their determination that permanent peace and friendship is hereby established throughout Samoa, beginning from this day.

2. All the war parties scattered throughout these islands shall each return to their respective homes.

3. Malietoa Laupepa is hereby made and appointed King.

4. Tupua Tamasese is hereby made and appointed Vice-King, and the length of their reign shall be left to the determination of the Government.

5. Nothing in this agreement shall interfere with any former treaty made by the Government of Samoa with foreign powers."

Then followed the signatures of eight chiefs representing each party with those of the witnesses, J. H. Gillis, U.S.N., Thomas M. Dawson, United States consul, J. Hicks Graves, Her Britannic Majesty's consul, and G. von Oertzen, acting German consul.[166]

[166] *Ibid.,* enclosure B 8 with Bates' report as above, pp. 208-209.

CHAPTER IX

GERMAN ENCROACHMENTS, AND INTERVENTION BY THE UNITED STATES

ALTHOUGH the United States government was not willing to enter formally into the convention of September 2, 1879, President Hayes in his fourth annual message to Congress declared that the interests of the three powers could be conserved by a diplomatic agreement. "In Samoa," he said, "the Government of King Malietoa[1] under the support and recognition of the consular representatives of the United States, Great Britain and Germany, seems to have given peace and tranquility to the islands. While it does not appear desirable to adopt as a whole the scheme of tripartite local government which has been proposed, the common interests of the three great treaty powers require harmony in their relations to the native frame of government, and this may be best secured by a simple diplomatic agreement between them. It would be well if the consular jurisdiction of our representative at Apia were increased in extent and importance so as to guard American interests in the surrounding and outlying islands of Oceania."[2]

No steps were immediately taken by the department to

[1] The President was referring to Malietoa Talavou. The news of his death on November 8 had not yet reached Washington. Dawson's despatch no. 200 notifying the department of the king's demise was not received until February 7, 1881.

[2] Richardson, vol. 7, p. 611. Fourth Annual Message to Congress from President Hayes, Dec. 6, 1880. (On November 13, 1880, the department notified Dawson that his jurisdiction had been extended to embrace the Marshall Islands. See Instructions to Consuls, vol. 97, p. 671.)

effect the diplomatic arrangement suggested by the president. The Washington authorities merely contented themselves with notifying Dawson on January 14, 1881, that it had never been the intention of the United States to regard the convention of September 2, 1879, as a treaty, but only as an arrangement from which the United States might withdraw at pleasure.³ To make more clear the policy of the United States toward the Samoan islands the department the next day enclosed a copy of the President's message referred to above.⁴

When the news reached the department on February 7, 1881, that King Malietoa Talavou had died the previous November, Secretary Evarts took immediate steps to have a conference with the German and British ministers at Washington.⁵ What the secretary intended to do at the conference is not clear, but it is quite possible that he had in mind to suggest the diplomatic arrangement for the government of Apia district referred to in the president's message. He may also have thought that the time was ripe for a tripartite agreement relative to the native government and concerning the successor to Malietoa Talavou. In any case this was the first time in the history

³ I.C., vol. 98, p. 331, to Dawson, Jan. 14, 1881.
⁴ *Ibid.*, vol. 98, p. 340, to Dawson, Jan. 15, 1881.
⁵ Notes to German Legation, vol. 10, p. 61. Evarts to Kurd von Schlözer, Feb. 9, 1881. Notes to British Legation, vol. 18, p. 447, Evarts to Sir Edward Thornton, Feb. 9, 1881. Evart's note to the British minister follows:

"Department of State,
Washington, February 9, 1881.
The R. H. Sir Edward Thornton, K.C.B.
Sir:
In view of official intelligence having reached the Department of the death on the 8th of November last, of King Malietoa, of the Samoan Islands, I have the honor to request that you will favor me with a conference upon the political situation in these Islands produced by this melancholy event. A like request is this day addressed to the Minister of Germany at this capital.
Wm. M. Evarts."

of the relations of the United States with Samoa that a diplomatic conference was suggested by the United States government. Secretary Evarts without a doubt thought that article V of the American-Samoan treaty put the United States under obligations to take the initiative in bringing about a peaceable solution of the new Samoan situation, as occasioned by the king's death.

The two ministers, Sir Edward Thornton and Herr Kurd von Schlözer, attended at the Department of State on February 10, the day after Secretary Evart's invitation had been sent to them. At the conference the secretary communicated to the ministers the news of King Malietoa's death and also laid before them a despatch from Consul Dawson giving the particulars of the political situation. Evarts then inquired whether the ministers had received "any instructions from their Governments or any information beyond what he had communicated." Both of the ministers replying, "that they were without information from their Consuls, and instructions from their Governments . . . the matter was postponed until they should have some instructions from their Governments relative to the subject."[6]

The Hayes administration came to an end within a month after the conference, and neither Secretary Blaine under President Garfield nor Secretary Frelinghuysen of President Arthur's cabinet seems to have followed up the step taken by Secretary Evarts. It remained for Secretary Bayard under President Cleveland to carry out the idea of a diplomatic conference for solving the Samoan problem.

On July 25, 1881, the department instructed Dawson to

[6] Memorandum, filed in vol. 106, Great Britain, Notes to Department of State. "Interview between the German and British Ministers and the Secretary of State, Feb. 10, 1881."

act in concert with the representatives of Germany and Great Britain in recognizing any change of government,[7] and on November 29, the consul was further instructed that he should not withdraw his support of the municipal regulations until so instructed by the department.[8] The position taken by the department with respect to the new native government under Malietoa Laupepa and also the municipal government under the convention of 1879 was prompted by the receipt of a number of despatches from Dawson from June to October.[9] The receipt also of a note from the British legation on October 20, advising the department that Great Britain had recognized Malietoa Laupepa as king, may have influenced the department not to withdraw its support of the municipal regulation.

In the British note it was explained that the only motive for the British government's recognition of Malietoa Laupepa was the desire to assist in the pacification of the islands, not because of any preference for one royal family there over another.[10] The department replied to the British note on November 19, stating that its contents would receive careful consideration but giving no intimation when Malietoa Laupepa would be recognized by the United States as more than king *de facto*.[11] On December 6, the department received information from Dawson that the German consul had been instructed to coöperate with the United States and British consuls in supporting King

---

[7] I.C., vol. 100, p. 219, to Dawson, July 25, 1881.

[8] *Ibid.*, vol. 101, p. 466, to Dawson, Nov. 29, 1881.

[9] C.D., Apia, vol. 9, despatches nos. 221 (March 24), 226 (March 29), 234 (May 19); Apia, vol. 10, despatches nos. 239 (June 2), 244 (July 12), 248 (July 16), 249 (July 18), 254 (July 25), 256 (July 27), 258 (Aug. 1).

[10] Notes from British Legation, Victor A. W. Drummond, chargé d'affaires, Oct. 20, 1881.

[11] Notes to British Legation, vol. 18, p. 641, to Sir Lionel S. Sackville-West, Nov. 19, 1881. (Sackville-West's credentials were presented November 14, 1881.)

Malietoa and, further, that the prospects for peace were good.[12]

Difficulties with the British acting consul, W. B. Churchward, relative to municipal matters arose in the fall of 1881. Churchward arrived in Samoa in the early days of October, having been nominated by Sir Arthur Gordon, now governor of New Zealand, as secretary to King Malietoa. Sir Arthur was still consul general and high commissioner for the Western Pacific and had also appointed Churchward as acting consul at Apia for the period the regular consul was to be absent from his post. Churchward was offered both positions during the course of a conversation at Wellington. Churchward records Sir Arthur's words as follows: " 'In taking over this duty, I must tell you that you will be in a position to do an immense deal of good.' A long pause ensued here, and, thinking the interview was finished, I was about to reply, when he added, in a severe tone, 'and a great deal of harm!' "[13]

This new move on the part of Sir Arthur appeared suspicious to Dawson and he reported to the department that the nomination of Churchward as secretary to the king would cause trouble.[14] Difficulties with Churchward as acting consul arose over the control of the municipal archives. Dawson refused to attend any meeting of the municipal board until the archives which were in the British consulate should be turned over to himself as the chairman of the board. The German consul general had intimated that Dawson could not prevent a meeting of the board by staying away, for the reason that the United States had not ratified the convention of 1879 and that Dawson therefore had no rights under the convention. Dawson reported his opinion that the British and German

---

[12] C.D., Apia, vol. 10, Dawson, Sept. 14, 1881, rec'd Dec. 6.
[13] Churchward, *My Consulate in Samoa*, pp. 2-3.
[14] C.D., Apia, vol. 11, Dawson Oct. 7, 1881, rec'd Jan. 3.

consuls were jealous of American influence in Samoa.[15] Dawson for the time being seemed to have more influence with the king, even though Churchward had come to be his secretary, and in December Dawson sent to the department a secret agreement he had made with the king that Malietoa would not permit any two foreign governments to carry on the local municipal government of Apia. In the same agreement the king made concessions in favor of United States citizens in certain contingencies.[16] Since according to the municipal rules a meeting of the municipal board could be held only with the unanimous concurrence of the three consuls, the government could not function until an understanding could be reached.

By December 20 the German and British consuls were ready to propose a meeting for the discussion of issues,[17] and on January 2, 1882, Dawson could report to the department that a compromise had been effected. The British consul was elected secretary of the board and American citizens were to have the right to elect their own representative on the board in addition to the consul. The extra American member could not, as theretofore, be elected by two foreign consuls against the wishes of the American consul.[18]

Dawson left Apia January 10, 1882, on a leave of absence, sailing for Yokohama. From Japan he went to China and thence to Australia, returning to Apia June 17.[19] Upon his return to his post he learned that he had been recalled and that one Theodore Canisius had been

[15] *Ibid.*, Dawson, Nov. 7, 1881, rec'd Feb. 1.
[16] *Ibid.*, Dawson, Dec. 1, 1881, rec'd Feb. 1.
[17] *Ibid.*, Dawson, Dec. 20, 1881, rec'd Mar. 6.
[18] *Ibid.*, Dawson, Jan. 2, 1882.
[19] *Ibid.*, nos. 313 (March 7), 314 (March 21), 315 (April 20), 320 (June 17).

appointed his successor.[20] Dawson delivered the consular archives to Canisius on August 31,[21] and the next day the new consul assumed charge of the post.[22] Dawson sailed for the United States September 13.[23]

The Lackawanna peace settlement of July, 1881, remained effective, and during the year 1882 nothing disturbing happened. In the beginning of 1883 a rebellion was again threatening, but it was averted by the settlement of the king question, the solution of the vexing problem being brought about by a compromise. The reigning king, Malietoa Laupepa, was to remain as ruler for seven years, when a new king might be elected. The consuls looked with favor upon the arrangement and Canisius in an address to the Taimua and Faipule advised them to maintain peace.[24] The action of Canisius was approved by the department.[25] The four-year period of the municipal convention of September 2, 1879, was approaching its end, and since it was not yet deemed possible to transfer the government of the foreign settlement of Apia to the native Samoan authorities, Canisius wrote to the department suggesting a continuance of the convention.[26] The day after the receipt of Canisius' despatch the department replied that a continuance of the convention on existing bases would be agreeable to the United States.[27] In other words, the informal arrangement whereby the United States through its consul participated in the tripartite government of Apia and district without ratifying the convention of September 2, 1879, would be continued

[20] C.D., Apia, vol. 11, Dawson, June 23, 1882, rec'd Sept. 11.
[21] *Ibid.*, Dawson, August 31, 1882, rec'd Nov. 22.
[22] *Ibid.*, Canisius, Sept. 6, 1882, rec'd Nov. 22.
[23] *Ibid.*, Dawson, Sept. 13, 1882, rec'd Nov. 22.
[24] *Ibid.*, Canisius, Feb. 15, 1883, rec'd April 28.
[25] I.C., vol. 106, p. 629, to Canisius, April 20, 1883.
[26] C.D., Apia, vol. 12, Canisius, May 10, 1883, rec'd Aug. 15.
[27] I.C., vol. 108, p. 107, to Canisius, Aug. 16, 1883.

by the United States, subject to the withdrawal of the United States at pleasure.[28]

Canisius could not wait for the department's instructions to reach him, as the convention of 1879 would expire by limitation September 2. Consequently, he participated in several meetings of the consuls for the purpose of determining upon what course they should take with regard to the convention. On September 1, six chiefs from the Taimua and Faipule met the consuls as representatives of the king. Said Canisius in his report of the negotiations: "There can be no doubt that the Samoan Government is not in a sufficiently stable condition to take over the Municipality. The natives have not yet learned to govern themselves, and much less white men. The Samoans resident within the Municipality are in general favorable to its continuation on the same basis as heretofore, and probably very few who live at any distance from the foreign settlement know, or care, anything about it at all. It is only the chiefs who compose the Taimua and Faipule who covet possession of the Municipality. They regard it as a source of revenue, and some of the oldest residents here, well acquainted with their customs and mode of thinking, say that some of these chiefs, knowing there to be several thousands of dollars, the taxes paid by the white residents, are simple enough to believe that this money would be turned over to them at the same time with the Government of the Municipality. Even if it were, they would not expend it in improving the town or in making any improvements whatever, but would at once begin to purchase arms and ammunition with which to slaughter one another at some future time."[29] The convention was prolonged indefinitely by the unanimous agreement of the three consuls and on October 1, Canisius

[28] I.C., vol. 98, p. 331, to Dawson, Jan. 14, 1881.
[29] C.D., Apia, vol. 12, Canisius to Adee, Sept. 3, 1883, rec'd Dec. 6, 1883.

transmitted an agreement between the consuls and the king concerning the continuance of the municipality.[30]

In reply to Canisius' despatch of September 3 relative to the prolongation of the municipal convention, the assistant secretary, John Davis, wrote on December 8 as follows: "I have to remark that the files of your Consulate show that we have uniformly declined to put ourselves on record in favor of a foreign or tripartite control over the Samoan Islands. The municipal Government of Apia so far controls the native Government, and upholds the power of the King, that it may be hard to draw the line between local municipal control, and exerting a preponderating influence in the affairs of the Samoan Government. Still the need of adequately protecting foreign interests in Samoa, and of maintaining a decent and stable Government for the district in which foreigners reside makes it very advisable that the arrangement agreed upon by you and your colleagues should continue so far as the United States is concerned, on the same basis as heretofore. Therefore, your acts to this end are approved, but you must be careful always to bear in mind the separation which should be marked between local self administration and the general control of the Samoan Government."[31]

In the early summer of 1883 native disturbances in Samoa were expected. In fact the political situation was assuming so threatening an aspect that Canisius had an interview with the king. The king informed him that he had been promised the support of the German government and he desired to know if the United States would coöperate.[32] The United States had not yet formally recognized Malietoa Laupepa as king *de jure* since the Lackawanna peace agreement of July, 1881, although

[30] C.D., Apia, vol. 12, Canisius, Oct. 1, 1883, rec'd Dec. 6.
[31] I.C., vol. 109, p. 131, to Canisius, Dec. 8, 1883.
[32] C.D., Apia, vol. 12, Canisius, July 11, 1883, rec'd Oct. 8.

GERMAN-AMERICAN RIVALRY 273

both consuls, Dawson and Canisius, had been instructed to recognize his government as *de facto*. Shortly after the receipt of Canisius' despatch, however, the department wrote in reply that the United States recognized Malietoa Laupepa as king. The government would not use force to sustain him but would not object to other governments lending him aid in case of an outbreak.[33]

On October 1 the consul sent a long despatch stating that rumors were current "that the Government of New Zealand is urging the Imperial Government of Great Britain to grant it permission to annex this group of islands." If this proved to be true, wrote Canisius, it was a revival "of the old effort of 1870 to 1875 when the Hon. Julias Vogel, Premier, Sir G. Bowen, Governor, and his successor, the Hon. Sir James Furgusson, so strongly pressed the matter." Canisius wanted to draw the department's "attention to the efforts on the part of British subjects in the Australian Colonies to secure, in some way possession of Samoa. We have obtained Pago Pago by the treaty of 1879 [1878], it is true, but this treaty expires in about five years, when the Samoan Government may not desire to renew it, so that this harbor may fall into the hands of British colonists in New Zealand, who would spare no effort to accomplish what they formerly intended. . . . The American residents in Samoa, who have become quite numerous, would have to retire before the advance of British colonists, and the universal opinion among them convinces me of this. The United States should never consent to the Samoan group falling into the hands of a foreign power. The future of these magnificent islands is very bright, and, with a good native Government may, before long, become a second Hawaii."[34]

On October 28 Canisius transmitted to the department

[33] I.C., vol. 108, p. 496, to Canisius, Oct. 23, 1883.
[34] C.D., Apia, vol. 12, Canisius, Oct. 1, 1883, rec'd Dec. 6.

correspondence he had had with King Malietoa anent the proposed annexation by New Zealand. The king, he said, opposed the scheme, but there were some chiefs who favored it in order to defeat and injure the king.[35] Throughout the month of November the agitation for annexation continued, Canisius transmitting to the department British colonial press articles containing alleged circular petitions and comments.[36] The British warship *Miranda* was in Samoan waters and Canisius sent the department correspondence between the king and its commander and between the king and the consuls relative to fighting that had begun between rival chiefs at Pago Pago on account of the New Zealand movement.[37]

Upon the receipt of Canisius' first despatch concerning the New Zealand annexation project, the department immediately on December 12 sent instructions to Canisius, enclosing also a copy of a note to H. A. P. Carter, Hawaiian minister at Washington from Secretary of State Frelinghuysen, dated December 6. John Davis, assistant secretary of state, wrote to Canisius that for the present it was only necessary to send him this note and Carter's note of October 18 to which Frelinghuysen's note was a reply. "As will be seen by the terms of the Secretary's letter," wrote Davis, "this Government would object to the destruction of the independent existence of any insular community to which we are bound by treaty."[38]

The Hawaiian minister had enclosed a protest drawn up by the Hawaiian government against the agitation going on among British colonists in Australia and New Zealand and among French colonists in New Caledonia "having as its object," in the words of Carter, "to induce

[35] C.D., Apia, vol. 12, Canisius, Oct. 28, 1883, rec'd Jan. 7, 1884.
[36] *Ibid.*, Canisius, Nov. 15, 1883, rec'd Jan. 31, 1884.
[37] *Ibid.*, Canisius, Nov. 24, 1883, rec'd Mar. 3, 1884.
[38] I.C., vol. 109, p. 147, to Canisius, Dec. 12, 1883.

their respective Governments to extend their dominion in the Pacific by the forcible annexation of islands whose native inhabitants have neither sought the protection of these nor other powers, nor given any reasonable cause for the threatened subjugations.'' The Hawaiian government had sent the protest to the United States for the reason that "the uniform policy which has been pursued by the Government of the United States towards Hawaii leads to a confident belief that its sympathies will be entirely in favor of the sentiments to which expression has thus been given."[39]

Among the "sentiments" expressed in the protest was the following: "His Hawaiian Majesty's Government responding to the national will and to the especial appeals of several Polynesian chiefs, has sent a special commissioner to several of the Polynesian chieftains and states to advise them in their national affairs; And His Hawaiian Majesty's Government, speaking for the Hawaiian people, so happily prospering through national independence, makes earnest appeal to the Governments of great and enlightened states, that they will recognize the inalienable rights of the several native communities of Polynesia to enjoy opportunities for progress and self-government, and will guarantee to them the same favorable opportunities which have made Hawaii prosperous and happy, and which incite her national spirit to lift up a voice among the nations in behalf of sister islands and groups of Polynesia."[40]

In answer to the protest and Carter's covering note Secretary Frelinghuysen made it clear that while it was

[39] Notes from Hawaiian Legation, Carter to Frelinghuysen, Oct. 18, 1883; *Foreign Relations, 1883*, p. 574.

[40] *Ibid.*, enclosure, protest, dated Iolani Palace, Honolulu, Aug. 23, 1883, signed by Walter M. Gibson, Minister of Foreign Affairs; *Foreign Relations, 1883*, p. 575.

unnecessary to assure Hawaii "that the sympathies of this Government and the people of this country are always in favor of good self-government by the independent communities of the world," and while the United States "could not, therefore, view with complacency any movement tending to the extinction of the national life of the intimately connected commonwealths of the Northern Pacific, the attitude of this Government towards the distant outlying groups of Polynesia is necessarily different." The New Hebrides group and the Solomon Islands, to the absorption of which by the Australian colonial system it was understood the protest referred in particular, were "geographically allied to Australasia rather than to Polynesia." These islands had at no time "so asserted and maintained a separate national life as to entitle them to entrance, by treaty stipulations and established forms of competent self-government, into the family of nations, as Hawaii and Samoa have done . . . The President, before whom the protest has been brought, moved by these considerations, does not regard the matter as one calling for the interposition of the United States, either to oppose or support the suggested measure."[41]

In sending the above quoted correspondence to Canisius it is clear that the department intimated thereby that while the government felt no concern about the annexation of such groups as were located within the so-called Australasian political system, the Samoan group as well as the Hawaiian Islands were regarded differently for the reason that the treaties between the United States and these archipelagos placed the United States government under peculiar obligations to them. As it turned out, it was not necessary for the United States to take a decided stand in opposition to the New Zealand agitation.

[41] Notes to Hawaiian Legation, Frelinghuysen to Carter, Dec. 6, 1883; *Foreign Relations, 1883*, pp. 575-576.

GERMAN-AMERICAN RIVALRY

The disturbances on the island of Tutuila referred to above could not be regarded as the beginning of another civil war, but they were symptoms of what was to happen at the end of the next year when Germany intervened in Samoa in earnest. The so-called revolution of Pago Pago was put down easily for the reason that the three consuls intervened together. For this action Canisius was commended by the department.[42] Apparently the rebellious chiefs were not supported by any foreign political interests at the beginning of 1884, for when it was reported that rifles and cartridges were being illegally imported into the neutral territory of Apia they were seized by the native government at the request of all three of the consuls.[43] In fact, at a political meeting of the Taimua and Faipule, the leaders of the Tupua (Tamasese) party announced that they would adhere to the promise they had made not to bring forward the "king question" until the end of seven years.[44] This was confirmed about six months later in July when Canisius reported that the principal agitator, Chief Masua, was at the point of death.[45]

During the autumn of 1883, when the rumors flew thick and fast concerning a possible annexation of Samoa by New Zealand, Canisius expressed concern about the rights of the United States in Pago Pago harbor and desired instructions.[46] The department replied in January, 1884, that the United States claimed the right to establish a coaling station at Pago Pago but did not claim exclusive jurisdiction over the harbor there.[47]

In the autumn of 1884, the reversal of Prince Bismarck's policy with reference to colonies was quite ap-

---

[42] I.C., vol. 109, p. 638, to Canisius, March 6, 1884.
[43] C.D., Apia, vol. 12, Canisius, Jan. 25, 1884, rec'd March 3.
[44] *Ibid.*, Canisius, Jan. 14, 1884, rec'd March 3.
[45] *Ibid.*, Canisius, July 23, 1884, rec'd Sept. 15.
[46] *Ibid.*, Canisius, Oct. 28, 1883, rec'd Jan. 7.
[47] I.C., vol. 109, p. 341.

parent in Samoa as well as in New Guinea and Africa. Dr. Stübel, the acting German consul, was instructed to draw up an agreement with King Malietoa for the establishment of a governmental régime in Samoa wherein German officials would be dominant in the interests of the Germans, particularly the firm headed by Theodor Weber. A convention was signed on November 10, the signatures on the instrument being those of Malietoa as king, Tupua as vice king, Dr. Stübel representing Germany, and Theodor Weber as witness. The convention contained eight articles and, according to the preamble, it was negotiated "for the purpose of securing the benefits of good government to Germans residing in Samoa and in execution of Article VII of the German Samoan treaty of friendship of January 24, 1879," which article contained provisions for future arrangements between Samoa and Germany in relation to crimes and misdemeanors of Samoans against Germans.

Moreover, the new treaty, Articles I to III, provided for the appointment of a German-Samoan commission which should consult and agree upon laws for the mutual benefit of the government of Samoa and the German residents. This was thought necessary since the native government had proven too weak to take the required measures effectually to protect the lives and property of German subjects, and of the colored laborers of other South Sea islands, living outside of the municipality of Apia. The council should consist of the German consul with two German residents appointed by the consul, and two Samoans, one each appointed by the king and vice king. Articles IV, V, and VI provided the means for enforcing the laws. The king should "appoint with the advice and consent of the German consul, a German officer [as a member] of the Samoan Government." This officer should "be the secretary and the adviser of the King in all matters in which

German residents of Samoa are concerned." The German officer should also serve as judge in criminal cases where German subjects were involved and when the punishment was not more than two years imprisonment. The more serious criminal cases were to be tried by the German consul as in the past. In cases against Samoans charged with crimes against Germans and their property, a Samoan judge should be associated with the German; also in cases where colored laborers were guilty of crimes against Samoans. In cases again where colored laborers were guilty of crimes against other colored laborers the German judge should act alone.

The money necessary for the execution of the agreement was to come from commercial taxes, fines, the proceeds of the labor of prisoners, and from general taxation of the German residents. The taxes were to be imposed by the German-Samoan council, and a representative of the German taxpayers was to be entrusted with the funds. The agreement was to go into effect immediately subject to the approval of the imperial German government, which government could also withdraw from the agreement on six months' notice.[48]

Correspondence between the American and British consuls and the German consul was immediately begun relative to the German designs, and Canisius received a statement from King Malietoa that the treaty was signed under duress. Canisius was of the opinion that the Germans planned to set up a new king if Malietoa proved intractable.[49]

Five days before the agreement was signed with the

[48] C.D., Apia, vol. 12, Canisius, Nov. 26, 1884, rec'd Feb. 2, 1885, enclosure, German-Samoan agreement, Nov. 10, 1884. For agreement see also H. Ex. Doc. no. 238, pp. 5-7, encl. in encl. no. 3, note from von Alvensleben to Frelinghuysen, Feb. 24, 1885.
[49] *Ibid.*, Canisius, Nov. 26, 1884, rec'd Feb. 2, 1885.

German representatives, King Malietoa, the vice king, and forty-eight chiefs, had signed a petition to Her Majesty, Queen Victoria, praying for a British annexation to prevent "other Governments" from taking Samoa. Reference was made to a petition sent "now nearly a year ago" to Her Majesty by the king for the same purpose.[50] Said the present petition: "It is entirely at the disposal of your Majesty as to whether it is better for us to become an English Colony or be connected with the Government of New Zealand." The petition was sent to the governor of New Zealand with the request that it be forwarded by cable to the Foreign Office in London. In the meantime the Foreign Office had not assented to a law passed by the New Zealand parliament in 1883 for the annexation of Samoa and it was questioned whether this petition would meet a more favorable fate.

The German encroachments were being felt by the British colonies at several points in Australasia, but especially with respect to New Guinea. Despatches between the Colonial Office in London and the governors of the various colonies were numerous in the year 1884, and in order to protect themselves a convention of the colonies was held in Sydney to protest to the mother country. In the meantime negotiations were going on between Prince Bismarck and Lord Granville for a settlement of the New Guinea problem, and on November 19, 1884, Lord Derby of the Colonial Office received a despatch from the governor of New Zealand that the latter's ministers hoped that Great Britain might be able to secure Samoa and Tonga to New Zealand. They would undertake, he assured Derby, to

[50] This petition, according to the report of George H. Bates, United States Special Commissioner to Samoa in 1886, was "mainly the result of unauthorized New Zealand agitators, as there was at that time nothing in the condition of Samoa to press him [Malietoa] into this position [fear of German encroachments], as there was at the time of his application, a year later." (H. Ex. Doc. no. 238, p. 160).

propose the next year to the New Zealand parliament that the cost of government would be guaranteed by the colony.[51]

In the course of the negotiations at Berlin Sir Edward Malet, the British ambassador, reported to Lord Granville on December 1, that Prince Bismarck had heard of King Malietoa's petition for a British protectorate. "The Chancellor said that this step," wrote Malet, "would create a very bad effect in this country [Germany] as the Germans had for some years past been interested in the island, and the Reichstag had already had before it for consideration the question of a subsidy to a Hamburgh house trading with Samoa. The Prince added that he trusted that I should be able to give him an assurance that Her Majesty's Government had no intention of annexing the island. I am informed by Mr. Meade that there are apprehensions in New Zealand that the Imperial German Government may, sooner or later, annex both Samoa and Tonga. Will your Lordship authorize me to state to Prince Bismarck that Her Majesty's Government will give positive assurances that the independence of both places will be respected by them provided that reciprocal assurances are made to the Queen's Government by that of His Majesty the Emperor?"[52]

Pauncefote sent this information to Lord Derby by direction of Lord Granville together with a copy of a telegram sent by the Foreign Office to Malet dated December 4 as follows: "Your despatch of the 1st has been received, and Her Majesty's Government authorize your Excellency to give assurances that they will respect the independence of Samoa and Tonga provided that they receive reciprocal

[51] Parliamentary Papers, vol. 54, 1884-1885 (Serial no. 46-C-4273-Feb. 1885).

[52] *Ibid.*, (Serial no. 57-C-4273-Feb. 1885), Foreign Office to Colonial Office, Dec. 4, 1884. Enclosure, Malet to Granville, Berlin, Dec. 1, 1884.

assurances from the German Government. You may add that pending the result of the discussion which has been agreed to by the two Governments, Her Majesty's Government do not contemplate any fresh arrangements in the Pacific."[53] Two days later, December 6, Lord Derby received a telegraphic despatch from the governor of New Zealand forwarding King Malietoa's petition for annexation.

On December 19, the Foreign Office informed Lord Derby that a telegram just received from the British ambassador at Berlin stated that Prince Bismarck had informed him (Malet) that the German flag had been hoisted at three places on the north coast of New Guinea, and at ten places in New Britain, New Ireland, and Sable Island.[54] On January 3, 1885, Lord Derby telegraphed the governors of New South Wales, Victoria, Queensland, and South Australia that the German annexation in New Guinea had "not been made in concert with the Government of this country." He added: "Her Majesty's Government are in communication with the Government of Germany on the subject."[55]

On the same day Lord Derby sent a long telegraphic despatch to the governor of New Zealand concerning Samoa to the effect that Her Majesty's government regretted "that they are unable to meet [the] wishes of New Zealand Government." He referred to a telegram of December 24, in which he reminded the governor that foreign interests in Samoa and Tonga impeded British annexation. He added: "German Government has given and received assurance within last few days that independence of these islands shall be maintained. If, therefore, Colonial Government should unfortunately send

[53] Parliamentary Papers, vol. 54, 1884-1885 (Serial no. 57-C-4273-Feb. 1885).
[54] *Ibid.*, (Serial no. 72-C-4273-Feb. 1885).
[55] *Ibid.*, (Serial no. 108-C-4273-Feb. 1885).

Colonial Secretary [to] Samoa, German Government would have strong justification for annexing islands accordingly. Her Majesty's Government hope that New Zealand Government will not preclude internationalization of the islands, which is obviously best course for British interests at present juncture.''[56]

The sending to Samoa of a colonial secretary, referred to in the above despatch, had been suggested by the New Zealand governor as a means of circumventing the German encroachments in Samoa as envisaged in the German-Samoan agreement of November 10, 1884. The governor of New Zealand replied immediately to the despatch from Lord Derby: "In reply to yours 3rd January decided not to send the Colonial Secretary to Samoa. . . . New Zealand has large interests in Samoa. My ministry consider that if Germany keep New Guinea and adjacent islands Samoa and Tonga should become British. They hope compact will be maintained with France about New Hebrides.''[57]

The negotiations between Prince Bismarck and Earl Granville over New Guinea continued until April 25, 1885, when the latter offered Count Münster, the German ambassador, a division line whereby the German part of New Guinea, later known as Kaiser Wilhelm Land, was definitely marked off from the British part to the southward, both German and British portions lying east of Dutch New Guinea. The offer was acceptable to Germany.[58] This peaceful solution of the New Guinea problem led to an agreement the next year, April 6, 1886, for the separation of British and German zones of influence throughout the Pacific.

The narration of the above events has been a digression from the main story of the policy of the United States

[56] *Ibid.*, (Serial no. 114-C-4273-Feb. 1885).   [57] *Ibid.*
[58] *Ibid.*, (Serial no. 1-C-4441, New Guinea, June, 1885).

with reference to Samoa, but it has been thought necessary to include it here in order to make clear the position of the two other treaty powers in the general field of colonial enterprises in the Pacific so as better to understand their relations toward one another, first antagonistic, and later friendly, as affecting the policy of the United States. It is obvious from the brief recital here of Anglo-German relations in 1884 and 1885 that at first Great Britain and the United States would be bound to act more or less in harmony, whereas later, when a complete understanding would be reached with Germany, as happened in 1886, Great Britain might be expected to withdraw from her close understanding with the United States and leave the latter to oppose alone the German encroachments in Samoa in 1887.

On December 1, 1884, King Malietoa sent Canisius a note explaining his course with respect to the petition to Great Britain for protection, and requesting that the facts be laid before the government of the United States.[59] On December 29, he sent an appeal to the emperor of Germany informing His Majesty of the manner in which the treaty of November 10 was procured; that he and the vice king were compelled to sign it without knowing its contents, the German consul having declined to furnish the Samoan government with a copy of the same until it was signed. Having assented to the agreement "on account of intimidation by threats," the king wrote to inform His Majesty of the Samoan government's "withdrawal from the agreement on account of its containing many impracticable clauses." Malietoa also requested His Majesty not to assent to the agreement. The Samoan king, moreover, complained of the actions of Theodor

[59] C.D., Apia, vol. 12, Canisius, Dec. 3, 1884, rec'd Feb. 2. King's letter of Dec. 1, 1884, enclosed. See also enclosure D 4 of report by George H. Bates, appendix A, H. Ex. Doc. no. 238, p. 211.

GERMAN-AMERICAN RIVALRY

Weber, the agent of the German firm. "He is continually scheming," wrote Malietoa, "and offering bribes to some Samoan chiefs to induce them to comply with his wishes and thus cause a rebellion in my country."[60]

For various reasons but principally because the Samoan government declined to execute the agreement of November 10, 1884, Dr. Stübel on January 23 seized the town and district of Apia as a "reprisal." He informed Malietoa that because he had "maligned" Germany he (the consul) would "in the name of the Imperial German Government and subject to the approval of the same, take possession of, as security, all the land which now constitutes all the municipality of Apia, as far as your highness' and your Government's sovereign rights are concerned, and the Imperial Government will so long assume these sovereign rights until an understanding has been successfully arrived at with the Government of Samoa which will make German interests secure in Samoa and will make difficulties such as have heretofore arisen impossible in future."[61] In a proclamation to the Samoan people by Dr. Stübel appeared the following: "During the long period that Malietoa has been King the Government of Germany has been treated with unkindness and injury, and all agreements that have been made between the Governments of Germany and Samoa have been repeatedly violated." War against Samoa, he said, was not intended, and when a peaceful solution should be effected between Malietoa and the German government the territory now taken would be given up.[62]

Consul Stübel informed Churchward and Canisius of

[60] Encl. E 9 in report by George H. Bates, appendix A, in H. Ex. Doc. no. 238, p. 225.

[61] Encl. in encl. 5 with report by John B. Thurston, appendix C, in H. Ex. Doc. no. 238, p. 290. Stübel to Malietoa, Jan. 23, 1885.

[62] Encl. in encl. no. 5 as above. Proclamation to Samoan people by German consul, Stübel, Jan. 23, 1885.

his contemplated step. As a public manifestation of the attachment of the Apia municipality, Captain Pluddeman of the German warship, *Albatross,* was to hoist the German flag at Mulinuu.[63] The British and American consuls protested against the action of Stübel and in a proclamation said: "It having been made public that the German Consul has assumed the right of rule in the municipality in contravention of the convention of 1879, and renewed by the three powers, we, the Consuls of the United States and Great Britain, do hereby make known that they insist upon the rights of the convention, and deprecate force consummating such assumption."[64] In reporting the attachment of the municipality by the German consul, Canisius stated that he had protested against the action as an infringement of rights of the United States under the treaty of September 2, 1879, and that he intended in conjunction with the British consul to continue the municipal government until he learned the wishes of the department, even if the German consul should withdraw therefrom.[65] It seems that the German consul at first actually withdrew from the municipal board,[66] but reconsidered and then threatened to have the Samoan flag removed from the government house by force if the American and British consuls insisted on its floating over the place of meeting of the board. Canisius and Churchward yielded pending reference of the matter to their respective governments.[67]

Abetted by the German consul and by Theodor Weber, a rebellion against Malietoa broke out simultaneously

[63] Encl. 5, Stübel to Churchward, Jan. 23, 1885, with report by John B. Thurston, appendix C, in H. Ex. Doc. no. 238, p. 289.

[64] Encl. in encl. no. 5, notice by the United States consul and acting British consul.

[65] C.D., Apia, vol. 13, Canisius, Jan. 28, 1885, rec'd March 2.

[66] *Ibid.,* Canisius, Jan. 28, 1885, rec'd March 2.

[67] *Ibid.,* Canisius, Jan. 28, 1885, rec'd March 2.

with the seizure by Dr. Stübel of Apia district. Malietoa was ordered by German naval officers to leave his own home, but this act was disavowed by Dr. Stübel.[68] The rebels soon appointed Tupua Tamasese as king and according to Canisius were furnished arms by Theodor Weber. King Malietoa requested the consuls to order the German and English men-of-war, then in port, to disperse the rebels. The consuls refused to comply but ordered both parties to stop hostilities.[69] By the end of the month of February, 1885, however, the situation had become decidedly worse on account of large accessions to the forces of the rebels. The British and American consuls and the commander of the British war vessel, *Miranda,* promptly issued a notice to the Samoans stating that their governments recognized Malietoa as king, and that the treaties were still in force. Canisius reported that Dr. Stübel refused to sign the notice, and that he continued his efforts to embarrass King Malietoa.[70]

On April 3, Canisius informed the department that news had arrived from New Zealand to the effect that the German government would repudiate the action of its consul, a report that greatly weakened the rebel cause. The German consul nevertheless continued to interfere with the Samoan government.[71] On April 10, he sent a letter to Malietoa forbidding his government to have *tololos* (large popular assemblies) at Mulinuu.[72] This step was taken with the idea of preventing government warriors from endangering the German control of the district of Apia. Malietoa replied sharply, "Do you want to drive me off Mulinuu? If so, tell me and I will go, and my Gov-

[68] *Ibid.,* Canisius, Feb. 3, 1885, rec'd March 2.
[69] *Ibid.,* Canisius, Feb. 14, 1885, rec'd April 1.
[70] *Ibid.,* Canisius, Feb. 23, 1885, rec'd April 1.
[71] *Ibid.,* Canisius, April 3, 1885, rec'd April 28.
[72] Encl. E 12 with report by George H. Bates, appendix A, in H. Ex. Doc. no. 238, p. 226.

ernment, but shall set it up in another place.' "[73] Canisius sent to the department a copy of the letter to Malietoa from the German consul, to whom he attributed all the troubles in the islands.[74]

On May 18, Malietoa sent another letter to the German emperor complaining about the actions of Weber, "who has been continually scheming to cause trouble and rebellion against my Government, and has led astray the mind of the Imperial German Consul here, and has made him so ill-disposed as to lead him to cast aside with contempt myself and my Government.' "[75] The king desired the removal of Dr. Stübel and the appointment of some official as "upright" as was Captain Zembsch to act as consul. The king recalled that when Captain Zembsch was consul general in Samoa, Theodor Weber had no influence over the German consulate.[76] A week later, May 25, the king wrote another letter to the German emperor again protesting against the actions of Dr. Stübel.[77] Copies of the two letters from Malietoa were sent to the department by Canisius on May 27.

The department received Canisius' despatch dated November 26, on February 2, 1885. This communication contained the first information to reach the department concerning Germany's change of policy in Samoa and the German-Samoan agreement of November 10. In this despatch the consul advised the department that he had endeavored to learn whether Germany was recognizing and countenancing the revolutionary movement. The depart-

[73] Encl. E 11 with above report.
[74] C.D., Apia, vol. 13, Canisius, April 28, 1885, rec'd May 29.
[75] *Ibid.*, Canisius, May 27, 1885, rec'd June 22; enclosure, King Malietoa to Emperor William, May 18, 1885. Letter is printed as encl. no. 3 in encl. no. 8, Bayard to Pendleton, June 25, 1885, in H. Ex. Doc. no. 238, p. 12.
[76] *Ibid.*
[77] *Ibid.*, Encl. no. 2. King Malietoa to Emperor William, May 25, 1885. Letter is printed as above.

ment approved the consul's action.[78] Ten days after the receipt of the Canisius despatch the German minister at Washington, von Alvensleben, informed Secretary Frelinghuysen that Dr. Stübel had telegraphed to his government that he had been obliged to hoist his flag to make reprisals, but that the consul's meaning was not understood and that Germany did not intend to interfere with the *status quo* in Samoa.[79] Five days later Frelinghuysen communicated with John A. Kasson, the United States minister at Berlin, and, referring to von Alvensleben's note, said that he should like to have any information which might be secured informally on the subject. "Should a suitable occasion offer," he added, "you may inform the Imperial German Government that Mr. Von Alvensleben's communication was very gratifying to the President."[80] The department also disclosed to Canisius the tenor of the German note, advising him that the German minister had said that Germany did not intend to interfere in any way in the affairs of Samoa.[81]

The German minister transmitted to the Department of State on February 24 a translation of the convention, which had been signed on November 10, he being charged by the German government also to explain that the agreement had been drawn up in accordance with stipulations in the German-Samoan treaty of 1879 in the application of new laws and statutes to German subjects in Samoa. "The benefits of better protection by law and of an improved criminal justice," the note continued, "will also be shared in by the citizens of the other treaty-powers resident in Samoa, while the expenses of the institutions

[78] I.C., vol. 112, p. 618, to Canisius, Feb. 6, 1885.
[79] Notes from German Legation, vol. 18, Alvensleben to Frelinghuysen, Feb. 12, 1885.
[80] Instructions, Germany, vol. 17, p. 474, no. 98 Frelinghuysen to Kasson, Feb. 17, 1885; H. Ex. Doc. no. 238, p. 4, encl. 2.
[81] I.C., vol. 113, p. 58, to Canisius, Feb. 20, 1885.

made in accordance with Article VII will be defrayed only by the Germans interested therein." The note, moreover, notified the United States that the imperial government intended to ratify the convention, and would "see to it that the provisions of the same are carried out." In informing the government of the United States of the convention, Germany expressed "the hope that its efforts to introduce order in Samoa and to obtain guaranties for a peaceful development of this group of islands will meet with that appreciation and assistance on the part of the American Government which the inter-communication of our interests in the islands and the friendly relations between the German Empire and the United States lead us to expect."[82]

As already stated, the department received a translation of the convention from Canisius on February 2 with the information that the king had signed the document under duress. Such a circumstance would, of course, prejudice the department against the treaty from the beginning. The new arrangement led to the suspicion that Germany not only thereby intended to destroy the triconsular government of Apia and district by removing Germans from its jurisdiction and withholding the taxes which the Germans would ordinarily pay for the support of the municipality, but, what was more serious, sought to obtain practical control of the Samoan government itself by means of the German-Samoan commission and the German adviser to the king. If the Washington authorities had any doubts concerning the attitude of the Samoan government toward the convention of November 10, these disappeared entirely with the receipt, four days after the German note reached the department, of a communication direct from the secretary of state of the Samoan govern-

[82] Notes from German Legation, vol. 18, Alvensleben to Frelinghuysen, Feb. 24, 1885; H. Ex. Doc. no. 238, pp. 4-7, encl. 3.

ment, complaining that the German consul had forced the king to sign the agreement without the consent of the Samoan government and people. The agreement, moreover, was a violation of Samoa's treaty with the United States, since under the latter the United States had undertaken to settle Samoa's difficulties with foreign powers. In conclusion the secretary requested that an American man-of-war be sent for the protection of Samoa.[83]

The end of the Arthur administration was at hand, and not desiring to commit the incoming Cleveland administration to any hastily conceived decision, Frelinghuysen on February 28 merely sent von Alvensleben a note of acknowledgment, contenting himself by saying: "The interesting points presented in this communication will doubtless receive full consideration at the hands of my successor in office, to whom I take pleasure in leaving it, inasmuch as it is deemed inopportune to prejudge the future course of events in this relation during the brief remaining term of the present administration."[84]

That Frelinghuysen was leaving a difficult problem to his successor, Thomas F. Bayard of Delaware, the retiring secretary knew full well, for when he wrote the above note to von Alvensleben, he had the Samoan government's protest before him, the latter communication having arrived that very day, February 28. Four more despatches reached the department from Canisius before the Arthur administration closed, all of them giving the department first-hand information concerning the attachment of the Apia municipality and district on January 23 by Dr. Stübel, and the last of the despatches—dated February 3

[83] Miscellaneous Letters, Department of State. Secretary of State of Samoa to the Department of State, Dec. 24, 1884, rec'd Feb. 28, 1885.
[84] Notes to German Legation, vol. 10, Frelinghuysen to Alvensleben, Feb. 28, 1885; H. Ex. Doc. no. 238, p. 7, encl. 4.

—containing a request from Canisius for a man-of-war to protect American interests. These despatches arrived on March 2.[85] On March 3 a despatch from Kasson in Berlin dated February 9 was received. It contained merely the information von Alvensleben had transmitted to the department on February 12, namely, that Prince Bismarck wanted it understood by the English and American governments that the German government "was wholly ignorant" of the reason for Dr. Stübel's hoisting the German flag in Apia by way of "reprisals". The Chancellor had instructed his son, Count Herbert von Bismarck, to say that the German government "had no intention to violate the understanding with the United States and England, but on the contrary would maintain it. They neither intended to take possession nor to establish a protectorate there, but would adhere to the *status quo*." Kasson concluded his despatch by saying: "He desired my Government to know promptly that if the Consular Act signified either, it was unauthorized and would be disavowed."[86] On April 6 the department received another despatch from Kasson enclosing a German newspaper account of the landing of the men from the *Albatross* and the hoisting of the German flag in Apia on January 23. "The present account," wrote Kasson, "leaves the transaction to be considered as an unwarranted assault on the independence of the islands."[87]

In view of the discrepancy between Prince Bismarck's remark concerning the flag-hoisting exploit of Dr. Stübel, and his intention to have the German consul's treaty of November 10, 1884, ratified by Germany, both the United

[85] C.D., Apia, vol. 13, from Canisius, nos. 144 (Jan. 28), 145 (Jan. 28), 146 (Jan. 28), 147 (Feb. 3).

[86] Despatches, Germany, vol. 37, no. 165, Kasson to Frelinghuysen, Feb. 9, 1885, rec'd Mar. 3; H. Ex. Doc. no. 238, p. 4, encl. 1.

[87] *Ibid.*, vol. 38, no. 210, Kasson to Bayard, Mar. 23, 1885, rec'd April 6; H. Ex. Doc. no. 238, encl. 6, p. 8.

States and Great Britain were mystified by what seemed a clear case of duplicity on the part of the German chancellor. It has already been noted that the British Colonial Office warned the New Zealand government not to persist in their efforts to acquire Samoa, as Great Britain and Germany had exchanged mutual promises not to disturb the *status quo* in Samoa. To disavow the German consul's seizure of Apia while at the same time supporting treaty negotiations which contemplated even more than the control of Apia, namely, the political control of all Samoa, was an inconsistent procedure. Great Britain opposed the agreement as giving Germany a preponderance of power, and on April 1 Sackville-West, the British minister in Washington, transmitted to the department for its confidential use correspondence of the British foreign office relative to the German consul's action in negotiating the agreement.[88]

The British minister continued to keep Secretary Bayard fully informed throughout the spring and summer concerning correspondence in the possession of the Foreign Office relative to German encroachments in Samoa.[89] Kasson, in Berlin, also wrote the department on April 13 that Great Britain threatened to make a similar convention with Samoa if the German agreement were ratified by Germany.[90] By the end of the month Kasson could say, however, that the German ambassador at London had been instructed to transmit a note to the British Foreign Office modifying the attitude of Germany and assuring the *status quo*.[91] Yet Kasson, on the same day this des-

[88] Notes from British Legation, vol. 111, Sackville-West to Bayard, April 1, 1885.
[89] *Ibid.*, Sackville-West to Bayard, April 17, May 5, May 11, June 9, June 23, July 7, and August 5, 1885.
[90] Despatches, Germany, vol. 38, no. 230, Kasson to Bayard, April 13, 1885.
[91] *Ibid.*, no. 251, Kasson to Bayard, April 30, 1885.

patch was sent, April 30, transmitted another communication dealing with the policy of Prince Bismarck and its bearing upon American interests and warning the department of possible future developments.[92]

Three despatches sent by Canisius in February were received on April 1. In one of these, dated February 23, Canisius informed the department that he and the British consul had posted a notice recognizing Malietoa as king. This action was approved by the department in a communication dated April 6, and indicated clearly that the United States would take no cognizance of the revolutionary movement abetted by the German consul.[93] The last communication sent to Canisius by the department commended him for his industry in keeping the department so well advised of political events in Samoa.[94] Canisius left Apia on June 6 on account of poor health.[95] Berthold Greenebaum, his successor, arrived at his post on July 28.[96]

Newly entered upon the duties of secretary, Bayard was not long in formulating the policy which the United States would assume with reference to the recent developments in Samoa. In a letter, dated June 19, 1885, instructions were given to the newly appointed American consul for his guidance,[97] as it was considered by the department that his position at the time was "one of some delicacy."[98]

[92] Despatches, Germany, vol. 38, no. 255, Kasson to Bayard, April 30, 1885, rec'd June 8.

[93] I.C., vol. 113, p. 349, to Canisius, April 6, 1885.

[94] *Ibid.*, p. 684, to Canisius, May 15, 1885.

[95] C.D., Apia, vol. 13, Canisius, Sept. 5, 1885.

[96] *Ibid.*, Greenebaum, July 28, 1885, rec'd Sept. 15.

[97] Although Greenebaum was appointed consul April 28, 1885, his name does not appear on the official list of the Bureau of Appointments of the Department of State for the reason that his appointment was never confirmed by the Senate. He served at Apia from July 28, 1885, to October 18, 1886, and was suspended by the President on October 4, 1886.

[98] I.C., vol. 114, p. 269, Bayard to Greenebaum, June 19, 1885; H. Ex. Doc. no. 238, pp. 9-11.

GERMAN-AMERICAN RIVALRY

In the first place, Bayard did not consider the fact that our consuls in the past had coöperated with the German and British representatives in the administration of the municipal government of Apia, as giving the United States a valid reason for opposing alleged German encroachments upon the local institutions of the town. He pointed out that although the municipality convention was signed by our representatives, it was never ratified by the United States government. "It may, therefore, be an open question," Bayard said, "whether our tacit acceptance of that convention and the entrance *de facto* of our consul into the municipal council of Apia give us any right to resent supposed German interference therewith." That is to say, as long as German interference in the municipal government had only a local significance there was nothing upon which our government could base any complaint, because the municipal convention of Apia was not a tripartite protectorate for all the islands, but merely "a compact for the administration of a settlement largely peopled by aliens whose established interests there are entitled to the security which such an arrangement affords." If German encroachments upon the municipal government should militate against the interests of American citizens we would have no redress unless we ratified the treaty and assumed our rights thereunder. If, on the other hand, Germany, under cover of local encroachments, was actually concealing an ulterior purpose of establishing a single protectorate for the islands, we would have the right to object, for "a single protectorate is as distasteful to our ideas of right in the premises as the tripartite protectorate which, on a former occasion, this Government was invited to consider the propriety of forming." Therefore, while we recognized that the framing of the municipality convention had as one of its purposes the exertion of "a moral influence in favor of a stable and good Government in the islands" the American consul should "be careful to distinguish between its special and local aims and any idea of a tripartite protection to which this Government may be deemed a party."

Yet there were good reasons for this government to take independently a lively interest in the free status of the Samoan islands. "The moral interests of the United States," the secretary continued, "with respect to the islands of the Pacific, necessarily dependent in greater or less degree on our American system of commonwealths, would counsel us to look with concern on any movement by which the independence of those Pacific nationalities might be extinguished by their passage under the domination of a foreign sovereign; and this would be equally true of possible English as well as possible German protection."[99] Whatever dynastic changes might occur in the native administration of the group, the neutrality of the islands should be upheld and respected "with the benevolent assurance of the powers most directly interested in the intercourse of that group." Hence, while we were "to a certain extent morally concerned" in the conservation of the government of Malietoa, in the "interests of peace" we "could not take the responsibility of interfering with the right of revolution, if the popular will shall be manifested adversely to the existing native Government." But on the other hand we had the "moral right to expect that no change of native rule shall extinguish the independence of the islands, and if such a change should be brought about by foreign interference and with the ulterior purpose, or result, of transferring the domination over the Samoan group to a single foreign flag, we would feel bound to dissent from such a proceeding."[100]

Whether Bayard, in writing the foregoing, actually con-

[99] I.C., vol. 114, p. 269, Bayard to Greenebaum, June 19, 1885.
[100] *Ibid.*

sidered the possibility of an extension of the Monroe Doctrine to the islands of the Pacific can only be an interesting speculation, but he stepped upon firmer ground when further on in his letter he called attention to the fact that our interests in Samoa were based upon the treaty of 1878. "The main point to be borne in mind is," he said, "that by a formal international treaty, the first which Samoa concluded with a foreign sovereign power, the United States set the precedent of recognizing the independent nationality of the native Government of the group; and, moreover, acquired certain definite rights of commercial intercourse and a concession for a naval station. By that treaty, also, the Samoan Government stipulated that this country might be called upon to extend its good offices to harmonize any difficulties which might arise between the native Government and any foreign Government." Under "the most favored nation clause" we had, moreover, "a full and identical right" to all the additional advantages stipulated in subsequent treaties between the Samoan government and the governments of Great Britain and Germany. "No change of native Government during the stipulated existence of those treaty rights could affect them or annul them, and any passage of those islands to a foreign domination under cover of a local change, with annulment of the treaty as a consequence, would be a manifest impairment of our treaty rights."

Bayard concluded his instructions by stating that Germany had offered "positive assurances, voluntarily given, that it has no desire or intention to interfere with the autonomy of the group, or with the relations which the other powers bear thereto in common with Germany." The English government had "publicly expressed its reprobation of any native movement looking toward the annexation of Samoa to the Fiji system under the British flag." As for ourselves "our policy in respect of transmarine possessions has been so long and so widely known as to require no declaration that we have no design upon Samoa for our aggrandizement. Any partial or selfish motives on our part would be, moreover, inconsistent with that attitude of perfect neutrality which we should maintain in order to render acceptable and effective any tender of our good offices under the clause of our treaty with Samoa looking thereto."

Greenebaum was advised, therefore, to "avoid any appearance of taking part in the existing questions there, against Germany," and that he should not "appear to share in what seems to be a general impression of the existence of ulterior plans of control on the part of Germany, which are authoritatively denied by that Government." His "efforts should, however, be directed to the maintenance of harmony and good-will, when these may be threatened, and to their restoration, if by any untoward course of events they should be disturbed. To your discretion and tact (a fitting opportunity arising)," wrote Bayard, "may be due a satisfactory exit from the present embarrassing situation in Samoa, with credit and honor to all parties concerned."[101]

For Greenebaum's information there was enclosed with Bayard's letter of instructions a copy of a despatch from the British acting counsul at Apia, W. B. Churchward, to Earl Granville, which, Bayard suggested, would show "the tenor of frequent communications in regard to affairs in the Samoan Islands," that had been made to our government by that of Great Britain.[102] The despatch, dated March 23, 1885, stated that the rebel party had been "strongly re-enforced" from a province on the island of Savaii, which had "always been in opposition to Malietoa." Churchward had also learned that Weber was ac-

[101] I.C., vol. 114, p. 269, Bayard to Greenebaum, June 19, 1885.
[102] *Ibid.*, pp. 11 and 12.

tively fomenting the rebellion and was urging the rebels to "appoint without delay their government officials so that when the two German men-of-war, which he tells them are daily expected, come, they will be found in a fit state of recognition." In the opinion of the British consul, only foreign intervention could prevent a civil war, and he concluded by saying: "There is not the slightest doubt that the rebels thoroughly identify Germany with their movement, that without German incentive it would never have existed, and that if German encouragement were discontinued it would fade away."[103]

On December 7, 1885, von Alvensleben's return to Washington, after an extended leave in Germany, was announced. He had an interview with Bayard on December 9 for the purpose, as he stated, of giving the United States government information concerning the intended policy of Germany in Samoa, a policy which it was expected would meet with the approval of the United States. He stated that Germany intended to assume political control only, and not interfere with any American rights. Secretary Bayard replied definitely that the United States government was not prepared to concede the position of Germany.[104] This was the first direct stand taken by the United States government against German encroachments in Samoa, and presaged friction if Germany should not find it possible to retreat from her position. For Germany to assume political control in Samoa was not exactly a violation of article V of the American-Samoan treaty, but under that article the United States had assumed the position of a benevolent protector, and German intervention would mean the virtual displacement of the United States from that preferred status.

At the time von Alvensleben had his interview with

[103] *Ibid.*
[104] Notes from German Legation, vol. 18, Alvensleben to Bayard, Dec. 9, 1885, memorandum of interview, rec'd Dec. 10.

Bayard, the latter of course knew nothing of what the German consul at Apia was planning to do. Dr. Stübel was waiting for a pretext to assume control of all Samoa as well as Apia district, and found it when King Malietoa moved his capital from Mulinuu to Apia proper. This act appeared to the German consul to be an invasion of what was to him virtually German territory, and on December 31, 1885, he ordered the hauling down of the Samoan flag.

The United States consul at Apia, Greenebaum, immediately advised the department of the act by cable,[105] and on January 9 the British minister in Washington transmitted a note to Bayard informing him that the British consul had telegraphed the Foreign Office to the same effect. The British consul had also said that he and the United States consul had protested, since it was rumored that Germany contemplated annexation.[106] The German minister also wrote Bayard on January 11 that there were rumors about a seizure of Samoa by Germany, but that he had no information. He had communicated to his government the views of the secretary of state as expressed at the interview in December.[107] The next day the United States intervened for the first time in the history of American-Samoan relations. On that day Bayard cabled to Pendleton, American minister, at Berlin, the intelligence received from the consul at Apia, namely, that the king of Samoa had been driven from his seat of government and the Samoan flag hauled down by forces from a German man-of-war. The British and American consuls had protested against the German action, "but in

[105] C.D., Apia, vol. 13, Greenebaum, Jan. 1, 1886, enclosing telegram, rec'd Mar. 2.

[106] Notes from British Legation, vol. 112, Sackville-West to Bayard, Jan. 9, 1886.

[107] Notes from German Legation, vol. 18, Alvensleben to Bayard, Jan. 11, 1886.

GERMAN-AMERICAN RIVALRY 301

what terms I am not yet informed" said Bayard. He further instructed Pendleton to advise the German foreign office that the United States expected that nothing would be done which would "impair the rights of the United States under [the] existing treaty with Samoa." The United States indeed anticipated a "fulfillment of solemn assurances heretofore and recently given that Germany seeks no exclusive control in Samoa." The relations of the United States with Samoa were those "with an independent treaty power, and our consul there [was] accredited to Samoan Government." The cable concluded with the statement that the German minister in Washington "has no instructions and is unable to communicate definite intentions of his government. Important you should ascertain precisely what they are."[108]

On the sixteenth Pendleton advised Bayard of an interview he had had with Count von Bismarck at twelve thirty o'clock on that day pursuant to instructions received. In reply to Pendleton's relation of the facts concerning German actions in Samoa the foreign minister said that "his Government was absolutely without information from its officials or people in Samoa." He remarked that on the same day, December 31, on which the British consul as well as the American had cabled "information of the same general tenor, the admiralty had received a despatch from the commander of the German vessel in those waters, whose troops [marines] are said to have landed and taken part in these alleged acts of violence, but that no mention was made in it of any such occurrences or of any cause for, or probability of, its happening, . . . and

[108] Instructions, Germany, vol. 17, telegram, Bayard to Pendleton, Jan. 12, 1886; H. Ex. Doc. no. 238, p. 15, encl. 9. The cable was sent to Phelps in London and by him forwarded by mail to Berlin immediately upon its receipt at 4 A.M. Jan. 13. (See Despatches, Great Britain, vol. 153, no. 191, Phelps to Bayard, Jan. 14, 1886, rec'd Jan. 27; H. Ex. Doc. no. 238, p. 15, encl. 10.)

he could not understand why the Government had heard nothing of the occurrences from either its consul or commander, if the facts be indeed as they were represented to the Governments of the United States and of Great Britain." To quote Pendleton further, "Continuing, he [the German foreign minister] said: 'While, therefore, I can give you no information as to the facts, only conjectures, which may, perhaps be entirely without foundation, I can say to you, as I said already a week ago to the British Ambassador that whatever may have occurred, we intend to maintain the status as it has heretofore existed. We have been satisfied with that; it has been satisfactory to the three Governments; we have neither interest nor desire to change it; but if we had, we would take no step, make no movement, without frankly consulting in advance the United States and Great Britain. If any wrong has been done it shall be righted, and reparation shall be made; and nothing shall be allowed to change the relative positions of these Governments.'"

Count Bismarck further informed Pendleton that he had instructed the German minister in Washington, von Alvensleben, to explain the situation to Secretary Bayard "freely and frankly" and to give him "all assurances". As soon as he received "authentic information regarding these events in Samoa he would communicate it to the Governments, and in the meantime hoped that these assurances as to the wishes and intentions of the German Government would allay all feeling which would naturally arise from these reports." Concluding his despatch Pendleton said: "He went so directly into the subject that I had no opportunity to say earlier, as I did say at this stage of the conversation, that the United States have a treaty with Samoa antedating that of Germany or England, securing to their citizens great advantages in the way of trade and whatever further benefits might at any time be granted to the most favored nation, and would not look with composure on an attempt from any quarter whatsoever to interfere with the provisions of that treaty, or to acquire any exclusive rights or privileges of occupancy or trade, to all of which he assented very appreciatively."[109]

On February 1, 1886, Bayard received from Phelps, the American minister in London, a despatch dated January 18 referring to Bayard's instructions of the twelfth to Pendleton, and enclosing a copy of a note from the Marquis of Salisbury on the subject of Germany's action in Samoa, the contents of which he said "will already have been communicated to you by Her Majesty's Minister at Washington." Salisbury's letter was dated January 16, and was in answer to one from Phelps of January 13 enclosing a copy of Bayard's instructions to Pendleton, and confirmed the intelligence received from Count Bismarck by Pendleton, namely, that the British government had brought to the German foreign minister's attention through Sir E. Malet the information telegraphed by the British consul at Apia, Mr. Powell, about the German actions there. Her Majesty's ambassador at Berlin had been directed at the same time to call the German government's attention "to the conventional arrangements between Great Britain, the United States and Germany regarding the independence of the Samoan Islands, and to express the confidence of Her Majesty's Government that the violent measure reported by Mr. Powell had not received the sanction of the Imperial Government." Salisbury's letter further corroborated the information given to Pendleton by Count Bismarck, in stating that the German foreign minister had said in reply to Malet's representations, that the German government had received "no

---

[109] Despatches, Germany, vol. 40, no. 168, Pendleton to Bayard, Jan. 16, 1886, rec'd Feb. 1; H. Ex. Doc. no. 238, pp. 15-16, encl. 11.

corresponding intelligence from Samoa" and that the German government "were the more surprised at the news because the commander of the *Albatross* had telegraphed on the 30 ultimo, but had made no mention of those grave incidents, and that Count Bismarck had assured him [Malet] that the Imperial Government would maintain all previous agreements with the treaty powers."[110]

On February 16, Bayard received a communication from the British representative in Washington, Sackville-West, enclosing, at the direction of the British foreign office, extracts from a despatch from the British consul at Apia, Mr. Powell. The consul reported that he urged upon the Samoan king "the necessity of keeping peace" and that his advice appeared "to have borne very desirable fruit, for during the following week 300 of Tamasese's men (rebels) returned to their allegiance to Malietoa. This, however, was immediately met by German intrigue." He had learned from "several reliable witnesses that Mr. Weber sent a large sum of money to the rebel chiefs, who then commenced to fortify their position." Powell had, however, received the pledged word from King Malietoa that there would be no "action of his to bring on the war which seems to be imminent; but he [Malietoa] remarked that 'almost the breaking of a stick might cause hostilities to commence.'" Powell was of the opinion that Malietoa deserved "the highest praise for the able manner in which he has restrained his warriors, from revenging the many insults and provocations received from the Tamasese faction, continuing over twelve months."[111]

[110] Despatches, Great Britain, vol. 153, no. 196, Phelps to Bayard, Jan. 18, 1886, rec'd Feb. 1; H. Ex. Doc. no. 238, p. 17, encl. 12.

[111] Notes from British Legation, vol. 112, Sackville-West to Bayard, Feb. 16, 1886, rec'd Feb. 16; H. Ex. Doc. no. 238, pp. 17-18, encl. 13.

GERMAN-AMERICAN RIVALRY 305

The British legation, in a note on March 30 to Bayard, stated that the secretary of state for foreign affairs wished the three treaty powers each to send a warship to Samoa to institute an inquiry and to make a joint report with suggestions as to the future government of the islands under the protection of the treaty powers.[112] Prince Bismarck was quick to oppose this move, for the next day, March 31, the British legation transmitted another note stating that Germany declined to accede to the proposal, and that therefore the matter had been abandoned by the British Foreign Office.[113]

On April 24 Pendleton sent Bayard a despatch in which he enclosed translations of articles from the *Norddeutsche Allgemeine Zeitung* and the *Berliner Tageblatt* giving the German version of the proceedings of the German consul and the men of the cruiser, *Albatross*, at Apia about the first of January. Pendleton explained that the former journal was the semi-official paper of Prince Bismarck, while the latter was in semi-opposition. The *Norddeutsche Allgemeine Zeitung* article on April 22 stated: "Our correspondent in the Samoan Islands reports: The official and private information of the 'entanglements' in the Samoan Islands, which appear in the English and American newspapers, and the complaints of the consuls of both these nations about the arbitrary and treaty-breaking conduct of Germany in these islands, need an earnest correction." The correspondent attributed the prevailing newspaper reports and editorials to a consular origin and referred to them as "these lying reports which surpass in shamelessness all that has heretofore happened in this domain." The German correspondent's version of the Stübel incident at Apia then appeared in full.

[112] *Ibid.*, vol. 113, Sackville-West to Bayard, March 30, 1886.
[113] *Ibid.*, March 31, 1886.

The *Berliner Tageblatt* of April 23 referred to charges made several weeks before in English papers, namely, "that the commander of the German cruiser, *Albatross*, had committed a great breach of international law in the Island of Apia (Samoan Islands) by the forcible seizure of the flag hoisted by King Malietoa. It was easy to see that the news originated in a purpose. In a correspondence of the *Nord-deutsche Allgemeine Zeitung* from the Samoan Islands the facts are now correctly set forth." Here followed a repetition of the account in the *Norddeutsche Allgemeine Zeitung,* and the article concluded: "The whole affair shows that the treaty relations on the Samoan Islands need urgently a more precise regulation."[114]

That Bayard also thought the time had arrived for a "more precise regulation" of the relations of the powers to Samoa as well as of their rights in those islands is evident from what soon transpired. For the moment, events in Apia again got beyond the control of the three governments concerned. While Bayard was confidently awaiting a happy solution of the recent troubles, the United States consul, Greenebaum, whom Bayard, the previous year at the time of his appointment, had expressly warned not to intervene, now complicated the situation still more by raising the United States flag over that of the Samoan government and taking the Samoan islands under American protection on May 14.[115]

The British legation on June 1 informed the State Department that the commander of the German squadron in Samoan waters, Admiral Knorr, had recognized Tamasese, and that in defense of Malietoa, Consul Greenebaum

[114] Despatches, Germany, vol. 41, no. 249, Pendleton to Bayard, Apr. 24, 1886, rec'd May 10; H. Ex. Doc. no. 238, pp. 18-19, encl. 14.
[115] H. Ex. Doc. no. 238, appendix C, report by J. B. Thurston, encl. 6, p. 291.

had declared an American protectorate over Samoa.[116] This seems to have been the first news the department had received concerning Greenebaum's exploit, but it was enough to impel the secretary of state to advise Germany and Great Britain that the act was unauthorized. In his identical instructions to Pendleton and Phelps the secretary of state declared further: "No separate protectorate by any nation desired. Suggest that German Minister here be authorized to confer with British Minister and me, and arrange that order be established. A competent and acceptable chief to be chosen by natives and upheld by three powers. Joint declaration to be made against annexation or protectorate by any of the three powers."[117]

The day after Bayard sent the instructions, he received a telegram from Phelps advising him that Lord Rosebery would assent to the conference proposed by Bayard if Germany also assented and that he (Rosebery) would confer with the German ambassador immediately.[118] On the following day, June 3, a telegraphic reply was received from the United States legation in Berlin also informing Bayard "that the German Government had confidently expected that this Government would disapprove the action of its consul at Apia, and was gratified that such was the case." Bayard's proposal for a conference in Washington was being considered.[119] Coleman, United States chargé d'affaires, also wrote a despatch on the third supplementing his telegram from Berlin of that

[116] Notes from British Legation, vol. 113, Sackville-West to Bayard, June 1, 1886.

[117] Instructions, Germany, vol. 17, telegram to Pendleton; Instructions, Great Britain, vol. 28, telegram to Phelps; H. Ex. Doc. no. 238, pp. 19-20, encl. 15.

[118] Despatches, Great Britain, vol. 153, telegram, Phelps to Bayard, June 2, 1886; H. Ex. Doc. no. 238, p. 20, encl. 16.

[119] Despatches, Germany, vol. 41, telegram, Coleman to Bayard, June 3, 1886; H. Ex. Doc. no. 238, p. 20, encl. 17.

date. In this communication he stated that although that day was a public holiday, Count Berchem, the under secretary, had received him in the place of Count Bismarck, who was absent from the city. Bayard's suggestions relative to a conference etc., "were listened to with marked interest, and I believe," said Coleman, "with satisfaction. Although Count Berchem informed me that the suggestions submitted must of course be taken *ad referendum*, yet a remark he made, viz., that the Imperial Government might perhaps prefer that the discussion of the same should take place at Berlin rather than at Washington, seemed to indicate at least his personal acceptance of the principle of your suggestion. I expressed the hope that in the event of its adoption Washington might be selected as the place for the discussion."

Count Berchem desired to know what was meant by the word "competent" in Bayard's instruction of June 1st, and "whether the three powers were to *cause* a choice of the chief to be made." To this Coleman replied that he understood the word "competent" to mean "possessing suitable personal qualities" and that his instruction from Washington "contained no suggestion as to the method of bringing about such a choice by the natives." Coleman added "that this latter point might perhaps be with propriety regarded as a matter of detail, with respect to which, as also to details connected with other of your suggestions, serious difficulties could hardly arise, if the contemplated discussion could be had upon the main points presented."[120]

On the same day that Bayard received the above despatch, June 21, he received another from Coleman, dated June 7, containing the information, that having been requested to call at the Foreign Office that day, Sunday, he

[120] Despatches, Germany, vol. 41, Coleman to Bayard, June 3, 1886, rec'd June 21; H. Ex. Doc. no. 238, pp. 20-21, encl. 18.

had been informed by Count Berchem that Prince Bismarck (then sojourning at Friedrichsrühe) had accepted the suggestions tendered in Bayard's instruction to Pendleton of June 1st. Count Berchem added that it could not be decided as yet when the proposed discussion at Washington could take place, as, owing to the lack of telegraphic communication with Samoa, some time must elapse before his government could instruct its consul there to avoid further complications and preserve the *status quo*. It would also be necessary to obtain full information as to the existing status on those islands. Instructions must also be sent to von Alvensleben at Washington. Count Berchem concluded his remarks by saying, according to Coleman, that "the Government of the United States would probably also want time for similar purposes."[121]

While these negotiations were going on, the American consul in Apia apparently had continued his independent course, for he informed Bayard by telegraph that the German consul had hauled down the German flag and acknowledged the flag of the United States. In advising on June 15 by cable the United States representatives in Berlin and London of this event, Bayard desired them to inform the German and British governments that this bare intelligence was all he had and that the consul's "unexplained action cannot prejudice course advised by this Government."[122] On the same day, June 15, Bayard wrote to the German and British representatives in Washington informing them of the contents of Greenebaum's telegram. "As I have no explanation from Mr. Greene-

[121] *Ibid.*, no. 270, Coleman to Bayard, June 7, 1886, rec'd June 21; H. Ex. Doc. no. 238, p. 21, encl. 19.

[122] Instructions, Great Britain, vol. 28, telegram, Bayard to Phelps, June 15, 1886; H. Ex. Doc. no. 238, p. 22, encl. 20. The same, *mutatis mutandis*, was sent to legation in Berlin.

baum, and have been able to send him no instructions, I am not in a position to add anything to his telegram, which, however, I at once communicate to you with the remark that nothing contained in it could appear to interfere with the plan of conjoint arrangements between the three powers, the United States, Great Britain and Germany, which I had the honor to submit to those Governments and to receive from them intimations of their satisfaction therewith.'"[123]

On June 18, Coleman informed Bayard that he had had an interview with Count von Berchem on the morning of that day when he verbally communicated the contents of the telegram from the secretary of state which he had received on the 16th. Count von Berchem "expressed his thanks," wrote Coleman, "for the information it conveyed." He said that the fact of the hauling down of his flag by the German consul had not until now been made known to him, but he was not surprised to learn that he had done so, "as instructions to that end had been sent him by his Government before the communication to the Foreign Office of the suggestions concerning Samoan affairs contained in your telegram of the 1st instant." The German government "had been willing to make this sacrifice of their prestige in the eyes of the natives which the hauling down of their flag involved, as soon as it should become possible to do so; that is to say, when the German fleet should have taken its departure." The German government was willing to do this because it was "actuated by a friendly spirit toward the Government of the United States and that of Great Britain and in the interest of the preservation of the *status quo* and the avoidance of further complications." Count von Berchem

[123] Notes to British Legation, vol. 20, Bayard to Sackville-West, June 15, 1886; H. Ex. Doc., no. 238, p. 22, encl. 21. The same, *mutatis mutandis*, was sent to the German minister.

had added: "The attitude of the British Consul, who appeared to be animated by a desire to maintain the *status quo*, was satisfactory; that of our consul [Greenebaum] alone afforded ground for concern. He hoped that instructions conducive to the preservation of the *status quo* and the avoidance of future friction had been, or would be, sent by the Government of the United States to their consul."

Coleman expressed to Count von Berchem his conviction that the secretary of state "shared his desire that all further complications should be avoided." He had "little doubt that special instructions" from Bayard had been sent to the United States consul at Apia to that end, "which might not, however, as yet have reached that officer, owing to the difficulties which existed in communicating with the Samoan Islands." Count von Berchem remarked further that Bayard's "disavowal of the claim by our consul [Greenebaum] of an American protectorate at Samoa was, of course, entirely satisfactory and conclusive on that point."

Count von Berchem further advised Coleman that instructions had been forwarded from the Foreign Office to the German minister at Washington directing him "to suggest that commissioners be sent by the three powers to Samoa to obtain for their Governments full information respecting the status there, as a preliminary to the discussion at Washington proposed by yourself [Bayard] and accepted by the German and British Governments. The German Government would, in any event, send such commissioner."[124]

Although meager advices had reached Bayard from the American consul, he was not left long in the dark after sending his communications to Germany and Great Brit-

[124] Despatches, Germany, vol. 41, no. 276, Coleman to Bayard, June 18, 1886, rec'd July 6; H. Ex. Doc. no. 238, pp. 22-23, encl. 22.

ain on the 15th. Only a few days later he received from the secretary of the navy a report sent in by Captain Day of the U.S.S. *Mohican,* giving a full account of the situation at Samoa up to May 29. The secretary of state hastened, June 22, to place in the hands of both von Alvensleben and Sackville-West copies of the report "in promotion of our proposed co-operation . . . in order that we may intelligently and harmoniously proceed in making an arrangement in behalf of our respective Governments, and with due consideration for the equal rights and privileges of all, which shall assist in the preservation of the autonomy of Samoa and secure peace and order for the inhabitants of that island group." In his note to von Alvensleben Bayard praised the recent action of Dr. Stübel, the German representative at Apia, which action, he said, "seems to have been dictated, throughout the occurrences reported by Captain Day, by a sense of liberality, justice and good feeling which can not fail to aid materially his Government, as well as that of the United States and Great Britain, in furthering a settled order in Samoa, with good understanding on all sides."[125]

Commander Day's report was dated May 28, the *Mohican* having arrived in the port of Apia on the 19th of the same month. "Much to my surprise," wrote the commander, "I found that the United States Consul, Mr. Greenebaum, had, upon the application of the King, Malietoa, and his Government, accepted the protectorate of the Samoan Islands on the 10th."[126] The king had based his application to the United States consul for protection upon article V of the American-Samoan treaty of 1878. The letter of application was dated May 10 and sometime

[125] Notes to German Legation, vol. 10, Bayard to Alvensleben, June 22, 1886, enclosure; H. Ex. Doc. no. 238, pp. 23-28, encl. 23. A similar note was sent to the British minister.

[126] *Ibid.*, enclosure, Commander H. F. Day's report, U.S.S. *Mohican,* Apia, May 28, 1886.

between that date and May 14 Greenebaum complied with the request.[127] On May 13 Malietoa requested Greenebaum to cause his opponents to disperse and return to their homes. To effect this the consul issued a proclamation on the same day.[128] Commander Day did not think that article V of the treaty justified the course taken by Greenebaum. Protection, however, was granted subject to approval by the United States, "but no one in Apia believes," wrote Day, "that approval will be forthcoming." The German admiral, according to Day, had close relations with the rebels and "took the trouble . . . to go down the coast some 15 miles to visit Tamasese." In addressing Tamasese, Admiral Knorr had encouraged that chief in the belief that Germany would soon take Samoa under her protection.[129]

While Admiral Knorr made no effort to do Malietoa honor but merely addressed him in his formal communications as "The Head Chief Malietoa," the British and American naval commanders recognized him as king. The German squadron, which had been in Samoan waters more than a month, left on May 16. On the same day the British man-of-war, *Diamond,* arrived. Her commanding officer called on Malietoa and on the following day the king was received on board with a twenty-one gun salute. "During the firing of this salute Mr. Greenebaum again hoisted the Samoan flag," wrote Day, "with the flag of the United States over it, on the Government house, where it is now displayed daily." Two days after the arrival of the *Mohican,* May 21, Commander Day arranged to receive Ma-

[127] Commander Day stated that the so-called protectorate was established on May 10. Other evidence points to the fact that the proclamation was written on May 14 but not published until May 16, the day the German squadron left Samoan waters.
[128] Notes to German Legation, vol. 10, Bayard to Alvensleben, June 22, 1886, enclosure, Exhibit B with Commander Day's report.
[129] *Ibid.,* enclosure, Exhibit C with above report.

lietoa on board his ship and gave him a twenty-one gun salute and all the other honors befitting his station.

On the same day, Dr. Stübel issued a "notice to all men" protesting against the American protectorate over Samoa proclaimed by Greenebaum.[130] "It is well known by all Samoa," he declared, "that negotiations are at present being carried on between the three powers with a view to bringing about that which will conduce to the prosperity of Samoa. These negotiations are not yet complete. For this cause German ships-of-war have left Samoa without inquiring into the transgressions of treaties and other violations of law recently committed by Malietoa. But these have been made known to the Government of Germany, in consequence of which the German flag has been kept flying at Mulinuu." The German consul added: "On this account nothing done by Malietoa during recent days is of any value whatever. It is quite impossible that protection can be extended over the Government of Samoa by the American Consul before such instructions have been received from his own Government; hence the hoisting of the American flag over the flag of the Government in Apia is of no value whatever. I emphatically protest against that act, and I exhort all Samoa to place no reliance upon it. It is of no value whatever, for they are committing acts which will cause serious trouble, since Samoa alone will be held responsible for the consequences of such acts."

On May 22, Malietoa came on board the *Mohican* and suggested that the United States consul and Captain Day "go down with the ship and have an interview with Tamasese and see if we could not bring him to Apia to talk matters over and try to reach an amicable settlement. He [Malietoa] would at the same time move his forces to the

[130] Notes to German Legation, vol. 10, Bayard to Alvensleben, June 22, 1886, enclosure, Exhibit H.

boundaries of Tamasese's province (he is governor of Aana), in order to show that he had the greater number, but promised that there should be no attack made on his part." Captain Day agreed, and Tuesday, May 25, was fixed for the demonstration. The British consul, Wilfred Powell, was invited to accompany the Americans and he accepted. "Tamasese was not inclined to see us," declared Day, "and when we appeared off his town he sent out a letter saying that we were accompanied by Samoan men, and he could not allow them on his territory. We replied that we would leave the Samoans on the boat. After we landed he tried to evade an interview, and it was only by sending a demand that he should come at once that we got him. We tried to make a satisfactory arrangement with him, but had no success. This rebellion of Tamasese was set going and has been kept going by the Germans, the principal man amongst them being one, Weber."

When Captain Day returned to the ship he found the German consul and vice consul on board. He invited the gentlemen to take passage in the *Mohican* to Apia, "and it was arranged that there should be a meeting of the consuls and commanding officers, with a view to devising some means by which the threatened civil war would be averted." The meeting was held on board the *Mohican*, and a proclamation was agreed upon.[131]

[131] *Ibid.*, Exhibit D with Commander Day's report. The proclamation follows:

"We the consuls of Germany, Great Britain and the United States of America hereby give notice that we, and our Governments, do not, and never have, in any way recognized Tamasese as King of Samoa, and order all Samoans to return to their houses and remain quiet and peaceable.

And we further demand the continued enforcement of the convention especially with regard to the neutral territory of Apia.

Apia, May 27, 1886.   Dr. Stübel,
                                Imperial German Consul-General
Wilfred Powell, H.B.M. Consul,   B. Greenebaum, United States Consul.''

On the same day that the proclamation was issued, May 27, Malietoa (according to Day's report) requested a meeting of consuls and commanding officers at the government house. The German consul did not attend, but signified his willingness to join in whatever was agreed on that was reasonable. "Malietoa told us that he had called the meeting to inform us that his Government had resolved on war. He had restrained his anger for eighteen months in the hope that in some way peace could be maintained, and he now saw no other course left. Still he was ready to receive and consider any advice that we might have to offer. It was suggested that the proclamation agreed on by the consuls had not yet been circulated, and it would be well to wait and see if it would not have the effect of causing Tamasese's followers to drop away from him. Malietoa said he was willing to do anything reasonable, and it was agreed that the German consul should be requested to write a letter to Tamasese urging him to withdraw his men from their forts on the border within twenty-four hours by noon of June 2—five days' notice. The alternative would be immediate war."

Greenebaum evidently communicated the decision of the meeting to Dr. Stübel, for on May 29, the German consul general replied to him as follows: "Sir: In acknowledging receipt of your letter of yesterdays' date, with inclosure, I have the honor to inform you that I shall proceed this morning to Leulumoega[132] in order to inform Tamasese personally of our decision, and to try to bring about in accordance with the same the peaceable settlement of the existing troubles. I shall not fail to communicate with you immediately after my return on Sunday afternoon."[133]

[132] The residence of Tamasese and ancient capital of the district of Aana.
[133] Notes to German Legation, vol. 10, Bayard to Alvensleben, June 22, 1886, Exhibit F with Commander Day's report.

On the same day, May 29, the German consul released his attachment of the municipal rights of Malietoa and hauled down the flag hoisted January 23, 1885. He informed Greenebaum of his act, saying that it was done "with a view to contribute as much as is in my power to the preservation of peace" and in conformity with instructions from his government.[134] A proclamation to the same effect was issued. There was "no desire," said the proclamation, "on the part of the Government of Germany to give any cause to anyone to say that the German flag has been the cause of war in Samoa."[135]

Thus had Germany retraced her steps in Samoa. This was due no doubt to the fact that both Great Britain and the United States were opposing the German encroachments, and until Prince Bismarck could win over Great Britain the *status quo* would be maintained. A year later when Great Britain and Germany were aligned against the United States, Prince Bismarck made another bid for German ascendancy in Samoa.

On July 7, the day after Bayard received Coleman's despatch of June 18, he communicated to Phelps in London his approval of Germany's suggestion "that the three powers should each send a commissioner to Samoa, to gain full information prior to the contemplated discussion" at Washington. The suggestion, he added, was in line with the original suggestion of the United States government, "that the existing representation of the three Governments at Apia should be replaced by officers having no connection with past events and able to view the situation impartially."[136] He concluded by requesting Phelps "to inform the British foreign office that this Government will in all probability be able to send out a

[134] *Ibid.*, Exhibit E.   [135] *Ibid.*, Exhibit G.
[136] Bayard might have added that the suggestion was also in line with the British proposal of the previous March.

special agent by the steamer leaving San Francisco, July 31, which will touch at Samoa en route for Auckland.''[137]

On July 22, the secretary of state wrote his instructions to George H. Bates of Delaware, whom he had appointed to go to Samoa as a special agent of the department.[138] Bayard recalled the fact that the Samoan islands were "almost the sole remaining neutral territory in Oceanica. The movement towards annexation or protection, of which the absorption of the Fiji islands by Great Britain was an early and striking example, has progressed until Tahiti, the New Hebrides, the Marshall, and the Gilbert groups have passed under the more or less immediate domination of particular European flags. Hawaii remains autonomous because possessing a complete and stable native government and independent treaties; these establish its place as a sovereign state in the family of nations. Samoa, while not possessing a stable, native, and autonomous sovereign Government such as that of Hawaii, enjoys, nevertheless, a guaranteed neutrality under the separate treaties which several of the maritime powers have concluded with the native Government."

Bayard pointed out further that the first of these treaties was concluded between the Samoan islands and the United States in 1878, and was followed by similar, although fuller treaties with Great Britain and Germany. The Samoan community not being wholly civilized these treaties retained full extraterritorial rights in favor of each of the contracting parties. "To administer the principle of extra-territorial jurisdiction," Bayard continued, "concerted action sprang up between the three treaty powers. It found expression in the municipality conven-

[137] Instructions, Great Britain, vol. 28, no. 348, Bayard to Phelps, July 7, 1886; H. Ex. Doc. no. 238, p. 29, encl. 24.

[138] Special Missions (Instructions) vol. 3, pp. 451-464, no. 1, Bayard to Bates, July 22, 1886; H. Ex. Doc. no. 238, pp. 29-32, encl. 25.

tion of 1879, establishing a local government for the town and adjacent territory of Apia. Although for reasons connected with their general foreign policy, the United States are not formally signatories to this convention, they have joined in executing its terms, and the consular representative of the United States has been and still is a member of the joint municipal government of Apia."

Bates was authorized "to disavow the action of Consul Greenebaum in assuming a protectorate over Samoa." The government was "unwilling to assume such a protectorate, either for itself alone, or under any joint arrangement whereby the native autonomy of Samoa would be replaced by a permanent tri-partite Government of the powers. It recognizes, however, that the temporary situation in the islands may prove to be such as to require the joint effort of the treaty powers to preserve order and insure stable government, in which native interests shall be under autonomous native control, while foreign extraterritorial interests shall remain, without clashing, under the joint care of their several representatives. The present municipal arrangement, by which the presidency of the board is held in turn by each one of the three consuls, appears to offer a clue to the problem of administration of foreign interests in the whole group. With such interests native dissensions and disturbances should not be allowed to interfere in any way."

Bates was however further advised "that the concern of the three powers with the neutral existence of Samoa is not limited by their joint municipal control of the foreign interests there established. Each has its treaty with the native government, and their several rights run side by side, so that any predominance of one would clash with the interests of the others. This is admitted by the treaties themselves. Those of Germany and Great Britain each recognize the prior treaty with the United States, and both, by implication and in terms, bind those powers to respect it. This is especially true of the right to maintain coaling stations on the islands, which was first secured by the United States by their treaty of 1878, a portion of the harbor of Pago Pago being set apart for the purpose. The British and German treaties followed with similar provisions, the former expressly recognizing the prior right of the United States in the premises by providing that their national stations should not encroach on that portion of the harbor already secured to the United States. We have here the principle of neutralization distinctly enunciated, and this circumstance has had an important influence on all that has since transpired. It is of special importance to the United States, for in no other part of Polynesia is a right of this nature possessed by them. In this relation I may draw your attention to the recent treaty arrangements between Great Britain and Germany of the 6th of April last, concerning acquisition of territorial or administrative rights over the unattached islands of the Pacific, by the sixth article of which it is declared that the arrangement does not apply to the Samoan Islands in view of the treaty rights therein, not only of the several contracting parties, but of the United States as well.''

Bates proceeded to Samoa shortly after he received his instructions, arriving at Apia on August 17. He found that Herr G. Travers, the German consul general at Sydney, had arrived before him to act as special commissioner for Germany. Dr. Stübel had been recalled from his post pending the investigation, and the duties of the German consulate had devolved upon the vice consul, Sonnenschein. The acting governor of Fiji, John B. Thurston, arrived in Apia, August 24, on board the British ship, *Miranda*. He had received telegraphic instructions to go to Samoa to act as special commissioner for Great Britain. Several meetings were held by the three representatives but their investigations were held separately and separate reports were made. The report by Bates, dated December 10, was very detailed. It contained a historical sketch of the Samoan relations, and recommended foreign control, suggesting that the United States might take a mandate.[139]

[139] Special Agents, vol. 2, report by George H. Bates, Dec. 10, 1886. Taken from portion not printed in H. Ex. Doc. no. 238, appendix A.

CHAPTER X

THE WASHINGTON CONFERENCE, 1887

THE special commissioners of the three treaty powers having reported their findings in Samoa and made their recommendations for the future guidance of their respective countries, the suggestion came from Germany that extracts of these reports be exchanged among the powers. This occurred late in February, 1887, when the German minister in Washington transmitted to the State Department an extract from the report of the German special commissioner, Travers, at the same time expressing the hope that the American government would reciprocate. According to von Alvensleben's note a copy of the extract was also being sent to the British government.[1]

But in the midst of preparations for the conference, which was to be held on the basis of the *status quo* in Samoa, Bayard received a despatch from the American vice consul at Apia dated January 31, which caused considerable uneasiness and speculation in official circles. This was manifest from Bayard's note to von Alvensleben just a week after the German minister had transmitted the above mentioned report. Indeed, the new development seemed to be a preliminary step, even before the conference assembled in Washington, to secure that preponderance of power in Samoa upon which Germany in the years 1887 and 1888 was particularly bent. Bayard wrote in part as follows: "It is stated in substance that a Mr. Brandeise, lately connected with the German Con-

[1] Notes from German Legation, vol. 18, Alvensleben to Bayard, Feb. 23, 1887; H. Ex. Doc. no. 238, p. 42, encl. 35a.

sulate at Apia, has been sent under pay and with the title of general to give military instruction to Tamasese in promotion of his rebellion against the Government of Malietoa. The vice consul further states that this action has been made the subject of earnest remonstrance by Malietoa to the Imperial German Government. I trust that the just and benevolent plan of co-operation by the three Powers will not be allowed to be impeded by any such inconsistent and maleficent action as has been so reported, and if any such steps have been taken that your Government will promptly check such action by its officials or under color of their approval.''[2]

No reply to Bayard's note was received until April 15, when a note from von Alvensleben stated that the German government was "not aware that a certain Mr. Brandeise at Apia sustains, or has sustained relations with the German consulate at that place, or that he has become associated with Chief Tamasese. The Imperial Government, moreover, has received no information concerning any representations made by Chief Malietoa on account of what has been done by Mr. Brandeise.'' Granting the statement made by von Alvensleben to be true, we see here an example of how badly informed the German Government was at this juncture, showing, moreover, how consuls could act at distant posts without the knowledge of their home governments due to the lack of cable communications or the failure on their part to inform their governments promptly by mail of important steps taken. Becker, the German consul, as a matter of fact, had acknowledged, on February 10, the receipt of a letter dated January 31 from the Samoan government complaining about the relations of Brandeis with Tamasese, and if he had written the home government about it, his

[2] Notes to German Legation, vol. 10, p. 482, Bayard to Alvensleben, Mar. 2, 1887; H. Ex. Doc. no. 238, p. 43, encl. 36.

letter could have easily reached Berlin before von Alvensleben's note of April 11.[3]

In the German note exception was taken to Bayard's reference to Tamasese's alleged rebellion against Malietoa, showing conclusively that the two governments were diametrically opposed to each other concerning the native government of Samoa and what the *status quo* implied. While the United States was consistently recognizing Malietoa as sole king of Samoa, Germany was just as consistently taking the ground that Malietoa and Tamasese were merely two chiefs contending for the kingship with Tamasese enjoying her especial favor. In fact, no change in German policy had taken place since the signing of the truce, June 8, 1886, on board the U.S.S. *Mohican*. Germany was merely marking time for the Washington Conference to grant her a mandate over the Samoan islands, meanwhile keeping Tamasese in view as a possible puppet king.[4]

In support of Germany's objection to Bayard's reference to Tamasese as a rebel, von Alvensleben enclosed a tabular statement prepared by Travers designed to show that Tamasese's adherents were nearly four times as numerous as those of Malietoa. Von Alvensleben concluded his note, however, by saying that the imperial government shared the view "that all propositions looking to a settlement of the question of sovereignty in Samoa,

[3] H. Ex. Doc. no. 238, p. 47, encl 5 in encl. 38, Carter to Bayard, April 2, 1887.

[4] In his note to Malietoa of Feb. 10, Becker referred to a previous note dated Nov. 12, 1886, in which he had informed Malietoa that the imperial government had instructed him upon assuming his consular duties to recognize the Tamasese government as well as that of Malietoa. Therefore the reference in the Samoan government's note of Jan. 31 to Tamasese's adherents as "rebels" had "greatly surprised" Becker, and he informed Malietoa that if any future communications contained such references, he would inform the imperial government, with dire consequences to follow for Malietoa. (See encl. 5 in encl. 38 in H. Ex. Doc. no. 238. p. 47 as above.)

should be reserved for the consideration of the Conference of the three treaty Powers which is to meet at Washington, and that there is no occasion for anyone of the treaty Powers to interfere, without the co-operation of the others, in existing party questions."[5] This was a promise that only by joint action or intervention would Germany seek to secure her rights; the future was to show how she kept that promise.

While difficulties with Germany over Samoa were still to be seen on the international horizon in the spring of 1887, other complications appeared in the most unexpected quarter. During his visit in the United States following the flag raising episode of the previous May, Greenebaum had been given to understand that his services would no longer be needed as a United States representative in Samoa, and it was understood at the State Department that he would resign from his post at Apia before his departure from Washington or soon thereafter.[6] But Greenebaum did not resign, and, while in Honolulu early in September on his return to Samoa, actually persuaded the Hawaiian government to give him an appointment as vice consul of Hawaii at Apia. This action by Hawaii was all the more plausible for, as the Hawaiian minister of foreign affairs in a conversation with Mr. Merrill, the American minister, explained, "as Mr. Greenebaum was now United States consul at that point [Apia] and lately having visited Washington was presumably fully informed as to the views and policy of the United States Government respecting the islands, it had been deemed expedient to grant him vice consular powers in order that Hawaii might be in accord with the

[5] Notes from German Legation, vol. 19, Alvensleben to Bayard, April 11, 1887, rec'd April 15; H. Ex. Doc. no. 238, p. 50, encl. 39.
[6] Instructions, Hawaii, vol. 3, p. 24, no. 32, Bayard to Merrill, Oct. 15, 1886; H. Ex. Doc. no. 238, p. 39, encl. 32.

United States Government respecting the policy to be pursued toward the Samoan group.'"[7]

Thus Greenebaum returned to Apia ostensibly representing two governments, the United States without authority, and Hawaii with his new commission. His presence in Samoa, however, occasioned considerable irritation in German official circles, for immediately upon receipt of intelligence from Australia that Greenebaum had returned and had resumed charge of the American consulate, Count Bismarck on October 2 showed Pendleton the telegram and said that if Greenebaum's reported action were by authority of the United States it seemed "to conflict with von Alvensleben's report of [a] very satisfactory understanding with Mr. Bayard that Greenebaum should no longer hold the post in Samoa." As Pendleton could give no explanation, Count Bismarck had asked him to telegraph Bayard. "This reported action," said Pendleton, "though believed to be without authority, evidently causes annoyance.'"[8] When Pendleton's telegram was received, the president immediately suspended Greenebaum, who placed his resignation in the hands of Bates, the United States special commissioner to Samoa, for transmission to Washington.[9]

The intelligence that Greenebaum was no longer consul of the United States was communicated to the Hawaiian minister of foreign affairs at Bayard's request, and our representative at Honolulu was thereupon given to understand that it was "the intention of [the Hawaiian] Government to send at an early day either a diplomatic commissioner or a consul to reside permanently at the

[7] Despatches, Hawaii, vol. 22, no. 79, Merrill to Bayard, Sept. 6, 1886, rec'd Oct. 9; H. Ex. Doc. no. 238, p. 37, encl. 50.

[8] Despatches, Germany, vol. 42, Pendleton to Bayard, Oct. 2, 1856, telegram; H. Ex. Doc. no. 238, p. 38, encl. 31.

[9] Instructions, Hawaii, vol. 3, p. 24, no. 32, Bayard to Merrill, Oct. 25, 1886; H. Ex. Doc. no. 238, p. 39, encl. 32.

Samoan Islands, and that on the appointment of such representative Mr. Greenebaum's functions as vice-consul will cease."[10]

The Hawaiian government was not long in making the change, and, incidentally, in causing more complications. On January 31 Bayard received a despatch from Honolulu, dated December 27, informing him that on December 22, King Kalakaua had commissioned the Honorable John E. Bush (a half-caste Hawaiian) as "Minister plenipotentiary to the Kings of Samoa and Tonga and the independent chiefs and peoples of Polynesia." Bush had left for Samoa on December 26 with a secretary of legation and two attachés. The "tenor of the instructions given to Mr. Bush" would be communicated to the United States government "through the Hawaiian minister at Washington." Meanwhile, King Malietoa had informed King Kalakaua "that he will not receive or recognize Mr. B. Greenebaum as a representative in any capacity of the Hawaiian Kingdom."[11]

But Bush, on the other hand, was received with open arms. The official reception occurred on January 7. In handing the Samoan king an autograph letter from the Hawaiian king, Bush expressed his sovereign's deep interest in the welfare of Malietoa and his people, "recognizing in them a people of a kindred race closely allied to the Hawaiians by blood, by language and by historical traditions." King Kalakaua had "viewed with solicitude," Bush continued, "the internal difficulties that have encompassed the Government of Samoa and the possibility of foreign intervention affecting its independence" and he (Bush) was instructed to express the king's "sym-

[10] Despatches, Hawaii, vol. 22, no. 91, Hastings to Bayard, Nov. 13, 1886, rec'd Dec. 20; H. Ex. Doc. no. 238, p. 39, encl. 33.

[11] Ibid., no. 93, Hastings to Bayard, Dec. 27, 1886, rec'd Jan. 31; H. Ex. Doc. no. 238, p. 40, encl. 34.

pathy and hope that you may succeed in maintaining peaceful stability and perfect autonomy, and should you desire the friendly advice and encouragement of His Majesty Kalakaua it will be freely given.'' Then the Hawaiian representative to Samoa announced that ''as a further token of friendship'' his sovereign conferred upon King Malietoa the ''Grand Cross of His Royal Order of the Star of Oceania, an order specially instituted to decorate the kings and chiefs of Polynesia and those who may in any way contribute to the welfare and advancement of Polynesian communities.'' The Samoan king replied in part as follows: ''It is true that the Hawaiians and Samoans are related by blood and other ties. I have in my possession genealogical records which prove that your kings and people and myself are related. We have often met here representatives of America, England and Germany, but this is the first time I have had the pleasure to meet an envoy from Hawaii, though we are so near to each other and a similar people.''[12]

About ten days later King Malietoa wrote an autograph letter to King Kalakaua: ''And now with great pleasure and delight I welcome Your Majesty's plenipotentiary in the person of Mr. John Edward Bush, Knight Grand Cross of Your Royal Order of the Crown of Hawaii, etc., to these my islands, for the purpose of meeting together with us. I am much pleased, and especially because it seems to me now, from the way you have remembered me, that your love for us is unchanged. By traditions we have learned the truth that your people are of one blood with us.''[13]

---

[12] Despatches, Hawaii, vol. 23, no. 105, Merrill to Bayard, Feb. 15, 1887, rec'd March 3. Speeches published in *Hawaii Government Gazette*, Feb. 14, 1887; clipping enclosed with despatch; H. Ex. Doc. no. 238, p. 42, encl. in encl. 35.

[13] *Ibid.;* H. Ex. Doc. no. 238, p. 41, encl. in encl. 35.

WASHINGTON CONFERENCE, 1887

In sending the newpaper clipping containing the above quoted letter, Merrill informed Bayard that the Hawaiian government had by recent mail from Samoa received a request from Malietoa that Mr. Carter, the Hawaiian envoy at Washington, be permitted to act as a representative of the Samoan Islands as well. Mr. Gibson, the Hawaiian minister of foreign affairs, had consented thereto, and Malietoa's full authority and personal instructions had been forwarded to Carter by Gibson with his (Gibson's) instructions to act as representative of Samoa "in the event the exercise of such authority as has been granted by King Malietoa meets with encouragement by the proper authorities in Washington."[14] In point of fact Bayard was not averse to receiving Carter as the spokesman of Samoa but informed him at first that it seemed better to regard him as charged provisionally with Samoan affairs. In the same way Bayard would like to see him represent Tonga as well.[15] Three weeks later Bayard informed Carter that he was recognized as the representative of the Samoan Islands, and that he would be pleased to receive communications from him in that capacity.[16]

These Hawaiians and Samoans, however, went further than merely making pretty speeches and writing sympathetic letters, for soon after his arrival in Samoa, the Hawaiian envoy was informed that the Samoan government "had determined to ask for some immediate agreement for a confederation with Hawaii."[17] A treaty was signed by Malietoa on February 17, with the approval of the Taimua and Faipule and accepted in the name of the Ha-

[14] *Ibid.;* H. Ex. Doc. no. 238, p. 40, encl. 35.
[15] Credences, vol. 6, p. 465, Department of State.
[16] *Ibid.*, vol. 6, p. 470.
[17] Notes from Hawaiian Legation, vol. 3, Carter to Bayard, Apr. 2, 1887, rec'd Apr. 4, encl. 1; H. Ex. Doc. no. 238, p. 46, encl. 1 in encl. 38, extract from letter no. 11, Bush to Hawaiian minister of foreign affairs, dated March 1.

waiian government by Bush, whose action was ratified by King Kalakaua on March 20. The treaty is a short one and reads as follows: "By virtue of my inherent and recognized rights as King of the Samoan Islands by my own people, and by treaty with the three great powers of America, England, and Germany, and by and with the advice of my Government, and the consent of Taimua and Faipule, representing the legislative powers of my Kingdom, I do hereby freely and voluntarily offer and agree, and bind myself to enter into a political confederation with His Majesty Kalakaua, King of the Hawaiian Islands; and I hereby give this solemn pledge that I will conform to whatever measures may hereafter be adopted by His Majesty Kalakaua, and be mutually agreed upon to promote and carry into effect this political confederation, and to maintain it now and forever."[18] In approving the treaty on March 20, the Hawaiian king expressly did so "subject to the obligations which His Majesty Malietoa may be under to those foreign powers with which he and the people of Samoa and the Government thereof have at this time any treaty relations."[19]

That the Hawaiian government did not take its responsibilities relative to Samoa lightly, is clear from the instructions received by its minister in Washington. On April 2, Carter addressed a note to Bayard enclosing the proposed treaty with Samoa and other documents.[20] The

[18] H. Ex. Doc. no. 238, encl. 2 in encl. 38.

[19] Despatches, Hawaii, vol. 23, no. 111, Merrill to Bayard, Mar. 29, 1887, rec'd April 23, encl. Clipping from *Hawaii Government Gazette*, Mar. 28; H. Ex. Doc. no. 238, p. 44, encl. in encl. 37.

[20] At that time neither Carter nor Bayard knew that the treaty had been approved by the Hawaiian government on the 20th of the previous month, and consequently Carter's note and Bayard's reply on April 12 referred to the treaty as being merely proposed. Bayard first received the information of the Hawaiian approval on April 23 in Merrill's despatch no. 111, dated March 29.

treaty was "entirely spontaneous on the part of King Malietoa and his chiefs," said Carter, "and was the prompt and not unnatural result of the appearance in Samoa of a Hawaiian Embassy representing as it did, a king closely allied in blood to the Samoans, and holding his throne under a constitution such as the Samoans would be glad to accept for their own." The Hawaiian cabinet wished to assure themselves, however, "particularly as to the treaty obligations which Samoa is under with foreign powers, and those which those powers may be likely to desire to impose on that country under new circumstances." It was hoped, moreover, that the powers would "see a solution of all their difficulties with Samoa in the attitude now assumed by her toward Hawaii." Bayard was assured that "the Hawaiian Government is quite prepared to assist the Samoan people in the work of organizing and administering government, in the formation of a proper police, and the establishment of proper courts of law, in the settlement of land tenure, and in making arrangements for a revenue and for the expenditure of the same for the public benefit."

The lack of public revenue in Samoa was "one serious difficulty which must have obstructed attempts at proper government" and since in the treaty of 1878 with the United States the Samoan government had bound itself not "to levy either import or export duties on goods conveyed to or from the kingdom in American vessels," the Hawaiian government requested to know whether "the United States Government would be disposed to retire from a stipulation which would prevent so greatly the development of the revenue of the country, leaving it entirely dependent on internal taxation." In conclusion the Hawaiian minister referred to certain documents enclosed with his note "relating to the sale of arms to Samoans who are in rebellion against the acknowledged King of

Samoa." The Hawaiian government wanted "to draw attention to this matter, in the hopes that the Governments of the powers interested will use their influence in preventing such sales."[21]

Considerable space has been devoted to recounting the development of the fantastic Hawaiian-Samoan rapprochement, not because it resulted in anything tangible, but because of its pathos. Here were the Samoans grasping at what seemed to them the only means left to ward off the political encroachments of Germany. While they had invited American and British protection from time to time, there is no record of their ever having approached Germany with a view to obtaining such a political relationship. There can be no gainsaying the fact, of course, that some of their appeals to the United States and to Great Britain were the result of influence brought to bear upon them by interested consuls, business men, and missionaries, but at no time can it be said that Weber or the German consuls obtained from any large representative group in Samoa a request for a German protectorate. Rebels, such as the Puletua back in the late seventies, might buy guns from the Germans and a Tamasese might permit himself to be set up as a puppet king by them, but even Tamasese never requested German annexation.

The reason for this unwavering antipathy toward things German can only be understood if it is remembered that in the minds of the Samoans in general the German empire was from the very first synonymous with the name of Theodor Weber, German consul, and the firm which he represented, Godeffroy & Sons of Hamburg. In these latter days, also, the empire was still confused with the name of Weber and the "Old Firm's" successor "Die Deutsche Handels und Plantagen Gesellschaft für Süd-

[21] Notes from Hawaiian Legation, vol. 3, Carter to Bayard, April 2, 1887, rec'd April 4; H. Ex. Doc. no. 238, p. 45, encl. 38.

See Inseln zu Hamburg," which in popular parlance was called the "D.H. and P.G." No German missionaries had ever come to Samoa to live among the natives with a view to educating them and assisting them in various other ways as the English had done. In fact, the only opportunity the natives had had of forming any opinion of Germans was through the business operations of Weber and his associates. These operations appeared to the Samoans as bordering on the predatory, and it seemed to them, moreover, that German warships came and went merely "to fetch and carry for the firm" as Robert Louis Stevenson so aptly characterized the relationship between the German empire and German trade in Samoa. There was nothing unusual in this situation, of course. The British empire protected British traders also; but with a difference. British law, while it protected British traders in all the out of the way places, also restrained them from committing palpable offenses against defenseless natives, and in consequence the British trading methods were usually less open to criticism. The origin of the German colonial empire was too recent to have enabled the Germans to work out a code for the natives in the Pacific similar to that enforced by the British high commissioner for the Western Pacific. The German firm in Samoa was interested in a strong government for Samoa, it is true, but its efforts in that direction were conditioned solely upon its desire for protection for its plantations, and not because of any paternal care for the Samoans themselves. It owned, moreover, the choicest lands of the island of Upolu, and this fact also was held up to the Samoans by jealous competitors as a crime against their inalienable rights. "Even from the deck of an approaching ship," wrote Stevenson, "the island is seen to bear its signature . . . zones of cultivation showing in a more vivid tint of green on the dark vest of forest. The total area in use is near ten thousand acres. Hedges of fragrant lime enclose, broad avenues intersect them. You will walk for hours in parks of palm tree alleys, regular, like soldiers on parade; in the recesses of the hills you may stumble on a mill-house, toiling and trembling there, fathoms deep in superincumbent forest.'' The firm was successful but at the sacrifice of peaceful relationships with the natives. Stevenson summed up the situation partly when he wrote: ". . . the true center of trouble, the head of the boil of which Samoa languished, is the German firm."[22]

The tradition of kinship between Samoans and Hawaiians had existed in both groups of islands for many centuries, and if the interest in the tradition had become somewhat weakened as the era of a common homeland receded more and more into the background, ethnological researches by the American and English missionaries in these groups of islands had in later years served to revive the interest to a considerable extent. Education for the Hawaiians, moreover, and the assistance to the Hawaiian government provided by the American missionaries, had its counterpart in similar services rendered the Samoans by the English missionaries. It was natural, therefore, for the natives of Hawaii or Samoa to look to America or to England for protection at certain periods of crisis. This was particularly true of the Samoans, an impressionable people, whose credulity was proverbial, and who would believe almost any American or Englishman when he talked to them of a possible protectorate. Unauthorized flag hoistings by American consuls would, of course, raise the hopes of the Samoans also, only to be dashed to the ground by the recall of these offending officials. Such a condition existed when Greenebaum was no longer permitted to serve as a representative at Apia.

[22] Robert Louis Stevenson, *A Foot-Note to History*, etc., pp. 393-400.

WASHINGTON CONFERENCE, 1887

When therefore, it seemed to the Samoans that the promise made in the treaty of 1878 by the United States to employ its good offices for the purpose of adjusting their difficulties was apparently never going to be fulfilled, the Samoan king seized the opportunity of asking aid from Hawaii. He was aware that Hawaii sustained a unique political position in relation to the United States, and it is not at all unlikely that he looked upon an alliance with Hawaii as bringing Samoa under the political aegis of the United States indirectly, if not directly, as he would have preferred.

The immediate cause of Malietoa's spontaneous appeal to Hawaii was in all probability the simultaneous appearance in Samoa's public life of the picturesque Bavarian ex-officer and adventurer, Brandeis, and the Hawaiian minister, Bush. The reception of Bush occurred on January 7. Malietoa's letter of protest to Becker, the German consul, concerning the relations of Brandeis with the rebel, Tamasese, was dated January 31. Becker's reply was dated February 10, and Malietoa's meeting with Bush and signing the treaty with Hawaii took place just one week later, February 17. Becker had, as a matter of fact, written Malietoa in a severe tone, and Malietoa easily discerned that Germany was in no mood to recognize his exclusive claims to the kingship. Becker's note read in part: "I am in receipt of the letter stamped with Your Government Seal, dated 31st of January, from Mr. William Coe, complaining about Brandeis, a German gentleman, gone to Leulumoega, in a military character, now in seditious relations to the Samoan Government and attempting insurrections, requesting me to do something to Brandeis. . . . Be it well known by your Majesty relative to the above létter, the Government of the Emperor-King of Germany is in friendly relations with the Government of Leulumoega, as it is with Your Government. The letter, with the seal, sent to the German consulate, greatly surprised me in calling the Government of Leulumoega 'rebels.' " Becker concluded his note by warning Malietoa that drastic action would be taken by the German government if he should send any more communications similar to the one received.[23]

Bush took up the cudgels for Malietoa as soon as the Hawaiian-Samoan treaty was signed, and already on February 28 wrote to Gibson, the Hawaiian foreign minister, in part as follows: "In view of the insulting tenor of the letter [Becker to Malietoa, Feb. 10] and its decisive recognition of the rebel party, in violation of the treaty stipulations and other agreements, Mr. Coe,[24] in behalf of the Samoan Government, has requested me to ask Your Excellency to assist them in this way. If Mr. Carter has been allowed to accept the commission as Minister Plenipotentiary for Samoa at Washington, will Your Excellency instruct him to ask as may be necessary to seek explanation of the German Minister at Washington or otherwise in regard to this matter, also as to the illegal acts of Mr. Weber in supplying firearms to the party in rebellion. I further inclose a copy of an affidavit in proof of the sale of firearms by Mr. Weber's agents. Many more affidavits of a similar nature could be obtained if required. The Samoan Government have often with substantial proofs protested to the German Consul against Mr. Weber's illicit trade but never obtained satisfaction, as all the German Consuls since Mr. Weber's time have been under his dictation and control."[25] Bush's correspondence with Gibson was forwarded to Carter in Washington and by

[23] Notes from Hawaiian Legation, vol. 3, Carter to Bayard, April 2, 1887; H. Ex. Doc. no. 238, p. 47, encl. 5 in encl. 38.

[24] Samoan assistant secretary of state and Malietoa's interpreter.

[25] Notes from Hawaiian Legation, vol. 3, Carter to Bayard, April 2, 1887, rec'd April 4; H. Ex. Doc. no. 238, p. 47, encl. 4 in encl. 38.

him sent to Bayard in the Hawaiian minister's note of April 2, quoted above.

On April 12, while still ignorant of the favorable action taken on the Hawaiian-Samoan treaty by the Hawaiian government, Bayard replied to Carter's note of April 2. "The serious responsibility which, apparently, would be entailed upon the Hawaiian kingdom by such an alliance as that now proposed [he wrote] and the close commercial relations under the existing treaties of Hawaii with the United States, cause me hesitation before giving encouragement or approval to a step which may involve important results. The remoteness of Samoa from Hawaii would render communication difficult, and the expense of a naval force commensurate with the obligations incurred would be a heavy burden upon the pecuniary resources of Hawaii. . . . Affairs at Samoa are now, and have been for some time past, the subject of co-operative and friendly consideration by the Governments of the United States, Germany and Great Britain; and to interpose the authority and responsibility of the Hawaiian Government would necessarily entangle the latter in pending questions of which the origin was beyond Hawaiian discretion and control, and, to an appreciable extent, embarrass the action of the three powers in reaching a solution of problems affecting native as well as foreign interests in Samoa. It would seem, therefore, from every point of view which is accessible to me, to be ill-advised for Hawaii to take any ground at the present time, and during the pendency of issues in the origin of which the Government of Hawaii could have had no concern, which might tend to bring that kingdom into conflict in Samoa with other interests directly concerned."[26]

In his instructions to Phelps and Pendleton, our minis-

[26] Notes to Hawaiian Legation, vol. 1, p. 119, Bayard to Carter, April 12, 1887; H. Ex. Doc. no. 238, p. 51, encl. 40.

ters in London and Berlin, respectively, Bayard referred to the possible consequences to the United States if the treaty went into effect: "The proposition advanced, involving an 'alliance and confederation' between the King Kalakaua and King Malietoa, is capable of such far-reaching consequences to Hawaii and, indirectly, to the United States, to whose system the Hawaiian Islands commercially hold close relation (with a political importance added—a natural result of their geographical position), that I cannot bring myself to regard it with favor, if, as I apprehend, it represents an expansive policy of King Kalakaua looking to the acquisition of political control in the outlying island groups of the Southern Pacific." Neither Phelps nor Pendleton was instructed to make any formal communication to the government to which he was accredited. The information was merely sent to them in case the subject should be brought up by the secretary or minister of foreign affairs in one or the other country.[27]

When Merrill's despatch of March 29 was received on April 23, Bayard learned that the treaty had been confirmed and ratified by the Hawaiian government on the twentieth of March. Bayard wrote Merrill a reply on April 28, in which he observed that the treaty was "expressly made 'subject to the obligations which His Majesty Malietoa may be under to those foreign powers with which he and the people of Samoa and the Government thereof have at this time any treaty relations.' It is quite impossible at present to forecast the effect of so vague an engagement to operate *in futuro,* and conditioned upon so comprehensive a proviso." Bayard also informed Merrill that he had communicated with Carter "that such an

[27] Instructions, Great Britain, vol. 28, p. 302, no. 594, Bayard to Phelps, April 12, 1887. The same, *mutatis mutandis,* was sent to Mr. Pendleton; H. Ex. Doc. no. 238, p. 52, encl. 41.

alliance is at present inexpedient; that it does not receive the sanction or approval of this Government." Carter had no doubt informed his government, continued Bayard, of "the surprise and . . . disquietude with which the Government of the United States learns of the proposed alliance." Therefore, the correspondence was sent to Merrill for his own confidential information only, and was not to be communicated to the Hawaiian government by him.[28]

Having learned the attitude of the United States toward the Hawaiian-Samoan alliance, the government at Honolulu recalled its representative in Samoa the following July, and the new Hawaiian minister of foreign affairs, Godfrey Brown, also informed Merrill that His Majesty's training ship, *Kaimiloa,* then in Samoan waters, had been ordered to return to Hawaii. "This will terminate," wrote Merrill, "what is commonly known as the Hawaiian-Polynesian policy."[29] Thus had the American administration by its prompt action prevented the Hawaiian problem from becoming entangled with that of Samoa. Our position in Hawaii remained unweakened by our Samoan relations, and neither Germany nor Great Britain were therefore able—which very well might have happened—to negotiate with us at Washington on a purely trading basis, that is, give us a free hand in Hawaii in return for a mandate for Germany in Samoa. It was no mere coincidence that we hastened to consolidate our position in Hawaii this same year (1887), by negotiating a treaty for Pearl Harbor, thus increasing our advantages there on the basis of our preferential treaty of 1875.

[28] Instructions, Hawaii, vol. 3, p. 36, no. 45, Bayard to Merrill, April 28, 1887; H. Ex. Doc. no. 238, p. 54, encl. 44.
[29] Despatches, Hawaii, vol. 23, no. 130, Merrill to Bayard, July 13, 1887, rec'd Aug. 15; H. Ex. Doc. no. 238, p. 58, encl. 52.

In compliance with the German request, the United States communicated to the Berlin government an extract of the Bates report on March 23,[30] and sent another copy on the same day to the British minister. On the nineteenth of April Sackville-West, in obedience to instructions from the Marquis of Salisbury, communicated an extract of the report of Mr. Thurston, at the same time calling attention to the fact that the German and British reports were not in accord "as to the areas of land respectively held by owners of various nationalities." According to the report of Mr. Travers, German subjects held "almost twice the amount of uncultivated land and six times the amount of cultivated land held by British and American subjects together," whereas Thurston's report showed that "the area of lands claimed by Germans amounted to 135,122 acres; that claimed by British subjects to 283,600, and that by Anglo-Americans to 276,000; making a total of 694,722 acres; showing that apart from the value of improvements, the interests in land of German subjects are comparatively small." The British minister was instructed also to call the American government's "attention to the fact pointed out by Mr. Thurston that the land claimed by foreigners in Samoa exceeds its whole area by 24,092 acres, and to the consequent importance of the land question being settled before any change is effected in the form of government, for the resources, if not the very existence, of that government must greatly depend on the decisions arrived at." Therefore Her Majesty's government considered "it essential in the coming negotiations, before a permanent land court be established, to provide for the disposal by a commission of the enormous mass of claims by foreigners, which, if admitted, would deprive

[30] Notes to German Legation, vol. 10, p. 491, Bayard to Alvensleben, Mar. 23, 1887.

the whole Samoan population of the land.'' The British minister was instructed, moreover, to request information from Bayard when the conference was to meet, ''and to express the hope of Her Majesty's Government that it may be at an early date.''[31]

At an interview a few days later, Bayard expressed himself to Sackville-West in so friendly a tone concerning the future relations between the powers in Samoa, that the British minister was moved to express to him the British government's appreciation of his ''friendly sentiments, and their belief that the establishment of a firm government in the Navigator's Islands, capable of maintaining order and securing to all flags freedom of commerce and equality of treatment, is the common object of the three treaty powers.''[32]

Simultaneously with the movement among the powers for holding a conference to settle the Samoan muddle, the native Samoan government under Malietoa was planning to hold a meeting with the rebel party under Tamasese in an effort to induce the latter again to recognize the rule of Malietoa. This information was sent in a despatch to the Marquis of Salisbury by the British acting consul at Apia, H. F. Symonds, on the same day that Sackville-West expressed the above quoted sentiments to Bayard. ''This meeting has been arranged by Malietoa,'' wrote Symonds, ''in order to satisfy the most turbulent of his chiefs, who are constantly urging him to put down the rebellion by force, and who are becoming impatient of his passive policy.'' Symonds believed that the meeting would end quietly and peaceably, but still there was a

[31] Notes from British Legation, vol. 114, Sackville-West to Bayard, April 19, 1887; H. Ex. Doc. no. 238, p. 53, encl. 42.

[32] *Ibid.*, Sackville-West to Bayard, April 25, 1887, rec'd April 26; H. Ex. Doc. no. 238, p. 54, encl. 43.

danger of a clash and of the meeting's having just the opposite effect from promoting peace.[33] More than a month elapsed, of course, before this despatch could reach Downing Street, but it nevertheless moved Salisbury to instruct Sackville-West to propose to Bayard "that telegraphic instructions should be sent to the Consuls of the three treaty powers to endeavor to maintain peace on [a] basis of *status quo* pending [the] decision of [the] conference."[34] Sackville-West's note was received by the State Department June 16, just nine days before the opening of the Washington Conference, and on June 21 Bayard informed the British minister that he was pleased to express his concurrence in Salisbury's suggestion[35] and enclosed a copy of his telegram to H. M. Sewall, the American representative at Apia, dated the twentieth, and reading as follows: "Treaty powers endeavoring to secure permanent native government for Samoa. Strongly advise natives to avoid resort to force, which would endanger Samoa's best interest."[36]

The same information was communicated to von Alvensleben the same day, Bayard expressing the understanding that such action was taken "to endeavor to maintain peace in Samoa on the basis of the *status quo* pending the decision of the conference lately initiated here for the friendly consideration of the state of things in those islands, and as being in the line of the views developed in the conferences so far held with yourself and

[33] Notes from British Legation, vol. 114, Sackville-West to Bayard, June 16, 1887, enclosing despatch, Symonds to Salisbury, April 25; H. Ex. Doc. no. 238, p. 55, encl. in encl. 46.

[34] *Ibid.*

[35] Notes to British Legation, vol. 20, p. 504, Bayard to Sackville-West, June 21, 1887; H. Ex. Doc. no. 238, p. 56, encl. 48.

[36] I.C., vol. 121, Bayard to Sewall, June 20, 1887; H. Ex. Doc. no. 238, p. 56, encl. in encl. 47.

WASHINGTON CONFERENCE, 1887   343

Sir Lionel West."[37] Von Alvensleben replied the next day that he had "not failed to bring [the instructions of Bayard to Sewall] to the knowledge of the Imperial Government,"[38] and on the twenty-fifth Sackville-West wrote Bayard that the British consul at Apia had been "instructed to continue to do his best to maintain peace between Malietoa and Tamasese on the basis of the *status quo* pending the decision of the conference now being held on the affairs of Samoa."[39]

It has been pointed out in the previous chapter that in order to facilitate the work of the conference the three treaty powers had agreed to send to Samoa special commissioners who were to collect facts and, on the basis of these facts, to reach conclusions and give advice for the benefit of their respective governments. We saw above that extracts of the reports were exchanged among the three powers for comparison and study with a view to enabling them to get together on some workable plan of affording the natives as much autonomy as possible while assuring to the powers concerned equality of opportunities in trade.

The first session of the Washington Conference took place on June 25, Secretary Bayard, Herr von Alvensleben, and Sir Lionel Sackville-West representing the United States, Germany, and Great Britain respectively. Just prior to the formal opening of the conference, an informal meeting was held between the two ministers of Germany and Great Britain and Secretary Bayard, at the request of the ministers, for the purpose of learning the

[37] Notes to German Legation, vol. 10, Bayard to Alvensleben, June 21, 1887; H. Ex. Doc. no. 238, p. 56, encl. 47.

[38] Notes from German Legation, vol. 19, Alvensleben to Bayard, June 22, 1887, rec'd June 23; H. Ex. Doc. no. 238, p. 57, encl. 49.

[39] Notes from British Legation, vol. 114, Sackville-West to Bayard, June 25, 1887, rec'd June 27; H. Ex. Doc. no. 238, p. 57, encl. 51.

views of the United States, the meeting ending with a further request of the ministers that these views be reduced to writing. This was done, and at the first formal session of the conference, Bayard inquired of these gentlemen whether they "had received his note inclosing a draught of a plan for the settlement of Samoan affairs, and whether they had prepared any comments upon it." Both of the ministers had received the plan, but von Alvensleben, though he had prepared a memorandum, could not give it out of his hand, stating as his reason, that his government had sent him general instructions before receiving Bayard's suggestions, and these had brought up more points than the instructions covered. He was willing, however, to let his government's views be put down in the protocol as he read them. Sackville-West for the same reason "decided not to give a copy of the memorandum which he had prepared," but, like von Alvensleben, was willing that his statements, as he read them, "should be taken down by a stenographer and embodied in the protocol of the conference." Secretary Bayard, previously to von Alvensleben's and Sackville-West's statements, had remarked that since he had handed them, at their request, the plan suggested by the United States, "it seemed proper that the views of the other two Governments should be handed to him in the same way."[40] Their refusal indicated no auspicious beginning of the conference for the United States, and foreshadowed obstacles for Bayard which might prove difficult for him to surmount. To his discerning eye it appeared as though for once Downing Street were deferring to Wilhelmstrasse and that Prince Bismarck and Lord Salisbury had really struck a bargain over Samoa, leaving the United States entirely out of the reckoning. Such, in fact, was

[40] Protocols MSS, Samoan Conference at Washington, 1887, Department of State; S. Ex. Doc. no. 102, 50 Congress, 2 session, p. 5, encl. 5.

the case, but almost two years elapsed before the United States government came into possession of information corroborating its suspicions.[41]

There were six formal sessions of the Washington Conference, the last being held on July 26, just a month and a day after the first session. Two subjects loomed large in the conference, namely, the constitution of the Samoan government and the land question. Other points were brought up at the beginning, but since an agreement seemed possible on these questions, most of the discussion revolved around the two subjects named. On both of these von Alvensleben and Sackville-West were in agreement, except for certain minor details, and the conference reached no formal conclusions for the reason that Bayard remained adamant in his opposition to their proposals. The German representative, with the support of his British colleague, developed a logical scheme for German domination in the islands although he paid lip service to the proposals for the neutralization and independence of the islands and for equal opportunities for the three treaty powers; while Bayard just as logically contended for the latter proposals and at the same time mercilessly laid bare the purport of the German plan. From a careful study of the protocols it is quite clear, however, that Bayard's plan was less practicable, due to its lack of simplicity. His tripartite arrangement could not have solved the knotty problems that had afflicted Samoa ever since the coming of the Europeans and Americans; on the contrary, it might very well, like Pandora's box, have in-

[41] On November 30, 1886, Lord Salisbury had enjoined upon Sir Philip Currie the necessity of "sitting upon the Colonial Office" with regard to the Samoan question. He wrote: "We shall get into a new Angra Pequena trouble if we do not look out. That is to say, we shall force him [Bismarck] into a menacing position upon a matter upon which we are not prepared to resist him to the end and the result will be a discreditable 'skedaddle.'" (Quoted from G. Cecil, *Life of Robert Marquis of Salisbury*, IV, 36.)

creased them. Moreover, Bayard's plan would have brought about a definite reversal of our traditional policy of "no entangling alliances," and paradoxical as it may seem, the very arrangement that we fought for in 1887 and succeeded in securing in a somewhat modified form in 1889, was repudiated in 1899, for the obvious reason that it was a reversal of our traditional policy. And yet we see in Bayard's stand the adoption of a firmer tone in our foreign relations with especial reference to our interests in the Pacific, and but for his preference for a tripartite arrangement in 1887, it is difficult to conceive of any other result than that Germany would have soon annexed the whole of the Samoan islands or at least extended her protection over them with the consequent loss of Pago Pago harbor to the United States. In 1899 Germany finally annexed Western Samoa, to be sure, but the United States acquired the coveted harbor for a naval station.

The American plan, which Bayard had previously sent to the other members of the conference, was put in the protocol of the first session as if read at the conference.[42] It consisted of fifteen points:

(1) The independence and autonomy of the kingdom of Samoa were to be preserved free from the control and preponderating influence of any foreign government.

(2) The three treaty powers should assist the natives of Samoa to form and administer their government.

(3) A native king should be recognized. The United States favored Malietoa Laupepa as king and Tamasese as vice king.

(4) There should be a written constitution adopted by the king and his council composed of chiefs from the various districts. The constitution should pro-

[42] Protocols MSS, Samoan Conference at Washington, 1887, Department of State; S. Ex. Doc. no. 102, pp. 6 and 7, encl. 5.

WASHINGTON CONFERENCE, 1887

vide for a legislature consisting of the Taimua and Faipule. The former should be made up of the king, vice king, the king's council and three ministers to be nominated by the three treaty powers. The chiefs in the Taimua should be elected for life. The members of the Faipule should be elected in the ratio of one for every 2000 inhabitants and for a term of three years.

(5) The three ministers should be nominated by the powers and appointed by the king. They might hold such offices as chief secretary and minister of foreign affairs, the treasurer, and the minister of the interior. They should be appointed for a term of years and should have the right to seats and debate in the Faipule.

(6) A municipal government should be formed for Apia without interference by the foreign consuls.

(7) Foreign consuls were to retain criminal jurisdiction over their own countrymen, respectively, as before.

(8) A court for the administration of justice among the natives should be constituted, the judges to be appointed by the king and council.

(9) The constitution should prohibit the imposition of pecuniary fines upon the natives. Sentences for criminal offenses should be terms of imprisonment with labor on public roads, etc.

(10) Sale of firearms, ammunition and intoxicating liquors should be prohibited.

(11) A land commission ought to be organized before whom all claims for title to land by foreigners should be submitted, and whose judgment should be final. The land commission should consist of five members; three foreigners, nominated by the powers and appointed by the king, and two natives appointed by the king. Wherever liquor or firearms

or some other trivial consideration had been given for land by foreign individuals or companies, such sales should be considered by the commission as void.
(12) The judges of the land commission should be paid their salaries out of the revenues of the kingdom.
(13) The land commission should be required to survey and set apart of unclaimed or unoccupied land, one-tenth thereof to be rented for the use and support of public schools.
(14) For raising revenue for the support of the government, customs and tonnage dues should be levied at the several ports of entry, and to this end each of the treaty powers would negotiate identic treaties with Samoa in which the rates of said duties should be established.
(15) Each of the treaty powers should alternately keep a man-of-war in Samoan waters for four months to assist in maintaining the government so to be established and to preserve peace and order.

The German memorandum[43] read at the first session by Herr von Alvensleben consisted of eight points:
(1) "King Malietoa having notoriously violated his treaty obligations toward Germany, and having even among the natives comparatively but few partisans, while a completely organized counter-government has been formed under Tamasese, a new election of king would have to take place according to the customs of the country."
(2) For purely native affairs the administration of the country could be carried on as before by the king, assisted by the native council composed of prominent chiefs.

[43] Protocols MSS; S. Ex. Doc. no. 102, pp. 7 and 8, encl. 5.

(3) A foreign adviser to the king should be appointed in order to strengthen the king's authority and maintain order and peace in the country. This adviser should act as mandatary of the three treaty powers and should be nominated by the treaty power having for the time being the preponderating interests in Samoa, the nomination to have the approval of the other two powers, and each appointment to be made for a term of five years. The adviser should be virtually the prime minister of the country and should discharge, under the nominal responsibility of the king, the government affairs. He would have to control all necessary measures with regard to the maintenance of public order in general, and especially to the security of any kind of property of foreign residents.

(4) "To avoid every misapprehension of the situation by placing the representative of one of the treaty powers in the most prominent position of the Samoan administration," the principles of absolute "equality of treatment in respect to commerce, navigation," etc., should be secured to the three powers by a renewal of formal acknowledgments already contained in the existing treaties.

(5) A special international court should be established to adjudicate claims and disputes relating to land. For the composition of this court due consideration would have to be given to the nationality of the parties to the dispute.

(6) For the purpose of regulating the finances and drawing up a budget in accordance with the needs of foreigners and natives, the question of levying taxes on foreigners with the consent of the three treaty powers would have to be considered.

(7) "As the German interests in Samoa outweigh actually those of the two other powers, Germany is entitled to nominate the first adviser in accordance with the provisions established above under point No. 3."

(8) "The existing treaties with Samoa to be maintained, and the declarations made previously by Germany, the United States, and Great Britain with regard to the independence of Samoa to be confirmed, in order to avoid the appearance as if the present interference in the Samoan administration implied an intention of the annexation of Samoa by a foreign power."

Then followed the reading of the British memorandum by Sir Lionel Sackville-West.[44] "It is understood that the three powers have no desire to found colonies in Samoa or to obtain commercial monopolies. Their sole wish is to establish the right and equality of commerce and navigation for their respective subjects and citizens. Assuming then that the three powers have no desire to destroy the independence of Samoa but only seek to establish the right and equality of their commerce and navigation, a declaration to this effect might be made by them as a preliminary step. It was, however, deemed expedient to ascertain the exact state of affairs in the islands by sending special commissioners, who should report thereupon." From the reports of these commissioners it was clear "that the Samoan natives are incapable of forming, independently, a stable and efficient administration for preserving their own independence and for securing to each power full freedom of commerce, navigation and jurisdiction of all matters affecting their respective subjects and citizens." The British government was, therefore, pre-

[44] Protocols MSS; S. Ex. Doc. no. 102, pp. 8 and 9, encl. 5.

pared to enter into an agreement providing for a mandate to one of the powers. The British government found support for such an intervention, the memorandum went on to say, in the United States commissioner's report where Mr. Bates said: "The real function of the intervening powers in Samoa will of necessity be actual administration of government. Nothing short of this, at least for a time, will remedy the existing condition of things." A mandate was thought necessary because it was generally agreed that a tripartite control was impracticable. The solution of the difficulty, therefore, according to the memorandum "would seem to be an alternate control for a limited period of either one of the three powers." Since all three commissioners had, moreover, concurred that Germany possessed the preponderance in commercial interests, the British government was "prepared to consent to the mandatory power being exercised by the German representative for the first term of five years, absolute equality of treatment in respect to commerce, navigation and jurisdiction, and all other matters whatsoever, to be secured to the three powers and to their subjects and citizens." The British government also proposed the establishment of a permanent land court to take cognizance of land claims, with a land commission to carry on preliminary work for the court. The levying of taxes on foreigners should also be considered. As for the consular jurisdiction of the three powers, it should remain unaltered. The British memorandum stated further that a new election of a king was necessary for the reason that Tamasese had not submitted to Malietoa after the three consuls had recognized Malietoa. Finally, the British government expressed itself in favor of maintaining the existing treaties with Samoa.

Nothing more was done at the first session than the

presentation of the various memoranda, as Mr. Bayard desired to study the propositions submitted by Germany and Great Britain. At the second conference,[45] held on July 2, Bayard outlined the points on which there seemed to be agreement, namely, "that there should be no annexation of the islands by any of the treaty powers; that the independence and autonomy of the islands were to be preserved with equality of rights of commerce and navigation for the citizens or subjects of the treaty powers; that a native government was to be established and assisted to maintain itself; that the present jurisdiction of consuls over their own countrymen should be preserved; that the present treaties be maintained, so far as the rights of the three powers under them are concerned; that means of raising revenue for the support of the Government should be devised, and that the question of taxing foreigners should be considered; that import and tonnage duties should be established by identic treaties between the three powers and the Samoan Government; that a land court should be formed to settle titles and holding lands in the group. It had been admitted that the claims of foreigners to lands exceeded the entire area of the islands, and this was the best proof that the claims required overhauling by a court whose decision should be final."

The United States differed with Germany and Great Britain relative to the details of the native government to be established, the form suggested by the latter two governments being simpler in outline. While these had stated that the government should consist merely of a king and a council of chiefs, Bayard's plan provided also for "a legislative assembly composed of representatives elected by the people of the islands," but in order to "facilitate agreement" and thinking it not unadvisable to

[45] Protocols MSS; S. Ex. Doc. no. 102, pp. 9-21, encl. 6.

simplify the government, Bayard said he would defer to Germany's proposal of the omission of the legislative assembly.

Bayard then pointed out that "there were some other points on which the propositions of the powers did not run so closely together." With respect to the kingship, the United States wanted Malietoa Laupepa continued as king and Tamasese as vice king, whereas the British and German governments proposed a new election. But again, for the sake of agreement, Bayard was willing to adopt the proposal of Great Britain and Germany with the one condition that the election should be "free and unawed" and according to the customs of the Samoans. There should be no participation by the consuls, except that they should issue a declaration of the results of the election after receiving the announcement from the natives. There then ensued a discussion between von Alvensleben and Bayard relative to the extent of participation by the powers in the election. To the suggestion by the former that the natives might nominate and the powers confirm, Bayard replied that such a procedure "would virtually give the powers the control of the choice of a king." It was desirable to have "a virtual neutralization" of the group, "and this was to be secured by the abstention of the three powers from seeking any special control."

At this point Bayard referred to the proposition of Germany and Great Britain that the nation "having a preponderance of present commercial interest should exercise a preponderating influence," and that since Germany enjoyed a preponderance in commerce and according to her claim a preponderance in land holdings as well, it had been agreed between Germany and Great Britain that the former "should therefore have a preponderance of weight in the counsels." This, Bayard thought, ran counter to the principle upon which the three treaty powers had first agreed to proceed, namely, equality, and that if carried forward to its logical conclusion, would inevitably result in reducing "the islands into a German possession." Germany's plan provided for one prime minister, whereas the plan of the United States, Bayard pointed out, embraced "three Ministers—a Minister of Foreign Affairs, a Minister of Finance and Treasury, and a Minister of the Interior."

Bayard then proceeded to show why the United States was interested in the islands. The main reason was the geographical location of the islands, lying, as they did, on the pathway of a commerce which was just in its infancy. The United States had also negotiated the first treaty with Samoa by which was ceded to this country the right of establishing a coaling station at Pago Pago. The fact that only a few years before the west coast of North America had been opened up to civilization by the completion of a transcontinental railway, made the control of such a coaling station in the Pacific the more necessary to afford protection to America's growing trade. The contemplated cutting of the isthmus by a ship canal would, moreover, increase the importance of such a station. The European powers had acquired practically all of the islands in the Pacific; Great Britain, France, Germany, and Spain, each controlled considerable areas, while the United States, "with a great ocean front on the Pacific . . . has not acquired a foot of land in that region." Furthermore, Bayard thought the position of the United States in Samoa was more disinterested by reason of its political policies; that because the policy of the United States "in respect to acquisition of remote points had been pretty well defined" there could be no fear of the United States wanting to annex the islands.

A considerable discussion ensued concerning the land claims of foreigners in Samoa, and the machinery of gov-

WASHINGTON CONFERENCE, 1887

ernment that should be set up for the adjudication of these claims. Von Alvensleben asserted that "the whole amount of German property in cultivated land exceeded six times the land owned by other nations," whereas Bayard was not certain that the German title to all this land was good. Bayard, moreover, proposed a land court "to consist of three foreigners, one to be nominated by each of the powers, and two natives," whereas von Alvensleben proposed three foreigners to constitute a commission which should pass on all claims with a court to have appellate jurisdiction in cases not finally decided by the land commission. Bayard objected to two bodies, arguing that it would be simpler to have the court decide all land claims. The British minister, however, supported von Alvensleben, saying that "it was intended to facilitate the action of the court by the creation of the commission."

The conference then resumed its discussion of the mandate scheme proposed by Germany, and in support of this Alvensleben read a memorandum pointing out that the history of the last ten years had proven that the native Samoans could not support a government, and that the simultaneous attempts of consuls to assist by intervention had only increased the evil. The only alternative to a tripartite arrangement for foreign aid to Samoa was to invest in a single individual the power of running the government. This so-called adviser should be the real ruler and should not be appointed by the king but by the powers. The memorandum concluded with the German contention that, in view of its greater interests, Germany should receive the mandate, for "It can not . . . be expected that she [Germany] should consent to remain more or less excluded from the efficient control of the country and have it pass to one of the two powers who has less interests."

Bayard then indicated that the plan proposed by Germany entirely eliminated the principle upon which the conference had originally agreed, namely, the independence of the native government and the equality of the treaty powers. Von Alvensleben retorted that Bayard's three-minister scheme only legalized and perpetuated the unsatisfactory three-consul method of intervening in Samoan affairs, and that the three-party government would lead to trouble. The British minister fell back upon the reports of Bates and Thurston as indicating that some sort of foreign control was necessary. Bayard then reiterated the position of the United States that "foreign assistance and native government should be combined."

To facilitate the work of the conference, von Alvensleben laid before it a draft of a convention between the three powers consisting of nine articles, a memorandum relative to land disputes, and a memorandum on the financial question. The convention provided for a German mandate, the election of a king, the settlement of land disputes, the question of revenue, the equality of treatment in respect to commerce, navigation, jurisdiction, etc., for the three treaty powers.

The third session,[46] held on July 9, indicated more clearly than before how closely allied Germany and Great Britain were on the two outstanding questions that disturbed the conference—the land problem and the mandate. Again the two foreign representatives favored a land commission and a court of appeal, whereas Bayard saw no need of the former. Sackville-West then read a memorandum explaining his views of the work of the proposed commission and court. "It appears to me," he said in part, "that the labors of the commission, which it is proposed to appoint, should be directed to the collection and classification of all existing claims, which cannot

[46] Protocols MSS; S. Ex. Doc. no. 102, pp. 21-25, encl. 7.

WASHINGTON CONFERENCE, 1887

be adjusted by compromise, for submission to the land court, which, after pronouncing upon them, would, for the future, be free to deal with all land questions arising upon their own merits. It must be borne in mind that not even a basis of a land system prevails in Samoa at present, and it is this basis which it is sought to establish by the preliminary labors of the commission." After a further protracted discussion, no agreement was reached, Bayard's final word being that "the object of the commission appeared to be only to make business for the court, which could, however, call all the cases into its cognizance and settle them." Sackville-West then read a paper concerning his view of the mandatory scheme. "It is admitted by the three powers," he said, "that foreign intervention can alone insure the stability of the native government which it is sought to establish in Samoa, and that the tripartite control which has heretofore been exercised has proved abortive. . . . The argument in favor of the mandatory scheme is that it will prevent the control from falling into the hands of those connected with local interest and do away with the tripartite control which has been the cause of so many disputes, and which has, in fact, led to the present conference."

The fourth session,[47] held on July 16, was largely taken up with a discussion of the same two subjects—the plan of government (either the mandate or the tripartite control) and the question whether there should be a land court alone, or a land commission and a land court. Sackville-West opened the discussion by correcting what might have been a misapprehension about the phrase "alternative control" in the British memorandum handed in at the first session. "The phrase 'alternate control for a limited time' does not imply that the representative of

[47] Protocols MSS; S. Ex. Doc. no. 102, pp. 26-31, encl. 8.

each power shall be elected the mandatary in rotation, but merely indicates that the mandatory scheme bears an alternate character; for should German preponderance cease at the end of the first five years the next power possessing it in succession would, according to the German plan, exercise the mandatory power.''

Von Alvensleben then wanted to know if Bayard's objection to the mandatory scheme was based on general principles or on an unwillingness that Germany should have the mandate, "that if, for instance, under the proposed conditions and terms the United States were called upon to make the nomination, Mr. Bayard would raise the same objections, for the reasons that these islands could not be prevented from becoming an American possession." To which Bayard replied that "there was not the slightest meaning in the illustration made by him of the deposit of this power [mandate] in the hands of the German which would not have been equally applicable to the vesting of the power in an American on the same principle."

At this juncture Bayard's language seems to imply that he might be in favor of a compromise whereby the mandate should be held by the three powers in rotation, indicating that there would be small opportunity for the king's adviser nominated by the American government, for example, to be partial toward his countrymen if he knew that after a five-year period he would be succeeded by an adviser of another of the treaty powers. But when von Alvensleben at that point inquired whether Bayard "still maintained No. 5 [three ministers] of his original proposition, or whether he made a new proposition that the mandatary should be chosen by the powers alternately," Bayard replied that "he still believed in the subdivision of powers; that if there were only two Ministers, one of Foreign Affairs and Commerce and the other of the Interior and Treasury, there would still be a check upon the disposition to misuse power."

Then von Alvensleben read into the protocol a paper of considerable length in relation to Bayard's proposal No. 5. By adopting this proposal the powers would merely follow a plan which had been proven unsatisfactory already in the case of the municipal board at Apia. Such a plan should under all circumstances be avoided when setting up a government for all of Samoa. It would only add to the troubles in Samoa, for the reason that there would be three foreign officials in the island in addition to the consuls, if three ministers were to be in the king's council. Von Alvensleben concluded: "The purpose of this conference is to secure lasting peace and order, and in this respect the interests of the natives and the foreigners are identical. However, by adopting Mr. Bayard's plan the conference would lay the germ of death at the very bottom of its reformatory work and incur the grave responsibility of having done so deliberately, that is to say, without paying due attention to the experiences made in Samoa, nor to the warnings which are contained in the reports of the special commissioners, forming the basis of our negotiations. . . . I therefore conclude that it is not the German but the American plan which is inconsistent with the principles of this conference."

The remaining part of the fourth session was devoted to the question of the land commission and the land court. In bringing this matter up Bayard said he did not see the use of having a land commission when the court might just as well determine whether the foreigners' titles to the land were good or not. "If there should be a question of title between two claimants, involving questions of fact, it would be in the power of the Court to appoint commissioners to ascertain facts; but that was not the thing meant by the word commission in the proposition of either of the other members of the conference." When it was explained by both Alvensleben and Sackville-West, that the work of the land commission was to be a preliminary study of the general claims and that its work, if not final, would at least facilitate the work of the court, Bayard "said he should not stand in the way of this piece of machinery if it was considered, upon reflection, desirable to the end." If, in other words, the final control would be lodged in the court of record "his object would be reached."

In the fourth conference some progress was made toward an agreement, Bayard having shown an inclination to agree with the other representatives on the land commission and land court, and also for a moment as it seemed, disclosing a willingness to compromise on the mandatory system provided the principle of rotation was adopted, allowing for an equality between the powers instead of a perpetual mandate to Germany which the German-British plan would surely have brought about. Certainly Bayard would have placed von Alvensleben and Sackville-West squarely on the defensive had he adopted the mandatory system with the principle of rotation included; and in the end he might have forced them to accept the compromise and thus saved the conference. But when questioned by von Alvensleben if he wanted to substitute the mandatory system with rotation for his tripartite arrangement, he failed to grasp the opportunity, modifying his own original proposition somewhat by saying "that if there were only two Ministers . . . there would still be a check upon the disposition to misuse power." Then von Alvensleben put Bayard on the defensive by showing that even the American special commissioner to Samoa, Mr. Bates, had reported adversely on the plan for a three-party control.

WASHINGTON CONFERENCE, 1887

The fourth session showed signs of an agreement, even though attained by means of compromise. The fifth session,[48] on July 21, began auspiciously, but soon disclosed a wide difference of opinion between Bayard and von Alvensleben when the constitution of the land court was brought up for discussion, with Sackville-West supporting von Alvensleben. As summarized by Bayard, the points of agreement so far effected, were the following: "there should be a free and unawed native election of a king, without the interference of foreigners"; there should also be an election of a vice king; there should be an election of a Faipule "without any further definition as yet of the Faipule power"; and, fourthly, the election of the king and vice king should be at large by the "aggregate vote of the whole group" while "each district should elect its own representatives to the Faipule."

Then Bayard turned to the land question and said there were three propositions before the conference with respect to its solution. As proposed in the first session, the American plan for the constitution of the land court provided for "a single land commission or court, of original and final jurisdiction, who should inquire into the nature and extent of each and every land claim by foreigners." This commission "should consist of five members, appointed by the King, three to be appointed on the nomination of the powers, and the remaining two to be selected by the King, in order to recognize Samoan customs in relation to land." The British plan provided for an international land court, and "that in order to facilitate its workings, 'the existing land claims of foreigners should be disposed of by a commission' previously to the establishment of the international land court." The German plan proposed the establishment of a commission before

[48] Protocols MSS; S. Ex. Doc. no. 102, pp. 31-39, encl. 9.

any court should be set up, the commission to consist "of three members, each of the three treaty powers naming one." In commenting on this plan Bayard thought that two natives should also be put on the commission so "that the natives would feel that whatever the decision, they had a voice in making it, and they would pay greater respect and more voluntary obedience to the tribunals in which their customs and people had been fairly represented." Bayard then announced his willingness to agree with the other two members of the conference in establishing a land commission as well as a land court "with the understanding that the final decision rests with the court." This concession was made, he explained, even though "he had been unable to change his opinion that there is no function which the two bodies, the commission and the court, can perform, that the court could not efficiently perform with more directness and less complication."

Bayard then discussed the constitution of the land court as outlined in the German plan. It was "to be 'composed of a judge nominated by the Samoan Government, and of a Consul or of one of the prominent countrymen of the litigant.'" This plan, Bayard thought, was creating "a special court in each case," and would not bring about that uniformity of decision, which was so necessary in order to guard against "hopeless injustice." Why, he asked, should the consul of the litigants be introduced into the tribunal when "the interference of the Consuls in other matters was deemed inadvisable on account of their partisanship"? Von Alvensleben thought that the principal concern of the conference was the "formation of the government, because all these discussions in the settling of land disputes seemed to him at present but preliminary." When the government was formed the conference could provide for the appointment of the Samoan

WASHINGTON CONFERENCE, 1887

judge by the government. It was then that the American proposal of the separation of powers led Bayard to remark that "he did not leave the composition of the land court as a separate body to depend upon the composition of the executive branch of the Government. If it did, the executive power would control the judge," a statement that brought forth from von Alvensleben an assertion that indicated clearly the German plan for controlling not only the executive but also the judiciary department of the native government. The protocol reads: "Mr. von Alvensleben said the mandatary or adviser would have to appoint the judge and the King would have to confirm him." The reason for the German reticence about discussing the composition of the land court in detail was now quite evident; and Bayard shrewdly retorted that "it seemed to him that that reduced the matter to an absolutism," and he concluded his comments with a withering exposé of the whole German plan.

The powers "embarked upon the conference," he said, "with a declaration of the absolute equality of the three powers, and that they were acting in an advisory capacity towards the Samoan people, and that they desired to preserve the independence and autonomy of the islands and absolute equality of treatment in respect of commerce, navigation, jurisdiction, etc.; and it is further stated that it was intended that there was to be no inequality whatever in respect to the influence to be exerted by the three Governments upon this community; that, whether their interest was little or large, the basis of their approach to this question was the equality of the three powers in dealing with the subject of Samoan Government." All this had been lost sight of in the German proposal for a mandate because of the reasons assigned for the mandate. Bayard went on to say "the executive power should not be given to protect the largest interests in Samoa at all;

it was to protect all the interests of Samoa. If a German agent, or governor, or mandatary was appointed, he should be appointed just as much in the interest of the American people as the German." Then quoting von Alvensleben to the effect that "It can not therefore be expected that she [Germany] should consent to remain more or less excluded from the efficient control of the country and have it pass to one of the two powers who have less interests," he added: "That was a clear proposition of inequality on its very face. If Germany could not be expected to consent to remain more or less excluded, how could she expect another power to remain so? There was upon the very proposition of exclusion the mark of inequality which is in contradiction to the idea with which the conference began." The German plan, he thought, proposed "to make the preponderating interests the beginning, end, and middle of the whole scheme of government." To this Sackville-West answered that he did not see it in that light. Whereupon Bayard replied that he had looked upon the land court as the corner stone of the whole arrangement but as the German minister had brought forward again the question of the form of the government "which was to appoint the land Court" it was clear to him that "preponderating interests" were to dominate the court decisions as well. The session ended abruptly with Bayard announcing that he would endeavour to show at the next meeting in writing that such was the case.

The sixth and last session[49] was held five days later, July 26. There was little or no discussion. Von Alvensleben began the deliberations by reading a paper in which he sought to show that Mr. Bayard was laboring under a misapprehension when he thought Germany was bent on

[49] Protocols MSS; S. Ex. Doc. no. 102, pp. 39-45, encl. 10.

asserting her rights in Samoa to the detriment of the other treaty powers. If the German mandatory scheme "would seem to create any appearance of inequality of rights," he said, "this would, however, be merely an appearance, as naturally the establishment of the whole government can only be made in this conference by the cooperation of the three treaty powers on a thoroughly equal footing."

Bayard then read a long paper explaining the reason for holding the conference, the history of the conference itself, including the points of agreement reached, and finally his objections to the German mandatory scheme. His keen powers of analysis probably never were more effective than when he exposed the German plan with the aid of the German minister's statement at the second session, which he had already quoted, but to which he now returned for the purpose of summarizing his whole position. But he did not object to the scheme merely because it failed to provide for an equal position of the powers in Samoa; it also involved, in his opinion, "the virtual displacement of native government, and, instead of native government with foreign assistance, [it] means the absolute and undefined control of the affairs of the islands by a single foreigner." He then came back to the American plan of the executive council of five (the three foreign representatives and the king and vice king), and cited a precedent in the mixed tribunals in Egypt in support of this plan, "which far from having been found to contain the 'germ of death,'[50] have operated for the promotion of justice and to the great and acknowledged satisfaction of all concerned." The further the conference had progressed, and the more the plan of Germany had been

[50] Reference to a statement made by von Alvensleben at the fourth session on July 16.

unfolded by the German minister, the further had they found themselves "departing from any substantial recognition of a native autonomy for Samoa, and the consequent independence of that island group." And continuing along this line he added, "The plan proposed and explained by Mr. von Alvensleben is substantially a foreign autocratic government, based on mercantile interests, and all experience has shown what must necessarily result from such an attempt and that under it the defeat of the objects we have all distinctly proposed is certain."

Bayard then proposed that the conference adjourn until autumn in order that the ministers of Germany and Great Britain might submit the protocols to their respective governments with a view to securing more definite instructions so as to enable the conferees to reach an agreement. Sackville-West thought that under the circumstances there was no other course than to adjourn and that he would inform his government of Bayard's proposal, to which statement von Alvensleben added the reason for the adjournment, namely, that the mandatory scheme was not acceptable to Mr. Bayard.

While there was no vote taken on the proposal for adjournment, no objection to it was advanced by von Alvensleben, and the conference came to an end. It had been doomed to failure from the very beginning, owing to the close agreement which existed between the British and German plenipotentiaries on every vital point. Von Alvensleben, moreover, was ably advised by Theodor Weber, who had come from Apia to represent the German mercantile interests. It is hardly likely that that domineering individual would have consented to any compromise on the mandatory scheme that would have jeopardized German control and the possible loss through an independently functioning land court of some of the German land holdings.

CHAPTER XI

THE BRANDEIS-TAMASESE RÉGIME

WITH the closing of the Washington Conference German intervention in its most serious form began in Samoa. It will be recalled that King Malietoa protested on January 31 to the German consul, Becker, concerning the aid that a Captain Brandeis was giving the rebel government of Tamasese at Leulumoega in the district of Aana. At that time it was alleged that Brandeis was drilling the Tamasese warriors in preparation for war upon King Malietoa. No war broke out in the spring of 1887, however, for the reason that Germany was awaiting the outcome of the Washington Conference, but on several occasions King Malietoa wanted to fight before the rebel party became too strong. He was kept from so doing by the promises from the consuls that the great powers would solve the Samoan problem at the approaching conference and that his rights would be protected. As a matter of fact, just as the conference was about to begin, it will be remembered, the three consuls received instructions simultaneously to "advise [the] natives to avoid resort to force" as the treaty powers were endeavoring to secure a "permanent native government for Samoa."[1] Malietoa, though his chiefs were straining at the leash to fight Tamasese, kept the peace, thus affording the Germans time after the close of the conference to prepare to support Tamasese in the open and to declare war upon Malietoa. Sewall carried out his instructions faithfully in advising Malietoa to re-

[1] Quoted from Bayard's telegram to Sewall, June 20, 1887.

main quiet, but later he regretted having done so when the German plan began to unfold.

When Sewall arrived in Apia to take up his work as the first consul general of the United States,[2] he found a trying situation confronting him. Although the British acting consul would have preferred to work with Sewall, he was obliged to act against his personal judgment on account of positive instructions from the Foreign Office in London to coöperate with the German consul, Becker. There had been no meeting of the municipal board or of the court of appeal for Apia following Sewall's arrival, and since the rules prevented a meeting of the board if any one of the consuls remained away, the German consul could easily prevent any business being transacted. The German consul wanted a municipal magistrate chosen from among the German residents in Apia.[3] It was known that Sewall favored an American for municipal judge, and moreover, it was Sewall's turn to be chairman of the municipal board. But he was given to understand that the Germans would never yield him the position.[4]

Sewall wanted the court of appeal, composed of the three consuls, to meet on account of a case that had arisen between an Englishman, named Gurr, and a German subject, named Marquandt. The case was tried before the municipal magistrate, Martin, but after a two hours' session the German defendant left the court and sought the protection of the German consul. Sewall, who was present at the trial, received an appeal from the English plaintiff

[2] The grade of the United States post at Apia was that of commercial agent until 1875, excepting the short period when Jenkins was at Apia. Jenkins' appointment was that of consul. Foster was the first to be appointed consul after Jenkins, 1875. Sewall went out as consul general in 1887.

[3] C.D., Apia, vol. 15, Sewall to Porter, Aug. 15, 1887, rec'd Sept. 12; H. Ex. Doc. no. 238, p. 61, encl. 56.

[4] *Ibid.;* H. Ex. Doc. no. 238, pp. 63-64, encl. 57.

THE BRANDEIS-TAMASESE RÉGIME 369

for a trial of the case in the consular court of appeal. The German consul refused to recognize the jurisdiction of the consular court of appeal in the case, and Sewall cited article V of the municipal convention of 1879, which provided that all offenses against the laws of the municipality, by whomsoever committed, should be tried by the magistrate appointed by the board.[5] Here, then, was a case where consular jurisdiction once surrendered by Germany to a common tri-consular jurisdiction, was taken back by Germany despite the convention of 1879. But Sewall, himself, was in an anomalous position also, for the reason that he was trying to enforce a convention which the United States Senate had never ratified, and which had been accepted only informally by the United States government. He was informed of his real status by the Department of State as soon as his despatch narrating the above events arrived in Washington. On October 10 Bayard sent the following telegram to the consul at Auckland for transmission to Sewall: "Do not assume jurisdiction over German subject in suit by Englishman for criminal assault, German consul having claimed right and assumed duty to try defendant under German laws." In sending a confirmation of this telegram, Alvey A. Adee, second assistant secretary, explained to Sewall that while the department recognized "the force of your reasoning, which is based upon the language of the fifth article of the convention," it was also necessary to point out that by article VI of the same convention it was provided that " 'If a subject or citizen of any of the contracting parties in Apia be charged with an offense against the laws of his own country, he shall be tried according to the jurisdiction provided therefor by the legislation of the nation to which he belongs, or according to the stipula-

[5] *Ibid.*, Sewall to Porter, Aug. 16, 1887, rec'd Sept. 12; H. Ex. Doc. no. 238, pp. 64-65, encl. 58.

tions of treaty concluded between his nation and Samoa.'" Then Adee continued: "It thus appears that while the convention gave the municipal board the general regulation of municipal matters and the power to enforce municipal regulations, yet this power was not intended to exclude, but, on the contrary, was limited so as to preserve the jurisdiction of the consuls over their respective countrymen for infraction of the laws of their own nation. Whatever advantage accrues from this jurisdiction comes equally to all nationalities, and is impartial in its effect.'"[6]

But there was another reason why the department had "not thought it advisable," said Adee, "to take an extreme position in assertion of the jurisdiction of the municipal board against a claim by another Government of a right under its treaty with Samoa, and that is, that this Government is not formally a party to the municipality convention, which has never been ratified by the Senate. The municipal government of Apia has been recognized in practice by the United States as a local police power.'"[7]

While Sewall was realizing in a very definite way that the German consul was not going to coöperate as in the past with the United States representative, he learned within a week after writing his despatch of August 16 the real reason for this attitude. Prince Bismarck had already decided upon war against King Malietoa and the establishment of a strong German régime in Samoa with Tamasese as the puppet king. The German squadron, which had been ordered to assemble at Sydney to be prepared to proceed to Samoa at a moment's notice should news arrive of the failure of the Washington Conference, was

[6] I.C., vol. 122, no. 22, Adee to Sewall, Oct. 13, 1887; H. Ex. Doc. no. 238, pp. 83-84, encl. 68.
[7] I.C., vol. 122, no. 22, Adee to Sewall, Oct. 13, 1887, p. 84.

THE BRANDEIS-TAMASESE RÉGIME 371

now on its way to Apia at the time Sewall complained to the department of Becker's actions.

The squadron of four ships under the command of Commodore Heusner arrived in Apia harbor on August 19.[8] No immediate action was planned for the reason that a Sydney mail steamer was expected to call at Apia, and no quick news to the outside world was desirable. The revolution must be a *fait accompli* before the rest of the world, especially Washington, should have any inkling of what was transpiring in Samoa, and before any preventive measures could be undertaken. The Sydney steamer left port on August 23, and Apia was cut off from any means of communication for at least three weeks. Then was the time to act.

On the same day, namely, August 23, the German consul, Becker, demanded an indemnity from King Malietoa[9] amounting to $13,000, of which $1000 was asked because of an alleged insult to the German emperor on His Majesty's birthday. The remainder of the money "was demanded for fruit alleged to have been stolen from the German plantations during the preceding four years." In addition to the money, Becker demanded from King Malietoa an *ifu*, the most degrading form of personal humiliation known to Samoans.[10]

The king replied immediately and asked for three days time. "It will be obvious to you," he wrote Becker on the twenty-fourth, "that it is essential for me to consult my Government and chiefs before replying to the grave charges and heavy demands contained in your communi-

[8] C.D., Apia, vol. 15, Sewall, Sept. 10, 1887, rec'd Oct. 10; H. Ex. Doc. no. 238, p. 67, encl. 60.
[9] *Ibid.*, encl. 1; see also H. Ex. Doc. no. 238, pp. 70 and 71, encl. 1 in encl. 60.
[10] In Samoa the *ifu* was a form of abject apology. The penitent would crawl toward the injured person on his stomach in the most humiliating manner.

cation.'"[11] The letter was sent to the German flagship at seven o'clock in the morning and a half hour later war upon Malietoa was declared. About seven hundred marines and six guns were landed and the German flag run up over the government house. Sewall protested to Becker "in the name of the Government of the United States" against the action taken,[12] and Becker replied: "I have the honor to inform you that His Majesty the Emperor of Germany has declared war against the Chief Malietoa. Germany does not intend to make any alterations in the existing relations between the three treaty powers and the Samoan Islands, but adheres to the conventions concluded between the three treaty powers.'"[13] The next day, August 25, Becker informed Sewall that the German government had recognized Tamasese as king of Samoa,[14] whereupon Sewall and W. H. Wilson, the British proconsul, issued a proclamation stating that their governments had never recognized Tamasese as king of Samoa, and that they would "continue as heretofore to recognize Malietoa."[15] On the same day Sewall issued a proclamation enjoining all American citizens "to offer no opposition to the German forces, but immediately to report . . . any molestation of person or property."[16]

On the twenty-fifth also, the *de facto* king, signing himself as Tuiaana Tamasese, informed Sewall that he had charge of the government and promised "to carry out and protect all treaties that have been made between Samoa and the great powers.'"[17] To this communication

[11] C.D., Apia, vol. 15, Sewall, Sept. 10, 1887, rec'd Oct. 10, encl. 2; H. Ex. Doc. no. 238, p. 71, encl. 2 in encl. 60.
[12] *Ibid.*, encl. 3; H. Ex. Doc. no. 238, p. 71, encl. 3 in encl. 60.
[13] *Ibid.*, encl. 4; H. Ex. Doc. no. 238, p. 71, encl. 4 in encl. 60.
[14] *Ibid.*, encl. 7; H. Ex. Doc. no. 238, p. 72, encl. 7 in encl. 60.
[15] *Ibid.*, encl. 8; H. Ex. Doc. no. 238, pp. 72-73, encl. 8 in encl. 60.
[16] *Ibid.*, encl. 9; H. Ex. Doc. no. 238, p. 73, encl. 9 in encl. 60.
[17] *Ibid.*, encl. 10; H. Ex. Doc. no. 238, p. 73, encl. 10 in encl. 60.

THE BRANDEIS-TAMASESE RÉGIME 373

Sewall made no reply.[18] Tamasese also issued a call for an assemblage of the Taimua and Faipule to be held at Mulinuu on September 15 and announced the retention of the governors of all the districts in Samoa with the exception of one in the island of Savaii.[19] Commodore Heusner proclaimed martial law on the twenty-seventh and Sewall warned Americans to stop when challenged by sentries.[20] Sewall protested to Becker on August 29 "against the continued presence of armed men within this town and district." He regarded the military occupation as a "direct violation of the neutrality of this town and district, guaranteed by the treaty convention of 1879."[21] Becker favored Sewall only with a formal acknowledgment of his letter.[22]

On the day of the declaration of war Sewall had been appealed to by Selu, the Samoan secretary of state, who requested help from the United States on the basis of article V of the American-Samoan treaty.[23] Sewall immediately communicated with Becker informing the latter that he had "granted the request of the Samoan Government" and was "ready to proceed to settle the difference on a satisfactory basis."[24] Becker gave Sewall "no formal reply" but they had "many interviews in this connection." Becker informed Sewall during these interviews "that the instructions from his government were that Malietoa should be taken into custody." After this object had been attained "he agreed," wrote Sewall, "to certain conditions upon which . . . hostilities would

[18] *Ibid.;* H. Ex. Doc. no. 238, p. 68, encl. 60.
[19] *Ibid.*, encl. 12; H. Ex. Doc. no. 238, pp. 73-74, encl. 12 in encl. 60.
[20] *Ibid.*, encl. 11; H. Ex. Doc. no. 238, p. 73, encl. 11 in encl. 60.
[21] *Ibid.*, encl. 13; H. Ex. Doc. no. 238, p. 74, encl. 13 in encl. 60.
[22] *Ibid.;* H. Ex. Doc. no. 238, p. 69, encl. 60.
[23] *Ibid.*, encl. 14; H. Ex. Doc. no. 238, p. 74, encl. 14 in encl. 60.
[24] *Ibid.*, encl. 15; H. Ex. Doc. no. 238, p. 74, encl. 15 in encl. 60.

cease.'"25 Sewall said further that he was inclined to advise Malietoa "to give himself up," but when Tamasese came to Mulinuu "bloodshed was inevitable, provided the Germans continued to support him. Left alone, he and his followers would immediately withdraw to their homes."26 Sewall continued: "To ascertain, then, whether the Germans intended to follow up the capture of Malietoa by the enforced submission of his followers to Tamasese, I asked Mr. Becker, in the interests of peace, to sign a paper which I drew up and put before him. This he refused to do. My mission now was useless. Malietoa might have been induced to give himself up to the Germans, but neither he nor his followers would consent to this if it meant their submission to Tamasese."27

At this time Captain Brandeis stepped forth in his real character, and the next year and a half may be very aptly called the Brandeis-Tamasese régime. In many respects Brandeis reminds one of Steinberger. He was just as able as the American, but whereas Steinberger, despite his title of colonel, was not a military man, Brandeis added a martial prowess to his many accomplishments.28 The Brandeis régime was a strong man's government just as was Steinberger's, the only difference between the two being that Brandeis remained in power longer than Steinberger. Whereas Steinberger had no support from Hamilton Fish, Brandeis could look to Prince Bismarck as the author of the whole movement and in consequence could depend upon German warships to support and protect him.

With the arrival of the German squadron Malietoa fled to the bush, and in the beginning of September the Ger-

[25] C.D., Apia, vol. 15, Sewall, Sept. 10, 1887, rec'd Oct. 10, encl. 15; H. Ex. Doc. no. 238, p. 69.
[26] *Ibid.;* H. Ex. Doc. no. 238, p. 69.   [27] *Ibid.;* H. Ex. Doc. no. 238, p. 70.
[28] Steinberger depended upon Major Latrobe for the military force that was developed during his régime.

THE BRANDEIS-TAMASESE RÉGIME 375

man ships were sent up and down the coast to search for him.[29] It was realized that with that chief at large the Tamasese régime would fall the moment the German warships should leave Samoan waters. Mataafa, the great chief in Atua, refused to accept Tamasese's appointment of himself as governor of that district. This in itself was no good omen for the success of Tamasese. According to Sewall the *fono* of the chiefs, called for September 15, was not propitious for the future. The Malietoa chiefs who had come in from the bush to learn Tamasese's and the Germans' terms, were told by Commodore Heusner "that Germany had made Tamasese King of Samoa and that they were then to sign a paper which had been prepared for them." "There was nothing for the chiefs to do but to submit," wrote Sewall. "They were unarmed in the camp of Tamasese, whose followers were armed to the teeth, and five German warships lay before them in the harbor. Accordingly, after the Commodore's speech, led by Brandeis, the German premier of Tamasese, they were brought before him, where they signed their names to a paper of the contents of which many of them are to this day ignorant." On this occasion Mataafa, who the next year was to become a thorn to Germany, informed Commodore Heusner that Tamasese was not entitled to the kingship; that Malietoa had first claim and then he himself. "This was bold talk," wrote Sewall, "and the beginning of dissension in the Tamasese ranks."[30]

At this *fono* four hundred and sixty-two chiefs signed the documents whereby Tamasese was recognized as king, but as most of them signed under duress, their signatures did not count for much. Scanning the names, Sewall found that two hundred and seventy-six of them repre-

[29] C.D., Apia, vol. 15, Sewall, Sept. 10, 1887, rec'd Oct. 10; H. Ex. Doc. no. 238, p. 70, encl. 60.
[30] *Ibid.*, no. 30, Sewall, Oct. 8, 1887, rec'd Nov. 5; H. Ex. Doc. no. 238, pp. 75-76, encl. 61.

sented Malietoa adherents and one hundred and eighty-six belonged to Tamasese and Mataafa. Malietoa's majority therefore, over the combined strength of rival claimants to the kingship was ninety.[31] Malietoa's main support was to be found in his home district on Upolu, namely, Tuamasaga, where all the chiefs were his adherents; in the district of Aana, where almost half of the chiefs were loyal to him; on the island of Manono; and in the districts of Itu-o-fafine and Faalsaleleaga, on the island of Savaii, where all the chiefs regarded themselves as his followers. Half of the chiefs on Tutuila were also Malietoa supporters. Mataafa's main strength was in his own district of Atua and on the island of Tutuila. Tamasese looked to Aana, his home district, where about one-half of the chiefs supported him, and to the district of Itu-o-tane on the island of Savaii for additional aid.[32]

On September 17 Malietoa voluntarily came in from the bush and surrendered himself to Becker, the German consul, and was taken on board the *Bismarck,* the flagship of the German squadron.[33] Before he entered Apia he signed a proclamation of abdication, saying that he would rather give himself up to the Germans than that blood should flow again on his account.[34] Meanwhile, the German commodore had postponed beginning hostilities, some of Malietoa's adherents promising to go to Malietoa and persuade him to come into Apia. This they preferred to do rather than see Malietoa taken prisoner.[35] Before surrendering himself, however, Malietoa wrote a letter to Sewall explaining his contemplated action. He reminded Sewall that he had yielded to his and the British consul's

[31] C.D., Apia, vol. 15, no. 33. Sewall, Oct. 8, 1887, rec'd Nov. 5; H. Ex. Doc. no. 238, p. 77, encl. 62.
[32] *Ibid.*, encl. 1; H. Ex. Doc. no. 238, pp. 77 and 78, encl. 1 in encl. 62.
[33] *Ibid.*, Sewall, Oct. 10, 1887, rec'd Nov. 5; H. Ex. Doc. no. 238, encl. 63.
[34] *Ibid.*, encl. 1; H. Ex. Doc. no. 238, encl. 1 in encl. 63.
[35] *Ibid.;* H. Ex. Doc. no. 238, pp. 79 and 80, encl. 63.

advice not to fight Tamasese when the rebellion was in its infancy. "Relying upon these directions," wrote Malietoa, "I did not put down the rebellion. Now war has been raised against me by the Emperor of Germany, and they have made Tamasese King of Samoa. The German forces and the adherents of Tamasese threatened to make war on all my people who do not acknowledge Tamasese as king. I do not know what wrongful act I have done, and do hereby protest against the action done by Germany. But the German Government is strong and I indeed am weak, therefore I yield to their strength that my people may live and not be slaughtered. . . . I desire to make known to you this: I fear, indeed that Germany will desire to compel me, as they are now making my people, to sign papers acknowledging Tamasese as king. If I write my name on paper it will be under compulsion and to avoid war being made on my people by the German forces."[36] On the day after Malietoa went on board the *Bismarck* he was transferred to the corvette *Adler* and taken away from Samoa, his destination being unknown at the time.[37]

Because the *fono* of September 15, referred to above, was called to meet at Mulinuu within the limits of the municipal district, Sewall called the magistrate's attention to municipal regulation no. 29 and requested Judge Martin to prevent the meeting being held there.[38] The article in question forbade "public assemblies of Samoans from outside the Tuamasaga territory . . . without special permission from the municipal board," and was designed not only to prevent chiefs hostile to Malietoa from invading his home district but also to preserve the neu-

[36] *Ibid.;* H. Ex. Doc. no. 238, pp. 80-81, encl. 2 in encl. 63.
[37] *Ibid.*
[38] *Ibid.,* Sewall, Oct. 10, 1887, rec'd Nov. 5; H. Ex. Doc. no. 238, p. 81, encl. 64.

trality of the foreign zone during civil wars. Sewall was quick to discern the ulterior purpose of the move, namely, that the triconsular government of Apia and the surrounding area should receive another blow, which eventually would mean the dissolution of the municipal government and the assumption of control in Apia by the Tamasese government, including the collection of the revenue. The German firm desired no longer to be subject to a tripartite government in Apia. With Tamasese's laws in force in Apia, which in turn were the laws of Brandeis under the inspiration of Theodor Weber and the German firm, Sewall and the British consul would be reduced in power and would have jurisdiction only over their own nationals. "The Firm" would then rule Apia as well as the rest of Samoa.

The magistrate, a German subject, though "he admitted the applicability of the regulation," wrote Sewall to the department, ". . . was disinclined to enforce it." Sewall then addressed a letter to Becker the day before the meeting saying in part as follows: "In view of the fact that Tamasese has been brought here by your Government, which has recognized him as king, and that his commissions are countersigned by one Brandeis, a German subject, I deem it my duty to request of you that the convention, and municipal regulations framed under it, will not be disregarded in respect to the gathering tomorrow."[39] Consul Becker made a verbal answer to Sewall to the effect "that while he also admitted the applicability of the regulation, he could not aid in its enforcement."

The American and English residents in the last quarter of the year 1887 refused to pay taxes to the municipal government. Their reason was that the German magis-

[39] C.D., Apia, vol. 15, enclosure, Sewall to Becker, Sept. 14, 1887; H. Ex. Doc., no. 238, pp. 81 and 82, encl. in encl. 64.

THE BRANDEIS-TAMASESE RÉGIME 379

trate, Judge Martin, who in addition to his judicial functions appointed the police and controlled the public expenditures, had, according to Sewall, shown subservience to "the Firm." While the roads in the German section of the town were well kept, those in the English and American sections were neglected. The English and Americans preferred to forego lighted streets and police protection, said Sewall, "than to pay their money into hostile hands which have usurped the direction of affairs in which all have an equal interest."[40]

On October 14 the triconsular government of Apia and the surrounding district, which had been established by the convention of September 2, 1879, ceased to exist. In the afternoon of that day armed sailors were landed from the German squadron and guards stationed at all important points in the town. A detachment was also sent to Mulinuu to guard the headquarters of Tamasese, and the German flag was raised.[41] This done, Becker informed Sewall by letter that he was "obliged to consider the municipal government to be provisionally in abeyance." The German consul sought to place the blame for the step upon Sewall, alleging that he (Sewall), having withdrawn his "consent to the continuation of Mr. Martin in his position as magistrate" and having, moreover, "refused to take part in the meeting of the municipal board agreed to for the purpose of electing a magistrate," the municipal government could no longer function. During the suspension of the municipality, therefore, the government of the town and district would be assumed by the Samoan government. This government, having requested aid from Commodore Heusner, added Becker, the commodore had

[40] *Ibid.*, Sewall, Oct. 10, 1887, rec'd Nov. 5; H. Ex. Doc. no. 238, p. 82, encl. 65.
[41] *Ibid.*, Sewall, Nov. 8, 1887, rec'd Dec. 3; H. Ex. Doc. no. 238, p. 91, encl. 75.

"provisionally occupied Apia for the protection of life and property of the German inhabitants."[42]

Sewall immediately replied to Becker denying that he had withdrawn his consent to the continuance in office of Judge Martin and also stating that he had not refused to attend the meeting of the municipal board. On the contrary, he was already on his way to the meeting of the board when Becker left the place of meeting, although he, Becker, had been informed by the British representative, Wilson, that he (Sewall) was coming. "I protest in the name of my Government," added Sewall, "against the action of the Imperial German Commodore in assuming control of this municipality delegated to the representatives of the three treaty powers by the convention of 1879."[43] The next day, October 15, Sewall issued a proclamation to American citizens that thenceforth they were subject only to his "control and protection."[44] By the Sydney mail steamer Sewall forwarded a cablegram to Bayard reading: "Tamasese German aid usurps municipal government. Americans unprotected."[45] The U.S.S. *Adams* arrived six days later, October 20, but until that time Americans had only the protection which the consulate could afford them.[46]

Sewall, in explaining to the department the reasons for the sudden turn of events, stated that "the time had come when a change in the municipal magistrate could no longer be delayed."[47] Judge Martin's term had expired six months before; therefore it was the turn of an Ameri-

---

[42] C.D., Apia, vol. 15, encl. 1, Becker to Sewall, Oct. 14, 1887; H. Ex. Doc. no. 238, pp. 93-94, encl. 1 in encl. 75.

[43] *Ibid.*, encl, 2, Sewall to Becker, Oct. 14, 1887; H. Ex. Doc. no. 238, p. 94, encl. 2 in encl. 75.

[44] *Ibid.*, encl. 3; H. Ex. Doc. no. 238, p. 94, encl. 3 in encl. 75.

[45] *Ibid.*, encl. 4; H. Ex. Doc. no. 238, p. 94, encl. 4 in encl. 75.

[46] *Ibid.;* H. Ex. Doc. no. 238, p. 91, encl. 75.

[47] *Ibid.*

THE BRANDEIS-TAMASESE RÉGIME 381

can to be appointed to the office. However, because of instructions from London to the British vice consul that he support the German's continuance in office for six months dating from April 1, and because his (Sewall's) predecessor, acting consul Hamilton, had agreed to the arrangement until he could get instructions from Washington, no American had been appointed to succeed Judge Martin.[48] An answer to Hamilton's inquiry came addressed to Sewall in which the latter was instructed "to support the American claim."[49] Sewall was never able to do this, however, for the reason that the German consul steadily refused to attend a meeting of the board for the purpose of electing a new magistrate. Finally a meeting was agreed upon for October 14. But the time had now expired during which British support for the German candidate could be expected, "and even with this support," added Sewall, "my dissent would prevent an election [of a German]." But, as Sewall explained further, "The municipal organization, even under the German magistrate, was an obstacle in the way of German supremacy and the establishment of Tamasese, for here the king had ceded his power."[50] It will be recalled that in the agreement prolonging the convention of 1879, it was stated "that the convention shall remain in force without change until such time as the internal state of Samoa will happily admit of the District again passing under the control of the Samoan Government as conditioned in Article X." The German authorities in Samoa evidently felt that with a strong régime

[48] Hamilton's despatch no. 162, April 18, 1887, requested instructions. (See Consular Despatches, Apia, vol. 15.)

[49] C.D., Apia, vol. 15, no. 43, Sewall, Nov. 8, 1887, rec'd Dec. 3; H. Ex. Doc. no. 238, p. 92, encl. 75.

[50] The power of government was transferred for four years to the three powers by Malietoa Talavou in the municipal convention of September 2, 1879. The transfer was prolonged indefinitely by Malietoa Laupepa on September 29, 1883.

under their inspiration, the time had actually arrived when the tripartite government of Apia and district was no longer necessary. Moreover, as Sewall wrote to the department, in order to obtain adequate revenue for the new Brandeis-Tamasese administration it was necessary to govern that area of the Samoan islands where most of the money wealth was concentrated. For all these reasons, therefore, the German consul, Becker, seized upon the technicality that Sewall was not present on time at the meeting called for the 14th, and he took the steps narrated above. The technicality was, of course, a very trivial one. As a matter of fact, Sewall had started for the meeting in company with Wilson, his British colleague, when he was obliged to return to the consulate for a document he had forgotten, telling Wilson that he would come to the meeting immediately. "Never since the convention was made," wrote Sewall in conclusion, "not even during the peace and quiet of the years preceding the revolt of Tamasese, has it been suggested from any quarter that the time had arrived when the municipal town and district could revert to the Samoan Government without prejudice to the interests of the foreign residents—the conditions provided in Article X of the convention. Certainly the present is no more favorable a time, when the country is in a state of war, and the only government is one forced upon the Samoans against their will, already deserted by the greater part of the natives who once supported it, opposed by the American and English residents, and not recognized by their Governments. And yet it is the interests of these that Mr. Becker would intrust to the government he seeks to establish; for the protection of German life and property he deems it insufficient, and the German commodore occupies Apia."[51]

[51] Sewall's despatch no. 43 as above; H. Ex. Doc. no. 238, p. 93, encl. 75.

THE BRANDEIS-TAMASESE RÉGIME 383

On October 24 Sewall wrote Becker a note referring to the latter's notification on August 24 of the declaration of war upon Malietoa, and requesting information "whether peace has yet been concluded, and if not, whether the German forces at present occupying Apia are here in the prosecution of war or for the police purposes mentioned in your communication of the 14th instant."[52] To this note Becker replied the next day that the conclusion of peace could "only take place by order of the Imperial German Government, and that as yet no instructions in respect to same have arrived here." The "provisional occupation of Apia," he explained, had "taken place for the purpose of assisting the Samoan Government in the preservation of order, and for the protection of the German inhabitants."[53]

But Sewall was not satisfied with Becker's answer, and again on November 19 he wrote him a note wherein he denied Becker's "right even to temporarily place in abeyance the municipal government delegated to the representatives of the three treaty powers." Sewall desired Becker, moreover, to define what he implied by the word "provisionally" in his communication of October 14 when he said Commodore Heusner had "provisionally occupied Apia."[54] In his reply Becker protested "against the insinuation" implied in Sewall's note that he had claimed the right to place in abeyance the municipal government. "The actual suspension of the municipal institution was caused through your non-appearance at the meeting called together for the election of a magistrate, and through the impossibility caused thereby to continue the

[52] C.D., Apia, vol. 15, Sewall Nov. 7, 1887, rec'd Dec. 3, encl. 1, Sewall to Becker, Oct. 24, 1887; H. Ex. Doc. no. 238, p. 96, encl. 1 in encl. 77.

[53] *Ibid.*, encl. 2, Becker to Sewall, Oct. 25, 1887; H. Ex. Doc. no. 238, p. 96, encl. 2 in encl. 77.

[54] *Ibid.*, Sewall Nov. 30, 1887, rec'd Dec. 31, encl. no. 1, Sewall to Becker, Nov. 19, 1887; H. Ex. Doc. no. 238, p. 105, encl. 1 in encl. 80.

municipal business." As for the conditions upon which he would consent to the revival of the municipal government and what he meant by the word "provisionally," he informed Sewall that he was "not authorized to induce the Samoan Government to withdraw from the administration of the municipal district which it has taken over, and to lay down conditions for the reëstablishment of the municipality." This matter would rest with the treaty powers and with the Samoan government and until a decision had been reached by them it would "remain the duty of the Government of Samoa to provide for the preservation of order within the municipal district." In other words, as long as the Brandeis-Tamasese control desired German naval protection in Apia that protection would be available.[55]

While the warlike events in Samoa were taking place, communications between Washington and Berlin became more frequent. On August 7, less than two weeks after the close of the Washington Conference, Prince Bismarck wrote a memorandum to von Alvensleben, which in effect contained his views on the question of adjournment of the conference and Bayard's contentions at that time. Von Alvensleben was instructed to leave the memorandum at the office of the secretary of state. This was done on August 29.[56] Bismarck said that although Germany would have preferred to see the United States agree to the German-English proposition of only *"one* adviser to the Samoan Government to act at the same time as the representative of the treaty powers," the imperial government, in view of Bayard's objections, was ready "to drop

[55] C.D., Apia, vol. 15, encl. 2, Becker to Sewall, Nov. 20, 1887; H. Ex. Doc. no. 238, p. 106, encl. 2 in encl. 80.

[56] Notes from German Legation, vol. 19, memorandum, Prince Bismarck to von Alvensleben, Varzin, Aug. 7, 1887, rec'd at Department of State, Aug. 29, 1887; H. Ex. Doc. no. 238, pp. 59-60, encl. 54.

THE BRANDEIS-TAMASESE RÉGIME 385

that point." He could not, however, see in the American proposition of an executive council with three foreigners "any redress of the now existing evils." Nevertheless, the United States being unwilling to grant Germany the mandate, although her commercial interests were preponderant and Great Britain had accepted the arrangement, the imperial government agreed "to the adjournment of the conference proposed by Mr. Bayard and will, jointly with the British Government, take into close consideration the American counter-proposition of a common control of the Samoan Government, to be exercised by the three treaty powers." Yet, while acknowledging as a fixed principle the equal rights of the three powers under the treaties, Germany felt constrained to proceed against King Malietoa for past offences, as it could not "renounce an immediate reparation for the insults against His Majesty the Emperor and the national honor committed by partisans of Malietoa on the 22d of March last on the occasion of His Majesty's birthday, by the ill-treatment of German citizens in Samoa and by violence inflicted upon them." If Malietoa should be unwilling or unable to make reparation Germany would declare war upon him. Bismarck, evidently fully advised of the rumored confederation of Hawaii and Samoa, informed Bayard, moreover, that in case the king of Hawaii should go to the assistance of Malietoa, Germany would declare war upon him also. The action against Malietoa was to be carried out independently of the other foreign consuls at Apia for the reason that Bismarck was convinced "that our representatives in Apia do not enjoy the expected support of their colleagues in case of disagreements and disputes with Malietoa."

As was noted, the German memorandum was received by Bayard on August 29. At the time of Bismarck's writing the memorandum, orders to the German ships at

Sydney were undoubtedly already sent, for when Bayard received the memorandum, the squadron of four ships under the command of Commodore Heusner had been anchored in Apia harbor exactly ten days.

Bayard made no answer to the memorandum. In fact, he may very well have felt that in view of the recent stand taken by himself in the Washington Conference against Germany's receiving the mandate for Samoa, Bismarck would hesitate before actually declaring war upon King Malietoa. This opinion was all the more plausible for the reason that all three powers had agreed upon the *status quo* in Samoa pending the outcome of the Washington Conference, and because in this very memorandum Bismarck had agreed "to the adjournment of the conference proposed by Mr. Bayard." In so doing, moreover, he had stated that the German Government would "jointly with the British government, take into closer consideration the American counter-proposition of a common control of the Samoan Government, to be exercised by the three treaty powers."

Sewall's despatch of September 10, recounting the events from the arrival of the German squadron until the declaration of war upon King Malietoa, was received in Washington one month later, October 10. The Secretary of State had already on September 23 been notified by the German minister that war had been declared upon Malietoa "personally," and on the very day of his receipt of Sewall's despatch he cabled the consul at Auckland to transmit to Sewall the following: "Am notified by German Minister that Germany has declared war against Malietoa personally for stated causes. Abstain from interference by favoring or opposing either party. The United States reserves all its rights in Samoa, and has received explicit assurances from Germany that Samoan independence and neutrality will not be impaired; that as soon as peace is restored Germany will continue co-operation with United States and Great Britain to establish stable and just government in Samoa." In sending Sewall a confirmation of the cablegram, Alvey A. Adee, second assistant secretary, wrote on October 13 that it was "gratifying to say that your action as so far reported by you, in the trying and delicate position in which you have been placed, has been dignified and discreet, and is fully approved."[57] It was the day after this communication was sent that Consul Becker announced to Sewall the suspension of the municipal government and of course all that transpired then and on the following days was not known in Washington until the arrival on December 3 of Sewall's despatch relating those events.

On the same day when the foregoing commendatory letter went forward to Sewall, Adee sent the instructions, already referred to, wherein he informed Sewall that he should not assume jurisdiction over the German subject in the suit by the Englishman, since the United States had not formally ratified the municipal convention. Had Sewall known on October 14 what Adee wrote on October 13 with reference to the rights of the United States relative to the municipal convention, it is highly improbable that he would have made such strenuous objections to the suspension of the municipal government. For after all, Germany was not violating a treaty with the United States in declaring war upon Malietoa or in causing Tamasese to be set up as king and the municipal government suspended. There was no joint treaty between Germany, Great Britain, and the United States guaranteeing the independence and neutrality of the Samoan islands, and as far as the municipal government was concerned, the United States was in a weaker position than Germany

[57] I.C., vol. 122, no. 23, Adee to Sewall, Oct. 13, 1887; H. Ex. Doc. no. 238, pp. 84-85, encl. 69.

and Great Britain for the reason, as Adee wrote Sewall, that the convention of 1879 had not been ratified by the Senate. The rights of the United States were incorporated in the treaty of 1878, and the right to intervene in Samoan affairs was expressly implied in article V. The question that naturally would occur to the United States government would be whether or not the independence of Samoa was endangered.

The news coming from Sewall concerning the German actions against Malietoa caused Bayard to cable Pendleton on October 11, stating that although Sewall had been instructed to preserve strict neutrality, the government was "anxious, in pursuance of its treaty with Samoa, to secure a peaceful adjustment of the difficulties and a considerate treatment of Samoans." Pendleton was instructed "to suggest to the German Government the advisability of the immediate election of a king and vice king, as agreed to in the conference, and the issuance of identical instructions to the representatives of the treaty powers at Apia to favor such an election, leaving other matters discussed in [the] conference for subsequent consideration."[58]

In submitting Bayard's proposal to Count von Bismarck, Pendleton said "that the Government of the United States was anxious, in the spirit of its treaty with Samoa, to urge peaceful adjustment and fair treatment of the Samoans, and that in this spirit I was instructed to propose to the German Government an immediate election of a king and vice king as agreed in the conference." The count replied "that there had already been an election of a king; that the last telgram from Apia had notified him of the fact." Pendleton reported: "I

[58] Instructions, Germany, vol. 18, telegram Bayard to Pendleton, Oct. 11, 1887; H. Ex. Doc. no. 238, p. 83, encl. 66.

THE BRANDEIS-TAMASESE RÉGIME 389

expressed some astonishment, saying that I had no intimation of the fact from the Department, or in the newspapers, and that the knowledge of the fact by the Department seemed inconsistent with the proposal which I had just been instructed by telegraph that day to present to him."[59] Pendleton was shown a telegram from Becker in which the German consul stated "that all the important chiefs had been called to meet on the 15th of September, and that coming together they had recognized Tamasese as king." A telegram from the German commodore had corroborated Becker's statement. Count von Bismarck, moreover, was not aware, reported Pendleton, that any agreement had been reached at Washington concerning a king and vice king for Samoa. "He rather felicitated me," said Pendleton further, "that the laudable purpose of my Government in proposing the immediate election of a king, as a means of preserving the peace and order of the islands, had been anticipated by the Samoans, and that this, having been so readily accomplished and with happy results, there was nothing for the Governments to do in that direction."[60]

Up to this point the German Foreign Office had been more promptly informed than had our department. Due probably to lack of communications, Sewall did not write his despatch concerning the *fono* of September 15 until October 8 and it was not received until November 5. Consequently Bayard did not have in his possession, at the time he instructed Pendleton to confer with Count von Bismarck, the information which he received on November 5 from Sewall, namely, that when at the meeting of September 15 a majority of the chiefs signed the docu-

---

[59] Despatches, Germany, vol. 45, no. 518, Pendleton to Bayard, Oct. 13, 1887, rec'd Oct. 26; H. Ex. Doc. no. 238, p. 85, encl. 70.
[60] *Ibid.*; H. Ex. Doc. no. 238, p. 86.

ment recognizing Tamasese, they did so under duress. With this information Pendleton could have replied to Count von Bismarck that an election under the guns of the German squadron could not be regarded as a free election, and Bayard's instructions to Pendleton would have appeared to the latter as consistent throughout. As it was, the United States minister seems to have been somewhat disconcerted by the information Count von Bismarck gave him, and the same day he cabled Bayard the substance of the interview.[61]

On November 2 Bayard received Sewall's cablegram forwarded by ship to Auckland concerning the assumption of authority in Apia by Tamasese, and he immediately cabled Pendleton to advise the German government that since Sewall had been informed that "his powers with regard to American citizens and their interests do not depend upon the municipal government," it was "confidently hoped that in the discharge of his functions Mr. Sewall will not be interfered with by the representatives of Germany."[62] Mr. Coleman, the chargé d'affaires in the absence of Pendleton, had an interview with Count von Bismarck on November 4, and stated Bayard's views with respect to Sewall's jurisdiction. In these views the German secretary of state for foreign affairs "wholly acquiesced" and said "that as a matter of course Germany would not interfere." Count von Bismarck informed Coleman, moreover, that "on the previous day" he had "visited Prince Bismarck, [his father] who regretted that the two nations should differ as to affairs on those remote and unimportant islands, while their relations elsewhere were so friendly, and suggested that a

[61] Despatches, Germany, vol. 45, telegram Pendleton to Bayard, Oct. 13, 1887, rec'd Oct. 13; H. Ex. Doc. no. 238, p. 83, encl. 67.

[62] Instructions, Germany, vol. 18, telegram, Bayard to Pendleton, Nov. 2, 1887; H. Ex. Doc. no. 238, p. 90, encl. 73.

THE BRANDEIS-TAMASESE RÉGIME 391

dispatch should be sent on the subject from the foreign office."[63]

On the same day that Coleman had his interview with Count von Bismarck at the Foreign Office in Berlin, the German chargé d'affaires, Baron von Zedtwitz, in Washington, called upon Secretary Bayard and handed him a memorandum from Count von Bismarck.[64] He said the document "contained a counter project of the German Government to the proposition of Mr. Bayard at the conference." The memorandum was dated September, 1887, and took up Bayard's proposition of an executive council for Samoa as contained in the protocols of the Washington Conference. The objection to this plan, stated the memorandum, was that "the appointment of three white ministers would entail too great expense. Moreover, three ministers, each looking after his own nation's interests, would only accentuate the evils of rivalry as already shown in the tri-consular government of Apia.[65] The participation of the king and vice king in the proceedings of the Executive Council," said the memorandum further, "will continue to be a mere matter of form as long as the two chiefs remain ignorant of the English language, and unfamiliar with European ideas relative to government and finance." Although Bayard based his views of an executive council "on the principle that the independence and autonomy of the country are to be kept free from the control and the preponderating influence of any foreign government," it did not appear to the German government "how these principles could be maintained if the Executive Council were to be composed in the manner

[63] Despatches, Germany, vol. 45, telegram, Coleman to Bayard, Nov. 4, 1887; H. Ex. Doc. no. 238, p. 90, encl. 74.
[64] Notes from German Legation, vol. 19, memorandum dated Berlin, September, 1887, rec'd Nov. 4; S. Ex. Doc. no. 31, 50 Congress, 2 session, pp. 6-9, encl. 2.
[65] Ibid.; S. Ex. Doc. no. 31, p. 6.

suggested." The three foreign ministers would outvote the king and vice king and not only "the prestige of the royal office" would be impaired, but all the governmental authority would be placed in the hands of the three members.[66] "The conclusion can not be avoided," continued the memorandum, "that what is now regarded as the independence and autonomy of the natives of Samoa, is nothing but absolute anarchy, and, as was the unanimous opinion of the special commissioners recently sent to Apia by Germany, England, and the United States, that native self-government without foreign assistance is now impossible and must be so for a long time to come."[67]

The German government was of the opinion that the future government of Samoa, in order to be effective, "must have two sides: first, that of a modern state in relation to foreign countries and to everything that concerns foreigners; and, secondly, that of a patriarchal government for the proper development of existing domestic institutions." The memorandum continued: "The objections that were stated in the conference by Mr. Secretary Bayard (which were discussed at length) to the appointment of *one* executive officer, appear to be rather of a theoretical than of a practical nature, since they are based upon the view that such an arrangement is at variance with the acknowledged equality of the treaty powers."[68]

However, if "the American Government can not be convinced of the practical advantages of the German-English proposition," concluded the memorandum, "and if it regards the carrying out of the same as dangerous to the independence and neutrality of Samoa, and as a

[66] Notes from German Legation, vol. 19, memorandum dated Berlin, Sept., 1887, rec'd Nov. 4; S. Ex. Doc. no. 31, p. 7.
[67] *Ibid.;* S. Ex. Doc. no. 31, pp. 7-8.
[68] *Ibid.;* S. Ex. Doc. no. 31, p. 8.

deviation from the traditional polity of the United States in the Pacific Ocean, the Imperial Government has no desire to adhere to the plan and to renew the discussion thereof." The counter proposition of Secretary Bayard as expressed in the conference was regarded on the other hand as impracticable and the German Government was therefore "unable to regard the same as sufficient ground for further negotiations."[69]

On December 9, 1887, the German chargé d'affaires at Washington, called upon Secretary Bayard and read to him a long despatch from Prince Bismarck dated November 18. Having recalled the fact that on a former occasion he had brought to the attention of Bayard the anti-German attitude of Sewall, the American consul general at Apia, during the recent German hostilities against Malietoa, he now complained about anti-German actions of Sewall's predecessors as well. The American representatives mentioned by Bismarck were consuls Dawson, Canisius, and Greenebaum. Consul Dawson, to be specific, had protested in 1881 against the landing of a force from the German warship, *Möwe,* when the German consul had thought this procedure necessary to protect the foreign settlement. Consul Canisius was charged with having inspired the two letters addressed by King Malietoa to the German emperor on the eighteenth and twenty-eighth of May, 1885, demanding the recall of the German consul, Dr. Stübel. Greenebaum was blamed for acting in opposition to the German representative, and of finally proclaiming an American protectorate over the islands, an act which Prince Bismarck admitted was disavowed by Bayard and resulted in the recall of Greenebaum.

Bismarck observed further in the memorandum how remarkable it appeared to him that after friendly relations had "continued undisturbed for more than a century

[69] *Ibid.;* S. Ex. Doc. no. 31, p. 9.

between Germany and the United States," they should become strained "on that remote realm of islands, where neither America nor Germany has any political interests to defend" by the "continual ill-will of a series of American representatives." There were no local commercial rivalries which could explain such a fact. He continued: "In this regard, our relations to Great Britain are by far more difficult. The contiguity of the English and German possessions at the Cape, in Zanzibar, in West Africa, New Guinea, and in different parts of the South Sea leads to rivalries which can not always remain free from frictions. Great Britain has much more occasion to be jealous of the extension of German influence, and has, besides, to take into consideration the claims and prejudice of her colonies, which, grown up under the idea of a British monopoly of ruling in transatlantic countries, are inclined to look upon foreign neighborship as an interference with the sphere of their interests, or as a menace to their security. Especially in the case of Samoa the British Government has, on account of the covetousness repeatedly shown by the New Zealanders of obtaining possession of those islands, to contend with unusually great difficulties with regard to a just and benevolent settlement of the existing difficulties with us. Nevertheless we are there in much better relations to England than to America, although the commercial interests of Great Britain in Samoa, though smaller than ours, are more considerable than those of the United States." Bismarck concluded his memorandum by comparing the commercial interests of Germany with those of America in Samoa to the great advantage of the former, though Germany had not sought for herself commercial privileges such as the United States had recently secured in Hawaii "by the ratification of the lately renewed reciprocity treaty of January 30, 1875." Germany had "always maintained the princi-

THE BRANDEIS-TAMASESE RÉGIME   395

ple of equality of rights of nations in Samoa, and never aspired to political advantages." Even though Malietoa had been deported by the German authorities, that fact did not change the "relations of the treaty powers to Samoa."

Finding no reason *"in the facts themselves"* which "could explain the continual ill-will" shown toward Germany "by the American representatives of the past and of the present," Prince Bismarck requested Bayard's assistance "in the investigation of this strange fact." Should his supposition prove correct, namely, "that those difficulties have their origin in the personal disposition of the American representatives in Apia, and not in their instructions," Bismarck was "convinced that the American Government will cause the necessary redress to take place."[70]

A little over a month after Bayard received the above memorandum from Baron von Zedtwitz he replied to Bismarck in a communication to Pendleton of approximately nine thousand words.[71] A more masterly presentation of the policy of the United States with reference to Samoa was never made. The note was a detailed summary of events of the past with Bayard's comments interspersed. It was especially designed to show that Germany had violated her agreement with the United States and Great Britain, namely, that matters be left in Samoa *in statu quo* until the three powers could reach an agreement for joint control. The Washington Conference was held on that basis and the adjournment was agreed to on that

[70] Notes from German Legation; H. Ex. Doc. no. 238, pp. 96-98, encl. 78; *Foreign Relations, 1888*, part I, pp. 662-664, Prince von Bismarck to Baron von Zedtwitz, Nov. 18, 1887, copy and translation left at the Department of State, Dec. 9, 1887, by Baron von Zedtwitz.

[71] Instructions, Germany, vol. 18, no. 280, Bayard to Pendleton, Jan. 17, 1888; H. Ex. Doc. no. 238, pp. 107-121, encl. 83; *Foreign Relations, 1888*, part I, pp. 594-608.

basis. By declaring war upon King Malietoa Germany was guilty of a breach of faith.

The secretary of state instructed Pendleton to say that the president shared the regrets of Prince von Bismarck "that the relations of traditional friendship which have subsisted between the United States and Germany unbroken for so many years should be, in any way or degree, disturbed or affected by occurrences in remote islands in which the material interests of both Governments are comparatively insignificant." As a matter of fact the United States government had "manifested in the most unmistakable manner its desire to avoid all possibilities of difference with the other treaty powers in Samoa." This policy had been "pursued with consistency and good faith, actuated not so much by the idea of any present or probable future commercial interest in that quarter of the globe in which the islands lie, as by a benevolent desire to promote the development and secure the independence of one of the few remaining independent territories and autonomous native governments in the Pacific Ocean." The United States might easily have acquired political control in Samoa "with much satisfaction to a majority of the natives" long before the treaties of Germany and Great Britain were negotiated with Samoa, if our government had "entertained any designs of territorial aggrandizement." However, "another and widely different policy has guided the action of the United States in respect to the native communities in the Southern Pacific." This "disinterested position of the United States is strongly emphasized by the promptitude with which the action of Mr. Greenebaum was disavowed by this Government, when he proclaimed an American protectorate over Samoa."[72]

In regard to Canisius's authorship of the two letters

[72] Instructions, Germany, vol. 18, no. 280, Bayard to Pendleton, Jan. 17, 1888; H. Ex. Doc. no. 238, p. 109.

THE BRANDEIS–TAMASESE RÉGIME 397

sent by King Malietoa to the German emperor, Bayard said the department had never received any information, but the documents possessed by the department relative to the *Möwe* affair "lead to a very different impression of that incident from that which Prince Bismarck has been led to entertain." The action of the German consul in requesting the landing of the German force from the *Möwe* was not only "not in agreement with the Samoan government and the municipal administration, but it was taken without consultation with the acting head of the municipal government [Mr. Dawson], after the disturbance had actually been quelled by the local police and was complained against by the Samoan King." Bayard denied that the lack of harmony between the German and American consuls had been "due to hostility to Germany on the part of the consuls of the United States" and, supporting this contention, he recalled certain incidents prior to the landing of the forces from the *Möwe*.[73]

When, for example, Sir Arthur Gordon arrived in Samoa in August, 1879, to negotiate a treaty between Great Britain and Samoa, he "consulted the foreign consuls and captains of the men-of-war then present upon the point whether he ought to treat with Malietoa as King of Samoa." He was "unanimously advised to do so," the German consul, Theodor Weber, who later as the head representative of the German company actively supported Tamasese, being one of the representatives concurring in that advice. "On the following day the German and American consuls joined with Sir Arthur Gordon in proclaiming the government of Malietoa as the only real government in the islands. At the same time the municipality convention was entered into by the American, British, and German consuls with Malietoa as representing the Government of Samoa. The consular repre-

[73] *Ibid.*; H. Ex. Doc. no. 238, p. 110.

sentative of the United States then consistently supported the government of Malietoa, and it is understood that the German consul was under instructions from his Government to pursue the same course."[74]

The instability of the native government of Samoa Bayard attributed to the "failure of the German consular representatives to give consistent support to existing native government," especially so during the past two years, rather than "to any action on the part of the consular representative of the United States." The German official attitude, thought Bayard, was naturally a reflection of the "desire of the local German element for such a native government as would be disposed to advance its commercial and landed interests."[75] "On no other hypothesis," continued Bayard, "am I able to account for the support given, especially during the past two years, to the natives in rebellion against the existing government, for, whatever may have been the grounds for complaint on the part of Germany against Malietoa personally, the support of Tamasese, or of any other opposing chief, could certainly form no part of a plan of redress against Malietoa."[76]

Bayard then proceeded to state: "Moreover, I am wholly unable to share in Prince Bismarck's impression that the efforts of Germany to establish a lawful and orderly condition of affairs in Samoa have generally, not to say without exception, met with the opposition of American consular representatives. I could readily point to many instances of co-operation of American consular representatives with those of Germany, when the efforts of the representatives of the latter were directed simply to the maintenance of peace and order."[77] The attitude of

[74] Instructions, Germany, vol. 18, no. 280, Bayard to Pendleton, Jan. 17, 1888; H. Ex. Doc. no. 238, p. 110.
[75] *Ibid.*; H. Ex. Doc. no. 238, p. 111.   [76] *Ibid.*   [77] *Ibid.*

THE BRANDEIS-TAMASESE RÉGIME 399

the United States relative to upholding the independence of Samoa was accentuated, when viewed against the background of the acquisitions of Great Britain, France, and Germany of the various island groups.

The secretary then proceeded to enumerate the islands acquired and the dates of their acquisition, and said that in view of this practical partition of the Pacific it was "unnecessary to emphasize the importance attached by this Government to the maintenance of the rights to which the United States has become entitled in any of the few remaining regions now under independent and autonomous native governments in the Pacific Ocean."[78] The policy of the United States in Hawaii was not subject, he said, to the same criticisms as that of Germany in Samoa, for "although the geographical and historical relations of the group [Hawaii] to the United States necessarily give this Government an interest in the future of the islands such as no other foreign government can possibly possess," yet the United States had not at any time since the reciprocity treaty of 1875 was concluded "sought to use it to control the native government of the islands or to regulate their internal affairs against the wishes of the inhabitants." On the other hand, the action of the German representatives in Samoa, "especially during the last three years, has been such as to raise grave doubts in regard to the future relations of the treaty powers respecting the islands, and these doubts have only been relieved by expected assurances from Berlin of the absence of any intention on the part of Germany to unsettle former understandings, and take control of the native Government and assume a protectorate."[79] He cited as an example of German encroachments the signing of the treaty of November 1, 1884, by the German con-

[78] *Ibid.;* H. Ex. Doc. no. 238, pp. 111-113.
[79] *Ibid.;* H. Ex. Doc. no. 238, p. 113.

sul general, Dr. Stübel, and King Malietoa, with Theodor Weber as witness, "under which substantially the entire control of Samoan affairs was to be handed over to the Germans." He admitted that the subsequent action of Dr. Stübel in seizing or attaching the sovereign rights of Malietoa to the municipality of Apia, had been disavowed by the German government, "but the causal connection of the act and of the long-existing and active local influence by which it was doubtless inspired, with subsequent disorders in the islands, needs no argumentative exposition."[80]

In reciting the more recent events and in stating the alleged causes for Germany's war against Malietoa, Bayard made the point that these causes "existed long prior to the meeting of the conference in this city, and some of them even anterior to its proposal, the acceptance of which was followed, as I was informed, by appropriate action to maintain the *status quo* in the islands." Nothing was said in the conference to disturb the impression that the *status quo* would be maintained until an agreement was reached. His "first intimation of belligerent intent on the part of Germany against Malietoa," therefore, was given to him "by the German Minister on the 29th of August last, five days after war was actually declared against him [Malietoa], and necessarily several weeks after it was determined upon," and Bayard's "first notification that war had been declared and that Germany intended to depose Malietoa was also *post factum,* being given to me by the German Minister on the 23d of September last, six days after the Samoan King was taken on board of the *Bismarck.*"[81]

Bayard then observed that the new government in Samoa was not considered as having satisfied the conditions

[80] Instructions, Germany, vol. 18, no. 280, Bayard to Pendleton, Jan. 17, 1888; H. Ex. Doc. no. 238, p. 114.
[81] *Ibid.;* H. Ex. Doc. no. 238, p. 118.

THE BRANDEIS–TAMASESE RÉGIME 401

laid down in the conference to the effect that a new election of king should take place in Samoa, " 'a native election, free and unawed.' " The signing by the chiefs on September 15 of the document whereby Tamasese was recognized could not be regarded by the government of the United States as "a native election, free and unawed" since the whole ceremony took place "under the eye and direction of German representatives." The government of Tamasese was "far more objectionable" than the mandate government proposed by Germany in the conference, for that government would at least have "carried with it the guaranties of the Imperial Government." The new régime "can be regarded," continued Bayard, "as nothing else than the government of the islands by the local German commercial and landed interests, through Herr Brandeis, Tamasese's sole minister."[82]

In reviewing the incidents leading up to the suspension of the municipal government, Bayard admitted that the United States had not ratified the convention of 1879. Yet the government "had always given the municipal organization the fullest practical support and recognition, as an existent local government." Moreover, "the American consul, being clothed by the laws of the United States and our original treaty with Samoa with judicial powers, had discharged through that organization, from its commencement eight years ago, judicial functions for the common advantage of all the treaty powers, and with their full assent and co-operation; and Americans, as well as the members of other foreign nationalities represented in Apia, had paid taxes to support the municipal government."[83]

In conclusion Bayard said "that in the opinion of this Government, the course taken by Germany in respect to

[82] *Ibid.;* H. Ex. Doc. no. 238, p. 119.
[83] *Ibid.;* H. Ex. Doc. no. 238, p. 120.

Samoa upon the temporary adjournment of the conference in this city . . . can not be regarded as having been marked by that just consideration which the ancient friendship between the United States and Germany entitles this Government to expect; that the present condition of affairs in the islands can not, in view of the circumstances under which it was brought about and is still maintained, be regarded by the United States as satisfactory; and that to the end of creating a more acceptable situation in the islands, the native government should be placed upon a basis more compatible with independence and impartiality in the discharge of its duties to all the treaty powers.''[84] Bayard summed up the difference in the attitudes of Germany and the United States toward the Samoan problem in the following words: ''Owing, doubtless, to her commercial preponderance in the islands, to Germany the primary object has seemed to be the establishment of a stronger government. To the United States, the object first in importance has seemed to be the preservation of native independence and autonomy.''[85]

The long memorandum was handed to Count von Bismarck, imperial secretary of state for foreign affairs, by Pendleton on February 7, 1888.[86] On December 21, 1887, and March 8, 1888, resolutions were passed in the Senate and House of Representatives, respectively, requesting the president to transmit the correspondence in the possession of the government relative to Samoa.[87] In order to present as complete a report as possible to the president for transmission to these bodies, Secretary Bayard sug-

[84] Instructions, Germany, vol. 18, no. 280, Bayard to Pendleton, Jan. 17, 1888; H. Ex. Doc. no. 238, p. 121.
[85] *Ibid.*
[86] Despatches, Germany, vol. 46, Pendleton to Bayard, Feb. 7, 1888, rec'd Feb. 25; H. Ex. Doc. no. 238, p. 123, encl. 85.
[87] Richardson, *op. cit.*, VIII, 612.

THE BRANDEIS-TAMASESE RÉGIME 403

gested to both Germany and Great Britain that in view of what had transpired since the Washington Conference and "pending further consideration of the Samoan question, each Government be at liberty to publish the joint protocols."[88] Both governments replied within a few days, declining to act on the suggestion. Sackville-West said that "Her Majesty's Government are of opinion that, pending the re-assembling of the conference, its proceedings should be considered confidential and that the publication of them at present might prejudice the satisfactory solution of the question."[89] Baron von Zedtwitz, German chargé d'affaires, wrote that the imperial government was "rather of the opinion that those protocols, in view of the interruption and hitherto fruitless course of the conferences, which have consequently yielded no definite result, are not suited for publication."[90]

The American press devoted much space to the Samoan affairs with the sudden turn of events in those islands in August and September. Presently attacks by the Republicans upon the alleged weak-kneed policy of Bayard began to be heard. These continued for over a year and at times the criticisms became bitter partisan diatribes. The resolutions in the Senate and House were inspired by the feeling that all was not well with the Department of State, and since Bayard was still pledged to secrecy relative to the protocols of the Washington Conference, this erroneous impression continued to dominate the minds of the Republicans. The year 1888, moreover, was a presidential campaign year and no possible criticism of the Cleveland

[88] Notes to British Legation, vol. 20, Bayard to Sackville-West, March 19, 1888; H. Ex. Doc. no. 238, p. 123, encl. 86. A similar note, *mutatis mutandis*, was sent to Baron von Zedtwitz.

[89] Notes from British Legation, vol. 115, Sackville-West to Bayard, Mar. 22, 1888, rec'd March 23; H. Ex. Doc. no. 238, p. 123, encl. 87.

[90] Notes from German Legation, vol. 19, von Zedtwitz to Bayard, March 24, 1888, rec'd Mar. 24; H. Ex. Doc. no. 238, p. 124, encl. 88.

administration in general was neglected. What became almost an obsession with some was the notion that Germany had broken a treaty with the United States, and that Bayard did not defend the rights of the country in a sufficiently vigorous manner to prevent German aggression. Bayard's firm stand against both Germany and Great Britain at the Washington Conference the previous summer was, of course, unknown, and as long as the protocols of this conference remained a secret within the Department of State and the two foreign offices of Germany and Great Britain, the Republican attacks upon Bayard for his alleged determination to keep from the people the knowledge of his "defeat" remained unanswered. Had Great Britain and Germany consented to the publication of the protocols, excellent campaign material for the Democrats would have been provided.

As a matter of fact there was no joint treaty with Germany or Great Britain relative to the islands as a whole. The convention of 1879 concerning the government of Apia had not been ratified by the United States Senate; hence there could be no violation of treaty rights of the United States with regard to that treaty. The United States had a treaty with Samoa, it is true, but so had the other two powers, and no primary position was enjoyed by the United States in Samoa by the treaty of 1878, as obtained, for example, in Hawaii by the treaty of 1875. Hence there was no violation here. What Germany did violate, however, was her agreement with the United States and Great Britain, made before the Washington Conference was held, namely, to maintain the *status quo* in Samoa until an understanding could be reached for a joint control in the islands by the three treaty powers. Perhaps it was this breach of faith that was interpreted as a violation of a treaty. Only when the protocols were published in February, 1889, were the Republicans finally

THE BRANDEIS-TAMASESE RÉGIME   405

deprived of their powerful weapon against the Cleveland administration and especially against the Department of State.

The *New York Times* at this time represented the moderate opinion on the subject. When Sewall was about to leave for Samoa to take up his work as the first American consul general and hence the ranking officer in Apia, the *Times* said: "The disturbed position of affairs in Samoa is seriously menacing American interests in that island. . . . His [Sewall's] hands would be much further strengthened if it were practicable to station a United States naval vessel at that point until the present disturbed condition of affairs subsides, but there are none available."[91] On October 30 the same newspaper stated editorially "Commodore Harmoney's views regarding the Mare Island Navy Yard will receive additional weight from the fact that they are given simultaneously with the announcement that King Malietoa has been transported from the Samoan Islands in a German man-of-war, and his kingdom is now practically under the control of the German Empire. . . . This seizure of a group of Pacific islands is but one of a series of similar transactions upon which the United States has looked with becoming tranquility in the past, but it is possible that in the near future this Government may find it expedient to object to the absorption of all the Pacific islands by European powers, and in that event the Mare Island Navy Yard, as our only naval station on the Pacific coast, will assume an importance which it has hitherto lacked."[92]

After the publication of the Samoan correspondence in the first days of April, 1888, the *Times* said editorially: "It appears from the diplomatic correspondence upon

[91] *New York Times*, July 27, 1887 (page 5, column 5). News dispatch from Washington dated July 26.
[92] *Ibid.*, October 30, 1887 (page 4 column 1) editorial.

the Samoan question which has been made up for Congress, that Secretary Bayard by no means looked upon the German usurpation of authority last year at Apia with the indifference then imputed to him. On the contrary, he expressed his surprise at this conduct in strong terms to Mr. Pendleton, our Minister at Berlin, and authorized him to make known his sentiments to the German Government.'"[93]

In May, 1888, the *Times* published a long article in which it was asserted that the cause of the German aggression in Samoa in the previous year was the renewal of the United States-Hawaiian reciprocity treaty with Senator Edmund's amendment. The amendment provided for a grant by Hawaii to the United States of Pearl Harbor as a naval base. "The mischief-making propensities of the Republican Senators," said the article, "have never been held directly responsible for the embarrassing circumstances of the Samoan Islands dispute, yet there appears to be reason for believing that the determination of those Senators to embarrass the administration was very successful in that direction. . . . As the United States had indicated a desire to acquire Hawaii, Germany fixed its eyes upon Samoa. . . . Of course no intimation has been thrown out that Germany has simply followed the example set by the United States, but that such is the fact, and that the trouble at Apia was brought on by the amendment of Mr. Edmunds to the Hawaii treaty is believed by persons who have known the talk of diplomatic circles about these matters.'"[94]

Shortly after the Brandeis-Tamasese régime was established, American property owners began to experience difficulties with Theodor Weber of the German firm. One H. J. Moors complained to Sewall in October that a

[93] *New York Times*, April 5, 1888 (page 4, column 2) editorial.
[94] *Ibid.*, May 20, 1888 (page 2, column 1).

THE BRANDEIS–TAMASESE RÉGIME

certain piece of property, which he had bought in December, 1885 from a New Zealander, named D. H. McKenzie, and on which he had paid the municipal taxes ever since, was claimed by E. Weber, attorney for Theodor Weber, his brother, who was then in Germany. Moors informed Sewall that he was certain Weber and Becker were at the time of writing "formulating a set of laws, and that Tamasese will accept them without amendment, and that a land court will be established with the express understanding that all claims made by the German firm will be engineered through." Moors continued: "Thus my property and the property of other persons is liable to be taken from us on the most slender pretext, unless we defend it rifle in hand, and I assure you that I will do so before I will be forced into such an iniquitous court." Moors said further that he had also been "compelled to see my trade reduced to nothing." It was not possible for him, therefore "to sit idly by and be despoiled of that which I have bought and improved at a large expense." Moors' interests in Samoa were the most important of any individual United States citizen, his taxes being one-half of the total paid by Americans in the islands.[95] In forwarding Moors' communication to the State Department, Sewall said: "It puts plainly the case of Americans whose land titles are endangered by the installment of Tamasese as king of these islands, and the consequent control of the Government by the Germans."[96] Moors left for the United States later in order to present the case of the Americans directly before the government. His interests were valued by Sewall at $40,000.[97]

[95] C.D., Apia, vol. 15, Sewall, Oct. 8, 1887, rec'd Nov. 5; encl. 1, Moors to Sewall, Oct. 5, 1887; see also S. Ex. Doc. no. 31, pp. 4-5, encl. 1 in encl. 1.
[96] *Ibid.;* S. Ex. Doc. no. 31, p. 4, encl. 1.
[97] *Ibid.*, Sewall, Feb. 29, 1888, rec'd Mar. 24; S. Ex. Doc. no. 31, p. 28, encl. 16.

In February, 1888, Sewall reported that a meeting of forty of the most reputable American and English residents of Apia had been held to protest against arbitrary and illegal methods of the *de facto* government in levying and collecting taxes. The chairman of the meeting was Thomas Crawford Johnston of the firm of A. Crawford & Company, of San Francisco, the largest American trading firm in the South Seas. One of the clauses of the resolutions drawn up at the meeting read: "That those present at this meeting pledge themselves to unite for the purpose of resisting by all lawful means the illegal demands and aggressive and despotic action of those persons who have illegally seized the municipal property and assumed to exercise jurisdiction over European and American residents."[98]

In April Sewall reported that the latest act of the German firm was to claim "a large strip of valuable land" belonging to an American citizen, named W. Blacklock, manager for H. J. Moors. The reason for this step, Blacklock thought, was the fact that Moors' visit to Washington had aroused the firm to take this action of reprisal. "The confidence on the part of the Germans in securing a settlement of their land claims favorable to them," wrote Sewall, "alarms our citizens, and the titles here is the subject of anxious inquiries at this office."[99]

If one were to set down one word which, more than any other, would explain the reason for the strenuous efforts of Theodor Weber and his firm to get control in Samoa it would be "copra." The German firm, known since 1880 as "Die Deutsche Handels und Plantagen Gesellschaft für Süd-See Inseln zu Hamburg," experienced financial

---

[98] C.D., Apia, vol. 15, Sewall, Feb. 29, 1888, rec'd Mar. 24, encl. 1, resolutions adopted Feb. 9, 1888; S. Ex. Doc. no. 31, p. 29, encl. 1 in encl. 16.

[99] *Ibid.*, vol. 16, Sewall, April 27, 1888, rec'd May 19; S. Ex. Doc. no. 31, p. 57, encl. 39.

THE BRANDEIS-TAMASESE RÉGIME 409

difficulties at its very inception, and except for the year 1884, when a dividend of four per cent was paid to its stockholders, no regular dividends were forthcoming until 1898. As a matter of fact, its original stock of five million marks, four-fifths of which represented the value of the Godeffroy assets, was as early as 1881 contracted to 2,750,000 marks divided into 2,750 shares of 1000 marks each.[100]

Throughout the eighteen eighties this "Long Handle Firm," as humorists were prone to call it, otherwise popularly known as the "D.H. and P.G.," attempted to dominate the commercial and political situation in Samoa. This was especially true after Prince Bismarck reversed his colonial policy in 1884. After that, as was seen, the German flag protected German trade in Samoa as well as in Africa and New Guinea, and the arrival of a German war vessel was always looked upon by the natives as having come to aid "Misi Ueba," that is, Mr. Weber. The following characterization written by Robert Louis Stevenson in 1892 perhaps is the best description of Weber in print. "John Caesar Godeffroy himself had never visited the islands; his sons and nephews came, indeed, but scarcely to reap laurels; and the mainspring and headpiece of this great concern, until death took him, was a certain remarkable man of the name of Theodor Weber. He was of an artful and commanding character; in the smallest thing or the greatest, without fear or scruple; equally able to affect, equally ready to adopt, the most engaging politeness or the most imperious airs of domination. It was he who did most damage to rival traders; it was he who most harried the Samoans; and yet I never met anyone, white or native, who did not respect his memory. All felt it was a gallant battle, and

[100] Dr. Heinrich Schnee, *Deutsches Kolonial Lexikon*, I, 300.

the man a great fighter, and now when he is dead, and the war seems to have gone against him, many can scarce remember, without a kind of regret, how much devotion and audacity have been spent in vain. His name still lives in the songs of Samoa. One, that I have heard, tells of Misi Ueba and a biscuit box—the suggesting incident being long since forgotten. Another sings plaintively how all things, land and food and property, pass progressively, as by law of nature, into the hands of Misi Ueba, and soon nothing will be left for Samoans. This is an epitaph the man would have enjoyed.''[101]

At the time under discussion the German firm made a bold bid for the monopoly of copra. When taxes were levied the natives would mortgage their whole crop at times to pay the government. Weber would pay the money to his own government, which would in turn expend the money in the interest of the firm by building good roads to its plantations. Whole villages, and in one case a whole district, that of Aana, would mortgage their crops of copra to ''the Firm'' to obtain the money at high rates of interest to pay these taxes. The governors appointed by Tamasese were instructed to forbid the selling of copra or the mortgaging of copra or lands to any other firm. As a matter of fact, the new government had been in power scarcely a month, wrote Sewall, ''when it levied a tax and collected under it $21,000, of which $11,100 was borrowed on mortgages; $9,100 of this was borrowed from the German firm 'payable in coprah.' ''[102] Hence when the new government announced in February, 1888, that the tax bill of that year which the natives were expected to pay, would be $47,000, or more than twice the amount of the

[101] Robert Louis Stevenson, *A Foot-Note to History*, etc., pp. 397-398.
[102] C.D., Apia, vol. 16, Sewall, Mar. 27, 1888, rec'd April 21; S. Ex. Doc. no. 31, p. 37, encl. 24.

THE BRANDEIS-TAMASESE RÉGIME 411

one for the previous year, the Brandeis-Tamasese régime was only raising up trouble for itself.[103]

The practical effect of the firm's attempt to monopolize the copra output as far as American traders were concerned is perhaps best seen in the case of one William Wallwork, who lived on the island of Savaii. He reported to Sewall in May that he had found it impossible to purchase copra, the German firm having secured a monopoly of the supply. The natives, he informed Sewall, had no voice in the disposition of their produce, being afraid of the governor of their district, who had gone to Apia some time before "and made arrangements with Brandeis and Weber for all the copra, barring out American and British traders." Sir John B. Thurston had been in Samoa investigating British complaints, however, and in consequence a Samoan, who had been imprisoned for selling copra to the British firm of McArthur and Company, was released. The American rights were not being protected and were "placed at the mercy of the government of a rival firm." Sewall asked how they were to be protected. Commander Day of the *Mohican* had instructions "not to interfere with matters on shore." The same instructions had been sent Commander Kempff of the *Adams*, which ship was at Apia before the *Mohican*. Sewall was indeed in a predicament. He had no relations with Brandeis, since the *de facto* government was not recognized by the United States, and there was no use in sending a complaint to Becker, the adviser of Brandeis, since he steadily disclaimed "any connection with the 'Samoan Government', in the name of which Brandeis assumes to act." Sewall therefore suggested cutting the gordian knot by a temporary occupation by the United States of

[103] *Ibid.*, vol. 15, Sewall, Feb. 29, 1888, rec'd Mar. 24; S. Ex. Doc. no. 31, p. 29, encl. 16.

the islands and the abolition of the Brandeis government. "I am aware," Sewall concluded, "that such a course here has never been contemplated by the Department, but the situation has never been before what it is now."[104]

Sewall became the chief opponent of the Brandeis-Tamasese régime, ably assisted by two other Americans, Moors and Blacklock. Robert Louis Stevenson wrote about these men some three or four years later as follows: "From the moment of the declaration of war against Laupepa, we find him [Sewall] standing forth in bold, consistent, and sometimes rather captious opposition, stirring up his government at home with clear and forcible despatches, and on the spot grasping at every opportunity to thrust a stick into the German wheels. For some while, he and Moors fought their difficult battle in conjunction; in the course of which, first one, and then the other, paid a visit home to reason with the authorities at Washington; and during the consul's absence, there was found an American clerk in Apia, William Blacklock, to perform the duties of the office with remarkable ability and courage. The three names just brought together, Sewall, Moors, and Blacklock, make the head and front of the opposition; if Tamasese fell, if Brandeis was driven forth, if the treaty of Berlin was signed, theirs is the blame or the credit."[105]

In May, 1888, Sewall reported that the great chief of Atua, Mataafa, was planning to assume the leadership of a movement directed against Tamasese.[106] In June the Atuan had not as yet made a demonstration, but it was reported that "he and some of the Malietoa leaders are

[104] C.D., Apia, vol. 15, Sewall, May 24, 1888, rec'd June 19; S. Ex. Doc. no. 31, pp. 67-68, encl. 46.

[105] Stevenson, *A Foot-Note to History*, etc., p. 433.

[106] C.D., Apia, vol. 16, Sewall, May 24, 1888; S. Ex. Doc. no. 31, p. 69, encl. 47.

eager for war." The German ships were still in Samoan waters supporting the Brandeis-Tamasese régime, but the Mataafans expected aid against them. Brandeis was organizing an army, since trouble was expected.[107] The *de facto* government began making wholesale arrests of chiefs.[108] Events were developing so fast that Sewall concluded to go immediately to Washington and report personally on the situation in Samoa. He was not gone from Samoa many days before war broke out. Blacklock, who had been left in charge of the consulate as vice consul, sent a cablegram dated September 4 via Auckland September 15, as follows: "Samoans at war. General revolt against Tamasese. Affairs more serious than ever."[109]

Immediately upon receipt of the cablegram Bayard suggested to the secretary of the navy, W. C. Whitney, that a ship be sent to Samoa to protect American interests,[110] and on September 17 telegraphic instructions were despatched to Rear Admiral Kimberly carrying this suggestion into effect.[111] During the whole period of disturbance an American naval vessel had, as a matter of fact, been stationed in Samoan waters. It has been noted that the *Adams*, Commander Kempff, arrived at Apia on October 20, 1887, six days after the suspension of the municipal government. On January 29, 1888, the *Mohican*, Commander Day, relieved the *Adams*, but on June 1 the *Adams* returned, relieving the *Mohican*, this time commanded by Commander Leary. The reason for the above

[107] *Ibid.*, Sewall, June 19, 1888, rec'd July 16; S. Ex. Doc. no. 31, p. 89, encl. 57.
[108] *Ibid.*, Sewall, Aug. 17, 1888, rec'd Sept. 10; S. Ex. Doc. no. 31, p. 112, encl. 77.
[109] *Ibid.*, telegram, Blacklock to Bayard, Sept. 4, 1888, via Auckland, Sept. 15, rec'd Sept. 15; S. Ex. Doc. no. 31, p. 113, encl. 78.
[110] Domestic Letters, Department of State, Bayard to Whitney, Sept. 15, 1888; S. Ex. Doc. no. 31, p. 114, encl. 79.
[111] Executive Letter Book, Navy Department, Whitney to Bayard, Sept. 17, 1888; S. Ex. Doc. no. 31, p. 114, encl. 80.

order from Secretary Whitney was the fact that instructions had been sent to the *Adams* to leave Samoa, and the department did not desire any long period to elapse with no ship in Samoan waters. When the Mataafa rebellion broke out, however, Commander Leary was still at Apia, his instructions being received only on September 4, and on September 9 he sent a detailed report to Secretary Whitney concerning the new turn of events. He attributed the revolt of the natives to "excessive taxation, deprivation of their freedom, abolition of native time-honored customs, confiscations of their goods, and imprisonment of their respective chiefs." He reported that he could not leave for San Francisco, as instructed, immediately, as he was expecting coal and stores from Auckland. When these arrived he would depart "unless a temporary delay should be absolutely necessary for the protection of American citizens."[112] The *Adams* remained in Samoa indefinitely and its commander became one of the outstanding figures during these troublous days. He sent a protest to Captain Fritze of the *Adler* on September 6, against a contemplated bombardment by the *Adler* of anti-Tamasese villages on the island of Manono. On the ninth he actively intervened in behalf of an American citizen, Captain E. L. Hamilton, on whose property depredations were being committed by the Tamasese warriors.[113]

The revolutionists elected and installed Mataafa as king of Samoa, and on September 11 the opposing forces met in what Commander Leary described as "the greatest battle that has ever taken place in the group, the Tamasese men firing the first shot." The battle continued until the next day and ended with a complete rout of the

[112] Leary to Whitney, Sept. 9, 1888. Extract transmitted to Department of State, Oct. 9, 1888; S. Ex. Doc. no. 31, pp. 115-116, encl. 83.
[113] *Ibid.*

THE BRANDEIS–TAMASESE RÉGIME 415

Tamasese forces.[114] Blacklock, in reporting the news that Tamasese was overthrown, stated that Germany had not yet declared a protectorate, but he feared it might happen. He concluded his telegram: "Could not the United States get in ahead till things are settled? Must act at once. Please telegraph instructions via Sydney."[115] Bayard, upon receipt of the telegram from Blacklock, immediately cabled Pendleton, stating that the United States would "respect the choice of the Samoan people, and assumed that the other treaty powers, in pursuance of their joint understanding, would take a similar course."[116] On October 3 Bayard was informed by Coleman, chargé d'affaires at Berlin, that Prince Bismarck had instructed the German consul at Apia by telegraph "to restrict his action to what was necessary to secure the safety of the lives and property of German subjects and to report by telegraph if they seemed in danger."[117]

On October 1 the British war vessel, *Calliope,* bearing the flag of Rear Admiral Fairfax, arrived in Apia accompanied by the cruiser, *Lizard.* The admiral immediately called a conference "to discuss the necessity of having neutral ground." The commander of the *Adams* wrote on October 8 that he would delay his "departure to allow opportunity to receive telegraphic instructions." He had had very unsatisfactory relations with the captain of the *Adler* because he evaded "the question at issue by taking shelter under the wing of the German consul."[118]

---

[114] *Ibid.,* Sept. 13, 1888. Extract transmitted to Department of State, Oct. 11, 1888; S. Ex. Doc. no. 31, p. 124, encl. 86.

[115] C.D., Apia, vol. 16, telegram Sept. 14, 1888, via San Francisco Sept. 29, rec'd Oct. 1.

[116] Instructions, Germany, vol. 18, telegram, Bayard to Pendleton, Oct. 1, 1888; S. Ex. Doc. no. 31, p. 127, encl. 89.

[117] Despatches, Germany, vol. 47, telegram, Coleman to Bayard, Oct. 3, 1888; S. Ex. Doc. no. 31, p. 131, encl. 91.

[118] Leary to Whitney, Oct. 8, 1888. Extract transmitted to Department of State, Nov. 3, 1888; S. Ex. Doc. no. 31, p. 133, encl. 94.

The department informed Blacklock on October 11 that the policy of the United States with reference to Samoa was one of non-interference. No protectorate could, therefore, be considered. Blacklock's duties during the hostilities should be confined to protecting, with the aid of the naval forces, the property and lives of American citizens. Blacklock was commended for his energy and efficiency during the critical period he was going through.[119] The department also desired to convey its thanks to Commander Leary for his "zeal and diligence."[120] The next day (October 12), Commodore Harmony, acting secretary of the navy, informed Secretary Bayard that Rear Admiral Kimberly, in command on the Pacific Station, had instructions "to continue to keep one of the ships of his command in Samoan waters and to give full instructions to her commanding officer to intervene vigorously, should occasion arise, to protect the persons and property of American citizens there residing."[121]

The serious situation in Samoa as far as American citizens were concerned was illustrated in Blacklock's despatch of November 5. "I am pleased to note," he wrote, "that a naval vessel has been ordered here, and I look for her daily. Her presence here is absolutely necessary for the safety of Americans and their property. Had the commander of the *Adams* not been induced to remain by the citizens' request and mine, also his own knowledge of the serious state of affairs existing, I am sure we would all be in a very unenviable position now (unless some of us had been killed). Captain Leary's actions here are

---

[119] I.C., vol. 127, to Blacklock, Oct. 11, 1888; S. Ex. Doc. no. 31, pp. 135-136, encl. 96.

[120] Domestic Letters, Rives to Whitney, Oct. 11, 1888; S. Ex. Doc. no. 31, p. 136, encl. 97.

[121] Executive Letter Book, Navy Department, Commodore Harmony to Bayard, Oct. 12, 1888, rec'd Oct. 13.

THE BRANDEIS–TAMASESE RÉGIME   417

very highly praised by our citizens and the British subjects, and I sincerely trust that the Department will uphold him in all he has done. The British Admiral [Fairfax] was much pleased with his actions here.'"[122]

With the defeat of Tamasese, Becker disappeared from the Samoan stage. He left in the middle of November for Sydney and was succeeded by Dr. Knappe. The British government had been represented by a new consul named Colonel de Coëtlogen since the previous summer, and during the hostilities he and Blacklock acted together.

On November 19 Count von Arco-Valley, the German minister at Washington, called upon Secretary Bayard and informed him that the German squadron had been ordered back to Samoa. This had been found necessary, he said, on account of certain injuries which "had lately been committed by warring natives to German subjects and property." He complained also of Blacklock's actions in Apia and of Sewall's expression of ill will toward Germany since his return to the United States. Bayard replied that Sewall had disavowed the sentiments attributed to himself and as for Blacklock he said instructions had been sent him to abstain from interfering in Samoan affairs.[123]

The American naval vessel *Nipsic*, under command of Commander D. W. Mullan, arrived in Apia on November 7 and found the U.S.S. *Adams*, the English ship *Lizard*, and the German man-of-war *Adler*, in port. The German ship *Eber* arrived in Apia on November 22.[124] The two American war vessels were kept busily engaged in pro-

---

[122] C.D., Apia, vol. 16, Blacklock, Nov. 5, 1888, rec'd Dec. 1; S. Ex. Doc. no. 31, p. 139, encl. 105.

[123] Instructions, Germany, vol. 18, no. 384, Bayard to Coleman, Nov. 21, 1888; S. Ex. Doc. no. 31, pp. 161-162, encl. 111.

[124] D. W. Mullan to Whitney, Nov. 25, 1888. Transmitted to Department of State, Jan. 9, 1889; S. Ex. Doc. no. 68, 50 Congress, 2 session, p. 10, encl. 2.

tecting American interests during the month of November and only in the first days of December did Commander Leary think it possible for the *Adams* to leave Samoa. "My stay here has been somewhat prolonged," he wrote to Secretary Whitney, "but it was necessary for the protection of American rights. Commander Mullan now understands the situation, and I shall leave the Samoan-American matters in his charge as soon as I can get away."[125] The *Adams* sailed for San Francisco on December 7.

On December 18 the Germans began to war upon Mataafa in earnest and tried to capture the chief. Dr. Knappe, the German consul, explained to Blacklock that it was the intention of the German men-of-war to put an end to the civil war and disarm both the rebels and the forces of Tamasese. A detachment of German sailors clashed with Mataafa's men but the natives finally repulsed the Germans, killing twenty and wounding thirty. The German men-of-war shelled villages the remaining days of December, and Blacklock thought the situation so serious that he sent a special messenger to Auckland to cable the department and answer any questions that the department might wish to ask.[126] The cablegram was received at Washington via Wellington on January 5, 1889, and read: "Three German war ships [have] undertaken to disarm Mataafa . . . Mataafa's men fired on and forced to fight. Germans routed. Twenty killed, thirty wounded. Germans swear vengeance. Shelling and burning indiscriminately, regardless of American property. Protests unheeded. Natives exasperated. Foreigners' lives and property in greatest danger. Germans respect no neutral territory.

[125] Leary to Whitney, Dec. 2, 1888. Transmitted to Department of State, Jan. 9, 1889; S. Ex. Doc. no. 68, p. 13, encl. 3.

[126] C.D., Apia, vol. 17, Blacklock, Dec. 31, 1888, rec'd Jan. 26; H. Ex. Doc. no. 118, 50 Congress, 2 session, p. 2, encl. 1.

THE BRANDEIS–TAMASESE RÉGIME 419

Americans in boat flying American flag seized in Apia harbor by armed German boat, but released. Admiral with squadron necessary immediately. Officer accompanying dispatch can be questioned at Auckland.'"[127]

The same day that Bayard received the cablegram from Blacklock he forwarded the information to Pendleton and Phelps with instructions to learn from the German and British governments their reaction to the situation.[128] The same day, also, Bayard sent a note to the German minister, Count von Arco-Valley, saying that it was "with great regret that I have to inform you of the news just received at this Department of the dangerous and deplorable condition of affairs at Samoa.'"[129] In her reply to Bayard's note Germany through the minister at Washington sought to place the blame for the attack of the Mataafans upon the Germans upon the shoulders of an American correspondent named Klein. He, it was claimed, directed the charge and Germany had declared war upon Mataafa as a result of the attack. At the same time Germany made complaint to the United States of the action of Klein. Bayard, in a note to Arco Valley on January 12, declared that he knew nothing of Klein and that he was not in the public service of the United States. Bayard reiterated the policy of the United States as expressed in the protocols of the Washington Conference, and as contained in his memorandum to Prince Bismarck on January 17, 1888. He informed the German minister that Rear Admiral Kimberly, commanding on the Pacific Station, had been ordered to proceed to Apia in his flagship, the *Trenton*, and he hoped it would be possible for the com-

[127] *Ibid.*, cablegram, Blacklock to Bayard, rec'd Jan. 5; S. Ex. Doc. no. 68, p. 17, encl. 6.

[128] Instructions, Germany, vol. 18, cablegrams, Bayard to Pendleton and Phelps, Jan. 5, 1889; S. Ex. Doc. no. 68, pp. 17-18, enclosures 8 and 9.

[129] Notes to German Legation, vol. 10, Bayard to Arco-Valley, Jan. 5, 1889; S. Ex. Doc. no. 68, p. 18, encl. 10.

manders of the ships of the three nations to restore order on a satisfactory basis.[130]

The day before Bayard sent the above note to the German minister, orders were sent from the Navy Department to Admiral Kimberly at Panama to proceed at once to Samoa. Whitney telegraphed him in part: "Protest against the subjection and displacement of native government of Samoa by Germany as in violation of positive agreement and understanding between treaty powers, but inform the representatives of the German and British Governments of your readiness to co-operate in causing all treaty rights to be respected and in restoring peace and order on the basis of a recognition of Samoan rights to independence."[131]

On January 31 Bayard received a cablegram from Blacklock stating that the German consul had declared Germany at war with Mataafa and that Samoa was under martial law.[132] Bayard immediately requested the German minister to state what was implied by the martial law said to have been declared, and he desired assurances that American rights would not be interfered with.[133] He instructed Pendleton the same day, January 31, to say that "since no declaration of martial law could extend German jurisdiction so as to include control of American citizens in Samoa," he assumed that the German authorities in Samoa "would be instructed carefully to refrain from interference with American citizens and property there."[134] The next day, February 1, the German minister informed Bayard that Prince Bismarck was "of the opinion that our military authority has gone too far in

[130] Notes to German Legation, vol. 10, Bayard to Arco-Valley, Jan. 12, 1889; S. Ex. Doc. no. 68, pp. 19-21, encl. 13.
[131] Whitney to Admiral Kimberly, Jan. 11, 1889; S. Ex. Doc. no. 68, pp. 21-22, encl. in encl. 14.
[132] H. Ex. Doc. no. 119, 50 Congress, 2 session, p. 2, encl. 1.
[133] *Ibid.*, p. 2, encl. 3.   [134] *Ibid.*, p. 2, encl. 2.

THE BRANDEIS–TAMASESE RÉGIME 421

this instance." That part of the proclamation concerning martial law over foreigners would therefore be withdrawn. The German consul's request to Mataafa "that the administration of the islands of Samoa might be temporarily handed over to him" was also disavowed as the demand was not "in conformity to our previous promises regarding the neutrality and independence of Samoa."[135] Pendleton in Berlin was given the same information. The German government regretted the action of Dr. Knappe and he had been rebuked.[136]

In the meantime President Cleveland sent a message to Congress on January 15, which placed the Samoan problem in the hands of the legislative branch of the government. "Acting within the restraints which our Constitution and laws have placed upon executive power, I have insisted that the autonomy and independence of Samoa should be scrupulously preserved according to the treaties made with Samoa by the powers named and their agreements and understanding with each other." The president informed Congress, moreover, that Admiral Kimberly, in the flagship *Trenton*, had been ordered to join the *Nipsic* at Samoa, the situation there being, as a result of the collision between Germans and natives, "delicate and critical."[137]

[135] *Ibid.*, encl. 4, p. 3.
[136] Despatches, Germany, vol. 48, telegram Pendleton to Bayard, Feb. 1, 1889; S. Ex. Doc. no. 102, p. 2, encl. 1.
[137] S. Ex. Doc. no. 68, p. 2. President Cleveland to Congress, Jan. 15, 1889.

CHAPTER XII

PREPARATIONS FOR THE BERLIN CONFERENCE

PRESIDENT CLEVELAND submitted the Samoan problem to Congress on January 15 for further action. This event hastened Prince Bismarck's willingness to concur with the administration in the necessity of resuming the deliberations among the three powers—suspended since July, 1887—and of returning to the *status quo* existing before Germany declared war upon Malietoa Laupepa in the fall of the same year. The concluding words of the president's message, while not a threat, showed conclusively that the patience of the executive had practically been exhausted.[1] Bismarck realized also that Great Britain could not continue much longer to oppose the American position, in view of criticisms emanating from Australia and New Zealand of Downing Street's alleged secret agreement with Germany concerning the disposition of the Pacific islands.[2] The attack of the liberals in Germany upon the government's colonial policy contributed to the same end. Therefore, in his next message to Congress, on January 30, the president was able to say in confidence "that a proposition from [the German Government] to that of the United States for a conference on the Samoan subject was on its way by mail, having left Berlin on the 20th instant." The president added that "in reply to an inquiry from the Secretary of

---

[1] Senate Ex. Doc. no. 68, 50 Congress, 2 session, pp. 1 and 2.
[2] Prince Bismarck was seeking an alliance with Great Britain, and actually offered it in November, 1889.

State whether the proposition referred to was for a renewal of the joint conference between the United States, Germany, and Great Britain which was suspended in July, 1887, that is, the Washington Conference, or for a consideration of Samoan affairs *ab novo*, the German minister stated his inability to answer until the proposition which left Berlin on the 20th instant should have been received."[3]

That Bismarck contemplated making his proposal for a conference before Cleveland's message to Congress was published in the German papers on January 16 is quite probable, but to send the proposal to the United States only four days after the publication of that message was perhaps more difficult in view of the inevitable criticism from certain German quarters to the effect that Bismarck had backed down in the face of a "threat" by the United States.[4]

The president concluded his message with the significant statement: "I shall hereafter communicate to the Congress all information received by me in relation to the Samoan status."[5] Congress was not kept waiting long,

[3] H. Ex. Doc. no. 118, 50 Congress, 2 session, pp. 1 and 2.

[4] Bismarck refers to this reversal of position in the following statement concerning his general foreign policy:

"It has always been my ideal aim, after we had established our unity within the possible limits, to win the confidence not only of the smaller European states, but also of the great Powers, and to convince them that Germany's policy will be just and peaceful, now that it has made good the *injuria temporum*, the division of the nation. In order to produce this confidence it is above everything necessary that we should be honourable, open, and easily reconciled in case of friction or *untoward events*. I have followed this recipe not without some personal reluctance in cases like that of Schnäbele (April 1887), Boulanger, Kauffman (September 1887); as towards Spain in the question of the Caroline Islands, towards the United States in that of Samoa, and I imagine that in the future also opportunities will not be wanting of showing that we are appeased and peaceful." (Quoted from *Bismarck: The Man and the Statesman*, II, 293.)

[5] H. Ex. Doc. no. 118, 50 Congress, 2 session, pp. 1 and 2.

for on February 8 he sent another message—his fifth communication to that body concerning Samoa since shortly before Christmas,[6] in which he said that Germany was not only willing to resume the conference of 1887, but in conjunction with Great Britain, was ready to publish the joint protocols of the conference.[7] This was a signal victory for the United States and a complete reversal of Bismarck's policy. Moreover, it was now possible for the administration, especially Bayard, to answer violent partisan attacks by proving conclusively that there was nothing in the records of the Washington Conference to indicate a surrender by the United States of any of its rights in Samoa. Witness to this effect is clearly shown in a letter from Carl Schurz to Bayard five days before the latter went out of office. "I have read the protocol with keen interest," wrote Schurz, "and cannot refrain from saying that the American side of the question has been represented by you with the most decided and unquestionable superiority in point of argument as well as vigor of debate. I do not wonder that those among your adversaries who still have some respect for the truth were silenced by the appearance of this document."[8]

In a memorandum of instructions from Bismarck to the German minister at Washington, Count von Arco-Valley, which the latter read to Secretary Bayard on February 4, the German chancellor proposed that the "best remedy for stopping the war in Samoa seems to be a resumption of the consultation which took place between the representatives of Germany, England, and the United States

[6] The fourth message, dated Feb. 1, 1889 (H. Ex. Doc. no. 119), enclosed further correspondence concerning events in Samoa.

[7] S. Ex. Doc. no. 102, 50 Congress, 2 session, pp. 1 and 2.

[8] *Speeches, Correspondence, and Political Papers of Carl Schurz* (Frederic Bancroft, editor), V, 15. Schurz to Bayard, New York, Feb. 27, 1889.

BERLIN CONFERENCE PREPARATIONS 425

in the year 1887, at Washington, and at that time adjourned without any possibility of their representatives coming to any agreement." However, since the three governments enjoyed equal rights in Samoa, he thought "the place for the negotiations should change in regular turn," and the German government, therefore, invited the government of the United States and that of Great Britain "to a conference regarding Samoa, to take place at Berlin." To assure the American government that Germany made no claims for a position of priority in Samoa, Count von Arco-Valley concluded the reading of the memorandum with the following statement: "I am also directed to declare that any supposition that Germany would not feel satisfied with a neutral position in the Samoan Islands is unfounded. As we have already declared in the last Conference [of 1887], it is neither our intention to put in question the independence of the island group nor the equal rights of the treaty powers. We simply desire to create a condition which offers permanent security for bringing to an end bloodshed and decapitation, and which grants permanent safety to the commercial interests of the three treaty powers in Samoa."[9]

That Bismarck's proposal was very favorably received is indicated by its immediate conditional acceptance by the United States government. Already on the next day, February 5, Bayard, under instructions from the president, sent a note to Count von Arco-Valley stating that he (the president) "fully shares in the desire expressed by the Prince Chancellor to bring the blessings of peace and order to the remote and feeble community of semi-civilized people inhabiting the islands of Samoa; and that he clearly recognizes the duty of the powerful nations of Christendom to deal with these people in a

[9] Notes from German Legation, vol. 20; S. Ex. Doc. no. 102, p. 3, encl. 3.

spirit of magnanimity and benevolence." The United States wished that the deliberations of the conference would be, as in the Washington Conference, "for the purpose of establishing peace and an orderly government in the Samoan Islands on the basis of their recognized independence and the equal rights of the three treaty powers, [and] as the assurance of Prince Bismarck that the pacification of the Samoan group and the occupation of a neutral position are his only objects . . . it is suggested in furtherance of the desired result of the conference that instructions to suspend belligerent action and await the action of such conference should at once be telegraphed to their respective officers in Samoa by the three treaty powers." The administration thought the announcement of the conference between the treaty powers would "at once cause a cessation of hostilities among the natives," and that a speedy election of a king by the natives "would certainly be a long step towards harmony." It was necessary, however, "that affairs in Samoa should remain *in statu quo* pending the conference." Indulging the hope that these suggestions would be adopted and that their adoption would bring about a successful issue of the conference, Secretary Bayard concluded by stating that the United States would "at once take steps to be properly represented at the meetings of such a conference in Berlin."[10]

In response to Bayard's note, the German minister called at the State Department on February 21 and, under instructions from Prince Bismarck, said that as soon as the United States informed Germany when the American representatives would arrive in Berlin, the day of the opening of the conference would be fixed. As for the suspension of hostilities suggested by Bayard, it was un-

[10] Notes to German Legation, vol. 10, pp. 621-624; S. Ex. Doc. no. 102, pp. 4-5, encl. 4.

necessary, since an imperial order for the ending of military measures by Germany was sent on January 12.[11] Only in case no agreement were arrived at by the three powers concerning satisfaction for the killing of German soldiers, or in case the holding of the conference were considerably delayed, would "Germany proceed to take satisfaction according to their own judgment." "Germany does not wish to create armed contention in Samoa, but Germany intends to punish criminals, and cannot renounce this right." Referring to the sending of Admiral Kimberly to Samoa, the statement adds: "In spite of the reinforcement of the American Squadron in Samoa, which could only be intended to be directed against Germany, the Imperial Government has until the present not given any order for any new ships to join the Squadron at these islands, because it is the desire of the Imperial Government to keep away from any responsibility of diminishing the reciprocal confidence between the two nations."[12] In commenting on this memorandum, Bayard in his communication to the president said: "It will be observed that, with certain ultimate reservations, this is a substantial acceptance of the suggestions of a conditional nature contained in my note of February 5 to Count von Arco-Valley accepting the German proposal to resume the Conference of 1887 on the same lines."[13]

[11] As late as March 7 Sir J. Fergusson, the parliamentary under-secretary of state for foreign affairs, in answer to a question by Mr. W. McArthur relative to Samoa, said, "We have no information of the conclusion of a truce between the German Consul in Samoa and the Chief Mataafa." (Reported by London *Times*, March 8. See enclosure, despatch no. 942, White to Blaine, March 8, 1889, in Despatches, Great Britain, vol. 161. See also *Correspondence respecting Affairs in Samoa. Printed for the use of the American Commissioners to Berlin*, p. 72, document no. 27, in Kasson Papers).

[12] Report Book, vol. 17, Department of State; see also Confidential Document, Executive E, to Senate from President, Feb. 27, 1889, 50 Congress, 2 session, p. 2.

[13] *Ibid.*

The intense popular feeling aroused in Germany by the serious losses inflicted upon German officers and men by the Samoans under Mataafa in the attack of December 18 prevented the government from renouncing its right to take measures for retribution or reprisal if necessary. But the fact that it wished to hasten the conference so that this question might be settled in consultation with the other powers is conclusive evidence that Bismarck had wearied of his attempt to secure for Germany a preponderant place in the government of Samoa and was willing to return to the proposal first made by Bayard on June 1, 1886, and accepted at that time by Germany and Great Britain. This proposal called for coöperative action with reference to Samoa by the three powers concerned, the guarantee of independence of the islands, and the maintenance of equality of the three treaty powers. Prince Bismarck and Lord Salisbury still held the opinion that a tripartite arrangement, whereby no nation should have a preponderant influence in the Samoan government, would not be as effective as one giving a single nation a mandate for the others, but they realized that a Republican administration, soon to assume power, would be in no mood to pursue a weaker foreign policy than its predecessor. Therefore they were willing to consider the acceptance of Bayard's plan.

The close of Cleveland's administration being at hand, the president addressed a confidential message to the Senate on February 27, saying that, in response to an inquiry of the German minister whether the names of the proposed representatives of the United States at the conference in Berlin could be given to him at once, he informed him that the appointments in question would be made by his successor (Harrison), "and that in coming to this decision the expedition desired by Germany in the work of the conference would, in [his] judgment, be pro-

BERLIN CONFERENCE PREPARATIONS 429

moted.'"[14] Bayard felt somewhat chagrined that he was not able to bring the Samoan question to a successful solution, due to the change of administration, and he made this clear in a letter to Carl Schurz the day after President Cleveland's last message to the Senate concerning Samoa. *"Entre nous,* I have been crippled a good deal," he wrote, "by poor Pendleton's invalid condition, and but for that, I believe the Berlin Conference *in re* Samoa would have been now progressing or even probably the matter settled. As it is, Harrison (Blaine! alas!) must appoint the American envoys—but I do not see how they can fail to follow the lines of the protocols as stated by me.'"[15]

On March 14, President Harrison nominated, and on the 18th of the same month appointed, John A. Kasson, of Iowa, William Walter Phelps, of New Jersey, and George H. Bates, of Delaware, to be commissioners of the United States to the conference at Berlin.[16] On March 22 the German minister in Washington wrote Blaine that the chancellor proposed to nominate Count Herbert von Bismarck, the secretary of state for foreign affairs, as chief of the German plenipotentiaries, and Count von Berchem, assistant secretary of state, as his son's substitute. Baron von Holstein and Privy Counselor Krauel, both of whom were connected with the German Foreign Office, were the other German commissioners.[17] Blaine in

[14] Report Book, Department of State, p. 355; see also Confidential Document, Executive E, 50 Congress, 2 session, p. 1.

[15] *Speeches, Correspondence, and Political Papers of Carl Schurz,* V, 16-17, Bayard to Schurz, Feb. 28, 1889.

[16] Confidential Document, Executive B, 51 Congress, 1 session, Blaine to Harrison, Jan. 7, 1890; see also Senate Miscellaneous Document no. 81, vol. 2, 51 Congress, 1 session.

[17] Notes from German Legation, vol. 20; see also *Correspondence respecting Affairs in Samoa. Printed for the use of the American Commissioners to Berlin,* p. 69, document no. 23, in Kasson Papers.

turn informed Count von Arco-Valley on April 3 the names of the American commissioners.[18] The next day the German minister laid before the secretary of state a proposal from Prince Bismarck "that, until the close of the Samoan Conference, which is soon to be held at Berlin, or until some other understanding shall be reached, but one war vessel shall be stationed at Apia by each of the three treaty powers, and that no reinforcements shall be ordered there." The corvette *Sophie,* which then lay off Zanzibar, had been ordered to Samoa "for the purpose of assisting in saving His Majesty's ship *Olga,* which latter will be removed in case it shall be found possible to get her afloat."[19] Secretary Blaine readily agreed, and on April 6 informed Count von Arco-Valley that an arrangement similar to that of Germany would be made. The *Nipsic* being so disabled that she would have to be taken to Auckland for repairs,[20] the gunboat *Alert,* then on her way to Samoa, would be retained there. The *Monongahela,* "a vessel used exclusively for the purpose of storing supplies," would remain at Apia, but, as she was an unarmed sailing vessel, "it is understood that her presence will be not at all in conflict with the amicable understanding reached by the two Governments."[21]

Full powers were conferred upon the American commissioners on April 12.[22] Of the three men, Kasson and Phelps had each held the post of minister to Austria-

[18] Notes to German Legation, vol. 10, p. 633; see also *Correspondence* etc., *in re* Samoa, p. 70, document no. 24, in Kasson Papers.

[19] Notes from German Legation, vol. 20; see also *Correspondence* etc., *in re* Samoa, pp. 70-71, document no. 25, in Kasson Papers. The *Olga* and other German and American ships of war had been disabled or destroyed in the hurricane of March, 1889.

[20] The *Nipsic* started out for Auckland but was obliged to turn about and go to Honolulu.

[21] Notes to German Legation, vol. 10, p. 634; see also *Correspondence* etc., *in re* Samoa, p. 71, document no. 26, in Kasson Papers.

[22] Credences, Department of State, vol. 6, p. 591.

BERLIN CONFERENCE PREPARATIONS 431

Hungary.[23] Kasson had likewise held the post of minister to Germany during the last months of President Arthur's administration, and had represented the United States at the Congo conference in Berlin in 1884-1885. In accepting Kasson's resignation as minister to Germany, Bayard commended him for having restored the good relations between Germany and the United States which during the time of Kasson's predecessor[24] had become disturbed on account of German restrictions upon the importation of American pork and the Lasker Resolution incident.[25] Although not designated as chairman of the delegation, Kasson's former residence in Berlin and his acquaintance with the German officials, as well as his experience as delegate to the Congo Conference, naturally caused the attention of the German and British delegates to be focussed upon him as the first among equals.

George H. Bates, a well-known attorney of Wilmington, Delaware, and the third commissioner, was perhaps more familiar with the Samoan problem than either Kasson or Phelps. Having been sent by Bayard as special agent to Samoa in 1886, he had furnished the latest data by which his chief had been guided in the negotiations of the Washington Conference the year following. His appointment, however, aroused considerable criticism in the German press and made it difficult for the German government to receive him upon his arrival in Berlin. Bates had written an article on Samoa for the *Century Maga-*

---

[23] Kasson was minister to Austria-Hungary during Hayes' administration from June, 1877, to February, 1881. Phelps was appointed minister to the same empire by Garfield in May, 1881, and served about a year. After the Berlin Conference, Phelps was appointed minister to Germany, and held that post during the remainder of Harrison's administration.

[24] A. A. Sargent, United States minister to Germany, March, 1882 to June, 1884.

[25] Instructions, Germany, vol. 17, p. 490, no. 123, Bayard to Kasson, March 21, 1885.

zine of April, 1889, and, since that article was not altogether complimentary to German policy in Samoa, the German press and officials regarded the appointment as inopportune.[26] Kasson in a personal letter to Blaine reported the difficulty he had at the opening of the conference in securing the recognition of Bates, but added, "The Bates incident is happily closed. It required no little personal and careful handling. The last week the German papers had been set upon him violently, and official hostility was patent. Mr. Coleman, in anticipation of our arrival, had the day before made the usual application for our visit to the Foreign Office, asking the hour for the reception of the American Commissioners, without mentioning our names. Count Bismarck replied that he would be happy to renew his acquaintance with Mr. Kasson, and to make the acquaintance of Mr. Phelps; and there stopped. Mr. Coleman saw the situation was becoming awkward, and addressed a note to Count Bismarck requesting him to consider the notes as withdrawn." Through the intervention of Sir Edward Malet, the British ambassador at Berlin and a member of the British delegation to the conference, and by skillful maneuvering on the part of Kasson, the recognition of Bates at the first reception was effected, the latter having made an explanatory statement to Count Bismarck that an exaggerated importance had been attached by the press to his article, which had been published before his appointment. "He was somewhat nervous," continues Kasson, "which may excuse his failure to choose his

[26] Secretary Blaine, on April 12 and before the American commissioners left the United States for Berlin, wrote Kasson and Phelps that the German minister had called the attention of the State Department to the article by Bates. "I asked him," wrote Blaine, "if he proposed to object to Mr. Bates' service on the Commission, but he replied that he had no instruction from his Government on that point." (Letter to be found in Kasson Papers.)

BERLIN CONFERENCE PREPARATIONS 433

words so wisely as I could have wished. He certainly went *far enough,* as you will see by the official report of it in the German paper sent from the Legation yesterday. On our departure, the Count shook hands with me, and bowed to the other gentlemen. When, the next day, he returned our visit, he shook hands with all and the 'Bates incident' was ended.''[27]

Another American appointment disagreeable to the Germans was that of Harold M. Sewall, former consul general at Apia, as special disbursing agent[28] to accompany the commissioners.[29] German animus against the United States had been aroused by Sewall's vigorous opposition to German encroachments during his stay in Samoa from July, 1887 to August, 1888, and Bayard had not permitted him to return to Apia after his examination before a subcommittee of the Senate committee on foreign relations in January, 1889. Therefore, his appointment as one of the American agents appeared to the German press a reversal of Bayard's more diplomatic methods, and another inept act on the part of the new administration. As a matter of fact, no American as able as either Bates or Sewall had been in Samoa up to that time, and their presence in Berlin, despite the German opposition, seemed to the administration absolutely necessary. The work of Bates proved particularly effective at the conference. It was only unfortunate that his and Sewall's statements and actions prior to their arrival made the reception of the American commissioners less spontaneous and cordial than it ought to have been.

[27] Samoan Conference at Berlin, 1889, MSS, Kasson to Blaine, April 30, 1889, personal letter.

[28] Sewall's duties embraced the disbursing of the fund appropriated by the Diplomatic and Consular Act, approved February 26, 1889, for the protection of the interests of the United States in Samoa.

[29] Instructions to Special Missions, vol. 4, p. 11, Department of State.

General instructions to the American commissioners were given by Blaine on April 11, with the added statement that as soon as the protocols of the several sessions of the conference were received from time to time from Berlin, more specific instructions would be sent them. They were to examine carefully the protocols of the Washington Conference and the report of Special Commissioner Bates, in order to familiarize themselves with the position taken by the former administration. Further on in the instructions Blaine said, that in consenting to the request of the German government "to reopen the adjourned proceedings of the Conference of 1887 at Berlin, instead of at Washington," the president was "anxious to manifest his entire confidence in the motives and purposes of the German Government," but that the delegates were to look upon it as an adjourned conference, in continuance of the conference at Washington in 1887, and not a new one on another basis.[30]

In taking this position, Blaine was merely following President Cleveland when he instructed Bayard to accept the German proposal in the latter's note to Count von Arco-Valley on February 5. He quoted extensively from this note and underscored the following words: " 'such consultation to be renewed, as it was undertaken, for the purpose of establishing peace and an orderly, stable government in the Samoan Islands, on the basis of their recognized independence and the equal rights of the three Treaty Powers.' "[31] Thus it is clear that the United States would recognize the legality of no changes since the Washington Conference such as the arrest and deportation of Malietoa and the setting up of the govern-

[30] Kasson Papers, Department of State, instructions to American Commissioners, April 11, 1889, pp. 3-4.
[31] *Ibid.*, p. 5.

BERLIN CONFERENCE PREPARATIONS 435

ment of Tamasese with Brandeis as his premier. Blaine referred to the fact—using the report of Bates as his authority—that the arrangements under the so-called Lackawanna Peace of July, 1881, had been remarkably successful and that for a period of three and a half years comparative peace had been enjoyed in Samoa.[32] It was not necessary, he thought, to enter into the events of 1885 and 1886, as the actions of both the German and American consuls had been disavowed by Prince Bismarck and Mr. Bayard respectively, and the agreement to send out special commissioners and later to hold a conference in Washington had left the two powers in similar positions.[33]

Relative to the Washington Conference, Blaine said: "After a very full and able discussion of the business before it, in the course of which some points of agreement were reached, and certain points of difference developed, the Conference, on the 26th of July, 1887, adjourned, in order, as stated in the proposition of adjournment, that further instructions should be at once obtained by the representatives of the Treaty Powers from their respective Governments, with a view to the reassembling of the Conference in the ensuing autumn."[34] Continuing, he said: "It would be a source of great satisfaction to the President, if the only duty incumbent on him now were to review the proceedings of the first Conference, and with proper regard to the views of Germany and Great Britain, reach such modified conclusions as would be entirely satisfactory to the honor and interests of all the Treaty Powers, and at the same time secure for the Samoan people a stable and orderly government. He firmly believes that such a result is possible, but since the ad-

[32] *Ibid.*, p. 6.   [33] *Ibid.*, p. 7.
[34] *Ibid.*, p. 10.

journment of the Conference certain events have occurred which require explanation.''[35]

The "war" against "Malietoa personally" and his deportation, while not considered by the president as "intentionally derogatory either to the dignity or the interests of the other Treaty Powers," could only be interpreted "under all circumstances, as an abrupt breach of the joint relations of the Treaty Powers to each other and to the Government of Samoa." He therefore found "it impossible to reconcile such action with this frank and friendly language of the German Government preliminary to the meeting of the Washington Conference: 'We intend to maintain the *status* as it has heretofore existed. We have been satisfied with that; it has been satisfactory to the three Governments; we have neither interest nor desire to change it; but if we had, we would take no step, make no movement, without frankly consulting in advance the United States and Great Britain.' ''[36] Having disposed of the question of the *status quo,* it became necessary to instruct the commissioners "as to the views and wishes of the President upon the conclusions reached and the difference developed in the deliberations of the first conference.''[37] Blaine then outlined the two opposing plans for the government of Samoa, which were brought forward in the Washington Conference, the one by Germany and supported by Great Britain, the other by Secretary of State Bayard, and proceeded to give the views of the president relative to both plans. It was plain from a reading of the protocols that the three treaty powers entered the Washington Conference with identical views of the purpose of the conference, and that the in-

[35] Kasson Papers, Department of State, instructions to American Commissioners, April 11, 1889, pp. 10-11.
[36] *Ibid.,* pp. 12-13.   [37] *Ibid.,* p. 16.

dependence of the native Samoan government and a perfect equality of the commercial rights and privileges among the treaty powers were the bases on which that conference had rested its deliberations.[38]

Commenting on the plan advanced in the Washington Conference that Germany be given the mandate over Samoa, Blaine continued his instructions: "It is unnecessary here to repeat the objections to this plan which were made by the representative of the United States, Mr. Bayard, with great acuteness and force, and which have the entire approval of the President. It is sufficient, in this instruction, to say that the President cannot accept this plan as satisfactory." By giving Germany the right to nominate the adviser because of its supremacy in commerce, "would be simply encouraging that power to maintain and extend such supremacy and to make it the basis for a perpetual reappointment and ultimately of absolute possession." By such an arrangement, moreover, the equality of the three powers could not be maintained and controversies would inevitably occur. Instead of making for peace, it would make for trouble, especially with Germany. "It would be far simpler and conduce more to frank and well understood relations to recognize this assumed superiority as real and to hold direct communication with Germany in our transactions with what would be practically her colonial possession."[39]

Then Blaine reiterated what Bayard had said concerning the interests of the United States in the harbor of Pago Pago and that on account of our need for a naval station in the South Pacific the United States could not "accept this scheme of subordination." Continuing, he said: "We cannot consent to the institution of any form of government in Samoa subject, directly or indirectly,

[38] *Ibid.*, pp. 16-19.   [39] *Ibid.*, pp. 24, 25, 26.

to influences which, in the contingencies of the future, might check or control the use or the development of this American right. Nor can the Government of the United States forget what we are satisfied the other Treaty Powers will cordially recognize—that our interest on the Pacific is steadily increasing; that our commerce with the East is developing largely and rapidly; and that the certainty of an early opening of an Isthmian transit from the Atlantic to the Pacific (under American protection) must create changes in which no power can be so directly or more durably interested than the United States. And in any questions involving present or future relations in the Pacific, this Government cannot accept even temporary subordination, and must regard it as inconsistent with that international consideration and dignity to which the United States, by continental position and expanding interest must always be entitled.''[40]

The stand taken by Bayard in 1887 against the German plan of government for Samoa was thus adopted by Blaine without any change. Germany and Great Britain must have sensed the consistency of the American policy at this point, for neither of these powers broached the subject in open conference at Berlin. A German mandate was abandoned before the first plenary session was held, and the principal point for which Bayard had contended so earnestly at the Washington Conference was thus sustained.

But what of Bayard's own plan of government for Samoa? Was the Republican administration ready to follow the Democratic policy here also? It will be remembered that the plan provided for—in addition to the king and vice king—an executive council consisting of three foreign secretaries, who, with these native rulers, would

[40] Kasson Papers, Department of State, instructions to American Commissioners, April 11, 1889, pp. 28, 29, 30.

form the executive government. These three secretaries were to be appointed by the king on the recommendations of each of the treaty powers, and, of course, would represent their respective countries, their salaries, however, to be paid by the Samoan government. Under Bayard's plan the consuls of the treaty powers were still to retain their extraterritorial jurisdiction over the citizens and subjects of their respective governments. "This scheme," wrote Blaine, "goes beyond the principle upon which the President desires to see our relations with the Samoan Government based, and is not in harmony with the established policy of this Government. For, if it is not a joint protectorate—to which there are such grave and obvious objections—it is hardly less than that and does not, in any event, promise efficient action."

Blaine stated further "that if the existing troubles were the result, not of any action of the Samoan Government, but of the rivalries and misunderstandings of foreign consuls and residents, the presence in the Government of three officers, representing the same differing nationalities and interests, would only transfer the scene of dispute to the executive council, and that these three Secretaries, being officers of the Samoan Government, would not be less partisan, but would be only further removed from the control of the Treaty Powers than are the consuls whom it is now found so difficult to keep within their strict line of duty. It is evident, moreover, that the different views which the representatives of colonial powers, like Great Britain and Germany, and a representative of the United States, would hold towards the natives and a native government, scarcely promise as a result the harmonious coöperation of these varied and variant interests."[41] Yet the president was impressed with the opinions expressed by all of the special agents

[41] *Ibid.*, pp. 3, 32.

to Samoa, including Bates, that (to quote from the Bates report) "The material question now to be determined is the character, extent and methods by which the expressed desire of the three powers to coöperate in the establishment of stable government in the Islands may be most effectively carried out. . . . The central government must be, for a time at least, administered by the three Treaty Powers, or through such agencies as they may select."[42]

At this point the president and Blaine were placed upon a two-horned dilemma. They did not favor Bayard's plan because it went too far and was "not in harmony with the established policy of this Government." On the other hand, they agreed with Bayard in repudiating the German mandate scheme because by adopting such a plan they would virtually turn the islands over to Germany as a protectorate or colony. What could the instructions say on this point? To become "entangled" or not to become "entangled," that was the question. As a matter of fact, the president had no alternative plan to offer and the burden of solving the problem was, with certain reservations, placed squarely upon the shoulders of the commissioners. "Under these circumstances," said the instructions, "and in view of these opinions of those best qualified to judge, the Government of the United States cannot refuse to give weighty consideration to whatever plan the Conference may suggest." If it were found absolutely necessary "that the three Treaty Powers should administer the Government of Samoa," the president wanted the intervention to be only a temporary one, and "avowedly preparatory to the restoration of as complete independence and autonomy as is possible in the Islands." A second reservation required "that the intervention of the three Treaty Powers must be on terms of

[42] Kasson Papers, Department of State, instructions to American Commissioners, April 11, 1889, pp. 33, 34.

BERLIN CONFERENCE PREPARATIONS 441

absolute equality" and that an arrangement whereby the consular officers could "be the most efficient intermediaries between the Treaty Powers and the native government would be the most acceptable."

The third subject upon which instructions laid stress was the land question. Too much importance could not be given to that question "in any arrangement for the establishment of order and civilization in Samoa." This was important for foreign landowners as well as for the natives, but especially for the latter, who must be "protected from those acts of interference and oppression to which the cupidity of foreigners has heretofore exposed them." Moreover, the consideration of the subject of land claims naturally suggested "that of the prohibition or regulation of the importation and sale of firearms and alcoholic liquors. . . . Many of these claims have, without doubt, been obtained by ministering to weaknesses and passions of the natives, by furnishing them with the articles above mentioned. It is thought that this reproach to civilization should be removed, by each of the Treaty Powers adopting stringent regulations on the subject."[43]

Two other matters remained: first, no subject not covered by the instructions should be discussed at the conference. Should any such "be submitted either by Germany or by Great Britain," the commissioners were instructed to "courteously but firmly decline all discussions."[44] Finally, although the president did not desire to embarrass the "discussion of the restoration of the *status quo* by reference to the incidents which accompanied the declaration of martial law by the German authorities," these incidents could not "be passed over in silence, if such silence is to be interpreted as acquiescence in either the rightfulness or the necessity of that measure. So trenchant were the invasions of the rights of

[43] *Ibid.*, pp. 34, 35, 36, 37, 38. [44] *Ibid.*, pp. 38, 39.

American citizens in Samoa, and so apparent was the purpose to disregard the dignity of the flag which protected them, that if immediate resentment of such treatment had provoked forcible resistance, this Government, while deeply regretting so unfortunate an occurrence, would have found it impossible not to sympathize with the natural indignation which prompted such a course. . . . Had the Government of the United States not believed that these objectionable proceedings were due to the hasty and too pronounced zeal of German naval officers, and not to the orders or wishes of the authorities at Berlin, an earnest and vigorous protest would have been made against the assumption of such power. In this belief, the President is content to overlook the offense and refers to it now lest silence on his part might be misconstrued by the German Government. You will, therefore, be careful, in any reference which you may make to the subject, to employ a friendly tone, and to assume that the proceedings referred to were at no time authorized by the Imperial Government."[45]

The American commissioners and Sewall sailed from New York, April 13, on the *Umbria,* arriving in London on Monday afternoon the 22nd. Only at midnight, Monday, did they learn exactly when the Berlin Conference would meet, namely on Monday, April 29. In sending them this information Blaine requested them to hasten on their way. They arranged, therefore, to leave London on Thursday the 25th, giving Kasson time to have an interview with Lord Salisbury on Wednesday afternoon.

To complete the story at this point it is necessary to revert briefly to conditions in Samoa. It was noted in the last chapter that orders were given to the commander of the Pacific fleet, Rear Admiral Kimberly, to proceed at

[45] Kasson Papers, Department of State, instructions to American Commissioners, April 11, 1889, pp. 39, 40, 41, 42.

BERLIN CONFERENCE PREPARATIONS 443

once to Samoa on account of the martial law established by Dr. Knappe, the German consul. Admiral Kimberly arrived on the *Trenton* in Apia on March 11 and found two other American ships of war already there, the *Nipsic* and the *Vandalia*. Three German ships were also in port, namely, the *Olga,* the *Adler,* and the *Eber*. One English ship, the *Calliope,* was also anchored there. By the time Admiral Kimberly arrived in Samoan waters the plans for the Berlin Conference were well under way, although the time, as indicated above, had not yet been determined upon. Considerable friction had existed between the German and American captains prior to Admiral Kimberly's arrival, and the most insignificant provocation might have brought on a battle in the harbor.

It must be remembered that much that happened at Apia occurred in spite of efforts of the authorities at home to prevent trouble. This situation was due for the most part to the difficulty of communication. Certainly, neither Bismarck nor Blaine would have countenanced any fighting after an agreement had been reached for the resumption of negotiations in Berlin. Within four days of the arrival of the *Trenton* in Apia harbor, however, a hurricane began without giving the slightest warning, and on the next day the *Trenton* and the *Vandalia* were totally wrecked, and the *Nipsic* was run ashore to escape the fate of her sister ships. Four officers and forty-six enlisted men were drowned, one of the officers being Captain C. M. Schoonmaker of the *Vandalia*. All three of the German ships were lost in the hurricane, but the English ship *Calliope,* on account of her superior engines, was able to steam against the winds and waves in the shallow inner harbor, and thus attain comparative safety in the outer harbor.[46] Many officers and men were wounded, and a hospital was established in a church and, later, in a

[46] H. Ex. Doc. no. 1, part 3, 51 Congress, 1 session, vol. 8, pp. 35-36.

school house belonging to the London Missionary Society. The natives, especially those under the chief, Mataafa, rescued many seamen from the churning waters.[47]

[47] L. A. Kimberly, U.S.N., "Samoa and the Hurricane of March, 1889" in Military Historical Society of Massachusetts Papers, 12, *Naval Actions and History 1799-1898*, p. 336; see also H. Ex. Doc. no. 1, part 3, report of the Secretary of the Navy, Nov. 30, 1889, vol. 1, pp. 95-123, enclosing the official reports of the disaster at Apia. In popular accounts of the relations at this period between the United States and Germany, one is almost invariably told that war between these powers was narrowly averted by the hurricane destroying or disabling the German and American ships of war in Apia harbor. It is quite true that, ignorant of the German and American governments' plans for a resumption of negotiations at Berlin, the German and American naval vessels were on the point of clashing before the arrival of Admiral Kimberly. That officer, however, exercised a moderating influence on the situation, which had therefore become less tense when the hurricane arrived. But even if the clash had occurred, it is quite doubtful if it would have led to war, in view of the concessions previously made by Prince Bismarck and of the approaching conference.

CHAPTER XIII

THE BERLIN CONFERENCE, 1889

GREAT BRITAIN's attitude at this juncture was somewhat enigmatical. Certainly for about three years, that is, since the agreement between Germany and Great Britain concerning their respective spheres of influence in the Pacific,[1] the policy of Downing Street toward German encroachments in Samoa had been a tolerant one despite the constant criticisms of this policy emanating from New Zealand and Australia, and from British missionaries and other British subjects in Samoa itself. This understanding to give Germany a more or less free hand in Samoa was patent in the Washington Conference where Bayard was blocked by von Alvensleben with the aid of Sackville-West. Subsequently, during the German war against Malietoa, and while the Brandeis-Tamasese régime was dominant in Samoa, it was equally clear from the instructions sent to the British representative at Apia that the British were still pursuing a "hands off" policy in those islands. The general understanding reached by Prince Bismarck and Lord Salisbury relative to European affairs in 1887,[2] coupled with the agreement effected

---

[1] The agreement of April 6, 1886, fixing a line in the Pacific separating British and German zones of islands.

[2] Bismarck succeeded in persuading Salisbury to enter into an understanding with Austria-Hungary and Italy in the year 1887 against the aggression of Russia. "I believe," wrote Salisbury to Bismarck on November 30 of that year, "that the understanding into which England and the other two powers are now prepared to enter, will be in complete accordance with her declared policy, and will be loyally observed by her. The grouping of states which has been the work of the last year will be an effective barrier

the previous year concerning Germany's "place in the sun" in colonial affairs in the Pacific, were outstanding events in Anglo-German relations during those years. Consequently, it is not surprising to learn that the German ambassador in London, Count Hatzfeldt, after the Berlin Conference had been determined upon, endeavored to retain the British support in the forthcoming meeting of the three powers.

Although the general instructions to the American commissioners of April 11[3] proposed no interview with Lord Salisbury, Henry White, American chargé d'affaires *ad interim* at London, with a view no doubt to counteracting the influence of the German ambassador, and to securing as friendly an understanding with Great Britain as was possible before the opening of the conference, thus preventing perhaps a repetition of the experience of the United States at the Washington Conference, arranged an interview between Lord Salisbury and Mr. Kasson for Wednesday, April 24, the day before the commissioners departed for Berlin, and five days before the conference was scheduled to convene. In his despatch to Blaine from London on the day of the interview, Kasson stated: "The object of the interview had been previously intimated to him. After some agreeable general conversation we came to the Berlin Conference. I expressed the hope that we should find the English members of the Conference disposed to exercise a little more latitude in discussing the pending questions than that which characterized Lord Sackville-West's participation in the Conference at

against any possible aggression of Russia and the construction of it will not be among the least services, which your Serene Highness has rendered to the cause of European peace.'' (Quoted by J. V. Fuller, *Bismarck's Diplomacy at its Zenith*, 1922; first publication of letter in German translation appeared in Hammann's *Zur Vorgeschichte des Weltkrieges, Erinnerungen*, 1919.)

[3] Kasson Papers, Department of State.

THE BERLIN CONFERENCE, 1889

Washington. His Lordship burst into laughter, remarking that Lord Sackville certainly was a man not famous for talking.[4] I made some remark to the effect that the English-speaking race seemed better adapted to promote civilization and peace among nations than were our German friends, whose arguments had too visible a force with sword and helmet. I thought we ought naturally to have a concurrence of opinion on this subject. He replied that England had too little interest in Samoa to take an active part in the Islands. In Australia they had taken some especial interest, and he would be glad, of course, to meet their views to some extent; but the German was greater than the English interest in the Islands."[5]

In the course of the conversation Salisbury and Kasson agreed that much of the trouble in Samoa had been caused by the "singular aggressive and dictatorial conduct of Consuls there," but when Kasson alluded to the land question as a fundamental one "in its effect upon the peace of the population" the British prime minister "disclaimed any great English interest there."[6] When Kasson referred to the question of political control and suggested that the control over the Samoans' internal affairs by strangers should be "moral rather than material," Lord Salisbury "avowed disbelief in the practicability of any form of divided control, and acknowledged his own responsibility for Lord Sackville's assent to the proposition of the German Government at the Washington Conference, under which the German control of the King's Government was assured.'"[7] And further we read in Kasson's

---

[4] This was a humorous reference to Sackville-West's "Murchison" letter in 1888, on account of which President Cleveland dismissed him curtly, thereby causing considerable irritation between the governments of Great Britain and the United States.

[5] Samoan Conference at Berlin, 1889, MSS, Department of State, Kasson to Blaine, April 24, despatch no. 2.

[6] *Ibid.*   [7] *Ibid.*

interesting communication: "In the course of our conversation, however, he made two avowals: (1) that, in view of our opposition to that proposition [German], he supposed it would have to be abandoned; (2) he thought Prince Bismarck was tired of the whole thing. He expressed no opinion upon any substitute proposition."[8] He thought, however, "that one of the best means of keeping order there [in Samoa] would be for the three powers to guarantee the interest on the cost of a cable to the Islands, either from San Francisco or New Zealand— New Zealand he believed was the nearest—by means of which the Governments could directly interfere to prevent such troubles as had occurred."[9]

Kasson "concluded the conversation with an expression of the hope that his [Salisbury's] instructions would leave the British representatives free to consider propositions which might be offered without being bound by any hard and fast rule. England being situated, as he had suggested, indifferently, might be able to aid materially in a proper compromise of differences." Salisbury seemed to concur in this "and remarked that he had not yet written his instructions."[10]

In his first despatch from Berlin, the day after his arrival there, Kasson recalled that Lord Salisbury had

[8] Samoan Conference at Berlin, 1889, MSS, Department of State, Kasson to Blaine, April 24, despatch no. 2.
[9] *Ibid.*
[10] Kasson concluded his despatch to Blaine thus: "I had met in the ante room my friend, the German Ambassador Count Hatzfeldt, who had precedence, which he insisted on waiving in my favor. After a persistent contest of courtesy, as to which of us should first enter Lord Salisbury's room, I was obliged to yield to his declaration that he would be a long time finishing his business, and could not think of detaining me so long. (!!) Lord Salisbury was very amiable and spoke with a frankness for which I am his debtor."

Following his interview with Kasson and presumably after his interview with Count Hatzfeldt, Lord Salisbury on the same day (April 24) sent the following communication to the British ambassador at Berlin, Sir Edward Malet: "I hope to send out your instructions in good time before the open-

made another suggestion at their interview in London, namely, that perhaps the best solution of the Samoan problem would be the division of the three largest islands among the three powers.[11]

Kasson reported also on the 28th that on that day he had visited Sir Edward Malet, the British ambassador, at Sir Edward's request, having gone to the British embassy even before the American commissioners called on Count Bismarck. The principal object was Malet's desire to assist Kasson in smoothing out the Bates difficulty, but he did not neglect to revert to the suggestion made by Lord Salisbury concerning the division of national influence among the islands, although he modified the suggestion considerably by intimating the desirability of American influence in Hawaii, English influence in the Tonga islands, and German influence in Samoa, with the exception of the island of Tutuila with its harbor of Pago Pago, which he thought might be separately managed by the United States. The suggestion was made, however, as a personal opinion and not officially.

The Kasson papers leave us in the dark concerning ing of the Samoan Conference. I have seen one of the American Plenipotentiaries and gather that your deliberations will not be long or difficult and will result in a victory for the Americans. But as a settlement of the question, this issue will be quite valueless. The fundamental difference between their view and that which we and the Germans have supported is that we think some one European power must lead in the Government of the islands, whilst the Americans think that all three Governments must be on a precisely equal footing. I understand that on this point the Germans mean to give in. We cannot fight it alone but the Government by three equal Consuls will not work smoothly for three years together. They are talking of having a majority arrangement by which two of the Consuls shall outvote the other. To this I have a strong objection. Samoa matters very little to us and I strongly demur to an arrangement under which, for Samoa's sake, we shall quarrel either with the Germans or the Americans once a month. . . . The greatest reform of all would be to lay a cable from Auckland to Apia. So, and so only, we should get rid of the *furor consularis.*'' (Quoted from G. Cecil, *Life of Robert Marquis of Salisbury*, IV, 127-128.)

[11] Samoan Conference at Berlin, 1889, MSS, Department of State, Kasson to Blaine, April 27, 1889, despatch no. 3.

Kasson's reply to Lord Salisbury at London, but his answer to Sir Edward was definite and unequivocal. The American instructions did not touch any other islands, he said, and the United States could not accept a mandate for Tutuila for the reason that under the American-Samoan treaty the government was bound to use its "good offices for the benefit of the natives of all the Islands." At this first meeting with Malet, Kasson succeeded in securing the British commissioner's consent to act as an intermediary in cases where the American and German views were at variance. Malet also agreed that the German proposal made at the Washington Conference and supported by England, namely, that the premiership should be vested in Germany, would have to be abandoned in view of the determined opposition of the United States.[12]

But difficulties with Berlin were more apparent than real. What Kasson feared as the greatest obstacle was a probable objection on Germany's part to the restoration of Malietoa and a return to a genuine *status quo*. Yet, if it were a question of restoring Malietoa in order to displace Mataafa (the latest culprit in the eyes of Germany), the difficulty might not be so great after all. In Blaine's instructions it was plainly stated that the proposal for the restoration of the *status quo* should not be submitted "as an ultimatum," for in the event of its non-acceptance by Germany, the president would want to be in a position to consider any substitute plan, although the rejection of the American proposal should only be accepted by the American Commission "*ad referendum.*"[13] Nevertheless, the president was "painfully apprehensive" that without the restoration of conditions in Samoa under which the

[12] Samoan Conference at Berlin, 1889, MSS, Department of State, Kasson to Blaine, April 27, 1889, despatch no. 3.
[13] Kasson Papers, Department of State, instructions from Blaine to Kasson, Phelps, and Bates, April 11, 1889, no. 2, pp. 14 and 15.

THE BERLIN CONFERENCE, 1889   451

natives could freely choose their king, there would be danger of the powers not reaching any general solution of the Samoan problem at all.[14] The question before the American commissioners was, therefore, how to proceed so as to secure Germany's adherence to the president's wishes without making it appear as though Germany were surrendering her position in the face of American demands. How it was done was explained by Kasson in his next despatch to Washington. But the mandate question was disposed of first.

The American delegation had been received on Saturday, the 27th, at the German foreign office by Count Bismarck, on which occasion the German secretary of state for foreign affairs announced the abandonment of the German mandatory scheme as advanced by von Alvensleben at Washington and supported by Sackville-West.[15] But in surrendering its claims to a mandate, Germany was not ready at the beginning of the conference to substitute the American plan of a tripartite control as suggested by Bayard in the Washington Conference. It was clear from the first formal statement by the German chief plenipotentiary that Germany wanted no arrangement made at Berlin which might make joint intervention the sole legal method, and which might diminish German influence over the native Samoan government. This will be discussed more fully when the deliberations of the conference are analyzed. Suffice it to say here that the rock upon which the Washington Conference was wrecked, namely, Germany's demand for a mandate, was removed by Germany herself even before the formal meetings of the Berlin Conference began, a step foreshadowed by Lord Salisbury's remark to Kasson in London.

[14] *Ibid.*, p. 13.
[15] Samoan Conference at Berlin, 1889, MSS, Kasson to Blaine, April 28, despatch no. 4.

When Count Bismarck returned the call of the American commissioners on Sunday, the 28th, the day before the conference was formally opened, Kasson in private conversation raised the question of Malietoa's release. "I desired Germany to offer it [the release of Malietoa] without open demand in conference, to avoid suggestion of humiliation," wrote Kasson. When Count Bismarck expressed the fear that such an interpretation would be made, Kasson assured him that the contrary would be the case if the release of Malietoa was "spontaneously done because past punishment was sufficient."[16] In a personal letter to Blaine written on the 30th, Kasson gave further particulars concerning his confidential talk with Count Bismarck anent Malietoa. He said that Count Bismarck had "quickly understood" the "serious importance" which the United States attached to the request. Consequently, in the same letter he was able to report that before the opening of the formal conference the German government had yielded "on the most dangerous point." It was necessary, however, to keep secret the manner in which the concession was secured, to prevent the German press from charging the Bismarcks (father and son) with having backed down under pressure.[17]

As indicated in the above letter, Germany did not keep the American commissioners waiting long for her answer. That it was as much of a concession as Kasson supposed, is doubtful. Moreover, as has been stated, Germany had perhaps already, before the Bismarck-Kasson interview, seriously considered the return of Malietoa as a lesser evil than Mataafa (since the United States would not recognize Tamasese), and Count Bismarck may have been clever enough to make Kasson feel that he had gained a considerable concession from Germany in order that Ger-

[16] Samoan Conference at Berlin, 1889, MSS, Kasson to Blaine, April 28, despatch no. 4.
[17] *Ibid.*, Kasson to Blaine, April 30.

THE BERLIN CONFERENCE, 1889   453

many might come back later and seek a return of the favor in another direction. The method pursued by Kasson in bringing the matter up privately rather than in an open session was highly commendable, and naturally made the relations between Germany and the United States favorable for a successful conclusion of the deliberations.

At the opening session on Monday, the 29th, the day following the Bismarck-Kasson interview, Count Bismarck read the following statement: "We have recently received an official report from the Commander of the German Naval vessel[18] to the effect that Malietoa, the former Samoan King, has expressed regrets and the earnest wish to be reconciled with the German Government. His Imperial Majesty, the Emperor, after having taken cognizance of this report, has ordered his release. Consequently Malietoa is at liberty to go wherever he pleases."[19] Kasson immediately expressed the pleasure with which the United States government would receive the German declaration, and the "English Ambassador joined in thanks on the part of England."[20]

Whether the president wanted Malietoa returned merely "as a Samoan wrongly deported or as a King to displace Mataafa" seems not to have been clear to Kasson while he was in England, and therefore, he had cabled Washington for further instructions.[21] On the 30th (the day after the opening of the conference), Kasson received a long cable from Blaine concerning Malietoa in answer to his inquiry. "The United States asks," said the instructions in part, "that the legitimate King temporarily deposed by German authority shall be allowed to return and be a candidate for restoration." Blaine reverted to

[18] The man-of-war, *Olga*.
[19] Samoan Conference at Berlin, 1889, MSS, Kasson to Blaine, April 29, despatch no. 5.
[20] *Ibid.*   [21] *Ibid.*, Kasson to Blaine, April 24, despatch no. 1.

the illegality of the deposition further on in the instructions. "You must not admit, however, in any discussion, that this Government recognizes the deposition of Malietoa to have been legitimate action by Germany, nor must you admit that Germany could declare war against Samoa without full consultation with the treaty powers, especially under the circumstances connected with the Washington Conference. It is the course of the German authorities immediately after the Washington Conference of which the President is of the opinion that this Government has just cause of complaint, and the President has hoped that the German Government, while not disavowing, might pass over the seizure of King as the overzealous act of a German Naval officer and a German Consul. You must ask the return of Malietoa not because he has been exiled long enough, but because he ought never to have been exiled at all. If you admit the German right to punish the King you must admit their right to fix the degree of punishment. The President's objection is fundamental."[22]

In response to Kasson's cable concerning Germany's action relative to Malietoa, Blaine immediately inquired whether the German government proposed to return Malietoa to Samoa or if he was to provide his own method of return. If the former procedure were to be adopted, the secretary of state said it was "important to know at what time" and that Kasson should "endeavor to obtain authentic and exact information on these points."[23] Evidently Kasson's "victory" in Berlin was regarded in Washington as a preliminary advantage but nothing more.

[22] Samoan Conference at Berlin, 1889, MSS, Kasson to Blaine, April 30, despatch no. 6, confirmation of cipher cable, Blaine to Kasson.
[23] *Ibid.*, Kasson to Blaine, May 1, no. 7, confirmation of cable Blaine to Kasson.

At this point it were best perhaps to give a short account of the assembling of the conference at Berlin. The American, German, and British plenipotentiaries met for their opening session at 2:30 Monday afternoon, April 29. In addition to Sir Edward Malet, the British delegates were Charles Stewart Scott, minister to Switzerland, and Joseph Archer Crowe. Count Bismarck, having welcomed the plenipotentiaries, said that he considered the harmony of feeling that had been manifested by the three friendly governments as a good omen for the success of their labors and proposed that the conference be organized, whereupon Kasson, speaking for the members of the conference, thanked Count Bismarck "for the kind words just addressed to them . . . and proposed that His Excellency be chosen to preside over the conference." This was done, and Count Bismarck thereupon introduced as secretaries, with the consent of the plenipotentiaries, Dr. Arendt, consul general of Germany in Belgium, and Mr. Beauclerk, British embassy secretary at Berlin.[24]

After some preliminary measures relative to procedure had been taken, the president of the conference read a statement concerning the German position on the Samoan question. The recent events in Samoa imposed upon the three treaty powers the duty of taking into consideration measures for the protection of life and property of foreigners in Samoa. As necessary preliminaries in ironing out the difficulties of the situation and to give sufficient guarantees for the future, the German government considered the maintenance of the existing treaties, the parity of the rights of the three treaty powers, and the independence and neutrality of the Samoan state. In the opinion of the imperial government the conference should

[24] Later in the opening session, when it was decided to use the English language instead of the French, W. Stemrich was substituted for Dr. Arendt.

not try to establish a government acceptable to the natives, but a solid base for the protection of life, property, and commerce for the nationals of the three treaty powers and to proceed toward this end by common action of the powers. The conference should concern itself with arranging the domestic affairs of Samoa only in so far as this seemed necessary to safeguard the security of the lives, property, and commerce of the subjects of the three treaty powers. But before the details of the conference were taken up it was necessary to learn the views of the other governments. Sir Edward Malet thereupon read the declaration of the British government. This referred particularly to the adjournment of the Washington Conference and the satisfaction that the British government found in the resumption at Berlin of the work of that conference. The government accepted cordially the bases for negotiation outlined by Count Bismarck, namely, the maintenance of the existing treaties, the equality of the rights of the three treaty powers, and the independence and neutrality of the Samoan islands. On these bases the British plenipotentiaries would do all within their power to arrive at a satisfactory solution, and create, with the aid of their colleagues, a system of administration for the Samoan islands, which could assure them peace and the benefits of a prosperous tranquillity.

Up to this point the speeches and deliberations had been carried on in the French language but when Kasson arose to speak he asked for permission to state the views of the American government in English. Speaking of the pleasure with which the United States received the German proposition for the resumption of the negotiations of the Washington Conference, Kasson said the president had instructed the American commissioners "to give the most earnest assurance of his desire for a speedy and amicable solution of the questions relating to Samoa, upon the principles accepted at its earlier meeting." The American government accepted and reciprocated the assurances of the German government concerning the neutrality of the Samoan islands and the equal rights of the treaty powers, and the president shared "the common desire of the powers to apply these principles to protect the Islands against a repetition of bloody wars and to secure all the just interests of foreigners engaged there in lawful business." Since the American statement was the only one mentioning the *status quo* in Samoa, it is perhaps well to quote this part of Kasson's speech in full: "So far as the *status quo* existing before the violent disturbances which have occurred since the adjournment of the conference at Washington, can be restored, the Government of the United States earnestly desires it, as the initiation of permanent peace and order among the natives." At the conclusion of Kasson's statement, Count Bismarck agreed to substitute the English language for the French, merely reserving the right to resume the French language if the German representatives found it necessary to do so. Count Bismarck also accepted Kasson's suggestion that the protocols be drawn up in the English language.

At the suggestion of the president of the conference, a "sub-committee" of three representatives—one for each power—was delegated to prepare an agenda for the conference. This committee consisted of Dr. Krauel, Mr. Bates, and Mr. Scott, the understanding being that all other members of the conference might attend their discussions. At the further suggestion of Count Bismarck the land question was the first to be submitted to the sub-committee, "as being perhaps the most important of all the questions to be dealt with by the conference." The meeting then adjourned with the understanding that the next meeting of the plenary conference should be called by the president.²⁵

On May 2, Kasson cabled Blaine in code that at the first session of the conference, Germany proposed that the conference should take no action "on the question of a government suitable to the natives, but should provide a solid basis for the protection of life, property, and trade of the foreigners, leaving natives to govern themselves in their own way."²⁶ The next day Kasson received Blaine's answer which stated clearly the American position as opposed to the German and at the same time showed that the United States was committed to a tripartite arrangement for joint intervention in Samoa in case of need. Again it was the United States which insisted on the "entangling alliance" and not Germany and Great Britain. Again we reiterated our position based on article V of our treaty with Samoa, so definitely stated by Bayard, and consistently maintained by him, in the Washington Conference of 1887. Furthermore, the reasons for our stand at this early date of the Berlin Conference were the same as those advanced by Bayard: first, that without some such arrangement any of the three nations might secure a preponderance in the Samoan government; and second, any one nation could declare war upon Samoa without reference to the rights of the other treaty powers. In short, it was our desire to effect a real neutrality in Samoa and the only way to do so was to establish a tripartite arrangement for the protection of Samoa or for joint intervention.²⁷

²⁵ Kasson Papers, Department of State, certified copy of the protocol of the first session, Monday, April 29, 1889; S. Misc. Doc. no. 81, pp. 17-21, encl. 3.

²⁶ Samoan Conference at Berlin, 1889, MSS, confirmation of cipher, Kasson to Blaine, May 2, 1889, despatch no. 9.

²⁷ *Ibid.*, Kasson to Blaine, May 3, despatch no. 11, confirmation of cipher, Blaine to Kasson.

THE BERLIN CONFERENCE, 1889

The second session of the conference was held on Saturday, May 4, with all the plenipotentiaries present. Count Bismarck presented the report on the land question, drawn up by the subcommittee, and requested Bates to read it after an agreement had been reached, "that the recommendations, submitted by the sub-committee to the Plenipotentiaries, should be taken by them *ad referendum* for the approval of their respective Governments." The first conclusion of the subcommittee was that the natives should be strictly prohibited in the future from selling any land to foreigners, a prohibition similar to those in the Tonga, Hawaiian, Fiji, and other Polynesian groups. On the other hand the natives might lease land "with the approval of the Executive Department of the Samoan Government and the Land Court."

Mr. Scott explained that both he and Bates had in committee expressed the doubt whether the putting into effect of such a prohibition would be "in strict conformity with one of the bases laid down by the President, namely, the recognition of the independence of the Samoan Government" and also whether "legitimate enterprises" would not be interfered with, but when it had been explained "that the prohibition would be enforced by the Samoan Government as a party to the contemplated treaty, and that the power of leasing left to the natives would give every necessary facility to foreign enterprise, he finally concurred in recommending the foregoing suggestion to the consideration of the conference."

The discussion concerning the first conclusion of the subcommittee thereupon became general, the main point upon which it turned being the practicability of leaseholds to encourage foreign investments, and the length of time for leases. When nearly all the commissioners had expressed themselves, but had reached no conclusion, Count Bismarck pointed out "that the question of the duration of leases was not very important for the present moment" since by confidential exchanges between the delegates it was his understanding that whatever arrangements for the Samoan islands would be drawn up would necessarily be for a limited period "of three or five years in order to put them to the test," after which period "the treaty powers would have to reconsider the said arrangements." To this Bates agreed and Kasson brought the discussion of the first suggestion to a close by proposing the acceptance of the principle that "it is necessary to restrain the disposal of land to foreigners in Samoa."[28]

The second proposal from the subcommittee suggested the setting up of a commission of three members to be appointed and paid by the three treaty powers respectively, for the purpose of investigating all land claims as between foreigners and between foreigners and natives, and reporting its findings to a land court. The commission among other things should investigate whether the land had been sold by its rightful owner, whether there had been "sufficient consideration," and whether the land sold could be identified. Moreover, the commission should "endeavor to effect just and equitable compromises between litigants and to make recommendations to the Land Court about granting or refusing the recognition and registration of titles."

It will be remembered that the German plan at the Washington Conference provided for a land commission in addition to a land court and that Bayard had opposed it because he thought that the functions of the proposed land commission could be carried on effectively by the land court, which was to be in any case the final court of appeal. No discussion took place at the Berlin Conference

[28] Kasson Papers, Department of State, certified copy of the protocol of the second session, Saturday May 4, 1889; S. Misc. Doc. no. 81, pp. 22-24, encl. 3.

THE BERLIN CONFERENCE, 1889   461

on the proposal of a land commission, and the suggestion coming from the subcommittee that a land commission be provided for, was adopted unanimously. This was a strong indication that the United States had accepted the German plan as more efficacious.

The third suggestion from the subcommittee referred to native representation in connection with the land commission. Although the committee thought it impracticable to have a native representative on the commission, it recommended that the Samoan government be empowered to appoint, with the approval of the land commission, "an assistant native commissioner or natives' advocate." Dr. Krauel apparently was responsible for this suggestion, for immediately after the reading of the same, he referred to arrangements made in Fiji, and "suggested that perhaps a suitable 'natives' advocate' could be found in the person of a foreign resident missionary." Bates seconded Dr. Krauel's suggestion and the subcommittee's proposition evidently was immediately adopted, although the protocol is silent on this point.

The next proposal was adopted without debate, namely, that the expenses of the land commission "should be paid equally by the three Governments." Then followed the fifth proposal, which provided for a "Land Court" consisting of "one judge learned in the law to be appointed by the Samoan Government upon the nomination of the three treaty powers, his decision to be final in all land cases." To this court should be referred by the land commission all disputed claims for final decision, while "undisputed claims or such as were determined by the unanimous vote of the commission should be confirmed by the Court without reëxamination."[29]

At the suggestion of the president of the conference, a "Committee of Revision" was elected to formulate the

[29] *Ibid.;* S. Misc. Doc. no. 81, p. 24, encl. 3.

final resolutions agreed upon by the plenary conference. Baron von Holstein, Mr. Kasson, and Sir Edward Malet were named to serve on this committee. The above quoted resolution (no. 5) was then accepted and referred with all others to the committee of revision.

Questions of the salary and tenure of office of the land court judge evoked a little discussion. Count Bismarck suggested that the salary be paid by the Samoan government, while Kasson thought that the three powers might pay the salary at the outset or that they might at least guarantee it. Sir E. Malet then called attention to the necessity of deciding whether the judge should be removable and whether he should be removed from office only with the consent of the three powers.

Proposals numbers six, seven, eight, and nine were then read by Bates and referred to the committee of revision. The sixth proposal provided for the production before the land commission within a specified time, not exceeding six months, of all deeds, mortgages, claims of liens, or interests in lands claimed by foreigners. Moreover, application to the land commission for its "recognition and equitable adjustment of such claims and the registration of such title" had to be made. Proposal number seven stated that "all lands acquired before the 28th of August, 1879 (the date of the Anglo-Samoan treaty) must be held as validly acquired if purchased from Samoans in a customary and regular manner." It will be remembered that the German-Samoan treaty of January 24, 1879 evoked strong criticism from natives and whites, because in article VI it guaranteed the possession by the Germans of all lands acquired prior to the treaty "from Samoans in a regular manner and in accordance with the custom at the time." At the Washington Conference Bayard made it plain, though without direct statement to that effect, that some of the land claimed by the Germans had

THE BERLIN CONFERENCE, 1889   463

been acquired fraudulently and that the principal work of the land court, if it were left untrammeled, would be to restore this land to the natives. At the Berlin Conference the principle of the German treaty was upheld, although the date before which all lands acquired should "be held as validly acquired if purchased from Samoans in a customary and regular manner," was fixed at August 28, 1879, the date of the last of the three-power treaties.

The eighth proposal stated that "the undisputed possession and continuous cultivation of lands for ten years or upwards shall constitute a valid title," but the ninth proposal provided that "where lands have been improved or cultivated upon a title which proves to be faulty, the title may be confirmed upon the payment, by the occupant, to such person or persons as the Commission may find entitled to the same of an additional sum to be determined upon principles of equity and justice."

Proposal number ten was then considered. It provided that "Recognition and registration shall be refused in the following cases: (a) promises to sell (or options); (b) when deed or mortgage contains no description of land; (c) if no consideration is expressed in deed or mortgage—or if expressed has not been paid in full to seller; (d) conveyances or mortgages of land made since Jan. 1, 1880, upon an actual consideration of the sale of firearms or munitions of war or of intoxicating liquors, in violation of Samoan law of Oct. 25, 1880, or Municipal Regulations of Jan. 1, 1880." An eleventh proposal provided for the organization of a native commission in local government districts to determine the sellers' right of ownership and to lay the results of investigation before the land commission.

The land question was then set aside for the time being and Count Bismarck submitted the following additional proposals:

"We propose that the conference may devise means by which the interests of the foreign residents in the Samoan Islands can be protected.

"The treaty powers agree to take steps to prevent the importation and sale of arms and munitions of war as well as the sale and gift of intoxicating liquors to natives of Samoa."[30]

On May 4, the day on which the second session of the conference was held, Kasson cabled Blaine that immediately after the receipt from the latter of the instructions of May 3, referred to above, Count Bismarck had called upon him, and that an agreement had been reached on the propriety of a tribunal to decide on a contested election or disputed authority of a chief. It was thought, too, by Kasson—after a conversation with the British ambassador—that the conference might make the land court judge also the arbiter of disputed elections. This was Kasson's suggestion, and he explained to Blaine "It may be possible to vest him with authority to settle foreign disputes with Samoa, reserving appeal if necessary to mutual arbitration, thus avoiding war."[31]

Thus, due to the demands from Washington, the initial position of Germany in the conference, namely, that there should be no machinery set up for the native government, was being gradually abandoned. Should the proposal for a disputed elections tribunal be carried through, the validity of Tamasese's right to the kingship would be the first to be determined, and Germany's recognition of Tamasese as king might, in consequence, be rendered null and void. That Germany expected this eventuality, and

---

[30] Kasson Papers, Department of State, certified copy of the protocol of the second session, Saturday, May 4, 1889; S. Misc. Doc. no. 81, pp. 24-26, encl. 3.

[31] Samoan Conference at Berlin, 1889, MSS, Kasson to Blaine, May 4, despatch no. 12, confirmation of cipher telegram sent same day.

THE BERLIN CONFERENCE, 1889

that it was felt necessary to prepare the German public for a probable change in the Samoan kingship are indicated by the suggestions made in the German press for possible secret arrangements with Malietoa, under which he might return to Samoa and be king as a friend of Germany. This intelligence was cabled to Blaine on May 5,[32] but on May 9 Kasson cabled, "I do not credit the report of a private agreement between Malietoa and Germany."[33] At the same time he wanted an expression from Blaine as to "the expediency of restoring the *status quo* with Malietoa as king and Tamasese vice king as either permanent or temporary arrangement preliminary to a free election." He wanted instructions before the question was raised in the conference so as to avoid confusion in Samoa.[34]

Immediately upon the receipt of instructions from Blaine that steps be taken for setting up some sort of tripartite foreign authority for the establishment and maintenance of a native government, another telegram was received from Washington suggesting that the commission "take every judicious step to obtain if possible full recognition by treaty of our exclusive right to the great harbor [Pago Pago], the concession of which is already so nearly complete."[35] Samoa might be paid a sum not exceeding twenty thousand dollars if such a condition were "absolutely necessary."[36] Kasson immediately re-

[32] *Ibid.*, Kasson to Blaine, May 5, despatch no. 17, confirmation of cipher telegram sent same day.

[33] *Ibid.*, Kasson to Blaine, May 9, despatch no. 22, confirmation of cipher telegram sent same day.

[34] *Ibid.*

[35] On Jan. 16, 1884, the Department of State in reply to an inquiry from Consul Canisius at Apia stated that the United States claimed the right to establish a coaling station at Pago Pago, but did not claim exclusive jurisdiction over the harbor there. (Instructions to Consuls, vol. 109, p. 341.)

[36] Samoan Conference at Berlin, 1889, MSS, Kasson to Blaine, May 5, despatch no. 14, confirmation of cipher, Blaine to Kasson, received same day.

plied: "It seems very difficult if not dangerous to raise, in the conference, a question as to our right to the harbor of Pago Pago in view of the harbor concessions to England and Germany which would then be brought also before the conference. . . . Is not actual possession and full ownership of shores more imperatively necessary now than everything else."[37] To this Blaine immediately replied: "You are right. Better make no reference whatever to Pago Pago. Instructions cancelled and withdrawn."[38] Thus we see Blaine pressing for more advantages than Kasson deemed it possible to secure. The exchange of cables concerning Pago Pago is nevertheless important as it reveals that our interests in Samoa were primarily based on a desire eventually to have our full control of Pago Pago recognized by the other powers. The demands of the navy for a naval station there in view of the probability of our building an Isthmian canal were definitely set forth by Bayard in the Washington Conference and again by Blaine in his instructions to the commissioners.

In another cipher received in Berlin May 5, Blaine advised the American commissioners to use their discretion relative to export and import duties for Samoa, but with respect to importation of liquors he said: "You must stand firmly against permitting the importation, under any circumstances, of spirits, wine, or malt liquors. If the use of intoxicating liquors is allowed among the natives, they are doomed."[39] To this Kasson replied that while all parties were agreed on prohibiting the sale or gift of liquors, arms, and ammunition to natives, there was a

[37] Samoan Conference at Berlin, 1889, MSS, Kasson to Blaine, May 5, despatch no. 17, confirmation of cipher sent same day.
[38] Kasson Papers, Department of State, Blaine to Kasson, received May 6.
[39] Samoan Conference at Berlin, 1889, MSS, Kasson to Blaine, May 5, despatch no. 15, confirmation of cipher, Blaine to Kasson, received May 5.

THE BERLIN CONFERENCE, 1889

feeling that the importation and use of these commodities by foreigners should not be prohibited.[40]

That the conference was reaching a critical stage is indicated by another telegram sent by Kasson to Blaine on May 9, wherein the American commissioner stated that at the American official banquet given to the German and English delegates the night before, he had had a conversation with Count Bismarck on the most delicate and difficult points. From the conversation the following desires of Germany appeared clear, and he requested Blaine's instructions concerning them. First, Germany wanted the exclusion of Mataafa as a candidate in the proposed election of the king, on account of his war and the mutilation of dead German sailors. This appeared necessary, as some satisfaction of national honor was required. But Kasson thought that if Mataafa were excluded, Germany might be willing to exclude Tamasese as well. The second demand was compensation out of the taxes raised for losses by war to white planters and the families of slain sailors. "I objected to this double satisfaction," said Kasson. "War was defensive, and war damages should be treated like damages by cyclone. That it was better not to raise these old war questions." Count Bismarck evinced no objection to Malietoa or any other candidate with the exception of Mataafa, added Kasson, and the "tone is conciliatory on both sides."[41] This conversation was confidential, and since Kasson probably failed to inform the other American delegates, they, especially Bates, became very critical of Kasson's methods and a crisis developed within the commission before the third session of the conference.

On the 11th, the day of the third plenary session, Kas-

---
[40] *Ibid.*, despatch no. 16, confirmation of cipher sent same day.
[41] *Ibid.*, Kasson to Blaine, May 9, despatch no. 23, confirmation of cipher sent same day.

son received a long despatch from Blaine in which the latter stated that the president could not "regard with favor an election in which certain candidates are to be pronounced ineligible in advance." But if Mataafa was to be ineligible "Tamasese should also be considered so." The reason for the president's objection to the elimination of these candidates was the suspicion that, despite Kasson's disbelief in any understanding between Malietoa and Germany, "the assent of Germany to Malietoa's candidacy is strongly suggestive of a secret understanding between that chief and Germany." This suspicion was supported, thought Blaine, by the fact that Malietoa had been "for a long period exclusively under German control, having been deported from Samoa as prisoner of war in eighteen eighty-seven." But in the president's view the graver question was the proposed indemnity to Germany. "If an indemnity of any magnitude is granted," continued Blaine, "German influence in the Islands will be predominant for many years." The suggestion appeared to Blaine "to be a skilful diplomatic move," and although it "should not be asserted to prejudice harmony and friendly compromise, yet in the judgment of the President," the secretary added, "we cannot assent to any settlement, which, as a necessary result, reduces natives to penury and dependence."[42]

At this point the question of the *status quo* and indemnity for Germany became complicated with the plan for disbanding the native factions. At the beginning of the conference Germany had made it clear that only if satisfaction for losses were not secured, or if the conference were delayed, would she use force in Samoa to obtain satisfaction. Now she was agreeable to a disbandment of the Tamasese forces as well as those of Mataafa, but just

[42] Samoan Conference at Berlin, 1889, MSS, Kasson to Blaine, May 11, despatch no. 25, confirmation of cipher, Blaine to Kasson, same day.

as Blaine was suspicious of Germany's newly formed friendliness toward Malietoa, so now there developed suspicion within the American delegation of some hidden motive behind Count Bismarck's willingness that the factions be disbanded, and, as we shall see, this suspicion was communicated to Blaine, who reversed himself on the proposal within a few hours after having taken his first position.

On the 10th Kasson informed Blaine that, at his suggestion, it had been agreed by Germany and England that he should propose at the next plenary session (May 11) "that identical instructions be telegraphed immediately to our Consuls and Naval Commanding officers in Samoa, to urge all Samoa natives to lay down their arms immediately and to return to their homes peaceably, there to await and abide by the resolutions to be adopted by the conference." Kasson added that Count Bismarck had called upon him "again to-day for private conversation" and had "indicated to exclude Tamasese as well as Mataafa from the coming election."[43] At the third plenary session, due to the objection of Phelps and Bates,[44] Kasson failed to carry out his plan for proposing a general disbanding of the two contending Samoan forces. He informed Blaine that Germany and England were willing and he wanted to know by telegraph if Blaine agreed to his proposition.[45] Kasson received Blaine's reply the same day as follows: "Movement of treaty powers for general peace in Samoa heartily approved by the President." But

[43] *Ibid.*, Kasson to Blaine, May 10, despatch no. 24, confirmation of cipher telegram sent same day.

[44] Kasson misinformed Blaine as to the number of American commissioners opposed to his plan. His cipher to Blaine (no. 13) reads: "Owing to one American objection I did not to-day present order for identical German, American and English instruction" etc.

[45] Samoan Conference at Berlin, 1889, MSS, Kasson to Blaine, May 11, despatch no. 26, confirmation of cipher sent same day.

Blaine added: "Be on your guard against exclusion of all candidates except Malietoa. Circumstances strongly point to the conclusion that to regain his liberty, he has pledged himself to coöperate with all German designs."[46] The next day, however, a cipher was received from Blaine, addressed to all the commissioners, suspending all action on his last instruction. In other words, Kasson's proposal that all three nations should send identical notes calling for a disbanding of the warring factions in Samoa was not yet approved.[47]

The reason for this sudden reversal was no doubt the receipt by Blaine of two cipher despatches, one from Phelps and the other from Bates, sent the same day as Kasson's despatch (May 11), and without Kasson's knowledge, but not received before the sending of Blaine's reply to that communication. Phelps' despatch read as follows: "Reluctant without President's explicit instructions to assent to Kasson's proposition for both sides to lay down their arms, unless Germany first withdraws the recognition of Tamasese. Proposition is unequal; we disarm a large regular force, they a small irregular force. General disarmament leaves Tamasese still recognized as sole king and he needs then no army. Remember during the Washington Conference we advised Malietoa to inaction, and the sad result, and there are now four German Naval vessels at Sydney as then. Why cannot we wait the result of the conference before we disarm Mataafa's forces. Such delay is short. Bates, Parker and Sewall share these views."[48]

[46] Samoan Conference at Berlin, 1889, MSS, Kasson to Blaine, May 11, despatch no. 27, confirmation of cipher, Blaine to Kasson, no. 9, received same day at 9:43 P.M.

[47] *Ibid.*, Kasson to Blaine, May 12, despatch no. 28, confirmation of cipher, Blaine to Kasson, no. 10, received same day at 6 A.M.

[48] *Ibid.*, Phelps to Blaine, May 11, despatch no. 34, confirmation of cipher sent same day. Lieutenant John F. Parker, U.S.N., was ordered to Berlin after the opening of the conference to assist the American commissioners.

Bates sent the following cipher to Blaine on the same day: "Kasson insists on proposing in the conference withdrawal of Mataafa's forces against the wish of the other two American Commissioners. This is an old scheme often attempted by the Germans, well known by those familiar with the situation, and caused bloodshed last December." Then he outlined the method pursued by Kasson at Berlin. Only one despatch from Kasson to Blaine had been submitted to the other two members of the commission thus far, and he believed that Kasson was carrying on secret negotiations, and refusing assistance from those sent over to advise the commission.[49] They had overlooked much "to avoid rupture" but if such tactics were continued there was danger that all that had been accomplished would be lost.[50] On the 12th Phelps again cabled: "Please remind the President in any decision our best information is that Tamasese would have no substantial native support, and all feel Mataafa represents sacrifice, nationality, patience and heart of Samoa."[51] On the same day (May 12), and after the receipt of Blaine's instructions cancelling his consent to the disbandment of the Samoan factions, Kasson sent a message explaining his proposal which, he asserted, was based upon a report from Rear Admiral Kimberly.[52]

It is clear from the above quotations that Phelps and Bates, as well as Sewall, were in favor of Mataafa being a candidate for the kingship. It is also quite clear that Germany would, under no circumstances, agree to Mataafa's candidacy, and consented to the elimination of Ta-

[49] Evidently a reference to Sewall, disbursing officer, and Lieutenant Parker.
[50] Samoan Conference at Berlin, 1889, MSS, Bates to Blaine, May 11, despatch no. 35, confirmation of cipher sent same day.
[51] *Ibid.*, Phelps to Blaine, May 12, despatch no. 36, confirmation of cipher sent same day.
[52] *Ibid.*, Kasson to Blaine, May 12, despatch no. 30, confirmation of cipher no. 15, sent same day.

masese, only on condition that Mataafa should not be a candidate.

Count Bismarck had informed Kasson the day before the third session, that Tamasese would be excluded, and it was on the basis of this elimination of Tamasese that Kasson, no doubt, intended to propose in the session on the morrow the disbandment of the Samoan factions. By the same cable in which he informed Blaine of his intention (May 10) he also informed him of Count Bismarck's call for a private conversation and of his "indicated willingness to exclude Tamasese as well as Mataafa from the coming election." Whether Kasson informed the other American commissioners of Germany's willingness to eliminate Tamasese is doubtful. But even if Kasson had informed the others of Germany's willingness to abandon Tamasese, they might still have been sceptical for the reason that all Kasson himself could say as late as May 13 was: "When I intimated that the exclusion of Mataafa from the candidacy on their protest would present the necessity on our part of objecting to Tamasese as the author and supporter of the present civil war, it was replied that it would be hard for them to abandon the man whom they had recognized, and exclude him from the candidacy. Later, however, Count Bismarck allowed me to understand that it might possibly be done, if we made it a condition of Mataafa's exclusion."[53]

In his despatch of May 13, Kasson defended his method of conducting the negotiations, and intimated that he regarded himself as the ranking commissioner. His previous diplomatic service in Berlin made it natural for the Germans to consult him more freely than the other two commissioners.[54] It is evident, too, that Count Bismarck

[53] Samoan Conference at Berlin, 1889, MSS, Kasson to Blaine, May 13, despatch no. 31, pp. 9 and 10.
[54] *Ibid.*, pp. 15 and 16.

THE BERLIN CONFERENCE, 1889

accepted Kasson as the chief commissioner and that an agreement with him would virtually mean an agreement with the others. Certainly Count Bismarck and Sir Edward Malet were considered the heads of their respective commissions, and to facilitate the work of the formal plenary sessions of the conference and even of the work of the subcommittees, understandings had to be reached by Count Bismarck with Kasson at informal meetings. In other words, a "Big Three" had of necessity been formed within the conference. It may be added that the Bates incident, though officially closed, made it difficult for the German representative to have any spontaneous and confidential talks with Bates. Kasson was perhaps too willing to believe that the German Foreign Office was entirely purged of ambitious imperial schemes with respect to Samoa and that Germany had "laid all her cards on the table," but on the other hand constantly to entertain suspicions of every move made by Germany, as Bates, Phelps, and Sewall seemed to do, would sooner or later have paralyzed the work of the American commissioners and have destroyed the goodwill between Germany and the United States which was so necessary for a successful conclusion of the conference.

It was a mistake that the administration had not appointed Kasson as chairman of the commission in the beginning; in the middle of the conference it was impossible to do so without appearing to take Kasson's side against Phelps and Bates and thus offend these latter and possibly force them to resign. A break-up of the American delegation would have jeopardized the American position, no doubt, and had to be prevented. Hence, on the 13th a cipher was received from Blaine as follows: "I hear with deep regret of differences in Commission. There must be cordial co-operation, and to that end perfect frankness should prevail between Commissioners. No representation binding the Government must be made without full knowledge of all three Commissioners. . . . The three Commissioners are of equal power one with the other. Their joint action is necessary to secure desirable results. Hereafter shall address telegrams simply to American Commissioners."⁵⁵ Blaine's rebuke elicited an immediate reply from Kasson. "Your eleven," he cabled, "must be responsive to some secret despatch. Every telegram and despatch received from you, or sent by me to you, has uniformly remained on file with the secretary accessible to all. No binding representation has been made by me without the knowledge of all the Commission. I do not understand the justification of all this. Pray remember always that my wish has been and is to withdraw and so escape tricephalous jealousies."⁵⁶

On the 14th the American commissioners were instructed not to take up the question of disbandment immediately but have it postponed until a later date or as long as the German government recognized Tamasese as king. Blaine suggested that instead the conference should proceed with other matters for the present, although "each Government in the meantime, might approve [the] action of [the] Naval officers and Consuls to obtain [a] truce."⁵⁷

Kasson's plan for immediate disbandment was, therefore, not approved, and principally for the reason that the American government did not take very seriously Count Bismarck's intimation to Kasson, namely, that

⁵⁵ Kasson Papers, Blaine to Kasson, Phelps, and Bates, instructions no. 11, received 1:30 A.M., May 13.

⁵⁶ Samoan Conference at Berlin, 1889, MSS, Kasson to Blaine, May 13, 1889, despatch no. 37, confirmation of cipher no. 16, sent same day.

⁵⁷ *Ibid.*, Phelps to Blaine May 14, despatch no. 38, confirmation of cipher no. 12, received same day.

THE BERLIN CONFERENCE, 1889   475

Tamasese would also be eliminated from the kingship. But Blaine was anxious that the commission should not become permanently divided on the matter, and, therefore, on the same day cabled Kasson personally as follows: "Your colleagues who cabled me personally should in turn frankly show you their despatches. We must have absolute frankness and confidence all around."[58] When Phelps saw this communication from Washington, he cabled Blaine: "Have seen only recently telegrams and no despatches from Kasson. Mine are with the secretary and are equally open to his inspection." Incidentally, this information was in flat contradiction of Kasson's representations to Blaine the day before. There is no clue as to who was telling the truth in this instance, Kasson or Phelps, but probably it was Phelps.

On the 14th in the subcommittee it seemed that the powers might come to an agreement concerning the election of the king, and also the vice king if the natives should want one, the question of the restriction of candidates, if any, being left to the conference. It was also suggested that the election might be decided by the land judge. Moreover, it was thought that one executive representative might be named by the three powers to be the "President of the Municipality and [to] have charge in [the] government of all international interests, subject to appeal to [the] land judge," who would be the "judicial representative of the powers and nominated by them." Phelps informed Blaine that Bates preferred two executive officers who, with the judge, would secure representation for each power, and equality of influence. Bates feared that only one executive officer would "open the way for German domination" and Phelps advised Blaine

[58] *Ibid.*, Kasson to Blaine, May 14, despatch no. 39, confirmation of cipher received same day, Blaine to Kasson.

that if the proposition could carry in the conference he did not object to the Bates plan.[59]

Here were two of the American commissioners assuming a stand similar to that taken by Bayard in the Washington Conference. He, it will be recalled, wanted a council of three, one member appointed by each power, to advise the king. In the last chapter we noticed that Blaine in his instructions expressly stated the president's refusal to adopt this part of Bayard's program, giving as his reasons that it went too far in the direction of an entangling alliance and was a reversal of the traditional policy of the United States. But in trying to apply the "no entangling alliance" doctrine to their specific problem, the American delegates in Berlin found it impracticable as long as the rights of the three powers were kept on an equal basis and no one power secured a preponderance of influence. Coöperation of some sort was necessary in Berlin as in Apia, and just as Consul Dawson in earlier years had found it necessary to enter into agreements in Apia providing for joint control of the municipality of Apia, so the American delegates in Berlin were bound to accept some kind of entangling alliance so long as no power either claimed or possessed, in a legal way, a preponderance of influence over the whole Samoan government.

The third session of the conference was held on May 11. In transmitting a press copy of the protocol to Blaine, Phelps offered suggestions and criticisms. The conference had determined to place restrictions on the importation of arms and spirits, and had accepted the principle of import and export duties for Samoa. Phelps thought the import duties "absurdly low," and stated that although in the subcommittee the Americans had persuaded the Germans to agree to a two and a half to three per cent

[59] Samoan Conference at Berlin, 1889, MSS, Phelps to Blaine, May 14, despatch no. 40, confirmation of cipher no. 17, sent same day.

THE BERLIN CONFERENCE, 1889

duty, the "good-natured refusal of the English Plenipotentiary to accept any but a one per cent statistical duty lost us the higher rate." The most important advantage gained that day, thought Phelps, was the tripartite representation in the municipal government. Scott of the British delegation had argued feelingly for only one foreign representative, but had been outvoted.[60]

To get an adequate idea of what transpired in the third plenary session, however, it is necessary to turn to the protocol.[61] Count Bismarck presented three reports coming from the subcommittee, one on the importation and sale of arms, munitions of war, and intoxicating liquors, one on revenue and taxation, and one on the special administration of the town and district of Apia. All three reports were read by Crowe of the British delegation, who, together with Phelps of the American delegation, had attended the sessions of the subcommittee. In considering the question of the importation and sale of arms and munitions of war, the subcommittee had agreed that all arms and ammunition should be excluded under all circumstances, exceptions to the rule to be made only in the case of foreigners for sporting purposes, and for the defense of the native government, which might import arms under special license. In the plenary session some objections were raised to making any exceptions with reference to the native government, Count Bismarck remarking that there was no danger of an attack upon the native government by a foreign state "since the three treaty powers had virtually already pledged themselves by agreement to protect the future of Samoa." Crowe explained that the subcommittee had suggested the ex-

[60] *Ibid.*, Phelps to Blaine, May 14, despatch no. 42.

[61] Kasson Papers, certified copy of the protocol for the third session, May 11, 1889; S. Misc. Doc. no. 81, encl. 3, Blaine to Harrison, Jan. 7, 1890, pp. 26-36.

ception in favor of the native government with a view to making it possible for it to put down civil disturbances, and when Malet interjected that "it was equally undesirable that facilities should be reserved for the natives to obtain weapons for use on such occasions," Phelps said that the subcommittee had kept in mind what constitutes one of the attributes of an independent government, namely, self-defense. "The Government," thought Phelps, "would need possibly to defend itself against disorderly persons or against an insurrection on a small scale." By making it possible for the government to import arms by special permission only, Phelps was of the opinion that all the necessary precautions had been taken. With only a slight change in the wording of that part of the first report from the subcommittee, it was referred to the committee of revision for its final editing. The change made was the substitution of the words "for purposes of the Government" for the words "for national defense."

The remainder of the first report dealt with the importation of intoxicating liquors. The subcommittee had come to the conclusion that the prohibition of the sale of intoxicating liquors to Samoans was an absolute necessity. When the new municipal organization for Apia should be established, it would be necessary to forbid unlicensed persons to sell liquors in the same way as under the former municipal regulations. As for the rest of Samoa the committee was in favor of allowing the Samoan government to make the necessary regulations in this matter. In the case of intoxicating liquors as with arms and ammunition, the restrictions by the native government could, however, be strengthened by treaty provisions with the three protecting powers, or the powers might undertake by treaty to secure these restrictions without any action by the native government. The two alternative proposals were left to the committee of re-

THE BERLIN CONFERENCE, 1889   479

vision to make a choice, and to report at a plenary session.

The second report dealt with revenue and taxation. The subcommittee had thought it necessary to ascertain as soon as possible the amount of income that might be available for the Samoan government to be established. But article III of the treaty of January 17, 1878, between the United States and Samoa, stood in the way of making a fair estimate for the reason that American nationals were exempt under that article from paying any duties whatever. However, the American delegates in attendance at the meeting of the subcommittee, Bates and Phelps, thought that the article might be waived, and on the basis of that understanding a schedule of rates was drawn up under nine heads. These categories were import duties, export duties, taxes, licenses, pilot dues, quarantine dues, judicial fees, fines, and postal receipts. The committee thought there should be only one port of entry for the whole group, namely, Apia, except that the three powers might each ask for one additional port of entry for general use at the points named by them. When Malet asked why the last suggestion had been made, Phelps explained that since the United States would have coal ships coming to Pago Pago, and Germany and Great Britain likewise to their naval stations, it would be well to have these points made separate ports of entry. Kasson objected to any taxation on coal imported for the use of naval vessels, and when Malet and Crowe of the British delegation both thought that no exceptions should be made, and when Phelps and Bates of the American delegation agreed with them, Kasson nevertheless continued to oppose the proposition and offered the following amendment to the report: "No duties shall be levied on coal and naval stores imported for the use of either of the treaty governments." Upon agreeing that this amendment should be taken into consideration by the committee of revision, it was further agreed that the paragraph under discussion should merely read: "One port of entry, which shall be Apia, to be allowed for the islands." In other words, if it should finally be determined that coal for naval stations should be admitted free of duty no other port of entry would be necessary.

The import duties suggested by the committee were divided into nine schedules, the first four relating to liquors for foreigners, the fifth and sixth relating to tobacco and cigars, the seventh and eighth to firearms and ammunition for foreigners, and the ninth schedule a statistical duty of one per cent *ad valorem* on all merchandise imported excepting the foregoing. With the exception of the duty on arms, the rates fixed by the subcommittee were adopted for the time being. With reference to arms Kasson suggested doubling the duty from two dollars per piece to four dollars. This suggestion was seconded by Crowe and agreed to by the conference. Phelps objected to the small duty on merchandise in general. A duty of one per cent *ad valorem* would yield very little revenue, and he suggested in the conference, as he had done in the committee, that the rate be raised to five per cent. Crowe then said that such a duty with only one port of entry in Samoa would encourage smuggling, to which Kasson replied, in support of Phelps, that import duties were the best source of revenue, and that a moderate duty, say of three per cent, would not encourage smuggling since "it was better to pay a moderate duty than to run the risks of confiscation of goods." Phelps then "desired that it should be recorded that the majority of the sub-committee was not averse to a duty of two and one-half to three per cent, and he trusted that this point would be borne in mind in all subsequent consideration of the matter." It is interesting to note that the three American delegates at this juncture in the discussion betrayed their party affiliations at home. While both Kasson and Phelps agreed "that an import duty was the best method of obtaining revenue," Bates informed the conference that "he was opposed to import duties upon general economic principles, and favored freedom of trade." However, since the duties in question were for revenue and not protection, and "in view of the necessity for revenue and the meagre resources of the islands, he was willing to make the so-called statistical duty at least two and one-half per cent." The question was then referred to the committee of revision.

The second category of revenue in the committee's report was that of export duties. There was to be an *ad valorem* duty on three articles of export, two and one-half per cent on copra, one and one-half per cent on cotton, and two per cent on coffee. This occasioned no discussion in the plenary conference and Crowe passed on in his reading of the report to the third category, namely, taxes. Under this head were nine schedules, the first two embracing capitation taxes on Samoans, colored plantation laborers other than Samoans, and other Pacific islanders. The third schedule related to trading boats, the fourth to firearms, the fifth to houses and lands used for commercial purposes, the sixth to registry of deeds of sale, the seventh to stamp taxes in transfers of property, the eighth to traders' taxes (the amount being regulated according to the total annual sales), and the ninth to trading ships.

A general discussion ensued with reference to capitation taxes and there was agreement that the Samoan government should endeavor to prevent the natives from mortgaging their communal lands and produce to pay these taxes. After a debate occasioned by Kasson's question whether schedule five relating to houses included all houses, "it was unanimously stated as the desire of the conference that the huts belonging to Samoan natives should not be subject to taxation." When Kasson wanted to know "whether the stamp tax included both real and personal property and was to apply to ordinary sales of merchandise," Bates "explained that it was not intended that the stamp tax should have such an application, and suggested that as a stamp tax only properly applied to written documents it had not been considered necessary to express it, but there could be no objection to amending it to apply only to writing." During the discussion relative to the category of taxes, Phelps inquired whether, since there was to be a tax on land and houses used for commercial purposes, there should not also be a tax on agricultural lands. To this inquiry, Crowe replied that "it would be unfair to lay additional charges on agricultural property or plantations, burdened as these would be with other dues and taxes on traders and export produce."

The fourth category of revenue and taxation was then read by Crowe. It related to licenses, that is, taxes upon tradesmen, artisans and professional men, tavern keepers, laborers and domestics, and others. For example, tavern keepers were to pay a license of from ten to twelve dollars per month; attorneys, sixty dollars, physicians, thirty dollars, butchers, twelve dollars, blacksmiths, five dollars, and carpenters, six dollars, per year. This part of the report elicited no discussion, although earlier in the session Kasson had said that the levying of import duties was a far more preferable method of obtaining revenue than "the taxing of useful artisans." The fifth category, namely, pilot dues, provided for the collection of one dollar per foot-draft per year for pilotage. The sixth category, quarantine dues, merely provided for the collection of a nominal sum of fifty cents to one dollar for vessels of 100 tons and under, and one dollar extra "for every further 100 tons or fraction thereof." The seventh, eighth, and ninth categories (judicial fees, fines, and postal receipts) were not outlined by the committee, and the report on revenue and taxation concluded with some general observations.

The duties and taxes suggested for Samoa were much lower, said the report, than those levied in Fiji, and, with the exception of the duties on ale and porter, "much lower than those levied under the tariff of Hawaii." As a matter of fact the only high duties related to articles which for the most part would be imported for the use of foreigners, such as liquors, tobacco, firearms, and the like. The statistical duty, so-called, of one per cent would be the only import duty affecting the natives. Since the Samoans had not been used to any import duties at all in the past, it was thought that if smuggling were to be prevented, this duty could not be raised. With respect to the export duties, although the committee had regarded them as undesirable, nevertheless it found it impossible to dispense with them in view of "the peculiar circumstances in which the islands were placed." The capitation tax of one dollar also was much lower than a similar tax in the Tonga islands. The duty of ten dollars on trading ships was the same as "habitually levied up to the present time." The committee thought the amount of income that would be realized from these duties and taxes would be difficult to estimate, but judging from the estimates presented in a draft-budget by Germany at the Washington Conference, the total might "well reach the amount of ninety thousand dollars."[62]

[62] At the second session of the Samoan Conference at Washington von Alvensleben presented a memoradum on Samoan finance, which included an estimate of annual revenue. The report of the committee at Berlin was based largely on this earlier German memorandum.

The remaining part of the third session was devoted to the reading and discussion of the third report from the subcommittee, namely, that concerning the municipal government of Apia. The committee reported that before arriving at any conclusions with respect to a distinct municipal government for the town and district of Apia, Dr. Krauel, in giving a short history of the former municipal government as organized under the treaty of September 2, 1879, had in committee made the observation that the United States had never ratified that treaty. To this statement Bates had agreed, but "added that that power had accepted it, and the consuls had entered *de facto* into the municipal council under it, and united in executing it as a convenient arrangement for conducting a local administration for the benefit of citizens of all the treaty powers." Attention was called to the fact that the municipal convention had been renewed for an indefinite period by the consuls on September 3, 1883, and that it had continued to be executed under that extension until the municipal government was abruptly terminated in October, 1887. Dr. Krauel had also stated that the municipal government had not functioned satisfactorily, and expressed the opinion that it was found undesirable to have the foreign consuls on the board. Scott of the British delegation concurred in this statement, as did Bates, though the latter expressed the opinion that the municipal board had given Apia a reasonbly good local administration.

After the general discussion of the municipal government problem had clarified the situation for the members of the subcommittee, they arrived at the following conclusions, which constituted their third report:

1. A special local government was to be provided for

Apia "without impairing the territorial rights of the Samoan Government."

2. This municipality should have conferred upon it "clearly defined powers over all residents and persons for the time being within its territory."

3. The limits of the municipality should be the same as under the treaty of September 2, 1879.

4. The treaty stipulations between the three powers and Samoa should include provisions for the establishment of the municipal government. This was necessary because under the present treaties the consular jurisdiction embraced the police jurisdiction with respect to the citizens and subjects of the respective powers.

As to the structure of the municipal government and the eligibility of foreigners to vote and hold office, the following conclusions were reached by the committee:

1. A municipal council should be established consisting of six members, three of whom should be appointed by the consuls and three elected by the taxpayers within the municipality paying not less than five dollars per annum. To be eligible to membership on the council, candidates must likewise have paid no less than five dollars per annum in taxes, and the term of office should be two years.

2. The chairman of the municipal council should be an officer of the Samoan government with the right of vote.

3. The powers of the council were to be two-fold, executive and legislative. Regulations and by-laws which did not conflict with the Samoan laws or the treaties could be made by the council and enforced by it. As to the control of the harbor, pilotage, and quarantine, though the old municipality had had charge of these matters, the committee thought that the new Samoan government should

assume the responsibility. The regulations of the former municipality which were applicable to the limited powers of the new government should be considered as in force until repealed or amended. The police and all other minor officers should be appointed by the council.

4. The judicial functions of the government should be lodged in a municipal magistrate appointed by the Samoan government with the approval of the chief justice of that government. Appeals from the decision of the municipal magistrate to the chief justice might be made under certain conditions.

In submitting these recommendations the subcommittee expressed the conviction: first, that no adequate measures could be devised for the protection of the lives, commerce, and property of the foreign residents in Samoa unless they included the security of a Samoan government sufficiently stable to restore and preserve tranquillity in those islands, and, second, that under present circumstances no native government could be expected to fulfil this necessary condition without foreign assistance. The subcommittee therefore thought that the conference should consider in what form that assistance should be rendered.

In the discussion that followed upon the completion of the reading of this report by Crowe, the composition of the municipal council immediately became a subject that caused a division of opinion. When Kasson "observed that the composition of the municipal council was a matter of no small importance," Scott revealed the fact that the committee report on the composition of the council "was practically the result of a compromise between two conflicting opinions which had been advocated in the subcommittee." The American representatives believed that the consuls should be represented in some way on the council as in the old municipal government, but Scott and others had thought that the consular corps "should be kept entirely aloof from it, so as to avoid the danger of imparting an international color to possible disputes on purely municipal and local questions which ought to be decided solely in accordance with local requirements and interests." Malet in the plenary conference took the same view as Scott, whereupon Bates explained why the matter had given rise to so much discussion in the subcommittee. Although he was equally desirous with the others of separating "the consuls from the purely local administration as much as possible," he felt that there were "good reasons for giving them the right to appoint one member each." Police power over nationals constituted part of the extraterritorial jurisdiction of consuls, and when this was surrendered to the municipal council, the consuls should have authority in some measure, at least, to determine the membership of the council. In the old government the consuls had been responsible for the entire membership of the council, and they had done their work well. To permit the foreign residents to elect three members was a concession to their desire "to have a voice in the selection of the council, and it was sufficient for the present." Phelps thereupon explained that the compromise in the subcommittee had been due to him. The municipal council would in effect exercise consular rights over foreigners, and therefore, the consuls should have the right to nominate one member each to act, so to speak, as their agents.

The real reasons for the position of Phelps and Bates in the matter of the composition of the municipal council are evident when we remember that the number of American residents in Apia was smaller than that of either of the two other nationalities, the British and the German, so that the chances of electing an American on the council were almost *nil*. The result might easily be that where all police power over American citizens, ordinarily under the jurisdiction of their consul, was exercised by a council composed of six foreigners, none of them an American, trouble might ensue. At the conclusion of Phelps' remarks, the plenary conference agreed to the clause providing for the appointment of three members of the municipal council by the consuls—one by each—and the clause was referred to the committee of revision.

In order to avoid the rule of the old government which said that no business could be transacted if one member were absent, Malet suggested that the new council be allowed to function with a stated quorum. Count Bismarck suggested that a "decision by majority would be advisable, which would exclude the necessity of a quorum," to which the conference agreed. To provide means for the setting in motion of the new municipal government Phelps "proposed the nomination of a 'second subcommittee' to consider the form of the future Samoan Government and its connection with municipal affairs." Count Bismarck, as president, thereupon appointed a second subcommittee to consist of Dr. Krauel and Messrs. Phelps and Scott.

The day before the fourth plenary conference was held, the American commissioners received a cable from Blaine stating the president's disapproval of the disagreements in the commission. He reported the president as expressing "chagrin and deep disappointment that there should be any lack of unity in counsel and in action among the Commissioners," and added, "There is no justification, in the President's judgment, for personal differences on a subject which is official and patriotic, and he specially desires that the public should know nothing of disagreements."[63] Upon receipt of this rebuke the commissioners

[63] Samoan Conference at Berlin, 1889, MSS, no. 46, Phelps to Blaine, May 16, confirmation of cable no. 14, received.

immediately replied that the president and Blaine had conceived an exaggerated idea of the differences in the commisson,[64] a reply that could hardly be true if Bates meant what he had said in his letter to Blaine just the day before. In that letter he criticized the methods of the conference and asserted that although at the opening Germany was "notoriously ready for yielding almost anything for agreement," the anticipation of the German government's demands had "complicated the situation and produced a noticeable change in their tone."[65] He added that "from a clear field we have changed to doubtful; Germans are united, we are not." Referring to the proposal to have only one foreigner as adviser to the Samoan government, he thought it was "too dangerous." Furthermore, the "exclusion of Mataafa or any native" would be a "fatal interference with [the] avowed basis of negotiation—Samoan independence." Bates thought the "proposed exclusion of Tamasese a trifling concession" and that Germany cared "very little for him except as an instrument." In order to regain its lost position, therefore, Bates suggested that "the United States could set up claims for the acknowledgment of the wrong deportation of Malietoa; unjustifiable war on natives; interference with Americans; using Samoan taxes for improvements on German property." Bates' final observation was that an indemnity in favor of Germany would be unjust; that "Samoa rather has occasion for it."[66]

On the same day that Blaine rebuked the commissioners for their lack of solidarity, he sent another telegram asking to know the amount of indemnity Germany would

[64] *Ibid.*, no. 49, Kasson to Blaine, May 16, confirmation of cipher telegram no. 21, sent same day.

[65] A reference to Kasson's view that Germany would never agree to Mataafa's candidacy for the kingship.

[66] Samoan Conference at Berlin, 1889, MSS, no. 45, Bates to Blaine, May 15.

demand for the families of the German sailors killed and mutilated by Mataafa's men in the attack of December 18. This was an important matter and should not be "left hanging over the Samoans indefinitely." Nor should Germany seek to do the collecting. The duty of discharging the indemnity "should be left to Samoa."[67] Still another cable was received from Washington on May 16 giving the president's views concerning the government of the islands. The "largest practical measure of self-government should be conceded to the natives," and no particular chief should be forced upon them by the Berlin Conference for the kingship. The natives should be permitted a perfectly free election. To insist on that ought not to cause the commissioners much trouble, as the president considered that as "settled by request of the German Government." Moreover, the president insisted that whatever jurisdiction outside that of the natives' was necessary to restrain and regulate the conduct of affairs where foreign interests were involved, should "be equitably shared between [the] three powers." In referring to the jurisdiction of the chief justice, Blaine said further that the president "would consider it unwise to refer settlement of all land questions to one judge unless impartially selected from a neutral nation." With reference to the municipal executive, who should also be the adviser to the king, the president thought that having only one municipal executive would invite "irritation and discontent" on account of the fact that one of the treaty powers would "always be excluded from influence in the Government." In conclusion Blaine warned the commissioners that every step at this point in their negotiations "must be watchfully guarded."[68]

[67] Samoan Conference at Berlin, 1889, MSS, no. 47, Phelps to Blaine, May 16, confirmation of telegram no. 15, received.

[68] *Ibid.*, no. 48, Phelps to Blaine, May 16, confirmation of telegram no. 16, received same day.

THE BERLIN CONFERENCE, 1889   491

At the opening of the fourth session[69] of the conference, held on May 17, Sir Edward Malet reported "that the Committee of Revision had met three times and had finished as much of their work as was possible with the matter which had hitherto been referred to them by the Conference, but that to formulate definitely all the conclusions already come to by the Conference must still depend in some measure upon its future decisions." At one of the meetings of the committee of revision the decision had been reached to refer to the conference the suggestion that the lord chief justice of England should nominate the chief justice of Samoa. The British government had expressed willingness to accede to the wishes of the representatives of the United States and Germany, but was "disinclined to be in any way responsible for the actions of the Chief Justice of Samoa." Kasson expressed himself at the plenary conference as in favor of the proposal, as did also Count Bismarck. The suggestion was thereupon accepted. Bismarck thought "that an analogous system might well be adopted in the appointment of the executive representative" because, speaking for his own government, he could say that Germany "would not willingly assume the responsibility of nominating this officer." As a mater of fact, in his opinion it would be better if a neutral subject, say a Dutchman or a Scandinavian, were appointed for this office.[70] To this suggestion Malet readily assented, but Kasson wanted time to study the proposal and suggested that it be referred to the subcommittee on the Samoan government, which was done.

[69] Kasson Papers, certified copy of protocol for fourth session, May 17, 1889; S. Misc. Doc. no. 81, pp. 36-42, encl. 3.
[70] This was an indication how far removed Germany then was from her former position at the Washington Conference, when she allowed that conference to break up on account of her demand for a mandate to appoint the adviser herself.

The report from this committee on the "Form of the Future Samoan Government" was then read by Scott. The committee had agreed unanimously, first, "That an independent and stable native government is a necessary condition to the security of foreign interests"; second, "That the forms of authority now existing on these islands could not be considered as fulfilling these conditions or even be recognized as governments at all"; third, "That, to secure both the independence and the stability of the native government to be established, it is necessary that the Samoans should choose and construct their own form of government, after their own native fashion, and administer it themselves, receiving from the treaty powers conjointly only such counsel and aid as they might ask and need." Having come to this understanding, the subcommittee had formulated five proposals containing advice which might be given to the Samoans with respect to their government. The first two related to the kingship, the Samoans to be advised to elect a king, and also a vice king if that were desirable. The question of excluding any candidates for the kingship was referred to the general conference. In view of the fact that there was still uncertainty as to the expediency of the second proposal, namely, the election of a vice king, Kasson thought both questions might be taken up at the next plenary conference. This suggestion was agreed to.

The committee's third proposal was that election disputes be decided by a chief justice to be appointed by the three powers. This was thought a better arrangement than for the consuls or naval commanders to intervene from time to time, as they had done in the past, when disputes arose among the natives as to who was to be king. In addition to the functions of umpire, the chief justice was also to preside over the land court, hear appeals from the municipal magistrate, and act as an "appellate judge and final umpire, in any misunderstanding between the Samoan Government and the representatives of any of the treaty powers." The fourth proposal was that the Samoans "might reconstitute their old Taimua and Faipule or adopt such other legislative machinery as they might prefer." The fifth proposal was a suggestion "that the foreign powers have an executive representative who shall be the adviser of the Samoan Government in all matters that concern foreign interests." This executive representative should be appointed by the Samoan government upon the nomination of the three treaty powers. His specific duties were to be the following: president of the municipal council of Apia, comptroller of the income and expenditures of the Samoan government and of the municipal government, and superintendent of "the harbor and quarantine regulations and other measures connected with foreign trade and shipping."

The day after the fourth plenary session, the American commissioners informed Blaine that it had been determined that the chief justice of Samoa should be nominated by the chief justice of England (Coleridge), and that the committee had recommended a "neutral appointee perhaps Scandinavian or Hollander to be chairman of [the] municipal council."[71] Kasson and Phelps previously on the same day had telegraphed to Washington a definite proposition from Germany, namely, that she would consent to the restoration of the *status quo* with Malietoa as king and waive indemnity if Mataafa were eliminated from eligibility as a candidate for election. Blaine was also informed that England supported the exclusion of Mataafa, and that Germany would not recognize Mataafa if elected. Then, as if to clinch their

[71] Samoan Conference at Berlin, 1889, MSS, no. 53, Kasson to Blaine, May 18, confirmation of telegram no. 24, sent same day.

evident desire to meet Germany's terms, Kasson and Phelps referred to the Lackawanna Peace Agreement of July 12, 1881, as the basis for the assertion that Malietoa was already elected at that time and that the United States need not demand another election.[72]

On the same day, Bates sent a telegram signed by himself alone, stating that only extreme measures would make Germany forego Mataafa's exclusion.[73] Four days before, on the 14th, the commissioners had warned Washington of what was brewing when they advised Blaine that it was the intention of the English to propose the restoration of a complete *status quo,* should any exclusion of a candidate for the kingship be insisted upon.[74] In other words, the English were going to propose that no election of a king or vice king be held, but that Malietoa be declared king by the conference if Germany continued to oppose the eligibility of Mataafa, and if the United States maintained her stand of permitting him to be a candidate for the kingship. Great Britain had thus stepped into the breach between the United States and Germany and was suggesting a common ground on which both powers might meet. There was of course the contingency that the United States might object to a complete *status quo* in view of the administration's fear that Malietoa in return for his release from captivity should commit himself to a pro-German policy. Furthermore, Mataafa's rebellion against Tamasese in the absence of Malietoa had won for him the sympathy of the American naval officers in Samoan waters and of the authorities in

[72] Samoan Conference at Berlin, 1889, MSS, no. 51, Phelps to Blaine, May 18, confirmation of telegram no. 22, signed Kasson and Phelps, sent same day.

[73] *Ibid.*, no. 52, Bates to Blaine, May 18, confirmation of telegram no. 23, sent same day.

[74] *Ibid.*, no. 43, Phelps to Blaine, May 14, confirmation of telegram no. 19, sent same day.

THE BERLIN CONFERENCE, 1889

Washington. The latter frankly feared that Malietoa, if restored to the kingship, might no longer represent the wishes of the majority of Samoans in view of Mataafa's popularity among them, and that, consequently, the powers might only invite more trouble in an effort to support him.

The position of the United States with reference to the *status quo* problem was clearly stated by Blaine in reply to Kasson's inquiry from London, and showed how far the United States had moved from its position in Bayard's day as a result of the changed conditions in Samoa. While Bayard, subsequently to Malietoa's deportation, had consistently insisted upon his restoration to the kingship as a *quid pro quo* to a complete understanding with Germany, Blaine was not in favor of restoring Malietoa as a matter of necessity to his former position. Said Blaine to Kasson before the latter reached Berlin: "Demand the return of Malietoa as individual with unprejudiced right of candidacy in free election to be promptly ordered. Your instructions indicate that free choice should be made by Samoans and negative the presumption that Malietoa should return as king."[75]

Between the 14th and the 18th Great Britain's attempt as intermediary had borne fruit as far as the German government was concerned. That government had finally decided to forsake Tamasese and support Malietoa for the kingship with the understanding that Mataafa would be eliminated, and as another gesture toward conciliation, was willing to forego an indemnity if the United States would agree to the elimination of Mataafa. The next step was in the hands of Washington. Would the president and Blaine accept Germany's offer? On the

[75] *Ibid.*, no. 50, Kasson to Blaine, May 17, confirmation of telegram, Blaine to Kasson, received at London, April 25.

19th the commissioners received the president's answer. Blaine informed them that the president consented to the restoration of Malietoa, and the return to a complete *status quo,* provided the three powers be equally represented in the executive government and an impartial judge be assured.[76] The communication was not clearly understood by the commissioners, who inquired immediately: "Must we understand from your seventeen that you veto English judge as reported in our twenty-four. Entire United States Commission in Berlin and attachés prefer this to judge of any other nationality. No other would have our ideas and methods of justice and law. It was accepted as American proposition."[77] Evidently the commissioners mistook what Blaine had tried to convey, for the next day they were told that the appointment of an English judge was acceptable to the president.[78]

The fears expressed by Bates and Phelps that a government with only one adviser might easily come under the domination of Germany were evidently responsible for the new attitude of the United States. In fact the proposal for two advisers which Bates had advanced in the subcommittee, and which was supported by Phelps, apparently was now adopted at Washington. Only one adviser for an enthroned Malietoa, himself perhaps imbued with pro-German ideas, would not do. Moreover, with the chief justice chosen from England, the United States would very likely be the one power unrepresented in the Samoan government. In returning to Bayard's position with respect to Malietoa, Blaine was also approaching his idea that the three powers should have equal representa-

---

[76] Samoan Conference at Berlin, 1889, MSS, no. 54, Commission to Blaine, May 19, confirmation of telegram no. 17, received same day.

[77] *Ibid.*, no. 55, Commission to Blaine, May 19, confirmation of telegram no. 25, sent same day.

[78] *Ibid.*, no. 56, Commission to Blaine, May 20, confirmation of telegram no. 18, received same day.

THE BERLIN CONFERENCE, 1889   497

tion in the Samoan government. How the new proposal from Washington was received in the conference the protocol for the fifth session will show.

At the fifth session of the conference, which was held on May 22,[79] the question of the election of the king came up for settlement. Count Bismarck stated that "the principle of the election of a King was . . . acceptable, but he was bound to make one exception, in the person of Mataafa, on account of the outrages committed by his people and under his authority upon dead and wounded German sailors lying on the field of action." Malet thought that this exception was a reasonable one to make, and then proceeded to read a statement the purport of which was that if the powers left the matter of electing a king entirely in the hands of the Samoans themselves "the result will be that they will have given the signal for civil war." If a peaceful election were possible, the statement continued, Malietoa, it was thought, "would be returned by a large majority." Hence, the British government proposed that the three treaty powers intimate "to the Samoan people that if they will take Malietoa as King, such act on the part of the Samoans shall receive the sanction of the treaty powers." This solution was all the more reasonable, according to the statement, since Kasson in the first session of the conference had pleaded for the restoration of the *status quo,* and Count Bismarck on the same occasion had announced the release of Malietoa from captivity. Both Count Bismarck and Kasson agreed to the proposal, and the latter suggested that it be referred to the committee of revision, which was done.

The question of the nationality and mode of appointment of the adviser to the Samoan government was then brought up from the subcommittee. Dr. Krauel stated

[79] Kasson Papers, certified copy of protocol for fifth session, May 22, 1889; S. Misc. Doc. no. 81, pp. 42-47, encl. 3.

that the committee had considered the matter, but had come to no conclusion. As a matter of fact, the American member, Phelps, had stated in the committee that the United States, although recognizing the advantages of one executive, preferred two advisers of nationalities different from each other and from the judge. This preference he again stated in the plenary conference. Both Baron Holstein and Count Bismarck objected to having two advisers on account of the expense, and Sir Edward Malet "said that he had heard with regret this new proposal of the United States plenipotentiaries, which appeared calculated to alter an entire scheme which the conference had been on the point of completing." He thought that the United States government might recognize in the scheme already advanced "a happy expedient for the avoidance of disputes between the representatives of the three powers," when the whole plan of government should be presented for adoption. If the assignment of the nomination of the chief justice of Samoa to the lord chief justice of England had caused the government of the United States to advocate two executive advisers, one perhaps a German and the other an American, in order to give representation to all three powers in the Samoan government, Sir Edward wished it to be remembered that the arrangement for the judge-nomination problem "was agreed to by Her Majesty's Government as a concession in order to solve difficulties, and that, in agreeing, they repudiated all responsibility for the acts of the Chief Justice and all representation on his part of the British Government." In case the two advisers should disagree the matter would then be decided by the judge, who would have to take the side of one or the other and thus "revive all the former difficulties and jealousies in Samoa," which, the British delegate said, could not be admitted by his government.

In the opinion of Count Bismarck what Sir Edward had said "was most reasonable," but "if the United States Government were not willing to accept the proposal the matter might be arranged later between the three powers." Phelps then said that he would press the proposal no further "in view of the disfavor" with which it had been received, and accepted the suggestion to leave the matter for final decision to a later period. Phelps, therefore, proposed that the conference "proceed to consider the method of appointment of the executive officer in case only one should be chosen," and added that it would be agreeable to his government to have some neutral power nominate a Dutch or Swiss subject for the position. "The nomination might be made by the President of the Swiss Republic," he added, to which Scott replied that in his opinion "the Swiss Government were not sufficiently acquainted with the interests of distant colonies to enable them to make such nominations." Count Bismarck supported Scott's remarks, and expressed pleasure that Phelps had met "more than halfway the views expressed by other plenipotentiaries." He proposed that the point at issue should be referred to the committee of revision "for examination by them in its present form."

Scott then brought up again the matter of the composition of the municipal council. At the third session of the conference he had suggested that the elective members of the council represent two or three districts or wards of Apia and not be elected from the municipality at large. This suggestion had not been considered by the committee of revision, and Scott had ascertained that the reason for this was that the German plenipotentiaries were unable to support the suggestion unless all six of the members of the council were elected "and the proposal for three consular nominees were abandoned." He then introduced a resolution amending the original proposal of the subcommittee, which provided for the election of all six members, three from that part of Apia which lay west of the Mulivai River and three from the district east of that river. In order to meet the wishes of the United States plenipotentiaries, that the consuls be given some influence in the municipal government, Scott proposed to add to the original proposal the amendment that all regulations passed by the municipal council, before becoming law, be referred to the consular board, who should either approve and return such regulations or suggest such amendments as might be unanimously deemed necessary by them. In case there should be no unanimity in the consular board in approving the regulations, or should the board's amendments not be acceptable to a majority of the municipal council, the regulations should then be referred to the chief justice of Samoa for final decision.

Kasson then said he "believed it to be the opinion of the Committee of Revision that it was not advisable to create too elaborate a machinery for simple working purposes. It would be better to define and limit the powers of the municipal council; and then trust to its discretion, subject to the revision and sanction of the Chief Justice." Kasson was otherwise agreeable to the plan suggested of making all the members of the council elective, and evidently Phelps had given up the proposal of having three of the members appointed by the consuls, for the protocol states that he "proposed that the subject should be referred to the Committee of Revision." Malet, however, thought it should be referred to the subcommittee of which Phelps was a member, "giving them power to come to a decision and to submit the same to the Committee of Revision." This suggestion was agreed to.

Before the conclusion of the session Phelps felt constrained to revert to the statement made by Count Bismarck relative to the exclusion of Mataafa from the right to be elected king "on account of the outrages committed by his people and under his authority upon dead and wounded German sailors lying in the field of action." Phelps said "that the silence of the American plenipotentiaries was not to be construed as assenting to those views, except as they expressed an indignation at the atrocities mentioned, with which the United States heartily sympathized." In other words, the right of Mataafa's taking up arms against Germany was not questioned by the United States.

The work of the Berlin Conference was nearing its close, and at the sixth session,[80] held on May 27, Count Bismarck was ready to read the *projet* of the general act as laid before the conference by the committee of revision. The document comprised eight articles covering the following subjects:

"First. A declaration respecting the independence and neutrality of the islands of Samoa, and assuring to the respective citizens and subjects of the signatory powers equality of rights in said islands; and providing for the immediate restoration of peace and order therein.

"Second. A declaration respecting the modification of existing treaties and the assent of the Samoan Government to this act.

"Third. A declaration respecting the establishment of a supreme court of justice for Samoa and defining its jurisdiction.

"Fourth. A declaration respecting titles to land in Samoa, restraining the disposition thereof by natives and providing for the investigation of claims thereto, and for the registration of valid titles.

[80] Kasson Papers, certified copy of protocol for sixth session, May 27, 1889; S. Misc. Doc. no. 81, pp. 47-59, encl. 3.

"Fifth. A declaration respecting the municipal district of Apia, and providing a local administration therefor.

"Sixth. A declaration respecting taxation and revenue in Samoa.

"Seventh. A declaration respecting arms and ammunition, and intoxicating liquors, restraining their sale and use.

"Eighth. General dispositions."

The first article, which provided for the independence and neutrality of Samoa and the restoration of Malietoa Laupepa to the kingship, was adopted without discussion. The election of Malietoa as king on July 12, 1881, having been recognized at that time by the three powers, he was again recognized as king, as though there had been no war against him and deportation by Germany after the conclusion of the Washington Conference in 1887. In other words, a complete *status quo ante bellum* was effected.

The second article with reference to the modification of existing treaties wherein their provisions were inconsistent with the general act of Berlin was adopted without debate, whereupon the third article respecting the establishment of a supreme court of justice for Samoa was read and debated. Bates considered that "the provision permitting the removal of the judge upon the simple request of a majority of the three treaty powers" was unwise. Kasson thought that there should be no change in the provision, however, and it remained as it was reported from the committee of revision. When Bates "called attention to the fact that although in section seven there was a provision for arbitrating differences between any one of the treaty powers and Samoa, there was no agreement on the part of the signatory powers that they would respectively accept and abide by the result of such arbitration," Malet, Kasson, Count Bismarck, and Phelps all "were of the opinion that the clause admitted of no ambiguity," and stated that "they would prefer to let it remain as it stood in the text."

Article IV in relation to land titles and the prevention of the alienation of Samoan lands occasioned very little discussion in the plenary conference. Bates "thought that the compensation of the natives' advocate should be paid by the powers and not put upon Samoa," but both Baron Holstein and Count Bismarck opposed this, the latter saying that "he felt sure the German Government would not be inclined, on principle, to pay the salary of the natives' advocate." The section remained unchanged.

Article V, providing for the government of Apia, was then read, the first three and fifth sections being adopted without debate. The fourth section, which in the final treaty became the fifth section, was passed over for future consideration as Kasson said that the "American Plenipotentiaries were not prepared to act finally upon it without further instructions from their Government." The part of section five, as renumbered, which awaited the decision of Washington, related to the nationality and method of selection of the president of the municipal council. It read as follows: "He shall be agreed upon by the three powers; or, failing such agreement, he shall be selected from the nationality of Sweden, The Netherlands, Switzerland, Mexico, or Brazil, and nominated by . . . and appointed by the Samoan Government upon certificate of such nomination."

Article VI, relating to taxation and revenue in Samoa, occasioned no discussion except section one with reference to the exemption from duties of coal and naval stores at the naval station. Count Bismarck, agreeing with the purport of the section, thought there should be a more precise statement concerning coal and naval stores landed for governmental purposes. Kasson thought the section, which he himself had drawn up, covered the situation and objected to any change in the wording. The section remained as it was, but Count Bismarck summed up the unanimous opinion in the following words: "If any article so imported should afterwards pass from government control into private ownership and be introduced for sale or consumption into other parts of the islands, they shall be subject to the statistical import duty as in the case of private merchandise imported."

When article VII, relating to arms and intoxicating liquors, was read by Count Bismarck, Bates observed that the powers had no right "to deprive the Samoan Government of the use of arms for its defence unless they were guaranteed against war." Kasson took the same position, pointing out that "it would be difficult to allow foreigners to import arms and at the same time to deny this privilege to the Samoan Government." When Phelps suggested "that all importation of arms for the use of the Samoan Government should be reported through the consular board," Count Bismarck thought that it was "necessary to place a certain limit upon this importation of arms, as it seemed to him to constitute a dangerous element for the natives." To this Kasson answered that "it was perhaps as dangerous to allow arms to foreigners as to give them to natives." Kasson then suggested the addition of the following at the end of section one: "But all such arms and ammunition shall be entered at the customs (without payment of duty) and reported by the president of the municipal council to the consuls of the three treaty powers. The three Governments reserve to themselves the future consideration of the further restrictions which it may be necessary to impose upon the importation and the use of fire-arms in Samoa." The proposal was adopted.

THE BERLIN CONFERENCE, 1889

Article VIII provided for the continuance in force of the treaty for three years, after which time it might be changed by the three powers upon the request of any one of them. Special amendments, however, could in the meantime be adopted by the three powers, which would go into effect upon the adherence thereto by the Samoan government. The general act should also be assented to by that government.

The seventh plenary session was held on May 29.[81] At the request of Baron Holstein, Kasson "read the emendations and additions proposed by the Committee of Revision, which were agreed to by all the plenipotentiaries and the general act ordered to be printed with the amendments." The American plenipotentiaries not having yet received final instructions relative to "section 5 of article V, it was agreed that this section should be reserved for consideration at the next session." When Kasson referred to section 3 of article V, and inquired whether it had been decided at the last session "that the appointment of the municipal magistrate should be confirmed by the Chief Justice," both Phelps and Scott explained that in the committee it was understood that the municipal magistrate should be appointed by the council subject to the approval of the consular board. But when Malet observed the appointment "would necessarily be referred for final approval to the Chief Justice," agreement was reached that although no change would be made in the wording of the section, the protocol should state "that section 3 of Article V intended that the appointment of the municipal magistrate should be made by resolution of the council, and thus be subject to approval, as in the case of other resolutions."

Thereupon Dr. Krauel called attention to the fact that

[81] Kasson Papers, certified copy of protocol for seventh session, May 29, 1889; S. Misc. Doc. no. 81, pp. 60-69, encl. 3.

section 9 of article III, as it appeared in the *projet* adopted at the sixth session, made no adequate provision "for the guidance of the Chief Justice of Samoa as to what laws he should enforce in judging cases to be tried by him." He thought that for the present the judge might "follow the procedure and rules employed by the British high commissioner for the western Pacific—a code which was known to be very well adapted for the purposes for which it had been created." Kasson observed that it would be a serious matter to adopt a system of laws which might not be well known and perhaps not suitable for Samoa. It was necessary to find a system to meet local needs. Count Bismarck, however, came to the support of his colleague and "remarked that if the Chief-Justice were not to be bound to administer the laws of any civilized country it might lead to serious difficulties, because he would be at a loss to decide what special system of laws out of the many in existence he should adopt in giving his judgments." The conference finally adopted section 10 of article III as follows: "The practice and procedure of common law, equity, and admiralty, as administered in the courts of England, may be, so far as applicable, the practice and procedure of this court; but the court may modify such practice and procedure from time to time as shall be required by local circumstances. The court shall have authority to impose, according to the crime, the punishment established therefor by the laws of the United States, of England, or of Germany, as the chief-justice shall decide most appropriate; or, in the case of native Samoans and other natives of the South Sea Islands, according to the laws and customs of Samoa." Section 9 of the same article as a substitute for the section in the *projet* provided for the supreme court's exclusive jurisdiction in: "1. All civil suits concerning real property situated in Samoa; 2. All civil suits of any

THE BERLIN CONFERENCE, 1889

kind between natives and foreigners or between foreigners of different nationalities; 3. All crimes and offences committed by natives against foreigners or committed by such foreigners as are not subject to any consular jurisdiction."

Count Bismarck then announced that the conference had adopted all the articles with the exception of section 5 of article V, dealing with the nationality and method of selecting the president of the municipal council, "which awaited the receipt of further instructions on the part of the American plenipotentiaries from their Government." He suggested that the conference adjourn until the time when all the members were ready "to sign the complete general Act with the approval of their Governments," and in bringing the session to a close he thanked all members of the conference for the "amicable manner in which each and all . . . had facilitated the labors of the conference." He hoped "that the final results of the conference would be to the advantage of the Samoans themselves and for the benefit of all the inhabitants of that part of the world."

Immediately upon the conclusion of the seventh session, Blaine was informed that the work of the conference was completed except for the question of the nationality and method of selection of the municipal executive officer and adviser to the king. The weather in Berlin was getting almost unbearably hot and the commissioners were anxious to complete the negotiations so that they might leave the city. But on the same day Blaine cabled the commissioners that the president wanted to examine the treaty very closely before any part of it was made public, and that the whole commission should stay in Berlin until the agreement was signed. It was impossible for the president to know from the despatches received from the commission "how far his suggestions have been embodied in the agreement and therefore does not as yet know whether all the provisions will be acceptable to this Government."[82]

The delay of the president in consenting to the signing of the act by the American commissioners caused irritation among the English and German plenipotentiaries, and the commission informed Blaine to that effect on June 9.[83] On the same day a reply from Blaine revealed considerable dissatisfaction with the terms of the *projet*. "In what essentials the United States gains under project I am unable to determine. This Government will never consent to absolutely rob Samoa of all autonomy and to instal an English judge as the ruler of the Islands. The modifications in detail which the United States demand will be sent you at once. If you will read my number Eighteen you will learn that the President would much have preferred a judge selected from neutral nation to one from England. I now learn for first time that the English proposition originated with you. Had the Commission informed us of successive steps in Conference, modifications could have been suggested during deliberations. Irritability on the part of your English and German associates is not a determining factor with the Government of the United States."[84] It is obvious that Blaine was as much irritated by the course of events at Berlin as were the English and German plenipotentiaries at the delay in signing the pact. The sending to Berlin of a tricephalous commission resulted in confusion in Washington as well as in Berlin. Kasson's and Phelps' favorable reports to Blaine were countered by the unfavorable

[82] Samoan Conference at Berlin, 1889, MSS, no. 69 Crosby to Blaine, May 30, confirmation of telegram received on May 29, no. 24, Blaine to Commission.

[83] *Ibid.*, Crosby to Blaine, June 9, confirmation of telegram sent same day.

[84] *Ibid.*, no. 85, Crosby to Blaine, June 9, confirmation of no. 31, Blaine to Commission, received same day.

ones of Bates and the disbursing officer, Sewall. In his displeasure with the work of the commission Blaine even forgot that his consent for an English judge had been obtained in the very communication—number eighteen—to which he now referred as having been intended to convey just the opposite meaning. Although the commission knew from a previous communication that the president and Blaine preferred a neutral judge to one from England, they had nevertheless received Washington's consent that an English judge be named in the communication referred to by Blaine, and that provision had remained undisturbed in the *projet*. It was curious that a proposal originating with the commission and practically the only one of importance upon which all three commissioners as well as Sewall agreed, should have caused such an outburst of criticism from Blaine.

Blaine's "modifications in detail" were sent to Berlin on the twelfth. His instructions were as follows: "The President directs me to say if it be the matured opinion of the Conference that the greatest good will be promoted in Samoa by endowing the Supreme Judge with the political powers embraced in the Act, he would be willing to have King of Sweden and Norway appoint the Supreme Judge, and the President of Switzerland appoint the Adviser, or the reverse, if preferred. The President thinks that political power in the hands of a Minister of Sweden and Norway, or Swiss Judge, could be exercised in Samoa without creating the slightest jealousy between the Treaty Powers. His first desire is for an adjustment that will be cordially received by all."[85]

It now became the unwelcome duty of the American commissioners to approach the English and the Germans and reveal the fact that the president had vetoed their

[85] *Ibid.*, no. 90, Parker to Blaine, June 12, confirming telegram no. 34, received same day.

own proposition, namely, that the government of Great Britain permit the lord chief justice to nominate the chief justice of Samoa. If the matter had not gone as far as it had, Downing Street having consented to the proposition with the understanding that the British government be not held responsible for the lord chief justice's acts, it would not have been so difficult to ask the British to withdraw from their commitment. However, Sir Edward Malet, a true diplomat of the old school, sensing the awkward situation the Americans were in, solved the problem at once, so that on the next day, when the eighth plenary session of the conference was held, a formal change in the act to meet the president's wishes in regard to the selection of the judge was all that was necessary.

The eighth session of the conference met on June 13.[86] Count Bismarck said that the plenipotentiaries having received instructions from their respective governments, it would be well to consider any modifications which members of the conference might wish to suggest. As for Germany, he was ready to announce that the emperor "had approved of the general act in its present form and that the German plenipotentiaries were prepared to sign it as it stood." Sir Edward Malet was of the opinion "that the general act in its present form might be acceptable to Her Majesty's Government, but that the British plenipotentiaries had no authority to accept any alterations therein without the previous consent of their Government." Thereupon Kasson stated that the decision of the United States government concerning the general act had been necessarily delayed on account of "the distance of communication." However, he could inform the conference "that the American plenipotentiaries were now authorized to sign the same with only two modifica-

[86] Kasson Papers, certified copy of protocol for eighth session, June 13, 1889; S. Misc. Doc. no. 81, pp. 69-71, encl. 3.

tions." The first of these related to the jurisdiction of the judge, namely, that it should not extend to "questions arising between masters and seamen," which questions should remain within the jurisdiction of the respective consuls, and that no *ex post facto* or retroactive jurisdiction should be assumed by the court. There was no objection to this modification by either Bismarck or Malet and it was incorporated in a new section—section 11 of article III. Then Kasson "stated that the United States Government had had some hesitation in accepting all the terms of article III respecting the jurisdiction of the chief justice of Samoa, whose powers they had found to be much larger than they had expected. They were also disinclined to give to one of the three signatory nationalities an appointment entailing so much political importance." The proposal that the king of Sweden and Norway nominate the Samoan chief justice instead of the lord chief justice of England was thereupon made by Kasson, and this was agreed to by both Malet and Bismarck subject to the approval of their respective governments. Section 2 of article III, as finally framed, read in part: "With a view to secure judicial independence and the equal consideration of the rights of all parties, irrespective of nationality, it is agreed that the Chief Justice shall be named by the three signatory powers in common accord; or failing their agreement, he may be named by the King of Sweden and Norway."[87]

The English and Germans declined to change the manner of nominating the adviser, leaving section 5 of article V as it stood in the *projet*, except for "filling up the lacuna" of the section with the words, "the chief executive of the nation from which he is selected." The section then read in part as follows: "He shall be agreed upon by the

[87] See enclosure no. 2, Blaine to Harrison, Jan. 7, 1890, S. Misc. Doc. no. 81, p. 8.

three powers; or, failing such agreement, he shall be selected from the nationality of Sweden, The Netherlands, Switzerland, Mexico, or Brazil, and nominated by the chief executive of the nation from which he is selected, and appointed by the Samoan Government upon certificate of such nomination."[88]

Blaine suggested later that the conference should limit the choice for judge by the king of Sweden and Norway to a Swedish subject but the German and English delegates declined to accede. When Blaine insisted on the matter, the commission telegraphed on the 14th as follows: "Our last proposition sent in forty-four is utmost they will concede. We are all united in the belief, and so was every other member of the Conference, that choice should not be restricted to any one nationality. Please answer to-night."[89] To this urgent communication Blaine answered immediately as follows: "Forty-five received. No objection, concede the point."[90]

The conference thereupon assembled for the ninth and last plenary session in the afternoon of the same day. Count Bismarck stated that all the plenipotentiaries had received instructions to sign the general act, and when Kasson "expressed the desire of his Government that secrecy should be observed as to the contents of the general act until it should be ratified by the respective Governments," Count Bismarck said "that such a course would be entirely in accordance with established precedents," but he thought "it would be very desirable, if the three powers would agree, to send identic instructions to

[88] See enclosure no. 2, Blaine to Harrison, Jan. 7, 1890, S. Misc. Doc. no. 81, p. 13.

[89] Samoan Conference at Berlin, 1889, MSS, no. 101, Parker to Blaine, June 14, confirmation of telegram no. 45, sent early in the morning of the same day.

[90] Ibid., no. 103, Parker to Blaine, June 14, 1889, confirmation of telegram no. 39, received from Blaine on morning of the same day.

THE BERLIN CONFERENCE, 1889   513

their consuls in Samoa in order to communicate to the Samoans such provisions of the general act as could be properly made known to them previous to ratification." Malet and Kasson believed this would be both desirable and possible.

Kasson now arose and, alluding to the approaching end of the conference, complimented Count Bismarck for his fairness and impartiality as the presiding officer of the conference. Sir Edward Malet on behalf of the British plenipotentiaries concurred in what the American representative had said, whereupon Count Bismarck in expressing his thanks for the complimentary remarks, said that the success of the conference had been "mainly due to the loyal and conciliatory attitude of each and all of the plenipotentiaries and to the large amount of good work which they had done." He hoped, furthermore, that the results of the conference would have "immediate and permanent benefit to the natives of Samoa, as well as to all foreigners residing in that quarter of the globe." All the plenipotentiaries then signed the general act and the Berlin Conference came to its close.[91]

In consonance with the views expressed in the last plenary session that certain portions of the general act be communicated by the three powers to their respective consuls at Apia to be by them conveyed to the Samoan leaders, the latter were informed that Malietoa Laupepa had been recognized by the powers on the basis of the Lackawanna Peace agreement of July 12, 1881. The notice from the consuls was dated November 8, 1889, and was signed by Dr. Stübel, German consul general, H. de Coëtlogen, British consul, and W. Blacklock, United States vice consul. The notice concluded with the words: "We . . . invite the people of Samoa to take without de-

[91] Kasson Papers, certified copy of protocol for ninth session, June 14, 1889; S. Misc. Doc. no. 81, pp. 71-73, encl. 3.

lay such measures as according to Samoan custom are necessary to reinstate the High Chief Laupepa as King of Samoa.'"[92] Tamasese, now repudiated by Germany, could do nothing else than submit, and on November 12 he wrote the consular representatives from Lufilufi that he was agreeable to the settlement of the king question in favor of Malietoa.[93] The accredited representatives from the several districts of the Samoan islands met on December 4 and formally elected Malietoa as king, and on the morning of the fifth he hoisted his flag over his residence and assumed control of the government. The U.S.S. *Adams,* being then in the harbor of Apia, Lieutenant Commander J. J. Hunker reported that he "considered the event of sufficient importance to justify me in dressing the ship with masthead flags, Malietoa's flag at the main, and firing a royal salute." In the afternoon of the fifth the consular representatives met at the American consulate "and issued a joint proclamation to the effect that the Governments of the United States, Great Britain, and Germany recognize Malietoa Laupepa King of Samoa, with an appeal to the two opposing parties to reconcile their differences and to contribute to a peaceable management of the Samoan Government under King Malietoa.''[94]

Secretary Blaine, in submitting the treaty on January 6, 1890 to President Harrison, wrote: "The protocols of the several sessions, herewith submitted, show the discussion which took place on each of the important heads, and indicate the successive stages by which the views of the three Governments thereon came into harmony. The result is, in the main, entirely in accord with the instruc-

[92] S. Misc. Doc. no. 81, p. 73, encl. 4.
[93] *Ibid.,* p. 75, enclosure C in enclosure 5.
[94] *Ibid.,* p. 74, enclosure 5, J. J. Hunker to B. F. Tracy, Secretary of the Navy, Dec. 5, 1889.

tions under which the American plenipotentiaries acted. It is proper to observe that the matters in respect of which an agreement seemed most difficult were the restoration of the *status quo,* the formation of a stable government, without preponderance of influence on the part of any of the treaty powers, and the raising of revenue for the maintenance of that government.'' Blaine explained how the conference had come to determine upon Malietoa for king and then in connection with the second problem said that ''the danger of preponderating influence on the part of any one of the three powers is obviated by taking the chief foreign adviser and judge from a neutral nation.'' In referring to the matter of revenue he said: ''The revenue question has been adjusted, with a due regard to the limited resources of the natives and the obligation of the three powers to share in the burden which, by force of circumstances, it has been necessary to impose in protection of their common interests and for the maintenance of peace and order.''[95]

The president transmitted the treaty to the Senate the same day he received it. ''I am pleased,'' he wrote, ''to find in this general act an honorable, just, and equal settlement of the questions which have arisen during the past few years between the three powers having treaty relations with and rights in the Samoan Islands.''[96]

The newspapers of the country commented extensively upon the treaty when it was released for publication. These comments ranged from the most laudatory estimates in the Republican press to denunciation by the Democratic organs. Exceptions there were, of course, the *Baltimore Sun,* Democratic, being one of them. A well written article appeared in that journal on January 20, under the caption, ''The provisions of the Samoan

[95] *Ibid.,* Blaine to the President, Jan. 6, 1890, p. 5.
[96] *Ibid.,* Harrison to the Senate, Jan. 6, 1890, p. 1.

Treaty." In summarizing the terms of the treaty the paper said: "The Samoan treaty, concluded at Berlin in June last between representatives of the United States, Germany and England, is distinctly an abandonment by Bismarck of the unjust and insolent attitude he assumed at the outset in respect both to Samoans and to the United States."[97] The *New York Herald* essayed the rôle of the non-partisan journal, and in a long article on "The Samoan Treaty" on January 25, it said: "We see with regret that the treaty about Samoa is discussed in the main by the press from a merely partisan standpoint. Republican journals praise it without stint; Democratic papers denounce it. It is, or it will be if the Senate ratifies it, in at least one respect an extremely important act, and it ought to be discussed by the press, as we hope it will be by the Senate, on far higher than partisan considerations." The newspaper then pointed out the important provisions in the treaty and in the main approved of them. With regard to the "entangling" feature of the treaty the *Herald* said: "We see but one serious fault in the treaty. It is that it involves us in agreements with European Governments which are contrary to the fixed policy of this country. That is a grave fault which it would have been easy to avoid. Our Government might have proposed to the other two separate treaties with Samoa, all three alike in terms and guarantees. In that way we should have maintained that policy of independence from complications with European Governments which has been our consistent policy from the foundation of the Union. Even this may not matter in the present case, if the Senate shall make it clearly understood that the present agreement shall not stand as a precedent."[98]

As was stated above, the treaty was transmitted to the

[97] Quoted in *Public Opinion*, Jan. 25, 1890.
[98] *Ibid.*, Feb. 1.

THE BERLIN CONFERENCE, 1889 517

Senate by the president on January 6, 1890. On the next day it was referred to the committee on foreign relations and ordered to be printed for the Senate's confidential use. The injunction of secrecy was removed by the Senate on January 27 and the treaty was taken up by the committee of the whole in the Senate on February 4. Senator Edmunds on that day introduced a motion to amend the general act by adding an additional article to make certain that nothing in the convention should "be deemed to impair the rights of the United States in and respecting the port of Pago Pago, as secured by the treaty of the United States with the Government of Samoa by article II of the treaty of January 17, 1878, between the United States and the Government of Samoa." The proposed amendment was debated and then voted down by thirty-five nays to sixteen yeas. Thereupon the convention was reported to the Senate by the committee of the whole, and there being no further amendments offered, Senator Sherman, chairman of the committee on foreign relations, submitted the customary resolution for the ratification of the treaty without any amendments or reservations. In other words, the treaty as it left the hands of the president had been reported favorably by the committee on foreign relations and by the committee of the whole without change.

The Senate proceeded by unanimous consent to consider Senator Sherman's resolution and the resolution was agreed to. Senator Edmunds, however, then took the floor and moved that the vote be reconsidered and submitted a resolution almost identical with his previous amendment.[99] The resolution was taken up the next day, February 5, and pending debate, a vote was taken on Senator Sherman's motion that Senator Edmunds' reso-

[99] Executive Journal, United States Senate, February 4, 1890, vol. 27, pp. 422-424.

lution lie on the table. This motion was carried, but when Senator Edmunds demanded the yeas and nays and it was found that the number of senators voting did not constitute a quorum, the Senate adjourned for the day without further action.[100] On the next day, February 6, Senator Sherman again moved that Senator Edmunds' resolution lie on the table, which was decided in the affirmative. But again the yeas and nays were called for, and when it was found that there was no quorum the president of the Senate directed that the roll be called. A quorum then being secured, Senator Sherman's motion was agreed to.

The Senate then proceeded to consider the motion of Senator Edmunds that the resolution of ratification be reconsidered. This was defeated by a vote of twenty-nine to thirteen. It was then ordered that the treaty be returned to the president with the resolution of ratification.[101] As no minutes of debates in the committee of foreign relations or in executive sessions of the Senate were taken, there is no way of penetrating the veil of secrecy to learn what was said on either side. Although there was a strong minority against the treaty, the fact that the Republicans controlled the Senate made certain its ratification.[102] The treaty was ratified by the president February 21 and the ratifications exchanged on April 12. It was assented to by Samoa on April 19 and proclaimed by President Harrison on May 21, 1890.[103]

Thus was launched the *condominium*,[104] which was de-

[100] Executive Journal, United States Senate, February 5, 1890, vol. 27, pp. 424-425.

[101] *Ibid.*, February 6, 1889, vol. 27, pp. 434-435.

[102] For complete record of action in Senate see *ibid.*, vol. 27.

[103] The original of the General Act is deposited in the Department of State. See printed treaty in Malloy's *Treaties, Conventions, etc.*, II, 1576-1589.

[104] "*Condominium* (droit internationale). Droit de souveraineté ou de protectorat exercé en commun par deux ou plusieurs puissances sur un pays

THE BERLIN CONFERENCE, 1889

signed to guarantee the independence and neutrality of the Samoan islands and at the same time to preserve the rights of the United States, Germany, and Great Britain secured by these powers in their separate treaties with Samoa of January 17, 1878, January 24, 1879, and August 28, 1879, respectively. In entering the *condominium* the United States reversed its historic policy of "no entangling alliances." It had been a party to no such treaty since the revocation of the treaty of alliance with France in 1800. But since the *condominium* only lasted ten years, from 1889 to 1899, and the reversal of policy was only a temporary one, the general act would not have been so important as it was, except for the fact that the American policy with reference to Samoa as reflected in the treaty was the confirmation of that imperialism which many have been prone to think had its origin in the annexation of the Philippines. American imperialism was twenty years or more old when President McKinley decided to take the Philippines and Guam from Spain. This imperialism had its beginnings in Samoa in 1877.

Apropos of America's significant step in relation to Samoa, John Bassett Moore, in lecturing before the Johns Hopkins University, said: "While the acquisition of the Philippines was wholly unpremeditated, can it after all be said to have disclosed symptoms or tendencies with which the entire previous conduct of the United States was at variance? What is to be said of the case of Samoa? The part played by the United States in the opening of Japan is so well known that it would be superfluous here to narrate it. Still, it did not involve the exercise of political control; but this cannot be said of the

. . . Dans les îles Samoa dont l'indépendance et la neutralité sont garanties, l'Allemagne, les États-Unis et l'Angleterre ont en vertu du traité du 14 juin 1889, des privilèges particuliers communs aux trois Etats." (*La Grande Encyclopédie*, XII, 354-355.)

course of the United States with reference to the Samoan Islands. The significance of the Samoan incident lies not in the mere division of territory, but in the disposition shown by the United States long before the acquisition of the Philippines, to go to any length in asserting a claim to take part in the determination of the fate of a group of islands, thousands of miles away, in which American commercial interests were so slight as to be scarcely appreciable."[105]

Dismissing the interesting question whether or not it had not been a wiser course for the United States, as a world power, to have limited its sphere of political interests strictly to the Western hemisphere by expanding the doctrine of our non-interference to embrace the Pacific area as well as the European continent, as a matter of fact we did not permit ourselves to be inhibited by any such implications of the Monroe Doctrine in our relations with Samoa and in our annexation of the Philippines.[106] No precedent for this departure could be found in our an-

[105] John Bassett Moore, *Four Phases of American Development, Federalism, Democracy, Imperialism, Expansion*, pp. 187-188.

[106] A French writer is of the opinion that the Monroe Doctrine hampered the freedom of the United States in relation to Samoa. He says: "Ce fut à propos de la question de Samoa que les Etats-Unis sentirent pour la première fois la gêne que leur imposait la doctrine de Monroe. Sans doute elle avait retenu l'Europe loin de l'Amérique; mais elle enfermait les Etats-Unis en Amérique. Tout territoire situé dans l'Amérique tombait sous le contrôle des Etats-Unis; mais réciproquement tout territoire placé en dehors du continent américain devait rester étranger aux Etats-Unis. Les îles Samoa étaient hors de l'Amérique, il ne fallait pas y songer." (H. Petin, *Les États-Unis et La Doctrine de Monroe*, p. 375.) Further on in his book Dr. Petin declares: "Les Etats-Unis ont compris que la doctrine de Monroe, dans son sens absolu, embarrassait leurs mouvements. . . . Au fond, les Etats-Unis se sentent vaincus et vaincus par la doctrine de Monroe. En 1872, alors que les Allemands n'étaient point à Samoa, la doctrine de Monroe a empêché le président Grant de donner suite à la prise de possession du capitaine Meade; en 1889, elle a fait adopter une solution équivoque permettant à l'influence allemande de s'exercer." (*Ibid.*, p. 391.)

nexation of Alaska or in our early relations and final annexation of Hawaii because these steps were natural ones, seeing that our "manifest destiny" and a strict interpretation of the Monroe Doctrine had caused us to insist on having Oregon and on annexing California. Alaska was a part of the North American continent and Hawaii could not be regarded as outside of our political interests since that group of islands strategically must serve as an outpost of defense for our Western coast. When we went beyond Alaska and Hawaii, however, we embarked upon an imperialistic career in the Pacific for, as Judge Moore says, our dealings with two great powers in relation to Samoa showed a tendency to go beyond our political ken which found its further confirmation in our annexation of the Philippines. Since we disengaged ourselves, however, with reference to Samoa in 1899 when the *condominium* came to an end and since it is a fact that there has never been a very strong feeling in the United States for retaining the Philippines, perhaps it can be said without serious contradiction that American imperialism beyond the Western hemisphere has never attained much importance simply because it has not been a natural development.

CHAPTER XIV

THE *CONDOMINIUM,* OR TEN YEARS OF ENTANGLEMENT

AT the end of the year, 1889, the political affairs of the natives in Samoa seemed to be amicably settled. At least so Captain Hunker of the U.S.S. *Adams* reported to the secretary of the navy on December 30. On December 18, Hunker, accompanied by the United States consul and a considerable number of the officers of the *Adams,* had made an official call upon King Malietoa and congratulated him upon his accession and upon what appeared then to be the final settlement of the Samoan troubles. Two days before, a large party of the Tamasese chiefs had come to Apia "and formally acknowledged their allegiance to Malietoa as their lawful sovereign," and on the same day of the visit of the Americans to Malietoa's official residence, the Tamasese chiefs wrote a letter to Malietoa expressing their intention to inform their followers of what had transpired and to advise them to return to their homes and be loyal to the new régime.[1]

That the political conditions in Samoa remained peaceful for a number of months is borne out by Sewall's despatches to the Department of State immediately upon his return to Apia in May, 1890. The king had expressed only one fear, namely, the danger to Samoa in the long and unaccountable delay in the appointing of the chief justice and the president of the municipal council.[2] With this ex-

[1] S. Misc. Doc. no. 84, 51 Congress, 1 session, together with three enclosures, pp. 1-3.

[2] S. Ex. Doc. no. 97, 53 Congress, 3 session, p. 53, Sewall to Wharton, May 22, 1890.

ception quiet prevailed, and Malietoa was recognized everywhere as king. Moreover, a better feeling prevailed among foreigners than had existed for some time past, and the consular representatives were coöperating in the management of the affairs of the municipality and in the discharge of other duties pending the arrival of the new chiefs of government.

For two reasons Sewall deplored the delay in appointing the chief justice. The Samoans were beginning to distrust the sincerity of the powers, and thus opportunity for intrigue against Malietoa presented itself. Moreover, the bane of Samoan politics in the past had been the assumption of political power by the consuls. Their exclusion from this power by the Berlin Act was one of the most salutary steps taken by the conference, and it was necessary, therefore, that the chief justice and president of the municipal council should come to Samoa as soon as possible to take over the affairs of government.[3]

Sewall was right. Peace in Samoa did not last for long. Perhaps the chief reason for this was the fact that the new government aroused the same inveterate reluctance of the natives to accept a centralized government, which they had always displayed. Their objections to the payment of capitation taxes, making it necessary for the government to use coercive methods to collect these taxes, also contributed to the general dissatisfaction with the new régime.

All arrangements which the Berlin Conference had made with such painstaking care for the benefit of the natives seemed to the latter as only so many instruments of oppression.[4] This government, as we saw in the preceding chapter, consisted first of a supreme court with a for-

[3] *Ibid.*, no. 97, pp. 57-59, Sewall to Wharton, May 30, 1890.

[4] *Foreign Relations, 1894, Appendix I;* S. Ex. Doc. no. 93, 53 Congress, 2 session, Secretary Gresham to President Cleveland, May 9, 1894.

eigner as chief justice. The chief justice had jurisdiction both original and appellate and his decisions were final. All questions arising under the general act were submitted to the chief justice, such as the question of the election of a king, what powers the king should enjoy, and any differences which might arise between Samoa and the treaty powers. His powers extended to the field of legislation also, for we find that he could recommend the passage of laws. His jurisdiction in criminal cases made it possible for him to impose the punishment prescribed by the laws of any one of the three powers which he deemed most appropriate when the criminal was a foreigner, whereas when a native criminal was on trial, he should follow the laws and customs of the islands. The chief justice had exclusive jurisdiction in all suits involving real property in Samoa and in all suits between foreigners of different nationalities and between foreigners and natives.

Next in importance to the supreme court was the municipal council of Apia, consisting of six members and a president. The president was also to be a foreigner in accordance with the terms of the general act, and in addition to his strictly municipal functions, he was to be the chief adviser of the king. The municipal council had the power of appointing the municipal magistrate and other subordinate officers, and of passing all ordinances, which, however, in order to be effective, must have the approval of the three foreign consuls. In case the consuls failed to agree, the ordinances were submitted to the chief justice for approval.

The general act further provided for a system of revenue consisting of important export duties and capitation taxes as well as license taxes. Finally, there was the temporary provision for a land commission consisting of three members, one to be appointed by each of the treaty powers, whose duties embraced the examination of claims and titles to land. The findings of this commission were subject to ratification by the chief justice.

By the above provisions a permanent government was set up to aid the native régime. It was hardly correct to say, therefore, that the native government was an autonomous one. In fact, it was, as Secretary Gresham reported to President Cleveland, "in substance and in form a tripartite foreign government, imposed upon the natives and supported and administered jointly by the three treaty powers."

Since the three powers failed to agree on a candidate for the office of chief justice for Samoa, the task of selecting one, according to the Berlin Act, fell to the king of Sweden and Norway, who chose a member of the Swedish judiciary named Conrad Cedercrantz. Cedercrantz arrived in Samoa in the latter days of December, and proclaimed his assumption of the duties of chief justice on January 2, 1891.[5] Though received with due courtesy by the natives, he evidently lacked the tact necessary for the successful carrying out of the delicate task which the powers had given him, for very soon there developed a difference of opinion between himself and the land commission "with regard to the method which should be adopted for the payment of the expenses entailed by the labors of the land commission."[6] The United States agreed with Germany and Great Britain that the expenses should be paid in equal sums by the respective powers, since this was regarded as necessary in order to bring to completion the labors of the commission. It was suggested that each consul be instructed by his govern-

[5] S. Ex. Doc. no. 97, p. 68, Sewall to Wharton, Jan. 26, 1891, with enclosure.
[6] *Foreign Relations, 1894, Appendix I*, pp. 629; S. Ex. Doc. no. 93, p. 126, von Mumm to Blaine, Aug. 24, 1891.

ment to inform the chief justice that the items of expenditures stated in the land commissioners' letter to the chief justice were "reasonable and necessary expenses of the Commission for taking evidence and making surveys." Should the chief justice decline to approve such expenditures, the American consul general, Sewall, was instructed to pay the American share of them if the consular representatives of the other two powers would do likewise. This authority was given the consul general in order to prevent the temporary stoppage of the labors of the land commission which, according to the Berlin Act, was limited to two years service.[8]

Another dispute arose between the land commission and the chief justice over the question of making an accurate map of the islands.[9] The latter wanted such a map made, the expenses to be borne by the commission. The commissioners declined to accede to the wishes of the chief justice, and were upheld by the powers.[10]

Another difference of opinion between the land commissioners and the chief justice, which required the intervention of the powers, arose over the intention of the chief justice to make the registration of land titles in the Samoan islands "dependent on a previous survey to be carried out at the cost of the parties interested."[11] The German and British governments agreed (September, 1892) to overrule the chief justice, and on October 4, Secretary Foster informed the German and British min-

[7] F.R., 1894, App. I, pp. 629-630; S. Ex. Doc. no. 93, pp. 126-127, Wharton to von Mumm, Sept. 9, 1891.

[8] F.R., 1894, App. I, pp. 515-516; S. Ex. Doc. no. 93, pp. 17-18, Wharton to Pauncefote, Sept. 18, 1891.

[9] F.R. 1894, App. I, p. 528; S. Ex. Doc. no. 93, p. 30, Pauncefote to Blaine, March 23, 1892.

[10] F.R., 1894, App. I, p. 528; S. Ex. Doc. no. 93, p. 30, Blaine to Pauncefote, April 6, 1892.

[11] F.R. 1894, App. I, pp. 569-570; S. Ex. Doc. no. 93, pp. 71-72, Herbert to Foster, Sept. 27, 1892.

isters that the United States government concurred with their governments.[12] About the same time, the powers again overruled the chief justice when they declined to allow him to charge a fee of five dollars for the registration of every single land title.[13]

Friction also developed between the chief justice and the municipal council. A difference of opinion arose as to the apportionment of import and export duties leviable under article VI of the Berlin Act, and the chief justice decided on March 28, 1892, that these revenues were to be paid to the Samoan government, not to the municipality of Apia.[14] The question was appealed to the treaty powers through their consular representatives in Apia, and by May of the next year the United States joined the other two powers in not accepting the decision of the chief justice, and requested him "to concert with the consular representatives of the three treaty powers to carry into effect the understanding heretofore reached by them."[15]

The president of the municipal council, Baron Senfft von Pilsach, did not arrive in Samoa until the spring of 1891. This officer was appointed by the German chancellor on February 2, and came to Samoa some time in May. The German consul general in Apia was instructed, in conjunction with his American and British colleagues, to arrange for Baron Senfft's inauguration immediately upon his arrival in Apia.[16] The municipal president had

[12] F.R. 1894, App. I, p. 649 and p. 573; S. Ex. Doc. no. 93, p. 146, Foster to Ketteler, Oct. 4, 1892; p. 75, Foster to Pauncefote, Oct. 4, 1892.

[13] F.R. 1894, App. I, pp. 568-569; S. Ex. Doc. no. 93, pp. 71-73, Herbert to Foster, Sept. 27, 1892, with enclosures.

[14] F.R. 1894, App. I, pp. 543-545; S. Ex. Doc. no. 93, pp. 45-47, Herbert to Foster, Aug. 26, 1892, with enclosures.

[15] F.R. 1894, App. I, p. 589; S. Ex. Doc. no. 93, p. 91, Gresham to Pauncefote, May 13, 1893.

[16] F.R. 1894, App. I, pp. 627-628; S. Ex. Doc. no. 93, pp. 124-125, Count von Arco-Valley to Blaine, Feb. 26, 1891.

not, however, been in Samoa long, before he got into a dispute with a German member of the municipal council, who had essayed to give advice to the king contrary to the advice from Senfft, who was the official adviser.[17] In this instance the municipal president felt aggrieved that he had not been supported by the three consular representatives.

Friction between Baron Senfft and the Samoan government had previously occurred over the matter of the proper coinage for circulation in Samoa. The Samoan government had decided that the gold currencies of the United States and Great Britain should be admitted as of equal value and that the silver money of the United States and Great Britain should be the only silver currencies admitted. Baron Senfft von Pilsach insisted that German silver marks should also be admitted. In August the municipal council of Apia passed an ordinance admitting United States, Chilean, British, and German silver as legal tender up to the amount of ten dollars. Since such a provision would in the opinion of Cusack-Smith, the British consul at Apia, "have enabled the German silver mark to flood the country," as had occurred in Tonga, "to the great inconvenience of all British traders," that officer proposed an amendment at a meeting of the consular board, securing his German colleague's adhesion thereto as well as that of his American colleague, "That the currency in use and the rates of exchange be for the present—the United States gold coinage; the British gold coinage—the sovereign to be equal to $4.86 United States coin; the German gold coinage—the 20-mark piece to be equal to $4.76 United States coin; and only United States silver and Chilean at the rate of $7 to the $5 United States coin, to be accepted, and without

[17] F.R. 1894, App. I, p. 516; S. Ex. Doc. no. 93, p. 18, Blaine to Pauncefote, Oct. 28, 1891.

limit." The amendment was adopted by the municipal council in lieu of its own resolution, unanimously with the exception of the president, and the Samoan government was also advised to accept this arrangement.[18]

In the following spring the acting secretary of state, Wharton, informed the British ambassador that the American consul general at Apia, Sewall, had been instructed to join with his colleagues in representing to the authorities of Samoa that the German coin be admitted into Samoa as well as those of the United States and Great Britain, the 20-mark gold piece being equivalent to $4.76.[19] Although it seems that at this time the United States government had reached an understanding with the German chargé at Washington that the German 20-mark gold piece was to circulate in Samoa as equivalent to $4.76, it came to be accepted immediately in Samoa as equivalent to $5, when duties were paid into the Samoan treasury, and as equivalent to $4.75 when received by merchants in Apia in payment for goods sold. This situation elicited a protest from the secretary of state to the British representative as being in contravention of section 4 of article VI, which forbade the use of other currencies at more than their equivalent in "the standard money of the United States of America." The note went on to say that Baron Senfft von Pilsach not only was receiving the pound sterling and the 20-mark gold piece at more than their equivalent value, but that he had substantially made them "units of value which the treaty precludes." It was hoped that the British government would coöperate with the United States "in securing an observance of the treaty," which had clearly established

[18] F.R. 1894, App. I, pp. 517-526; S. Ex. Doc. no. 93, pp. 19-28, Pauncefote to Blaine, Dec. 24, 1891, with enclosures.

[19] F.R. 1894, App. I, p. 528; S. Ex. Doc. no. 93, p. 30, Wharton to Pauncefote, March 24, 1892.

the coin of the United States as the unit of value in Samoa and permitted "other coin to be taken at their equivalent only."[20]

Another matter, which caused trouble between the president of the municipal council and the other council members, was his insistence that the revenues of the municipality and of the Samoan government be kept together. At a meeting of the council on November 25, 1891, the council had passed the following resolution: "That the treasurer be instructed to withdraw the municipal moneys from the Union Bank of Australia, Sydney, as soon as the terms of deposit have expired, and to deposit the same, in United States gold, in the municipal treasury." The consular board having approved the resolution, Baron Senfft von Pilsach was duly informed by the chairman *pro tempore*. When by his letter of December 23, the president of the municipal council declined to accept the instruction, the matter was referred by the council on December 30 to the chief justice for settlement.[21] The president maintained that the action of the council was in violation of article V, section 3, of the Berlin Act, according to which there existed "neither a special treasurer nor a special treasury of the Municipal Council of Apia." According to the act all the revenues were to be received by the treasurer "appointed, not by the municipal council, but by the Samoan Government upon the previous agreement of the signatory powers." There was no separate municipal treasury, therefore, except insofar as the municipality's accounts appeared in the ledgers of the common treasury.

The decision of Chief Justice Cedercrantz upheld the

[20] F.R. 1894, App. I, p. 571; S. Ex. Doc. no. 93, p. 73, Foster to Herbert, Sept. 28, 1892.

[21] F.R. 1894, App. I, pp. 573-575; S. Ex. Doc. no. 93, pp. 75-77, Herbert to Foster, Oct. 5, 1892, with enclosures.

THE *CONDOMINIUM* 531

position of the president. He declared the resolution by the council of November 25 to be void because in conflict with the Berlin Act. In order to reach an amicable settlement of the dispute, the municipal president addressed a letter to the three powers suggesting that the difficulty could be met by keeping the revenues of the municipality distinct from those of the Samoan government. The British and American governments were disposed to regard this as the better course, and the German government decided to remain neutral in the matter, even though it accepted the decision of the chief justice, for the reason that it regarded the question as of no great importance.[22]

Thus far the three powers had evinced a genuine desire to coöperate fully in making the new régime in Samoa a success, but the same misunderstandings among the local officials as had arisen in Samoa before the Berlin Conference were bound to recur. Already in his first year as president of the municipal council (October 5, 1891), Baron Senfft von Pilsach requested the powers to relieve him from his duties. When they declined to accede to his wishes, he repeated his request, and again they refused to accept his resignation. In reporting to the Department of State the agreement of the Marquis of Salisbury with the German government in this matter, the British chargé d'affaires in Washington represented the British prime minister as adding that should the municipal president's resignation "appear to be periodical, he would be disposed to reconsider the question in the light of later information."[23]

By the spring of 1892 the foreign residents in Apia were strongly of the opinion that the Berlin Act should

[22] F.R. 1894, App. I, pp. 579-580; S. Ex. Doc. no. 93, pp. 81-82, Herbert to Foster, Nov. 2, 1892, with enclosures.
[23] F.R. 1894, App. I, p. 577; S. Ex. Doc. no. 93, p. 79, Herbert to Foster, Oct. 8, 1892.

be materially modified in order to eliminate the defects of the instrument. They held a public meeting on February 29 and adopted several important alterations which, through the chairman, Robert Louis Stevenson,[24] were forwarded to the British consul with a view to their submission to the three treaty powers. One suggested change had reference to the functions of the chief justice during a vacancy. Whereas the Berlin Act stipulated that the powers of the chief justice during a vacancy should be exercised by the president of the municipal council, the meeting adopted the suggestion that "the consular representatives of the three signatory powers acting together" should fill the vacancy, or in the event they declined, they should have the power with the consent of the Samoan government to appoint an acting chief justice. This suggested change was in all probability prompted by the situation which arose the year before when Chief Justice Cedercrantz, without notifying the consuls, had gone to Australia, and had left the powers of his office in the hands of the president of the municipal council, Baron Senfft von Pilsach, who had used them in a rather dictatorial manner.[25] On the other hand, the president of the council had also recommended changes in the organic act, as had the consular representatives of the United States.

Since according to section 1 of article VIII it was possible after three years following the signature of the Berlin Act for any one of the three powers to request the consideration by them of any changes, the American secretary of state, on December 9, 1892, handed the German and British ministers a memorandum suggesting "that some amendment of the Act, if only for explanatory pur-

[24] A very critical account of the new régime is to be found in Stevenson's *A Footnote to History: Eight Years of Trouble in Samoa.*

[25] F.R. 1894, App. I, pp. 529-538; S. Ex. Doc. no. 93, pp. 31-40, Pauncefote to Blaine, April 28, 1892, with enclosures.

poses, [was] necessary." No formal conference was necessary, thought Foster; an informal conference in Washington would accomplish the purpose. Advice might be secured from the consular representatives and the land commissioners, and Foster proposed that instructions be sent to the consular representatives to hold a joint conference at Apia, and to "make a joint report as to recommendations which they [would] be able to agree upon respecting the more effective working of the Berlin General Act." With this information at hand, the informal conference at Washington could be held. Nothing, however, came of the suggestion, presumably because the Republican administration soon relinquished the reins of government.

The land commission, as it was first constituted under the Berlin Act, consisted of Bazett M. Haggard for Great Britain,[26] Carl Eggert for Germany,[27] and Henry C. Ide for the United States.[28] The German and British members arrived as early as February, 1891, but had to await the arrival of the American member.[29] The commission began its work on May 30, 1891, but owing to the fact that the German member was relieved in the spring of 1892 on account of ill health and the American member was later obliged to return to the United States, the work of the commission was considerably retarded. To be sure, the German government, when relieving Herr Eggert, in order to permit no loss of time, had by telegraph authorized the acting imperial consul at Apia to appoint a successor. An immediate choice was made in the appointment

[26] F.R. 1894, App. I, p. 740; S. Ex. Doc. no. 93, p. 204, Lincoln to Blaine, March 24, 1891.

[27] F.R. 1894, App. I, p. 626; S. Ex. Doc. no. 93, p. 123, von Mumm to Blaine, Nov. 2, 1890.

[28] F.R. 1894, App. I, p. 512; S. Ex. Doc. no. 93, p. 9, Gresham to President Cleveland, May 9, 1894.

[29] S. Ex. Doc. no. 97, 53 Congress, 3 session, p. 76, Sewall to Wharton, Feb. 17, 1891.

of T. Greiner, who was in the German consular service at Sydney. But at that time (March 3), of the 3,705 land claims that had been laid before the commission for its investigation, only 72 had been acted upon, and when Mr. Ide left for the United States, the final decisions on all cases not then acted upon had to await the arrival of his successor. E. J. Ormsbee was appointed in Ide's place,[30] but he remained in Samoa less than a year, his departure taking place on March 1, 1893.[31] The delay in the appointment of a successor to Ormsbee resulted in a suspension of the work. William Lea Chambers, who was finally appointed, arrived in Samoa in the fall.[32]

Already in January, 1893, the Department of State had communicated to the German minister the suggestion that since the land commission could not accomplish its task within the two-year period provided for in article IV, section 3, of the Berlin Act (that is, from May 30, 1891, to May 30, 1893), it was desirable to prolong the period. The German government was favorable to a prolongation of one year to the end of May, 1894,[33] but when Great Britain proposed shortening the period of extension to March 31, 1894, the other two powers acceded.[34]

After the arrival of Chambers, the work of the land commission was considerably hastened. By January 29, 1894, when Chambers made a report to the State Department, 1,094 claims had been disposed of since his arrival,

[30] F.R. 1894, App. I, p. 690; S. Ex. Doc. no. 93, p. 189, Adee to Saurma, Sept. 22, 1893.

[31] F.R. 1894, App. I, p. 603; S. Ex. Doc. no. 93, p. 105, Pauncefote to Gresham, Oct. 5, 1893.

[32] F.R. 1894, App. I, p. 602; S. Ex. Doc. no. 93, p. 104, Adee to Pauncefote, Sept. 21, 1893.

[33] F.R. 1894, App. I, p. 750; S. Ex. Doc. no. 93, p. 215, Phelps to Gresham, April 28, 1893, with enclosure.

[34] F.R. 1894, App. I, p. 750; S. Ex. Doc. no. 93, p. 215, Gresham to Phelps, May 16, 1893.

THE *CONDOMINIUM* 535

and only 986 were left on hand.[35] But when it was clearly seen that the work could not be completed by March 31, at the instance of the German government, both the British and American governments consented to a second extension of time to December 31.[36] Although the great acceleration of the work of the commission after the arrival of Chambers on November 3, 1893, was mainly due to him, and although urged by the Department of State to remain after March 31st to wind up the business as quickly as possible, he found it necessary to return to the United States, with about 500 claims yet to be disposed of. According to the British consular representative at Apia, Chambers had "been popular with all sections of the community" and it was desirable that he return to Samoa to assist in the closing of the work of the commission.[37] Chambers did return,[38] and on September 12 he reported from Samoa that the labors of the commission could easily be concluded within sixty days from that date. This information caused the department to suggest to the German and British governments that the three governments should cable identic instructions to their respective commissioners that the work must be completed and all reports and papers forwarded to the supreme court of Samoa by December 31.[39] The last meeting of the commission was held on December 5. At this time the secretary

[35] F.R. 1894, App. I, p. 616; S. Ex. Doc. no. 93, p. 118, Gresham to Pauncefote, March 7, 1894.

[36] F.R. 1894, App. I, p. 614; S. Ex. Doc. no. 93, p. 116, Pauncefote to Gresham, Feb. 21, 1894.

[37] F.R. 1894, App. I, p. 620; S. Ex. Doc. no. 132, 53 Congress, 2 session, pp. 2-3, Pauncefote to Gresham, May 8, 1894, with enclosure, J. B. C. Smith to Earl of Rosebery, March 28, 1894.

[38] F.R. 1894, App. I, p. 623; S. Ex. Doc. no. 132, p. 6, Uhl to Pauncefote, June 13, 1894.

[39] F.R. 1894, App. I, pp. 727 and 624; S. Ex. Doc. no. 93, 53 Congress, 2 session, p. 452, Uhl to Saurma, Oct. 8, 1894; p. 442, the same to Goschen.

of the commission reported that he had delivered to the clerk of the supreme court all the reports on claims, 3,942 in number.[40]

A synopsis of a review of land claims examined by the commission shows that of the 134,419 acres of land claimed by German subjects, 75,000 acres, or about fifty-six per cent, were confirmed, whereas of the 1,250,270 acres claimed by Englishmen, only 36,000 acres, or about three per cent, were confirmed, and of the 302,746 acres claimed by American citizens, only 21,000 acres, or about seven per cent, were confirmed.[41] According to Chambers' report to the secretary of state, nearly all the 21,000 acres confirmed to Americans belonged "to a corporation composed of San Francisco stockholders, which, at the time the investigation took place, was insolvent . . . and the titles were confirmed to certain trustees." Not more than 2,000 acres "were confirmed to all other American claimants."[42]

Although the Tamasese forces had disbanded at the beginning of the new régime,[43] Mataafa and his followers were not reconciled, and soon became a disturbing factor.[44] Already in the summer of 1891, the British and German consuls with the concurrence of the Samoan government had decided to suggest to their governments the desirability of capturing Mataafa and disarming his warriors. The American consul general, Sewall, in view of the fact that there had been no outbreak or violence, was opposed to such a procedure, for he believed that with a single ship representing each power in the harbor, Ma-

[40] S. Ex. Doc. no. 97, p. 470, Exhibit A, as enclosure to "Report of W. L. Chambers, United States Land Commissioner to Samoa" to the Secretary of State, Washington, Feb. 3, 1895.
[41] *Ibid.*, p. 471, Exhibit B.   [42] *Ibid.*, p. 467.
[43] Tamasese died on April 17, 1891.
[44] When he took up his residence at Malie on May 31, 1891.

taafa would be sufficiently impressed, and the restoration of order and confidence would be the result. For the time being, therefore, the Department of State urged upon the other powers the less drastic course, as the president deemed "the measures suggested by the German vice-consul to be altogether unjustifiable and likely to destroy all the good results anticipated and partly realized by the Berlin Conference."[45]

When, however, a few months later, King Malietoa complained to the powers that Mataafa's forces were "defying and obstructing the authority of the Supreme Court of Samoa at Malie" and requested "the assistance of the foreign men of war at Samoa with a view to enable the court to execute its warrants,"[46] the United States government was prepared to accede to the king's appeal. In replying to a note from the British ambassador, the secretary of state said: "Assistance in support of the authority of the Supreme Court, if discreetly given, would seem to be well directed, and its moral and demonstrative effect might aid in quieting the existing troubles." On the same day Blaine wrote the German chargé d'affaires in the same vein. He suggested to both powers that similar instructions be given by the three powers "permitting any man-of-war of the three treaty powers, which for the time being may be present in Samoa, to render such aid as may be necessary in executing the warrants of the Supreme Court, such aid to be limited strictly to that purpose and to be rendered by the man-of-war at the request of the Consul of its country, who will act in the matter, if the Consuls of the three powers shall jointly decide in any particular case that there is

[45] F.R. 1894, App. I, pp. 514-515; S. Ex. Doc. no. 93, pp. 16-17, Wharton to Pauncefote, Sept. 8, 1891.

[46] F.R. 1894, App. I, p. 526; S. Ex. Doc. no. 93, p. 28, Pauncefote to Blaine, Jan. 27, 1892.

necessity for such aid and shall request the consul to have it rendered.''[47] The suggestion was agreed to by both the British and German powers,[48] and instructions were accordingly sent to their respective representatives in Apia.[49] The Department of State sent its instruction to the United States vice consul on July 11.[50]

In the fall the question of maintaining a strict concert of the treaty powers came up. The German government proposed to send one or two men-of-war to Samoa to protect life and property. Although the Earl of Rosebery saw no objection to the German proposal and was "disposed to recommend acquiescence in it,"[51] Secretary Foster saw nothing in the situation in Samoa which suggested the "necessity of more than one vessel of either power being dispatched to those waters." Otherwise the German proposal was entirely in harmony with the views of the United States as expressed at the first Samoan conference in Washington in 1887, when Secretary of State Bayard suggested that each power keep a warship in Samoan waters for four months alternately.[52] In a prompt reply to this note the Earl of Rosebery informed the State Department that Her Majesty's government was sending to Samoa one ship for the protection of life and property there. With respect to the point raised by Foster anent the desirability of limiting the number of

[47] F.R. 1894, App. I, pp. 633 and 527; S. Ex. Doc. no. 93, p. 130, Blaine to von Mumm, Feb. 20, 1892; p. 29, the same to Pauncefote.

[48] F.R. 1894, App. I, p. 529; S. Ex. Doc. no. 93, p. 31, Pauncefote to Blaine, April 19, 1892.

[49] F.R. 1894, App. I, p. 639; S. Ex. Doc. no. 93, p. 136, von Holleben to Wharton, June 6, 1892.

[50] F.R. 1894, App. I, pp. 540 and 640; S. Ex. Doc. no. 93, p. 42, Foster to Herbert, July 11, 1892; p. 137, the same to Ketteler.

[51] F.R. 1894, App. I, p. 576; S. Ex. Doc. no. 93, p. 78, Herbert to Foster, Oct. 6, 1892.

[52] F.R. 1894, App. I, p. 578; S. Ex. Doc. no. 93, p. 80, Foster to Herbert, Oct. 12, 1892.

THE *CONDOMINIUM* 539

ships to one for each power, the British note stated: "His lordship is very anxious that the concert of the three treaty powers should be maintained in Samoa and he is, therefore, not disposed to raise the point as to whether one or two ships of war should be sent there so long as joint action is taken and joint instructions are agreed upon by the three governments."[53]

By June the United States government was prepared to go further and to intervene together with the other powers. It was willing to "join in an active demonstration for the purpose of surrounding and disarming" Mataafa and his followers.[54] At the same time Secretary Gresham desired a conference with the British and German representatives as soon as possible, but when Germany objected, he waived his request for it.[55] The U.S.S. *Philadelphia* sailed immediately from New York (June 24) with orders to coöperate with the German and British ships,[56] but it had reached only the port of Callao on the west coast of South America when the Department of State received news from Blacklock, vice consul general at Apia, stating that the civil war was over, and that Mataafa and his chiefs had surrendered and were on board the British and German warships.[57] When Secretary Gresham inquired what disposition should be made of the prisoners, the German government proposed to take charge of them and keep them on the Marshall Is-

[53] F.R. 1894, App. I, pp. 578-579; S. Ex. Doc. no. 93, pp. 80-81, Herbert to Foster, Oct. 25, 1892.

[54] F.R. 1894, App. I, pp. 590 and 675; S. Ex. Doc. no. 93, p. 92, Gresham to Pauncefote, June 19, 1893; p. 172, the same to von Holleben.

[55] F.R. 1894, App. I, p. 591; S. Ex. Doc. no. 93, p. 93, Gresham to Pauncefote, June 23, 1893.

[56] F.R. 1894, App. I, p. 594; S. Ex. Doc. no. 93, p. 96, Gresham to Pauncefote, July 6, 1893.

[57] F.R. 1894, App. I, pp. 596 and 680; S. Ex. Doc. no. 93, p. 98, Gresham to Pauncefote, Aug. 9, 1893; p. 177, Gresham to Ketteler, same date.

lands, the three powers to share equally the cost of their maintenance.[58] To this both the British and United States governments readily acceded.[59]

By the end of the year 1892, the treaty powers were becoming convinced that the two offices of chief justice and president of the municipal council should be vacated. In a note to the German chargé, Secretary Foster suggested on October 6, that in view of von Pilsach's repeated requests to be relieved and because of the friction between himself and others in authority in Samoa, he (Foster) was disposed to believe it best for the three signatory powers to "accede to the Baron's request to be allowed to resign his office, in which for some time he [had] manifestly continued with great reluctance."[60] The German government indicated its willingness to accept the resignation of the president of the council provided the office of the chief justice was vacated also, for it attributed von Pilsach's troubles with the consular representatives to the influence over him by Cedercrantz. A successor to von Pilsach would come under the same influence, hence the desirability of dispensing with Cedercrantz's services as well. To fill the two vacated positions the German government suggested that the former American land commissioner, Henry C. Ide, be appointed chief justice, and a German merchant in Fiji, Wilhelm Hennings by name, be given the position of president.[61] The State Department was agreeable to the German proposal if the British government concurred in the two

[58] F.R. 1894, App. I, p. 598; S. Ex. Doc. no. 93, p. 100, Pauncefote to Gresham, Aug. 18, 1893.

[59] F.R. 1894, App. I, p. 600; S. Ex. Doc. no. 93, p. 102, Gresham to Pauncefote, Sept. 6, 1893.

[60] F.R. 1894, App. I, pp. 649-650; S. Ex. Doc. no. 93, pp. 146-147, Foster to Ketteler, Oct. 6, 1892.

[61] F.R. 1894, App. I, pp. 660-661; S. Ex. Doc. no. 93, pp. 157-158, Ketteler to Foster, Nov. 15, 1892.

THE *CONDOMINIUM*

nominations,[62] and on November 17 the secretary of state in conference with the British minister made known to him the American position.[63] Following an extended investigation, the British government decided not to accept the German proposal with reference to Hennings for the presidency of the council,[64] and in the following July the German government suggested E. Schmidt, formerly vice consul at Apia, as a suitable person for the position.[65] This nomination was acceptable to the other two powers.

Chief Justice Ide arrived at Apia on November 3, 1893, and the retiring chief justice departed by the same steamer, "having previously turned over his office to Mr. Ide."[66] The newly designated president of the council, Herr Schmidt, arrived on December 29, and on the next day received his appointment from King Malietoa and took the oath of office.[67]

Despite the fact that the first chief justice and the first president of the council did not prove satisfactory either to the Samoan government, the municipal council, or the

---

[62] F.R. 1894, App. I, pp. 661-662; S. Ex. Doc. no. 93, pp. 158-159, Foster to Ketteler, Nov. 18, 1892.

[63] F.R. 1894, App. I, p. 582; S. Ex. Doc. no. 93, p. 84, memorandum of conference between Secretary of State and British minister, Nov. 17, 1892.

[64] F.R. 1894, App. I, pp. 587-588; S. Ex. Doc. no. 93, pp. 89-90, Wharton to Pauncefote, March 3, 1893.

[65] F.R. 1894, App. I, pp. 677-678; S. Ex. Doc. no. 93, pp. 174-175, von Holleben to Gresham, July 8, 1893.

[66] S. Ex. Doc. no. 97, 53 Congress, 3 session, p. 319, Blacklock to Quincy, Nov. 7, 1893, received Nov. 29. It had been suggested that the consular board take over the duties of the chief justice as well as those of the president of the council. The United States government had objected to this and consequently Chief Justice Cedercrantz had remained in Samoa until the arrival of his successor, whereas the consular board exercised the functions of the president of the council between the departure of Baron Senfft von Pilsach and the arrival of Herr Schmidt. (See Gresham's note to Pauncefote, May 8, 1893, in *Foreign Relations, 1894, Appendix I*, p. 588.)

[67] S. Ex. Doc. no. 97, pp. 332-333, Blacklock to Uhl, Jan. 3, 1894, received Jan. 26.

consular board, the relations among the consuls themselves, after the Berlin Act went into effect, were excellent for several years, and consequently amity existed among the three signatory powers. Although the American consul general, Sewall, would not agree at first to any concerted action against Mataafa with a view to that chief's arrest and deportation, he eventually advised cooperation, an agreement that resulted, as we have seen, in the joint intervention of the three powers. Blacklock, the vice consul general, *ad interim,* also concurred to the fullest extent with his colleagues.

It was only after the arrival of the successor to Sewall, Consul General James H. Mulligan, in August, 1894, that friction arose sufficient to attract the attention of the powers. Arriving in Apia on August 9, he took over the consulate on August 13. A dispute occurred in the autumn between the German consul, Biermann by name, and Mulligan, over Mulligan's failure to unite with the consular board in ratifying certain resolutions adopted by the municipal council, thus bringing the legislation of the municipality of Apia to a standstill. The attention of the Department of State was called to the matter by a note from the German minister, who requested that the American consul general be given instructions "to act in harmony with his consular colleagues in political matters."[68] The secretary of state took the position that although Mulligan had good reasons for doing what he did, he would nevertheless "be instructed to desist from such method in connection with the work of the consular board, and to take part, in accordance with the spirit of the Berlin act in its deliberations."[69]

Thus during the first four years of the *condominium,*

[68] House Doc. no. 1, part 2, 54 Congress, 1 session, p. 1126, Saurma to Gresham, Feb. 23, 1895.
[69] *Ibid.,* pp. 1128-1129, Gresham to Saurma, March 5, 1895.

THE *CONDOMINIUM*   543

the United States government found it possible to act in entire harmony with the other two powers. In 1895, however, it firmly opposed two positions supported by Germany, one referring to the question of control of the Samoan finances and the other relating to the so-called "arms and ammunition ordinance, 1894."

During the year 1894, the German government had communicated with the State Department on four occasions regarding the first question and for the fifth time on March 13 of the following year.[70] Owing to the fact that the United States had consistently opposed, throughout its connection with Samoa, any attitude of the powers toward the island kingdom which would tend to deprive it of its so-called autonomy, the suggestion that the control of the Samoan finances be transferred to the president of the municipal council met with disapproval. In concluding his answer to the German government, Secretary Gresham said: "While this Government sympathizes with the general purpose of preventing the native Government from squandering its revenues, it cannot consistently consent that the president of the Municipal Council shall exercise arbitrary control over the revenues of which he is only the custodian."[71]

To prevent the natives from securing firearms for future civil strife, the municipal council passed an ordinance on August 14, 1894, for the suppression of the smuggling of arms into Apia. To secure a similar regulation for the territory outside of Apia, the chief justice and the president of the council, on behalf of the Samoan government, recommended that approval be given by the three governments through their consular representatives of a uniform law binding upon all. Germany favored such action, and Great Britain did likewise, though she

[70] *Ibid.*, p. 1130, Saurma to Gresham, March 13, 1895.
[71] *Ibid.*, pp. 1136-1137, Gresham to Saurma, April 25, 1895.

objected to the right of search by the president of the council of vessels belonging to British subjects, insisting that the power of searching such vessels should remain with the British consul.[72] In his reply to the German note Secretary Gresham said that the main provisions of the draft of regulations did not "materially differ from the Berlin act" but there were "ancillary provisions for insuring obedience to that act which [were] not contained in the act itself," and the department did not feel authorized to issue such regulations without additional legislation by Congress. There was ample legislation, of course, to enable the consul general himself to bring to trial and to punish American citizens for violating the terms of the Berlin Act, but neither the department nor the consul general could "require American citizens in Samoa to make reports to the president of the Municipal Council or to submit to his searching their premises." Moreover, such citizens could "not be subjected to punishment for refusing to make reports or for resisting search."[73]

Later in the year Germany came forward with another proposal with reference to the prevention of the smuggling of firearms. In September, 1894, the consular representatives in Samoa together with the senior officers of naval vessels then stationed in Samoan waters had reached a verbal agreement that to prevent smuggling of arms, all merchant vessels in Samoan waters should be subjected to search by any naval vessel belonging to any of the treaty powers. This agreement was made subject to approval by the treaty powers. The British and German governments subsequently approved the agreement and when the United States failed to take a similar step, the German government in September, 1895, requested the adhesion of the American government to the meas-

---

[72] H. Doc. no. 1, part 2, 54 Congress, 1 session, pp. 1130-1134, Saurma to Gresham, March 19, 1895.

[73] *Ibid.*, pp. 1134-1135, Gresham to Saurma, April 18, 1895.

ure.⁷⁴ Secretary Olney replied on November 7 that, in full agreement with the stand of his predecessor, Secretary Gresham, he was unable to accede to the wishes of the German government.⁷⁵

In May, 1896, the relations between Secretary Olney and the German minister became somewhat strained owing to Olney's irritation at the proposed assumption by Herr Schmidt of the functions of Chief Justice Ide during a five weeks' vacation the later planned to take in Australia. The German government assumed that the provisions of article III, section 2, of the Berlin Act permitted the president of the council to represent the chief justice at all times when the latter absented himself from the islands. Olney was unable to accept such an interpretation of the act. "The 'vacancy' contemplated hereby," he said, "is one that exists by reason of the death, resignation, or removal of the chief justice from office, whereupon a successor is to be appointed and qualified. Hence, the temporary absence of the chief justice for the purpose of taking a much-needed and well-earned rest does not constitute a vacancy within the spirit or the meaning of the act." It was hoped, therefore, that the German consul would be instructed to act in conjunction with his colleagues in representing to Herr Schmidt that he was not "authorized or empowered to discharge the duties of chief justice of Samoa, except in the express contingency provided by the Berlin General Act.'"⁷⁶ A few days later the German minister took issue with Olney and endeavored to show that in a previous case the United States government had approved the arrangement whereby the municipal president substituted for the chief justice, concluding his note in a rather serious vein, when

⁷⁴ *Ibid.*. p, 1143, von Thielmann to Olney, Sept. 19, 1895.

⁷⁵ *Ibid.*, pp. 1147-1148, Olney to von Thielmann, Nov. 7, 1895.

⁷⁶ *Ibid.*, 54 Congress, 2 session, pp. 537-538, Olney to von Thielmann, May 8, 1896.

he said: "If your excellency in your last note of May 8, 1896, abandons this standpoint (which has hitherto been approved by all parties) and takes the opposite one, you can not expect that I, as the representative of His Majesty the Emperor near the United States Government, shall adopt your view and make it the subject of a report to the Imperial Government. I am rather compelled most respectfully to leave it to your excellency to issue suitable instructions to the United States ambassador at Berlin if you wish your present view of the case, which is diametrically opposed to the understanding of 1893, to be brought to the notice of the Imperial Government."[77] In consequence of this statement Secretary Olney declined to take the matter to Berlin, and contented himself by noting that he had filed a protest with the German minister "against the action proposed by Mr. Schmidt, and until some overt act on his part [was] reported to the Department showing that he [contemplated] discharging the duties of Chief Justice during the latter's temporary absence, [he was] perfectly willing to permit the subject to rest as at present."[78]

Just as the first chief justice and the first president of the municipal council had got into many difficulties and had proved unsatisfactory both to the native government of Samoa and to the municipal council and the consular board, so the second incumbents of these offices, Ide and Schmidt, likewise failed to reconcile their conflicting interests. Trouble between Chief Justice Ide and the consuls arose in the spring of 1894, when he had been in the country only a few months. The chief justice claimed the right to attend meetings with the consuls when political matters were discussed, while the consuls retorted that

[77] H. Doc. no. 1, 54 Congress, 2 session, pp. 539-540, von Thielmann to Olney, May 13, 1896.
[78] Ibid., pp. 540-541, Olney to von Thielmann, May 23, 1896.

his duties were wholly judicial, and, consequently, far removed from issues that were purely political. The German government informed the United States that it thought the consuls were right, but the friction apparently was unavoidable and furnished "additional evidence that a many-headed administration of affairs in Samoa [was] in the long run untenable, and that it must lead to constant friction, even supposing the officials there to be guided by the most upright and conciliatory feelings."[79]

The course pursued by the president of the council, Schmidt, appeared dictatorial to the native government, so much so that King Malietoa sent a petition to Secretary Gresham, when Schmidt had held office only a year, requesting his removal. "The president," he wrote, "instead of confining himself to giving advice when requested to do so by the King, assumes the position of a dictator how distasteful, unwise or inexpedient it may be in the opinion of the Government." Further on in his petition he wrote: "Instead of endeavoring to increase the power and effectiveness of the King and Government his conduct has had the effect of diminishing its dignity and has inspired its subjects with contempt instead of respect."[80]

When Herr Schmidt had served three years as president of the council he, like Baron Senfft von Pilsach before him, was ready to surrender the office to some one else. The German government, again with the consent of the other two powers, nominated another German subject to take his place, namely, Dr. Raffel, but when the suggestion was made to Secretary Olney that since Herr Schmidt wanted to leave immediately after his three-year

[79] S. Ex. Doc. no. 97, 53 Congress, 3 session, pp. 459-463, Saurma to Gresham, Nov. 12, 1894, with two enclosures: "Chief Justice Ide to the Consuls," Aug. 24, and "The Consuls to Chief Justice Ide," Sept. 5, 1894.
[80] *Ibid.*, p. 473, King Malietoa to Gresham, Mulinuu, Apia, Dec. 31, 1894.

period of service had expired, that is, at the end of the year 1896, and that since several months would elapse before the arrival of his successor it would be desirable to turn the duties of the president of the council temporarily over to the consular board,[81] the secretary of state expressed disapproval, finding support for his action in the "unsatisfactory condition of affairs that arose in 1893 when the consular body, under instructions from the Governments concerned, relieved Baron Senfft von Pilsach." Both the British consul, Cusack-Smith, and the new United States consul, William Churchill, were opposed to the suggestion and were supported by their respective governments; but in declining to accede to Germany's wishes, Olney made it known that if Great Britain reversed her decision in the matter and adopted a common ground with Germany, a "deferential concurrence" of the United States government would be "feasible."[82] When, therefore, a few days later, Secretary Olney was informed by the German minister that for reasons of health it was imperative that Herr Schmidt be relieved immediately, and that the government of Great Britain had officially just communicated to the imperial government its consent thereto,[83] Olney promptly acquiesced in the arrangement and informed Baron von Thielmann that he had telegraphed "the consul general of the United States at Apia to act in harmony with his colleagues in performing the duties of the municipal presidency in the interim between Mr. Schmidt's departure and Dr. Raffel's arrival, which [he trusted would] be no longer delayed than [was] actually necessary."[84]

[81] H. Doc. no. 1, 55 Congress, 2 session, p. 449, von Thielmann to Olney, Dec. 18, 1896.
[82] *Ibid.*, pp. 449-450, Olney to von Thielmann, Dec. 21, 1896.
[83] *Ibid.*, p. 451, von Thielmann to Olney, Dec. 26, 1896.
[84] *Ibid.*, p. 451, Olney to von Thielmann, Dec. 28, 1896.

THE *CONDOMINIUM* 549

When soon after, Chief Justice Ide also desired to be relieved, the suggestion was made by the British government that the consular board or one of the consuls assume his duties until the arrival of the newly appointed chief justice, William Lea Chambers.[85] It became the duty of Olney's successor, John Sherman, to decide upon this point and we find him hewing close to the line of policy adopted by Olney in that the United States continued to object to any tendency to ignore the terms of the Berlin Act. In his reply to Pauncefote's note the new secretary of state pointed out that since under section 2 of article III only the president of the municipal council could act as chief justice during a vacancy, the government of the United States could "not assent to the suggestion of Her Majesty's consul, as expressed by Lord Salisbury, that the functions of the chief justice be temporarily confided to the consular body or a single member thereof." If such an obstacle had not confronted the powers, the suggestion would have been objectionable anyway, since, owing to the departure of Herr Schmidt and the non-arrival of Dr. Raffel, the consular board was still discharging the duties of the president of the municipal council,[86] and the government of Samoa as well as the municipality of Apia would thus have fallen back under consular control as completely as in the days before the Berlin Act, a situation that act was especially designed to prevent.

Mataafa and his chiefs were kept on the Marshall Islands for almost five years. When in the spring of 1898 the three consuls in Apia received notice of an uprising by certain chiefs, they decided on April 15 to recommend to the powers the pardon and release of Mataafa on the supposition that the return of that leader would be a source of strength to King Malietoa. In consequence of

[85] *Ibid.*, p. 454, Pauncefote to Sherman, March 9, 1897.
[86] *Ibid.*, pp. 454-455, Sherman to Pauncefote, March 15, 1897.

this recommendation, the British government made an inquiry whether the United States was disposed to concur in it on Mataafa's signing a protocol promising complete loyalty to King Malietoa.[87] Secretary Day promptly concurred in the recommendation, and informed both the British and German ambassadors that Consul General Osborn would "be instructed to coöperate with his colleagues in obtaining the signature of Mataafa to the protocol in question."[88] The German government also consented to the release of Mataafa on the stipulated terms,[89] whereupon the United States came forward with another proposal, namely, that Mataafa's chiefs also be released, provided they too signed a protocol of allegiance to the Samoan government.[90] This was also agreed to by the other two powers.

Meanwhile, the British government received information from its consul, E. Maxse, that Malietoa's health was precarious and that the question of the selection of his successor by the treaty powers might come up for consideration. Pauncefote was therefore instructed to inquire what view the United States government would take of the matter.[91] Secretary Day referred the British ambassador to the Berlin Act, which nowhere conferred authority "upon the treaty powers to appoint or agree upon a successor to King Malietoa." When the natives had duly elected a successor "according to the laws and customs of Samoa," as the act read, "the Government of the United States [would] be most willing to coöperate with the interested powers to recognize the natives'

[87] H. Doc. no. 1, 56 Congress, 1 session, pp. 604-605, Pauncefote to Day, June 14, 1898.
[88] *Ibid.*, p. 605, Day to Pauncefote, June 25, 1898. Note to von Holleben dated the same day contains the same information (see *ibid.*, pp. 605-606).
[89] *Ibid.*, p. 606, Sternberg to Day, July 7, 1898.
[90] *Ibid.*, p. 607, Day to von Holleben, July 7, 1898.
[91] *Ibid.*, p. 607, Pauncefote to Day, July 12, 1898.

THE *CONDOMINIUM* 551

choice and to do all that [lay] in its power to strengthen his hands for the preservation of peace and the maintenance of good government in the Samoan Islands.'"[92]

On September 1, Pauncefote wrote Secretary Day from New London, Connecticut, that word had been received of King Malietoa's death, and that the British government now desired to learn the views of the United States government relative to the desirability of delaying the return of Mataafa "until after the election of a new King."[93] A reply to this note was delayed on account of Secretary Day's going to Paris with the American commission to negotiate a treaty of peace with Spain, and on September 28, Pauncefote wrote another note recalling to the attention of the government the question of delaying Mataafa's return.[94] A long note from the new secretary of state, John Hay, was sent on October 5, wherein he expressed the willingness of the government to concur in the suggestion, "if it be not now too late," that Mataafa's return be delayed until after the election and installation of a new king. But he took the same position as had Secretary Day before him, that there should be no interference by the powers in the election of Malietoa's successor.[95]

As may be surmised, the tripartite control of the Samoan government was proving unsatisfactory to all parties concerned, and severe attacks for various reasons were launched against it in Germany and the British Empire, as well as in the United States.

The attitude of the British colonials of New Zealand and Australia was perhaps best expressed by Basil Thomson, an authority on South Pacific questions, when, in

[92] *Ibid.*, pp. 607-608, Day to Pauncefote, July 18, 1898.
[93] *Ibid.*, p. 609, Pauncefote to Day, Sept. 1, 1898.
[94] *Ibid.*, pp. 609-610, Pauncefote to Adee, Sept. 28, 1898.
[95] *Ibid.*, pp. 610-612, Hay to Pauncefote, Oct. 5, 1898.

describing the *condominium,* he called it a *modus vivendi,* and "one of the most fatuous schemes ever devised for governing a country." Continuing his criticism he wrote: "The natives were to be governed by a King whom the majority did not obey; the Whites by a German President of Municipality, who was also to act as adviser to a King that did not want his advice. The Consuls were to sit still and watch; and over all was set a Swedish Chief-Justice, to intervene in the disputes that were certain to ensue. On these disputes it is not necessary to enlarge here. Those who have not read the 'Footnote to History'[96] need only imagine the natural results of such a situation to get a fair idea of what actually happened.'"[97]

A more judicious estimate of the *condominium* was expressed by Henry C. Ide, first, American member of the Samoan land commission and, later, chief justice of Samoa. Writing a few months before the partition treaty was signed he said in part: "The weak point of the treaty [*condominium*] has always been its complicated character, a wheel within a wheel, a native government theoretically autonomous, a President to advise it, and try to control it, a Chief Justice to recommend legislation to the native government and to be the final legislator in the municipality of Apia, as well as a Court of last resort, and three Consuls with ill-defined boundaries of power. Thus instead of one King there were six. With such a subdivision of authority it has been extremely difficult to locate responsibility and for anyone to secure efficient and progressive action without finding some fatal clog or brake in another part of the machine. Then, too, the utmost tact and discretion and due respect to national prejudices and customs of others are requisite to any degree

[96] Reference to Robert Louis Stevenson's book.
[97] Basil Thomson, "The Samoan Agreement in plain English," in *Blackwood's Magazine,* December, 1899.

of success. A single act of impatience or disregard of the rights or dignity of another official, or contempt of native form and politeness, may create conditions destructive of all usefulness on the part of an official. Any act of injustice or oppression is sure to be quickly resented.

"In spite of drawbacks, fighting, difficulties and embarrassments, the Berlin Treaty can justly claim not to have satisfied the sanguine hopes of its distinguished authors, but yet to have given a better government to Samoa than ever existed there before, to have made Apia as well governed a Municipality as is often found, to have created more miles of good roads than had been there made in all time before, to have effectually prevented the sale of destructive intoxicating liquors to natives, to have settled finally all land titles and established an efficient system of registration, to have created a government that paid its own bills, to have secured equal rights, in all respects, to residents of all nationalities, to have established an international court of last resort that has earned the respect of all, and, what is more important than all else, to have established a rule of law to govern all the high contracting parties in their relations to Samoa. Before the treaty constant friction arose, but there was nothing to define the rights of either nation, and the troubles in Samoa were a constant menace to the peace of nations. The difference, internationally, is that between a new mining camp in the Klondike, where every man is his own judge, and the same community when organized under known written law."[98]

The main theme of the strictures in the United States against the *condominium* was that it was an "entangling alliance," and a reversal of our traditional policy. Although Secretary Blaine, in authorizing the delegates at Berlin to sign the general act, had in the main followed

[98] Henry C. Ide, "Samoa," in *The Independent*, Feb. 2, 1899.

closely in the footsteps of his predecessor, Thomas F. Bayard, secretary of state during Cleveland's first administration, the arrangement turned out to be unworkable, just as the German representative at the Washington Conference had foretold when opposing the American plan. President Cleveland in his second administration, did not hesitate to state his adverse opinion of the *condominium* in at least three of his four annual messages to Congress. In this position he found sympathetic support in the critical attitude of Secretary Gresham, who in concluding a long report to the president on the Samoan problem said: "Soberly surveying the history of our relations with Samoa, we well may inquire what we have gained by our departure from an established policy beyond the expenses, the responsibility and the entanglements that have so far been its only fruits. One of the greatest difficulties in dealing with matters that lie at a distance is the fact that the imagination is no longer restrained by the contemplation of objects in their real proportions. Our experience in the case of Samoa serves to show that for our usual exemption from the consequences of this infirmity, we are indebted to the wise policy that had previously preserved us from such engagements as those embodied in the general Act of Berlin, which, besides involving us in an entangling alliance, has utterly failed to correct, if indeed it has not aggravated, the very evils which it was designed to prevent.'"[99]

In submitting more information on the Samoan question Secretary Gresham on July 3, 1894, wrote the president: "The undersigned finds in these additional papers abundant confirmation of the views heretofore expressed by him touching the unsatisfactory character of the en-

[99] F.R. 1894, App. I, p. 513; S. Ex. Doc. no. 93, p. 10, Gresham to the President, May 9, 1894.

THE *CONDOMINIUM* 555

tanglements in which the United States have become involved by reason of their participation in the General Act of Berlin and the inadequacy of the engagements so made to remedy the evils it was sought to meet."[100]

The Mataafa incident in the earlier years of the *condominium* and the action that the United States was forced to take with reference thereto prompted President Cleveland, in his first annual message to Congress in December, 1893, to refer to the Samoan problem in part as follows: "Led by a desire to compose differences and contribute to the restoration of order in Samoa, which for some years previous had been the scene of conflicting foreign pretentions and native strife, the United States, departing from its policy consecrated by a century of observance, entered four years ago into the treaty of Berlin, thereby becoming jointly bound with England and Germany to establish and maintain Malietoa Laupepa as King of Samoa." In referring to the ordering of the U.S.S. *Philadelphia* to Samoa to assist in putting down Mataafa's rebellion, and the subsequent arrest of Mataafa and ten of his chiefs, the president continued: "This incident and the events leading up to it signally illustrate the impolicy of entangling alliances with foreign powers."[101]

In his second annual message to Congress President Cleveland expressed his conviction that the present arrangement concerning the government of Samoa would never succeed. He furthermore invited an expression of the opinion of Congress on the propriety of steps being taken by the United States government looking to the withdrawal from its engagements with the other powers

---

[100] S. Ex. Doc. no. 132, 53 Congress, 2 session, p. 1, Gresham to President Cleveland, July 3, 1894.

[101] Richardson, *A Compilation of the Messages and Papers of the Presidents*, etc., IX, 439.

on some reasonable terms not prejudicial to any of its existing rights.[102]

In his third annual message President Cleveland returned to the attack on the Samoan *condominium*, and, referring to his former statements, wished to emphasize the opinion he had "at all times entertained", that the position of the United States "was inconsistent with the mission and traditions of our Government, in violation of the principles we profess and in all its phases mischievous and vexatious." He again pressed this subject upon the attention of the Congress, and asked for such legislative action or expression as would "lead the way to our relief from obligations both irksome and unnatural."[103]

However, no action was taken by Cleveland, as there was little or no response to his call even in his own party. Moreover, the only alternative to a continuation of the *condominium* would have been a treaty for the partition of the islands. The president was in no mood to surrender the treaty rights secured from Samoa back in 1878 with especial reference to Pago Pago harbor in Tutuila, and at the same time he was just as anxious that the independence of the Samoans be maintained under the protection of the three powers as he was that the Hawaiians should remain independent under the protection of the United States. And there was no third solution of the muddle, for it would have been like jumping from the frying pan into the fire to permit Samoa to return to the status which obtained before the General Act of 1889. Anarchy would have soon resulted, and Germany would have intervened to protect her economic interests and probably would have annexed forthwith the whole group.

Therefore, when McKinley succeeded to the presidency the "entangling alliance" was still in force, and when he

[102] Richardson, *op. cit.*, IX, 477.   [103] *Ibid.*, p. 635.

THE *CONDOMINIUM* 557

announced that there would be no withdrawal from Samoa, he had the country back of him. Moreover, the Republican administration, the foreign policy of which found expression in the annexation of Hawaii, the Philippines, Guam, and Porto Rico in 1898, also had no compunctions about grasping, if necessary, the only practicable alternative to the dissolution of the *condominium*, and therefore supported the Samoan partition treaty of 1899.

CHAPTER XV

THE PARTITION OF SAMOA, 1899

THE partition of the Samoan islands was due partly to renewed troubles in Samoa itself and partly to complications among the European powers. Following the Spanish-American war, Germany, bent upon securing the Caroline Islands as well as other parts of the tottering colonial empire of Spain which had not been appropriated by the United States, felt the time also opportune for her reaching a final solution of the Samoan problem. She thought that the United States could easily be won over to her scheme of partition if we secured Tutuila with Pago Pago harbor. How to come to an agreement with Great Britain was another matter, for even though the British Foreign Office might be willing to surrender its position in Samoa in return for compensations elsewhere, there was always to be considered the prejudice in New Zealand and Australia against any increase of German power in the South Pacific. However, the "Fashoda Incident," with the possibility of Germany coming to an understanding with France against Great Britain, the kaiser's recent visit to the Turkish sultan, and the fast developing crisis in South Africa afforded Germany opportunities of fishing in troubled waters, and these opportunities she did not neglect.

Germany's first move with reference to Samoa came as a result of the sudden death of Malietoa Laupepa (August 22, 1898), king of Samoa under the protection of the three powers since the *condominium* went into effect

THE PARTITION OF SAMOA, 1899 559

in 1890. The report in Berlin, moreover, that the United States contemplated improving its coaling station in Pago Pago harbor furnished added impetus to Germany's desire to bring the Samoan problem to a head. But she must have an understanding with Great Britain first. The United States could be approached later. Accordingly on August 31 (only nine days after the death of Malietoa Laupepa), the German secretary of state for foreign affairs, von Bülow, instructed by telegraph the German ambassador in London, Count von Hatzfeldt, to "sound Mr. Balfour in confidence to learn if England would make a joint proposal with [Germany] in Washington" with a view to partitioning the islands between the United States and Germany, the former power to have the island of Tutuila with the harbor of Pago Pago and the Manua group and Germany the remaining islands, Upolu, Savaii, and a few smaller islands, while England might find her compensation in the annexation of the Tonga Islands to the southward of Samoa.[1] Although von Hatzfeldt answered von Bülow promptly that he would see Balfour, he had small hope that the latter would agree to any plan of division. Furthermore, the report that the Americans intended to improve Pago Pago harbor did not alarm the British, wrote Hatzfeldt, for the Australians, upon whose feelings in the matter the British policy would largely be based, showed little or no objections at this time "in having Americans as neighbors in Samoa, whereas a foothold on [Germany's] part would meet with decided opposition."[2] When von Hatzfeldt's forecast proved correct, von Bülow made another suggestion which, when brought to Balfour's attention at a second conference by von Hatzfeldt, seemed to interest

[1] *Die Grosse Politik*, vol. 14, part 2, serial no. 4028.
[2] *Ibid.*, serial no. 4029.

the British minister very much, namely, that the boundary lines between certain British and German territories in Africa might be rectified and that Germany would surrender her right to extraterritoriality in Zanzibar in return for British concessions in Samoa. Hatzfeldt stated, moreover, to Balfour, his opinion that no difficulty need be experienced with the United States in regard to the partition, if Great Britain and Germany would jointly sound Washington, especially since they could offer to the United States the whole island of Tutuila with its harbor of Pago Pago, whereas now the United States had only the right to establish a coaling station there. These negotiations came to an abrupt end, however, on September 8, when von Hatzfeldt informed von Bülow that the prime minister, Lord Salisbury, telegraphing from his retreat in the Vosges mountains, had expressed his unwillingness to continue the conversations, giving as his excuse that Australia would resent any change in the *status quo.*

On September 19, Mataafa, the old pretender to the Samoan kingship, returned with other exiled chieftains to Samoa. Having been given permission to leave his place of exile, the Marshall Islands, in July, his return, of course, had not been intentionally fixed to occur at the time when the kingship should become vacant. Nor did Mataafa take any overt steps to claim the throne. However, on November 12, a group of Samoan chieftains announced to the consuls and to the chief justice of Samoa that Mataafa had been duly elected king. On November 14, an opposing faction declared that Malietoa Tanu, son of the deceased king, had been chosen by them. Both parties then appealed to Chief Justice Chambers, who under the General Act of 1889, had the power to settle the dispute. The investigation was opened on December 19

THE PARTITION OF SAMOA, 1899

and on December 31 Judge Chambers ruled in favor of Malietoa Tanu. Thereupon civil war broke out, and the chief justice, as well as Malietoa Tanu, sought safety on board the British warship, *Porpoise*. On January 4, the three foreign consuls, Rose, Osborn, and Maxse, recognized a provisional government controlled by the Mataafa party, with Dr. Raffel, the German president of the municipal council, acting as executive officer. When Chief Justice Chambers later refused to recognize the provisional government, Dr. Raffel closed the supreme court, whereupon the British consul, Maxse, intervened, declaring Raffel's action contrary to the General Act of 1889. Then the chief justice, in agreement with Maxse and the American consul, Osborn, and supported by the British naval commander, Captain Sturdee of the *Porpoise*, reopened the court by force on January 7.

When the news of these events reached the United States, Admiral Kautz was ordered to proceed to Samoa in command of the *Philadelphia*. The British government also ordered the warship, *Royalist*, to join the *Porpoise*. Arriving in Apia harbor on March 6, the admiral, five days later, declared the provisional government deposed. American and British marines were landed on March 13, and on March 15 the American and British naval vessels bombarded Apia, their gun-fire damaging the German consulate as well as destroying some native houses. Although Malietoa Tanu was crowned king on March 23 under the protection of foreign guns, the civil war continued, Mataafa defeating his opponents again on April 1. The fighting progressed throughout the month of April, the American and British warships participating at times against the forces of Mataafa, although the three powers had already agreed to send a joint commission to settle the question on the spot. The difficulty of speedily communicating with the distant islands made it impossible to bring about an immediate truce after the decision of the powers was reached.[3]

The proposal to send a joint commission to Samoa was first made by Germany.[4] This proposal was promptly acceded to by the United States during the first part of April, and after a short delay, Great Britain likewise agreed to send a commissioner.[5] As a matter of fact, the German government was so pleased with President McKinley's willingness to assist in the solution of the Samoan problem that the German emperor summoned Mr. White, the American ambassador, on April 6, and in a

[3] This situation was a repetition of the circumstances which obtained ten years earlier in March, 1889. It will be recalled that at that time, although the three powers were making plans for a settlement of the Samoan question at Berlin, the naval vessels representing these powers were on the verge of a serious clash.

[4] There was much suspicion in German naval circles of the true intentions of Great Britain and the United States at this time, and von Bülow's conciliatory efforts seemed to them as futile. In the *Memoirs of Prince von Bülow*, a reference is made to this attitude. "I still remember an incident, small but significant," writes von Bülow "in the Reichstag debate of April 14, 1899, a debate which took place amid some excitement not only in the house but in many quarters in the country. Tirpitz was sitting next to me, and while the opener was proceeding with his interpellation the Admiral said to me *sotto voce:* 'You really can do no good by speaking. It is clear that the action of the British and Americans points to the determination to go to war with us, in order to destroy us before our fleet has been hatched out of its shell. Otherwise one would have to assume that both John Bull and Jonathan had gone mad.'" (See I, 331.)

[5] White wrote Hay on April 4 from Berlin as follows: "Baron von Richthofen, as Acting Minister of Foreign Affairs, called on me yesterday to express the satisfaction of the German Government at the President's willingness to accept the proposal to send high commissioners to settle matters in Samoa. He also informed me that there had been some difficulty with the British Government, probably due to unwillingness in London to take definite action in the absence of Lord Salisbury, but thought that these difficulties had been mainly cleared away though sundry minor points were still in doubt." (See Despatches, Germany, vol. 69, no. 813.)

THE PARTITION OF SAMOA, 1899

long interview with him expressed his personal pleasure at the new turn of events.⁶

The complete agreement of the three powers to send the commission to Samoa was based on a memorandum contained in identical telegrams despatched by Lord Salisbury to the British ambassadors in Washington and Berlin. Sir Julian Pauncefote handed the same to the secretary of state on April 13. It read as follows: "In view of the troubles which have recently taken place in Samoa, and for the purpose of restoring tranquillity and order therein, the three parties to the Conference of Berlin have appointed a commission to undertake the Provisional government of the islands. For this purpose they shall exercise authority in the islands. Every other person or persons exercising authority therein, whether acting under the provisions of the final act of Berlin or otherwise shall obey their orders, and the three Powers will instruct their consuls and naval officers to render similar obedience. No action taken by the Commissioners in pursuance of the above authority shall be valid unless it is assented to by all three commissioners. It will fall within the attribute of the Commissioners to 'consider the provisions which they may think necessary for the future government of the islands, or for the modification of the final act of Berlin, and to report to their Governments the conclusions to which they may come.' "⁷

---

⁶ Telegram received in cipher from Berlin, April 6, 1899: "Was summoned today by German Emperor and had a long interview. He asked me to tender the President his personal thanks for the kind terms of his cable despatch after the Samoa troubles, and for his friendly attitude towards heralded proposal to send Commissioners. He said that Great Britain, which has shown much reluctance to join in any practical arrangement, is now showing more willingness to do so; and that, what the Commissioners first of all need to do is to restore peace, and then make such amendments to the treaty as they find desirable." (See Despatches, Germany, vol. 69.)

⁷ *Foreign Relations, 1899*, p. 614.

The day following the receipt of the quoted memorandum Secretary Hay instructed Ambassador Choate "to inform Salisbury by formal note of acceptance by the United States of the joint agreement in the words [of] Lord Salisbury's telegram."[8] On the fifteenth Choate informed Hay that his instructions had been carried out.[9]

No time was lost in selecting commissioners. Mr. Bartlett Tripp was chosen to represent the United States. The British government chose Mr. C. N. E. Eliot, second secretary of the British embassy in Washington, as its representative. The German choice fell upon Freiherr Speck von Sternberg, counselor of the German legation in Washington. The commission sailed on the U.S.S. *Badger* from San Francisco, arriving in Apia on May 13.

The first task of the commissioners was to establish their authority as the provisional government. This was easily carried out, whereupon they proceeded to disarm both of the warring parties, the followers of Mataafa and those of Malietoa Tanu. After due investigation the three commissioners speedily reached a unanimous decision that Chief Justice Chambers' decree in favor of Tanu's claim to the kingship was valid under the Berlin Act, but the German representative, although he admitted that the decree was binding, felt unable to allow Tanu to assume the kingship. As all the commissioners were agreed that the kingship ought eventually to be abolished anyway, a compromise was reached whereby Tanu's abdication was secured. A proclamation was then issued on June 10, "signed by the three Commissioners stating that Chief Justice Chambers' decision was valid and binding, that Tanu had resigned the office of king and that the office was abolished."[10]

[8] *Foreign Relations, 1899*, p. 614.   [9] *Ibid.*
[10] *Correspondence respecting the Affairs of Samoa*, Eliot to Salisbury, Apia, July 26, 1899.

THE PARTITION OF SAMOA, 1899   565

The most significant statement made by Commissioner Tripp in his final report to the Department of State was that he doubted if the Samoan problem could ever be satisfactorily solved under the tripartite control of the powers.[11] This view of course coincided with those of the German and English representatives, and already in August we find Germany reviving the partition project, when the German special envoy in Washington, Herr von Mumm, in confidence, suggested such a procedure to John Hay, the secretary of state.[12] This proposal was formally

[11] Tripp to Hay, Aug. 7, 1899. Manuscript is in vol. 4, Special Agents; see also *Foreign Relations, 1899*, pp. 648-663, and Senate Miscellaneous Documents, vol. 6, no. 51, 56 Congress, 1 session. There are 28 enclosures with the manuscript. These are listed in Senate Misc. Doc. no. 51, but not in *Foreign Relations, 1899*.

[12] The following portion of a memorandum gives a full account of the interview between von Mumm and Secretary Hay which occurred in Washington on August 31, 1899: ''Mr. von Mumm, the German Minister, called this morning and read to me in confidence a telegram which he had received from Baron von Bülow, in regard to Samoa. Von Bülow expressed his gratification at the temporary lull in the troubles at Samoa, and his pleasure at the frank and magnanimous attitude of the Government of the United States in these matters, but he could not conceal his anxiety in regard to the future of the group. He thought that the measures which had been adopted, although probably the best that could have been attained, were only a palliative, and that the Act of Berlin was not to be considered permanently available for the peace and good order of the Samoan islands. He, therefore, renewed in a more formal manner, the suggestion which has been made verbally by Dr. von Holleben here and by the German Foreign Office to Ambassador White, of a partition of the group, the United States to retain the island of Tutuila, and Germany and England to divide Upolu and Savaii between them.

''I said to him that in the absence of the President and my colleagues in the Cabinet, it would be impossible for me to give him any intimation of the spirit in which this proposition would be received; that he was right in taking it for granted that we should be glad of some permanent settlement which would insure the peace and order of the Samoan islands to the satisfaction and with the assent of all the three powers, and when he asked my personal views in regard to it, I declined to give any indication of them until I could consult with the President and some of my colleagues.

''I asked him whether the Government of England had been approached in regard to this proposition. He said he had no information in regard to

presented in writing on September 20 when von Bohlen handed to Dr. Hill an aide-memoire of his oral communication of the same date in behalf of von Mumm.[13] In the meantime, Secretary Hay on September 5 had communicated with Bartlett Tripp, asking his advice, and the American commissioner immediately replied by telegraph that he strongly favored the plan of dividing the islands.[14] In a letter to Hay he gave further expression to his opinion as follows: "The joint report of the Commission expresses very emphatically the doubt of any permanent Government under a tripartite form, and in my individual report I went as far as I deemed it proper to advise the earliest possible withdrawal from the unprecedented alliance. My individual view is even stronger than finds expression in either report and I see at present no other solution of the problem than by a division of the islands."[15]

It was of course necessary for Hay to ascertain the British attitude and accordingly on September 7, he sent the following telegram to Ambassador Choate: "German Government strongly urges partition of Samoan Islands, the United States to retain Tutuila and adjacent islets, and England and Germany to divide the rest. The President is disposed to regard this proposition favorably if details can be satisfactorily arranged with due regard to the national interests and to the welfare of the inhabit-

that, but his personal impression was that the Government of Germany preferred first to get the view of the Government of the United States before submitting the scheme to the British Government, and thought it would stand a far better chance of being accepted by England if the American and German Governments were united in recommending it." (See Numerical File, vol. 547, 1906-1910, Department of State.)

[13] Notes, Germany, vol. 28, Department of State.

[14] Special Agents, vol. 4, Department of State. This advice had also been given to Hay almost a year before by John Bassett Moore, as he relates in his introduction to this book.

[15] *Ibid.*

ants. Ascertain discreetly the views of Her Majesty's Secretary of State for Foreign Affairs."[16]

In an interview with Lord Salisbury on the 22nd Choate endeavored to ascertain his views on the proposition of the German government as stated in Hay's inquiry. At this time Germany was anxious to have the United States press the British government to consent to the proposal, and the German ambassador had called on Choate on the 6th with this end in view. Lord Salisbury expressed his willingness to accede to the proposal with the understanding that the United States should get the island of Tutuila, whereas the remaining islands were to be allotted to Great Britain and Germany by an arbitrator.[17]

On September 27, our ambassador in Berlin, Mr. White, was informed that the Department of State had been advised by both the British and German ambassadors that an understanding had been "reached by their Gov-

[16] *Foreign Relations, 1899*, pp. 663-664.

[17] *Ibid.*, p. 664. The despatch from Choate to. Hay dated London, September 22, 1899, follows in part: "Lord Salisbury had no hesitation in saying that the present mode of governing the Samoan Islands could not succeed, and that he was inclined to favor the partition as the only means of securing good government there, if the details could be satisfactorily arranged, and that he was perfectly willing to give me the present state of the negotiation with Germany, which is that, assuming that the United States would be entirely satisfied with Tutuila, they had got so far as to agree that the terms on which they should divide the rest should be arranged by some sort of arbitration; that the King of Sweden should be the arbitrator; but that upon what rules and principles the arbitration should proceed they had not yet been able to agree. He said further that the fundamental difficulty was that there were three parties to divide and really only two islands to be divided; that after setting apart Tutuila for us the only other island of any value is that in which Apia is situated. Of course they consider that the United States is to be in no way a party to or concerned in the proposed arbitration. The main result so far is that both Germany and Great Britain seemed to be convinced that it is impracticable to continue to govern the islands by the present tripartite method—as he said the late Commission reported would probably be the case—and the welfare of the islands required a change."

ernments to refer to the arbitration of the king of Sweden and Norway the pending question of indemnity for alleged losses suffered in Samoa in consequence of unwarranted military action," and that the United States upon the request of these governments had "accepted in principle the proposed settlement of the question."[18] The question of indemnity had been raised by Germany due to losses sustained by her subjects in Samoa during the American and British bombardment on March 16, 1899, of Mataafa forces in and around Apia. The negotiations between the three powers for a convention relative to the arbitration of the claims of Germans and others were delayed during the month of October, but when the treaty of partition was assured, a claims treaty was signed in Washington on November 7. The ratifications of this convention were exchanged March 7, 1900.[19] By this act Oscar II, king of Sweden and Norway, was requested to arbitrate between Germany on the one side and the United States and Great Britain on the other. King Oscar accepted the trust and rendered his decision on October 14, 1902, wherein the governments of the United States and Great Britain were adjudged responsible for the losses caused by the military action of their naval vessels.[20] These governments then made an agreement whereby each would pay one-half of the sums that should be found due to the subjects of other governments.[21]

The original understanding between Germany and Great Britain to submit to the king of Sweden and Norway the arbitration of the question of the division of the Samoan group west of Tutuila was eventually abandoned,

---

[18] Instructions, Germany, vol. 21, Hill to White, Sept. 27, 1899.

[19] Malloy, *Treaties*, etc., II, 1589.   [20] *Ibid.*, p. 1591.

[21] For a full account of the Claims question see an article by Walter Scott Penfield entitled, "The Settlement of the Samoan Cases," in *The American Journal of International Law*, VII, 767-773.

due to Great Britain's unwillingness to accept the island of Savaii should the island of Upolu be allotted to Germany. The negotiations for the partition of Samoa moved slowly, therefore, and in October there was a strong opinion current in Germany favoring Germany's selling out entirely her interests, principally on the island of Upolu, to Great Britain. In fact on October 24, Ambassador White informed Hay that at a recent meeting of the colonial council, the members by a majority vote had expressed themselves in favor of such a course. But Count von Bülow had taken the opposite ground in stating to the council, according to White, "that whatever might be the pecuniary considerations, there were still stronger considerations of a sentimental sort, that the German people at large had come to think that honor required them to retain their interest in Samoa, and that he was therefore opposed to any such disposal of German rights as the Council had favored."[22] White, further on in his despatch, reiterated that in a conversation with Count von Bülow a few days before, the German secretary of state for foreign affairs had "dwelt on the sentimental side of the question; on the fact that the occupation in Samoa was at the beginning of German Colonial history; that the events which had occurred since had increased national feeling in favor of its retention; and that he was himself anxious to bring about some arrangement by which the United States should retain the Island of Tutuila with the harbor of Pago-Pago, and that Germany and Great Britain should make an arrangement regarding the remaining Islands."[23]

On October 25, Choate informed Hay that when on that day he had inquired of the British secretary of state for foreign affairs what "the present status of the negotia-

[22] Despatches, Germany, vol. 70, no. 1054.
[23] *Ibid.*

tions between Great Britain and Germany with regard to Samoan affairs was," the secretary had "replied that they [meaning Great Britain and Germany] had not come to an understanding, but that they might yet do so." Choate then told him what his understanding of the situation was, so far as the United States was concerned, namely that they (Great Britain and Germany) "were trying to see whether they could agree on the terms of division of the two remaining islands, assuming that we should be content with the one island on which we now have a coaling station; and that, if they found they could, he would open the whole matter to us of the proposed partition, so that the whole subject of the interests of the inhabitants, as well as the international relations, should be considered. He said *that* was his understanding, and that as soon as they came to any point—or, as he expressed it, 'as soon as he heard anything,' he would notify me. He said that they both [Great Britain and Germany] regarded 'our island', as he termed it, as the best of the three; and, assuming that we should be content with that, they did not suppose we should feel much interest in the settlement of the remaining questions between them. I told him that we feel a great interest in properly protecting the rights and interests of the natives, which of course would have to be provided for in any agreement."[24]

In the beginning of the month of November Hay exhibited some impatience with respect to the delay in coming to terms on the part of Great Britain and Germany, and on the 3rd of the month he cabled Choate: "If there is any doubt of the American attitude as to partition of Samoa, you may say to Lord Salisbury that we are favorable to it, provided that satisfactory terms can be made,

[24] Despatches, Great Britain, vol. 198, no. 188.

THE PARTITION OF SAMOA, 1899 571

and that we shall be content with that portion of the islands east of the one hundred and seventy-first meridian."[25] The next day Hay informed Choate (evidently in response to an inquiry from the latter) that the United States government had "no objection to England and Germany coming to a preliminary agreement about Samoan Islands west of the one hundred and seventy-first meridian, subject, of course, to concurrence of the United States."[26]

The Samoan problem now proceeded rapidly toward a solution. November 9, John B. Jackson, chargé d'affaires at Berlin, informed Hay that von Bülow the same day had told him of an agreement reached between Germany and Great Britain in regard to Samoa the day before in London, and that the whole agreement would be cabled to von Mumm, the German ambassador in Washington, for communication to Hay "as soon as the text was received from London." Von Bülow "expressed hopes," added Jackson, "that the agreement would meet with the satisfaction of the United States Government, and mentioned the fact that in accordance with the agreement not only the Island of Tutuila would become the property of the United States, but also the smaller islands, Rose and Manua."[27]

The actual signing of the agreement did not take place, however, until November 14. The agreement left Germany in possession of all the Samoan group with the exception of the islands allotted to the United States. In surrendering all her rights in Samoa, Great Britain obtained extensive compensations from Germany elsewhere. These embraced the transfer of all of the German rights in the Tonga group including that of establishing a naval

[25] *Foreign Relations, 1899*, pp. 664-665.
[26] *Ibid.*, p. 665.
[27] Despatches, Germany, vol. 70, no. 1070.

station and coaling station, and the right of extraterritoriality; the shifting of the line of demarcation between German and British islands in the Solomon group so as to give to Great Britain all the German islands to the east and southeast of the island of Bougainville; the division of the so-called neutral zone in West Africa by a definite boundary line between British and German possessions; the promise of Germany "to take into consideration, as much and as far as possible, the wishes which the Government of Great Britain may express with regard to the development of the reciprocal tariffs in the territories of Togo and of the gold coast"; the renouncing by Germany of her rights of extraterritoriality in Zanzibar, which renunciation, however, was not effectively to "come into force till such time as the rights of extraterritoriality enjoyed there by other nations shall be abolished." A copy of the treaty between Germany and Great Britain was transmitted to Hay by Pauncefote on November 27.[28] It only remained for the powers to negotiate a tripartite convention in order to secure the approval of the United States to the whole agreement.[29]

Now it happened, however, that the United States had a treaty of amity, commerce, and navigation with the king of Tonga, negotiated by George H. Bates in 1886, which gave "the United States the right of acquiring by lease ground in any harbour of the Tonga Islands which may be mutually agreed upon for the purpose of establishing

[28] *Foreign Relations, 1899*, pp. 665-666.

[29] When the negotiations of the treaty of partition had been completed, the news was hailed with considerable pleasure by those Germans interested in colonial expansion. The Prince of Wied, president of the German colonial council, telegraphed von Bülow as follows: "In its great pleasure at the good news of the happy acquisition of the two Samoan islands, Upolo and Savaii, the Colonial Council assembled here to-day feels it must offer you, as the well-tried director of the Empire's Foreign policy, its warmest congratulations on this splendid achievement in colonial policy, which is at the same

a permanent coaling and repair station" and which also gave "the Consuls and Consular Representatives of the United States certain constitutional rights, etc. in the Islands." On the same day that Pauncefote transmitted to Hay the British-German treaty, he also in another note suggested that in view of Great Britain's giving up her rights and claims in Tutuila, the United States might "agree to terminate Art. 6 of the United States treaty with Tonga as part of the general arrangement."[30]

To Lord Pauncefote's note Hay replied two days later: "Your Excellency is no doubt aware that the negotiations between Great Britain and Germany in regard to mutual compensations in the arrangement of the partition of Samoa were conducted without the participation of the United States, and that the abstention of this Government from those negotiations was based on the understanding that no interests of the United States would be involved in them. In the preliminary conversations which preceded the drafting of the tripartite Convention now under discussion, there never has been any suggestion of the renunciation by the United States of any rights they might have outside the Samoan group of islands. For these and other reasons, which I have had the honour to communicate to Your Excellency, it is thought by this Government inexpedient to introduce at this late day a clause such as is contemplated in Your Excellency's note of the 27th of November."[31]

---

time a genuinely popular one. Will Your Excellency permit the Colonial Council, in view of the great difficulties which German diplomacy had to overcome in securing the acquisition of the Samoa Islands, once more to assure you of the full and entire confidence in Your Excellency of all the colonial interests of the country. (Quoted in *Memoirs of Prince von Bülow*, I, 332.)

[30] Notes from British Legation, vol. 132, Pauncefote to Hay, Nov. 27, 1899.

[31] Notes to British Legation, vol. 25, Hay to Pauncefote, Nov. 29, 1899.

The tripartite convention was signed at Washington on December 2, 1899 by Hay, Holleben, and Pauncefote, and the ratifications were exchanged February 16, 1900.[32] Germany declared a protectorate over the Samoan islands west of 171° W. on February 17, 1900, and continued to hold Western Samoa until an expeditionary force from New Zealand seized the colony at the outbreak of the Great War.[33] Western Samoa was allotted to New Zealand as a mandate under the Treaty of Versailles.[34]

[32] *Foreign Relations, 1899*, pp. 667-669.

[33] Dr. Solf was administrator of Western Samoa for ten years, from which post he was promoted to that of Minister of Colonial Affairs, in the German imperial cabinet.

[34] A recent book by N. A. Rowe entitled *Samoa Under the Sailing Gods* gives a rather critical account of the administration of Western Samoa under the New Zealand mandate.

CHAPTER XVI

AMERICAN SAMOA

ALTHOUGH in writing this book the author has been mainly concerned with tracing the foreign policy of the United States in relation to Samoa, a word in conclusion about American Samoa may perhaps well serve as an epilogue.

On December 6, 1899, Commander Benjamin F. Tilley, captain of the U.S.S. *Abarenda,* who had been in Samoan waters since August for the purpose of directing the construction of a naval wharf at Pago Pago, communicated with High Chief Mauga at Pago Pago, announcing the partition of the Samoan islands and requesting him to advise the district chiefs to continue to maintain order.[1] On February 19, 1900, three days after the partition treaty had been proclaimed by McKinley, an executive order was signed by the president reading as follows:

"The island of Tutuila, of the Samoan group, and all other islands of the group east of longitude 171° West of Greenwich, are hereby placed under the control of the Department of the Navy for a naval station.

"The Secretary of the Navy shall take such steps as are necessary to establish the authority of the United States and to give to the islands the necessary protection."

---

[1] *American Samoa—A General Report by the Governor.* Transmitted to the Secretary of the Navy by H. F. Bryan, Governor of American Samoa, and Commandant Naval Station, Tutuila, Oct. 1, 1926, p. 45; see also H. Doc. no. 3, 56 Congress, 2 session, annual reports of the Navy Department for the year 1900.

The secretary of the navy on the same day issued an order as follows:

"The island of Tutuila of the Samoan group, and all other islands of the group east of longitude 171° West of Greenwich, are hereby established into a naval station, to be known as the naval station, Tutuila, and to be under the command of a Commandant."[2]

Commander Tilley, having been assigned to the command of the naval station, decided to hoist the United States flag at Pago Pago on April 17. On the same day the high chiefs of Tutuila ceded the islands of Tutuila and Anuu to the government of the United States. Although the official flag-hoisting for all of American Samoa had already taken place at Pago Pago, Commander Tilley, to gratify local sentiment, raised the flag in the Manua group on June 5 and at Leone at the western end of the island of Tutuila on June 21. On July 10, to make a good job of the flag-hoisting business, Commander Tilley visited Rose Island, an uninhabited coral atoll, about eighty miles to the eastward of Manua, and raised a flag there also, leaving it to fly until torn to tatters by hurricane winds.[3]

The actual cession of the Manua islands of Tau, Olosega, and Ofu, did not take place until July 14, 1904. The chiefs of these islands, although they had previously accepted the sovereignty of the United States, until that date had stubbornly refused to give a deed of cession for fear that by so doing they would lose their lands. The only action taken by the United States at the time was an acknowledgment by President Roosevelt of the receipt of the deed of cession and an expression of gratification in receiving such a token of the friendship and confidence of the chiefs and people of the islands.[4] As a matter of

[2] *American Samoa—A General Report by the Governor*, p. 46.
[3] *Ibid.*, pp. 46 and 48.   [4] *Ibid.*, pp. 49-50.

fact, no action was taken by Congress relative to the two cessions of 1900 and 1904 until 1929, and although in 1903 full information was furnished Congress concerning the islands, no act at that time was passed defining the political status of the inhabitants of American Samoa. In 1926 Senator Lenroot introduced a bill in the Senate providing for the acceptance of the cessions and the establishment of a civil government, but Congress adjourned without taking action. There have been, of course, certain acts by Congress on specific subjects, and also decisions by several departments of the United States government, which have to some extent affected the political status of the islands. So, for example, American Samoa is a domestic, not a foreign territory. On the other hand, Samoans, while they owe allegiance to the flag, are not citizens of the United States. Vessels owned by Samoans are entitled to fly the flag of the United States, but are not admitted to American registry. According to an opinion of the attorney general, "Neither the Constitution nor the laws of the United States have been extended to [the Samoans] and the only administrative authority existing in them is that derived mediately or immediately from the President as Commander in Chief of the Army and Navy of the United States."[5]

Since President McKinley turned the islands over to the Navy Department to administer, there have been nineteen naval governors of American Samoa. A codification of the "Regulations and Orders for the Government of American Samoa" was made in 1921. Since then there have been some amendments.[6] The administration of these so-called laws has devolved on American naval officers except those which are enforced by the secretary

[5] *Ibid.*, p. 55.
[6] *American Samoa—Codification of the Regulations and Orders for the Government of American Samoa.* (Washington, 1931.)

of native affairs, who is a civilian appointed by the secretary of the navy. The public health officer on the islands is the senior medical officer at the naval station; likewise the superintendent of public works is public works officer of the station. The naval chaplain serves as superintendent of education. Then there are the chief customs officer and the island treasurer, both naval officers. Finally there are the board of education, budget board, auditing board, comptroller, the board of directors of the bank of American Samoa, and the board of assessors.

There are three administrative districts in American Samoa. The Manua group of islands constitute one district, the other two being eastern and western districts of Tutuila. These districts are administered by native district governors, appointed by the governor, that is, the naval commandant. The districts are divided into counties and the native chiefs of these subdivisions are also appointed by the governor of American Samoa. Then there are village chiefs elected annually by village councils composed of family heads. The selection of village chiefs must, however, be approved by the governor. A *fono*, or general meeting, is held once a year, to which delegates come from all parts of the islands. The purpose of these meetings is to discuss questions of general interest, to recommend new laws or changes of existing laws to the governor, and to secure information from him with respect to various matters connected with the administration of the government.[7]

Owing to the fact that reports were coming to the United States from time to time, especially after the Great War, that the Navy Department was in effect administering a despotic government in Samoa, and since Congress had at last come to realize that its total dis-

---

[7] *American Samoa—A General Report by the Governor*, p. 59.

AMERICAN SAMOA

regard for almost a generation for the welfare of the inhabitants of the islands must be speedily remedied, a Senate concurrent resolution was introduced by Senator Bingham in 1927 providing for the appointment of a joint committee of Congress to investigate conditions in American Samoa. Joint hearings on this resolution were held before the Senate committee on territories and insular possessions and the House committee on insular affairs on January 17, 20, and 21, 1928. Another resolution (namely Senate Joint Resolution 110) was later substituted for the former resolution and was passed by the Senate in May, 1928. The House acted favorably in February, 1929. By this resolution Congress accepted, ratified, and confirmed the cessions of April 17, 1900, and July 14, 1904, respectively.[8] All civil, judicial, and military powers in American Samoa were left in the hands of the president until Congress should provide for the government of the islands. With a view to setting up a proper government for the islands, the resolution moreover provided for a commission of six members to be appointed by the president, two from the Senate, two from the House of Representatives, and two from among the native chiefs, to study the problem and "to recommend to Congress such legislation concerning the islands of Eastern Samoa as they shall deem necessary or proper."

Although President Coolidge, shortly before he went out of office, appointed the commission, it did not proceed to Samoa until the late summer of 1930. The American personnel of the commission consisted of Senator Bingham of Connecticut, chairman, Senator Robinson of

[8] Technically, the islands had not belonged to the United States by any legal act before 1929, because prior to the partition treaty, the United States, as well as the other powers, had acknowledged the independence of Samoa. In 1929 the United States legally annexed American Samoa when Congress accepted the deeds of cession.

Arkansas, Representative Williams of Texas, and Representative Beedy of Maine. Hearings were held by this commission in Honolulu September 18 to 20 and in American Samoa from September 26 to October 4.[9] The chairman of the commission transmitted to President Hoover the report of the commission on January 6, 1931. The commission recommended among other things that the Samoans be granted American citizenship; that the land in the islands be acquired and held only by citizens and residents of American Samoa; that the Samoan *fono* be permitted to determine the qualifications for *Samoan* citizenship, as distinct from American citizenship with the one restriction that the *fono* be not permitted to deny Samoan citizenship to any Polynesian of part blood, who is otherwise qualified. The report also recommended that the legislative power be placed in the Samoan *fono,* with the right of appeal to the president should the governor veto a measure and the *fono* pass it over his veto by a two-thirds vote. The report further recommended that the governor be appointed by the president with the approval of the Senate, and that the president shall be free to appoint naval officers, army officers, or civilians.

With reference to judicial matters, it was recommended "that in all important legal cases an appeal may be taken from the high court of Samoa to the United States district court of Hawaii," and "that one of the judges of that court [shall] go to Samoa from time to time as it becomes necessary to hear appeals."

Since the commission did not think it advisable to bring American Samoa under the constitution of the United States, it recommended that a bill of rights quite similar to the first ten amendments to the United States consti-

[9] *American Samoa—Hearings before the Commission appointed by the President of the United States.* (Washington, 1931.)

tution be incorporated in the organic act for American Samoa.

A proposed organic act was included in the report. It comprised five chapters with the following headings: General Provisions, The Legislature, The Executive, The Judiciary, Miscellaneous.[10]

At the time of writing no action has been taken by Congress with respect to the recommendations of the commission, but there is no doubt that that body will soon remove American Samoa from its present anomalous status in relation to the United States. That this is highly necessary is borne out by the facts adduced by the commission and by its conclusions.

[10] *The American Samoan Commission, Report.* (Washington, 1931.)

BIBLIOGRAPHICAL NOTE

BIBLIOGRAPHIES

THE primary material and secondary works in connection with the general subject of Samoa are so voluminous that no attempt is made here to list them all. For a more detailed bibliography the reader is referred to the author's doctoral dissertation, which is in the Yale University Library.

A useful guide to government manuscript material is the following: C. L. Van Tyne and W. G. Leland, *Guide to the Archives of the Government of the United States in Washington*. Second edition, revised and enlarged by W. G. Leland. Published by the Carnegie Institution of Washington, 1907.

The most complete list of printed documents, books, and articles on Samoa is one published in 1901 by the Library of Congress. Its title is *A List of Books (with References to Periodicals) on Samoa and Guam,* and it was compiled by A. P. C. Griffin, Chief of Division of Bibliography.

Another printed bibliography on Samoa is to be found in a publication entitled *Handbook of Western Samoa.* (Wellington, N. Z., 1925).

MANUSCRIPT SOURCES

The most important primary material for a study of American foreign policy with reference to Samoa, is to be found, of course, in the archives of the Department of State in Washington. This material includes instructions to United States ministers in Berlin, London, Honolulu, and at other capitals, and despatches from these ministers; notes to and from German, British, Hawaiian, and other ministers in Washington; instructions to United States consuls stationed at Apia, and despatches from them; domestic and miscellaneous letters; instructions to and reports and other papers of special missions and agents, particularly those of Steinberger, Bates, Kasson, Phelps, and Tripp; protocols of the

BIBLIOGRAPHICAL NOTE 583

Washington Conference of 1887 and of the Berlin Conference of 1889; report books containing communications from the Secretary of State to the President; and credences, containing letters of credence to ministers, special agents, and commissioners.

It should be remarked that although a considerable number of the Steinberger Papers were printed in Senate and House executive and miscellaneous documents, those that were not printed are to be found together with the former in the archives of the Department of State. This is true likewise of the Kasson Papers, some being printed in *Foreign Relations, 1889*, whereas others remain unprinted.

Supplementing the archives of the Department of State, the archives of the Navy Department have been found very helpful. The principal manuscripts used were those contained in the Executive Letter Books; General Letter Books; Pacific Fleet Books; Letters to Commandants of Navy Yards and Stations; Commandants' Letters, Navy Yard, Mare Island; Commanders' Letters; Letters to Commanding Officers; Officers of Ships of War; and the two volumes of MSS, relating to the Wilkes Exploring Expedition, which contain Wilkes' despatches during the time he was in command of that expedition in the Pacific from 1838 to 1842.

Many documents are deposited in the archives of the Territory of Hawaii at Honolulu relating to the attempt on the part of King Kalakaua to effect an *entente* with King Malietoa of Samoa.

AMERICAN PRINTED SOURCES

The Senate and House documents printed from 1857 to 1901 contain much consular and diplomatic correspondence relating to Samoa supplied to Congress by the Department of State, many reports from the Navy Department concerning activities of naval officers on the Pacific Station, and numerous reports from the Bureau of Foreign Commerce from 1856 to 1900 with respect to commercial relations with Samoa.

The principal documents of the United States Government which have been found useful are the following: 43 Congress, 1 session, Senate Ex. Doc. no. 45; 44 Congress, 1 session, House

584   UNITED STATES POLICY IN SAMOA

Ex. Doc. no. 161; 44 Congress, 2 session, House Ex. Doc. no. 44; 46 Congress, 1 session, Senate Ex. Doc. no. 2; 50 Congress, 1 session, House Ex. Doc. no. 238; 50 Congress, 2 session, Senate Ex. Docs. nos. 31, 68, 92, 102, Senate Misc. Doc. no. 58, House Ex. Docs. nos. 118, 119, and House Misc. Doc. no. 108; 51 Congress, 1 session, Senate Misc. Doc. no. 81 (the same document appeared first as Executive B of the same session), Senate Misc. Doc. no. 84, House Ex. Doc. no. 1, part 3; 53 Congress, 2 session, Senate Ex. Docs. nos. 93, 132; 53 Congress, 3 session, Senate Ex. Doc. no. 97, House Ex. Doc. no. 242; 54 Congress, 1 session, House Doc. no. 1, part 2; 54 Congress, 2 session, House Doc. no. 1; 55 Congress, 2 session, House Doc. no. 1; 56 Congress, 1 session, House Doc. no. 1, Senate Misc. Doc. no. 51, Senate Doc. no. 157; 56 Congress, 2 session, House Doc. no. 3.

The printed material relative to Samoa in *Foreign Relations*, issued by the Department of State, are to be found in the volumes for the years 1878, 1879, 1887, 1888, 1889, 1894 (Appendix I), 1899. Much of the correspondence, however, is the same as in the Senate and House documents listed above.

Other collections of printed material are the following: (1) James D. Richardson, *A Compilation of the Messages and Papers of the Presidents, 1789-1897*. (Washington, 1896-1899). Volumes VII to X inclusive contain messages with references to Samoa. (2) *The Statutes at large of the United States of America, from December, 1899, to March, 1901, and recent treaties, conventions, executive proclamations, and the concurrent resolutions of the two houses of Congress,* volume XXXI. (Washington, 1901). (3) *Senate Committee on Foreign Relations. Compilation of treaties in force.* (Washington, 1899). (4) *Journal of the Executive Proceedings of the Senate,* which contains minutes of the Senate in executive sessions in connection with the Meade treaty of 1872, the American-Samoan treaty of 1878, and the General Act of 1889. (5) William M. Malloy, *Treaties, conventions, international acts, protocols, and agreements between the United States of America and other powers, 1776-1909.* (Washington, 1910).

In the *Congressional Globe* and the *Congressional Record* will be found the debates on the treaties of 1878, 1889, and 1899 as well as on other questions relating to Samoa.

BRITISH PRINTED SOURCES

For a study of British foreign policy in relation to Samoa the following official documents are indispensable: (1) George P. Gooch and Harold W. V. Temperley, editors, *British Official Documents on the Origins of the War, 1898-1914.* (London, 1926 ff.). In volume I entitled "The End of British Isolation" is a chapter entitled "Great Britain, Germany, and Samoa", which "deals with Anglo-German friction in Samoa, and incidentally throws light on the Manila incident between Germany and the United States in 1898. The last part of the chapter describes the conclusion of the negotiations and the colonial concessions to Germany under the stress of the South African War at the end of 1899." The negotiations in London and Berlin are clearly set forth in the printed despatches, instructions, notes, and memoranda. (2) Parliamentary debates commonly called *Hansard's Debates.* (London, 1812 ff.). These debates contain parliamentary discussions of British relations with Samoa. (3) *British and Foreign State Papers* issued by the Foreign Office of Great Britain from 1841 to 1900. (4) Parliamentary *Accounts and Papers* containing British consular reports etc., from 1854 to 1901. (5) *Great Britain, Sessional Papers* from 1881 to 1899, containing British diplomatic correspondence respecting the affairs of Samoa. (6) Lewis Hertslet and Edward Cecil Hertslet, *A Complete Collection of the Treaties and Conventions, and Reciprocal Regulations at present subsisting between Great Britain and Foreign Powers.* (London, 1827 ff.). Volumes XV, XVII, XVIII, and XIX contain treaties etc., relating to Samoa. (7) *Votes and Proceedings of the Legislative Assembly of New South Wales, 1883-'84.* Volume IX, pp. 95-96, contains report of the Intercolonial convention of 1883, called to consider the subjects of the annexation of neighboring islands and the federation of Australasia.

GERMAN PRINTED SOURCES

For the student of German foreign policy with respect to Samoa the following official documents and publications are of primary importance: (1) Johannes Lepsius, Albrecht Mendelssohn Bartholdy, and Friedrich Thimme, editors, *Die grosse Politik der europäischen Kabinette, 1871-1914: Sammlung der diplomatischen Akten des Auswärtigen Amtes.* (Berlin, 1922-1926). Vierter Band, Kapitel 23: Deutsch-Englische Beziehungen 1885-1888 (Annäherung von 1885, Koloniale Schwierigkeiten und ihr Ausgleich). Dokumente nr. 779-819. Kapitel 29: Bismarcks Allianz-angebot an England. Verhandlungen über Helgoland 1889. Dokumente nr. 942-955. Achter Band, Kapitel 54: Die Bedeutung der Kolonialfragen für die Gruppierung der Mächte. B. England und Deutschland: Samoa-Kongo; Vierzehnter Band, Kapitel 96: Das Abkommen über Samoa und die Deutsch-Englischen Beziehungen 1899. Dokumente nr. 4028-4117. (2) Bernhard Schwertfeger, *Die diplomatischen Akten des Auswärtigen Amtes, 1871-1914: ein Wegweiser durch das grosse Aktenwerk der deutschen Regierung.* (Berlin, new edition, 1927). A summary and guide for *Die Grosse Politik* etc., referred to above. In "Erster Teil" entitled "Die Bismarck-Zeit," on pp. 115-119, appears a summary of chapter 23, and on pp. 131-133, is a summary of chapter 29 of volume IV. In "Zweiter Teil" entitled "Der Neue Kurs", on pp. 70-73, appears a summary of chapter 54, part B, of volume VIII. In "Dritter Teil" entitled "Die Politik der Freien Hand", on pp. 72-79, appears a summary of chapter 96 of the second part of volume XIV. (3) *German Diplomatic Documents, 1871-1914.* Translated by E. T. S. Dugdale. (New York, 1928-1931). (4) *Stenographische Berichte der Verhandlungen des Reichstags.* (5) *Anlagen zu den stenographischen Berichten der Verhandlungen des Reichstags,* which contain public documents of the German Reichstag including *Denkschriften,* or official accounts of the German Government's diplomatic negotiations etc., and *Aktenstücke,* or extracts from official correspondence. (6) *Weissbücher,* containing official correspondence of the German Government, including instructions to German diplomatic officers and consuls, and despatches from these officers; also notes to and from foreign governments. Parts V, VI, and VIII relate to Samoan affairs. (7) *Reichs-Gesetzblatt,* containing a collection of statutes and proclamations of the German Government.

CONTEMPORARY LETTERS AND MEMOIRS

William Roscoe Thayer, *The Life and Letters of John Hay*. (Boston and New York, 1915). In volume II, 220, appears a letter from Hay to Henry White (Sept. 9, 1899), wherein the Secretary of State reveals Germany's desire to work in harmony with the United States relative to Samoa. On pp. 281 ff., in the same volume, appears a letter from Hay to Joseph H. Choate (Nov. 13, 1899), informing the American ambassador in London how news of the partition treaty was received in America.

Carl Schurz, *Speeches, Correspondence, and Political Papers*. Edited by Frederic Bancroft. (New York, 1913). This work contains interesting letters passing between Thomas F. Bayard and Carl Schurz after the publication of the Washington Conference protocols.

Frederick William Seward, *Reminiscences of a War-Time Statesman and Diplomat*. (New York and London, 1916). Gives an authoritative account of the negotiation of the American-Samoan treaty of 1878.

Robert Louis Stevenson, *A Foot-Note to History: Eight Years of Trouble in Samoa*. (New York, 1892). Contemporary observations of the workings of the *condominium*, or tripartite arrangement for the government of Samoa.

Robert Louis Stevenson, *Vailima Letters, being Correspondence Addressed by Robert Louis Stevenson to Sidney Colvin, November, 1890-October, 1894*. (Chicago, 1895). Political troubles in Samoa are related in volume two.

Prince Otto von Bismarck, *Bismarck: The Man and the Statesman*. Translation by A. J. Butler. (New York and London, 1899).

Prince Bernhard von Bülow, *Memoirs of Prince von Bülow*. Translation by F. A. Voigt. (Boston, 1931). In volume I the German statesman reveals the importance of Samoa as a *"point d' appui"* for German trade and the German navy. He also refers to his attitude toward Great Britain and the United States as conciliatory despite Admiral von Tirpitz's feeling that the British and American naval tactics in Samoa early in 1899 could only lead to war with Germany.

Freiherr Hermann von Eckardstein, *Ten Years at the Court of St. James', 1895-1905.* Abridged translation by G. Young. (London, 1921). Having been a member of the German embassy in London, von Eckardstein gives an authoritative account of Anglo-German relations with respect to Samoa before the partition of 1899.

Otto Hammann, *Zur Vorgeschichte des Weltkrieges, Erinnerungen.* (Berlin, 1919). This book is one of a series of works by the same author, comprising the memoirs of a man who for many years was the director of the press bureau of the German foreign office. This volume covers the period from 1897 to 1906. Another book by Hammann, *The World Policy of Germany, 1890-1912,* translated by Maude A. Huttman, pp. 84-87, discusses the Samoan settlement of 1899.

G. Cecil, *Life of Robert, Marquis of Salisbury.* (London, 1922-1932). The fourth volume, the latest published, contains correspondence relating to Samoa until 1889.

A LIMITED LIST OF SECONDARY WORKS

Reference Works

The Annual Register, Appletons' Annual Cyclopaedia and Register, The Statesman's Year-Book, The Encyclopaedia Britannica, La Grande Encyclopédie, and *Meyers Konversations-Lexikon.*

General Works and Books

The significance of the Samoan problem as a landmark in United States history has been stated most clearly in the works of John Bassett Moore, ablest of interpreters of American foreign policy. In volume VII (pp. 661-663) of *The Cambridge Modern History* (Cambridge, Eng., and New York, 1902-12), Judge Moore considers the Samoan problem in a chapter entitled "The United States as a World Power." He discusses the problem at considerable length in his *A Digest of International Law* (Washington, 1906), volume I, chapter IV, section 11, pp.

536-554. In two later books by Judge Moore the problem again receives adequate attention: namely,

Four Phases of American Development: Federalism, Democracy, Imperialism, Expansion (Baltimore, 1912), and *Principles of American Diplomacy* (New York and London, 1918).

S. F. Bemis, editor, *The American Secretaries of State and Their Diplomacy* (New York, 1927-29). Volumes VII and IX have short references to Samoa. In volume VIII the chapters relating to the secretaryship of Thomas F. Bayard, written by Lester B. Shippee, include one on Samoa covering the period of Cleveland's first administration.

Erich Brandenburg, *From Bismarck to the World War. A History of German Foreign Policy 1870-1914* (New York, 1927). Translated by Annie Elizabeth Adams. In this book appears the best German single-volume secondary account of German foreign policy in relation to Samoa that has been written since the publication of *Die Grosse Politik* documents. In chapter VI will be found an account of the Samoan partition settlement of 1899.

James Morton Callahan, *American Relations in the Pacific and in the Far East, 1784-1900* (Baltimore, 1901). [Johns Hopkins University Studies in Historical and Political Science].

André Cheradame, *La Colonisation et les Colonies Allemandes* (Paris, 1905).

William B. Churchward, *My Consulate in Samoa etc.* (London, 1887), an excellently written history of the rivalry of Germany, Great Britain, and the United States during the years, 1881-1885, by a British consul stationed at Apia.

William M. Crose, *American Samoa, A General Report by the Governor. 1913.* Revised edition by H. F. Bryan. (Washington, 1927) [Navy Department]. Includes an historical sketch since the partition of 1899.

Alfred L. P. Dennis, *Adventures in American Diplomacy, 1896-1906* (New York, 1928). Discusses Samoan question on pp. 106-111. In three appendices to chapter IV the author reproduces two memoranda and one despatch showing the importance of reaching a solution of the Samoan problem in 1899.

Davis Rich Dewey, *National Problems*, volume 24 of *The Ameri-*

can Nation series, edited by A. B. Hart (New York and London, 1904-'18). On pp. 203-205 the Samoan question is briefly discussed.

Foster Rhea Dulles, *America in the Pacific* (Boston and New York, 1932). Chapter VII entitled "The Navy Discovers Samoa" is a good summary of American relations with Samoo to 1889. Chapter VIII, "An Entangling Venture", continues the story from the Berlin Conference to the partition of 1899.

Carl Russell Fish, *The Path of Empire*, volume 46 of the *Chronicles of America* series, edited by Allen Johnson. (New Haven, 1919).

John W. Foster, *American Diplomacy in the Orient* (Boston, 1903). The Samoan question is treated in chapter XII.

Heinrich Friedjung, *Das Zeitalter des Imperialismus, 1884-1914.* 3 volumes (Berlin, 1919-22).

Joseph V. Fuller, *Bismarck's Diplomacy at its Zenith.* (Cambridge, Mass., 1922) [Harvard Historical Studies]. The period regarded by the author as the one when Bismarck exercised greatest influence in international affairs was embraced within the years 1885 to 1888. It may be remarked that during this period occurred the so-called "honeymoon" in Anglo-German relations. The friendly attitude of the British prime minister, Lord Salisbury, toward the German chancellor was reflected in the understanding with reference to Samoa as well as in other fields of international relations, and but for the stubborn resistance of the American secretary of state, Thomas F. Bayard, to the plans of Bismarck, who was abetted by Salisbury, Samoa might perhaps have been annexed by Germany shortly after that time.

G. P. Gooch, *History of Modern Europe, 1878-1919* (London and New York, 1923). Discusses Samoan partition settlement on pp. 305-306, showing the strained relations between Great Britain and Germany in the summer of 1899.

John B. Henderson, Jr., *American Diplomatic Questions* (New York and London, 1901), contains a survey of the international rivalry with regard to Samoa from 1872 to 1900.

Willis Fletcher Johnson, *American Foreign Relations* (New York, 1916).

BIBLIOGRAPHICAL NOTE 591

Jeannette Keim, *Forty Years of German-American Political Relations* (Philadelphia, 1919). Chapter V deals with diplomatic relations with respect to Samoa from 1872 to 1899.

L. A. Kimberly, U.S.N., "Samoa and the hurricane of March, 1889." Printed in vol. XII of the papers of the Military Historical Society of Massachusetts.

Robert M. McElroy, *Grover Cleveland, the Man and the Statesman*. Two volumes (New York and London, 1923). Chapter X is entitled "Cleveland, Bismarck, and Samoa."

Elizabeth van Maanen-Helmer, *The Mandates System in Relation to Africa and the Pacific Islands* (London, 1929).

Reuel S. Moore and Joseph R. Farrington, *American Samoan Commission's Visit to Samoa, September-October, 1930* (Washington, 1931).

Julius Obermüller, *Zur Geschichte der deutschen Colonien in der Süd-See mit besonderer Rücksicht auf die Kämpfe um dieselben und die Ereignisse von 1888-1889* (Leipzig, 1889).

C. O. Paullin, *Diplomatic Negotiations of American Naval Officers, 1778-1883* (Baltimore, 1912).

H. Petin, *Les États-Unis et la doctrine de Monroe* (Paris, 1900). Pp. 375-391: "La nouvelle politique des États-Unis, Samoa."

Felix Rächfahl, *Deutschland und die Weltpolitik, 1871-1914*. Volume 1, "Die Bismarck'she Ära" (Stuttgart, 1923). An excellent treatment of German foreign policy from 1870 to 1890.

N. A. Rowe, *Samoa under the Sailing Gods* (London, 1930).

Clare Eve Schieber, *The Transformation of American Sentiment toward Germany, 1870 to 1914* (Boston, 1923). Chapter II deals with German-American relations with respect to Samoa from 1870 to 1899.

Guy H. Scholefield, *The Pacific, Its Past and Future, and the Policy of the Great Powers from the Eighteenth Century* (London, 1919). Includes the most authentic account of British imperial and colonial policy with reference to Samoa.

Freeman Snow, *Treaties and Topics in American Diplomacy* (Boston, 1894).

Mary Evelyn Townsend, *Origins of Modern German Colonialism,*

1871-1885 (New York, 1921). [Vol. IX of Columbia University Studies in History, Economics, and Public Law.]

Mary Evelyn Townsend, *The Rise and Fall of Germany's Colonial Empire, 1884-1918* (New York, 1930). On pp. 198 ff., there is a brief discussion of the partition treaty of 1899 from the German point of view.

Alice Felt Tyler, *The Foreign Policy of James G. Blaine* (Minneapolis, 1927). Chapter IX is an excellent account of the Berlin Conference of 1889, based primarily on manuscript material in the archives of the Department of State.

Veit Valentin, *Deutschlands Aussenpolitik von Bismarcks Abgang bis zum Ende des Weltkrieges* (Berlin, 1921). A scholarly treatment of German foreign policy.

Sir A. W. Ward and G. P. Gooch, *The Cambridge History of British Foreign Policy, 1783-1919* (New York, 1923). In volume III, the authors discuss the question of the Samoan Islands.

Robert Mackenzie Watson, *History of Samoa* (Wellington, N. Z., 1918).

Francis Wharton, *A Digest of the International Law of the United States* (Washington, 1886). In volume I, section 63, pp. 436-441, the author discusses "Samoa, Caroline, and other Pacific islands."

Charles Wilkes, *Narrative of the United States Exploring Expedition during the years, 1838, 1839, 1840, 1841, 1842* (Philadelphia, 1844). The *Narrative* embraces the first five volumes of the printed Wilkes Report. The remaining volumes of the Report relate to scientific observations.

Quincy Wright, *Mandates under the League of Nations* (Chicago, 1930).

Alfred Zimmermann, *Geschichte der Deutschen Kolonial Politik* (Berlin, 1914). An excellent history of German colonial politics. The author presents on pp. 288-299, a full account of the German policy in relation to Samoa from 1883, when New Zealand urged annexation by Great Britain, to the partition of Samoa in 1899.

INDEX

Abarenda, United States war ship, stationed at Pago Pago, 575

Adams, United States war ship, in Samoan waters, 189, 203, 205, 206, 207, 208, 380, 411, 413, 414, 415, 417, 514, 522

Adee, Alvey A., second assistant secretary of state, explains position of United States on municipal convention, 369-370

Adler, German war ship, in Samoan waters, 414, 415, 443

Afrikaanshe Galei, ship of Dutch East India Company, makes first known expedition to Samoa, 5 n

Agate, A. T., artist, member United States Exploring Expedition, 14

Alaska, attitude of United States toward acquisition of, 195; a natural expansion, 520-521

Alaska, United States war ship, in Samoan waters, 259

Albatross, German war ship, in Samoan waters, 235, 286, 292

Alert, American gun boat, retained at Samoa during Berlin Conference, 430

Alvensleben, Herr von, German minister to Washington, reassures Department of State of Germany's desire to maintain *status quo*, 289; explains convention of 1884 to Department of State, 289-290; announces Germany's desire to assume political control in Samoa, 299; denies knowledge of Brandeis's activities in Samoa, 323; declares Germany will interfere only in conjunction with other powers, 324-325; represents Germany at Washington Conference, 343; actions suspicious at outset of conference, 344, 345, 445; argues for land commission, land court, and German mandate, 355, 356, 358; opposes tripartite control, 356, 359; advised by Weber at conference, 366

American administration in American Samoa, placed under Navy Department, 575-576, 577-578; anomalies of Samoan status under, 577-581; method of, 578; commission appointed to study, 579; civil government recommended for, 580-581

American Philosophical Society of Philadelphia, interested in United States Exploring Expedition, 15

American-Samoan treaty of 1878, initiated by Samoan authorities, 183 n, 191; mission excites warnings from American press, 191, 192-193, 200, 213; Le Mamea presents credentials to Department of State, 192; President Hayes bespeaks consideration of mission, 193-194; annexation or protection sought, 194; Seward explains expansionist policy of government, 194-195, 196; proposals presented to president and cabinet, 195; opposed by members of Congress, 195-196; treaty of commerce and friendship drafted, 196; terms relating to rights in Pago Pago, 197, 233 n; to commercial regulations,

197; to extraterritorial rights, 197; to intervention, 198; submitted to Senate and ratified, 196, 198-199; hailed in press, 199-200; acclaim and celebration of, in Samoa, 203-206; subsequently ratified by new Samoan government, 241, 246; compared with British and German treaties with Samoa, 231-232; subsequent action on, by Department of State, 245-246, 246 n, 266, 297-298, 301, 302-303, 338, 388-389, 450, 458; Samoan representations under, 334-335, 373

Anglo-Samoan treaty of 1879, terms of, relating to British equality with other nations, 230-231; relating to land claims, 231; relating to extraterritorial rights, 231; relating to naval base and coaling station, 232; relating to municipal government for protection of British subjects, 235; compared with American-Samoan and German-Samoan treaties, 231-232

Annexation, or Protectorate:

――――United States, policies relating to, of business interests, 51, 54-55, 67, 68, 69, 71, 73, 83-86, 87, 96, 99, 100, 103, 108; of consuls and special commissioners, 52-53, 60, 61, 67, 68, 93, 94, 98, 99, 102, 107-108, 110-111, 112, 113, 115, 117, 119, 125, 126, 127-128, 147, 165, 186-187, 190, 306-307, 415; of foreign residents, 51, 52, 54-55, 71, 97, 98-99; of government departments or officials, 52, 53-54, 63, 66, 67, 69, 71, 72, 73-75, 83, 85, 86, 87-89, 90, 109, 110, 115, 118-119, 120, 127, 129, 130, 134, 147, 173-174, 195-196, 307, 416; of missionaries, 104-106, 133; of natives, 55, 60, 70, 79, 83, 84, 85, 91, 93, 96, 97, 99-100, 103, 104, 106, 107, 108, 139, 141-142, 162-163, 183 n, 184, 192, 334-335

――――English, policies relating to, of the Foreign Office, 75, 78-81, 137, 160, 164, 183, 201, 202, 216, 225, 229, 235, 238; offers to respect independence of Samoa, 281-282; warns New Zealand against demonstrations, 282-283, 293; of New Zealand, Australia, and Fiji, 75, 76-78, 81-82, 136, 137, 160, 273-274, 277, 280 n; New Zealand passes law annexing Samoa, 280-281; urges deal with Germany to obtain Samoa and Tonga, 283; native desires for, 160-162, 162-164, 233, 274, 280, 334-335; rumors of, 224, 225

――――German, policies relating to, of business interests, 51-52, 52-53, 54, 58, 59, 68, 70, 75-76, 76-77, 98-99, 212-213, 215, 217, 252-253, 332-334; of government, 53-54, 55, 79, 160; native desire for, never expressed, 332; native antipathy toward Germany, 332-334; colonial expansionist sentiment aroused by failure of Godeffroy Company, 253; opposition prevents subvention to company, 253-254; Bismarck *vs.* Windhorst in Germany's Samoan policy, 254; United States fears aroused by, 255-256; reversal of Bismarck's policy becomes apparent in Samoa, 277-278; arouses fear in British and American circles, 279, 280, 283, 286, 287, 289, 290-291, 292-294, 399

――――Joint protectorate, by three powers, native petitions for,

INDEX

233-234; urged by United States representatives, 225, 238, 241, 249, 257-258; favored by English and German representatives, 234; instructions for, from English and German governments, 248, 283; convention for, entered into by consuls of three powers and natives, 249-250; uncertainty of United States' attitude toward, 235, 244, 250-251, 255, 272; attitude of United States due to fears of single protectorate by England or Germany, 251-256; decision of United States to coöperate informally, 256-257; established under *condominium*, 518-519, 523-525

Apia, post of United States consular representatives, see Williams, J. C.; Pritchard, George; Chapin, V. P.; Van Camp, Aaron; Jenkins, J. S.; Swanston, R. S.; Dirickson, J. C.; Wolfe, S. M.; Ketchum, Daniel; Gardner, E. W.; Coe, J. M.; Foster, B. S.; Griffin, G. W.; Parker, D. S.; Colmesnil, J. G.; Dawson, T. M.; Canisius, Theodore; Greenebaum, Berthold; Sewall, H. M.; Blacklock, W.; Mulligan, J. H.; Churchill, William; Osborn, L. W.

"L'Archipel des Navigateurs," 8

Arco-Valley, Count von, German minister to Washington, complains of anti-German activities of Americans, 417, 419; conveys Bismarck's invitation to Berlin Conference, 424, 425; receives conditional acceptance from Bayard, 425, 434; learns American plans for Berlin Conference, 430

Arend, flagship of first known expedition to Samoa, 5 n

Arendt, Dr., German consul general in Belgium, secretary to Berlin Conference, 455

Ariadne, German war ship, in Samoan waters, 215, 217

Arms traffic, with native factions, 152, 159; embargo on, by British government, 170; provided against in Deinhard agreement, 243; in convention for tripartite protection, 257; checked by native government, 277; prevention of, urged by Hawaii, 331-332, 336; prohibition of, suggested at Washington Conference, 347; regulated by Berlin Act, 464, 477-479, 504; causes friction among powers under *condominium*, 543-545

L'Astrolabe, French vessel, in La Pérouse's expedition, 8

Aube, Captain, French naval officer, protects United States flag and consul from British attack, 175-176; relieved of command by French government, 178; informs American minister in Paris of removal, 179; reinstated by French government, 179

Augusta, German war ship, in Samoan waters, 162, 182

Australia, location with reference to Samoa, 1; first called "New Holland," 4 n; agitation of, for Samoan annexation, 136, 137, 273-274; opposes partition, 560

Badger, United States war ship, takes tripartite commission to Samoa, 564

Balfour, A. J., English minister, confers with von Bülow and Hatzfeldt on partition of Samoa, 559, 560

Baltimore Sun, United States newspaper, on Berlin treaty, 515-516

Bancroft, George, United States minister to Germany, reports of, in Germany's Pacific policy, 53-54

Banishment, severe penalty among natives, 22

Barracouta, British war ship, in Samoan waters, 137, 138, 141, 142, 143, 144, 157; see Barracouta affair

Barracouta affair, facts of, 142-144; referred by British commodore to home government, 143; Department of State presents claims to British government, 145-146; responsibility for, disclaimed by Great Britain, 146; report on, requested by Congress, 146-147; object lesson to Department of State, 148; British naval officer and consul removed on account of, 146, 156-157; indemnity for, demanded by British consul, 161, 163-164, 184, 187, 188; settlement of, checks interference by European consuls, 212

Bartlett, J. J., United States adventurer, recommended by Steinberger, 214; services sought in Samoan government, 215, 216; arouses suspicions of German consul, 217; premier of Samoa, 221; British and German consuls hostile to, 222; desires to strengthen military power of "Steinberger" government, 222, 224; arrest of, ordered by American consul, 238-239; wife of, sent to United States, 239; leaves Samoa after fall of "Steinberger" government, 246-247; enters suit against United States consul and naval officer for arrest, 247

Bates, George H., special United States commissioner to Samoa, on British moves for annexation, 201; on German treaty rights in land, 218, 219; on rival kingships, 261; instructions of, on American policy in Samoa, 318-320; enters upon investigations in Samoa, 320-321; reports on findings, 322, 340, 351, 360; appointed United States commissioner to Berlin Conference, 429; qualifications for post, 431; criticised by German press, 431, 432; makes explanatory statement to Count von Bismarck, 432-433; recognized at conference, 432; high regard for, by administration, 433, 434; participation of, in proceedings, 457, 459, 460, 461, 462, 471, 475, 479, 482, 487, 494, 496, 502-503, 504; negotiates treaty with Tonga, 572

Baumann, Cornelius, in Dutch expedition to Samoa in year 1722, 5 n

"Baumann's Land," 6 n

Bayard, Thomas F., United States secretary of state, launches diplomatic discussion of Samoan problem, 266; policy of, regarding participation in municipal convention, 295-296; respect for Samoan independence and neutrality, 296; maintenance of American rights under treaty of 1878, 297-298, 299; foreign encroachment in Samoa, 295, 296, 298-299; takes direct stand on German encroachments in Samoa, 299; intervenes for first time in Samoan situation, 300-303; favors "more precise regulation" of relations of powers in Samoa, 306; opposed to "annexation or protectorate by any of the three powers," 307; instructs United States ministers in London and Berlin to suggest tripartite conference on Samoan question, 307; disavows acts of

INDEX 597

United States consul in Samoa, 309-310, 319; gives British and German ministers official report on unwarranted activities of United States consul, 312; inquires of German minister the meaning of Brandeis's presence in Samoa, 322-323; informs Hawaii as to Greenebaum's status, 326; advises Hawaii in strong terms against alliance with Samoa, 337-339; becomes suspicious of Anglo-German accord in Washington Conference, 344-345; supports tripartite arrangement and land court, 345-346, 355, 358-359, 359-360, 362, 363, 364, 365; outlines points of agreement and disagreement with colleagues, 352-354; summarizes basis of American interest in Samoa, 354; exposes whole German plan, 362-364, 365, 366; proposes adjournment of conference, 366; experiences difficulties in tripartite municipal administration, 369-370, 387; advises neutrality in German war on Samoa, 386-387; attempts settlement under rights in American-Samoan treaty, 388; embarrassed in representations to Germany by lack of information from Samoa, 389-390; makes historical résumé of relations with Germany in Samoa, 395-402; attacked for "weak-kneed" policy, 403-404; defended by *New York Times*, 405-406; asks for war ship in Samoa, 413; notifies Germany United States will respect election of Mataafa, 415; inquires into German war in Samoa, 419-420; record in Washington Conference commended, 424; conditionally accepts German invitation to Berlin Conference, 425, 426; reaffirms United States recognition of Samoan independence and tripartite equality in Samoa, 426; chagrined that change of administration prevents consummation of plans for Berlin Conference, 429; indebted to Bates for assistance at Washington Conference, 431; appointment of Sewall as special agent at Berlin Conference called reversal of diplomatic policies of, 433; policies of, toward Berlin Conference, followed by Blaine, 434; as outlined in Washington Conference, 434, 435, 436; in regard to Pago Pago, 437; opposed to German mandate in Samoa, 438

Beach combers, menace of, to natives, 21; lawlessness of, 38, 215

Beagle, British ship, in Samoan waters, 160

Beauclerk, Mr., of British embassy at Berlin, secretary to Berlin Conference, 455

Becker, Herr, German consul to Samoa, fails to keep government informed on affairs in Samoa, 323-324; reprimands King Malietoa, 335-336; makes humiliating demands on Malietoa, 371; recognizes Tamasese as king, 372; instructed to seize Malietoa, 373; declines to enforce municipal convention, 378; puts an end to tripartite control, 379-380, 382, 383-384; and land claims, 407; disclaims connection with Brandeis-Tamasese government, 411; disappears after fall of Brandeis-Tamasese régime, 417

Beedy, Carroll L., member House of Representatives, on commission investigating government of American Samoa, 580

598   UNITED STATES POLICY IN SAMOA

Behrens, Karl Friedrich, explorations in South Pacific, 4-5 n; account of expedition under Roggewein in 1721-22, 4 n; description of discovery of Samoa, 5-7

Berchem, Count, German under secretary for foreign affairs, reports government's willingness to enter into conference on Samoa, 308-309; announces withdrawal of German intervention in Samoa, 310-311; represents Germany at Berlin Conference, 429

Berlin Conference, events force Bismarck into coöperation, 422-424; conference invited to Berlin, 424-425; accepted as continuation of Washington Conference, 424, 425, 427, 434, 435, 436; general basis agreed upon, 425, 426, 428; United States and German commissioners announced, 429-430; Germany objects to two United States representatives, 431-433; objections overcome with aid of English, 432-433; Blaine instructs United States commissioners to resume on *status quo* basis, 434-436; to refuse German mandate plan, 436-438; to assume responsibility, with reservations, in forming government, 439-441; to regard land question of prime importance, 441; to exclude subjects not covered by instructions, 441; to assume German interventions were unofficial, 441-442; United States seeks English support in advance, 447-448, 449-450; question of *status quo* not so formidable, 450, 452; Germany abandons mandate scheme in advance of conference, 451; Kasson provides way out for Germany on Malietoa, 451, 452-453; opens auspiciously, 455; positions of three powers on Samoan question given, 455-457; Malietoa-Mataafa-Tamasese triangle, 450-451, 452-454, 467-471, 471-472, 493-496, 497, 500-501, 502, 513-514; discord in ranks of United States delegates, 467, 470, 471, 472-474, 475, 480-481, 488-489, 508-509; discussion and agreements of, relating to: land question, 459-463, 501, 503; arms and liquor traffic, 464, 466, 476, 477-479, 502, 504; native government, 464-465, 467, 468, 469, 470, 471-472, 490, 492, 493-496, 500, 502; taxation and revenue, 476, 477, 479-483, 502, 503-504; municipal government, 475, 484-488, 490, 491, 493, 496-497, 497-498, 499-500, 502, 503, 505, 507, 511-512, 513, 524; discussions and agreements of powers on: organization and jurisdiction of supreme court, 490, 491, 492-493, 496, 498-499, 501, 506-507, 508, 509, 510, 511, 523-524; modification of existing treaties, 501, 502; duration and amendment of treaty, 460, 502, 505; Blaine and hot weather cause impatience, 507-508; English and German delegates accept general act as presented, 510; United States delegates accept with two modifications, 510-512; agreements kept secret, except on kingship, 512; native government, as provided by, 523-525; amendments proposed by foreign residents, 531-533; see *Condominium*, Tripartite government, Washington Conference

Berliner Tageblatt, German newspaper, on Stübel's activities in Samoa, 305, 306

Bingham, Hiram, United States

INDEX 599

senator, introduces resolution to investigate conditions in American Samoa, 579; chairman investigating commission, 579; makes report to President Hoover, 580

Bismarck, Count Herbert von, German minister of foreign affairs, conferences with United States representatives on hostilities in Samoa, 388, 389, 390; proposed as German commissioner to Berlin Conference, 429; reconciled to appointment of Bates as United States commissioner to Berlin Conference, 432; announces abandonment of mandate scheme prior to Berlin Conference, 451; yields on question of kingship, 452-453; opens Berlin Conference, 455; states German position on Samoan question, 455-456; participation of, in conference, 459-460, 462, 464, 467, 472, 477, 488, 491, 497, 498, 501, 503, 504, 506, 507, 510, 511, 512, 513

Bismarck, Prince Otto von, German chancellor, policy on territorial expansion, 54; policy reversed, 253, 254, 255, 278-279, 281, 282; effect on German-American relations, 256, 262-263, 290-291, 301; negotiates with England for settlement in New Guinea, 280, 283; knowledge of Stübel's encroachments in Samoa, 301; gives emphatic assurance of coöperation with England and United States in Samoa, 302, 303-304; opposes English move for investigation of Samoan situation, 305; strikes bargain with Salisbury in Samoa, 344, 345 n, 445-446; tempers expansionist policy, 302-303, 304, 310, 314, 316, 317, 324; returns to expansionism after failure of Washington Conference, 367, 370-371, 374; declares war on Malietoa, 372; submits memorandum on points at issue in Washington Conference, 384-385, 391-393; threatens war on Samoan and Hawaiian kings, 385; submits lengthy analysis of German-American ill-will in Samoa, 393-395; plan to call for tripartite conference on Samoa hastened by Cleveland, 422, 423; policy attacked by liberals, 422; reversal of policy toward conference diplomatic victory for Cleveland, 423 n, 424; England and Germany agree to publish protocols, 424; invites conference to Berlin, 425; orders suspension of hostilities pending conference, 426, 427; willing to lay aside preference for mandate, 428

Bismarck, German war ship, arrives in Apia during civil war, 240; ends civil war by show of force, 240; treaty of peace between native factions signed on board, 241-242; Deinhard government organized on board, 242, 244, 252; Malietoa imprisoned on, 376

Blacklock, W., United States acting consul at Apia, and land claims, 408; and Tamasese-Brandeis régime, 412; acting consul, 413, 415; instructed to confine activities to protecting lives and property, 416; arouses complaints from German foreign office, 417; sends messenger to Auckland to keep in touch with Washington, 418-419, 420; participates in restoration of Malietoa Laupepa, 513-514, 539; coöperates in *condominium,* 542

Blaine, James G., United States secretary of state, apparent indifference of, to Samoan question, 266; announces names of United States commissioners to Berlin Conference, 430; agrees to limit number of war ships in Samoa during conference, 430; approves Cleveland-Bayard policy, 434, 435, 437; lays down basis for resumption of conference, 434, 435; defines position of United States favoring tripartite control as opposed to mandate, 436, 437; on United States' rights in Pago Pago harbor, 437; on United States' interest in Pacific, 437, 438; expresses skepticism of tripartite government, 439, 440; on land question, 441; in constant communication with representatives at Berlin Conference, 453-454, 458, 464, 465-468, 469-471, 473-474, 475, 476-477, 488-490, 493-497, 507-508, 509, 512; submits Berlin treaty to President Harrison, 514-515; agrees to naval support for Samoan court, 537-538

Bohlen, Herr von, presents Germany's proposal for partition of Samoa, 566

Bougainville, Lewis Antoine de, second known discoverer of Samoa, 7; description of Samoan periaguas and native sailors, 8

Bounty, mutineers of, searched for by *Pandora*, 10

Bowen, Sir G., urges annexation to British Empire, 77, 273

Brackenridge, J. D., assistant botanist, member United States Exploring Expedition, 14

Brandeis, Herr, German agent in Samoa, sent as military instructor to revolutionary faction, 322-323, 335, 367; compared with Steinberger, 374; becomes premier of Samoa, 375; puppet of Weber, 378, 401; knowledge of, denied by German government, 323

Brandeis-Tamasese government, tool of German commercial interests, 378, 401, 407, 410-411; maintained by German naval force, 379-380, 381-382, 384, 398, 401, 409, 413; has coöperation of England, 364, 381, 445; opposed by United States consul and residents, 412; defeated by Mataafa, 414-415; Bismarck limits German interference to protection of lives and property, 415; United States unwilling to recognize legality of, 435

British high commissioner for Western Pacific, creation of office, 232 n; diplomatic functions of, 229; judicial functions of, 231, 235; legislative functions of, 231

Brown, Captain George, United States naval officer, interviews King Malietoa, 259

Brown, Rev. George, missionary, 98, 104; on conditions in Samoa, 105-106, 112

Brown, Godfrey, Hawaiian minister of foreign affairs, terminates Hawaiian-Samoan rapprochement, 339

Bülow, Count von, German minister of foreign affairs, negotiates with England for partition of Samoa, 559; reported to oppose selling out to England Germany's interests in Samoa, 569; reported to favor United States claims in Samoa, 569, 571

Bush, John E., Hawaiian minister to Samoa, received with enthusiasm, 327; instructed to extend "friendly services" of Hawaii,

INDEX 601

328, 331; takes up cudgels for Malietoa's government, 336; recalled by Hawaiian government, 339

California, land speculators of, 44, 84; attitude of members of Congress from, on Samoan protectorate, 75; see Polynesian Land Company

California and Australia Steamship Company, see Webb Line

Calliope, British war vessel, in Samoan waters, 415, 443

Campbell, J. A., third secretary of state, on German interference in Samoa, 153

Canisius, Theodore, United States consul at Apia, appointed to succeed Dawson, 269-270; urges Taimua and Faipule to maintain peace, 270; urges Department of State to continue participation in municipal convention, 271; interviews king regarding native disturbances, 272; reports rumors of agitation in New Zealand for annexation, 273-274, 277; advises Department of State of political events in Samoa, 286, 287, 288, 290, 291, 292, 294; requests man-of-war to protect American interests, 292; retires on account of ill health, 294; subject of complaint by Bismarck, 393; defended by Bayard, 396-397

Caribbean Sea, fears of German expansion in, 54

Carter, H. A. P., Hawaiian minister to Washington, presents protest to Department of State against forcible annexations in Polynesia, 274-275; acts as representative of Samoa, 329

Cedercrantz, Conrad, chief justice of Samoa, lacks tact, 525; disagrees with land commission on expenses and fees, 525-527; disagrees with municipal council on apportionment of revenues, 527, 530-531; leaves post without notifying consuls, 532; office vacated by powers, 540

Central American Transit Company, 45; see Webb, W. H.

Chambers, William Lea, land commissioner for United States, 534, 535; appointed chief justice of Samoa, 549; attempts to settle civil dispute in Samoa, 560, 561; seeks safety on *Porpoise*, 561; approves settlement by commission, 564

Chandler, Captain, United States naval officer, despatched to protect American interests, 225; stirs native factions to verge of civil war, 225-226; clears United States consul of part in Lackawanna affair, 227; enters into negotiations for municipal convention, subject to approval of government, 234, 235, 237; leaves in midst of civil war, 239; return of, urged by Dawson, 259

Chapin, V. P., United States commercial agent at Apia, appointed, 25; report of, on prospects in islands, 26; request of, for naval vessel, 26; protest of, to chiefs against civil war, 26; systematic consular records begun by, 26; acting consul, 29; losses of, attributed to Jenkins, 32-33

Chatham Island, 10

Chief justice of Samoa, as provided in Berlin treaty, 501, 511; delay in filling office complicates politics, 522, 523; see Berlin Conference; see also *Condominium*

Chiefs, Samoan, as native spokesmen, 20, 63, 65, 67, 84, 91, 92, 93, 95, 96, 97, 98, 99; as rulers and judges, 101; as legislators, 101-102

Choate, Joseph H., United States ambassador at London, informs Salisbury that United States is willing to participate in three-power agreement, 564; finds Salisbury willing to consider partition of Samoa, 567; communicates with Hay on negotiations for partition, 570, 571

Christiancy, I. P., United States senator, on treaty of 1878, 198

Christian missions, complaints of, against United States naval officers and consuls, 29

Chuden, Captain, German naval officer, witnesses peace treaty and natives' agreement with Deinhard, 242, 244

Churchill, William, United States consul general at Apia, opposes consular assumption of presidential duties, 548

Churchward, W. B., British acting consul and secretary to king, conflict of, with American consul over archives of municipal board, 268-269; protests activities of Stübel, 286; recommends intervention to end German encroachments in Samoa, 298-299

Cleveland, Grover, president of United States, more definite policy on Samoan question launched in administration of, 266; criticized on Samoan policy, 403-404; takes Congress into confidence, 421, 422-423, 428-429; on American position in *condominium*, 555-556

"Cocos and Verrathers," 4, 6, 6 n

Coe, Jonas M., United States commercial agent at Apia, appointment of, as commercial agent to Apia, 33; trouble of, regarding status of half-castes, 34; appeal from, regarding his position, 34-35; report of, concerning political and social conditions, 34-35, 37-38, 38-40; participation of, in Court of Foreign Residents, 36; requests of, for advice in international judicial complications, 37-38; report of, on German activities, 52, 70, 139-140, 144; arrested and deported by English naval officer, 142, 143; official interpreter to Samoan government, 163; appointed minister of justice in government under tripartite protectorate, 250, 256

Coëtlogen, Colonel de, British consul to Samoa, coöperates with his United States colleague, 417; participates in restoration of Malietoa Laupepa, 513-514

Cole, Cornelius, United States senator, on Samoan protectorate, 75

Coleman, Chapman, United States chargé d'affaires in Berlin, reports Bismarck as favorable to a conference on Samoa, 307-309; on German face-about toward coöperation in Samoa, 310-311; embarrassed by appointment of Bates as commissioner to Berlin Conference, 390-391, 415, 432

Colmesnil, J. G., United States vice consul at Apia, appointed, 157; warns American citizens against political meddling, 158; intervenes with English and German consuls to advise political factions, 158-159; withholds advice on petition for British annexation, 161; veers toward joint protectorate of Great Britain and United States,

INDEX 603

162-163; clashes with British consul, 163-164; consents to extend protection of American flag, 164-165, 165 n; secures neutral municipal zone in civil war, 170-171; agent for land company, 150, 169; removal requested by Griffin, 169; recognition of, refused by Department of State, 159, 169; accompanies Le Mamea to Washington, 191, 192, 193

Commerce, American, in Samoa, Wilkes treaty for, 20-21, 30; character of, 28-29; disadvantages of, as compared with English and German, 40-41; influence of, on efforts of navy to secure bases, 43, 73-74; negligible throughout century, 520

Communication with Samoa, early dependence for, 24, 45, 46, 48, 50; lack of, cause of internal complications, 190, 300, 309, 311, 354, 371, 389, 443, 448, 561-562

Condominium, foreshadowed in establishment of neutral municipal area, 223; failure of, predicted by German and English spokesmen, 448 n; as launched by Berlin Act, 518-519, 523-525; position of United States in, 519-521, 554-556; weaknesses and accomplishments of, 552-553; disrupted by civil war, 560-562; displaced by provisional government of commissioners, 563-564

Congress of United States, petitioned to send exploring expedition into Pacific, 12; act of, regarding powers of consuls in uncivilized or unrecognized countries, 35-36; authorizing deepening of harbor in Midway Islands, 42; authorizing survey routes for Isthmian canal, 42; opposition of, to insular expansion, 42, 47; indifference of, to naval expansion, 43; and Meade's treaty, 74, 111; and Samoan annexation or protectorate, 75, 110, 111, 195-196; and Steinberger mission, 110; requests president to submit correspondence on Samoa, 402; criticisms of Bayard heard in, 403; debates and ratifies Berlin treaty, 517-518; action on cession of American Samoa, 576-577; aroused by reports of despotic government, 578-579; no action on report of investigators, 581

Couthouy, J. P., member of United States Exploring Expedition, 14

Conway, British naval vessel, 21 n

Cook, Captain, English explorer, in Friendly Islands, 10

Coolidge, Calvin, president of United States, appoints commission to report on government in American Samoa, 579

Copra, importance of, to commerce with Samoa, 51, 115, 152, 408, 410, 411

Courts, of foreigners in Samoa, Court of Foreign Residents, 36, 37; Court of British High Commissioner of Western Pacific, 224; Consular Court of Appeal, 368; Supreme Court of Samoa, 523-524

Crawford and Company, United States firm in South Seas, 408

Crowe, Joseph Archer, represents England at Berlin Conference, 455, 477, 480, 481, 486

Cunningham, W. C., British vice consul to Samoa, relations with Wilkes, 17, 21

Cusack-Smith, Mr., British consul to Samoa, opposes consular assumption of presidential duties, 548

Dana, J. D., mineralogist with United States Exploring Expedition, 14

Danae, British war ship, sent to Samoa for joint protectorate over islands, 248; landed to punish Samoan rebels, 257

Dauntless, English schooner, in Samoan waters, 92

Davis, John, assistant secretary of state, instructs consul to distinguish between local administration and general control in Samoa, 272; sends consul correspondence with Hawaii relative to annexationist moves in Polynesia, 274

Dawson, Thomas M., United States consul at Apia, appointed, 189; delayed by storm, 190; *exequatur* held up by Samoan government, 207; Griffin and Goward hostile to him, 207 n, 208; goes before native assembly to obtain recognition, 209; legal problems of, in interpreting treaty, 209-211, 244-245, 246 n; judicial powers explained by Department of State, 211; assaulted by English beach comber, 215; requests war ship to protect American interests, 216, 225, 239-240; calls attention to land clause in German treaty, 218; transmits to Department of State native protests on German treaty, 219; refuses intervention to forestall Bartlett, 222; advises Malietoa Laupepa concerning, 222; agrees with European colleagues to maintain neutral municipal area in Apia during civil war, 223; actions approved by Department of State, 223-224; refuses to recognize jurisdiction of British high commissioner, 224; urges Department of State to joint protectorate, 225, 238, 241, 249, 257-258; reprimanded for consent to salute to opposition, 226; denies advising naval officer to salute, 227; describes consular government in neutral municipal area, 228; consents to conference with British high commissioner on proposed Anglo-Samoan treaty, 229; enters into municipal convention subject to approval of government, 234-235, 237; describes character of Samoan government, 237-238, 241, 257-259; summary attitude toward adventurers, 239; courtesy of, to Bartlett's wife, 239; elected first magistrate under municipal convention, 240; reports on Deinhard's activities to Department of State, 244; grants provisional recognition to new government, 245 n; frustrates schemes of the San Francisco land ring, 247; agrees to proposal for joint protectorate over all Samoa, 248; acts without instructions, though believes he follows desires of Department of State, 248-249, 251; appoints Coe as minister of justice for newly protected government, 250; reports bankruptcy of powerful German firm, 252; arouses jealousy of German consul general, 259; signs "Lackawanna Peace," 263; informs Department of State of his colleagues' instructions to coöperate in recognition of Malietoa Laupepa, 267-268; reports suspicious actions of British high commissioner and consul, 268-269; makes secret agreement with king to prevent American exclusion from municipal board, 269; recalled from consular post,

INDEX 605

269-270; subject of complaint by Bismarck, 393

Day, Captain B. F., United States naval officer, reports on American consul's unwarranted intervention in Samoa, 312-313, gives Malietoa salute for recognition, 314; cooperates with Malietoa and British and German consuls to end civil war, 314-316

Day, W. R., United States secretary of state, declines to interfere in election of king, 550

Deinhard, Captain, German naval officer, persuades native factions to sign peace treaty, 241-242; reestablishes government under new constitution, 242-244; English and American representatives not invited to negotiations, 244; provides in both instruments for settlement of damages to property during civil war, 242, 244; motives explained, 252; arouses suspicions in United States, 255-256

Democratic party, see Party politics in United States

Derby, Lord, correspondence of, with Samoan government, 157; in settlement of Anglo-German interests in Pacific islands, 280, 281, 282-283

Deserters, foreign, among United States seamen, undesirability of, 16, 20; rewards to natives for apprehension of, 21; power of consuls to deal with, 64-65

"D. H. and P. G.," German business firm, see Godeffroy Company

Dillon, Peter, explorer, 9 n

Diplomatic powers, of United States naval officers, 17-18, 19-20, 21, 22-23, 25, 43

Dirickson, James C., United States commercial agent at Apia, 32; report of, on case between van Camp and Jenkins, 32-33; report of, on character of foreign residents, 33; resignation of, 33

Downing Street, 75, 79, 180, 201, 342, 344, 445, 510

Drayton, Joseph, artist, member United States Exploring Expedition, 14

Dreadnought, American schooner, 168

Drinkwater-Bethune, Captain, British naval officer, drew up first port regulations for Apia, 21 n

Dumont-d'Urville, J. S. C., visit to Samoan archipelago in 1838, 11; observations, 12 n

Dutch East India Company, explorations of, in Samoa, 5-7

Eber, German war ship, in Samoa, 417, 443

Edmunds, George F., United States senator, on treaty of 1878, 198; and United States-Hawaiian reciprocity treaty, 406; and rights in Pago Pago harbor, 517

Edwards, Captain Edward, first English explorer to Samoan archipelago, 9-10

Eggert, Carl, land commissioner for Germany, 533

Eliot, C. N. E., second secretary to British embassy in Washington, represents British government in tripartite commission in Samoa, 564

Elloy, Father L., Roman Catholic missionary, 104, 105

Elvira, United States bark, seizure of, by United States consul, 29-30

Emma C. Jones, United States whaler, boats of, attacked by Samoans, 39

English, explorations of, in Samoa, 9-10

English policy in Samoa in relation to Germany and United States, coöperation with Germany, 280-284, 344, 345, 345 n, 445-446; coöperation with United States, 446-448, 449-450; comparative indifference of, 447-448, 448 n, 449; favors partition by other two powers, 565, 567-569, 571-572, 573-574; see Annexation, or Protectorate, English

"Entangling alliances," United States' Samoan policy, traditional attitude of United States toward, 354; *New York Times* warns against, 192-193, 199-200; American consular representative favors, 225, 234-235, 248-249, 257-258; form of, sanctioned by Department of State, 253-254, 270-271, 272, 345-346; insisted upon in Berlin Conference, 458, 476; *New York Herald* on, 516; in *condominium*, 519-521; Gresham on, 554-555; Cleveland on, 555-556

d'Entrecasteaux, Captain, French explorer, 9 n

Erben, Captain Henry, United States naval officer, in Samoa, 121-122, 122 n

Estafette, Paris newspaper, on German plans in Samoa, 212

Evarts, William, United States secretary of state, letter to, from Samoans, 175; receives Samoan commissioner, 192; on national expansion, 195; signs treaty of 1878, 196; holds conference with German and British ministers on kingship in Samoa, 265-266

Everett, Edward, United States secretary of state, appoints first regular consul, 25

Exploring Expedition, United States, authorized by act of Congress, 12-13; entrusted to Commodore Jones, 13; command of, transferred to Lieutenant Wilkes, 13; general instructions for, 13-14; instructions relative to the Samoa and Fiji groups, 14; names of scientists aboard, 14; vessels comprising, 15; route of, 15; extent of explorations, 15, 17; explorations of, and reports on Samoan group, 15-17, 18 n; return route of, 17-18; see Wilkes, Lieutenant Charles

Extraterritoriality, in Samoa, act of Congress, 1848, relative to, 31; as exercised in Samoa, 31, 35-36, 228; provided in German-Samoan treaty of 1879, 220-221, 232, 279; provided in English-Samoan treaty of 1879, 231, 232; provided in American-Samoan treaty of 1878, 197, 232; in German-Samoan convention of 1884, 279; maintained in Washington Conference, 347; in Berlin Act, 501, 523-524

Factions, native political, see Malietoa Laupepa, Malietoa Talavou, Malietoa Tanu, Mataafa, Mauga, Puletua, Taimua and Faipule, Tamasese

Fairfax, Rear Admiral, English naval officer, calls conference to establish neutral ground, 415

Fanny, United States schooner, in Samoa, 89, 90, 91, 107, 108

"Fashoda Incident," in relation to German policy in Samoa, 558

Faumuina, Chief, 93

Fiji Islands, distance from Samoa, 2; chiefs of, make commercial agreements with United States,

INDEX 607

Lieutenant Wilkes, 20-21; annexation to British Empire, 75; agitation in, for British annexation of Samoa, 136, 137, 160, 201

Fish, Hamilton, United States secretary of state, and early relations with Samoa, 47, 50, 71, 79, 80, 87, 88, 109, 110, 112, 114, 115, 117, 118-119, 120, 125, 126-127, 144, 145

Fishing, native industry, 3, 8

Flag of Samoa, 65, 99, 101, 107, 108, 242

"Fly-flap," emblem of Samoan nationality, 96, 114, 117, 118

Flying-Fish, tender with United States Exploring Expedition, 15

Fono, native assembly, meeting of, with Lieutenant Wilkes, 20; consent of, obtained for code of regulations, 20; described, 96-97; called together in German war, 375-376; utilized in United States administration, 578; extension of functions recommended, 580

Foreign residents, early contacts with Samoa, regulations for murder of, or crime against, 20; apprehension of deserters among, 21; number, 29; character of, 33; business interests of, 28-29

Foreign vessels, in early contacts with Samoa, protection of, by native government, 20; deserters from, 21; port charges on, 20-21, 28

Foster, J. W., United States secretary of state, suggests informal conference to amend Berlin Act, 532-533; on number of war ships in Samoa, 538

Foster, S. S., United States commercial agent and consul at Apia, report on disadvantages to American trade, 40-41; activities of, against Steinberger, 126, 128, 129, 131-134, 136, 137, 138, 139, 140, 141, 144-145; agent for Polynesian and Samoan land companies, 132, 135, 150; removed by Department of State, 148; investigated by Griffin, 150; aids Chief Mauga in war with Samoan government, 152-153, 182, 204-205

France, explorations in Samoan archipelago by de Bougainville in 1768, 7-8; by La Pérouse in 1787, 8-9; by de Freycinet in 1819, 11; by Dumont-d'Urville in 1838, 11, 12 n; becomes involved with United States and England over Aube affair, 175-179; annexationist policy in Polynesia alarms Hawaii, 274-275

Frazior, Mr., English resident in Samoa, estimates Samoan population, 11 n

Freemantle, Captain, British naval officer, 30

Frelinghuysen, F. T., United States secretary of state, fails to follow up diplomatic conference on Samoan question, 266; states position of United States relative to Samoa and Hawaii as distinct from other Pacific groups, 275-276; investigates German activities in Samoa, 289; leaves problem to successor, 291

Freycinet, Louis de, discoverer of Rose Island, 11

Friendly Islands, named by Captain Cook, 1-2

Fritze, Captain, German naval officer, plans bombardment of Samoan villages, 414, 415

Furgusson, Sir James, urges annexation to British Empire, 77, 273; fears United States interests, 81-82

608 UNITED STATES POLICY IN SAMOA

Gardner, Edward W., United States commercial agent to Apia, shipwrecked and lost en route, 34

Gazette, German newspaper, contradicts report that Germany sought annexation of Samoa, 213

German policy in Samoa, business and commercial interests of nationals in, 51, 54, 76-77, 180, 218, 220, 252, 253, 333-334, 536; attempts at domination by trade interests, 51, 54, 115, 152, 167, 408, 409, 410-411; early policy of Foreign Office, 54; expansionist sentiment develops, 253, 254, 255, 277-279, 281, 282; effect of expansionist policy on relations with United States, 256, 262-263, 290-291, 301; rapprochement with England sought, 280-284; strikes bargain with England on Samoa, 344, 345 n, 445-446; effects of combination obvious at Washington Conference, 345, 445; maneuvers for mandate over Samoa, 349, 355-356, 358, 359, 360, 363, 364-365; defeat by United States, 353-354, 355-356, 358-359, 363-364, 365-366, 385, 436, 437, 450; resort to intervention, 367; see Intervention, German; Bismarck analyzes friction with United States in Samoa, 393-395; Bayard replies, 395-402; compared with Anglo-German policy, 394; with Anglo-American, 397; entrance into Berlin Conference for settlement, 422-424; see *Condominium;* partition as final basis of, 558-560, 565-574; see Annexation, or Protectorate, German

German-Samoan convention of 1884, terms of, 278-279; method of obtaining signatures to and execution of, 279, 284, 285, 286, 287, 290-291; subject of inquiry between Department of State and Foreign Office, 289; causes despatch of United States man-of-war to protect Samoa, 291

German-Samoan treaty of 1879, terms of, 217-218; compared with British and American treaties with Samoa, 231-232

Gibbons, Henry, first United States commercial agent on island of Tutuila, 24-25, 26

Gillis, Captain J. H., United States naval officer, negotiates important peace treaty with natives, known as ''Lackawanna Peace,'' 262-263

Goat Island, United States flag raised on, 206

Godeffroy Company, German business firm, interests of, in Samoan islands, 51, 54, 76-77, 180, 218, 220, 252, 253, 333-334; secret negotiations with Steinberger, 115-117, 144, 147; through German consul seeks to establish government more amenable to its interests, 150, 151, 152; attempts to dominate trade interests, 167, 409, 410-411; falls into financial difficulties, 251-252, 408-409; schemes to overthrow tripartite control, 378; collapse of, brings expansionists and the opposition into sharp conflict in Germany, 253-254; subvention for, urged by Chancellor Bismarck, 253, 256; see Weber, Theodor

Gold, rumors of, in Samoa, 114

Gold coast, in relation to Anglo-German policy in Samoa, 572

Gordon, Sir Arthur, governor of Fiji and British high commissioner for the Western Pacific, 143, 161, 162, 163, 164, 172, 181-182; attempts to settle Griffin-Liardet case, 182-183; efforts to

INDEX 609

coerce Samoan government to sign an ''obnoxious'' agreement, 183-185; arouses suspicion in United States, 199, 200-202, 255-256; commissioned to negotiate treaty with Samoa, 229; confers with foreign consuls and naval commanders, 229-230; treats with *de facto* government of Malietoa Talavou, 230; terms of treaty arranged by, 230-233; announces offer from Malietoa of Samoan annexation, 233; favorable to tripartite control, 234; assists in drawing up municipal convention, 235; supports consular government during civil war, 240, 258; recognizes government set up by Deinhard, 246; appoints secretary to King Malietoa, 268

Gorrie, John, chief justice of Fiji and judicial commissioner for the Western Pacific, 182, 185

Goward, Gustavus, United States commercial agent at Pago Pago, appointment of, 189, 190; describes reception of American-Samoan treaty, 203-205; jealous of incoming United States consul, 207 n

Grant, U. S., president of United States, policy of, toward insular expansion, 42, 86, 88, 110, 195; policy of, toward naval expansion, 43-44, 88; on ratification of Meade's treaty, 71-72, 85, 110; on ship subsidies, 85, 110; and native petitions for protectorate, 109-110, 118; Pacific interest checked by domestic embarrassments, 145, 147; communications to, relative to *Barracouta* affair, 140, 141, 142, 145

Granville, Lord, negotiates with Bismarck for settlement of interests in Pacific islands, 280, 281, 283

Graves, J. Hicks, British consul to Samoa, draws up plan for joint protectorate with American and German consuls, 249; signs ''Lackawanna Peace,'' 263

Great sacred mat, of Tui Atua, 100, 101

Greenebaum, Berthold, United States consul at Apia, appointment never ratified by Department of State, 294 n; advises Department of State of German occupation of Samoan capital, 300; declares United States protectorate over Samoa, 306-307, 309, 312, 313, 314; actions disavowed by Department of State, 309-310, 311, 319, 393; refuses to resign, 325; appointed Hawaiian vice consul at Apia, 325; tenure short-lived, 325-326; subject of complaint by Bismarck, 393

Greiner, T., land commissioner for Germany, 533-534

Gresham, W. Q., United States secretary of state, characterizes *condominium*, 525; consents to concerted intervention in Samoa, 539; on control of native revenues, 543; on methods for suppressing arms smuggling, 544; on our entanglements in Samoa, 554-555

Griffin, Gilderoy W., United States consul at Apia, 148; instructed not to interfere in political affairs, 148, 149, 156, 167; refuses to support German consul in changing flag and government of Samoa, 149, 151, 156; refuses to aid British high commissioner to obtain agreement with Samoa, 183; investigates activities of ex-consul Foster, 150, 152-153; consistent supporter of Samoan government, 149-150, 150-151, 152,

154, 172, 174, 175, 181, 183, 184, 185, 186, 187-188; attempted bribery of, by business interests, 167, 168-169; efforts for treaty between Samoan and Washington governments, 154-155, 165-166, 172-173, 174-175, 186-187, 188, 191, 204; instructions to, modified, 167-168, 172, 173, 174; adopts policy of "intervention without entangling alliances," 174, 181, 183, 185, 186-187, 188; establishes consular court, 175; conflict with British authorities, 175-176, 183, 184-185, 186-188, 191, 201; echoes of, in French, British, and German foreign offices, 177-181; resides under protection of Samoan government, 176, 181, 184; transferred at own request, 176, 189; regrets request, 208; seeks to prevent successor from obtaining the consulate, 207-208; contrast in attitude toward, of natives and foreign residents, 208-209

"Groeningen," Dutch name for island of Savaii, 6, 6 n

Guano business, 45

Haggard, Bazett M., land commissioner for England, 533

Hale, Horatio, philologist, member United States Exploring Expedition, 14

Half-castes, definition of, 31; question as to status of, 31, 34; report of Department of State regarding, 34; status of, fixed by Congress, 34; citizenship of, in American Samoa, 580

Hamilton, Elisha L., appointed United States vice commercial agent on island of Savaii, 28; and land question, 116, 414

Hamlin, Hannibal, United States senator, on treaty of 1878, 198, 198-199

Harmony, D. B., Commodore, acting secretary of United States navy, orders "vigorous intervention" for protection of American lives and property, 416

Harrison, Benjamin, president of United States, submits Berlin treaty to Senate 515, 516-517; has no clear policy on Samoan government, 440

Haskins, Commodore, English naval officer, refers *Barracouta* affair to home government, 143; advises Taimua and Faipule, 149

Hatzfeldt, Count von, German ambassador in London, maneuvers for Anglo-German accord at Berlin Conference, 446, 448 n; sounds England on partition of Samoa, 559-560

Hawaii, distance from Samoa, 1; survey of, by United States Exploring Expedition, 18; regarded as link with Samoa, 43; interest of, in trade routes, 45; annexation of, proposed, 50; "observed" by Steinberger, 90; model for Samoa, 154-155, 273; protests to United States against forcible annexations of Polynesian groups, 274-275; seeks accord with United States in Samoa, 325-326, 326-327, 339; sends Bush as minister to Samoa, 327; forms treaty of political confederation with Samoa, 329-330; offers assistance in reorganization and administration of government, 331-332; war on, threatened by Bismarck, 385; America's relation to, compared to Germany's to Samoa, 399; American imperialism in, inspires German policy in Samoa, 406

INDEX 611

Hawaiian-Samoan confederation, efforts toward, 325-332; terms of, 330; pathos of, 332, 334-335; frowned upon by Washington, 337-339; terminated, 339

Hay, John, United States secretary of state, declines to interfere in election of king, 551; joins with Britain in accepting proposal for tripartite commission in Samoa, 564; approached by von Mumm on partition project, 565, 565 n, 566; favors withdrawal from *condominium*, 566; sounds England on partition, 566, 567; informed that Germany considers selling Samoan interests to Great Britain, 569; hastens partition by definite statement of United States' claims, 570, 571; negotiates with Pauncefote for partition agreement, 572, 573; signs partition agreement, 574

Hayes, Rutherford B., president of United States, receives Samoan envoy, 192; presents Samoan question in annual message, 193-194; on national expansion, 195; recommends to Congress tripartite diplomatic agreement for securing stability in Samoa, 264

Hennings, Wilhelm, appointed president of municipal council, 540; not acceptable to England, 541

Hertha, German war ship, in Samoan waters, 149, 152, 155, 261

Heusner, Commodore, German naval officer, arrives in Apia under German orders, 371; lands marines and hoists German flag, 372; proclaims martial law, 373

Hill, D. J., assistant secretary of state, receives Germany's proposal for partition of Samoa, 566

Hobbs, J. K., land claims of, 211

Holland, probable explorations in Samoa, 4-5; explorations in South Pacific, 4-7; known discovery of Samoa, 5-7

Holleben, Herr von, German diplomat, signs partition agreement, 574

Holstein, Baron von, German commissioner at Berlin Conference, appointed, 429; participation of, in proceedings, 462, 498, 500, 505

Hoover, Herbert, president of United States, receives report of commission investigating government of American Samoa, 580

Houghton, Sherman, United States congressman, on Samoan protectorate, 75

Huahine laws of Tahiti and Tonga, 98

Hudson, Captain W. L., United States naval officer, with United States Exploring Expedition, arrests native murderer at Apia, 22

Hunker, J. J., United States naval officer, gives official salute to Malietoa Laupepa, 514; reports on situation, 522

Hunt, W. J., English adventurer, deported by English high commissioner, 258

Hurricane of March, 1889, 443, 444, 444 n

Ide, Henry C., land commissioner for United States, 533, 534; becomes chief justice of Samoa, 540, 541; assumption of political powers by, annoys consuls, 546-547; resigns as chief justice, 549; on weaknesses and accomplishments of *condominium*, 552-553

Ifu, form of humiliation, explained, 371 n

Imperialism, American, begins in

Samoa, 519, 520-521; leads to partition, 557
Independence, United States frigate, in Samoan waters, 29
Independence of Samoa, attitude of three powers toward, maintenance of, consistent policy of United States, 276, 296-297, 298, 301, 318, 319, 346, 363, 365-366, 392-393, 396, 398-399, 402, 426, 436, 543, 556; respect for, assured by Germany, 289, 292, 293, 297, 302, 304, 425, 428; desire for, expressed by England, 281-282, 297, 303, 350; United States policy reversed, 557
Ingalls, J. J., United States senator, asked to intervene for Steinberger, 145
Intervention in Samoa:
——United States, suggested by foreign residents, 97, 105, 106; joint action with Great Britain proposed, 162, 163, 299; with Germany and Great Britain, 225, 234-235, 248-249, 257-258; agreed to by consuls to protect neutral municipal area, 240, 248; case of Foster in arresting and deporting Samoan premier, 141-142; case of Colmesnil in hoisting United States flag over Samoa, 164-165; case of Griffin in hoisting United States flag over Samoa, 184, 186, 187; act of Dawson in consenting to salute of rival king, 226; in entering agreement for tripartite control of islands, 248-250; case of Greenebaum in declaring United States protectorate over Samoa, 306-307, 309, 312, 313, 314; contradictory policy of Department of State in condemnation and removal of Foster, 148; in instructing Griffin for "intervention without entangling alliances," 172, 174; in tacit acceptance of Colmesnil's acts, 173; in rebuking Griffin for his later acts, 189; in alternate approval and reprimand of Dawson, 223-224, 226-227, 244-245, 250-251, 255, 257; in instructing representatives for negative intervention, 273; in suspending Greenebaum, 326; case of first diplomatic intervention by United States government, 300-301
——English, reversal of non-interference policy, 136-137, 201; conspiracy of consular and naval officers to overthrow government, 137-139; arrest and deportation of Samoan premier, 141, 142, 143-144; attack on Samoan capital, 142; denial of responsibility by British authorities, 146, 156-157; continued opposition of local groups, 149, 150-151, 152, 166, 168, 170, 171, 172, 181-182, 222; joint action with consuls of other powers, 158-159, 223, 228, 234-235, 240, 248-250, 262, 267-268; British consul seeks control of native revenues, 163-164; threats of Gordon against Samoan government, 183-185; attempts of consul to force treaty with Samoa, 185-188; see *Barracouta* affair
——German, by consuls and naval officers presumably uninstructed, 149, 150, 151-152, 157, 160-161, 166, 168, 182, 241-244, 248-251, 255; by official or semi-official agents: consul instructed to establish a government dominated by German officials and

INDEX 613

business interests, 278; convention entered into with native government, 278-279; native signatures obtained under duress, 279, 284; consul seizes municipal area to force execution of convention, 285; action protested by consuls as violation of municipal convention of 1879, 286; German Foreign Office professes ignorance of consul's motives, 289, 292, 300; but affirms policy of assuming political control, 299; German consul hauls down Samoan flag, 300; act provokes first intervention by United States, 300-301; German Foreign Office temporarily reverses policy, 302-303, 304, 310, 314, 316, 317, 324; failure of Washington Conference revives German encroachments, 367, 370-371; emperor declares war on Malietoa and recognizes Tamasese as king, 372, 375, 377; adherence of chiefs obtained by force, 375; puppet government maintained by German war ships, 379-380, 381-382, 384, 398, 401; United States government takes strong position on, 400, 402, 454; moral rather than legal breach, 387-388, 404; defeat of Tamasese, 414-415; Bismarck orders consul to act only to protect lives and property, 415; German squadron ordered back to Samoa, 417; Samoa becomes naval rendezvous, 417-418, 419; German forces war on Mataafa, 418; American authorities appeal to *status quo* agreement between powers, 419-420; Bismarck tempers policy, 420-421;

President Cleveland lays matter before Congress, 421-422

—— by joint action of three powers, urged by United States at Berlin Conference, 457, 458; employed under *condominium*, 537-540, 561-562

Isabel, a ship, bears "Tatooed Prince" to San Francisco, 191, 192

Isthmian canal, heightened interest in, 42, 43, 45; survey of routes for, 42; negotiations for, shelved, 195; linked with Samoa in United States policy, 354, 438, 466

Jackson, John B., American chargé d'affaires at Berlin, informs Hay of Anglo-German agreement in regard to partition of Samoa, 571

Jenkins, Jonathan S., United States consul at Apia, 30; involved in case against van Camp, 30; investigation and report of, by Dirickson, 32-33

Johnson, Andrew, president of United States, and national expansion, 195

Johnston, Thomas Crawford, United States trader in South Seas, protests against taxation methods of Brandeis-Tamasese government, 408

Jones, Captain Thomas ap Catesby, command of United States Exploring Expedition first entrusted to, 13; delay and resignation, 13; treaty with Hawaii, 60-61

Juno, British man-of-war, 30

Kaimiloa, Hawaiian training-ship, 339

Kaiser Wilhelm Land, designation of German New Guinea, 283

Kalakaua, king of Hawaii, sends representative to Samoa, 325, 327; bestows decoration upon Samoan king, 328

Kasson, John A., United States minister to Germany, instructed to sound out German policy on Samoa, 289, 292; warns Department of Bismarck's policy, 293-294; representative at Berlin Conference, 429; special qualifications for appointment, 430, 431; assists in overcoming German objections to Bates' appointment, 432, 433; seeks accord with England and Germany prior to Berlin Conference, 447-448, 449-450, 451-453; cables Blaine for further instructions, 453, 458; states views of United States government, 456-457; participation of, in proceedings, 458, 460, 462, 464, 465, 466, 467, 469, 471, 472-473, 474, 475, 479, 480, 481, 482, 486, 491, 492, 493, 494, 497, 500, 502, 503, 504, 505, 506, 510, 511, 512

Kautz, Admiral Albert, United States naval officer, participates in Samoan civil war, 561

Kearsarge, United States war ship, in Samoan waters, 38, 39

Kempff, Commander Louis, United States naval officer, in Samoa, 411, 413

Ketchum, Daniel, United States commercial agent to Apia, never assumed office, 33-34

Kimberley, Lord, on annexation of Samoa by England, 78-79, 80-81

Kimberly, Rear Admiral L. A., United States commander of Pacific Fleet, ordered to send war ship to Samoa, 413, 416; Germany objects to presence of, in Samoa, 427; ordered to proceed to Samoa, 442, 443; recommends disbanding native factions, 471

Knappe, Dr., German consul in Samoa, succeeds Becker, 417; declares intention of Germans to capture and disarm rebel chiefs, 418; establishes martial law in Samoa, 443

Knorr, Captain, German naval officer, refuses to salute "Steinberger" flag, 149; signs "Treaty of Friendship" with Tonga, 155; recognizes revolutionary government in Samoa, 306; embarrasses Malietoa government, 313

"Kordinoff," name given to Rose Island by Russian explorer, 10

Koster, Jan, with Dutch expedition to Samoa, 5 n

Kotzebue, Otto von, expedition of, to Samoan archipelago, 10-11

Krauel, Dr., German privy counselor, commissioner to Berlin Conference, 429; appointed to committee on agenda, 457; participation of, in conference discussions, 461, 484, 488, 497-498, 505-506

Krusenstern, Captain A. J. von, Russian naval explorer, circumnavigation of globe by, 10; memorandum and charts of, sent United States Navy Department, 14

Labor, native, prohibited on Sundays, 64; traffic in, 77; on plantations, 124; German treaty rights in, 218; protection for, provided in German-Samoan convention of 1884, 278

La Boussole, French vessel, in La Pérouse's expedition to Samoa, 8

Lackawanna, United States ship, despatched to Samoa for protection of American interests, 225;

untoward salute of, threatens civil war, 225-226; 235, 237; leaves in midst of civil war, 239; lands again during a civil war, 262; negotiations for peace conducted on board, 262

"Lackawanna Peace," important in diplomatic relations of three powers, 262-263, 513; terms of, 263; strength of, 262, 270; commended by Blaine, 435

Lamanon, de, M., French naturalist with La Pérouse's expedition, 9

Land alienation, during civil wars, 40, 84, 218; advice against, by United States government, 88, 94, 441; laws relating to, 102; provisions for, in German treaty, 218; source of friction among natives and foreign residents, 106, 131-133, 219, 333-334, 406-407, 408; extent of, estimated, 340-341, 355; prohibition of, in Berlin treaty, 459-460; see Godeffroy Company, Polynesian Land Company

Land claims and titles, attempt at regulation by Steinberger, 131; in German-Samoan treaty, 218; in English-Samoan treaty, 231; major issue at Washington Conference, 340-341, 345, 347-348, 349, 351, 354-355, 356-357, 359-360, 361-363; attempted regulation in Brandeis-Tamasese régime, 407; commission to investigate, set up, 460-461, 524-525; land court to adjudicate, provided in Berlin treaty, 461-462; number of, confirmed by land commission, 536, 553; see Godeffroy Company, Polynesian Land Company

Land commission, conflicts of, with chief justice over expenses and fees, 525-527; membership of, 533-534; period of work extended, 534, 535; review of claims examined by, 536

Land speculators, baneful practices of, 40, 44, 70, 84, 94-95, 98-99, 115, 116, 135, 167, 168-169, 218, 247, 464; see Godeffroy Company, Polynesian Land Company

Langle, de, M., French naval captain with La Pérouse's expedition, 9

La Pérouse, Jean François de Galaup, first known explorer to land in Samoan archipelago, 8; description of native life, 8-9; ill fate of expedition, 9; journal of expedition, 8 n, 9 n

Latrobe, John H. B., Jr., secret agreement of, with Steinberger, 120-121

Laws, Samoan, 97, 98, 102; priority of foreign, 220-221, 231, 232; English law, with modifications, adopted in Berlin Act, 506; efficacy of, under *condominium*, 553

Leary, Commander R. P., United States naval officer, in Samoa during Mataafa's revolt, 413; outstanding figure during Mataafa's revolution, 414, 415, 416-417, 418

Le Mamea, Chief, Samoan secretary of state, countersigns addresses and petitions to United States government, 154, 163, 171; sent as special envoy to negotiate treaty with United States, 183 n, 191, 193; described by Seward, 192; negotiates with Seward, 194-195, 196; disavows overtures with England, 200, 201; returns with treaty of 1878, 189, 190; efforts of, to bolster up government, 214-215, 216; informs Dawson of negotiations for treaties with other governments, 214

Lenroot, I. L., United States senator,

introduces bill providing for government of American Samoa, 577
Le Signelay, French war ship, in Samoa, 175; see Aube, Captain
Liardet, E. A., British consul to Samoa, 156, 157, 161, 162; demands control of government revenues and mortgage on lands, 163; defies United States authorities, 175; involves his government with those of United States and France, 175-176, 178-180; recalled for investigation, 177; sudden death prevents testimony, 182-183; supports opposition in civil war, 204
Liquor traffic with natives, forbidden or discouraged, 21, 64, 102; missionary efforts against, 124; joint action to prohibit, in municipal convention, 236; in Deinhard agreement, 243; in convention for joint protectorate, 257; at Washington Conference, 347; in Berlin Act, 464, 502, 504, 553
Lizard, English war ship, in Samoa, 415, 417
London Missionary Society, 17, 133, 141, 444
Lord, Thomas A., United States adventurer, arouses California land speculators against Dawson, 247

McKee, James, and Polynesian Land Company, 95
McKenzie, D. H., and land titles in Samoa, 407
McKinley, William, president of United States, announces "no withdrawal" from Samoa, 556-557; willing to assist in solution of Samoan problem, 562; orders American Samoa placed under Navy Department, 575
Malet, Sir Edward, British ambassador to Berlin, confers with Bismarck respecting independence of Samoa, 281, 303; helps secure recognition of Bates at Berlin Conference, 432; suggests partition of Samoa to Kasson, 449; consents to coöperate with Americans at Berlin Conference, 450; represents England at Berlin Conference, 455; reads declaration of British government at Berlin Conference, 456; appointed to committee of revision, 462; subsequent participation in conference, 478, 479, 487, 491, 497, 498, 500, 503, 505, 510, 511, 513
Malietoa Laupepa, nephew of elder chief, sends letters to president of United States, 100; king of united Samoa, 122, 131; adopts missionaries' ideas of dress, 124; appoints a minister to Washington, 134-135; supports Steinberger in trial, 139, 140; agrees to arrest of Steinberger, 141; abdication forced by Taimua and Faipule, 141, 245; favorite of missionaries and English and German factions, 142, 151, 161, 170; quarrel in ranks of Puletua as to who should be king, Malietoa Talavou or Malietoa Laupepa, 216; appointed regent, 242; signs consular agreement for joint protectorate by three powers, 235; wars with opposition after death of old king, 259; crowned king, 260; recognition of, urged by American and British consuls and by English local press, 260, 261; created king by "Lackawanna Peace," 263; successor to, subject of conference between United States secretary of state and British and German ministers, 265-266; recog-

INDEX 617

nized by England, 267; American recognition deferred, 267, 272-273; agreed upon as king for seven-year term, 270, 277; promised support of German government, 267-268, 272; forced to negotiate convention with Germany, 278, 279, 284; petitions England for annexation, 280; protests to German emperor against convention of 1884 and Stübel-Weber activities, 284-285, 288; explains petition for British annexation to American consul, 284; threatens to change capital as protest to German encroachments, 287-288; efforts of, to maintain neutrality 304, 341, 367; appeals to American consul for protection under terms of American-Samoan treaty, 312-313, 314-315, 316, 373; protests to Germany against Brandeis, 335, 367; forms treaty of political confederation with Hawaii, 329-330; supported by United States in Washington Conference, 346; opposed by Germany, 348; German government makes war on, 371-372; takes to the bush, 374; surrenders and goes aboard the *Bismarck*, 376; explains his actions to American consul, 376-377; deported by Germans, 377; Germany at war with, 422; United States denies legality of arrest and deportation of, 434; release of, pledged by Germany, 452; restored to power by Berlin Conference, 502, 513-514; asks powers to intervene against Mataafa, 536, 537; protests against policies of foreign adviser, 547; illness and death of, 550, 551

Malietoa Talavou, elder chief, elected king, 216 n; agrees with government to neutral municipal area in war, 223; courtesy but not recognition for, advised by American consul, 225; offended by military salute to opposition, 225-226; offers Samoan Islands as joint protectorate to England, Germany, and United States, 233-234; adheres to municipal convention, 235; appeals for protection during civil war, 240, 249; elected king for life by both factions, 241, 242, 249; recognized by foreign powers, 246, 249, 250, 251, 397; signs consular agreement for joint protectorate, 249; ill-advised by English adventurer, 258-259; death of, 259, 265; administration of, commended by President Hayes, 264

Malietoa Tanu, son of Malietoa Laupepa, opposes Mataafa in claim to Samoan throne, 560, 561; seeks safety on British war ship *Porpoise*, 561; crowned king under protection of foreign guns, 561; persuaded to abdicate by tripartite commissioners, 564

Malo, designation for Samoan government, 230

Mandate over Samoa, maneuvered for, by Germany, 324, 325, 349, 355-356, 358, 359, 360, 363, 364-365; recommended by England, 351, 356, 357, 357-358, 364; opposed by United States, 353-354, 355-356, 358-359, 436, 437; 363-364, 365-366, 385, 450; Germany and England willing to abandon policy in Samoa, 428, 438; Western Samoa allotted to New Zealand as, in Treaty of Versailles, 574

"Manifest destiny," not applicable to Samoa, 521

Marriages, registration of, 125
Martha, the, shipwreck of, 34
Martin, Judge, chief municipal magistrate, tool of Godeffroy Company, 379
Mataafa, Chief, pretender to Samoan kingship, 105; signs consular agreement for joint protectorate by three powers, 249; asserts right to succeed Malietoa, 375; leads revolt against Tamasese, 412-413, 414-415; installed as king, 414; defeats German forces second time, 419; intense feeling against, in Germany, 428; launches civil war on Malietoa government, 536, 537; captured and exiled, 539-540; pardon and release of, discussed by powers, 549-551; returns from exile, 560; elected king, 560; opposed by British and United States marines, 561
Matafao Peak, 2
Maudslay, A. P., British consul to Samoa and deputy commissioner for the Western Pacific, attempts to coerce Samoan government into agreement, 185-188; signs treaty with Samoa, 230; adheres to municipal convention, 235
Mauga, Chief, 63, 65, 70, 71, 91, 92, 93, 128; hostility of other chiefs toward, 101, 107; letter of, to president, 108; independence of, 111, 129; leader of Puletua in war against government, 182; famous "ransom mat" goes to United States, 204-205
Maxse, E., British consul general to Samoa, reports situation in regard to kingship, 550; recognizes Mataafa government in Samoa, 561
Meade, Commander Richard W., in Pacific waters, 56; dilemma over instructions, 56-57, 68; influenced by Peirce and Wakeman, 58-59, 61, 67; objects of cruise in Samoa, 60-61; concludes treaty for naval base, 63; concludes treaty of commercial regulations, 63-65; and new Samoan flag, 65; address of, to natives, 65-67, 80

Meade's Treaty, inspiration for negotiations, 59, 60, 61, 62, 68; negotiations with Chief Mauga, 63, 204; terms of treaty, 63-65, 233 n; effect of, on German-American relations, 69-70; on Anglo-American relations, 79-81; on agitation in New Zealand, 76-78, 81-82; on Anglo-German relations, 79; submitted to secretary of navy, 71 n; advocacy of, by secretary of navy, 71, 73-74; by secretary of state, 71; by president, 71-72; failure of Senate to ratify, 74; modifications by Steinberger, 91-92, 128

Menshikoff, American bark, 84, 156, 162, 164

Mensing, Captain, German naval officer, signs municipal convention, 235

Meredith, Thomas, United States consular agent on island of Tutuila, 139-140

Merrill, Mr., United States minister to Hawaii, reports on Hawaiian activities relative to Samoa, 329, 338, 339

Mervine, Commodore William, United States naval officer, protests against, by English missionaries, 29

Micronesia, survey of, proposed, 49

Midway Islands, act for deepening harbor of, 42; work on survey of, suspended, 43

Miller, Captain J. N., United States

INDEX 619

naval officer, despatched to investigate *Barracouta* affair, 142-143

Miranda, British war ship, in Samoa during New Zealand agitation for annexation, 274; at time of German intervention, 287

Missionaries, English origin of first, 77; and annexation or protection by United States, 83, 84, 104-106, 113, 334-335; and land alienation, 94; and Samoan laws, 98, 124-125; and the Steinberger mission, 98, 100, 101, 104-106; from London Missionary Society, 104; of Roman Catholic faith, 104, 105; of Wesleyan faith, 100, 105; native, 108; coöperation of, pledged, 105, 111; critical of British policy in Samoa, 445

Mohican, United States ship, in Samoan waters, 312, 313-314, 411, 413

Money and coinage, early conditions, 28; under *condominium*, 528-530

"Monroe Doctrine," of New Zealand, 77-78; as conceivable of extension by United States to the Pacific, 296-297; United States hampered by, in relation to Samoa, 520 n

Moore, John Bassett, on our Samoan policy, 519-520, 521; advises partition of Samoa, 566 n

Moors, H. J., United States resident in Samoa, dispute with Weber over land claims, 406-407; opposes Brandeis-Tamasese régime, 412

"Most favored nation" rights, in treaties, 213, 221, 231; embarrassment of, to native government, 234

Möwe, German war ship, subject of correspondence between Bismarck and Bayard, 393, 397

Mulinuu, capital of Samoa, included in neutral municipal zone, 170-171; refuge for American consul, 176, 181; scenes in, at celebration of American treaty, 205; protection for, pending civil war, 223

Mulinuu, Samoan war vessel, seized by British high commissioner, 184, 188; renamed *Elizabeth*, 187

Mullan, D. W., United States naval officer in Samoa, 417

Mulligan, James H., United States consul general at Apia, disrupts consular harmony, 542

Mumm, Herr A. von, German minister at Washington, takes part in negotiations for partition of Samoa, 565, 571

Municipal convention of 1879, grows out of native request for tripartite protectorate, 233-234; organized by consuls, 234-235; legal basis for tripartite control, 235; terms of, 235-237; agreed to, by American representatives subject to approval by government, 235, 237; approved by Department of State, with reservations, 235, 244, 256-257, 264, 265, 267, 270-271, 272, 401; never ratified by United States, 235, 237 n, 268, 295, 369, 370, 401; accepted by Germany, subject to conditions of German-Samoan treaty, 235, 237; accepted by England as formal treaty, 235; accepted by both native factions, 241; sanctioned formally or informally by powers, 244; amended, 248, 249-250; indefinitely extended at end of four-year period, 271-272; execution of, embarrassed by: informal participation of United States, 268, 271, 272, 295-296; 369-370, 387; German interference in internal politics, 278-280, 281-282, 285-287, 288-291, 298-299, 300; annexationist agitation in New Zealand, 273-274, 276, 280-281, 283; terminated by Germany, 379-380, 381-382; see Tripartite government

Municipal council of Apia, as organized by Berlin Conference, 502, 503, 512, 524; presidents of, 527, 541, 547; disputes with president of, over coinage and common treasury, 528-531; with chief justice over assumption of political powers, 546-547

Municipal government of Apia, as organized under consuls, 170-171, 223, 228, 235-237; under *condominium*, 518-519, 523-525; see Neutral municipal area, Municipal convention, Tripartite government, Berlin Conference, *Condominium*

Münster, Count, German ambassador to England, agrees to partition of New Guinea, 283

Murray, A. W., charges of, against United States consul and naval officer, 29

Narragansett, United States war ship, cruises in Pacific, 56, 57

Natives, of Samoan archipelago, description of, by first explorers, 6; skill as navigators, 8; arrangement of villages, 9; reputation damaged by fate of La Pérouse expedition, 9; as described by Lieutenant Wilkes, 16; women, 16; government of, 21; commerce of, with foreigners, 28

Nautilus, German war ship, in Samoan waters, 217, 242

Naval base, United States in Samoa, efforts of various interests to obtain, 43, 51, 55, 57, 59, 60, 61, 63, 66, 73-74, 88, 119-120, 126; American opinion on, 195, 196, 199-200; rights for, acquired in Pago Pago, 196-197, 205; exclusive rights sought, 466

"Navigators Islands," 4; named by Bougainville, 8; and United States Exploring Expedition, 14; referred to thus in Peirce's letter to Commander Meade, 60

Navy, United States, in early contacts with Samoa, surveying projects of, 13-17, 43, 59-60; diplomatic offices of, 17-18, 19-20, 21, 22-23, 25, 43, 60-61, 63-65, 66-67; judicial powers of, 21-22, 38, 39, 62-63; moral support of, to consuls, 22, 38, 39, 43, 44, 49; postal services of, 24; infrequent visits of, 38; lack of instructions for, 38, 39

Neutral municipal area, established by American consul, 170-171; tripartite guarantee by consuls, 223; see Tripartite government

New Guinea, annexed by Germany, 255; annexation not recognized by England, 282; Anglo-German negotiations over, lead to partition, 280-283

New Hebrides, position relative to Samoa, 1; United States refuses intervention to prevent annexation of, 276

"New Holland," Dutch name for Australia, 4 n

New York Herald, United States newspaper, on Berlin treaty, 516

New York Times, United States newspaper, on "entangling alliances" in Samoa, 192-193, 199-200, 213; on Samoan annexation or protectorate by England, 193, 199, 200; by Germany, 213, 217; on stronger United States policy in Samoa, 405; defends Bayard,

405-406; accuses Republicans of responsibility for Samoan situation, 406

New Zealand, visited by United States Exploring Expedition, 17; interest of, in Webb's proposed steamship service, 46, 47-48; agitation for Samoan annexation, 75, 76-78, 81-82, 136, 137, 201, 273-274, 277, 280-281, 280 n, 283

Nipsic, United States war vessel, in Samoa, 417, 430, 443

Nord-Deutsche-Allgemeine Zeitung, German newspaper, supports Bismarck's policy of colonial expansion, 254; on Stübel's activities in Samoa, 305, 306

North American Steamship Company, 45; see Webb, W. H.

North German Gazette, newspaper, on German activities in Samoa, 217

Noyes, E. L., United States minister to Paris, 178, 179, 180

Oertzen, G. von, acting German consul, signs "Lackawanna Peace," 263

Ogden, R. L., San Francisco ship builder, letter to President Grant, 144

Olga, German war ship, provision for saving, 430; lost in hurricane off Samoa, 443

Olney, Richard, United States secretary of state, disagrees with Germany on interpretation of Berlin Act, 545-546, 547-548

Oratory, native, 95, 96, 97; characterized, 219; see Tololos; see also "Talking man"

Ormsbee, E. J., land commissioner for United States, 534

Osborn, L. W., United States consul general at Apia, recognizes Mataafa government in Samoa, 561

Oscar II, king of Sweden and Norway, arbitrates Germany's claims against United States and Great Britain for losses in civil war in Samoa, 568

Pago Pago, distance from Panama, 1; harbor of, described, 16, 50-51, 60, 205; United States consulate established at, 24-25; resurvey of, 68; efforts toward United States naval base in, 43, 51, 55, 57, 59, 60, 61, 63, 66, 88, 119-120, 126; offered United States in return for protectorate, 195-196; United States rights in, under treaty of 1878, 197, 213, 220, 277; English rights in, under treaty of 1879, 197 n; United States flag raised in, 205-206; makeweight in United States policy in Samoa, 256, 273, 274, 277, 346, 354, 437, 466, 556, 558, 559, 560, 569; Blaine seeks exclusive rights in, 465-466; in Senate debates, 517; taken over by United States navy, 575; United States flag raised in, 576

Pall Mall Gazette, English newspaper, on German military actions in islands, 217

Panama, distance from Pago Pago, 1

Pandora, English ship, voyage to Samoa, 9-10

Parker, D. S., acting United States vice consul, 139-140, 155, 156, 157

Partition of Samoa, suggested by Salisbury and Malet, 449; as alternative to *condominium*, 556, 558; hastened by imperialism of Republican party, 557; Spanish-American War inspires Germany to definite move toward, 558; German efforts to overcome opposition in Australasia, 558, 559; England refuses to negotiate for, 560; hastened by civil war in Samoa, 561; Germany revives project, 565, 566; Great Britain and United States ready to discuss, 566, 567; von Bülow opposes plan of German colonial council to sell out, 569; United States takes definite stand on, 570-571; Germany and Great Britain reach an agreement, 571; terms of partition, 571, 572, 574; complicated by United States treaty with Tonga, 572-573; signing of agreement by tripartite convention, 574; American territory obtained by, 576; ratification by Congress, 579

Party politics in United States, as related to Samoan affairs, 196, 403-404, 404-405, 428, 438, 481, 515, 516, 556, 557

Paulding, J. K., United States secretary of navy, and United States Exploring Expedition, 15

Pauncefote, Sir Julian, British ambassador to Washington, in settlement of Anglo-German interests in the Pacific, 281; receives negative answer from United States relative to appointment of temporary chief justice, 549; seeks American attitude toward kingship, 551; reports Britain's willingness to take part in tripartite commission, 563; negotiates with Hay for partition agreement, 572, 573; signs partition agreement, 574

Peacock, in United States Exploring Expedition, 15

Peale, T. R., naturalist, member United States Exploring Expedition, 14

Pearl, English war ship, recognizes Steinberger government, 113

Pearl Harbor, United States naval base in, 406

Peerless, Steinberger's "yacht," 138 n, 144, 145, 150

Peirce, Henry A., United States minister resident in Honolulu, urges ship subsidy for Pacific lines, 46; influence of, on American expansion in Pacific, 49-50; urges treaty with Samoa, 60-61, 68; supports protectorate policy, 67-68; talks with Wakeman, 68

Pendleton, G. H., American minister to Berlin, instructed to remonstrate with Bismarck on Stübel's encroachments in Samoa, 301-303; reports to Bayard on attitude of German press toward Samoa, 305-306; instructed to confer with German government on Samoan situation, 388-390, 415, 419, 420; invalid condition of, blamed for delay in preparations for Berlin Conference, 429

Pensacola, United States war ship, in Pacific, 120, 121

Periaguas, description of native skill with, 8

Petin, H., quoted, 520 n

Phelps, E. J., American minister in London, reports on English overtures to end German intervention in Samoa, 303-304, 419

Phelps, W. W., United States representative at Berlin Conference, 429, 471, 475, 476-477, 478, 479, 480, 482, 487, 488, 494, 496, 503, 504, 505

Philadelphia, United States war ship, bombards Apia, damaging German consulate, 561

Pickering, Charles, naturalist, mem-

INDEX 623

ber United States Exploring Expedition, 14

Pilsach, Baron Senfft von, president of municipal council, friction with council, 527-531; tenders resignation, but refused, 531; becomes dictatorial, 532; resignation effective, 540, 547, 548

Platt, Frank, secretary to Steinberger, 140-141

Pluddeman, Captain, of German war ship, implicated in Stübel activities of 1884, 286

Polynesian Land Company, activities in islands, 84, 95, 132, 135, 167, 168-169

Poppe, Herr, German acting consul, 140

Population, statistics of, estimate for 1838, 11 n; estimate for 1855, 29; estimate of native, for 1871, 60

Porpoise, in United States Exploring Expedition, 15

Porpoise, British war ship, part in Samoan civil war, 561

Port regulations, for foreign vessels in Samoan waters, 20-21, 28, 29, 63-65, 91-93; in United States-Samoan treaty of 1878, 197, 219; in German-Samoan treaty of 1879, 219, 220; in Berlin Act, 476-477, 479-483, 503-504

Portugal, probable explorations in Samoa, 4; explorations in neighboring groups, sixteenth century, 4 n

Powell, Rev. Dr., 91

Powell, Wilfred, British consul in Samoa, reports on German encroachments in Samoa, 303, 304

Predpriatic, Russian ship, voyage of, to Samoa, 10-11

Pritchard, George, acting United States consular representative at Apia, 25; as an English resident supports the Puletua, 170

Products of islands, 28-29, 51, 121 n

Protectorate, see under Annexation

Pule, native political faction, 101, 122 n, 123

Pulepule, Chief, 122

Puletua, native political faction, 152, 157, 158, 159, 169, 170, 172; supported by English and German governments, 150, 159, 160-161, 170, 171, 172; German support withdrawn from, 212

Purvis, Captain, British naval officer, instructed by British government to recognize Malietoa and join naval forces of Germany and United States for protectorate of Samoa, 248, 251; intervenes in behalf of consuls to end civil war, 257

Quai d'Orsay, 178, 179

Racial relations, 31, 97, 106, 220-221

Raffel, Dr., appointed president of municipal council, 547; closes supreme court in Samoa, 561

Railways, transcontinental, link in communication, 46

Recognition of Samoa, by United States, 142, 174, 204, 276

Relief, in United States Exploring Expedition, 15

Religious freedom, 102

Republican party, see Party politics in America

Rich, William, botanist, member United States Exploring Expedition, 14

Ripley, E. V. C., appointed vice commercial agent for Tutuila and Manua, 28

Robeson, G. M., United States secretary of navy, 71, 73; letter of, outlining policy of Navy toward Pacific commerce, 73-74

Robinson, Joseph T., United States senator, on commission investigating government of American Samoa, 579

Rodgers, Commander Frederick, United States naval officer, and treaty of 1878, 203, 204; takes formal possession of rights in Pago Pago, 205-206

Roggewein, Jacob, in charge of expedition for Dutch East India Company, 5; first known discoverer of Samoa in 1722, 5; account of explorations, 5-7

Roosevelt, Theodore, president of United States, acknowledges cession of Manua Islands to United States, 576

Rose, Herr, German consul in Samoa, recognizes Mataafa government in Samoa, 561; closes supreme court, 561

Rosebery, Lord, on concert of powers in Samoa, 538-539

Rosendaal, Roelof, with Dutch expedition to Samoa, 5 n

Royalist, British war ship, part in Samoan civil war, 561

Ruge-Hedleman and Company (German), 159

Russia, explorations in Samoa by Kotzebue, 10-11

Saavedro, explorations of, in South Pacific, 4 n

Sackville-West, Sir Lionel, British minister to Washington, gives Department of State confidential use of Anglo-German correspondence on Samoa, 293, 304; friendly gestures prior to Washington Conference, 340, 341, 342, 343; veers to German position in conference, 345, 346, 355, 356-357, 357-358, 360, 361, 364; agrees to adjournment of conference, 366; declines to allow publication of protocols, 403, 446-447

"Sacred mat" of Tui Atua, presented to Steinberger, 100, 101

Saga, Chief, sends "staff" and "fly-flap" to United States president, 96

Saginaw, United States war ship, detailed for survey in Midway Islands, 42

St. Thomas, island of, attitude of United States toward acquisition of, 195

Salisbury, Lord, prime minister of England, remonstrates with Germany on the apparent violation of Samoan independence, 303; suggests tripartite protectorate for Samoa, 305; strikes bargain with Bismarck on Samoa, 344, 345 n; willing to lay aside preference for mandate system in Samoa, 428; receives Kasson, United States delegate to Berlin Conference, 446; states position on Samoa, 447-448, 448 n, 449; on resignation of Pilsach, 531, 549; unwilling to negotiate with Germany for partition of Samoa, 560; authorizes British participation in tripartite commission to Samoa, 563; consents to partition proposal, 567

Saluafata harbor, Germany acquires naval base in, 202, 220; rebellion breaks out in, 251

Samoan Islands, the fourteen islands of group named, 1 n; strategic position of, 1-2, 26, 43, 44, 55, 73, 354; vegetation and animal life on, 2-3, 6, 9, 16, 28-29; size of, 3; discovery of, 3-7

INDEX 625

Samoan Land Company, 150

Samoan native government, lack of centralization in, 22, 26, 27-28, 38, 39, 65, 66, 67; attempts at union, 67, 93, 97, 107, 110; flag of, saluted by foreign consuls, 99; adoption of constitution and laws, 101-102, 242-244; reorganized by Steinberger, 122-124; interregnum, 142; disintegration of, 213, 214, 215-217, 216 n, 230, 237-238, 245; places neutral municipal area under consular control, 223; reorganized by Deinhard, 242-244; accepts consular agreement for joint protectorate by three powers, 249, 250; disrupted by death of Malietoa Talavou, 259-262; reestablished by "Lackawanna Peace," 263; chaos, see Stübel; seeks confederation with Hawaii, 329-330; constitution of, major item in Washington Conference, 345; falls under Brandeis-Tamasese régime, 371-372; reconstituted in *condominium*, 523-525; ends in partition, 573-574

Samoan Times, quoted, 208-209

San Francisco, distance from Samoa, 1; proposal to connect with Australasia by steamship line, 45-46

San Francisco Alta, 200

San Francisco Chronicle, 191

Santa Cruz, island of, attitude of United States toward acquisition of, 195

Santo Domingo, attitude of United States toward acquisition of, 195

Sapphire, British war ship, in Samoa, 182, 183, 185, 187

Sateli, Chief, 107

Schlözer, Kurd von, German minister to United States, on American and German naval bases in Samoa, 202; confers with Secretary Evarts and British minister on Samoan question, 266

Schmidt, E., appointed president of municipal council, 541; assumes functions of chief justice in Ide's absence, 545, 546; dictatorial policies of, antagonize native government, 547; resigns, 547, 548

Schoonmaker, Captain C. M., United States naval officer, lost in hurricane at Samoa, 443

Schouten, Dutch explorer in Pacific, 4

Schurz, Carl, commends Bayard for handling of Washington Conference, 424

Scientific interest of United States in South Pacific, instructions to Exploring Expedition, 14; scientists in expedition, 14, 17, 19

Scott, Charles Edward, represents England at Berlin Conference, 455; participation of, in proceedings, 457, 459, 487, 492, 499, 500, 505

Sea-Gull, tender with United States Exploring Expedition, 15

Seamen, United States, early contacts of, with Samoa, 19; trade of, with Samoans, 28

Sewall, H. M., first United States consul general at Apia, instructed to advise peace among factions during Washington negotiations, 342, 367-368; confronted by German opposition, 368-369, 370, 379-381; advised of peculiar position of United States in tripartite municipal convention, 369-370, 387-388; protests against violation of neutrality, 372, 373; seeks action on basis: of United States-Samoan treaty, 373-374; of municipal convention, 378, 380, 383-384; reports on relative strength of Malietoa and Tamasese, 375-376;

assumes protection of United States citizens, 380; explains termination of tripartite government, 380-382; commended by Adee for discretion, 387; anti-German actions of, subject to complaint by Bismarck, 393, 417; describes prejudice to American property and trade rights by Germany, 407-408, 411; recommends American occupation of islands, 411-412; consistently opposes Brandeis-Tamasese government, 412, 413; appointed disbursing officer at Berlin Conference, 433, 509; favors Mataafa for king, 471; reports peace in Samoa, 522-523; opposes intervention against Mataafa, 536-537, 542

Seward, F. W., United States assistant secretary of state, receives Samoan commissioner for treaty, 192; explains American opinion on annexation and protectorate, 194-195; sounds out secretary of state, Navy Department, and Congress on treaty, 195-196, 198; draws up treaty of 1878, 196; suspicious of English intentions, 200, 201-202; see Treaty of 1878; see also Le Mamea

Sherman, John, as United States senator, steers Berlin treaty through senate, 517, 518; as United States secretary of state, favors strict interpretation of Berlin Act, 549

Ship subsidies, 46, 47; arguments for, 46, 48; attitude of administration toward, 85

Sine, Chief John, 90-91

Slave traffic, and depopulation, 113

Society Islands, position relative to Samoa, 1

Solomon Islands, United States refuses intervention to prevent annexation of, 276

Sophie, German war ship, in Samoan waters, 430

Spain, probable explorations in Samoa, 4; explorations in neighboring group, 4

Spanish-American War, inspires Germany to move toward partition of Samoa, 558

"Staff," emblem of Samoan nationality, 96, 114, 117, 118

Standard, London newspaper, quoted on British protectorate in Samoa, 200

Starbuck, Alexander, quoted, 12

Stearns, Norman W., appointed to serve as acting United States vice consul in certain contingency, 29

Steinberger, Colonel A. B., 81; friend of President Grant, 85; overtures to president for special commissionership, 85, 86, 112-114; relations with W. H. Webb, 85, 86, 109-110; correspondence with Secretary Fish, 87, 110, 112-114; appointed special commissioner, 87, 117; instructions: for first mission, 87-89; for second, 117-120; purposes of missions, real and assumed, 87-89, 93-94, 97-98, 103-104, 109-110, 116, 119, 120, 125; curiosity concerning, 81, 90, 109, 114, 121, 201; negotiations for rights and port regulations in Pago Pago harbor, 91-93; regarding land alienation, 94-95, 98-99, 115; for United States political primacy, 91, 93, 94, 96, 97, 98, 99-100, 102-104, 105, 106, 107-108, 109-111, 112-113, 114, 115, 116, 117; for setting up native central government, 93-94, 97, 98, 99-100, 101-104, 107-108, 113, 122-124; personal ambitions, 103, 104-105,

INDEX 627

111, 112-114, 115, 116, 117, 120, 123, 125-126, 132, 147, 214; support of, by natives, 91, 93-94, 95-97, 98, 99-101, 102-104, 107-108, 109, 111, 113, 119, 122, 126, 127-129, 130, 132, 135, 139, 141-142, 143, 149; and European consuls, 92, 93, 98, 99, 111, 125, 127, 128, 132, 136, 137, 137-138, 139, 140, 141; and President, 85, 86, 102, 110, 114, 115, 118, 140, 141, 145-146, 147; and Department of State, 87-89, 90, 109, 110, 112, 114-115, 117-119, 120, 125, 126-128, 129, 130, 134, 135, 139-140, 144, 147, 148; and Navy Department, 119-120, 130, 142-143; and Congress, 111, 113, 115, 120, 125, 126, 146-147; and foreign residents, 94-95, 97, 98-99, 104-106, 109, 130-131, 139-140; and missionaries, 98, 99, 101, 104-106, 111, 112, 113, 124-125, 131, 133-134, 136, 137, 139, 141; secret agreement with German firm, 115-117, 121 n, 144; secret agreement with Latrobe and Wilkinson, 120-121, 121 n; becomes premier of Samoa, 125-126; resignation as United States special commissioner, 125, 133, 134; rumors of filibustering expedition by, 160, 214 n; friction with United States consulate, 126-127, 129, 130, 131-134, 136, 137-138, 139, 140, 141, 144-145, 148; investigation, arrest, and deportation of, 138-139, 141, 142, 143, 144, 146; actions disavowed by Department of State, 144, 148, 149

Steinberger government, see Samoan government

Steinberger mission, criticized by *New York Times*, 192

Steinberger seal, 171

Sternberg, Freiherr Speck von, represents Germany in tripartite commission in Samoa, 564

Stevens, Captain, British naval officer, in Samoa, 137, 138, 139, 141, 142, 143, 144, 145, 146; see Barracouta affair

Stevenson, Robert Louis, residence in Samoa, 3 n; on German-Samoan relations, 333-334; characterizes Theodor Weber, 409-410; describes American opposition to Brandeis-Tamasese government, 412; seeks modification of Berlin Act, 532

Stewart, J. B. M., and petition for annexation, 83-84, 85, and Polynesian Land Company, 84, 156; attempts to undermine Griffin, 156, 166-167; takes Samoan delegation to Fiji aboard the *Menshikoff*, 162; coöperates with Colmesnil in flag-hoisting episode, 165 n

Stewart, Cooper and Company, 155-156

Stübel, Dr., German consul, negotiates convention for native government dominated by German interests, 278-279, 399-400; attaches municipality of Apia, 285, 400; hoists German flag in native capital, 286, 292; forbids native *tololos* in Mulinuu, 287; recall requested by King Malietoa, 288; intervention of, disavowed by German government, 289, 292, 300; orders Samoan flag hauled down, 300; reverses position in Samoa, under instructions from Berlin, 310, 314, 316-317, 513-514; action praised by Bayard, 312; recalled, 320

Sturdee, Captain, of British war ship *Porpoise*, supports supreme court, 561

Supreme Court for Samoa, established by Berlin Conference, 501, 523-524; delay in organization of, causes complications, 522, 523; chief justices of, 525, 540, 549; friction with land commission, 525-527; aided in execution of warrants by war ship, 537-538; encroaches on prerogatives of council, 546-547; dignity of, 553; fortunes of, in civil war, 561

Swanston, Robert S., United States acting vice consul at Apia, appointed, 30; inquiries of, concerning half-castes, 31, 34; concerning anomalous position of consular officer, 31-32

Sydney, distance from Samoa, 1; visited by United States Exploring Expedition, 17

Sydney Morning Herald, and American violations of Wilkes' treaty, 29

Symonds, H. F., British acting consul at Apia, reports on Malietoa's efforts to curb chiefs, 341

Taimua and Faipule, address letter to United States president, 102-103; terms explained, 122 n; premier to preside over Taimua and have privilege of floor in either assembly, 123; depose Malietoa, 141; request Steinberger's return, 149; intimidated by Germans, 151-152; protest against Germans to United States president, 152; Griffin offered commission to go to Washington to negotiate a treaty, 153-155; British change consul in answer to protest of, against Steinberger's arrest, 156-157; struggle with opposition (Puletua) to retain control of government, 158-162; negotiations with Colmesnil for United States protection against British and Germans, 163-165; inform Colmesnil that United States flag will be hauled down to avoid complications, 169-170; defeat of opposition, 170-171; Griffin welcomed by, 172; request president again for treaty, 174-175; threatened by English and Germans, 181-188; send commissioner to Washington to negotiate a treaty, 191; approached for English treaty, 201; acclaim treaty with United States, 203-205; urge return of Griffin by Department of State, 208; grant Dawson recognition, 209; announce disbandment of government, 214; weakness of, stirs opposition, 215-216; defend German-Samoan treaty, 219; seek consular protection for municipal area, 223, 227; officially recognized by United States in spite of weakness, 225; driven from capital, 230; reestablished by Deinhard, 242; representatives from, to conduct foreign affairs, 243, 244; cupidity of, described by United States consul, 271; suggested reorganization of, at Washington Conference, 347

"Talking man," 95, 100

Tamasese, Chief, crowned king by rival faction, 260; local English newspaper urges consular stand against, 261; created vice king by "Lackawanna Peace," 263; appointed king during Stübel intervention, 287; revolution of, supported by Germans, 278, 284-285, 286-287, 288, 298-299, 304, 306, 313, 315, 322-323, 324, 367; supported by Germany in Washington

Conference, 348; recognized as king by German government, 372; agrees to protect treaties with other powers, 372; repudiated by Germany, 514; acknowledges Malietoa Laupepa, 522

Tasman, explorations of, in South Pacific, 4, 5 n

Taxes and revenue, native dislike of, 331, 523; crops mortgaged for, 410-411; and foreigners, 221, 279, 290, 349, 351, 377-378, 382, 401, 407, 408; as provided in Berlin treaty, 479-483; disputes over apportionment of, 527, 530-531, 543; adequacy of, 553

Thielmann, Baron von, German chargé d'affaires at Washington, representations to Department of State regarding consular coöperation, 180-181; takes issue over interpretation of Berlin Act, 545-546

Thomson, Basil, on the *condominium*, 551-552

Thornton, Sir E., British minister to Washington, inquires into United States policy on annexation, 79-80; questioned by Seward on British policy in Samoa, 202; confers with Secretary Evarts and German minister on Samoan question, 266

Thurston, John B., acting governor of Fiji, sent as English special commissioner to Samoa, 321; reports findings, 322, 340, 356; investigates German copra monopoly, 411

Tienhoven, Dutch ship, in first expedition to Samoa, 5 n

"Tienhoven," Dutch name for island of Upolu, 6-7, 6 n

Tilley, Benjamin F., Commander of United States ship *Abarenda*, announces partition of Samoa, 575; made commander of naval station, 576

Tololos, held in celebration of treaty with the United States, 205-206

Transcontinental railroad, welcomed by New Zealand, 76; arouses British suspicions, 79; American link with Samoa, 354

Travers, Herr G., German consul general at Sydney, sent as special commissioner to Samoa, 320; reports findings, 321, 340

Trenton, United States war ship, in Samoan waters, 443

Tripartite government, stages in, begins in establishment of neutral municipal area, 170-171; tripartite guarantee of neutrality for Mulinuu requested by native government, 223; three consuls guarantee neutrality and protection for Apia municipality, 223; American participation in, approved by Department of State, 223, 227; administration of, in municipal area described, 228; natives request joint protectorate of all Samoa by three powers, 233-235; American representative urges tripartite protectorate, 225, 238, 241, 249, 257-258; preliminary convention for, entered into by local officials of three powers, 234-235; terms of preliminary convention for, 235-237; American participation in, approved by Department of State, 244; English and German representatives announce instructions for joint protectorate with United States, 248; tripartite treaty negotiated by consuls of three countries, with native chiefs, 249, 250; terms provide for triple ministry as executive council to king and government, 250; attitude of Department of State toward tripartite treaty uncertain, 250-251, 255; causes of uncertainty, 251-256; decision to coöperate informally, but not to enter entangling alliance, 235, 244, 256-257, 264, 265, 267, 270-271, 272; President Hayes recommends to Congress some tripartite agreement for maintaining stable government, 264; Secretary Evarts asks diplomatic conference with German and English ministers, 265-266; Department of State instructs consul on concerted action with his colleagues, 267; concerted action embarrassed by: Department's anomalous acceptance of convention, 268, 271, 272, 295-296, 369-370, 387; by agitation in New Zealand, 280-281, 283; England favors internationalization by powers, 283, 305; German activities produce chaotic situation, 278-280, 281-282, 285-287, 288-291, 298-299, 300, 377-378; Berlin government declares intention to maintain *status quo*, 289, 292, 293, 297, 302, 304, 317; but insists on execution of convention of 1884, 290, 292, 299; Bismarck's duplicity strengthens coöperation between England and America, 279, 292-294, 298-299, 300, 303-304, 317; embarrassed by activities of American consul, 306-307, 309-310, 311, 319; supported by United States at Washington and Berlin conferences, 345, 346, 347, 354, 358, 458, 465, 475, 490, 496-497; opposed by England and Germany at Washington Conference, 349, 350-351, 353-354, 355-356, 357-358, 359; suspended by Germany, 379-380, 381-382; reëstablished by Berlin Conference, 484-485, 503, 511-512, 523-525; friction of local officers presages ill, 525-531, 546-547; powers show coöperation, 531, 538-539, 542-543, 548, 563; changes in instrument of government suggested, 531-533; disturbed by civil war, 536, 537; intervention by concert of powers, 537-540; powers vacate offices of chief justice and president, 540-541; consular harmony disturbed, 541-542; Germany and United States disagree: over control of finances, 543; over suppression of traffic in firearms, 543-545; over assumption of judicial functions by president of council, 545-546; over assumption of presidential duties by consular board, 547-548; England and United States disagree over consular assumption of supreme court duties, 549; kingship becomes general concern, 549-551; regarded as ''fatuous,'' 551-552; unsatisfactoriness of, 551; criticisms of, 552-556; civil war upsets, 561; joint commission to ''settle on the spot'' decided on, 561-565; partition ends, 573-574; see Berlin Conference, *Condominium*, Municipal Convention, Washington Conference

Tripp, Bartlett, represents United States on tripartite commission in Samoa, 564; favors partition of Samoa, 565, 566

Tui-Manna, King, 108

Tuiteli, Chief, 107

Tupai, Chief, 95-96, 100

Turner, Dr. George A., medical missionary, 83, 100 n, 141

Turner, Rev. George A., missionary, 100, 100 n, 104, 112

INDEX

Turner, Rear Admiral Thomas, Commander United States Pacific Fleet, 50 n

Tuscarora, United States ship, in Samoan waters, 121, 122, 142-143

United States Exploring Expedition, sent to Pacific after repeated petitions, 12; delays in getting under way, 12-13; instructions for, 13-15; work of, 15-18; see Wilkes, Lieutenant Charles

van Camp, Dr. Aaron, United States commercial agent at Apia, difficulty of, in securing exequatur, 27-28; report to Department of State on conditions in Samoa, 28-29; sudden departure of, 29; charges against, 28-29; investigation of, 32-33

Vandalia, United States war ship, wrecked by hurricane off Samoa, 443

"Verrathers, Cocos and," 4, 6 n

Versailles, Treaty of, Western Samoa allotted to New Zealand as mandate under, 574

Vincennes, in United States Exploring Expedition, 15

Vogel, Julius, premier of New Zealand, urges annexation of Samoa to British Empire, 77, 81, 273

Waddington, Monsieur, French minister of foreign affairs, intermediary in Aube affair, 178, 179, 180

Wakeman, Captain E., agent of Webb Line, description by, of Pago Pago harbor, 50-51, and Upolu, 55; report by, on German activities in islands, 51-52, 54; arguments of, for annexation and naval station, 55; conversations with Peirce in Honolulu, 59; report to Webb, 71, 72

Wallwork, William, United States trader in Samoa, in difficulties with Weber's firm, 411

Washington Conference, precedent for, 265-266; proposed to British and German governments by Bayard, 307, 310; British and German governments favorable to, 307, 308, 309, 310; Germany suggests despatch of special commissioners to Samoa, preliminary to conference, 311; suggestion accepted by United States and England, 317, 320-321; United States commissioner instructed regarding: neutrality of islands, 318, 319-320; extraterritorial jurisdiction in, 318, 319; prior treaty rights of United States, 319-320; commissioners complete survey preliminary to conference, 320-321; further progress complicated by: German maneuvers in Samoa, 322-323, 324-325; United States consul's negotiations with Hawaii, 325-327; Hawaiian-Samoan rapprochement, 327-339; three powers exchange reports of their special commissioners, 340, 343; native factions urged to peace during negotiations, 342-343; conference opens, 344; British and German delegates refuse to submit plans of settlement, 344-345; German and British delegates in opposition to that of the United States (Bayard) on fundamental issues, 345, 445; terms of American plan, 346-348; German memorandum, 348-350; British memorandum, 350-351; points of agreement of three powers, 352, 361; conflicts over form of government to be established, 352-354, 355-356, 358-359, 363-364, 365-366, 385, 391-393; Bayard defines the interest of his government in Samoa, 354; disagreement over method of settling land claims, 354-355, 356-357, 359-360, 361-363; adjournment agreed upon, 366; Bismarck submits memorandum on, 384-385, 391-393; Germany charged with breach of faith relating to, 395-396, 400-401; England and Germany refuse to publish protocols, 403; part played in, by Bates, recalled, 431, 434; Blaine strongly favors continuation of United States policies outlined in, 434, 435, 436

Waters, George F., claims against Steinberger, 150

Webb, William H., United States ship builder, extensive interests in Pacific, 44-45, 64, 69; expansionist hopes of, 45; application of, to Congress for subsidy, 46, 47; aided by New Zealand government, 47-48; competition of, with English line, 46; sponsors survey of harbor facilities and trade possibilities in Samoa, 50-51, 67; reports data on naval base, 52; advocacy of, by secretary of navy, 85, 86, 110; recommends to President Grant appointment of Steinberger as special commissioner, 86, 109, 110; see Webb Line

Webb Steamship Line, its representative, Wakeman, visits Samoan Islands and makes report, 50-52; special favors of, in Meade treaty, 69; strong support of, by secretary of navy, 72-73; subsidized by New Zealand, 76; and Polynesian Land Company, 84

Weber, Theodor, German consul and agent of Godeffroy Company, plans of, for German priority in Samoa, 37, 51-53, 51 n, 54, 68; protests to Chief Mauga against Meade treaty, 70; attempts to change Samoan government and flag, 149, 151, 155, 157; Liardet's opinion of, 161; failure to bribe Griffin, 167; Pritchard's characterization of, 170; changes tactics toward government, 212; negotiates for treaty with Samoa, 202, 215, 217-218, 252; favors tripartite control, 234; adheres to municipal convention, 235; witnesses peace treaty between native factions, 242; participates in government reorganization: with Deinhard, 244; with Stübel, 278-279, 400; with Brandeis, 378, 401; loses political prestige in bankruptcy of Godeffroy Company, 252-253; continued intrigues in Samoa, 278, 284-285, 286-287, 288, 298-299, 304, 315, 336, 378, 406-407, 408-411; synonymous with Godeffroy Company in minds of Samoans, 332, 333, 409-410; attends Washington Conference to advise German delegate, 366; see Godeffroy Company

Wellman, B., land claims of, 211

Welsh, John, United States minister to London, 177, 180

Werner, Captain, German naval officer, negotiates for treaty with Samoa, 215, 217

West Indies, 195

Western Samoa, mandate of, 574

Whalemen, American, see Seamen, United States

Whaling industry, growth of, for United States, 12; influence of, on Exploring Expedition, 12; on es-

INDEX 633

tablishment of consulate in Samoa, 19, 25; on adoption of commercial regulations with Samoa, 19, 20, 40; use of Apia as port of refreshment, 28; difficulties of, with natives, 39

Wharton, William F., United States acting secretary of state, favors admission of German coins in Samoa, 529

White, Andrew D., United States minister to Berlin, reports to Department of State on German expansionist policy, 253-254, 255-256; influences policy of Department relative to tripartite control, 255, 256; informed of United States' consent to partition of Samoa, 567, 568; reports to Hay Germany's proposed sale of Samoan interests to Great Britain, 569

White, Henry, United States chargé d'affaires in London, seeks friendly understanding with Salisbury prior to Berlin Conference, 446

Whitmer, Rev. S. J., 104

Whitney, W. C., United States secretary of navy, sends war ship to Samoa, 413

Wilhelmstrasse, 344

Wilkes, Captain Charles, United States naval officer, commander United States Exploring Expedition, 13; appointment of, protested, 13; vessels under command of, 15; survey of Samoan group, 15-17; empowered to make regulations with natives, 21-22; code of regulations adopted, 20-21; punitive jurisdiction of, over natives, 21-22; views of, regarding punitive jurisdiction, 22; good-will gestures of, 22-23; on Pago Pago harbor, 200; see United States Exploring Expedition

Wilkinson, Walter S., secret agreement of, with Steinberger, 121 n; representative of Samoan government to draft treaty, 135

William Penn, United States whale ship, crew of, attacked by Samoan natives, 22

Williams, Guinn, member House of Representatives, on commission investigating government of American Samoa, 580

Williams, Rev. John, founder of English missionary work in Samoa, visited by Wilkes, 17

Williams, John C., provisional appointment by Wilkes as United States acting consul at Apia, 19; official appointment as commercial agent by Department of State, 19, 23, 24; objection of, to terms of appointment, 24; acting consul, 33-34

Williams, S. F., British consul, 92, 93, 97, 125, 128, 138, 140, 141, 149, 166 n

Wilson, W. H., British pro-consul to Samoa, instructed to coöperate with German consul, 367, 381; refuses to recognize Tamasese as king, 372

Windhorst, Dr., leader of Central party in Germany, opposes Bismarck in colonial expansion, 253, 254

Winslow, Rear Admiral John A., United States naval officer, commander of Pacific Fleet, 55, 56, 57, 58

Wolfe, Samuel M., United States commercial agent to Apia, recalled before sailing, 33

Women, prostitution of native, 64, 124

Wrecked vessels, protection of, 64; custodians for, 20

Young, Mr., English planter of Fiji, activities of, in Samoa, 136-137

Zedtwitz, Baron von, German chargé d'affaires at Washington, tenders Germany's counter proposal to that of the United States, 391; submits Prince Bismark's telegram to Bayard, 393-395; declines to permit publication of protocols, 403

Zembsch, Captain, German consul general for Samoa, announces instructions to recognize Malietoa and enter into joint protectorate by three powers, 248, 251; draws up plan for joint protectorate with United States and English consuls, 249; not connected with German commercial interests, 253, 288; adopts Weber's "divide and rule" policy, 259, 260; gives ostensible recognition to Malietoa Laupepa, 261

DATE DUE